they called it ROCK

The Goldmine Oral History of Rock 'N Roll 1950 -1970

Edited by Kit Kiefer

Published by

**krause
publications**

700 East State St.   Iola WI 54990
715-445-2214

Library of Congress Catalog Number: 91-61304
ISBN: 0-87341-170-6
Printed in the United States of America

Contents

To the past, present and future of *Goldmine*:
to Rick Whitesell, its first editor;
John Koenig, its longtime publisher;
and Jeff Tamarkin, its current editor.

Introduction

First an explanation, then an advertisement, and finally a caveat.

If you found yourself, as you picked this book, saying to yourself, "*Goldmine*? What's *Goldmine* got to do with anything?", an explanation. *Goldmine* is a magazine for record collectors. It comes out every two weeks and is a combination popular-music magazine and record/tape/CD/memorabilia trading guide. All of the interviews in this book except for three came from the pages of *Goldmine*. It's an incredible product; no other magazine covers the spectrum of modern recorded music the way *Goldmine* does. And if you buy a lot of recorded music, no other publication offers as much for sale and at such good prices as *Goldmine*. The magazine costs $35 a year and is available from Krause Publications, 700 E. State St., Iola, Wis. 54990. There is nothing else like it.

The caveat is that this book is not *the* history of rock 'n' roll. *The* history of rock 'n' roll has yet to be written, and shouldn't be written for a long time. Rock 'n' roll is an evolutionary medium, and even the influences, the music that was made in the '50s and '60s, are changing; songs are continually being unearthed and repackaged and careers are continually being re-evaluated. This book is simply *a* history of rock 'n' roll, told by the people who made it, as their stories appeared in the pages of *Goldmine* down through its 15-year history.

Those are stringent requirements for inclusion, and because of that, artists were excluded. Bob Dylan gets short shrift, because no Dylan interview has ever appeared in *Goldmine*. The same goes for the Velvet Underground, Smokey Robinson and the Miracles, the Hollies, the Temptations, Van Morrison, and Peter, Paul and Mary. Sam Cooke and Otis Redding, Jimi Hendrix and Johnny Ace were also slighted, for obvious reasons. Chapters on white doo-wop (Crew-Cuts, Diamonds, Tokens, Four Seasons) and black doo-wop (Frankie Lymon and the Teenagers, Five Satins, Orioles, Harptones, Cleftones); Texas (Roy Head, Doug Sahm, Johnny Winter) and country music (Buck Owens, Harold and Owen Bradley, Ernest Tubb); girl groups (Chantels, Angels) and instrumentalists (Les Paul, Lonnie Mack, Bill Doggett, Duane Eddy) were eliminated due to space restrictions. For that matter, so were groups from existing chapters: the Blues Magoos, ? and the Mysterians, the Leaves, the Honeys, Gene Chandler, the Association, the Buckinghams, John Cipollina, Blue Cheer, Gary Puckett and the Union Gap, the Deep River Boys, the Left Banke, the Delta Rhythm Boys, Tiger Haynes and the Three Flames, the Flamingos, and many more. I hope you'll forgive the omissions and realize that I am aware of the exclusions and the significance of those inclusions. I'd have loved to have included them.

What I've tried to do with this book is establish a framework, to try to take the words of these artists and arrange them in such a way that the whole of rock 'n' roll makes at least a little sense. But at the same time, I haven't tried to make any deep conclusions or overdo the sociological stuff. This book isn't about me, or what I think of these groups, or really where I think they fit in. It's just a concept album of three-minute anecdotes.

I've also tried to keep the factual errors on my part to a minimum, but I claim no responsibility for something Ike Turner or Huey P. Meaux might say that has absolutely no basis in fact. Some of these interviews will contain lies. But lies fit into the mosaic just as assuredly as the truth does.

There are many people who need to be thanked for their contributions to this book. If you'll bear with me, I'd like to thank them now.

First, thanks to all the writers who did the original interviews. Their names appear at the end of each interview, along with the issue where the original interview appeared. It is their work, not mine, that will make this book memorable. They have all my respect and deepest gratitude.

Thanks to Jeff Tamarkin for his patience, even when he didn't know exactly what I was up to (which was most of the duration of the book, actually). Thanks to Jeff also for lining up most of the pictures that appear here.

Thanks to Greg Loescher, publisher of Krause Publications' music division, for his support and cooperation, and for lending me the Animals album with "San Franciscan Nights" on it so I could figure out exactly what Eric Burdon is saying at the beginning of the song.

Thanks to John Koenig, former publisher of the division, for fighting for the project, and for me. If you like this book, thank him. It's his dedication and perseverance for nearly a decade that made it happen.

Thanks to Steve Ellingboe, publisher of the Krause Publications sports division, for allowing me to do the book. Steve also lent his vast knowledge of the Beatles, the British Invasion, and wimp rock in general (i.e., Gary Lewis and the Playboys, Freddie and the Dreamers, Tommy Roe) to the project.

Thanks to Bonni Miller and Julie Steumpfig of the *Goldmine* editorial staff for their patience, and for fishing my copy out of their baskets.

Thanks to former editors Trey Forester and Deb Kellom, wherever she may be. Thanks to Joe Schoeneman for lending me reference materials I never used. Thanks to Dana Jennings, Dan Gardiner (who also did the superb cover art), Brad Wernle, Paul Green and Mark Ingebretsen for saying the book is going to be a best-seller; now, let's see them do their part.

Thanks to Marge Larson and the rest of the typesetters for work above and beyond the call of duty. Thanks to the keyliners for the same. Thanks to book editors Pat Klug and Mary Sieber for putting up with me.

Thanks to my brother for insisting that Eric Clapton was definitely *not* a part of Derek and the Dominos, and for giving me the incentive to prove him wrong. Thanks to my parents for saying, "We don't mind if you spend money on music. It's better than a lot of other things you could spend your money on."

Thanks to Hal Hintze for consistent moral support (he publishes a science-fiction magazine called *Atopos* that's really worth your time and money), and Ann Alnes for the same.

And thanks to all the artists who made the music and then talked about it. It's their book.

Kit Kiefer
Iola, Wis.
June 1, 1991

1. Roots and Rhythm

The history of rock 'n' roll starts at a point too far back and too much buried to ever figure out to the month or day or second. You can trace rock back to the blues, and from there to African chants, and from there back to the first guttural sounds spoken by primitive man, the first songs of birds in the trees or cries of animals in the swamps. You can trace it back to country music, and from there to folk songs, and from folk songs to plainsongs and hymns, and from there all the way up to heaven. There's no point in trying to figure out the exact moment of genesis for rock 'n' roll, because there is no exact moment of genesis. "It ain't why," Van Morrison sang once, "it just *is*." And so it is.

But rock 'n' roll has its sources and its roots; jazz, blues and country are nearly equal contributors.

The three borrowed from one another freely; modern country-blues and jazz-rock pales to milk-white in comparison to the way Bob Wills threw together all three in his western-swing stew, or rural folk-blues performers like Sonny Terry and Leadbelly crossed paths and tunes with white folksingers like Woody Guthrie. The best American music in the days before rock 'n' roll mixed in a little bit of everything, because the best American musicians at that time knew a little bit of everything. The surprise isn't that rock 'n' roll developed but that once it developed it fed off itself, and encouraged jazz and blues and country to do the same. There weren't any more jazz-based solos on Hank Williams records, or folk inflections crawling back into the blues. Rock 'n' roll started the segmentation of popular music. The result has been the expected.

Rock 'n' roll is rooted in rhythm. The rhythm came from places like Jefferson County, Ala., and clubs like the Moravian in Philadelphia. It snaked through the call-and-response singing of the gospel quartets and the bluesy jazz of the trios and quartets. With a bigger guitar over the top and a thumpier bottom end it became rock 'n' roll.

The rhythm was there in the gospel recordings of Charles Bridges and the Birmingham Jubilee Singers. Bridges was one of the seminal figures in early gospel music. Even though his group sang a capella, there was a beat in the bass and a smoothness to the harmony that would later show up in many of the best doo-wop groups. Along with singers like Earl Malone of the Spirit of Memphis Quintet, James Allen of the Dunham Jubilee Singers, the Rev. Isaac Ravizee of the Ravizee Singers, and the Rev. Sam McCrary, they provided musical inspiration, and the beat, for what would eventually become rock 'n' roll.

Charles Bridges: We got to record through a white gentleman; his name was Mr. Simms. He got interested in us and had us to come to his home several times and audition, sing.

We sang in Atlanta, in Marietta, Georgia, in Lynch, Kentucky. We mostly gave our concerts by ourselves, the whole program. We played mostly churches and school houses. After we went to New York we played vaudeville houses. We were at the Keefe Palace in Chicago. They had us there for a week or two weeks.

Our rivals at the time were the Norfolk Jubilee Quartet. We never did meet them. We'd follow them or they'd follow us into a theatre, or something like that.

We were on the radio, out of Birmingham and Bessemer. That was back in the 1920s, WAPI and WVRC, and the one out of Bessemer, WILD. We'd sing at parties around town, up on the highland part of town, the aristocratic part of town. Mr. Crawford Johnson, he was the Coca-Cola man at that time, at the Coca-Cola plant. He'd ask us to come to his house and sing, at parties.

The Jubilees broke up. A few years later I joined the Blue Jays. I wasn't singing with any other groups in between. I was just singing in church, you know.

The Blue Jays came to my house and wanted to know would I like to sing with them. I told them, "Yeah, that would be nice." I think they were going on a tour at that time. We went off and toured all through Alabama, down to Texas.

Rev. Isaac Ravizee: Silas would beat him [Bridges] out with the public. Now, I wouldn't say he would beat him out with the elects, but with the public. Silas would beat him every time. Silas was a small man and thin, about 5'10". And he'd have that frock on; it wasn't a tux, but he had the tux collar. And when Silas would sing he'd lick out his tongue *[demonstrates]* like that! And just as sure, the people would be there! The people would be there. No, they were aroused when Charles was singing, they would say, the people would use the expression and say, "Oh, he's laying it." But he wouldn't bring about the enthusiasm until Silas get it. But Silas'd get it, and old Silas'd start stepping and dart that tougue out, and you had to carry 'em out of there! *(Doug Seroff; February 1980.)*

❦

Gospel groups found commercial success with white and black audiences in the '30s and '40s. White audiences listened to gospel acts as part of the rediscovery of American arts and artists that took place in the late '30s. Black audiences listened to gospel groups because they always had.

Groups like the Charioteers were mainstreamed. They sang everywhere from churches to clubs, with everyone from Baptist preachers to Rudy Vallee. From groups like the Charioteers, it was only a small step to the Mills Brothers and the Ink Spots — and from there, only a small step on the Platters, Clovers and Orioles.

Howard Daniel sang with the Charioteers.

Howard Daniel: As soon as I graduated from Northwestern in 1929, I went to teach at Wilberforce College. I was professor of music at the time, and I had charge of the Glee Club. When we went on tours, I wanted a quartet to sing along with the Glee Club, instead of just having choral numbers or solos. The Glee Club consisted of 26 men, and I organized the Charioteers so we would have another group to go along with it.

The school quartet was out of town and there was to be a statewide quartet contest in Columbus, given by the Knights of Columbus. The president of the school, Wilbert Jones, asked me if I would take my group up to Columbus in place of the other quartet.

They had about 28 quartets in the contest, and we only knew two songs — "Let The Church Roll On" and "Steal Away To Jesus." This was still in 1930. When you got up to Columbus you had to pick a number, and I picked number 13. You had to do one song on stage with the curtain up so the audience could see you. Then, when it came time for your elimination number, they dropped the curtain so the audience would not know who was singing.

There was a white quartet that was just about four groups ahead of us and man, they sang "Steal Away To Jesus" as their elimination number! We didn't know what to do for a while, so I said "Well, we'll just go on and sing our arrangement of 'Steal Away' "; that was all we could do. That is what we did, and we won the contest. When we sang it, there was a hush all over the audience. The Library Of Congress still has a recording of that, made that day and presented to the governor.

The music director at WLW in Cincinnati, Grace Raines, heard us and liked us. She asked us what we were going to use as a theme song; we sang "Swing Low Sweet Chariot," and she said, "That's it! Call yourselves the Charioteers!"

I continued to teach school. I lived in Xenia and I'd get up at four every morning, drive to Wilberforce and pick up the boys, and then we'd drive to Cincinnati — 55 miles one way. We had a show with Paul McCarmody at 7 o'clock in the morning. Then we'd have to come back and try to make classes. I had a 10 o'clock class. We did that for two-and-a-half years, and sometimes we'd have to go back in the evening for a show called *Moon River* that came on at midnight.

In December 1934, we were invited to broadcast on WOR in New York and the Mutual Network. Everybody agreed that this was our big chance, but at the time I had two babies — my sons — and at first I told the boys I couldn't come to New York with them and leave my wife behind. My wife, Jessie Clark Daniel, was professor of chemistry at Wilberforce; she had finished at Wilberforce and went right back to teach there.

We met Jean Goldkette at WOR. He had most of the black bands coming out of Ohio and Michigan, and he's the one who built the Greystone Ballroom in Detroit. All of our work had been a capella, and when we got to New York we found out we couldn't make any money doing that, singing spirituals. After we got with Goldkette, we got a studio in Carnegie Hall with a grand piano and we went to work. We would start about 9 o'clock in the morning and work until 12, then go across to Horn & Hardart, come back after lunch and rehearse until 6 or 7 at night. Jean got us a friend of his, a German boy, as a pianist and he played with us for a year or so, but he died. This left us in pretty bad straits.

We were desperate for a pianist for a while. In the interim, Teddy Wilson played for us about two years. Wilson didn't want to leave us. At the time, we were rehearsing "Glory Road" at Wilson's house when Teddy got a telegram from Benny Goodman in Hollywood. He asked Teddy to come and work with the band in their first motion picture. We told Teddy he should take the job, although he didn't want to go. All we asked was that he find us another pianist who could play exactly like him!

Bing Crosby had caught us in *Hellzapoppin* and asked us to come to Hollywood to audition for a two-week spot on his show. He sent us our fare, round-trip tickets. We went out there to stay two weeks and stayed with him until he went out of show business in 1947 — five-and-a-half years. After Bing left Kraft, he went with Philco for a year and we went to Philco with him. By then, he was making too much money and he gave up show business for awhile.

We used to do all the camp shows with Bing. We took a show to all the various camps in California like Pendleton and Young. Once a week we would visit the camps and entertain with Judy Garland, Bob Hope, Dorothy Lamour and a lot of stars. Bing would always send his station wagon down for me to take the boys in. A lot of performers would take the bus, but we used Bing's station wagon. During our time with Bing, we used to do a show at a club up in the valley. One night, Billy was sick and couldn't make it. Well, the Mills Brothers and I are good friends. I used to play golf with Donald all the time. I called him up and said, "Look here, man, come out and sing with us because Bill is sick." He went on out there and filled in. It was beautiful — the Charioteers, led by Donald Mills. That's the way the quartets would help each other then; it was a beautiful relationship. All the groups were very close during those times.

Our biggest hit was "So Long." It was played throughout the war years. After the war, a lot of guys came up to us when we were performing and said, "We wanted to shoot you guys!"

9

We asked why and they said, "You put out that 'So Long' record and we were falling in love with these chicks and marrying them and going into the war. And when we came back, we couldn't find them!" Those chicks had all said "So Long!" Man, they wouldn't let us come off the stage unless we sang that song.

After President Roosevelt died, all the stars did a show for Mrs. Roosevelt from Hollywood. This was taped and sent into Mrs. Roosevelt's house. We sang a couple of spirituals on the show. Bob Hope, Bing, Frank — everybody was on that thing. It's six of eight double records — 12" 78s — beautifully bound. They made one for each of the performers on the show. *(Peter Grendysa and Rick Whitesell; June 1980.)*

🦃

The impact of big-band R&B has been overlooked by a lot of the people who try to figure out rock 'n' roll and encapsulate its greats. They're perfectly willing to give Chuck Berry his due, and Ray Charles and Jimmy Reed — and rightly so — but they forget about performers like Bullmoose Jackson, whose "I Love You, Yes I Do" and "Big Ten-Inch Record" were R&B milestones; Wynonie Harris; honking saxophone great Big Jay McNeely; Texas boogie pianist Amos Milburn; Roy Brown; R&B shouter Gatemouth Moore; and the greatest of them all, jump-blues singer Big Joe Turner and bandleader Louis Jordan.

Jordan once said there was nothing in rock 'n' roll that he didn't do better and with a higher degree of musicianship, and he was right. His best records — "Saturday Night Fish Fry," "Is You Is Or Is You Ain't My Baby," "Ain't Nobody Here But Us Chickens" — mixed humor with a driving beat. It was hard swing with a rougher, bluesier edge, a little like Bob Wills playing R&B. The line between what Jordan did with eight or nine pieces and what Bill Haley and the Comets did with five or six was very narrow. Haley essentially took Jordan's music and subtracted a few instruments, brought up the beat and, as Jordan hinted, lightened up on the complexity. Sure, the kids could dance to Bill Haley and the Comets, but they never had any trouble dancing to Louis Jordan, either — when they could hear him.

Jordan recorded with Bing Crosby, thrived during World War II, then after the war was over, played a smaller and smaller succession of mostly black clubs and theaters. Ray Benson, one of the founders of the western-swing band Asleep At The Wheel, caught up with Jordan towards the end of his musical career.

Ray Benson: We saw him. It was in a little club in Berkeley called Ruthie's Inn, on San Pablo Avenue. It must have been 1972, maybe 1971. We had to play a show, so we only got to see four numbers: "Ain't Nobody Here But Us Chickens," "Caledonia," "Boogie Real Slow With The Lights Down Low," and one more. Anyway, we walk in and the guy says, "Ladies and gentlemen, Louis Jordan!" He walks out, and he looks just as young as he ever did. And this was just a year before he died. He looked young, he was jumping, he was standing up, he was playing his ass off, he was singing, and he walked onstage and there were all these older black women with mink stoles and big diamonds, and as soon as he got up onstage there they stood up and started *dancin' around.* It was amazing, because it wasn't at all full. It was mostly one table of us young hippies and the rest was really older black folks, because the younger folks didn't know who the hell Louis Jordan was. They were listening to *Superfly* back then. *(Kit Kiefer; April 21, 1989.)*

🦃

Bullmoose Jackson: I was a violin player from the time I was five years old, as long as I can remember. The other kids in the neighborhood weren't that fortunate to have that dollar a week for violin lessons, trumpet lessons or whatever. The majority of the kids I grew up with didn't get into music until they were in high school. I was way up at the top of the list as far as being able to read music, and the other guys would tease me out of envy. I really never had any formal training on the saxophone or clarinet, but being able to read music it was just a matter of getting a decent tone on the instruments. I had a few lessons for tone and whatnot from instructors around Cleveland. From the time I was five until I was 14, I had strict violin training. My mother and father wanted me to be a concert violinist, but in those days there were no openings for black musicians in symphonies.

10

I was working at the Cedar Gardens, 97th and Cedar in Cleveland, with Miss Sadina Walker's band in 1943, and Lucky Millinder came through. At that time Lucky Thompson was playing tenor, and he was leaving the band to go somewhere on his own. Someone told Lucky about me, and he came out to the Cedar Gardens to hear me play. It was on a Wednesday night and they were leaving on Saturday and going to Kansas. He was so impressed he said, "Can you leave?"

BULLMOOSE JACKSON: 'I tried not to sound like anybody else. That was my main thought and object with my saxophone and my singing.'

At that time you had to give two weeks notice, but Miss Sadina was the type that didn't want to hold anybody back, so she said, "Go on and play, I'll get somebody else." So I left that Saturday and we went to Wichita for our first stop. Then we went down through Texas and to the West Coast.

One night in Lubbock, Texas, Wynonie Harris got his habits on. He was the type of guy that would say, "Well, I'm not going to sing tonight; I don't feel up to it. I'm going home." They had to do a little coaxing to get me up there to sing, but I was always interested in singing since I sang in church with my momma. After I got there, I loved it. That night in Lubbock I sang "Hurry Hurry" and "Sweet Slumber." "Hurry Hurry" was a blues tune that Wynonie was doing, and Trevor Bacon had done "Sweet Slumber." Trevor had left the band to go with Tab Smith. The place we were playing was one of those that had chicken wire between the band and the audience to keep the whiskey bottles from hitting the musicians. To me, as a kid, it wasn't bad; it was just funny.

I tried not to sound like anybody else. That was my main thought and object with my saxophone and my singing. When you hear the first two or three notes, you can say, "Well, that's that sad old Bullmoose!" And of all the musicians, I always admired Chuck Berry and Lester Young, but I never wanted to sound like them in singing; I liked Nat Cole and Billy Eckstine. In fact, I worked with Billy when he was making $19 and we were making $22.50 just playing behind him. That was at the Club Moon Glo in Buffalo, New York.

I didn't go out with my own Buffalo Bearcats for a couple of years, until I really got myself together. It wasn't one of those things where you go out without any rehearsals or arrangements. I had a very good arranger, alto player Snooky Hulbert. He was the third sax player with Lucky, and when I left, Money Johnson, Sam Taylor, Bill Mann, and my bass player Jimmy Meard all came with me to the Bearcats.

At the time "I Love You, Yes I Do" was a big hit, we were being paid a straight salary; there were no royalties. I think we were getting $31.50 each per track. In those days they didn't have tapes; they'd record you on big discs. If you made a mistake, you'd have to start over again. I don't believe the companies were making a heck of a lot of money with the prices they were getting for records and the production costs with the big bands. Anyway, we toured for three straight years after "I Love You, Yes I Do."

If I would just get off my behind, I could be doing more. If someone would just plant his foot in my ass and say, "Come on, Bullmoose; we're going to make it one more time before you leave here," I think I could do it. But I'm going to go to my grave being myself. Just because the times change, I won't change. We can do some disco or whatever, but I get more applause and recognition just being Bullmoose Jackson. I need a good agent now, because with the band I have now, all you'd have to do is call me and tell me where to go and what time to get there and I'd know what to wear and what to play. And we'd be there. *(Peter Grendysa; November 1979.)*

Amos Milburn: I was born April 1, 1928, in Houston, Texas, to a family of 12. I was eighth from the bottom; we always counted up from the baby back then. My mother tried, but I'm sorry to say I didn't get much church in me. But I did go occasionally.

I had a brother who inspired me with tunes that were, as we called them, pop tunes ... oh, "Ashes In The Tray" and "Cocktails For Two" and lots of other numbers. I do remember as a very young kid, during the Depression, where the truck would back up to our house and throw the canned goods off. And when I was dancing on the truck, doing the buck dance, the first prize was a box of groceries and a case of beer. My big brothers would get the case of beer and Mama would get the groceries for us, and I'd get a whipping when I got home with the groceries because Mama didn't know where I was — and that's the truth! She just said, "Lord, what am I gonna do with that boy?"

I could imitate Erskine Hawkins and some early Louis Jordan numbers. I took piano lessons, but I was into things like Tommy Dorsey's "Boogie Woogie" and the Albert Ammons, Pete Johnson, Meade Lux Lewis stuff. In high school, they wanted another instrument, a French horn, but my heart was in the piano. I was told, "You know you can't go down a field with a piano!" I left school a little after that.

I went to work for a drug store, but I still played the piano. They used to have house parties, and you know you'd go there on Saturday nights — oh, man, as a little boy — and those big, fat women, they're drinkin', drinkin' their wine and their homemade brew. And at that time I didn't care for them things. It was later in my career I started drinkin' heavy.

I started learning to play in B-flat and A-flat; you know, when you first went to New York, if you couldn't play "Body And Soul" — wow! And I did learn the chords to "Sophisticated Lady" — the great Duke — "Jumping At The Woodside," all those jazz numbers. Lionel Hampton's "One O'Clock Jump," Tommy Dorsey's "Boogie Woogie" ... I really liked Will Bradley and took a liking to "Down The Road Apiece," and that was my chief song when I was playing little towns around Houston.

When I came back from the service, every little joint around Houston was somebody's chickenshack — "Mabel's Chickenshack," "Uncle Charlie's Chickenshack" — no windows, no doors, just a hole in the wall, but they stayed chuck full of folks. I never played in any 'cause they weren't really night clubs, more like beer gardens. You know, it was true what I said about "being careful when you took a seat" — 'cause they sure was places where the bad cats meet!

When I heard Fats' very first record, "The Fat Man," I noticed the piano. I said, "That sounds like me," and everybody else was telling me, "That guy sounds just like you on piano." We later played engagements together on the road.

I met Charles Brown in the '40s, down when it was the bitter end. I loved Charles' technique on the piano, and Charles' daddy used to be crazy about my style. He'd say, "That Amos could sure put on a show." His daddy would come and see me all the time. Charles and I are still good friends.

We worked together a lot. I worked with the Clovers, too. We did over 30 one-nighters once, the Clovers and I, back in 1952 or '52. I also liked the Five Keys. I gave them "Glory Of Love" to record. I had recorded it already, but it wasn't released. It stayed in the can 'til way later and I said, "Fellas, you want a hit? Record this song." And they recorded it for Aladdin Records. Then there was Floyd Dixon, he was our baby, and he was a guy that loved Charles Brown and Amos Milburn. He was such a sweet guy when he was growing up; we remember when he first appeared, wanted to go every place that we went.

I did "Bad, Bad Whiskey" in 1950. This was the time when there was a lot of money around and people were really boozin' it up heavy, so that's what I was getting — whiskey tunes. This went over very well in clubs, on records and everything. They even gave me a gimmick in "Juice, Juice, Juice" where they asked me what type of juice and I answered, "Why, orange juice, of course!" Old O.J. would've liked that!

In 1957 I got an act together with Charles Brown. We took a trip to Florida for a guy who almost had me in jail. They like to starved us to death down there, and in order to feed us he had us sign our name to a check. I went to the courthouse, and he'd already had us booked into Miami, Fla., and he's gonna put us in jail, like about a week before the engagement. He said we'd forged the check, and the only way he'd feed us was for us to sign our name. But we was dumb and didn't know we were signing our name to a check.

But when we got to the courthouse the judge straightened it all out. He said, "If ever I catch you treating any citizen that comes to visit Florida like this again, I'm going to put you in jail." After that, Charles left and caught a bus because there were some people up in Newport, Kentucky — Sin Town, U.S.A. — and they said for him to come up to Newport. So I stayed for a while in Tampa, and worked a little club. I left there on a bus and went to New Orleans and I worked at the Dew Drop Inn.

I had a stroke later on. I was playing a set at Satan's Den, and I couldn't play the notes no matter how hard I tried. The manager of the club came up to see what was wrong and told me to get off the bandstand; I was about to have a stroke. My mouth started to get all crooked and I didn't know what had happened. It didn't paralyze me, but the doctor did warn me I could have another one soon if I didn't ease up.

Then I had a second one, paralyzed my left side, then, in August 1972, my wife died. She was a sweet woman who thought of no one but me, and I hated to lose her.

Everything works for the good. Just 'cause I'm paralyzed doesn't mean that it's the end of the world. I don't feel sorry for myself. I can cook and do a lot of things.

I give my life to God, and this is a new life. But one thing about me, I know I can play — right now! You know they had a truck right outside my apartment, and a spiritual singer and a reverend, and I went out and they lifted me up on the truck, and I just went to it like it was nothing. I want to learn gospel piano. I dig it. I always liked the music. Like the Dixie Hummingbirds and those spirituals that Sam Cooke sang on with the Soul Stirrers, and the 5 Blind Boys. I start my day off with church."

You know, even the kids today — what happened? The kids never heard this music, and it's something ... I get letters from places like London, man, and they tell me all these things. I tell you, I ain't losing nothing. I've had more people contact me — just like I was a star all over again! *(George Moonoogian; December 1979.)*

❧

Gatemouth Moore: I wrote "I Ain't Mad At You" in Washington, D.C. A woman had just took her shoe heel and busted her husband across the head, and the police was going to arrest her.

The wagon was there and he was bleeding all over. I was on my way to the nightclub. I was playing at the Stardust at that time. They were putting her in and he was saying, "Don't put her in jail. I ain't mad at you, baby," and he was just bleeding all over. When I got to the nightclub that night, the band started playing and I started singing, "I Ain't Mad At You."

Rufus Thomas — I raised him in Beale Street. First fellow to make my song was Josh White. The next time I heard it was a group called the Flenoy Trio. The boy was a guitar player in the Carolina Cotton Pickers Orchestra. He did it. The next time, Rufus made my record. Rufus was a dancer and comedian, he never was a singer. Another famous version was by B.B. King.

I toured with the Mills Brothers, and with the Ink Spots. I was featured singer with Russell, what was his name, the piano player, who took Louis Armstrong's band — Louis Russell. In those days my records were out on National. I'm the first male blues singer to go to Small's Paradise. When I came up, the blues singers were all women. In my young days before I got famous on records, I traveled the United States with Ida Cox and the Darktown Scandals. From there I went to Winnipeg, Canada. I traveled all over the country as a straight man and a singer. The quartet was going then. Then I traveled with Irvin C. Miller's Brownskinned Models — it was a famous black show. And I was on another show — Charles Taylor and the Brown Mannequins. These were the famous black shows that played in those days.

Yeah, these were my days. Next they had Elk Rendezvous and Louis Jordan and the Timpany Five made their hit. There were three of us in the big nightclub days. T-Bone, Wynonie Harris and myself, and then there was another fellow who came with us to Chicago. He was a saxophone player called Cleanhead Vinson. Then there was another youngster that came up after us called Jimmy Witherspoon.

Can't forget the daddy. He was on 18th and Vine when I hit there in the '30s. He had been in Kansas City. Oh yeah, Joe Turner was before us, he was before *all* of us. 'Cause when I left Topeka and hit Kansas City, Joe Turner was there. So you see, there's nobody living now but me and a fellow that came up later. He wasn't in our class, but he came up through the years — Muddy Waters. But he sang the lowdown blues in those joints like the Club Delisa. We were in all the big clubs. Sir, I was in Washington when a fellow named Billy Eckstine won the contest, and before Earl Hines ever became great. Well, let me go back again. My brother is in New York. Look him up; he was one of the great sweet singers that every was. He sang with a band called Ernie Fields. He's been in the record business quite a while. His name is Melvin Moore.

Yeah, they tore the Chicago Theatre up. I come way back, sir. I don't know how I remember all this stuff, but it's my life. *(Aaron Fuchs; November 1982.)*

Bill Haley and the Comets made Big Joe Turner's "Shake, Rattle and Roll" a hit. Someone else hit with Turner's "Corinne Corrina." Throughout the big man with the big voice kept recording, as he had since the '30s, when he scuffled his way into the great Kansas City jazz scene. Big Joe Turner recorded with everyone from Count Basie to the Blasters. He provided great music for an endless roster of lesser artists, and provided an unique link between classic jazz and classic rock 'n' roll. He died in 1989.

Johnny Otis pulled R&B and rock 'n' roll together in those early years. The rhythms he put on records like "Willie and the Hand Jive" became rock's basic rhythms. And Otis brought R&B sounds to new audiences through his popular L.A. television show. He helped Leiber and Stoller write "Hound Dog," discovered Jackie Wilson and Ray Charles and Etta James, and fronted one of the tightest bands in history — all by his own admission. Otis did as much as anyone in forging the modern sound of R&B.

Big Joe Turner: Well, the blues is a type of music that tells about everybody's troubles and everybody's happiness and things. So we make up the songs about stories that go down through life, and we translate it into the music.

It was a long time ago. I used to listen to Ethel Waters' records and I used to sing them around the house, and I had a piano in the hall. My brother-in-law's brother played the piano in a nightclub, so he taught me all the songs that they played in the nightclub when he'd come home in the daytime, when he was up. He used to let me sing along with him, and that's how I learned how to keep time.

I met Pete Johnson in Kansas City on Independence Avenue. He was working a nightclub there, him and Merle Johnson. They just had a drummer and a piano player. I used to go down there. I was too young to go in. I used to slip down there and listen to 'em play! I was pretty tall when I was a young kid. One time I put on my daddy's long pants, made me a mustache with an eyebrow pencil and stuff and slipped in there. People was crowdin' around the door, so the bouncer overlooked me. So I got in and stood there a while. I used to tell them that I could sing, and they'd say, "Get outta here, boy! You can't do nothin'!" So I used to hang around until the men caught me and kicked me out, and I would slip back in every chance I got. I guess I was about 14, 15 years old.

BIG JOE TURNER: 'Everyone was singin' slow blues when I was young, and I thought I'd put a beat to it and sing it up-tempo.'

After I got older, I used to sing in a nightclub, and a friend of mine was a bartender, a school chum. He was little older than me, so I used to ask him to teach me how to tend bar. So they finally give me a chance. First they started me off by bringin' in the whiskey. That was back in bootleg days. I'd go back to the stash, get the whiskey and bring it in the nightclub in big pitchers, and when I got behind the bar I'd stay there and watch the bartenders. I'd mix the drinks and stuff, and stay back there and watch. They had a lot of waitresses, and I'd wash glasses and help around the bar and I learned how to mix up a few drinks, and then I started waitin' on the waitresses when they got crowded. So the boss saw me back there, and I used to come out from behind the bar, and go up to the bandstand and sing, and then come back down, get right back behind the bar 'cause I was interested in that, and that's where I learned. Then they trusted me, you know, and I was runnin' pretty fast. I wasn't readin' up on that stuff, what they mixed the drinks with, 'cause back in bootleg days they didn't have too many mixed drinks. They had red whiskey and white whiskey, and that red whiskey was what they called needle whiskey, and corn liquor was white, kinda yellow lookin'. That's how I learned to tend bar.

That was before the days of the Cafe Society. I wasn't even thinkin' of the Cafe Society then. Long time after that I worked a lot of nightclubs. I worked all over. I started travelin' on the road to St. Louis, Wichita Falls, Kansas, and different places singin' with the band.

John Hammond came to Kansas City talent-scouting, looking for different bands. He heard Count Basie over there. We had a radio station that had just opened up, and they didn't have nobody to work at it and so they used to come around to the different nightclubs and book up a set, and broadcast it. So we sang over the air, and they was able to carry it way up to New York and all around. It was a powerful station and they heard us on the air. So John Hammond finally came through there one time listenin' to Count Basie, and he wanted me to come with Count Basie's band to New York. I was workin' for Pete Johnson and I'd never sung with a 12-piece band with arrangements. I was a little awkward singin' with those arrangements, so I told him I'd rather not go over there; I'd rather wait until he came back here sometime and bring me and Pete Johnson to New York.

So he promised and finally, maybe four or five years later, he came back and got me and Pete Johnson and took us to New York. And that's when he recorded us. The first recording we ever made was for John Hammond.

Everybody was singin' slow blues when I was young, and I thought I'd put a beat to it and sing it up-tempo. Pete Johnson and I got together, and we worked at that pretty good for a long time, and we finally got pretty good at it. So we used to do it in a nightclub and it went over so good, we just kept it up.

I met Billie Holiday in New York City at the Cafe Society. I used to bug her all the time 'cause I used to go into her dressing room all the time and use her brown powder and put it on my face. She used to throw me out; I used to walk with her during the intermissions. She would walk up and down the streets to get some fresh air, so me and her got to be good friends. Finally she took me over to her house and I met her mother, and all the people that stayed at her house, and we got to be good friends, and I wrote her a song called "Fine And Mellow." It was the only blues song she ever sang.

Well, John Hammond put a concert together in Carnegie Hall called "Rhythm And Blues," and "Spirituals To Swing." He had a lotta quartets there. He had a lotta acts and we had Pete Johnson; that's when they introduced boogie-woogie to the world. They had Albert Ammons, Pete Johnson, and Meade Lux Lewis; they played boogie-woogie at the Cafe Society, downtown. They was on stage together with me in the middle. We had the Golden Gate Quartet on there; they sang spiritual songs. They used to work at the Cafe Society, and that was the first time I ever met them. I forget where they come from; they was from down South somewheres. And Big Bill Broonzy out of Chicago. He was a blues singer, played guitar. That's where I first met him. He took off his shoes and he's standin' up on the stage singin' and cryin'. So John Hammond asked him, "What you cryin' for? Ain't nobody gonna do nothin' to ya." He said his shoes was hurtin' his feet. He had bought him some new shoes, and the shoes was hurtin' his feet. He [John Hammond] said, "Well, take 'em off!" So he took his shoes off and he worked out like a champ.

At Cafe Society, first Albert Ammons and Meade Lux Lewis was there first, and then they brought in Pete Johnson and I. We got together, so they decided to make it a threesome instead of two and one. You see, Pete Hammond was playin' for me, so they decided that we'd have two pianos. They had an upright-type piano, so they put that out there with the baby grand, and I used to come out and sing in the middle of 'em. It went over so good we kept it up. We got to be famous with that crowd.

They was crazy 'bout "Roll 'Em Pete," "Cherry Red," " My Gal's A Jockey," and I used to do a lot of pop songs, too. I used to do the "Sheik of Araby," "Red Sails In The Sunset," and a lot of other I don't remember. It's been so long ago.

I worked at the Apollo Theatre way before Alan Freed was thought about. I had recorded with Decca, Columbia, RCA, National, a couple of more labels. I was singin' on the stage at the Apollo Theatre, and Ahmet Ertegun of the Atlantic Record Company heard me. Of course, he had heard me before. He always said he was going to record me, so he come up there one morning to catch the show. After the show he came backstage and talked to me. We went out to dinner, and he asked me how I would like to record for him. I told him it would be okay if he paid me my money. So I didn't know how much money to ask for. So he said he'd give me $500. I thought that was somethin'. I said, "Yeah, that's good!" That was for four sides. So about three to four weeks later we went into the studio and he recorded me, and it went over so good, he recorded me again.

I made a lot of records. "Sweet Sixteen," "Corrine Corrina," "Shake, Rattle and Roll," "Nightime Is The Right Time," "Up, Up And Away."

Elmore James was good. I had never heard of him before. I heard people talk about him, but I never saw him before. But I ran into him in Chicago when we were doing a session up there for Atlantic so they went and got him and I wrote the number "TV Mama." So they asked me how would I like for him to play the guitar? I hadn't heard him, so he came in and played a couple numbers. So I told him [Ertegun], "He sounds all right to me." We only made four sides, and that was the last I ever saw of him.

Well, our music caught on pretty good. They said it wasn't going to catch on, but it did. So it went along, up and down, up and down, people knocked it. They said we was hypnotizin' the white folks with that Negro music.

It never bothered me, because I worked in the white nightclubs in my hometown lots of times, and it wasn't nothin' new to me. I got over all right. I had a little stage fright there for a while, so I just figured they'd understand what I was singin' about. It went over so nice that I got confidence all over again. I said, "Well, they understand." It was kinda hard there for a while though 'cause it was when we was singin' over there in Europe, people can't speak a word of English, and you'd say, "What the devil did they come to the concert for? They don't know what the hell I'm sayin'." So they were here to hear the music and they'd buy the record and listen to the sound and they liked it.

I never heard of New Orleans, and a friend of mine, a fellow I met named Frank, had the Dew Drop Inn in New Orleans. Then I used to go down there all the time, so finally he sent for me to come and work in his nightclub. So I worked in the nightclub about a month and left. I went over real good. I had standin' crowds all out on the street. So he sent for me every month or so. So I kept runnin' back down to New Orleans. That's where I met Fats Domino, Roy Brown, and all the boys in New Orleans.

Music? I like it all. Music is a part of me and I enjoy music, period. But that long-hair stuff, I don't understand it so good; I don't know what's happenin'. Some of it they play is so far out that you don't know what the devil they doin'. You never know what they playin' and when they get through, you don't know what the song was. *(James Austin; November 1982.)*

Johnny Otis: One of the first things I did on record was "Double Crossin' Time," with the Robins. The Robins were a group I found called the Four Bluebirds. When I first found them at the Barrelhouse [Otis' club through the '40s and '50s], there were three, without Bobby Nunn, though Bobby was there. I put Bobby with them, with the bass voice, thinking in terms of a Ravens-type group. We called them the Bluebirds, but they didn't like that name, so we changed it to the Robins.

"Double Crossin' Blues" was based on an old vaudeville act I remember played called Apus and Estrellita. They didn't sing it, they just talked it. I put it to music; we were lucky with that. It launched Little Esther. A happy accident. I was leaving the old chicken ranch in Watts in my old '28. We were waving goodbye to Phyllis [Otis' wife], going to the Robins' first session. Mario, the bass player, was driving this old car and just as we were pulling out, Little Esther came running up — she used to help me catch chickens in the back yard — saying, "Let me go, let me go." I said to Ralph Bass, "We got 20 minutes. I've got a little song; let's teach it to these kids, let's do it." Ralph says, "Well, hurry up, do it!"

I said this could be like the Ravens and Dinah Washington thing. We made a take, but Esther giggled a little bit. So somebody said, "You need to do that again." But he said, "Time is up." They sent it back east; it sat on the desk of Herman Lubinsky [owner of the Savoy]. Bill Cook, who's a disc jockey, happened in one night about a week later and said, "Got anything new, Herman?"

"Well, I got some stuff Johnny Otis sent. You can listen to it," Lubinsky said.

He put it on, and Cook said, "What is this?"

"That's nothing. Just some girl, Little Esther."

"Man, that's great. Let me play it on the air."

He played it on the air and immediately it became the biggest record throughout the nation. People called it "Lady Bears."

When I was with Federal [Records], we did a talent show in Detroit that was supposed to have been an hour. It turned into three hours because there was so much talent in Detroit. When the talent show was over, we called King Records. I was one of their talent scouts then. I said, "I sure have found some people here."

I picked Jackie Wilson, Little Willie John, and Hank Ballard and the Midnighters. There were others with potential during that evening. I said, "They're not going to like Jackie Wilson because he's going to sing 'Trees' or 'My Buddy.' They're not going to hear him like I hear him, so I better write him something bluesy." Being very gifted, he picked it right up. It was "Every Beat Of My Heart." When they got there, they listened. They didn't like him, they liked the song. They didn't like Little Willie John, either. They chased their tails.

They had the Dominoes — suddenly it was all vocal groups — so they liked Hank Ballard and the Midnighters because they were a vocal group. They gave the song to the Midnighters because they were a vocal group, and the Midnighters recorded it. Not much of a record, didn't do much. Ten years later, Gladys Knight and the Pips recorded it and became a big hit.

I have a feeling that Jackie Wilson had a mental block about recording that song. He resented what had happened, that he was rejected by King Records. I kept haranguing the people at King, saying, "You ought to go get those two kids. And they did, as a matter of fact."

I'll tell you one they didn't get. We were in Cincinnati. We played a gig, and then the thing was to go down to Brewster Avenue to King Records. I went out on the porch, and I sat there waiting for the man to bring the car around so we could go. There was Ray Charles. He was unknown then. He was a singer with Lowell Fulson. He said, 'Hey Johnny, where you going?"

I said, "I'm going down to King Records."

"Could I ride with you there? I'd like to go down there, audition for them," he said.

He gets there and I take him in. I said, "Syd, listen. I want you to hear this young man." I'd heard him. Little Esther and I had gone and heard him sing, and he just blew our minds. He was marvelous. We're sitting in this part of the room where there's a grand piano. Young Ray goes in, sits down and starts singing. Syd Nathan turns to me: "I don't need any poor man's Charles Brown; I've already got Charles Brown."

A couple of years later, Ray Charles is eating up the world. There's a big disc-jockey convention in Miami and I said, "Syd, come here. Remember the kid I brought to sing for you and you said you didn't need no more Charles Browns?"

"Yeah, I remember."

"Guess what his name is?"

"I don't know and I don't care."

"Ray Charles."

He refused to accept that, never would.

We found Etta James in San Francisco. Somebody called me on the phone, we were asleep. We were to play that night and the little girl said, "Hey Mr. Otis, I want to sing for you."

"Come to the gig tonight. I want to sleep now," I said.

18

She said, "No, I want to sing now." She came up and knocked on the door. She had two little girls with her, came in, and even though she had that much nerve, still there was an element of shyness because she turned her face away. She faced into the bathroom when she was singing. It sounded so good, like an echo chamber. I said, "Wow!" We called her mother up, and I brought her right to Los Angeles with me. She lived in our home for awhile. She had this idea for a song. She had a crush on Hank Ballard at the time, and she had this little idea that went, "Roll with me, Henry." I wrote the words to "Roll With Me Henry" — also known as "The Wallflower" — and then "Dance With Me Henry."

If ever a song was about dancing with no sexual connotations, this was it. Not that there's anything wrong with honest sexuality ... it's a dance record. But try to tell that to the uptight establishment of 1954.

In 1955, I started Ultra Records. The main motivating factor was that when we started moving the blues-related songs into the major studios, we had problems with the engineers. They didn't like it when he asked them to crank the drums up or to make a twangier sound on the guitar; it was not their concept of a good balance. They didn't like the sound and the tones. First chance I got, I got me some money, I bought a board and said, "I can do that, too." They wouldn't let me sit there and do the dials, so we did it ourselves.

I also started the TV show that year. We were on 11 [KTTV] first, then 5 [KTLA], then 13 [KCOP], and then 22 [KJIX] for a minute. A live studio audience was part of it. They would come by the hundreds, and you'd let them in as you could because you don't want to start no riot out there. Those kids wanted to get in, we didn't have no special people. It was basically teenagers, 10 to one. There were industry people coming too, to see what this new thing here was. I leased a big building and we built a bigger studio, and that's where I rehearsed our television show and broadcast my KOFX radio shows with a telephone line; we did them live, but remote. That's where we did the Dig things.

There were a couple of people in town who were prominent who were anti-rhythm 'n' blues. It was virulent. I was invited to this television show. I didn't want to go; I was talked into it. Bardu Ali and I went there. A lady came in and gave me a list of questions, and that was fine. But she also gave me a list of answers.

"We'd kind of like you to stick to this," she said.

"You ask me a question and you're going to tell me what my answer is?"

Bardu kept nudging me. "Tell her yes. You do what you want when you are on the air, because if you tell her no you ain't gonna get on the air."

So when we got on the air, the guy asked me a question, I told him what I felt like and they tried to cut me off. But, you know, that was the same station I had my show on. All my guys were up in the booth and they wouldn't cut me off. So I said what I had to say, and it became a stinky mess.

We had a hit in England, "Ma, He's Making Eyes At Me." We recorded "Ma" thinking it would be a hit here, but it didn't make it here. So Hal [Zeigler] went over and set up a tour, and he said, "I saw kids in the venues where they couldn't dance, theaters and little concert halls were they had to sit, doing a thing you used to do in black show business. The big hands called it the Hand Jive."

"Oh, yeah, sure, I remember that," I said. When the trumpets were up playing the solos, the saxes might do this thing. Hal said, "Make a record on that, and we'll probably have a hit in England." So I did put a record together. He hated it; he didn't want us to release it. Capitol loved it, and said, "That's great; that's going to be a hit."

It's that beat again. If it were possible, we could trace that back to West Africa, but my first experience with that beat was with Count Otis Matthews and the West Oakland House Rockers when I was a kid in the late '30s. He would play in the gymnasium in West Oakland, and he would get little cans and fill them up with little rocks, and he'd sit them on the piano. At the end of the evening he'd pick cute little girls out of the audience and bring them up to shake — our little go-go girls — and he'd have them do "shave and a haircut, six bits." He'd sing "Mama killed a chicken, thought it was a duck."

Next time I encountered that beat was in not such frivolous circumstances, on a chain gang in Mississippi. We had stopped a bus on the highway and I heard this ching-ching-ching. They were taking a break, rattling those chains and singing that same thing: "Mama brought a chicken." It was a very heartbreaking scene, but it also spoke of the human spirit, refusing to give up.

One time Bo Diddley came up to me and said, "Say, man, what's this thing you made with my beat on it?."

"It's called 'Hand Jive,' and I got it from 'Hambone,' " I said.

He said, "Shh," because "Hambone" preceded his record. *(Steve Propes; March 25, 1988.)*

The most transcendent R&B artist of them all was a jazz pianist and bandleader who had his biggest hit with an ancient pop standard and had his biggest critical success with two albums of country covers. Ray Charles grew up at an Alabama school for the blind and had his first success in Seattle with a Nat King Cole-style trio. Charles liked big bands, favored strings and female backup singers, and mixed blues and big bands and call-and-response gospel into a powerful musical product that influenced a second generation of rock 'n' rollers. He fought a heroin addiction, had a major hit with "Georgia On My Mind," and brought R&B back to its country roots with his *New Sounds In Country And Western Music* album. His uplifting version of "America, The Beautiful" helped transform him from an R&B trendsetter to an American institution. Later in his career he cut an album with Willie Nelson, did Diet Pepsi commercials, and grew rich on his royalties.

Ray Charles: I travel because I can't stay in one city and really do what I wanna do. I truly enjoy goin' different places and seein' different people. True, sometimes it can bring about a little hardship, because sometimes it can go a little further, or can get a little more difficult to do than you want. But let's face it: When you're blessed doin' what you really truly love doin', I mean, my God, don't you know its gonna cost you something? You know what I mean? Really. I hear too many people who *have* to work. They gotta live. And every day of their lives they do jobs, and they really don't care about it. And yet I feel, honestly, the people are with me and they've been with me, they support me, and I'm doin' what I love doin'. So it's worth it for me to go and I meet people, and I guess I'm just vain enough to want to get as many people as I can.

I've never called myself a genius. I didn't give that title to myself. And truly, I think it's a great compliment. I mean, it's a wonderful thing to have people feel that way about you. That's really putting you on a high pedestal. But I never thought of myself as a genius. In fact, I know without a doubt I'm not a genius. I mean, I don't kid myself. But I feel good that the people love what I do so much that this is the kind of compliment that they bestow upon me. It's really beautiful. But I'm truly just a plain cat, man. I think I do what I do well, and that's proba-bly it. Of course, the main key to me is that everything I do, it's truly what I feel. And if people, as it turns out, just happen to feel what I feel, then it sort of works out nicely.

Even today I'm this way: I love good music. I don't care where it comes from. Whether it's classical ... and people misunderstand. They think just because it's classical, or just because it's an opera, that it's gotta be good. There's been some awful operas written; don't fool yourself. Some terrible classical music written. The thing of it is, music is such a big tree, with so many branches. And of course, as you know, you can find some good and bad in every art, whether it's painting, scupture, or whatever. And I think that for me, I enjoy good classical music. I enjoy the blues — love to sing the blues. I love to play good jazz. I love to take a country song — I'm not a Charlie Pride; I mean, I don't think of myself as a country singer — but I love to take country music and sing it my way. You know, put my own self into it and make it become *me*. That's what I enjoy doing.

As a youngster comin' up, there were things that I wanted to do. For instance, I wanted to make a record someday. Now can you imagine a kid, nine years old, sayin' "Oh, if I could just make a record"? 'Cause in my mind, that was really the ultimate of success. I mean, that would really be saying that you was really into what you was doing, you really was into music. And I thought if I could make a record, that would prove I was great. So the day when I made my first record was a big thing, number one. Or I'd tell myself, "Oh, if I could just play in Carnegie Hall one day," or, "If I could just have my own band one day, or my own trio." Which is what I first started with, a trio. Then I had a small band, and then I said, "Oh, I hear so much that could be done with a big band, I'd love to have a big band." You know, these are things that I wished for.

And then when I started making records, I said, "Wouldn't it be nice one day if I could honestly win a Grammy." And then one year Sinatra and I had a little thing where we were both nominated for the best male vocalist, or something, and I won by four votes. Isn't that great to do that? You know, to be in competition with the best in the world. That's *it* to do that.

Things have happened to me in my life, I have to tell you. In spite of tragedies — and I've had many tragedies in my life, truly — but on the other hand, I've had many things happen to me in my life that the public made me feel ... I would've never dreamed. There was no way I would've even thought about, truly. I had a thing that they did in Georgia for me, where they honored the song "Georgia" as the state song. They already had a state song, but they took it away and used my version. I mean, if anybody had told me this would happen in the state of *Georgia!* What can I tell you?

RAY CHARLES: 'Music to me is the same as my breathing. It's not separate. It's not something I do on the side. How can you stop breathing?'

When I write songs, I try to think about everyday. Because every day I see the lives of people. I'm among people. It's the same as someone who writes for soap operas. You see life, and you put it in your songs. It doesn't mean that everything you sing about has to necessarily have happened to you. But life is life. And the most common thing among people is love affairs. You know, falling in and out.

What has happened is that more people have become aware, not so much of my music, but of black music *period*. Because of many white artists who have taken black music and "presented" it — if you want to put it that way — to the masses. And these artists, of course, they said, "This is who I listen to. I listen to B.B. King, I listen to Muddy Waters, I listen to Ray Charles," and da-da-da-da-da-da. So naturally, the other populace began to say, "Maybe we'll start to listen, too." And so I think there was an evolution that did take place. You see, musicians get among themselves. I mean, blacks among whites and whites among blacks. And so what happened is, what I was doing, you had people come along like Elvis Presley, the guy that did "Blue Suede Shoes," and the Beatles and folks like that, and they made the masses more aware of the music.

I make music because I breathe. Music to me is the same as my breathing. It is not separate. It's not something I do on the side. When people ask me when am I gonna retire, there ain't no retirin'. I *can't* retire. How can you stop breathing? When I retire from music, I'll be gone. I mean, that'd be the end of me, truly. I just hope that I can continue to inspire young people to play good music. And I hope that I continue myself to make people feel good with my own music. And if I'm able to do that, then truly, that's the key to me. *(Jivin' Johnny Etheredge; Sept. 13, 1985.)*

❦

No one represents what R&B means like Ike Turner. He was a talent scout and record producer. He was there when Jackie Brenston cut "Rocket 88." He was at the Sun Studios when Howlin' Wolf recorded. In 1954 he recorded a song, "Boxtop," with Anna Mae Bullock. She was billed as Little Ann. Six years later she would be known as Tina Turner, and with Ike they would cut powerhouse R&B, everything from "It's Gonna Work Out Fine" to "Oo Poo Pah Doo" to "River Deep, Mountain High" (which Ike was credited for but did nothing on) to a remake of Creedence Clearwater Revival's "Proud Mary" that went top five in 1971. Ike and Tina split several years later. Tina went on to have a successful solo career. Ike went on to have scrapes with the law, drug convictions and no solo career. But that was the way of R&B.

Ike Turner: I was born in Clarksdale, Mississippi. Lots of people came from there: Washboard Sam, B.B. King, Johnny Ace, Roscoe Gordon, Howlin' Wolf, Willie Nix, James Cotton. I came up with a lot of these people. James Cotton.

I was a bad kid. I hit my stepfather behind the head with a two-by-four, man. He whipped me. I caught myself running off from home. I hitchhiked a ride to Memphis. I was nine years old, something like that. I got a job at the Hotel Peabody in Memphis, a hall boy, cleaning doors. Man, I was so hungry, I was snapping at the wind. I'm serious.

I went back to Mississippi. I went to West Memphis, and that's where I met Joe Bihari, and he was at Sam Phillips' studio. You heard of Phineas Newborn? They was recording somebody, trying to get the guy to do the piano part. Anyway, I went in there when they took a break. I was sitting there messing with the piano. I had some shorts on, a shirt hanging, looked like I didn't have any pants. I started playing the piano, he said, "That's what I want." That's how we got in. We cut "Rocket 88."

Jackie Brenston and His Delta Cats. It was [Sam Phillips'] idea to do that. He set it up. We went there that Wednesday; man, we got arrested three times going over there. Speeding, one time. We had the bass on top of the car, it blew off, the big basses. We had a lot of trouble that day. It was raining. We got to Memphis, we didn't record that day, and we had to stay there until that night. Anyway, we put that song together and cut it.

It's amazing, man, just listening to it. The drums, where they put the drops in there, man, they're doing that stuff today. I was really ahead of my time, man.

When I met the Bihari Brothers, Joe Bihari put me on a salary, man, and I was getting a check every Monday and Wednesday from out here at Modern Records Company. In those days in Mississippi, the highest job wasn't but $25 a week. I was getting $40 and sometimes $80 and $100, like twice a week. They bought me my first car, my first Buick, '49 Buick. I was doing great.

In those days, Leonard Chess was coming down to Memphis, we would cut a song like "Moaning At Midnight" on Wolf. Soon as Chess would leave town, we would send the same record to L.A., to the Bihari brothers. We would get money double. Nobody ever signed no contracts.

In 1954 I was playing 14 jobs a week. I went to St. Louis to do one show, went back to Mississippi, packed my clothes, moved back to St. Louis.

I met Anna Mae Bullock in St. Louis in 1956. Her sister, Aileen Bullock, was going with the drummer, Eugene Washington. She brought this girl over — "She can sing, my sister." I said, "Yeah," because everyone thinks they can sing around St. Louis. I never would give her the microphone. You play 45 minutes, rest 15. We took an intermission, man, while the band took 15, man, this girl took the microphone, gave it to Tina, I heard her sing, man, that's when we got to be friends. I took her to the house, listened to her sing.

After "Rocket 88" I finally — Jackie and I broke up — every time I get a hit record on somebody, they split. Then man, I was doing a song for Art Lassiter; he's a singer in St. Louis. I wrote "A Fool In Love" for him. Tina and I were buddies, man. I would take her with me everywhere I go. This guy came down and borrowed $90 to get some tires — Art Lassiter — and I gave him the money, man. I'd been working on the song at the house with him and he didn't show up at the studio, so we was out at the studio and they only had one or two tracks then. Tina knew the words just sitting at the piano with me, when I was doing it with him. The guy at the studio said, "Why don't you let me put her voice on it as a guide, and I'll put it on one track and I'll put the band on the other track." So that's what we did. When I put it on there, I carried it to the Club Imperial in St. Louis and all the kids said, "Put it out like it is." So I sent it to the record company.

Phil Spector was doing his thing with the *TNT* movie. He wanted us to do something on that; while I was doing that, he got the idea he wanted to cut Tina. I agreed to let him do that. I thought "River Deep" was great, man. It was a big record ... except America. White stations say it was too black; black stations say it was too white. That was a good record; you've got to play it loud.

"Proud Mary" came from messing around with Spector. That's when I got the idea — "rolling, rolling." We cut the record down there at United. I don't even like the record, man. I was just doing something to get a side. The other side, "Mosquito's Tweeter," the other side is what I was going with.

Tina and I weren't like man and wife. We were more like brother and sister. People say, "You husband and wives, brothers and sisters?" I say, "We're sisters."

When you don't agree, man, we'd never agree with nothin'. When I'd put, "Hey, hey, hey, wow," in "Fool In Love," they didn't want to do that. When I'd put in, "Gong, gong, gong," they didn't want to do that. In "Proud Mary," when I went to the fast part, they didn't want to do that. Everything I do, man, it's always right. They always laugh about it. I have a complex about that. *(Steve Propes; Nov. 3, 1989.)*

2. Goin' Down Slow

Rock 'n' roll descended — or ascended, if you prefer — from the blues. Rock borrowed the 1-4-5 chord pattern of rural folk blues, and most of its themes. It borrowed blues songs for material, and continues to do so. But mostly it borrowed the instrumentation and sound. The amplified guitar, bass and drums were the basic blues instruments. Country music added steel guitars and fiddles; R&B added horns. The blues kept things basic, and so did rock.

Blues records and blues artists either inspired rock artists or gave them most of their material outright. Eric Clapton grew up listening to Muddy Waters; the Rolling Stones were practically a Jimmy Reed cover band. Led Zepplin crunched Howlin' Wolf and didn't give him credit. Elvis Presley's first records included "Milkcow Blues Boogie" and Arthur Crudup's "That's All Right (Mama)." Robert Johnson influenced everyone. The impact of the blues on rock could be direct, as when Cream copped Sonny Boy Williamson, or subtle, as in the angular thwack and rough harmonica of the Beatles' "Love Me Do," or the vocal inflections in an early Roy Orbison song. But the impact was there.

Blues-record labels tended to be small and regional. Local performers would cut songs on local labels. If the songs were popular enough, they would be leased to larger labels. One of the most influential small labels was Trumpet. The label was based in Jackson, Miss., and cut some of the best Mississippi Delta blues performers: Sonny Boy Williamson, Elmo James and Willie Love. Trumpet cut big-city blues and dabbled in R&B and country. It lasted from 1950 to 1955 and cut about 100 records, but the impact of those records is still being heard, anytime someone puts the needle down on Cream's "Eyesight to the Blind" or the Hindu Love Gods' "Hoochie Coochie Man."

The co-founder of Trumpet Records was Lillian McMurry.

Lillian McMurry: My husband Willard was in the furniture business, and I was his book-keeper. In the early '50s, Willard bought out a hardware store at 309 North Farish Street, where the black and white downtowns intersected. Willard sent me down there to sell out all the stock. In the front were a few old 78s. There were no such thing as 45s or albums then.

Anyway, I'd never heard a black record before. But this white guy Campbell and two brothers that were black, named Green and Willard, were sent over to the store to help me, and started playing a record by Wynonie Harris. I'd never heard anything with such rhythm and freedom before. Campbell and the two brothers told me how prized the "race" records were to black people and how you had to order them from wholesale houses in New Orleans. Shortly thereafter, Willard and I were going to New Orleans on business and I had Campbell make up a list of records to buy. He listed some of the blues artists, and Sister Rosetta Tharpe for spiritual and Hank Williams for country. I didn't evey know who Hank was much less the others. I figured I could play the records through a speaker outside the shop and attract people off the street.

When I got to New Orleans, some of the distributors laughed, but they kindly told me where to get which labels I had listed and I only bought what Campbell had listed. When we got back to Jackson we sold those out pretty damn quick, along with all the old stock in our store. Before I realized what was happening, I was calling orders to New Orleans and Memphis and selling all the records I could get.

I went home and asked Willard if I could keep the store, running a combination record and furniture shop. He said, "Sure." So he stocked it with furniture and I had shelves built for records to nearly cover a whole wall. The storefront was painted a bright yellow, and an ad agency was hired to do our logo. The name painted on the window was "Record Mart — Furniture Bargains," with the outline of a couple jitterbugging with sparks and notes flying from their feet and a phonograph record.

This was the last days of race records before the mid-'50s and rock 'n' roll. There weren't many record stores at all, except in the big cities. White folks didn't buy enough records to put in your eye. Basically it was a black market. We bought a few hillbilly and pop records, but basically it was a black market.

I bought three hours a day on WRBC with Woodson "Woody" Wall — the "Ole Hep Cat." It went so well that I got in the mail-order business. I bought stuff like old RCA 78s. Large lots of old blues 78s like Tampa Red, Big Boy Crudup and Washbord Sam. Radio listeners could order out package deals made up of old and current blues. From the replies we made a mailing list and sent free catalogs. We sometimes has 1,500 orders a day; mostly they were to rural areas with no shops. We never had more than a 2 percent return on CODs, which is unheard of today. The Record Mart show beamed out to at least six states, sometimes more, even all the way to Cuba. I tried to buy time on other stations but all I got was, "We don't play black music."

All the big stars used to make personal appearances at the Record Mart promoting their local bookings. The whole street would be full of black people to see the stars. Then we'd load up and go on up to the radio station and do interviews on the *Record Mart* show. Sometimes there'd be so many artists on the air at one time that Woody would shove me on the air while he looked for records. I remember Joe Liggins, the Trumpeteers, Charles Brown, Lowell Fulsom and Ray Charles on the same show.

Most of the R&B artists were booked across the river from Jackson in the "dry bootleg" county on the infamous "Gold Coast," or at Willie Stevens' off Delta Drive. The spiritual groups worked at black theaters, Campbell College (now Jackson State) or in church. Willie Love told me that a church on Farish that booked quartets had moonshine stored underneath it and a restaurant next to the Record Mart was caught running booze out of the water faucets! I tended to my own business and the blacks knew it, and respected me and the Record Mart folks.

We had listening booths in the shop along with the record players on the counter. Groups of black men would crowd into the booths and I found out they were singing spirituals along with the records. Some of them were really good too! By the middle of 1950 I started thinking, "Why can't I make a record?" Gads, I didn't know what I was getting into.

I liked the singing of a group later named the St. Andrews Gospelaires and signed them to a contract. I got Woody Wall and an engineer at WRBC to record them one night after the station closed. After that session I started looking for other groups. The Southern Sons came along, so I signed them and recorded them at Scott's Radio Service Studio. Next I recorded the Earl Reed Orchestra and country artists Kay Kellum and Roy Harris at Scott's. We recorded old soft sonic discs without even a hot needle. If we made a boo-boo we had to throw it away.

The first contracts and recording were done in my name. Then Willard and our lawyer said we needed to incorporate and the Diamond Record Company Inc. was formed. We wanted to call the label Diamond, but we couldn't get the rights because somebody else had the name. So we decided to call the label "Trumpet," after Gabriel's trumpet in the Bible. People blow trumpets in all types of music, so it seemed logical.

I got six records together and hired a salesman to travel the South. He went out and blew money and ran up a big car bill in Memphis so I fired him. That was bad enough but then disaster really hit. All our masters burned in a fire at Master Record Co. in Chicago. After the fire we had to start over making Trumpet Records.

We made some new recordings including Sonny Boy's "Eyesight To The Blind" backed with "Crazy About You Baby," that were ready for the market. But we needed distributors. I spent a fortune trying to set up distributors, but to no avail. One distributor who'd been sent records told me he didn't want any blankety-blank Trumpet Records!

Well, I figured that if a mule won't go, you gotta get his attention — you hit him over the head with a board. So we sent letters with return postcards inside to all the radio stations so they could mark what they program and the DJs' names. We got over 3,000 replies and then sent them free records. The DJs played the records and got the distributors' attention, and they started calling us for Trumpet Records. We gave the distributors free samples with a 5 percent privilege every six months. We wound up with 36 distributors that way.

Diamond Record Company began signing and cutting sessions on other artists at Scott's, and we traveled a lot to try equipment at other studios but most were a disappointment. I tried sending Sonny Boy and Willie Love to Houston; they had a great time entertaining everyone on the train, but when they got to the session the engineer called me in the middle and he said he couldn't get anything. Then Sonny Boy and Willie got on the phone and begged me to come to Houston because they couldn't record without me. Finally I just told them to come on home.

So we set some recording equipment in the Cedars of Lebanon Club in Jackson and lined up all our artists. Bill Harvey, the great musician from Memphis, was hired to rehearse the musicians. We cut 42 sides working three days and two nights straight. We had eight hits out of the session even though I lost my voice for two months from the strain.

I had an advantage over some producers being so close to the record shop and hearing what sold. But then, if you had the No. 1 *Billboard* R&B hit, you'd be lucky to sell 50,000. We hardly did that well, but we did well with Sonny Boy's "Nine Below Zero" backed with "Mighty Long Time" — a double-barreled hit — "Too Close Together" and "Cat Hop." Willis Love Had "V-8 Ford Blues" backed with "Nelson Street Blues," which sold well over the R&B areas.

After Sonny Boy died, I finally found out from his two his two sisters that he was born in 1908 and that his real name was Aleck Rice Miller. He even married Mattie under the name Willie Williamson. His two sisters said he was just a teenager when he "borrowed" a man's mule, painted him another color and rode him off. But the paint washed off and Sonny Boy got caught and was sent to the pen. A guard let him slip off because he liked Sonny Boy and his harp playing. He changed his name from Rice Miller so he wouldn't have to go back to jail.

How I found him, one day Curtis Dossett told me about this harmonica player that sang the blues somewhere in the Delta. So my brother, Curtis and I took off looking for this black artist, I didn't even know his name. We started in Flora and drove all the way to Greenwood, but nobody would tell my brother or Curtis anything. They didn't know how to talk to black people. I wasn't scared but they wanted to do the talking.

Finally we got to Belzoni and stopped in front of a little shack that had a jukebox in it. Curtis and my brother went in and came back without finding a thing. So I said, "They think you're the sheriff looking for him. Let me get out and talk."

So this black lady came to the door, and I told her I was Lillian McMurry from the Record Mart in Jackson. She said, "Yes'um. I hears your show all the time; come right in." I told her who I was looking for and said, "He's a harmonica player and I don't even know his name. But they say he plays and sings the blues. I want him to make a record for me." So she says, "Yes'um; he's here." So she goes in the back room out comes Mattie [Sonny Boy's wife]! So I met Mattie and she said, "He's not here now but he'll be back shortly." I gave her my name and address and telephone number and Sonny Boy called the following Friday.

Sonny Boy picked the musicians and paid 'em what he could get 'em for out of his advances. Sonny Boy used Willie Love or Dave Campbell on piano. Elmo James or Joe Willie Wilkins on guitar, although B.B. also filled in on one session.

Willard would send a driver from the furniture store to get some "joy juice" demanded by the musicians, and things would get going. Sonny Boy, Willie and Elmo all could turn a fifth upside down and kill it like that! Then Sonny Boy would get an idea and work on it. Sometimes we'd be in the studio until 2 a.m. until we recorded it right. If he said "Let's get outta here" or made a few boo-boos while recording, that was alright as long as the feeling was in it because that's what sold records.

Sonny Boy was as hard on the musicians as he was on himself. He would get mad at musicians and tell 'em off. I didn't mind a few cuss words because I'd be in the mixing room with the pots open and they didn't know I could hear them. If it was funny, I'd get down behind the viewing window, until I stopped laughing.

One day Sonny Boy finished a session where he got real angry at this one musician. He and the musicians were coming through where I was sitting and Sonny Boy started yelling, "You mother------" at the musician. Well, I'd never heard anything like that before, even though I thought I heard everything. So I said, "Sonny Boy, you wait here." I wanted the rest of the musicians to leave, so I wouldn't embarrass him in front of the other musicians. So I told him, "Sonny Boy, you get your hat and your coat and anything that belongs to you and get out of here and don't ever come back!"

The next day Sonny Boy went down to the furniture store to see Willard and he was crying. He told Willard, "I'm awful sorry, Mr. Willard; I ain't slept a wink." So Willard told Sonny Boy, "Stay away from her for a few days and let her cool off. She'll kill you for sure because she's got your gun. She's liable to shoot you with your own gun."

Sonny Boy came back a few days later and Willard told him it was all right to come by the office, but to throw his hat in first to see if I'd shoot it! So Sonny Boy came to my office and told the bookkeeper that he was there to see me and to apologize. Sonny Boy threw his hat in and waited. Finally he came in and started apologizing all over the place. I said, "Sonny Boy, I told you before about cursing at people. I've been told that at personal appearances you've used such language. You denied it, but now I believe it." Sonny Boy swore he never used bad language, and I forgave him and he never used it in my presence again.

There's just no way explaining Sonny Boy. Whiskey, women and fancy clothes is the way Sonny Boy lived. Without my knowledge he used to order two or three fancy suits and have them delivered to the Record Mart for me to pay for! As for money, sometimes he'd get $100 in the morning, blow it, and get another $100 in the afternoon and not give his wife a dime.

Sonny Boy was always good to me and Willard. If he knew he was gonna have a record released he'd come from Chicago or wherever he was to pack the new release and he'd work just like a dog. Usually during this time Sonny Boy and me and sometimes Mattie would work on songs for the next session but, of course, Mattie and I never got credit.

We constantly searched for better ways and a different sound from everybody. After "Nine Below Zero" and "Mighty Long Time," two guys from RCA, Don Law from Columbia and Ted Black called me to ask how I got that sound. I guess it didn't pay off monetarily, but it was rewarding.

Sonny Boy brought Elmo to me, but he got a big head and you couldn't tell him anything. He couldn't get any original material together. I didn't even know until a few years ago that he didn't write "Dust My Broom." We even lent him money against his royalties. All those records he cut after he left us sounded like "Dust My Broom." A night-club owner in Canton told me that when Biharis' got through riding Elmo around Canton in their Cadillac, Elmo demanded that all blacks call him "Mr. James." Biharis even tried to get Sonny Boy and Willie too. My lawyer and I caught two of the Bihari brothers in the act of cutting Lonnie Holmes and his Dark Town Boys that I had on contract.

Sonny Boy and Willie were real close friends. They used to jam together and have fun. Oh, how I wish I'd taped some of those things. They used to do a thing like the "Two Black Crows Minstrel Show," battling lines at each other. Willie would dance in unison with Sonny Boy while they played their instruments. Then they'd sing together and shuffle all over the studio. They'd just go back and forth shufflin' and buck dancing, big Sonny and little Willie with his spats on. It was so joyously funny you just couldn't believe it.

I tried to warn Willie about drinking too much, but he didn't listen. He got sick and had to go to the hospital. We paid our private doctor to care for him and cathetherize him or he'd have burst. The day he died [Aug. 19, 1953], I went to see him and he said, "Miss Lillian, you and Mr. Willard were better to me than my own people."

Our distributors started demanding more return privileges and more promotion records. Some started getting into us for huge bills on hit records, paying slowly and, worst of all, declaring bankruptcy on which we'd get paid about one cent on a dollar, or nothing at all. I couldn't do business that way, no matter how much I enjoyed the work. If Trumpet couldn't get its money, there was no use operating. You can't imagine how much money went down the drain. I worked several years paying off bills rather than going into bankruptcy.

I never realized what I was getting into when I started in the music business. There was lots of fun, but there were so many heartbreaks, too. But I guess that's what the record business is all about. *(Almost Slim; July 6, 1984.)*

☙

Chicago was, is, and will be one of the hotbeds of blues recording. The sound of Chicago blues is urban — steamy, gritty, city-smoke-in-your-nostrils blues. Chicago blues features guitar powerhouses and big shouting vocalists. Chicago produced Magic Sam and Buddy Guy and Jimmy Reed and Chess Records.

Jimmy Reed recorded many sides for a Chicago label called Vee Jay. Vee Jay, along with Chess, was Chicago's most prominent blues and R&B label. It launched the careers of the Spaniels, Eddie Taylor and Betty Everett, but along the way also wound up with Little Richard, the Four Seasons, Arthur Godfrey and the Beatles. Vee Jay was a family-run label, and one of the most curious labels in rock or blues.

Sid McCoy and Vivian Carter started it, and later Betty Chiappetta took it over. Calvin Carter was the label's A&R man, Jimmy Butler recorded R&B for the label, and "Red" Holloway was part of the house band. Bob Crewe brought the Four Seasons to the label.

Sid McCoy: Vivian Carter and I started out together in radio. There's a man in Chicago by the name of Al Benson, probably the biggest black disc jockey in the history of the business. He controlled 10 commercial hours a day. Benson came up with a contest to find a young, deserving fellow and girl to put on the air. Vivian was the girl that won, and I was the fellow.

Vivian Carter: There must have been 800 or a thousand people there to get an audition. You had to write a commercial and read it for him. I had never thought about writing a commercial, but I heard him announce this contest about 10 minutes before he went off the air. He said he was looking for a girl and boy disc jockey, and if you would like to enter, write a one-minute commercial and be at one of the hotels at seven o'clock. That was like 10 minutes to six when I heard about it. I hadn't even thought about a commercial, but I listened to his commercial on a clothing store and jotted down notes while he was talking, and I wrote my commercial that way. Winning the contest gave me a radio show, a 15-minute program from 1:00 to 1:15. We each got a 15-minute shot, and that's how we both broke into radio.

Jimmy Butler: There's a man by the name of Calvin Carter. He did A&R for Vee Jay Records, a company man. His job was to get out and cut hits. Today, he would be called a promoter. Calvin did it for 12 years, and when you list the acts he signed, using no other ears to depend on but his own, it reads like a Who's Who in the music business. He covered every base. For example, gospel acts he signed: Five Blind Boys, the Staple Singers, the Swan Silvertones, Maceo Woods, the Raspberry Singers. In the blues field, he signed Jimmy Reed and John Lee Hooker. In R&B, the Dells, the Spaniels, myself, the El Dorados. Female singers such as Priscilla Bowman and Betty Everett. The jazz artists included Eddie Harris and the MJT+3.

Unfortunately, the only industry people knowing him today are those who came in contact with him back in those days; but I think he deserves a place in R&B music on the same level as Phil Spector.

Calvin Carter: Vivian and Jimmy borrowed $500 to produce the first record, borrowed it from a pawnshop.

When we first met Jimmy Reed in 1953, he was actually working in Chicago in the stock-yards, where he was cutting up cattle. He was in Chicago and he was playing harmonica for a guy called King David that we were interested in. So we were having a rehearsal with them one day, and we heard Jimmy play. We asked him, "Say, let me ask you a question. Do you have any songs that you've written?" And he says, "No, but I've got some I've made up." And that was how we got Jimmy Reed.

Sid McCoy: Even before I started A&Ring things for Vee Jay, I used to go down to Universal and just sit there, sit in on the sessions, because they were really so fabulous. Calvin did the recording sessions with Jimmy Reed, which were always a gas. There was first of all the music that came out, and then there was the color. Jimmy Reed would sit there on a drum case, with the mike adjusted to it. Next to him would be his wife, Mama Reed, and Mama Reed would have to speak the lyric to him. He'd say, "Speak the lyric to me, Mama Reed!" And they would be things that he had composed himself, in many instances. She would be there to lay it on him phrase by phrase as he went through it. Just fantastic.

Calvin Carter: Jimmy Reed was something else. He'd get drunk the day of the session, so I had a police officer that I'd get to "arrest" him the night before and take him to jail. I'd come down the next morning and pick him up and take him right to the studios. He never knew that, I never told him that, because I don't think he would have appreciated it that I put him in the tank overnight. *[Laughs]* Well, that's the only way that I could get him down to the studio sober.

In most of his dates, he was drunk, he was dead drunk. If you notice, he slurred so very badly. But that's because he felt so insecure. He could read, but he was playing guitar and harmonica at the same time, so his wife would have to whisper the lyric in his ear. Sometimes you could hear her leaking through the microphone, because at that time we didn't have vocal isolation, a single channel for all the vocals. One day Jimmy Reed was singing a song called "You Don't Have To Go." And you know how the old blues used to be: "Oh, baby, you don't have to go; oh, baby, you don't have to go." So he starts off the song and she gives him the first line, "Oh baby, you don't have to go ...," and he sings, "Oh baby, you don't have to go." Then she says, "Now repeat it." And he threw the guitar down and says "Damn it, repeat, hell; you tell me what to sing. If you're going to sit up there and tell me, then, damn it, you better tell me!"

When he finished the song, we would always tell him, "Don't talk at the end of the song," because it would spoil the take." So we'd say, "Sshhh!" or, "Keep silent and we'll give you the cue when it's okay to talk." One song we'd done had taken a long time, and by the time we were done, just as we finished a good take, Jimmy popped a string and said, "Awww, man. That ain't the way that was supposed to went!" He said the funniest things on these record dates. I intended to put out an album of outtakes before the company went out of business, because I always kept the microphones open as soon as Jimmy came in for the date. We recorded every-thing that he did; I had a wealth of that kind of stuff. There weren't any curse words on there, but it was just like what Amos and Andy did. I don't think Jimmy Reed would have appreciated it. It wouldn't have been funny to him. He wasn't really trying to be funny; that's just the way he was. When he was being very serious and you thought that it was very funny, he would think that you were talking down to him.

Betty Chiappetta: In 1955, they also started recording Eddie Taylor, who never became the big artist that he should have been. They started recording Eddie as an individual artist, but he had been backing up Jimmy Reed on almost all his sessions.

Calvin Carter: Eddie Taylor was actually very important for Jimmy Reed; he really made the Jimmy Reed sound come out. Eddie played rhythm guitar and bass guitar, and he was the boo-gie. He would get a good roll; he was fantastic. He just didn't sing too well, and he was, like, well, in the background. We put a record out on him. "Just A Bad Boy" and "Big Town Playboy." Both sold pretty well, but he just didn't have the presence that Jimmy Reed or John Lee Hooker had in his vocal style. But he was actually the force behind the boogie feel that made Jimmy Reed famous. Jimmy played the single-note harmonica that was very outstanding, but to me it was that boogie of Eddie Taylor that really made it stand out.

We got John Lee Hooker out of Detroit. He was the guy who never rhymed. You know, he just didn't have the usual rhyme lines. We only did one take on everything he did; he'd never do it the same way. Of course, you know he couldn't read music, but nobody could play with him either. His timing was off; he could only play by himself. So I put some plywood on the studio floor on the tile floor, and that would be his drums, and I just used him on guitar. Sometimes I would use Eddie Taylor on some of John Lee Hooker's things that had a Jimmy Reed feel in the background music.

Sid McCoy: I can remember sitting around on Friday evenings at Vee Jay, after the work day, and sitting around having a taste, and telling stories. More often than not, Jimmy Reed stories would occur. Al Smith, who was a bass player and producer for Jimmy, went out on the road and kind of looked after Jimmy Reed. They were someplace playin' the chitlin' circuit, and Jimmy Reed wanted to drive, and of course Al was trying to prevent him from doing it, but Jimmy was insistent and so he gets behind the wheel anyway ...

Red Holloway: Well, he ran into a fellow's car. We were in Mississippi. This fellow jumped out and said, "Goddammit, I ain't had this car three months, and my wife puts one dent in it, and goddamn, here you put another one on this side!"

So Jimmy got out and said, "I's sorry. Look here, I pay for the damage. My name's Jimmy Reed and I ..."

"YOU Jimmy Reed?"

"Yeah, I'm Jimmy."

"Oh, man! I was just gettin' tickets for your dance tonight! Man, don't worry 'bout that dent. Hey George! Come look here; this is Jimmy Reed here."

"Well, I'll pay for ..."

"Oh, don't worry 'bout that fender; hell, I'll get it fixed!"

Another time we were down south, and that's during the time they had a lot of bootleg whiskey and stuff, and people were dying from this white lightning, because it was homemade and had all kinds of chemicals in it. Jimmy had bought two gallons of white lightning, and the next day after he bought them we saw the paper where about 12 people died, so we showed this to him and told him, "You better pour that stuff out." This particular state where we were was dry, and we were going to be there for a week, so that's why Jimmy had bought two gallons. Well, he started crying when he poured it out. "This breaks my heart. You don't think a shot would hurt me?"

"Well, it might kill you, I don't know. You can drink it and die." So he poured it out.

Boy, he was a funny cat. There were so many funny things that happened on the road. He was just a natural country blues singer, and the more he slurred his words, the better they like him. But he was one funny cat, believe me. It was quite an experience.

Calvin Carter; Aw, Jimmy Reed was something else. He had a hose in his harmonica rack, which led down to his inside coat pocket, where he kept a bottle. He could suck the whiskey up through that.

Let me tell you the craziest story ever. We were playing a club in San Francisco, and Jimmy Reed was getting bald, so he bought a wig. About five minutes before we went on, I told him, "Look, Jimmy, you better go in the bathroom, you know, because we don't want to have any problems." When Jimmy had to go, he had to go, know what I mean? So he says, "Where is it?", so I said, "Well, there it is."

Now, right next to the bathroom there's a big wall that was mirrored. So after about four minutes, Jimmy wasn't back, so I started getting nervous and I went to look for him. So when I got there, here he was just cussin' and tough, and I said, "Hey, Jimmy Reed, you been to the bathroom yet?"

And he says, "No," so I said, "Well what's the matter; man; c'mon!" And he says, "I been asking this cat for the last five minutes where the bathroom is, and he's too ugly to tell me!" And he'd been looking at himself in the mirror!

Betty Chiapetta: Randy Wood, who at the time was the West Coast sales manager for Vee Jay, was responsible for the Four Seasons coming to Vee Jay. Frankie Valli, who knew Randy, called him and played a dub of "Sherry" over the phone. Randy said that it sounded great, so Frankie sent him the dub. So Randy took the dub to Huggy Boy, one of the DJs in Los Angeles, who had a radio program that originated from a record store. They played the dub, and stores were getting calls like crazy — and there wasn't even any record yet!

Calvin Carter: At the time, we were pretty hot. We had the Four Seasons and we got a lot of airplay. There was a #1 record over in England at the time, and our lawyer, who represented us in other countries, was Paul Marshall. Trans Global, a company over there, had a #1 record and they asked us if we wanted it, and of course we wanted it. It was "I Remember You," by Frank Ifield. We took the record, and as a throw-in, they had a group and asked us if we would take them, too. The group turned out to be the Beatles, and we got a five-year contract on the Beatles as a pickup on the Frank Ifield contract.

We got into a little trouble financially because of the deal with the Four Seasons. We were giving them 16 cents per record including publishing, so therefore we were losing two points — 1.8 cents — for every record we sold with them. Now, the first three records sold in excess of 1 million each, so we got behind with them.

We were also set to release an album by the Beatles about that time [*Introducing The Beatles*], but we had too many items in our catalog already, and the distributors were complaining. So we eliminated some of these albums we were set to release, and the Beatles album was one of them, because the Beatles just did not sell very well the first time around. I kept the Beatles album in my desk drawer for several months after that.

We put the album out, and EMI, through Capitol, sued us to cease and desist. They got an injunction against us seemingly every week. They would get an injunction against us on Monday, and we would get it off on Friday, then we'd press over the weekend and ship on Monday; we were smooth, we had everybody alerted, and we were pressing records all the time on the weekends.

We finally made something out of the court settlement, because we just couldn't afford to fight that big a company. We kept what we had, and they had all future product. We were selling so many Beatles records, we just couldn't afford to fight for the five-year rights. At that point, we had even got a 10-year moratorium from our creditors on our outstanding bills, that we'd just keep them coming. There was a lot of pressure on us. We sold in one month's time about 2.6 million Beatles singles on Vee Jay and Tollie. Those were fantastic times. And right in the middle of this, we moved from Chicago to California. What a mess, what a mess. We got the Beatles and went from 15-20 employees to like 200 overnight. It was a Marx Brothers movie. *(Mike Callahan; May 1981.)*

❦

The sound of the blues that influenced so many rock musicians is the sound of Jimmy Reed and Muddy Waters. Willie Dixon was responsible for a good portion of that sound.

Dixon was a bass player by trade. He played in the legendary Big Three trio with Pianist Leonard "Baby Doo" Caston and Ollie Crawford. He launched the Chicago Blues All-Stars and played with Muddy Waters. Dixon was also a songwriter responsible for blues classics like "I Just Want To Make Love To You," "Back Door Man," "Hoochie Coochie Man," "You Shook Me," and "Wang Dang Doodle." He produced Koko Taylor and scores of other artists for Chess throughout the '60s and '70s. He also formed the Blues Heaven Foundation to preserve and encourage the blues and its players.

Willie Dixon did an album once called *I Am The Blues;* in many respects, he is.

Willie Dixon: You see, the blues is actually the root of all American music, and a lot of folks don't know this. The blues is the facts of life. And blues came from the various experiences that people have had in life all their life, and people decided they're going to sing about it. If a guy doesn't have a lot of education to work with, he has to sing it according to the way he feels. And a lot of times, a guy feels different from you but you don't know it, no more than just looking at it, and because if he can't explain it, he can't tell you. But I've been lucky enough — I don't

31

know if you'd call it lucky or unlucky — to have a bit of experience about all of it from my childhood days until the present day. And I know when a man is singing about something, what he's singing about and the ways he feels about it.

If a guy's singing about goin' up the country and he won't be back no more, and you say, "What does he mean he won't be back no more?" Well, he means what he says. He was probably in the South or somewhere where he wasn't getting the proper treatment or the proper understanding, and he feels like he's downtrodden. And he feels like it's the time to get the heck out of there because he's tired of this place. There was a fellow that asked me not long ago, "What do you mean by, 'Blues jumped a rabbit and jumped him for a salad now?' " Well, you see, if the guy had come along with me when I was in the South, there were many days when the dog didn't jump a rabbit or my old man didn't shoot a squirrel, and we didn't eat before we went to school. Then, when a guy says, "Goin' down slow," I know many people who could express that better if they could explain it. A fellow having enjoyed the best of his life in many places says, "I'm not going to be here much longer." And he starts thinkin' about it and says, "Someone write my mama and tell her the shape I'm in and tell her to don't send no doctor," and all these things. All

WILLIE DIXON: 'If the blues was better understood, the world would be a better place to live in.'

of these are the facts of life. And when the world understands this as the facts of life and quit trying to ridicule people because they think this is just something that they made up, then they'd make a better understanding. And a better understanding makes a better world all the way around.

I feel that if the blues were properly understood, the world would be a better place to live in. The average person that don't understand the blues can't realize what a position a person would be in when, in the first place, they took his country, in the next place, his language, the next place, his religion, and they took all of his traditions. And they forced him into other things that he disapproved of all around. It would be like you being forced to be an Indian or an African or something. You find you're doing the same thing your foreparents did. They brought them to the States to be a slave and work, and you're still being a slave and working. The other man supposed to be the boss; he's still the boss. So I feel people can be educated with what I call a blues education.

I was born in Vicksburg, Mississippi, July 1, 1915. Oh, yeah, it was a big family. My mother was the mother of 14 kids, but some of them died when they were babies. Her name was Daisy Dixon.

My mother wrote a lot of poems herself, but she was kind of spiritually inspired, with the biblical thing. And I can remember when I was in Jerusalem and I sent her back a Bible with one side of the page in Hebrew, the other English. They used to sing songs about Jerusalem in my happy home when I was a kid. And they just accepted biblical affairs as the word. And whatever anyone told them, that's what they accepted.

In the early '20s, I met Little Brother Montgomery. I used to follow Little Brother all up and down. One day they'd be on a wagon bed with horses and mules playing a piano up there and a clarinet with a guy with a megaphone. They're going to be playing a dance in the South Side Park in Marcus Bottom. Next two or three days, they'd come on with a Model T Ford truck bed and they'd have the same thing. I was just a barefoot kid. Every night I'd get a whippin' for being out all day and all night chasing this truck around. And Little Brother — he was little at that time!

The first time I ran away from home, I went out to this place in the country. I was about 12 years old and went to a place called Bovina, about 15 or 16 miles out of Vicksburg. My mother was looking for me, but I didn't know country kids had to work hard; I thought they had the same thing going for them that we had in Vicksburg, which was nothing. I'd go to school and maybe I'd go get slop for the pigs, and that was it. Anyway, I went out there and that's where I found out what work meant. Them guys out there were working like mad! I'd never seen the sun rise in my life. But they said they had to make money so they could come to Vicksburg. I was pretty fat and big, but I'd never done no work! I hadn't even cut wood with an ax. Eight or ten barrels of charcoal sold for 50 cents! That's when I started figuring my arithmetic — that's four of us got to split that. And I ain't got my money yet!

The first time I came to Chicago, I was 13. And then I had a sister living here named Katy Gibbs. She had married a guy named Ted Gibbs, and was living at 4716 South Forestville. I was working on an ice wagon here. They used to have a company called the L&N Ice Co. And at that time, they didn't have no Frigidaires, man, you had to put the ice on your shoulder and go all the way up to the fourth floor. Most buildings had three floors, but occasionally there'd be a fourth. And it seemed that everybody on a fourth floor wanted 100 pounds.

I grew up doing that. I thought I was making a lot of money, but I was making $20 a week. I'd go to school now and then, but my sister was trying to keep me in school, and I wouldn't go. They finally sent me back home after about a year, and I had to go back to school in Vicksburg. I went back to school there for a while. Thought I was going to be a fighter. And because I'd worked on the boats with those roustabouts — they pick up a barrel and truck it on off the gangplank. 'Cuz I was a big boy, I thought I was a man. I was pretty strong.

After I got to fighting, I fought at the YMCA two or three times, and I fought at four or five places around there, and then I came to Chicago. It was around 1936. I had a friend with whom I hoboed to New Orleans in 1935. And we didn't know where to find nothin' to eat but at the banana cart and the watermelon cart. I went with the steamer excursion boat going every night to St. Paul. I came back one day through Rock Island, Illinois, and caught a bus from Rock Island to Chicago. In Chicago, I met my sister, I lived with her, and then I decided I was going to finish my fighting career. I won the Golden Glove in 1937. Well, I did pretty good after I won the Golden Glove.

Yeah, the heavyweight champion in 1937! And then, after I won the Golden Glove, I got me a couple of managers. I had about five good fights, and turned pro in 1938. Anyway, after I turned pro I had three or four really good fights. They were taking a third of my money for management, and so much for my trainer, and I wasn't getting no money. And on top of that, people who'd fought less than me were getting $400 to $500 for their fights. I was getting $200 and thought I deserved more money. One day, we were discussing contracts — they had all the contracts written — but the contract that I hadn't signed! We got into a heated discusson, and wound up in a fight. We tore up the office and all got expelled. And at that time, I was training over at Eddie Nichols' gym. My manager really wanted us to cover up his dope racket; he didn't really care whether we won or not. But all the while, this fellow Baby Doo Caston was playing guitar around the gymnasium. We sat around all day when we wasn't practicing for a fight, singing.

I wasn't playing no bass at all. I was just singing. I used to sing bass all the time. So [Caston] said, "Hey, you ain't doing' nothin'. Why don't you come out nightclubbing with us?" I hadn't ever been in a nightclub in my whole life. So he and a guy called Evan Spencer, we got together and we went up and down Madison Street, all of 'em down Clark Street, everywhere. We used to sing the Ink Spots, the Mills Brothers and everybody.

Anyway, we went all the different places and I found out, hell, I was making more passing the hat than I was fighting! We'd wind up over in Jewtown [Maxwell Street] playing on Sunday with a water bucket and people would fill that water bucket up with pennies and nickels and a few dimes, you know. And we just put them in three piles, cuz we couldn't count all them pennies all day.

All along, I'd be writing songs. I'd try to turn them into popular tunes and nobody really cared. We was recording blues, even though we were playing a lot of popular things at the clubs, because when you go places playing, passing the hat, everybody's got a request for a different thing. And we had to spend a lot of time getting that together. But we recorded the blues: "Wee Wee Baby, You Sure Look Good To Me" and "The Signifying Monkey," "88 Boogie" and "Lonesome Blues."

That's when I started working at Chess, while I still had the Big Three Trio. Because I played pretty good bass. We was right out there on Madison Street, just gigging up and down there, me and Baby Doo. He made me a tin-can bass with just one string, and I played that thing all over Chicago. In fact, I've been trying to find somebody that has pictures of me on that tin can! Anyway, we used to jam with Muddy Waters when he first started out.

Well, Muddy wasn't on no label when we was jammin'! Him or Walter, either. And we went over there on 35th Street, over on the street where they cut the Dan Ryan Expressway, next to Jefferson. Anyway, we jammed with Muddy and one day he got to record, and he told Chess to call me up and see if I could play bass on his session. Well he recorded a couple things ahead of that time. They called me in Omaha, where I'd been working. That's right; Omaha, Nebraska. I was working at the Dundee Dell. So I came back and recorded with Muddy Waters and Robert Nighthawk. Nighthawk recorded that thing about "Sweet Black Angel." And then he had some girls singing behind him. Well, we'd already recorded "Wee Wee Baby, You Sure Look Good To Me" for both Delta and Bullet, which was the same company, and Columbia too. Then Baby Doo started having matrimonial trouble with his family. Every time we'd get onstage, there'd come the police and drag him off the stage! So we [the Big Three Trio] gave up for a while and I started working with Chess.

After they found out I was on the loose, I got a contract from Chess as a producer. And I was told the contract was as producer, songwriter and all like this. Chess started me and had me listen to the artists and see what I could make out of some of the songs they had, of if they didn't have songs that were properly sufficient, to try to write songs for them. I had a load of songs — I've had a load of songs ever since I was 10! And somehow or other, it looked as if some of them reached different [artists]. So as everyone came along, I had a song for them. Even Leonard Allen at the United States label wanted a few. And that's the way it went, up until Leonard [Chess] died. Then I worked with the company a while longer.

But the thing about it was that when Chess found they could use me more in the studio than as a would-be artist, they gave me a salary there. I figured it was a good thing because I got a pretty straight salary there. And I worked on salary 'til after Leonard died. At the same time, I was writing my own songs. I was with Arc Music; he and Chess had a deal. Under Arc Music, all my music was my own.

Leonard ran the company. There were a lot of understudies around there, but they really didn't understand the business like he did. After you've done business with the headman and then you have to do business with a substitute, you don't come up with the same agreement. It's that simple. Phil [Chess] took it over. Marshall [Leonard's son] didn't do much because he was on the move all the time and youngsters didn't have much time for it in the first place. I think they only reason Marshall was in it was because he was forced in it. It's like my kids; they wouldn't give a doggone about the music or nothin' else. They were forced in it because if you're going to eat around me, you got to play music. Or work. So they'd rather play music than work. *(Cary Baker; January 1982.)*

❦

The one thing above all others that attracted so many rock performers to the blues was the electric guitar. The electric blues guitar in the hands of Freddy King or a B.B. King sounded the way rock 'n' rollers wanted their electric guitars to sound — big and dirty, yelling and screaming with string bends and double-stops all over the place. It's the nature of blues to put the emotion of the song into the instrument as well as the voice. The best blues instrumentalists said as much with their instruments as the best blues singers did with their voices. And it was that emotion channeled through the guitar that was so appealing to rock 'n' rollers.

Freddy King was one of the biggest influences Jeff Beck, Peter Green, Jimmy Page, and Eric Clapton had. King's classic records included "Hideway" and "Have You Ever Loved A Woman" (which would later show up as a scorching cover version on Derek and the Dominos *Layla*). B.B. King became the blues' pre-eminent guitarist on the strength of records like "The Thrill Is Gone" and albums like *My Kind Of Blues*, though his songs have been covered less frequently than those of Freddy King or T-Bone Walker. B.B. King's role has been more as an ambassador, bringing the blues and the stinging, wide-vibrato sound of his electric guitar to the Fillmore, to prisons, to the Royal Albert Hall, to the rest of America and the rest of the world.

Freddy King: I know more about Chicago than anywhere else. See, I was born in Texas, went to school in Texas, then when I finished we went to Chicago to live. We'd often go there to visit, but after I finished school we went for good. Then, in 1963, I moved back to Dallas, made my home there. I've got investments there.

Well, as I said, I'd learned to play from my mother and my uncles. I was playing in Lightnin' Hopkins' style when I arrived then I started playing in Muddy Waters' style. Then, later on, I just started putting all those styles together with a bit of T-Bone Walker and B.B. King and made a style of my own. But I didn't start playing electric guitar until after we got to Chicago. I was 17. It was a Key guitar, then later it got stolen. After that I got a Sunnyland and that got stolen. I got my first Les Paul when I started work with Earlee Payton in 1956.

Sonny Thompson, who was A&R man for King at that time, came to check me out at Mel's Hide-Away Lounge, which is where I got the title "Hideaway" from. Sonny Thompson called me and said, "Do you want to record?" I said, "Yeah." So he said I should be there tomorrow. So I drove down, got out of the car, went into the studio and Smokey Smothers was recording. I helped him with his stuff and then got down to my session.

I guess I was more fortunate than a lot of the cats. I was a person who would always listen to older entertainers like Muddy Waters and Robert Jr. Lockwood. They'd say how they had been cheated, and I'd just sit there and take it all in. It was schooling me. During the '50s, a recording company would cut a session on you and they'd buy you a Cadillac. You never would pay for it, except you'd pay for it as long as you were with that company. But when I recorded I drove a Cadillac up to the recording studio and got out. A Cadillac didn't excite me.

Some of the older entertainers were only paid with a bottle of booze ...

Damn right, and some weren't paid with nothin'. How long can you go? That's it.

On those early cuts, I just went into the studio and done them myself. Wasn't nobody saying, "Do this one," or, "Do that one." They just said I should play how I feel. Then they got wise. They'd come down with songs and say, "Sing this," and I wouldn't feel it. Maybe it's right for someone else. Of course, they want you to sing it because they got the publishing on it. Say you want to record a song by Willie Dixon, who wrote "Hoochie Coochie Man." They'd say, "No, we don't want that! Sing this." So I quit for two years on account of that. I made up my mind that when I go into a studio, the producer and me would work together. If he's got a song I like, I'll do it. If I don't, throw it out. Now all the while I was on Shelter, I never turned down but one of Leon Russell's songs. But to force material on you just because they've got the publishing, I mean they wouldn't do that to Frank Sinatra.

Like I was saying, I always would listen. I don't want to give you the idea that the other cats are dumb, but maybe they just wanted to get a record out and were scared that if they said something then they'd be told, "No, man, we can't use you." I figure it like this: I know I can do my job and I can talk back shit to him, too, you know. If someone says, "We don't want your kind of music," then I can say, "Well, when I play, people dance, you know, they clap their hands, they give me a standing ovation. You're sitting behind a desk, you don't know nothing." *(Dave Booth and Colin Escott; June 22, 1984.)*

B.B. King: A preacher — my uncle's brother-in-law — who used to play in the church I attended first inspired my interest in the guitar. It was a Southern custom for adults to eat dinner earlier than the kids, and when this preacher came to visit he'd bring his guitar and lay it on the bed while he ate. It was challenging for me to get on the bed and fool with the guitar. One time he caught me playing it and I expected him to give me a real hard time. But he didn't; he showed me a few chords, and believe it or not, I still use them today.

I started to sing gospel music, using the guitar to tune up the group I played with. When I was introduced into the Army at age 18, I started playing around little towns, just standing on the corner. People asked me to play gospel tunes and complimented me real nicely: "Son, if you keep it up, you're gonna be real good some day." But the people who asked me to play the blues tunes normally tipped me, many times getting me beer. So that motivated me to play the blues, you might say. But I still feel the gospel all the time.

The roots of the blues is in the church. Most of us sang gospel before we did sing the blues. I went to those little towns to play blues, but I couldn't play in my hometown because the church people would have seen me.

I had a show called "The Sepia Swing Club" in Memphis, where I'd spin records for 55 minutes and gab inbetween. I wasn't restricted to playing any particular kinds of music, so I played everything from B.B. King to Bing Crosby. But I only played my own tunes if I had requests for them; I'm a little self-conscious about those things. Young and new players had a good chance with me because I'd spin their records. I didn't always take it as a personal thing like a lot of people [in radio] do today.

When I left Mississippi, my hometown of Indianola, I went to West Memphis, Arkansas, to get a job at a little cafe where they had food in the front and gambling in the back. The lady there told me that if I could go on the radio and advertise her place, then she would give me a job there, six nights a week, $12 a day. And $12 a day was more money than I ever heard of. I was making $22 a week! That was by driving tractors and doing everything to try and make ends meet. Now here I was making more than $22 in two days! That day they put me on the air, as a performer. Then about three months later they wanted a disc jockey.

The B.B. came from my radio show in Memphis, where they used to call me Beale St. Blues Boy. People would write in and call me either "Beale Street Boy" or "Blues Boy." Then they stopped writing it out and abbreviated it B.B. So I was B.B. King more than I was really Riley B. King.

Regarding the name of the guitar, I used to play in a place called Twist, Arkansas, every Friday, Saturday and Sunday night. It was a plantation town. I played a club that got really cold and they'd set a big garbage pail half-filled with kerosene in the middle of the floor for heating. Usually, people didn't disturb it. But one time two fellows started to fight and one knocked the other over onto this container. It spilled on the floor and it looked like a river of fire. Everybody started running for the front door, including B.B. King. But then I'd remember that I left my guitar inside so I went back for it. The building was wooden so it started falling in around me. I almost lost my life trying to save that guitar. The next morning we found two men trapped in one of the rooms burned to death. We also discovered that the two guys were arguing over a cook — a lady named Lucille. I never did meet her, but I named my guitar Lucille to remind me never to do anything like that again.

Believe it or not, it was harder to make records then. You didn't have 24 tracks as you do now. I've made records in the last 10 years and didn't even really know the song. I mean, you could sing it without really knowing it because they'd punching in this button and that button. Back in the early days you had to do it with the nitty-gritty. Going from mono to stereo was a big thing. Gosh, two tracks! Most of the time they'd put the rhythm, the horns and, say, the guitar, on one track and the vocal on the other. So it was actually harder to get a good record then.

The Fillmore itself had a special feeling and a real warmth to it. That was the first time I ever got a standing ovation before even going out. Just when they mentioned my name I got a standing ovation. Then when I came out onstage. I got another one. It was so emotional I cried. I couldn't help it.

Bill Graham had booked us in there and when I got there I thought maybe they had made a mistake because there was nothing out there but white kids. I used to play that auditorium before that and it was 80, 90 percent black. Now I was there and it was 98 percent white! I had never played like that.

When we pulled up in our old red bus, I sent my road manager out to find out if it was the right place, and, sure enough, Bill Graham came out and said that it was the right place. Man, I was shakin'! I had to go in there and walk over wall-to-wall kids.

So, yes, I was very happy that we had started to get white people, but I didn't understand it. When I first started, I thought that as an artist you should be able to play for anyone. It didn't happen like that at first, and then when it did start happening, I started to worry about why it was happening.

I don't think I've made as many [live albums] as I'd like to. I guess I've just been lucky to play in places that can be recorded well. Some of those events we really had to capture, such as when I played with the Crusaders and the Royal Philharmonic Orchestra. That's something that don't happen every day. Same thing as the Cook County Jail; those kinds of historical events should be available on record.

I try to make each day what it is and not try to make it like yesterday. That's what keeps it refreshing. You take a song like "The Thrill Is Gone," which was my biggest record, and every day someone wants to hear it. So if you try to play it every day like you recorded it, it would be so boring. So I try to play each day as I feel it.

In my early years, I used to think I was one of the best singers in the world. Then I started hearing people like Sam Cooke sing gospel and people like Roy Brown sing the blues and I thought that I wasn't such a good singer after all. Then I started to be praised in the later '50s and early '60s as a great guitarist, and I thought that I was. Then I started hearing people like Barney Kesel, Charlie Christian, Django Reinhardt, Kenny Burrell, and I found out that I wasn't really a great guitarist. So I think overall I'm a pretty good entertainer. So if you separated either one, I'd be mediocre. *(Jeff Tamarkin; June 1983.)*

3. Rockabilly Boogie

The first music you could take and say, "Now *that* was rock 'n' roll," was rockabilly. Bill Haley and the Comets were a rockabilly band; Elvis Presley was a rockabilly performer. So were Roy Orbison and Carl Perkins and Johnny Burnette and Johnny Cash and Conway Twitty. There were R&B groups and country groups that were precursors of rock 'n' roll, but rock 'n' roll really started with rockabilly — and rockabilly doesn't necessarily mean Elvis Presley. Elvis' first recording was in 1953. By that time Johnny Burnette, his brother Dorsey and Paul Burlison had been fooling around with rockabilly for more than two years, and Bill Haley and the Comets had been *recording* rockabilly since June 1951.

Bill Haley and the Comets are an interesting case. Haley was a fairly successful Philadelphia-based country singer. Hank Williams recorded one of his songs, "Too Many Parties And Too Many Pals," under his Luke the Drifter monicker. Haley was a slave to his record company (Decca) and later in his career insisted on recording songs from his own publishing companies instead of trying for all-out hits. He cut tunes like "Rockin' Rollin' Schnitzelbank" and never had a hit after 1960. But Haley cut Jackie Brenston's "Rocket 88" in June 1951 and followed that up with "Rock The Joint." It featured Al Rex's percussive slap bass out front in the mix and had the same guitar solo as "Rock Around The Clock." It sold 150,000 copies and was arguably the first rock 'n' roll hit record.

"Rock-a-Beatin' Boogie," a song Haley wrote for the Treniers in 1953, included the lines "Rock, rock, rock everybody/Roll, roll, roll everybody," that Haley felt gave Alan Freed the idea to call the new music rock 'n' roll.

While Bill Haley and the Comets were recording rock 'n' roll in Philadelphia, the elements of what would become the Johnny Burnette Rock and Roll Trio were playing the elements of rock 'n' roll. During the days they'd play country on the radio stations. At night they'd play blues and more country. By 1953, they were playing old Hank Williams tunes in a new rockabilly style. With Johnny Burnette as the trio's wild front man, they later went on to score smashes with "Tear It Up," "Oh Baby Babe," and "Honey Hush." Elvis Presley came to their early gigs. Bill Black and Scotty Moore were around and listening when the Burnettes first started recording. Bill Black's brother later joined the group as their bass player. If they weren't the biggest rockabilly group ever, they were one of the most influential.

Paul Burlison was the lead guitarist with the trio, and bassist Johnny Black and drummer Tony Austin joined later.

Paul Burlison: In 1951, I was playing on a little radio station, KWEM in West Memphis, Arkansas. I was playing country music with a country band with a fellow named Shelby Fowler. Shelby and I had an afternoon radio program over there from 5 'til 5:30 in the afternoon. Then I would come out of the radio program and Howlin' Wolf would come over there from the cotton fields in Arkansas. A guy named Smokey Joe Baught played the piano. He was with Sun Records and had a song out called "Signifyin' Monkey." He lived in West Memphis at that time, but would come over in the afternoons to hand around the studio just to play the piano with the Wolf. So the Wolf was standing outside the studio there after we got through with our country show at 5:30. Wolf came on from 6 to 6:30. He would stay outside the studio just grinning and smiling. And I'd walk out of the studio and he'd say, "How about playing a little blues with me?" I'd say, "Man, I'd love to." And we'd go to the next studio, which was behind the studio we played in. We'd go back there and play the blues. He'd just play the ol' harmonica. Smokey would play the piano and I'd play the ol' guitar. Just the three of us. He played the blues! This went on for — well, not a long time. He would do this to advertise where he was playing that weekend. He never announced our names because it was just kind of unheard of for blacks to be playing with whites at that time.

Wolf wasn't exactly a professional musician at that time. That's right. He'd come into the studio wearing a pair of khaki pants and a white T-shirt. he had these holes cut in his shoes for his corns to hang out! He'd slide right into the studio like that in the afternoon. He had a big old candy box that he'd set right down in front of him. He'd sit right down in a chair and have the mike right in front of him. He'd stick the harmonica in his mouth longways. The only time he was playing was on weekends. It was only for a short time, but I did enjoy playing with him.

Johnny Black: I think we all liked it. From the standpoint of rock and roll ... well, there was no rock and roll. The only up-tempo music was black. Even though we were playing country, we still liked it. And a neighbor of mine was a disc jockey at the same station y'all was just talking about. I'd go in with him a lot and he'd play different black groups and solo artists. We loved them.

In fact, B.B. King had a radio program on WDIA. He came on at 5:00. I know that in 1949 I was working and, hey, we'd bust out of that door at 5:00. He was billed as "The Beale Street Blues Boy." From 5:00 to 5:15 it was live. That was the highlight of our day — not our lunch, but just listening to B.B.

Paul Burlison: Rufus Thomas had a show at the Handy Theatre on Park Avenue called "Rufus & Bones." They used to bring the black revues in at the W.C. Handy Theatre on Park, and a lot of white people were going in. We're talking about the late '40s and early '50s. No ropes. And no problems, either. We went to enjoy the music regardless of what color it was. Rufus Thomas used to have kind of a comedy act with this guy named Bones. It was a minstrel show. We went out there to watch them whatever chance we'd get, even the honky tonks. We'd go down to the honky tonks and listen to them play.

We were playing Hank Williams-type stuff. In 1953, Johnny Burnette and Dorsey Burnette and myself recorded in Mississippi on the Vaughn label. A thing called "Go Along, Mule." That was a rockabilly, uptempo thing. This was 1953!

On this stuff there was just bass, a rhythm guitar and the lead guitar and the fiddle. [When we wanted loud drumming] we'd beat on the drum cases. We told the drummer we was gonna bust his head unless he played hard. We told him, "Don't play good; play loud." On "Tear It Up," we played on the drum cases instead of the drums.

We played at a little club called Neil's Hideaway. It was 20 miles north of Memphis. It was down a hill. Oh, man, that thing was packed every Saturday night, and them boys would get up there and start stompin' the dust. And I saw some fights there, man. I saw one guy get his ear bit off one night — plumb off! They fought for 45 minutes. They got so tired they couldn't finish the fight. They said, "Let's come back tomorrow at 2:00 and finish it."

I'm not kidding you. In those days, man, you had to duck a lot. They was bad. Them ol' boys would grab you by the arm and say, "Hey, man, play 'Clementine.' "

Tony Austin: When I started playing with the group I was about 14 or 15. They were going on the road with Carl Perkins in Jacksonville and with others, switching back and forth. I quit because I was too young at that time. I couldn't leave town. But Johnny and Paul came by one day and said, "Come on. Hey, we sure could use a good drummer. Come with us."

Paul Burlison: We didn't even try Memphis to make a record. We wanted to go someplace where we'd get more recognition by getting on a national television show. Memphis only had Sun Recording Services then. That was it. Sam Phillips was limited. He had a lot of black artists. And between them and Elvis, he just couldn't really handle anyone else.

So we went to New York to record and Elvis stayed in Memphis. Part of the reason, I would think, was Paul was married and I was married, and Elvis was single. He could stay home and do what he wanted. He had no overhead. And regardless of how bad you wanted to record, food, clothing and shelter fit in there somewhere for the family.

On our first trip to New York, we drove straight through to New York without even stopping to sleep. We had the worst storm New York had had in 12 years. Dorsey and Johnny were both asleep in the car and I drove. The snow was everywhere. We didn't have any money to buy chains, so we just let some air out of the tires. We stopped on this mountain — the highest of the Blue Ridge Mountains. I opened the doors and said, "Okay, you guys. Get up! Here we are in New York! Come get some of this fresh air!" Johnny got out. He was half asleep. He looked down and saw the drop and said a person would starve to death even before they hit bottom.

In '56, we didn't go up there to get on Ted Mack's. We went through the electricians' union to get jobs because we'd been laid off. Memphis didn't have any work at that time. Dorsey and I went up there as electricians and Johnny went along with us. That's the way it actually happened. Johnny just went along. John was working for a collection agency. He was repossessing people's cars. He used to come along to get me every Saturday and we would tow away people's cars for this mortgage company. When we got laid off, there were a lot of people ahead of us, and you had to work local for maybe three months before the union would send you out on another job. So we heard they had cleaning work at a stink plant. So the union hall called the New York union hall and they said, "Yeah, we can put 'em on."

Johnny and I went down there to the Ted Mack show one night. Dorsey had gone to the movies to see one of those weird movies up there. I don't mean that kind of weird. I'm talkin' about outer-space movies, somethin' like that. He loved that stuff. Johnny and I were just sitting in the audience at the Ted Mack how and I said, "We ought to get on that thing." So we went and asked one of the ushers at the door. "Hey, how do you go about getting on this show?" He said, "You see that fellow over in the corner? That's Oscar Shoemaker. Go over there and talk to him and he'll tell you all about it." So we walked over 'cross there and introduced ourselves and he said, "What do you do?" Johnny said, "I play the guitar and I sing. My brother plays bass and Paul plays the electric guitar." He said, "Well, come down to Nola Studios at 7:30 on Thursday night and we'll gie you an audition. If you're good enough, we'll put you on." And that's the way it happened. We didn't even have a bass fiddle with us. We had to go to a music store and rent one. Well, we got to the audition and there was a line going all across the lobby, all the way up a flight of stairs, and all the way down a hall to a door. People coming out said they were booked solid for the next few months and no one would get on till after that. When we finally worked our way in, a man said, "Okay, boys, you've got six minutes to do your stuff — and out. That's all you've got." I plugged the guitar and the amp in real fast. I looked up and saw some steps going up and a big glass balcony above us. There was a mike up there and a mike down by us so we could talk back and forth. The man said, "Okay, boys, let's hear it." So we took off on "Maybellene," the Chuck Berry song. I looked up there and the judges sitting up there were older-type people and I thought, "I don't think they're gonna like this much." But this little old lady started clapping her hands and movin'. The man called us back and said, "Okay, boys, can you do another one?" so John did "Tutti Frutti." He cut loose on that. They hadn't heard music like this up in New York. Then they said, "Can you do another?" and John said, "Yes sir, we'll do'em all night for you." They said, "I think one more will be sufficent." So we did one more.

Then the man said, "All right, boys, y'all got something there. It's fresh. It's new. We're gonna put you on in two weeks. But don't tell anyone outside waiting." We went back to the YMCA where we were staying and we called everybody back home and said, "Hey, we're going to be on the Ted Mack amateur hour in two weeks!" Soon as we got done with the calls, we hung up the phone and the Ted Mack people called to say they were moving us up one week. So we had to call everybody again and tell them we was gonna be on a week earlier.

So here's how it happened: We went on that first night and, luckily, there was a lot of young people in the audience and that applause meter just went over and stopped. Everyone came over and congratulated us and said, "Man, you'll get it." I mean to tell you, man — talk about happiness! I tell you, we was tickled to death. We walked off with first prize three times.

A disc jockey out in Cleveland, Ohio, named Bill Randall saw us and he called Eddie Jerome to tell him to be sure to sign us up if he could. He had a big orchestra that played at the Edison Hotel. We couldn't sign with anyone right at first, 'cause we'd signed a contract with Ted Mack to tour with him for three weeks. So when we got back to New York we had all these record companies that wanted to sign us up. Capitol Records followed us all over the country, trying to get us to sign with them. Coral Records wanted us, and ABC-Paramount, too.

We'd sit out on the edge of the stage after the show was over and sign autographs for an hour and a half. People lined up — adults, everybody.

Everybody liked it. It wasn't vulgar. It had catchy little words and guys like us acted like we were enjoying ourselves onstage, and it just grew into the crowds. It just generated something.

Dorsey was an excellent songwriter. He was really good with words. And he put the words to "Tear It Up." Johnny helped him on the words. The music? Well, they just started singing. There wasn't any arrangement. I put the only thing I knew at the time behind it.

"Tear It Up" was #1 in Boston and #1 in Mississippi. The record was there. But the distribution and the whole Coral setup wasn't there at the time. Coral didn't really get their stuff together on the rock and roll thing Buddy Holly, Brenda Lee and Waylon came along.

You know, when we went to a town, we had our own records in our car, and we would have to go to the disc jockeys ourselves and sit at the station to get them to play the record. They would play it while you were in town. There were so many labels coming out at the time. Certain areas would play the stew out of our records. Wherever they played it regularly, it would get to #1. But at this time, payola was going on, and whoever put out the money — that's how it got somewhere.

They wasn't pushing the records. Like I said, if it broke in an area, we'd play a lot of shows there. That's the way it was. We got tired. Nothing was happening with the record sales. We were playing seven nights a week — one-nighters. That gets old, y'know.

Dorsey left first. We'd gone to California. Dorsey was a great singer himself; he had a good voice. He wanted to branch out on his own. So that's how it was. And I stayed with Johnny.

He just wanted to do something on his own. so then I just got tired of the road. Just bone tired; just dead tired. I just decided that nothing was happening. Since I was an electrician, I knew I could make a good living back home and could be living with my family. We all stayed on real good terms. Just like brothers—always, till both of 'em died. Even after they had "Dreamin'" and "You're Sixteen," they still tried to get me to come back. I just couldn't do it. *(Aaron Fuchs; September 1982.)*

Shortly after the Burnettes began recording, another singer began cutting rockabilly in Memphis. Carl Perkins was a South Tennessee boy who grew up on Bill Monroe bluegrass and sang country music, gospel, and blues while he was growing up and working in the cotton fields. His version of "Blue Suede Shoes" predated Elvis' by four months and would have been a bigger hit had Perkins not been in a serious automobile accident in March 1956 that kept him from touring and promoting the record.

Perkins was a purer rockabilly artist than Elvis, and wound up being more of an influence on British Invasion Groups like the Beatles, who cut versions of Perkins' "Honey Don't," "Everybody's Trying To Be My Baby" and "Matchbox" and treated Perkins like a conquering hero when he toured England in 1963.

Perkins' classics included the songs the Beatles recorded and the songs that Elvis recorded, along with "Boppin' The Blues" and "Movie Magg." He still tours and occasionally records.

Carl Perkins: I started out when I was about four or five years old. I remember the first "guitar" I ever had was a thing my dad made for me. It was a cigar box with a broom handle for a neck, and I actually played around with that thing. I loved it, that little ol' box. And I learned my first few chords from my dad. He didn't actually play guitar, you know, but he did know three or four chords: G, C, D and F.

I got my first real guitar through an old black man, John Westbrook, who sold his guitar to my dad. I was really influenced by John's blues. As the years went on, I realized he wasn't that good of a guitar player, but to me, I loved the way he pushed the strings, especially the third string, and that just infiltrated my little soul! I would play Ernest Tubb's "Walking The Floor Over You" or Bill Monroe's "Blue Moon Of Kentucky" and add Uncle John's blues licks in it. And that is where my style came from.

Another thing that added to it were the gospel songs that we used to sing in the cotton fields. I grew up working in the fields with black people. In the afternoons, the hot sun would beam down, and they'd start singing. I loved the way they sang. I loved the rhythms they sang the old gospels to. When I first started playing, I mixed that black rhythm with the country songs I was hearing on the radio.

I remember my dad telling me, "Carl, you ain't playing that right, boy." I said, "I know it, dad, but this is the way that I like to do it." Then he would say, "Well, you'll never amount to nothin'. You're singin' 'Walking The Floor Over You' too fast. Slow it down." When I was growing up in the hills of Lake County, Tennessee, my dad listened strictly to country music, and that was all he allowed to be played on the radio. So I listened to the Grand Ole Opry and Bill Monroe; later on, Hank Williams definitely influenced me.

But it wasn't Sam Phillips who influenced any of the artists. I have read through the years where it's been said that he did, and he did not. Everyone that went to Sam Phillips' Sun recording studio already had their own style developed. Rockabilly music was very popular and had been for a long time in the cotton-belt area of West Tennessee, Eastern Arkansas and Northern Mississippi. It was influenced by the black rhythm and black spiritual songs. I think probably the first rockabilly record ever recorded was done by Elvis — Bill Monroe's "Blue Moon Of Kentucky." When he sang, "Oh, wellah, wellah, wellah, wellah Blue Moon, boom, boom, boom..." well, that's the black Southern spiritual music, and it was just a marriage between that and country music. Until they settled on the name "rockabilly" they called it a lot of different things that we can't repeat right now. But "rockabilly" was the first clean name we had.

And I must say, you know, that although we were among the first people to record our type of music, we were by no means the first to play it. There were a lot of guys back then who played the same type of music that we did, some of them better than we did. They pushed hard enough, but just didn't have the desire or dream to get on record.

I think rockabilly is a basic form of what has graduated into rock 'n' roll. I think if you tear the music apart to the roots you're gonna find four guys playing bass, guitar, lead guitar and drums. The rest has just been added; four and five-part harmonies and all the electronics to make up a big rock 'n' roll sound. But if you take away that basic beat — the rockabilly thing started back in the '50s — then you've torn the rock out of the roll music.

I get a little tired sometimes of playing "Blue Suede Shoes," but all I have to do is think back on what my life would have been without "Blue Suede Shoes," and suddenly I enjoy singing it again. You don't want to get so used to success that you forget the ladder used to climb there — what caused you to live in the house you're living in, drive the car you always wanted, and play the fine instrument you're working with. You know, these people who come to see you are the ones who are buying your records, and they deserve to hear what they want to hear. Anyway, if you don't like a song, why record it in the first place?

I wrote that song — well, it was in '55, about the middle of that year, and we were in Parkins, Arkansas. Presley was on that show, and Johnny Cash said to me, "Carl, you ought to write a song called 'Blue Suede Shoes.'" I said, "I like them shoes, John, but I don't know nothing to say about 'em." He said, "Well, in the Army, guys would line up for chow with their combat boots on and somebody would say, 'Hey man, don't step on my suedes,' you know."

Well, I thought about it but couldn't do anything with the idea. I really couldn't. About three weeks after that, I was playing a dance in my hometown, and I was watching this couple jitterbug. They danced right in front of the bandstand, every time. She was a really pretty girl, and I noticed that this dude had on suedes. Suedes were really beginning to be a hot footwear item in that part of the country, although I'd never owned a pair. And he put his up and said to her, "Uh, uh, don't step on my suedes." Right then the whole thing socked me, it really did. I thought, that's what I'll say about them: "You can do anything but don't step on my blue suede shoes."

That night, about three o'clock in the morning, I was lying in bed, thinking about that boy loving those shoes so much. And I thought, how am I going to get in to saying, "Don't step on my shoes." Then I thought about the old nursery rhyme, "One for the money, two for the show, three to get ready and four to go." We used to say that playing hide and seek. I got up out of bed, went downstairs, got my guitar and went, "One for the money, two for the show," and it was just flooding my soul. I really was excited. I knew I had something there.

My wife called downstairs and said, "Carl! You're playing too loud! You're going to wake the kids up! But whose song is that?" I said, "It's ours." And she said, "Well, that's a hit song. That is really good." I couldn't find any paper to write on, 'cause all our people lived around so close to us, we had no kids in school, and I was very poor; I guess I didn't have any reason to write. So I took three potatoes out of a brown paper sack and wrote "Blue Suede Shoes," exactly as it is today, right on the sack. I did it about three o'clock in the morning, never even stopping. The words just came. After the opening of "One for the money, two for the show, three to get ready," I wrote, "Go man go."

I didn't have a telephone, but a fella across the street from me did, so I called Sam Phillips the next day and read it to him over the phone. He said, "I like it, I really like it. When can you come down and record it?" This was like on a Saturday, so I told him we could come Monday. He said, "All right, be here then and we'll cut it." I had already cut a song called "Honey Don't" that he liked. So I went down and set up our little equipment, and he said, "I want you to do it like you did on the phone. Put it all there."

Sam had a technique of getting the very best out of you that you had. He would be in the control room and come out and say, "Carl, do you remember how good you feel when you're playing the last song on a hard night at a club?" I said, "Yes sir." Then Sam said, "Well, you probably put everything into it because you know it's the last one, right?" I agreed with him and then he would say, "Well, that's what I want you to do right now in the studio. I want you to imagine that you're doing the final song on a long four-hour night." And it was those little things that caused the artists to put out everything they had. So in his way, Sam Phillips was a genius.

So the tape began, and I completely drew a blank when I got to "Go man go" — I forgot the word "man." On the original record, there's a slight pause and then the word "cat" flies in there. I did it again later in the song, 'cause I thought, well, I said "cat" before, I'd better say it again.

We got through with that take and Sam came out of the engineer booth and said, "That's it. You can go home. You got your record." I said, "I made a mistake." He said, "I didn't hear one." I said, "*I* did. I said, 'go *cat* go,' and it's 'go *man*'." He said, "I heard that 'cat' and I like

43

that 'cat'." He played it back for me and said, "What do you think?" I said "Well, if you're satisfied with 'go cat go,' and think it's as good as I can do it." He said "That's all I want to hear from you. You'll never sing it any better."

So we went home. The record came out on Jan. 1, 1956, and it was the first song to top the charts in all three categories of music: country, pop, and R&B.

There I was, on my way to being the first rockabilly artist to appear on national television; at that time Elvis hadn't been. I was on my way to do the Perry Como show and "Blue Suede Shoes" was number one.

I didn't know it until after the car accident that Sam Phillips had flown ahead of me to New York and he was going to present me my gold record as a surprise on the Perry Como show. I had sold a million records from January 1 to March 22 when the wreck occurred. What would have happened, I guess, no one really knows.

It was while I was in the hospital that Elvis recorded "Blue Suede Shoes" in April 1956. Of course, he did very well with it and a lot of people don't realize it, but Presley never had a single record of it. It first came out on an EP and was also included in a few of his albums. But he certainly became identified with the song, and it came along just at the time that he was getting to be the star that he rapidly became. Even though the song became synonymous with, him I've never felt bitter about it. I was just thankful that I lived through the accident, because it was a very bad one. I lost a brother and another man was killed. But I did lay there and think what if it hadn't happened. I guess we'll never know, but I do know life has been awfully good the way things have turned out. There's no question that I have been a very lucky man just to have known and worked with people like Elvis, Buddy Holly, The Beatles and others. Again, I've been fortunate to have been around and that's good enough for me.

All the power on those songs came out of the pickers, really, if you'll listen. They slapped the bass with authority, man. It was pure power. I mean, we couldn't plan on going back and adding something. We didn't know from overdubbing or multiple tracks. They didn't have that. It was a one-shot thing, man. You picked your heart out. You flew down on that guitar and did things you didn't know you could do. And you did the same thing with your singing.

I did a film [*Jamboree*]. That's an interesting story. The film company owned part of a publishing company and they sent down two songs to Sam Phillips at Sun Records. I had my choice of the songs, one of which I could do in the movie. I listened to the demos and chose "Glad All Over." I thought it was the best song. Jerry Lee Lewis got the song I didn't want and had to sing that one in the movie. It was a little tune called "Great Balls Of Fire," and everybody knows what happened to him after that. He had a smash hit, and nobody ever heard of "Glad All Over" again.

I've always maintained that of all the guys who came out of the Sun Record stable, Jerry Lee is the most talented guy of the whole shebang. I don't think there's any doubt about it. If Presley were alive today, I'm sure he'd say that Jerry Lee's one of the most dynamite talents in the whole world. He really is, and always has been. Here's a guy that can just flat entertain you. I mean, that's all there is to it. Elvis always had sex appeal, and could twitch his little finger and get screams. Jerry Lee got the same effect by simply pounding out pure rock 'n' roll. It's a shame he doesn't straighten his act up and get rid of the things that are destroying his talent. He's old enough to know better. In fact, he's practically my age.

You mentioned the Beatles. Well, I did a tour in '63 of England and on the final night I was asked to go to a party. I never will forget. I said, "Man, I'm a little too tired for that. I'm going to America tomorrow." I had been over there for about six weeks, the longest I'd ever been away from home. I work with Chuck Berry and really had a great tour, but was just dead, you know, and ready to go home. But for some reason or the other I said, "I'll go to the party but I can't stay long 'cause my plane leaves at nine in the morning."

It took an hour to get to this party, winding through London and the outskirts, and up this kind of hill to a castle. I said, "Golly, nothing but Rolls-Royces, Mercedes — what are we doing in a place like this?" And I was told, "Just stay cool, man." We rang the doorbell and the butler said, "May I say who is calling, please?" And they said, "Tell them Carl Perkins." And I said,

"Man, that name ain't gonna get us in here, you know. This is class." But the butler came back immediately and said, "Yes. Right this way."

We walked into this big mansion and we were standing in the hall. I had never met the Beatles and, at the time, they had never been to America. I'd seen pictures of them because my kids had pictures of them. I saw this table all covered with food — turkeys, pigs with apples in their mouths — I mean, it was a big deal.

I said, "Hey, that cat looks like Ringo Starr, man, with the Beatles." And I was told that *was* Ringo Starr. About that time, Ringo saw me and stood up in a chair and said, "Ladies and gentlemen, he's here." Everybody broke out into applause. Out of the crowd came John, Paul, George and Ringo, and they were just the sweetest, nicest guys I had ever met.

CARL PERKINS: 'Until they settled on the name "rocka-billy" they called it a lot of different things we can't repeat right now. But "rockabilly" was the first clean name we had.'

We sat around and ate, and about three o'clock in the morning, out comes a guitar. The Beatles were sitting on a couch and I'm sitting on he floor and George is asking me, "How'd you kick off 'Honey Don't,' Carl?" I'm knocked down because I didn't realize that they had ever heard of me, you know — I'm serious. I knew they were going to be really big because the kids were going around, even then, saying, "I want to let my hair grow, just like them." It was really a great thrill for me to sit there as they called off all those old records. They'd say, "Let's sing this," and we sit and sing and play until four in the morning.

They took me back to my hotel, and on the way, Paul said, "What are you doing tonight?" And I said, "Well ..." This was one of the greatest moments in my life, when something inside me told me not to go home; these guys like you. I said, "Nothing." He said, "We'd love you to come to a recording session. We're recording tonight. Man, we'd love it." I said, "Well, man, I'd be glad to." And he said, "We'll send a car for you."

They sent a Rolls-Royce limousine to the little hotel I was staying at, and I will never forget how thrilled I was to go into the studio and find them there. Ringo said, "Mr. Perkins, do you mind if we record some of your songs?" And I said, "Son, I'd be thrilled to death." So I sat there while they recorded "Honey Don't," "Matchbox," and "Everybody's Trying To Be My Baby." We jammed and had a lot of fun.

Needless to say, it did a lot for me. I was ready to quit the music business. I had gotten me a farm and was kind of fed up. I just couldn't get anything to happen, record-wise. But those boys gave me a shot in the arm, so to speak. I came back home and was a new man — I really was.

Gosh, to my family, the woman I've been married to all these years, and to the boys who are playing with me with me now — I've got two more children, three grandchildren — I'd like to be remembered ... well, I've got a little plaque in my house and it says: "Within these walls I've written my songs. I've done you right and I've done you wrong. Let it be said when I'm gone away that he smiled and wasn't ashamed to play."

And I'm not. To my family, I want to be remembered as the man who went out there in the wilds of the music business and stuck it out, through the hard times and the good. To my fans and the people I've met along the way — well, it wouldn't have been possible if it hadn't been for them. Someday, on that old tomb rock out there in that little cemetery in Tennessee, I'd just like the word "lucky" to be put there, because really, that's what I've been. I've worked pretty hard at my trade, and I'm going to continue to. I feel like I'm climbing a mountain now and something big is going to happen. I don't know how big; I don't know what some people consider "big." To me, "big" would be to have one more really good record before I cash it all in. *(Wayne Jones, June 1980; and Colin Escott, Sept. 26, 1986.)*

❦

The most talented performer to come out of the rockabilly ranks was Jerry Lee Lewis. He was also the wildest, on and off stage. Lewis played boogie-woogie piano like he invented it, and could take any song and make it his own simply by sitting down at the piano and singing it. He cut some of the best songs of the rockabilly era and some of the worst, simply because he was recording on days he didn't feel like singing, and was singing bad material, poorly produced. He had a reputation of being impossible to handle, and he lived up to that reputation whenever he could. But he was also deeply religious, believed in the devil as the embodiment of sin, and believed in Jesus Christ as the One True Way. He sang and recorded gospel. He also was married twice before he was 21, and destroyed his career at its peak by marrying his 13-year-old cousin. As rockabilly expert Colin Escott put it, "He is the self-created Killer, tempting God to come and reclaim him alive, and tempting every other singer who fancies himself a showman to follow Jerry Lee Lewis on stage."

Lewis came to Sun Records after being kicked out of Southwestern Bible Institute in Wasahachie, Texas. He had drawn the ire of administrators there for playing piano in roadhouses, a talent he had learned still earlier, when he and his cousin, Jimmy Swaggart, would slip into black juke joints and watch the performers. (Swaggart later became a television evangelist; his ministry collapsed when a prostitute went public with her liaisons with Swaggart.)

Lewis started playing the piano when he was 10, and learned from everyone he ever saw or heard. Moon Mullican may have been an influence, as were many of the great boogie-woogie pianists, but the greater part of Jerry Lee Lewis was Jerry Lee himself.

When Lewis came to Sun, he just wanted a job playing piano. Lewis' father had sold 13 dozen eggs to get his son to Memphis. When Sam Phillips heard him, as Escott said, "Phillips saw an artist who could do all the things that Phillips *would* have done if he could have sung and played." Together they formed an unholy alliance and cut Lewis' best songs.

Lewis was never much of a chart force. His first song, "Crazy Arms," was a slight hit. His biggest song, "Whole Lotta Shakin' Goin' On," was eclipsed by two different version of "The Banana Boat Song" in 1957, and by the middle of the next year Lewis' career on the rock 'n' roll charts was essentially over. Lewis never had a No. 1 hit on the pop charts, though he did on the country and R&B charts.

The followup to "Whole Lotta Shakin' " was "Great Balls Of Fire." The followup to that was "Breathless," and then came "High School Confidential" — the movie and the song. In May 1958, as Lewis and his wife were touring England, the British press picked up on the age of

46

Lewis' bride. (The two had been married in late 1957.) The promoter, J. Arthur Rank, kicked Lewis off the tour and replaced him with a local teenager. Lewis, reading the papers after the scandal broke, said, "Who is this DeGaulle? He seems to have gone over bigger than us." It was essentially the end of the road for Jerry Lee Lewis as a rock 'n' roll star of the first magnitude.

Carl McVoy was Lewis' cousin. Jack Clement produced Lewis for Sun. Roland Janes played on Lewis' first Sun session. Jud Phillips and Cecil Scaife did promotion for Sun Records.

Carl McVoy: He worried the hell out of me, wanting me to show him things on the piano. I think I was instrumental in the way his style developed, because I got attention when I played. I rolled my hands and put on a damn show. When Jerry went back to Ferriday [Louisiana], he played everything I knew.

Jack Clement: I was working with Roy Orbison, and Sally Wilbourn brought Jerry Lee back to me. She said, 'I've got a fella here who says he plays the piano like Chet Atkins. I thought I'd better listen to that. He started playing things like "Wildwood Flower" and I believe he was playing piano with his right hand and drums with his left. I finally made a tape with him because he was different. We recorded "Seasons Of My Heart," but I told him to forget about country because it wasn't happening at that time. I took his name and told him I'd let Sam hear the tape when he got back. After Jerry left, I started listening to the tape and I found that I liked it. It really grew on me.

Roland Janes: Jack phoned me and said, "Man, I got this piano player, cat from down in Louisiana. He's pretty good. I'm gonna put a few things down on him. Do you want to come in and help us out?"

I said, "Yeah, sure."

He said, "Man, could you drop by and get [drummer J.M.] Van Eaton? Think you can get him to come out?"

I said, "Yeah, I'm pretty sure I can."

He [Van Eaton] didn't drive at the time; that's how young he was. So we went down to the session and cut "Crazy Arms." I don't think Jack was even in the control room. He was out in the studio and just left the machine running. Billy Riley had walked in about that time and he picked up my guitar. Right on the end of the song he hit a chord. I came out of the washroom about halfway through the song and picked up an old upright bass and started playing it — and I don't play upright bass. Fortunately, I wasn't close to a microphone. On that song, there were technically only two instruments, drums and piano.

Jud Phillips: [After he recorded "Shakin' "] I took him to New York and presented him to Jules Green, who was managing Steve Allen, and Henry Frankel, who was talent co-ordinator for NBC. I took a real gamble in terms of Sun Records to see whether a mass audience would accept this man. Our distributors made sure that every retail outlet in the United States had copies of "Shakin'." That represented a lot of merchandise that could have been returned.

Roland Janes: He's a very deep person. He could be hurting and never let it show. I don't think he ever quite understood why [the scandal involving his young bride] happened. He's such an honest person, and he didn't think he'd done anything that was unacceptable to anyone. He didn't think the public would be concerned about what he did if it didn't relate to his music, which was a total miscalculation on his part. The truth is that you've got the world and you've got Jerry Lee Lewis. He'll do things his way regardless of what anyone thinks. He felt betrayed, though — and he had every right to — but he held his head up and didn't cry.

Cecil Scaife: At that time, Jerry had his hair peroxided blond and it was extraordinarily long. That, and his 13-year-old bride, was the image that the cartoonists caricatured. She would be holding a teddy bear in her hand.

I had a very serious talk with Jerry about his image. We went to the restaurant next door to the studio and sat down in a booth. Jerry had one of his pickers with him. You could rarely get him one-on-one. I told him what I thought we should do in as much detail as I though he could absorb in one sitting. I wanted to get him out of typical rock 'n' roll regalia. Ivy League was in. I wanted him to get a crewcut. I wanted to hold a press conference where Jerry would announce that he was somewhat remorseful. He would take on an adult image.

We discussed it for over an hour. Jerry was very polite and listened. He would nod every once in a while, but he kept looking at his watch. Finally, he looked at his buddy across the table and said, "What time is it?" The guy said, "It's five before one." Jerry said, "Oh! The double feature at the Strand starts in five minutes. It's *Return of the Werewolf* and *The Bride of Frankenstein Meets Godzilla*!" Then he jumped up and left the table. That was the last time we discussed Jerry's image.

JERRY LEE LEWIS: After news of his scandalous marriage came and went in the British papers, Lewis said, 'Who is this DeGaulle? He seems to have gone over bigger 'n' us.'

Roland Janes: People are always trying to compare musicians, but I can't find anyone to compare with Jerry. What you hear him doing on records is only a small percentage of what he's capable of doing. I don't think even he knows who great he is. He can take a solo with either and and sing a song five different ways, every one of them great. I remember when we were working the package shows. Jerry would sit backstage after the show at the piano and all the big stars would gather around him and watch — Chuck Berry, Buddy Holly, the Everly Brothers and so on. Jerry would be leading the chorus and everyone would be having a ball.

Jimmy Van Eaton: Jack Clement had Jerry in for an audition, and at the time I was doing some studio work with some other musicians and he asked me to come in and just see what Jerry had, you know. That's the way it started. On his first record there was just drums and piano.

I wasn't that impressed with him [at first]. I was more impressed with his piano playing than his singing. As we played more, the people just really started liking what he was doing. That was what was really amazing to me — to see the people really enjoying it like they did.

The first session with Jerry was pretty easy to remember. I thought it was strange; he had a goatee that first time, and that was back before they ever became popular. "Crazy Arms" was the first one we did with him.

The way he plays and the way I play are an awful lot alike. With Jerry, you got it on the first or second time or you didn't get it. He wasn't one of those guys where you do over and over and over. You had to get it the first couple of takes.

The sessions that I did — and there were a lot of them — Jack Clement did most of them. Then they brought Bill Justis in and he started doing some. They did some together, but Justis never did do any engineering. He would do arranging and things like that or just bring the people in, but Jack Clement was really more responsible than anybody.

I like "High School Confidential" pretty good. There's a couple of others I thought were better. It's hard to say, really. "Down the Line" was pretty good and "Whole Lotta Shakin' Goin' On" was such a monstrous hit. There's some I think have really got a groove going better than that one, you know.

The sound was something pretty unique. There was just something about that studio. Also, at that point in time there were a lot of creative people on the scene. New fresh ideas. You know, Sam wasn't afraid to take a chance with that stuff. The timing was right.

A lot of times, Sam would just ask Jerry to play. You see, "Whole Lotta Shakin'" came about that way. It was a song that Jerry had been doing in the clubs where he was playing, you know, and it was a monstrous hit. And I think they were searching for something that might be in the back of his mind. They would just ask him, "Look, just do any of these old songs." None of them actually had the appeal that "Whole Lotta Shakin'" did. Jerry just had an enormous amount of songs. He could just sit down and do anything. Amazing. He's still an amazing entertainer. He could still be great if he wanted to be. *(Hank Davis and Colin Escott; July 14, 1989.)*

At the other end of the spectrum from Jerry Lee Lewis was Roy Orbison. College-educated, not good-looking and shy, Orbison sung in a melodramatic style that owed as much to opera as it did to rock 'n' roll. Not wanting to be typecast as another rockabilly singer, Orbison began specializing in dramatic ballads, and was able to prolong his career well into the '60s because of it. "Running Scared," "Crying," "Only The Lonely," "Dream Baby" and "Oh Pretty Woman" established Orbison as a distinctive, gorgeous voice in rock 'n' roll, and a particularly self-conscious one. As one rock journalist pointed out, "Oh Pretty Woman" is about what Orbison *might* have done with a pretty woman if he were to see one. It was mental and internal and ahead of its time.

Orbison's career experienced a renaissance shortly before his death in 1989. He recorded a new album, *Mystery Girl*, with Jeff Lynne producing. He joined Bob Dylan, Tom Petty, George Harrison and Lynne in the Traveling Wilburys. And he recorded a Home Box Office special with Elvis Costello, k.d. lang, Bruce Springsteen, James Burton, and T-Bone Burnett that later became the stunning album *A Black And White Night — Live*. Roy Orbison was unique.

Roy Orbison: The beginning of everything — it sounds trite — is that my father gave me a guitar when I was six years old. I told him I wanted a harmonica. He asked me if a guitar would be okay instead, and I said sure. Then we moved to Fort Worth, Texas, and my mother and father started working in a defense plant. This only has a bearing because every night a cousin or uncle or friends would come by, and play and sing. So I learned very quickly that if I learned to play this guitar and sing fairly well, I got to stay up later than the rest of the kids, and actually be a part of the festivities. It had such a profound effect on my life, because these people didn't know what was going to happen to them. So they partied heavy and played heavy.

I was six to seven. The topic of the conversation was either music or it was about the war. So, I'm still a historian and still a music maker. I then visited a radio station in Kermit, Texas, KVWC. I'd go down every Saturday to do their jamboree thing, and became a regular, me and a fellow called "Stan the Man." Then, when I was 10 years old, I won a medicine show contest, tied with a fellow who was 15 years old. I won $7.50 and he got $7.50. Then we moved to the oil fields of West Texas, and I played and sang for the school and things, and then formed a group.

Generally, it was country, but by the time I had the group, I guess when I was about 14, we were doing things like "Lady Of Spain" and "In The Mood," and pop stuff as well. Whatever was current in country, we had to do it. As soon as it faded away, we'd drop it. We toured for the principal of the school. He was running for Lion's Club governor. So, we played here and there, and some people asked us to play a dance one evening. I was going to say, "We've played all that we know," and they said, "We'll pay you $400 if you come play." So I said, "We'll be there!" I amplified the guitar, and we had a drummer already.

I'll make a jump from there. I went to college, and I did nothing at college except play the guitar, really, and learn that that wasn't what I wanted to do. There was North Texas University. Pat Boone was there at the time, and he'd made a record. So I wanted to make a record. Elvis Presley had started recording at that time. We were very close to Dallas, Texas and he [Elvis] would play a place called the Big D Jamboree. So, my second year of college, I went to Odessa Junior College, which was very near my hometown of Wink [Texas], and I started a couple of television shows. We would play honky tonks, and promote them on the television show. The fellow took the bar and we would take the door, and charge a dollar a person and make a little money. I had heard these boys at school who had written a song called "Ooby Dooby." So I took it to Clovis, New Mexico, and made a record of it at Norman Petty's studio, and then sent it to Sam Phillips.

I was the first to use [the Clovis studio], other than Norman, who used it for his own trio. He built it for them. We hired the studio to make "Ooby Dooby." Shortly after that, Buddy Knox and Jimmy Bowen recorded "Party Doll" and "I'm Sticking With You" there and that was a huge seller, 800,000 or so, and then Norman saw the possibilities. And, of course, the re-cut of "Ooby Dooby" sold 250,000. Basically, though, it was just the closest place to where Buddy Knox, Buddy Holly and myself lived.

Elvis and Johnny Cash came through Odessa, Texas, and they were with Sun Records at that time. They appeared on my TV show to promote their concerts and I called Sam Phillips on the advice of Johnny and said that Johnny had said that I might be able to get on his label. He said, "Johnny Cash doesn't run my record company," and hung up on me. Anyway, a little later I played my demo for Cecil Haughlafield and he played it for Sam Phillips on the phone. Sam said, "Send it to me. I can't tell nothing over the phone." So, Cecil sent it and Sam called back and said, "Can those boys be here in three days?" Then we dashed off to Memphis and recorded "Ooby Dooby."

The second time I met Jerry Lee, I told him that I had a session coming up and asked him to play piano on it. There weren't many players around, you know. Just a handful of us. Jerry had just played piano on one of Carl Perkins' sessions so I asked him if he would like to play on my session and he said, "No, I don't do that any more." He had just had his first record released and he felt that he had graduated beyond that, I guess.

We used to jump around all over the stage like a bunch of idiots. Well, wait a minute; Johnny Cash didn't. And I never toured with Elvis but he came backstage at a show I played in Memphis when "Ooby Dooby" was No. 1. That was at the Overton Park Shell. It was all very new then. I remember that we came through Canada in late '56 and no one knew quite what we were doing. They could identify a little with Johnny Cash but once you got more progressive than that, it was beyond them. Very frantic, hectic shows. We were trying to make stage shows out of one hit record, which is very difficult.

Sam wanted us to sound like everyone else he had been recording. He would bring out these old 78s. He would say, "This is the way I want you to sound." He'd play "Mystery Train" and those other big thick old 78s. He'd say, "Sing like that," but what he meant to say was, "Sing with feeling." Anyway, we'd try to please him and still stay ourselves, you know. That was all Sam knew and all he wanted to know.

Another thing was that the studio was a tiny place, about the size of this dressing room. If you had drums, you had to sing above all the music which meant that you had to sing loud and that gave you a powerful voice. We all developed powerful voices.

I think that Sam's contributions were to get us to sing with "soul" before the word was invented and to get us to project, otherwise it wouldn't be recorded.

My big ambition was to own a new Cadillac before I was 21 years old. A Cadillac and a diamond ring! That's what everybody wanted.

By the time I left Sun I was wanting to do the material that I eventually wound up singing a couple of years later. We all left and we all went on to sell literally billions of records.

I made two records with Chet Atkins in 1958. The first was "Sweet And Innocent" and "Seems To Me." The next was "Almost Eighteen" and then we recorded the first record I made at Monument, "Paper Boy," at RCA. Just after we cut it, I made the decision to move to Monument. That was on Chet's advice. He said that he couldn't do what he wanted with me at RCA, so it would be best if I went with someone who had freedom of action. Chet played on that first Monument record and helped us with it.

Rockabilly was a strange term to me. The first time I saw it written was on an import EP. There were four songs, and it had a picture of a hillbilly with a corncob pipe and a hillbilly hat. And it said "rockabilly" and "hillbilly rock." And of course, the country singers objected to being called hillbillies. We didn't object to it; we just didn't know what it was. We didn't know, for instance, that we were creating anything. We were doing our own thing, and didn't know that it was a small circle of some importance until 1970.

Joe Nelson and I wrote "Only The Lonely," and we were on our way to Nashville. We had two or three other songs. So I stopped by Elvis' house. He had just gotten out of the Army. It was early in the morning and I'd driven from West Texas. We got there about six in the morning, so I sent a note by the gateman, and he sent a note back saying that he had the whole troop in there, at Graceland, and they were all still asleep, that he would see me in Nashville. So I wanted to play him the song, and had it been later, and had he heard the song and wanted it, he could have had it. But he didn't get to hear it.

Then I played it for Phil Everly, and I'm not sure whether he thought I was pitching it to him or not. I just played it for him because I was proud of it. Had he wanted it, he could have had it. But he didn't say, one way or another. So, I went in and recorded it and two other songs, and it happened to be that big. So, in actual fact, I guess you could say that, as it happened, I had to record "Only The Lonely" myself to get it done, not properly, but to get it done. Everything was lovely after that; it was terrific.

All my songs were written after the event. You may have heard of people who, in the midst of a broken love affair, they'll write a great song; well, in my midst of broken love affairs, I can't sleep, I can't think, I can't eat. So how you gonna write a song? But later, when I'm content, I can write a happy song, sad song. I can reflect on what happened. So, like, "Working For The Man," that song was inspired by when I was working in West Texas, and "Crying" was a true experience. And so was "Running Scared." But it was years later.

It was a hit-and-miss proposition. "Only The Lonely" was super big. "Blue Angel" wasn't quite so big. "I'm Hurtin' " wasn't as big. Then, "Crying" got back to the top 10, "Running Scared" got to #12, and "Dream Baby" was #1. And by the time I got to England with the Beatles, I had "In Dreams," which was #3. I had a big log of hits, and they were very excited to see me. And they still are to this day. It's practically the same way in the States.

I had played a show in Alabama and flew back by private plane on the way to join the Beatles for a tour of England. I had left the clear pair [of glasses] aside because it was such a sunny day. Anyway, I left them on the plane and I had to open in England with the sunglasses. It wasn't a gimmick, it was a mistake and I was very embarrassed to go on stage in sunglasses. All these photographers were there and they took pictures that went around the world of me and the Beatles. Made them and made me, that tour did. After that I was stuck with the sunglasses.

My fan-club president said, "You'll be touring with the Beatles. They're the hottest act in England. So everybody will see how good you are." She was biased, naturally. I left my clear glasses on the plane, and I was very frightened to go onstage for many reasons. First of all, I was in a foreign country. Second of all, I'm always nervous before I go on. Then, I had these dark glasses. And I managed a dozen or so encores; in fact, they were still shouting for me as the Beatles were playing. For a while. Then it was one constant scream.

They came to me and said, "Look, since you're making all the money, let us close the show."

And I said, "Let's wait until after rehearsal." It was, in fact, my show. I said after we had equal billing — I've forgotten whether it was Roy Orbison/Beatles or Beatles/Roy Orbison — I said, "I'll let you know after rehearsal." I did my rehearsal, and then they did theirs. They were doing "Twist And Shout" and things like that; "Money." Every song they played was up. So it didn't make sense to me to go on after all this rocking music, and do ballads. I only had "Dream Baby" and "Candyman" to play up. I told them they could close the show. It helped them. They did overcome the, "We want Roy. We want Roy," after I had left. They were frightened each night, but it helped both of us, because it was the right set-up for them and for us.

In '64, "It's Over" was my first release that year. It was the first #1 single by an American in England since '62, I think. Then, "Pretty Woman" came out, and it was #1 here and there at the same time. That was the first time that had happened since 1961. So for the first years, '64 and '65, they were the #1 vocal group in the world, and I was the #1male vocalist in the world. So, their coming to America didn't do anything but help me, that year. Their biggest year was my biggest year in the States.

[After "Pretty Woman,"] the very next record didn't sell anything. In fact, nobody knows the title of the next record, on Monument. Then we released another on Monument. It had to be somebody's fault somewhere. The reason I say that is because you would have pre-orders of 100,000 coming off of that. But the next record didn't sell that. It didn't. Then when I re-signed, with MGM, I did have three or four more hit records. Not of the magnitude of "Pretty Woman," but then that was the biggest seller. I set a big precedent with "Only The Lonely" when it went 2 million. The next one after that was a million, and the one after that 600,000. And I said, "I'm on my way out again." Then "Running Scared" came out and hit it. So, I don't know what the reason would be for that. It's strange. If I knew the secret...

My voice is as strong as it ever was, even stronger now. I do realize that you have to warm up a little bit now. I never do. I just go out and sing. I think I'll always be a studio artist. And I think I'll do the touring thing for another four or five years, at least. Then I think, I think from what I know now, as opposed to what I knew 10 years ago or 20, that I would try to pass along some of the things I've learned, to younger talent; maybe be a producer. I think I could be great at that. That's what I'll probably do.

I'll never be an old man. My father called me the other day, on my birthday, and he said, "How old are you?" And I said, "Dad, you know how old I am." He said, "No, tell me how old." So I told him, and he said, "You're almost as old as I am." And I said, that's right. He learned to fly when he was 43, and got his pilot's license. And he bought a mini Harley Davidson when he was 51. So he's still rockin' and I'll still be rockin'. *(Dave Booth and Colin Escott, Feb. 1, 1985; Jeff Tamarkin, October 1979.)*

☙

Tragedy was no stranger to great rockers, and rockabilly had its share of tragedies. Both Eddie Cochran and Gene Vincent had their careers altered by a car wreck in England. Cochran died in 1960 when his sports car collided head-on with an oncoming vehicle. Vincent suffered painful injuries, and began drinking heavily to ease the pain. His career turned into a bitter shell of what it had been, and what it could have been. As a result of the crash, the two have been linked, and Vincent has been pushed aside a little in favor of Cochran. But while Cochran had his hits with "Twenty Flight Rock" and "Summertime Blues," Vincent had a bigger hit with "Be-Bop-A-Lula." Both were great rockabilly artists, and influences on everyone from Blue Cheer to Dave Edmunds to the Who.

Jerry Merritt was Gene Vincent's guitar player.

Jerry Merritt: I was born in a little town called Johnson which is about five miles outside of Fayetteville, Arkansas, on Dec. 25, 1933. I lived there until I was 10 years old, then my family moved out to Washington state in the Yakima Valley area. We came to Washington to pick apples because we were fruit workers — well, what I mean to say is we became fruit workers out of necessity as a means to survive. I lived in Yakima until I went into the Army in 1953. I did go back to Arkansas a few times. When I got out of the Army and went into show business, I lived and worked out of Kansas City and toured around Chicago and the Midwest.

I'll tell you what influenced me to get into the music business. It sounds crazy, but it was a necessity to keep from starving to death. I mean it was that bad because when I got out of the army I didn't have much of an education. I only went to the eighth grade. You couldn't get a job nowhere at that time. So, anyway, I could play guitar a little bit. I played in a small band over in France before I went in the infantry up in Germany. So one July fourth [1956] I went and seen this guy in a tavern. It was just a joint; it still is the same dive, it's still there. So I asked him for a job and he said he'd try me out. That was 29 years ago that I started playing music for a living, and since that time that's all I've done is show business.

The first time I ever saw Gene was at a show that me and the Pacers did at the Yakima Armory in 1957. We were on the same show with Gene Vincent and the Blue Caps. Gene never did remember that show because he played so many shows on the road. So me and my group played there and had the opportunity to work as the warm-up band, as they call them nowadays. Then later on, Pat Mason [Gene Vincent's manager] called because I had worked with acts like the Collins Kids and Carl Perkins and wanted me to go on the road with Bobby Darin, touring with him. So I worked backing up Bobby Darin for a while. Then I met Gene Vincent at a rehearsal in Centralia [Washington]. It was a kind of a coincidental type thing that worked out really good. Gene asked me if I wanted to work with him, so I did.

When I worked with Gene we worked just the two of us as a duo. When we went out on tour there would be backup bands that worked with us in each different area we were in.

Besides playing guitar for Gene I would sing too. We'd both sing together as a duet. When we went on stage, he'd enter from one side and I'd come in the other side, and it worked out really great.

If I remember correctly, the Blue Caps disbanded in the early part of 1958. Then Gene had another group for a while that he called the Blue Caps. I worked with Gene starting in the winter of 1958. In July of '59 I went on a Japan tour with Gene. In August of '59, we were back in the States and cut an LP [*Crazy Times*]. Then in 1960 I worked with him some. I worked with Gene a total of three years, it wasn't a full three years but kind of an off-and-on thing during that time. Then, after 1960, we kept in touch all the time because we were real good friends. When Gene went to Europe in 1960 on the tour that Eddie Cochran got killed in a car wreck, he wanted me to go with him but I didn't go because of domestic problems at the time. We kept in touch all through the '60s, and in 1966 he asked me to write a couple songs for him, so I wrote "Born To Be A Rolling Stone" and "Hurtin' For You Baby."

In July of 1959 I caught a plane out of Seattle and flew up to Anchorage, Alaska, to meet Gene. From there we flew on over to Japan, and when we got there we didn't even have to clear customs, as it was all taken care of ahead of time for us. There were over 10,000 people there to meet us. Then we had a parade all the way to our hotel. We stayed at one of the most modern hotels in Japan and had to eat our meals in our rooms because there were so many girls waiting for us outside in the hallway. In the theater we performed in we broke all attendance records. It held 20,000 people and we did three shows a day. It was packed for every show we did. In the five days we performed at this one theater we had almost 300,000 kids there! It was really the experience of a lifetime. They gave us the old V.I.P. treatment; we had bodyguards and limousines. I know that Gene always felt that the Japan tour was one of the biggest things to happen to him in his career.

He got homesick for his wife Darlene, and one day he just said, "That's it, I'm gonna take off for home." He left me sitting in Japan and I wouldn't leave. I said, "We gotta honor this contract because if we don't we're in trouble" — and we would have been! I was having too much fun to leave, anyway. I didn't *want* to leave.

I stayed for two more weeks after he left. I worked the shows by myself. Now, part of the shows — and this is what was really weird about it — I worked under my own name and part of the shows I had to work under his name. What I had to try and do was get it out of my mind that they were doing that, because it was really hitting me hard and I just wanted to be myself. I could do all of Gene's songs; I could lay it right out! I couldn't really believe that they'd do that; I just did it and got right offstage. I didn't really portray myself as him, because it was like I *was having* to do that show, but still I was me! I just couldn't get it through my head to be somebody else. I did the show and I think I did it pretty well. The promoters billed me as Gene Vincent, so I did the job exactly like they wanted me to and the audience thought I was him, because we did look a lot like each other. It didn't go on forever, I ended up doing my own shows in different towns, not in the same place.

GENE VINCENT: 'Gene Vincent was one of the greatest rock 'n' rollers of all time.'

We argued all the time. We argued 24 hours a day 'cause we had fun doing it. People thought we were mad at each other, but we never really were. There might have been a couple times when we got into it over little things, but we just had fun. We did things like call each other names and crazy stuff like that. One of the things about Gene was that he could get fired up if he thought someone said the wrong things, because he did have a temper.

It's really sad that Gene had to die at such a young age. We were really good friends and I miss him a lot. I do keep in touch with his family, his ex-wife Darlene, his daughter Melody, and his son. His girl and boy are a real lot like him. Gene Vincent was truly one of the greatest rock and rollers of all time. *(Don Kirsch; Feb. 21, 1986.)*

Rockabilly wasn't restricted to men. Women cut some of the wildest rockabilly sides of all. Wanda Jackson was the queen of rockabilly. She dressed in high heels and tight dresses and belted out wild rockers like "Let's Have A Party" and "Fujiyama Mama." While Jackson thought of herself as a country singer, and had hits on the country charts while she was cutting rock 'n' roll, she was completely convincing as a rock 'n' roller. She recorded rock with some of the best country musicians of the day: Chet Atkins, guitarist Joe Maphis and steel guitarist Speedy West. Buck Owens played guitar on one of her early singles, and Roy Clark played guitar on her all-rocking 1961 album *There's A Party Going On*. She later became a best-selling gospel artists, though she did dip back into secular music for an album in 1987.

Wanda Jackson: I signed my first contract with Decca in 1954. I was a junior in high school. I had a two-year contract with one two-year option. They were going to pick up the option, but I had the opportunity to sign with Capitol. That's the company I'd always wanted to be with, so I took that opportunity.

Hank Thompson was instrumental in getting me signed to Capitol. Rose Maddox is one of the girl singers I liked. You have to understand, there weren't many girls singers back then. Kitty Wells was another. I liked some of the girl singers that yodeled, Laura Lee and some others. I learned their songs because I learned how to yodel. I always thought that a girl singer had to be able to yodel, so that's the first thing I learned to do. Then there was Jean Shepard, who came along about the same time as me, or a little ahead of me. She had a great voice. I also did some of Hank Williams's songs. Then I tried to set my own style. When you first begin, you pattern after people and then it becomes a blend. Wanda Jackson is a blend of all of those.

Actually, I don't know if you know the story behind "Let's Have A Party." It kind of proves how reluctant I was to sing this type of music. I had done my first album and we just needed another song. I had been opening with this song of Elvis' on my shows. I thought it was a good song, so I said, "Let's throw it on the album," which we did. Then it wasn't for two or three years later that the disc jockeys started playing that song. People started requesting it, and then Capitol was flooded with questions of "Where is this single?" I called my producer, Ken Nelson, on the road to see how my latest record was doing and he said, "Well, congratulations, you've got a hit." I thought he meant my country song and he told me, "No, 'Let's Have A Party.' " No one was more shocked than I was. That gave me the opportunity to start singing that kind of song, and it really got me out of a protective shell. I kind of launched out in some new fields, got some new clothes. I was the first girl that I know of in country music to sing in a tight dress, more of a sexy-type outfit: high heels and long earrings and silk fringe dresses. I designed those and was wearing them long before the go-go dancers were popular in the '60s. It helped me to be innovative.

The first session for Capitol, Joe Maphis came in. I was excited that he was going to play on my record. He was really a laid-back person; he came in his house shoes. These guys recorded all the time, so it was no big deal for them, but it was my first session there so I was nervous. I couldn't believe somebody would wear their house shoes. Later on, Buck Owens played acoustic guitar on quite a few songs. He was so poor then that his guitar case had tape on it; it didn't have a handle. He put it under his arm like a fiddle or something. Then, of course, Roy Clark, he's my protege. When I formed my first band, the Party Timers, to go into Las Vegas, I knew I'd need somebody because we had to do five 45-minute shows a night. I had to have somebody to help me carry the load because I knew I couldn't stand up to that. He worked out beautifully and Ken Nelson and [manager] Jim Halsey were there that night and the rest, of course, is history. It really happened fast for him.

I love "Fujiyama Mama." I heard it when I was in high school, on the juke box at a little place where we went for Cokes. I played it every time I was in there, and finally I found the single, and then I recorded it later on.

What's confusing to a lot of fans is that I had been doing country before "Let's Have A Party." In the country field I had already had "You Can't Have My Love," "If You Don't Somebody Else Will," "Silver Threads And Golden Needles" and some other things on the charts that weren't as big as those. So the country fans knew me, but the bubblegum class didn't; that was the first time they had heard of me.

I've always felt that I'm just a country singer. That's really where I'm comfortable. Also, at the time, I got thrown into this rock 'n' roll scene and I didn't understand these people. I didn't live the lifestyle that they lived. I was just country folk, y'know? I loved the country artists because they were nice people. These other people, there wasn't anything wrong with them individually, it's just that I wasn't comfortable around the whole scene. So I said I wanted to get back to my roots. I'm glad that I did because I've stayed around longer because of that. Now, people are reflecting back so much and they're seeing what I did in those days and they appreciate it. But I'm afraid that if I had just stayed with rock 'n' roll I probably would've fizzled out before now. My voice would have, anyhow.

I became a Christian in June 1971. I recorded one gospel album for Capitol. They finally allowed me to do it; I'd wanted to do it before, but after I became a Christian my heart was in it and Ken Nelson agreed. Then in about six months I was wanting to do another one. Ken Nelson said, "Now, Wanda, we're not a gospel company. We can't do that many." I was pretty unhappy about that time, not with Ken Nelson, who was already getting ready to leave Capitol, but because every time I'd walk in I'd have a different producer. I'd never know who was going to be producing me. They were in a real turmoil. I still had a long-term contract and I didn't think you could get out of them — nobody asks to get *off* of Capitol Records! But I did and Ken Nelson agreed; he said he thought I'd be happier if I could record my gospel music. So he helped me get out of the contract. That wasn't real successful as a career concern, but it was what I wanted to do; it was very important to my spiritual life and growth. And it's proven to be good for my ministry. I go into churches and sing and give my testimony and my husband gives his testimony. So I had my career on one hand and my ministry on the other. *(Jeff Tamarkin; May 22, 1987.)*

Rockabilly evolved. It had to; it was inevitable. The music it became was country — again. Conway Twitty and Marty Robbins and Johnny Cash and Waylon Jennings reclaimed the sound and made country music out of it. Today singers like Marty Stuart and Emmylou Harris mine the same territory Carl Perkins mined almost 40 years ago.

Rockabilly became country-rock, in the hands of Gram Parsons and Chris Hillman. Rockabilly became roots-rock, in the hands of the Blasters and Los Lobos. It became power-pop, in the hands of Dave Edmunds and Nick Lowe. It became punk, in the hands of the Cramps. And it stayed rockabilly, in the hands of Robert Gordon and the Stray Cats.

It also became mainstream pop, in the hands of the Everly Brothers. The Everlys started from a country background, moved into rockabilly and then moved back out again, selling 15 million records a year for Cadence, and more than that over nearly 10 years with Warner Brothers. The Everlys' sound was based on almost telepathic harmonies that conveyed an incredible sense of yearning, combined with the wry, fresh songs of the songwriting team of Felice and Boudleaux Bryant. Their string of hits included "Bye Bye Love," "Take A Message To Mary," "Bird Dog," "Crying In The Rain," "All I Have To Do Is Dream," "Walk Right Back," "Cathy's Clown," "When Will I Be Loved," and "(So Sad) To Watch Good Love Go Bad." The brothers split up in 1973 but reunited in 1984 with a trimuphant concert tour and the Dave Edmunds-produced album, *EB '84*. The record included "On The Wings Of A Nightengale," a Paul McCartney-penned tune which *Rolling Stone* called "the best single of the year." It died on the charts.

Don Everly: Well, my mom and dad had a show for about 15 years off and on in Iowa and Tennessee. We were originally from Kentucky, but we moved around because we were in show business. That show entailed country music, gospel music and pop. I would do Pee Wee King's "Slow Poke," which I class as a pop song, and some Hank Williams songs, which I also class as pop because they were hits in the pop field for Tony Bennett. We did that right up to 1955.

Phil Everly: That's right. I was six years old when I started performing over live radio. Then, of course, live radio started dying out with the advent of television. The last radio show we did was in Knoxville, Tennessee, working the morning show. They finally fired us. The format of our show was much closer to the old Carter Family Show than, say, *The Adventures of Ozzie and Harriett*, where Ricky Nelson got his start. There was no situation comedy on our show.

Don Everly: You could send in and get rose bushes and things like that. It was a very legitimate radio-type show.

There [still is radio like that], but it's confined to places like Virginia, Tennessee and small stations. Now the larger radio stations will concentrate on big record deals instead of the little personal items.

Phil Everly: Well, our dad not only influenced us, but had a lot of influence on music generally. He taught Merle Travis to thumb-pick. He and another man, Mose Rager, who was also influenced by our dad, really helped to lay the foundations of the thumb-picking style which you hear everywhere today. The style originated out of Drakesburg, Kentucky, and if you really want to go back, my dad was influenced by a black man, Arnold Schulz. So, my dad has made an indirect contribution to a major proportion of the music you hear today. That's a fact.

Don Everly: "Bye Bye Love" was done on our first session. There were no real arrangements, and no one expected it to be a big hit. They expected it to be a country hit. Actually, Gordon Terry recorded it the same time we did and they expected his version to be a very big hit. They were counting on it.

Phil Everly: We would have sung anything at that time because we needed the money. We did it over the course of two days, and Donald devised the intro, which is a big ear-grabber. Oddly enough, he had put the same intro on another song six months earlier and Archie had turned it down. We were working a tent show in Mississippi when it became a hit.

The interesting thing is that Buddy Holly was in Lubbock, Texas, we were in Knoxville, Tennessee, Buddy Knox was in Oklahoma and so on. There were pockets of rock music all around the country. We were too pop to get on the Grand Ole Opry. We were too weird, our hair was too long and we didn't wear cowboy suits. We were different.

Don Everly: If you pinned it down, then I guess I'm classified as rock 'n' roll, but then we've also been classified as rhythm & blues and country. Now, there was a lot of fuss about Elvis in the early days, but I would have never bought one of his records. His image and charisma were more important. Ray Charles really knocked me out. When I recorded, I tried to do his music in the style I could do. Phil and I are really a strict mixture of rhythm 'n' blues and country. There's not too much dilution there.

How many hits do you think the English groups got off B.B. King before he was known? I loved that music. I worked with Howlin' Wolf at the Paramount years and years ago. Jimmy Reed is another one who's still forgotten. He didn't just influence me; he influenced Eddie Cochran, Buddy Holly and a lot of others. You hear shades of Jimmy Reed on records every day. I've felt that there's a lot of cheap copies of rhythm 'n' blues that I didn't care for. There's nothing worse than a bad copy of something that's good. You've got to digest your influences and come up with something that's valid. That's *you.*

Don Everly: We've been influenced a lot by the Beatles. Let's face it: the Beatles at their peak were one of the finest groups that there ever was and probably ever will be. People are still digesting what they've done.

Phil Everly: I think we may see a time of live recording again — live in the studio. The engineers were much more important back then. Originally we cut in monaural, then in two-track, then in four, etc. We had three hours to get down our performance, and if we didn't do it then it was a mess. The engineer had to catch it all. Like on "Bye, Bye Love" there's the part that goes "Bye, bye love — da, da, da da." He had to capture that punchiness. He couldn't whip that up later. The engineers back then were much more artistic in that sense. And, of course, now it's easier to go into a 16-track studio with no talent and still get something.

I have no hangup about living in the past, but touring was more fun. The large packages have gone. You'd be on tour for 80 days with your contemporaries, like seven or eight people out of the Top 10. The camaraderie was great, but that only lasted about three years.

Music comes out from what you are. A novice might say, "Hey, that's just the same as it was yesterday," but you can pick up differences just between two shows, the shadings and so on. Our music has changed as we've changed. It's hard to pinpoint specific changes. I'm older — much older. Basic maturity, you know. I think music has moved toward us. Look at it like a diagram. You have Buddy Holly, who could reach men in music, people who just liked music, you know. Then you had us with harmonies and Buddy had this guttiness, realness. It's moved toward us. Holly would be a giant if he were alive today. Individuality died out with the Fabian era; that just about killed the industry. Then you had the Beatles era, when people rushed over with pockets full of money to sign English acts ... it was absurd. Up until that time, everyone thought rock 'n' roll could stop any given day. No one projected into the future.

It's still what it was. Whenever we get together, we play and sing at home. It still feels good.
(Dave "Daddy Cool" Booth and Colin Escott; March 2, 1984.)

4. Reelin' and Rockin'

Chuck Berry, Bo Diddley and Little Richard took a lump of clay and made rock 'n' roll out of it. Among them they took the constituent parts of rock 'n' roll from the hands of the R&B bands and the country singers and the blues guitarists and made it a singular form of music, with styles of its own, and songs, and stars. Among them they cut the classics of rock 'n' roll, and established the riffs and chord progressions upon which almost everything else that would follow would be based. Among them they established the lexicon of rock 'n' roll and changed the course of music forever, and they did it on relatively small labels with little promotion or fanfare. And none of them had a #1 record in the '50s.

Charles Edward Berry was a reform-schooler who built cars, worked as a hairdresser, and played guitar. He joined the trio of pianist Johnnie Johnson on New Year's Eve 1952 at the Cosmopolitan Club in St. Louis, replacing a saxophone player. Berry thought of himself alternately as a suave singer in the Nat King Cole mold and a jazz guitarist, like Charlie Christian. With Johnson he played a country-tinged blues, like a shuffle but different, full of double-stops and bent notes.

In 1955 the trio went to Chicago and the offices of Chess Records. Chess was branching out, recording doo-wop vocal trios like the Flamingos and Moonglows in addition to the Muddy Waters and Howlin' Wolf blues that were the label's staples. Leonard Chess listened to the trio and heard something. He rushed them into the studio, where they cut "Ida Red," an up-tempo song, and a slow blues, "Wee Wee Hours." "Ida Red" was changed to "Maybellene," and the song was released. It was the first hit of the rock 'n' roll era, and the name on the label was not Johnnie Johnson. It was Chuck Berry.

"Maybellene" was followed by one classic after another: "Roll Over Beethoven," "School Day," "Rock And Roll Music," "Johnny B. Goode," "Sweet Little Sixteen," "Little Queenie," "Reelin' and Rockin'," "Around And Around," "Sweet Little Rock 'N' Roller," "Promised Land," "Back In The U.S.A.," and more. Many were based around the same chord progression, or even the same melody. The progressions were blues progressions, standard stuff. Similar or identical melodies were nothing new to blues. Berry wasn't doing anything that hadn't been done before — in that sense.

Berry appeared on TV, in movies and in concerts. He built an amusement park and bought big cars. But in 1959 he was arrested for violations of the Mann Act, which prohibited transporting a minor across state lines for immoral purposes. He was convicted and sent to prison.

When he was released, Berry resumed a somewhat productive career. He had hits with "Nadine," "You Never Can Tell" and "No Particular Place To Go," but the original licks were being outnumbered by the recycled ones, and the spark was gone. Berry kept touring — he continues to tour — but dropped his backup band and picked up whatever band was around in that town that night. Sometimes he was good with these bands, and sometimes he was awful. He just didn't seem to care one way or the other, as long as he was paid. He had his only #1 in 1972 with the ridiculous "My Ding-A-Ling."

Berry regained the limelight in 1986, when he published his autobiography and appeared in the concert film *Hail! Hail! Rock And Roll.* But the book and the film just further enhanced Berry's reputation as an enigma and his status as the father of rock 'n' roll.

Everybody has played a Chuck Berry song, and most everyone has cut one. Country singer Emmylou Harris had a hit with "You Never Can Tell." Classical rockers the Electric Light Orchestra had their first hit with "Roll Over Beethoven." They copied the Beatles, who also cut the song. Buddy Holly did "Brown-Eyed Handsome Man," a song that manages to fit Venus DeMilo and Willie Mays within two verses. Southside Johnny and the Asbury Jukes and Jerry Jeff Walker and the Lost Gonzo Band cut "Johnny B. Goode." The Beach Boys had hits with "Surfin' USA" and "Rock And Roll Music." British pub-rockers Ducks Deluxe and Cajun singer Johnnie Allan cut "Promised Land." So did the Grateful Dead.

Johnnie Johnson was Berry's piano player. Though it was Johnson's trio when Berry joined, Johnson doesn't seem to mind the turned-around way things worked out.

Chuck Berry: The music was here long before Louis Jordan, but to my recollection, Louis Jordan was the first one that I heard play rock 'n' roll. Louis Jordan's music was popular, but the white population didn't hear it until I came along. Not until I came along, but until the period when I came along, when the radio stations started lifting the ban on black music. There were radio stations in St. Louis that didn't play any black music. If they didn't play it, you didn't hear it. When Alan Freed started his exploitations, and he saw 'em dancin' and rockin' on the floor, doin' the barrelhouse roll, you know, so it was rock 'n' roll music. That's where the "brand" came from. But Louis Jordan was playin' it long before me, Fats, any of us.

I came up with Tommy Dorsey and Nat Cole and Glenn Miller. Swingman. Swing was my thing. And that's really what I'm playin' now. I'm only playin' it with three pieces, which makes it rock 'n' roll. Most of the stuff I do could've been wrapped up in Tommy Dorsey's "Boogie Woogie," Count Basie's "Tuxedo Junction," Flying Home," Lionel Hampton, Carl Hogan. [Carl Hogan played electric guitar with Louis Jordan's Tympany Five. Check out his solo on Jordan's "Blue Light Boogie."]

What I was playing was more blues than rock. You see, rock wasn't named rock. It got named rock during the time I was there. Little Richard had "Tutti Frutti" out before I had "Maybellene." And Bill Haley had "Rock Around The Clock" before I left. But I had recorded, and my record "Maybellene" was doing things up around WENY in New York.

I don't know how many gold records I earned. I don't know how many gold records anybody else earned. To earn a gold record, I don't know if any one person would know, because too many people have their hands in the pie. BMI and ASCAP are the only ones that really know how many gold records. They don't even really know. They know what's reported, how many records sold. But if they report a million, then you know you got a million. So far as BMI is concerned, there's more than one. And as long as they pay me the bread, it can stay one, the way I have problems with my taxes. *[At this point, Chuck leaned closer to the microphone, as if to make sure he would be heard.]* So, yes, there's been one, I.R.S. There's been one. *[Chuck laughs]* I'm payin' my taxes now, so it doesn't make any difference. There's been more than one, let's put it that way.

With about one-eighth of my wealth now, I could live to be 100 and have it pretty good. But I darn sure wouldn't be out there for the next 20 years doin' benefits. I don't know how many times I've been asked, "Doesn't it hurt you to see another artist doing your number, and making more than you made out it?" In the first place, he never gets it for nothing, because anything that you create, you get a royalty from it. But people think that should hurt me, because someone else made $2 million off something, and I only made two or three hundred thousand.

You'd have to be black to know what I'm gettin' ready to say now. That's happened to me so many times that it's just a passin' thing now. You become immune to hurt. It's an everyday thing, to be turned back so many times. The next turnback, you say, "Well, okay, it's one of those things." But if you've never been turned back, you can see where if I get my 15th turnback, and you happen to see it, and you've never been turned back, you should think it would kill me dead. But it's nothin' to be turned back, or turned down, or whatever.

It's not hurt that you're talking about. It's fear. There's no such thing as hurt. You're either in fear or you're in happiness. Fear is the father of all negative emotions. If you feared nothing, it couldn't hurt you. I haven't conquered it, but I've mastered it. I feel a little, but when I think of why I fear something, you can diminish it and squash it right out. You just have to analyze your hurt as you go along.

I'm livin' like a champ. Payin' my taxes. Boy, this tax thing that I was in was no bum rap. It was straight true. It was a bum rap in the sense that it was little more, it was about 15 percent that they added on, but that's nothing to kick about. In other words, they were 85 percent right and 15 percent wrong. But what made it so bad is, if I had known that there was more than just payin' it back, if I'd have know that there was a penalty to it ... No, I went that route. I've had some penalties. And every penny I still had in my safe. I didn't want nobody to find the dollar with the number on it. I just thought, "Well, whenever they catch up with ya ..." Six years I had it. Six years I held that bread. And I told them that I still had it. I was just lettin' 'em know, "If y'all want it back, y'all know where it is." *[Chuck laughs]* And they said, "Mmm, you mean you got $400,000 somewhere?"

Is rock 'n' roll comin' back? It never left, baby, if you wanna know something. People don't want to see 17 pieces up there in neckties. That's what they don't want. They wanna see some jeans out there, and some gettin' down, and some wigglin'. They don't want it just straight. Charlie Christian was the best guitar player, and he never looked up from his guitar. The greatest guitar player that ever was, Charlie Christian. And Carl Hogan, looked up from his guitar. Most of my licks came from Carl Hogan and Charlie Christian. But because I've put a little dance with it, I guess they appreciate hearin' somethin' along with seein' somethin'.

As for my colleagues, Bo's not makin' the money. Bo's really been clipped. His manager was clippin' him. And that ain't all. He clipped him financially and socially. Even had his wife move all the way to Florida. You see, Bo doesn't have too much education, and Bo's satisfied with a few little mature toys, like color cameras where he can take pictures and see 'em right back, and things like that that excite him. I love him. Here's a guy that's down and don't even know he's down, and he's good. He's good because he's down, I guess. You gotta love an ignorant person that's not belligerent. You gotta love him. He plays what he knows. So was Presley, playin' what he knows, but he got some backin' up and some guidance. Bo didn't have no guidance. It's a shame, too. Domino had schoolin'. Domino knew what he was doin'. He had a nice manager. And McPhatter, he ruined his stomach. Lloyd Price is a smart guy, but lawd, he didn't get the breaks that Domino got, or that Bo Diddley or I got. Larry Williams was very belligerent. Larry had a chance to do *American Hot Wax* and blew it. He wanted $700 instead of $500. And at that time, when he was down, it would have raised his exploitations, you know, among the public. I hate to talk about my colleagues like that. I just thought it was belligerent. Little Richard's so wishy-washy. That's a good artist, man. Boy, I liked his songs. Man, he sang. He had a beautiful voice for rock 'n' roll. Beautiful voice. I think Richard oughta get back in there.

I play about six to eight gigs a month. If I did more, I'd fall short on my administration. I have 26 pieces of property that I'm takin' care of, and nine of them are out here on the coast. It takes some time to keep up with what comes up, and get the answers back. It's just not all telephone work. You gotta look at some of these things. Commercial properties and aprtments. One's in Canada. It cost 28 grand in '71, and now it's worth 76 grand. Now this is an accomplishment to

CHUCK BERRY: 'Rock wasn't named rock. It got named rock during the time I was there. But Louis Jordan was playin' it before me, Fats, any of us.'

me as much as having written the song "Johnny B. Goode." I got a piece of property right in L.A., paid $90,000 for, and I was offered $250,000 for it.

I've done a thousand dates in the last five years. Two have been ridiculous, but still wound up with the audience hollering for "more, more, more." Because there's something behind that. People kind of like mistakes. When mistakes happen, you can make a joke out of them that's almost better than the music that they came expecting to hear. Because it's brand new. There's no two mistakes alike. And I doubt if there's ever any two handled alike.

I love the blues, and I played the blues tonight, but that's not makin' money. That's entertainin' the people. You put it on record, it'd sell 17 copies. But tonight I may have thrilled a thousand people with that one blues. But people think, "I know he's playin' the real thing because he knows what's happening — and if he don't, he should." *[Chuck laughs.]*

B.B. King has wrote the song: "The Thrill Is Gone." I enjoy it if I satisfy the people the people, which is accomplishing the mission; it's good. But as far as the thrill ... I'd have never gone out there tonight if they had been just $1,000 short. I don't think I deserve to have any less than what I'm accepting, which is less than the average act of my status.

I don't need to be out there. I turned down a $22,000 job because I should've made $30,000 on this particular job. Now you know the thrill ain't gone. If the thrill was really gone, I'd have took the 22, because that would be money sure enough. When you know you're bein' hit, forget it. Especially if you don't have to do it. Forget it. But I enjoy it.

People don't retire. My father, and all these people, they cut grass. They fix their porches. Is that retirin'? You might as well do something beneficial. I come out here and do my type of cuttin' grass. I can go back and have six cats to cut grass. Twenty cats to cut grass. So I'll do what they want me for, and get somebody else to cut grass. I'm satisfied. *(John Etheredge; November 1983.)*

❦

Johnnie Johnson: My mother bought a piano when I was about seven years old, and after the movers brought the piano in the house and left, I sat down and went to playing it. I was just playing a perfect tune, and my mother just went to crying. This is when she said my playing was a gift from God. So to bring it right to the point, I've been messing around and playing piano since I was about seven years old.

I was pretty much just playing the standards that were out at the time, like "Chopsticks" — the things that a little kid could learn by music. I was playing by ear. I could hear a piece of music and then just sit down and start playing it.

I can read chords, but I can't spot-read — that is, note for note. Like if somebody would bring a sheet of music into a club where were playing, I couldn't play it right off the bat. I'd have to play the chords on the music. So I can read chords, but that's my limit.

I never did have a teacher; what I learned was all self-taught. There were some instances where another musician would explain a chord or two to me, like, "This is a B-flat 7th" or, "This is a B-flat 9th," but that was about it.

I first started playing in clubs after I got out of the Marine Corps in 1946. I started playing in clubs in Detroit. Then I left Detroit and went to Chicago, where I got a little more experience playing in clubs and was making a little more money, and then eventually I left Chicago and came to East St. Louis.

I played in mostly black neighborhoods that had these dinner clubs and things. From 1953 on up, there didn't appear to be that much segregation going on, because I played in a lot of clubs where white and colored were having dinner or whatever together, so it wasn't real segregated. But some sections of the city or places I went were.

I remember being on the road with the first big show that I went out with, the Buddy Johnson Band. Sometimes we'd have to play two shows, one for the black audience and one for the white. Some places we went, we couldn't even get a hotel; we'd have to sleep with the families, black families, that lived in the towns where we'd play. So many of them would take a different band member into their homes and that's how we would spend the night.

I had a brother in East St. Louis, and he got me a job working with him at the Pennsylvania Railroad freight house. In time, I met a lot of musicians, and then I got on a bill at a club.

This particular club was called the Cosmopolitan, where I hired Chuck Berry to work with me because I was a man short. Chuck replied by coming to work with me, and we've been together ever since.

We were recognized as a group and were well liked, but adding this guitar and replacing the saxophone, it was something different, and Chuck had more of a flair for showmanship than the fellow he was replacing. Chuck came in there clowning; what I mean by clowning is he had this little thing he did called the "buggy ride." He would pantomime, in other words, and that held the people's attention. Then he came up with the duck walk and the type of music he was starting to write and all this was different, so it went over very big.

Chuck first did the duck walk at the Cosmopolitan in 1954, before "Maybellene" had come out, and he used to do this across the stage and the crowd of people in there would go wild.

Oh, I liked it, because it was funny to me. I had never seen anything like that, y'know; it was real comical to me.

When I hired Chuck he was playing shuffle boogies and guitar boogies, and he started this rock 'n' roll stuff, y'know, he started providing the songs almost immediately. Like there was this piece called "Ida Red." It was a western tune that Chuck wrote and we had been playing, but when we went over to see the Chess Recording Company in Chicago and Leonard Chess heard it, he liked the song, but not the name. There was a mascara box laying on the floor in the corner of the studio and Leonard Chess said, "Well, hell, let's name the damn thing 'Maybellene.' " That's how "Maybellene" got its name — off a discarded mascara box. You probably know the rest of the story from there.

Learning Chuck's songs was simple. It was just a shuffle, y'know, playing a blues and a shuffle, a rock 'n' roll tune and a shuffle, and the were practically patterned all the same. They would just be in different keys.

I almost knew what he was going to play before he played it. We had, I guess, what you'd call vibes. He could follow me when I'd take a solo and give it a background that really made the solo stand out. And when he was taking his solo or singing, I knew just what to play behind him so that it would blend in just right. That's the best that I can explain it.

In the studio, I had an old upright piano and they put the mike in back of it. The people at the Chess Recording Company would make all the arrangements for the amplifiers and the microphones and things like that, and they would adjust the mikes to where they would get the best sound.

When we were getting ready to record, they'd get a sound check on all this and adjust the balance for each instrument while we'd be running over the song two or three times to feel out what Chuck was saying in the tune or what he was thinking of. Then when we'd actually start recording, we'd try to take the least amount of cuts of it as we could. The idea was that they were trying to keep you from being tense.

I remember too well how nervous I was going in to do our first record, "Maybellene" and "Wee Wee Hours." I was scared I was going to hit the wrong key and mess up the recording, but after that session, once we established that we'd have this little rehearsal before, it became very relaxed and it would take maybe three or four cuts and the record would be made. Certain things would go down this time that didn't go down the last time, but generally speaking, it was just the same old routine when we'd be in recording. They were all just routine recordings.

My favorite has got to be "Johnny B. Goode," because Chuck specified in his autobiography that it was written for me. So, yeah, that's my favorite, and "Wee Wee Hours." Now that one is one of my pleasures.

One of the most exciting things that happened to me was back when I first came to St. Louis. I was a great fan of Earl "Fatha" Hines, the piano player, and he had put out this W.C. Handy thing, a boogie-woogie on the "St. Louis Blues." So I was sitting in the Musician's Hall one day and I was playing this piece when the manager of the hall came over and said, "Johnnie, this gentleman's band is playing at the Y tonight and they'd like to use this piano for rehearsal." So I said sure and jumped up and turned around, and found myself looking right into Earl Hines' face. He had been standing behind me for like 10 or 15 minutes while I was playing his song. He shook my hand and congratulated me on my playing and I just went out the door like I was in a trance or something. That's a memory that I'll have for the rest of my life. *(Danny McCue; Sept. 21, 1990.)*

❦

If Chuck Berry was the father of rock 'n' roll, Bo Diddley was the crazy uncle with the beat. Elias Otha Bates was born in the Mississippi Delta and raised by his mother's cousin, who changed his name to McDaniel and moved him to Chicago when he was five. Young McDaniel took violin lessons and played trumpet for awhile, but didn't take to any instrument until his sister Lucille bought him an electric guitar. He wired the guitar through an old radio, and soon had formed a blues and boogie group with his cousin and a friend. They called themselves the Langley Avenue Jive Cats and played on street corners and flea markets — anywhere they could make a few cents.

In the late '40s, McDaniel was driving a truck and working construction for a living, and playing guitar on weekends. His wife, Ethel Mae Smith, didn't approve of his staying out late and playing music. "She reportedly became adamant about the matter," Ed Heath wrote, "and decided that the couple's bed should be equipped with a razor, at which point McDaniel decided to forego the pleasures of matrimony for a while."

By the early '50s McDaniel had a solid, albeit unconventional, band. Jerome Green shook maracas and Frank Kirland played drums. McDaniel played guitar and sang. They were a blues and boogie band with a beat. But McDaniel still drove his truck, and boxed lightweight on the side.

McDaniel could have picked up the name "Bo Diddley" from a couple of places. Delta kids would make primitive stringed instruments out of boards, nails, a couple of empty bottles, and waste-cotton string, and call them "diddly-bows." "Bo Diddly" was a slang phrase for bully in Chicago. Whatever the origin of the name, it was also the name of the band's first record, made as a demo and hawked to local record companies. Leonard Chess liked it and decided to release it. And as Heath wrote, "At that point Elias McDaniel became Bo Diddley."

Diddley's first record was a two-sided hit. "Bo Diddley" was backed with "I'm A Man," a grinding blues in the Muddy Waters vein. They became an R&B #1 in 1955. Diddley only cracked the R&B top 10 twice more, and had only five records crack the pop charts. Only one made it as high as #20.

Bo Diddley was more of a rhythm generator than a singer or songwriter. The double-thumping, toe-tapping beats of "Who Do You Love" and "Bo Diddley" were not the same beat but an assortment of beats, all Delta-based and irresistible. They were the products of influences, and maybe some of those influences stretch all the way back to Africa, but mostly they were the products of Diddley himself.

BO DIDDLEY: 'Me, Chuck Berry, Gene Vincent, Carl Perkins, we all launched this thing, but my music was the first to be called rock 'n' roll.'

"What has always made the Diddley sound unique and immediately recognizable," Heath wrote, "is not a particular beat but the music's driving insistence from beginning to end. In

Diddley's best stuff, the rhythm and melody are one and the same, grabbing the listener/dancer within the first three bars and never letting loose until the last note has died away, and sometimes, not even then. The music has an urgency — that is the Bo Diddley stamp — and even when someone else is playing, there is never any doubt as to whom it belongs."

A thousand times more people have copied Diddley's rhythm than have ever covered his songs. "Who Do You Love" is a scary piece of music. The reclusive folk singer Townes Van Zandt covered it, and Diddley covered it himself on the soundtrack to the movie *La Bamba*. Buddy Holly covered "Bo Diddley" and brought the song and the singer out to a whole new audience. In 1974 Diddley returned the favor by cutting "Not Fade Away," a Holly song with a Diddley beat.

Warren Zevon, on his unjustifiably overlooked live album, *Stand In The Fire,* covers both "Bo Diddley" and "Bo Diddley's A Gunslinger." The songs are as fierce a couple of pieces of rock 'n' roll as have been cut in the last 15 years. And the songs have as much to do with the songs as the singer and the performance.

Bo Diddley: I changed my name to Bo Diddley in my earlier years when I was a boxer. I quit fighting, picked up a guitar and here I am.

I was there first when it all started, along with such other artists as the Flamingos, Moonglows, Little Walter Jacobs, Muddy Waters, Spaniels and others. And during that time, as I remember, there was basically only black and white music. Many white stations did not play the "new" thing in music called rock 'n' roll, and also rhythm and blues. Alan Freed was the man who had enough nerve to play the records of those various artists, including mine, and send this new music out over the nation. Many people put Alan down for this, but my hat's off to him, because he was a fighter and a believer. If it wasn't for him, we may have been a few years late getting a little taste of rock 'n' roll. I'm sure there would have been other DJs who would have played it, but the people who owned the radio stations just didn't understand, for it was something that was just too new.

Frank Kirland and Jerome Greene are both deceased now. That band broke up because Jerome got married; his wife took him off the road.

The Duchess was named Norma Jean Wofford, and she was in the group for three or four years. She's in Los Angeles County somewhere now.

Who came up with the idea of maracas in a rock 'n' roll band?

Bo Diddley.

Bo Diddley's A Gunslinger was my favorite album. That was my favorite cover, too. With the *Black Gladiator* album, that was all my idea. I used to go to movies all the time and see white gladiators on the screen. I said, "Well, shoot, I got a few muscles; I'm gonna be the black gladiator." And the thing about it was, I was very capable of backing up that name, if there was a confrontation, ya understand. I'm still the Black Gladiator. I was a light heavyweight around the neighborhood and Corpus Christi.

I feel that during the '50s I was unjustly handled. If I had had the manager that I have now, I would be a multimillionaire today. I never really used to tell anyone, but I was ripped off pretty bad by the people at Chess Records. I never thought they would do what they did to a lot of their artists. I am happy, though, about them giving me a chance, because I did have the opportunity to travel all over the world, make a lot of friends, and make a name for myself. This was all beautiful, but there was absolutely no reason for what they did to me and their other artists.

My music did not get the promotion after I started to wise up and figured out what was happening. That's when things started to decrease with Bo Diddley at the hands of the Chess organization. It was like they thought, "Uh-oh, the nigger's gettin' smart."

They might have pushed my records here, but they had this little black-and-white thing goin' during those years and it was just plain stupid that people disliked you because of the color of your skin, but they liked everything you did. I don't believe that most white people really hated blacks. I really don't believe that. Black people did most of the cookin' for a lot of white people. Now, the way I look at that is, if I don't like you, you ain't comin' in my house and do nothin', and you definitely ain't comin' in my damned kitchen!

So what was it? Economics, dollar bills. "Let's keep him here, give him a little money and a pat on the head, and keep him happy." This was the story that went down, and it was still goin' down in the '50s when rock 'n' roll started. And nobody knew what was happenin' until blacks and whites started talkin' to one another. This kind of shook people at that time, that black musicians were beginning to talk to white musicians. They didn't want this because we were getting too friendly, too chummy. We were not supposed to do that in "Old America." I call this "New America" now; it feels a lot better.

Seems to me like the concept of rock 'n' roll is for everybody, but you'll never get rid of all the fools because, as I've said many times, you can even find a fool in church, and there ain't supposed to be any fools in church. But the devil goes to church too. Sometimes the devil's onstage with you when you're playin', tryin' to make you fail. He might be a fellow in your band who really don't want to be there: "Just give me my check so I can leave." That's the devil workin' with you, and in him.

Chuck [Berry] and I used to be very far apart because I think there used to be some sort of hidden professional jealousy. It's not that we ever had words, but rather that we just didn't associate. Chuck, though, is a very strange man, very strange. Now, we're the best of friends. I'll tell you how tight we are; I'll go to Los Angeles, and Chuck will hunt me down 'til he finds me. Then we may go over to his house and look at some old films or stuff like that. Either that or he'll call me at 4 a.m. lost on the highway someplace, trying to find the way to my house. Then I'll have to get up out of bed and go to meet him and lead him back to my ranch. These are the little things that make me feel good. I really am so glad that we have become friends. Even though I thoroughly don't understand him, he is a beautiful cat.

Rock 'n' roll was not started by Little Richard, or Elvis Presley, or Chuck Berry, or, for that matter, not by Bo Diddley, alone. Me, Chuck Berry, Gene Vincent, Carl Perkins, we all launched this thing, but my music was the first to be called rock 'n' roll. Alan Freed used to introduce me on stage and say, "Here is the man with the original sound, and he's gonna rock 'n' roll you right outchyour seats." The name rock 'n' roll was invented by Alan Freed.

[Little] Richard don't bother me sayin' [he's the inventor of rock 'n' roll]. He's a very good friend of mine. He knows the truth, so we don't have to go too far with that. Richard's a show-man, and he's a good one. And what he is doin' is psychin' the public, but he knows that I was here two or three years ahead of him.

He's the same as Elvis. Elvis Presley was a very nice person, but he didn't invent anything either, ya know? To Elvis, rhythm 'n' blues was the same as rock 'n' roll. Rhythm 'n' blues was for black people, and when white people did the same songs, they called it rock 'n' roll. We later found out what the difference was: Rock 'n' roll carried a bigger paycheck than rhythm'n' blues. This was all geared to keep black people from gettin' their hands on any money. And that's the honest-to-God truth. If they'd wanted to pay me the kind of money they paid Elvis, then maybe I could have had me all the things Elvis had. *(Ed Heath, July 27, 1990; and Wayne Jones, issue #12.)*

If Chuck Berry was the father of rock 'n' roll and Bo Diddley the weird uncle with the beat, Little Richard was the good uncle, the mother and the favorite son all rolled in one. Someone less kind might say that if Elvis was the king of rock 'n' roll, Little Richard was the queen.

To hear him tell it, Little Richard had the prettiest face in rock 'n' roll, the tallest hair, the brightest teeth, the flashiest clothes, the highest scream, the best band, the loudest piano, the wildest stage act, the most bizarre sex life, and the craziest music in rock 'n' roll. To hear him tell it, Little Richard invented rock 'n' roll. To his detractors, Michelle Phillips had a prettier face, Wayne Cochran had taller hair, Sam Cooke had whiter teeth, and the rest was swiped from Esquerita. The truth is somewhere between, and probably closer to Little Richard than to his detractors.

Richard Penniman was a dishwasher who played piano in his spare time, and came up with the lyrics to songs while he washed dishes. By 1953 he was recording for the New Orleans-based Speciality Records, who wanted to make him a blues singer. The result of the first recording session was "Tutti Frutti," a song Penniman wrote with obscene lyrics but recorded with newly written, slightly cleaner lyrics. Its rhythmic punch and explosive "A-whomp-bomp-a-lu-bomp-a-whomp-bam-BOOM!" was undeniable. Along with "Maybellene" and "Bo Diddley" it was one of the first definitive records of the rock era.

"Tutti Frutti" was followed by a string of great songs for Speciality: "Rip It Up," "Long Tall Sally," "Keep A-Knocking," "Good Golly, Miss Molly," "Lucille," "Ooh! My Soul," "Ready Teddy." None of them were particularly big hits. All of them were insistent, pounding, driving rockers, with Richard screaming and shouting above the din of what might have been the wildest band in rock 'n' roll. They are good and powerful and indescribable, and absolutely essential.

By 1960 Little Richard had renounced popular music and enrolled in a Bible school. By the early '60s he was rocking again, appearing with the Beatles and cutting more up-tempo, piano-pounding sides. In the '70s he found religion again. In the '80s he varied between finding religion and cutting rock 'n' roll. He wrote an autobiography that told appropriately wild stories of his bisexual, debauched life at the top, and had a chart hit with "Great Gosh A' Mighty," from the movie *Down And Out In Beverly Hills.* In the 1990s he was playing a handful of concert dates and doing Nike and Taco Bell commercials. No one except for Jerry Lee Lewis has struggled as much with God and the devil. No one except for Jerry Lee Lewis was a more dynamic piano player. No one had been as wild as Little Richard and come out of it so unscathed.

Little Richard: I recorded for RCA in 1950. [Note: It was actually 1951.] That was for Camden. If you was black, it was called Camden Records, and if you were white it was called RCA Victor. I was with them before Elvis came to them. Elvis came to them in '55. I had already recorded rock for them but they didn't push me. Then from there I went to Peacock Records in Houston and did some work with Don Robey. John Otis was recording for him and Willie Mae Thornton. She did "Hound Dog" about three years after that. [Note: Thornton actually recorded the song in 1952, before Richard came to Peacock.] When I first got to RCA they were calling me the orginator of rock 'n' roll, the king of rock 'n' roll. I was the first person to record that kind of music. I had never heard that kind of music. I was so different there wasn't nobody that would want to touch me. The bands didn't want to play with me because they said, "Man, the way you play, there ain't nobody want to hear that." They wanted blues, and I was rockin'. Even Chuck Berry was playing blues at the time. He was playing stuff like Muddy Waters. I was the only one doin' all that ravin' and screamin', and everybody thought I was a lunatic. So they said, "This man is the architect; he's the orginator of rock and roll."

I was on Peacock, and he said, "Man, why don't you send a record to Specialty?" So I sent a blues. I said, "Maybe I'll just start singing the blues, 'cause there ain't nobody listenin' to this other stuff." So I sang a blues called "Wonderin' " and I sent it to Art Rupe at Specialty. He sent Bumps Blackwell a year later to meet me in New Orleans, at Cosimo [Matassa]'s studio.

Bumps Blackwell got Lee Allen and Earl Palmer and Red Tyler to play with me. This same band recorded with Fats, but they recorded a different type thing with Fats. Fats was more like country blues.

Larry Williams, Huey Smith, they never played piano on my records. I always played. In fact, I didn't know Huey Smith that well. And Larry Williams, I put Larry in show business. Larry, Jimi Hendrix, James Brown, Otis Redding, Joe Tex, the Beatles, Mick Jagger — those people started with me. I started them. I never knew that Larry Williams could play the piano like that. Or Huey Smith. They wasn't famous then and nobody was allowed in the studio. It wasn't but three tracks in like a little kitchen. We had to squeeze in to sing. No, that was a lie, the same as it was a lie that I got my hairstyle from Esquerita. That was a mistake in printing and we went back to the printing company on that. Esquerita copied me. Now, I did learn to play some things from Esquerita on the piano.

Back then a lot of the songwriting credits were taken from me. Like John Marascalco was my chauffeur, a white guy out of Mississippi. He came to me with a bunch of words and I wrote the songs, but I didn't have enough sense to get the crediting. Like "Rip It Up," I wrote the songs, I put the melody to all the songs but I didn't get no credit, I didn't know.

I didn't get the credit I should get, because of Bumps Blackwell. I'm a writer, and when somebody brings a song to me I change it. All they brought to me was words on paper. Now, "Slippin' And Slidin'," I did that by myself. They didn't have nothing to do with that. Same with "Tutti Frutti." She [Dorothy LaBostrie, who is credited with having changed Richard's obscene original lyrics to the familiar words] shouldn't have gotten any credit for that. But I couldn't do nothing about it. I did the writing. The record company had nothing to do with it [the co-crediting]. That was Bumps, the producer, and the writer. Art Rupe had nothing to do with it. At the time I don't think Bumps really knew at much about the business, either.

Back then you had to get broken on the black stations first. Then the Top 40 stations would pick you up, like Alan Freed, who was a great person and a good friend. Jocks like Dr. Jive, King Bee, Rodney Jones would have to start playing it first. A lot of black jocks and programmers and promotions men didn't get credit back then for what they did. Or black heads of record companies. Now they do, and I'm grateful to see it. I just hope they don't forget about their brother Richard.

I used to listen to a station out of Nashville called WLAC. It had a guy named Gene Nobles, and I listened to him. That's where I first heard "Tutti Frutti" after I recorded it. My mother didn't know that my name was Little Richard. It came on and I said, "Mother, that's me." I had snuck off and recorded it. That was a big thrill.

Of all my old songs I like "Lucille." It sounds like a choo-choo train. The train used to run in front of my house in Macon. I was glad to write about it.

Out of all the covers of my songs, I have two favorites. One is Paul [McCartney's] "Long Tall Sally" and the other was Otis Redding's version of "Lucille." And my other favorite was Sam Cooke with "Send Me Some Lovin'."

I was a creator in the studio, plus I was an innovator. I would take chances and try things. Which I'd like to do in this generation. I hope that some record company will give me that opportunity. And I'm still with God. I'm still a messenger and my music is the message sound and I thank everybody for everything, and I would appreciate if they would go and get *Lifetime Friend.*

We were like the Martin Luther Kings in music. You wouldn't hear people like Michael or Diana Ross if it hadn't been for me. I broke the ice for them and Prince, Whitney Houston, Janet Jackson, Tina Turner. I opened the door. I'd appreciate it if I could do a duet with one of them.

One last question before we go: When the history of Little Richard is written, how would you like to be remembered?

As the originator and creator of rock 'n' roll. And as someone who had God and kept the Sabbath. God bless you. *(Jeff Tamarkin; April 10, 1987.)*

Charles Connor: Richard, along with me, created a certain kind of beat. Richard wanted a whole lot of excitement! He wanted the drummer to do a lot while he was playing. At that time, we didn't have a bass player, so I had to play heavy with my kick drum. That type of energy had a lot of eighths and sixteenth notes. I never heard any drummer play like that before. Richard would be doing the same kind of energy and rhythm on the piano.

I started out backing Professor Longhair in New Orleans. His style was really interesting, and you noticed when you were doing a good job. If he was satisfied with your playing he would look at you and smile, maybe wink his eyes or something. So you knew you were in good company.

We met Richard at his hotel after we had seen him the night before. We were so nervous. Richard asked, "How would you like to play behind me? I want to form a band after I finish my

engagement here and go to Macon, Georgia. I need an ace drummer and a saxophone player."
We were so excited that he would pay us $15 each a night and guarantee us four nights a week. I
was underage, so my mother had to give her consent. She didn't want to, but she did.

In Macon one night, Lloyd Price told Richard that if he had any kind of demo tape or anything to send it to Specialty Records. So Richard sent them a demo tape, but months had
passed. They finally asked Richard to come down to Cosimo Studios in New Orleans to cut a
demo tape for Specialty Records. The thing about it is that Specialty didn't want Richard to sing
up-tempo stuff; they wanted him to be a blues singer! But Richard had so much energy and
everything!

After "Tutti Frutti" came out, Little Richard went to the West Coast to play some dates with
Johnny Otis and then left us in Georgia for about three weeks. During that time our manager,
Clint Bradley, had some dates to fill for Little Richard, and he didn't want to lose his deposits.
Richard wasn't there, so guess who took his place: James Brown! It had Little Richard's picture
on the placard, and when we were getting ready to call James out, we'd say, "We're now bringing out Litttlllllle ... ,' while the crowd screamed. We'd never say "Little Richard." Everybody
was saying, "That don't look like Little Richard!" So James would sing "Tutti Frutti" and
everything with his head down. This was before he had any hits.

With James we were going to some strange territories in places like Kentucky, where people
had never seen Little Richard. We filled 18 dates, but it still had Richard's name and picture on
the placard! James acted like Richard; he had a little dance step and all. You have to remember
in those days there wasn't too much communication and a lot of people didn't have television
sets. But nobody asked for refunds, because James was a good entertainer and he'd satisfy the
audience. We'd give them a longer show, but we'd hope and pray that we'd get out of that place.

On "Keep A-Knockin'," Little Richard wanted something different. First, he thought of a
four-bar piano solo and said, "That's not powerful enough!" Then he thought of a four-bar bass
intro and said, "That's not it, either." So I said, "Let's do something that's never been done
before. How about a four-bar drum intro?"

I believe that was the first rock 'n' roll drum intro on record, and it's still strong today. But it
was something different. I've heard different bands trying to do an imitation of it, and they just
couldn't handle it. You've got to come up with those accents in certain places.

"Lucille" was one of the most powerful tunes Richard did. It had jazz undertones because the
guys in the band loved jazz. You couldn't call them jazz musicians, but they loved Charlie
Parker, Coleman Hawkins, all those guys. Clifford Burke, the tenor saxophone player, was really
into jazz. Grady Gaines and Wilbur Smith also really loved jazz. That's why it has that flavor.

I liked "Ooh! My Soul" because I had a special little thing I could do with the drums, some-
thing like a little pickup with sixteenth notes or whatever. "She's Got It" was more of a New
Orleans French Quarter second line beat, sort of a Paris-type rhythm there. It has that New
Orleans gumbo flavor.

The Upsetters wasn't just a name; when we'd go into a place, we'd upset it! We were the first
band on the road to wear pancake makeup and eye shadow, have an earring hanging out of our
ear, and have our hair curled in the process. It was really gay-looking. Richard was the only guy
in the band that was actually like that, but he wanted us to be different and exciting. We played
big auditoriums, 10,000 to 12,000 people. That was a lot of people in those days.

We were going across the Pacific Ocean on our way to Sydney, Australia, on a four-engine
plane. One of the engines on the plane caught fire. I used to drink pretty heavy then. I actually
had to drink to build up my nerves to ride on it.

I was sitting by the window of the plane. Out of the sun. I thought, "It can't be the sun this
time of night." I looked on the left side, and one of the engines had caught on fire. All of the guys
in the band immediately started praying; I personally had an instant bowel movement. I got
nervous and went back to the bathroom and changed my clothes. Little Richard was praying,
asking the Lord to save us. That's when he made up his mind to come out of show business.
(Frank Beeson; April 10, 1987.)

☙ ☙ ☙

5. All Shook Up

Elvis Presley *was* the king of rock 'n' roll, for longer than most people thought either logical or prudent.

Elvis Presley was the king because he did new things to rock 'n' roll at a time there was scarcely such a thing as rock 'n' roll, and did them with more style and sex appeal than anyone else. Presley was the king because with his supple voice and steamy, hip-throwing style he could sing blues, country, pop, black doo-wop ballads, rockabilly, and everything in-between and make it his and his alone. Otis Blackwell was one of the true innovators in rock; Doc Pomus called him a genius. But Presley took Blackwell's "Don't Be Cruel" and made it an Elvis Presley song, once and forever. The Orioles did a marvelous "Crying In The Chapel"; Elvis covered it, and it was his. Carl Perkins' "Blue Suede Shoes" was a powerhouse; Elvis snatched it from him. And he did the same thing with songs as disparate as Bill Monroe's "Blue Moon Of Kentucky" or "Harbor Lights." Even "My Way" was conquered by Elvis, by siege, by sheer weight of bombast. The instant when Elvis Presley ceased to become the king of rock 'n' roll was not when he veered too far into the mainstream, because he was headed into the mainstream all along. Elvis Presley ceased to be the king of rock 'n' roll when the songs he was recording were tailored so expressly for him that there were no more chances to take, no opportunity to take that song and make it his, and not leave it as someone else's.

Elvis Aron Presley was born in Tupelo, Miss., to an obsessive mother and a less-than-obsessive father. Elvis was one of twins; the second child was stillborn. He grew up in the housing projects of Memphis, and later went to work driving a bakery truck.

One of his childhood acquaintances was Jimmy Denson.

Jimmy Denson: My daddy was a traveling evangelist. His revival tent had been blown away in a storm in Florida, and we were on our way to Oklahoma to hit the sawdust trail when our limousine broke down near Memphis in December 1932. For the first five years of my life we lived in 16 states before we settled in Memphis and founded the Poplar Street Mission.

After hearing my daddy for two weeks, Mrs. Presley said, "Sister Denson, I'd like for my boy to be able to play the guitar like Brother Denson." My mother said that her 15 year-old-son, Jessie Lee, was a much better guitarist than his daddy. She asked him to teach Elvis, and Jessie Lee said that everybody would laugh at him because Elvis was the biggest sissy in Memphis. My mother quoted the scriptures, "Whatsoever you do for the least of these children, you do for me" and Jesse Lee finally agreed.

I opened the door when Elvis knocked on it — February 1948. I had seen him once before that — in the mission, getting his toys and clothes. He started coming for lessons with Jessie Lee in March 1948. He'd come every day. Later, Jessie, Johnny and Dorsey Burnette and Elvis would play in the basement under Elvis' apartment. Jess and Dorsey had been in jail together for incorrigible truancy at a state training center in Nashville. Dorsey was a born fighter, a natural badass. He wasn't very bright — a bit psycho — and he drank a lot. Johnny had to get mean because Dorsey was always beating him up. It was the proudest moment of Elvis's life to join these badass boys.

I had seen Vernon, the neighborhood wino, the infidel. It hurt me to call him "Mister" Presley. I'd see him come home, and an hour later he'd come back out and walk down to Third and Poplar and drink all night. He was an illiterate. His IQ was between 40 and 50; Gladys had a normal IQ. Elvis' IQ was 68, even though they later said it was higher. He graduated from high school, but he was what they called an "up-and-out" student. He was so quiet and pious that the teachers gave him Cs and Ds so that he could get up and out of school.

They didn't have anything. Their furniture came from the Poplar Street Mission. The bed that Elvis and Grandma Minnie slept on was the brown iron double bed that my brother was born on. The table and hotplate were given to Grandma Minnie when she set up in Memphis after her husband left her.

Gladys wouldn't let him out of her sight. She walked him to work at Loew's and the Malaco Theater, she walked him to Lansky's clothing store and stood on the sidewalk. She had an illness called an obsessive-possessive disorder. We had to to get her permission to take Elvis anywhere. I asked my mother why Mrs. Presley always held Elvis's hand; and she said, "She can't help it." Gladys was always afraid something would happen to Elvis, probably because she had lost Elvis's brother at birth. One afternoon, Mrs. Presley held Jessie Lee to her and told him that God had sent him to replace her dead son — whose name was also Jesse — and to guide and protect Baby Elvis.

He was so helpless. Infantile. All the old women called him Baby Elvis. The kids called him queer — "Mama's Titty Baby." He never grew up from cradle to grave. He was always physically protected by other human beings. We had him seven years. We had wanted to take him to the YMCA, but Gladys wouldn't let us; she'd say, "My baby's too frail." Elvis was mute. You had to look directly at him and pull words out of him. It was a long time before I got an answer in sentence form out of him.

He had all different hair styles. His mother gave him a permanent that went awry, then he shaved his head in a Mohican fashion, and then he grew his hair long.

For seven years, I never heard a pretty sound come from his lips. We got him to sing on stage at school, it was the bravest thing I ever saw him do — stand up there in front of all the kids who had been bad-mouthing him. Two days later we carried him down to WMPS-TV for an audition, but it never led anywhere. He never sang in public until my sister Delores got him to sing "Keep On The Firing Line" at Brother Grubbs' revival. His first fan was an 80-year-old lady — a drunk — Mommy Massengill. Her two alcoholic sons, Hugh and Amos Massengill, were big hillbilly stars in the '30s and '40s on the flour shows. Mommy Masengill lived across the street from the Presleys after they moved to Alabama Street, across the street from Lauderdale Courts.

We took him to the Girls Club at Fourth and Jefferson. It was a club for the poor kids. Elvis was a wallflower. He would join Lee — sing behind him — like he did in the basement. Lee, Dorsey and Johnny Burnette, Bill and Johnny Black would get gigs out in Millington, over in Arkansas, but Gladys wouldn't let Elvis go.

He'd sing anything Eddy Arnold or Patti Page sang. What was big. We weren't restricted to shitkicker stuff. My older brother had a big collection of Bing Crosby, and we heard the big bands playing on top of the Hotel Peabody. All our neighbors played the shitkicker music; the first thing you'd hear every morning would be the flour bands.

When he was 17, he would slip away and Gladys would come looking for him.

He needed drugs to come out of himself. Dewey Phillips, the first DJ to play an Elvis record, gave them to him. I knew Elvis for seven years. He was lethargic. He took the amphetamines, benzedrine, to give him energy. Dewey would slip them to him in an alley bar near the Chisco Hotel. We warned Elvis because we'd seen our brother Delmer take every drug imaginable for years.

I'd moved to Houston over Christmas of '54, but we'd keep up with him. One time in the summer of 1955 I saw Elvis, Scotty and Bill. They'd outfitted the back of the Cadillac with pillows from floor up to seat level. I saw Elvis knock off two pieces [girls] there after one show. Bill Black told me that when he wanted to sleep, he'd just say, "Elvis, I want to be seen tonight when we go through these little country towns," and Elvis would pop a handful of benzedrine and drive all night — he didn't want nobody to be seen but himself — and Bill slept in the back on those pillows.

Gladys was disgusted when Elvis started wiggling his ass. She died a slow painful death that started when Elvis signed with Colonel Parker. She said, "I know this is a bad man." Colonel Parker wanted her out of Elvis's life so he could assume control. Elvis was the Colonel's prisoner; he was already a recluse and already on drugs. He made Elvis betray his mother, Bill Black, Scotty Moore, Jessie Lee and myself. The night Elvis was on *The Ed Sullivan Show*, we were there in the front row — Jessie Lee, Nick Adams and myself. We tried to see Elvis in his

ELVIS PRESLEY: 'I had no idea success would come to Presley. Frankly, I thought the boy would starve to death.'

dressing room but the Colonel answered the door and said, "No one can see Elvis." I was in a position to break his jaw, but Jessie stopped me. I gave Elvis to the Devil that night! January 7, 1957! *(Colin Escott; Aug. 10, 1990.)*

In 1953 Elvis made his first record. He went into a small recording booth at the Memphis Recording Service studios on Union Street with his guitar and cut two songs: "My Happiness," which had been a hit for the Pied Pipers, and "That's When Your Heartaches Begin," which had been a big hit for the Ink Spots and a smaller hit for country singer Bob Lamb. He later gave the acetate to Ed Leek, a high-school friend of Presley's who became a pilot for Trans World Airlines. Leek surfaced with the disk in August 1988 and told his story to *Goldmine*. Within a week, everyone from the *Times* of London to Fox Broadcasting to RCA Records wanted to know about the disk and its contents. After Sam Phillips originally denied the disk's authenticity, he listened to it and recanted; it was the genuine article, he said. It was eventually leased to RCA, and the songs showed up on an Elvis CD collection, *The Magnificent Performances*, in 1990.

Ed Leek: It's the original record Elvis made in the 12th grade, when he was in high school. There's something written on the middle of the record, under the label. And the record has what looks like a metal center. Underneath the label, which is just a typewritten thing, is a real Sun label. The label's typewritten with the title, and underneath it just says Elvis Presley.

Back then he'd sing for anybody who'd listen. He'd sing on street corners, wherever, and it was like this even back when he was in the second grade, third grade. This record is the kind — you know, you pay two or three bucks for to make it yourself. One side of it has "That's When My Heartaches Begin"; the other side is "My Happiness." He just plays his own guitar, strums along with it, and sings. At one point momentarily his voice cracks, so you know he's young, but there's no mistaking who it is. It's Elvis. And he didn't change all that much from the beginning.

He was very bashful starting out. I can remember going out to the first clubs he used to play, like the Eagle's Nest, and he'd be so nervous it'd be like he had a stranglehold on the mike and grab his ear, and damn near twist his ear off. We'd be sitting in the audience and you know how you can get a lock on someone, just stare them down, and I'd stare and start twisting my ear, and make him darn near forget his lines. When this stuff came out later about him twisting around on stage, I think somewhere along there someone found if they could get him to move around they'd stop that ear-twisting, nervous-tension thing of his, 'cause he looked kind of silly grabbing the microphone like that.

I met him in the 12th grade. We had the same home room. There were about 16 of us who hung around together and ran around together. You know: Whoever had the car'd drive, and everybody else would throw in a couple of dimes or whatever for gas. We'd go stand on the corner on Main Street. Some went to Snowden High School, some went to Treadwell. We palled around together, but we were only really in home room together.

I was selling cars then and going to medical school. I had a '54 Mercury, a demo I drove around, and I had a Jeepster. Elvis was always after me to borrow that Jeepster. He'd say, "I got a date. Let me borrow the Jeepster," and I'd see him a couple of times that night, with a different girl each time. The only thing he had was a '42 Lincoln coupe that Vernon had put a V-8 in. That would get him down to the theater, but then he'd always call me up and ask me to push it back. If he wanted a date he needed something that would run.

People always wonder about the Cadillac limousines. They know he liked the Cadillac limousines but don't know why. Well, the reason he bought Cadillac limousines was because he was afraid to fly. Most of them were used, too. He'd use those Cadillac limousines to go to the Louisiana Hayride and all those places he played, and Black would put that big bull fiddle of his up on top. There was this big football player I think we went to high school with. He ended up at the University of Alabama, I think, and once or twice I ran to him, and he had a Cadillac limousine, too, and he let me drive it. So I was driving down Main in this Cadillac limousine and I met Elvis, coming up the other way in a Cadillac limousine. I told him I won it in a crap game, and I really had him going.

I told him, "The way to get around is to buy an airplane, and I'd fly it for you." He said, "Well, if I do that then we'll die together." With an attitude like that, there's no way he's ever going to fly. And he had some experiences early on with flying that sorta scared him off. I put him on a flight in Detroit down to Toledo. He sat down next to the emergency exit, and he's just holding on to that thing, and he looks at me like some little kid, like he's just scared to death. In Texas the fool pilot took off without checking the fuel, and they ran out of gas and had to land in a farm field. Another time he was flying a Delta Convair out of Atlanta, and one engine went on V-2. They went around in the pattern on one engine. He was just like any other country boy: You scare him a couple of times, and he won't do that any more.

ELVIS IN THE STUDIO: 'He'd putter around and sing gospel songs for two hours, maybe three, and then he'd say, "Okay; let's go to work, let's make some records," 'cause he was ready.'

I was selling cars at the Lincoln place in Memphis. They always hired on salesmen so they could work at the big Cotton Carnival. They wanted someone out there to man the podium. That was the duty I drew. I was out there one night, right across from the Ford display. They had Slim Rhodes and his brother Spec — who always blacked out a couple of teeth in front, and wore a checkerboard suit — and the Rocky Mountain Boys. Well, I struck up a conversation with them and became friends with them, and mentioned I knew Elvis, which is what I knew about music at the time. They asked me, "Could you get him to sing?" Well, he'd sing for anyone. They played, he sung, and we packed that tent. And Slim bought a Mercury from me.

I saw how it was going. I always said, "You're going to get a gold record," and when he got a gold record, I said, "Now you're going to get some more." When he got those, and when he was just getting into the movies, I said, "Well, now; you win me an Oscar." I didn't realize he'd make so many millions and millions, but, of course, I wasn't really into records.

I was glad to see him make it, though. He was a nice guy, and things came hard to him. I still think the biggest thrill for him was to go out and get a cheeseburger and a shake and be able to pay for it. Even when he was big and we'd sneak out late at night, it'd always be to go get a hamburger and a chocolate shake. That was the main reason us guys would travel with him. Anytime he went out in public, girls mobbed him and their boyfriends tried to deck him.

I remember one time I wanted to borrow a sport jacket of his. And he was big then, and he had these real nice sport jackets. He had this white one that was just real good-looking, and I said I wanted to borrow it. He said, "No, I'm gonna wear it," and I said, "But I really want to wear it." He wore it, and when he got out he got all mobbed, you know, and all that was left of that jacket was one button. He turned around and said, "Ed, I wished to hell I would have let you wear it."

I told him once, "Man, I like the money you're making but wouldn't swap for that goldfish bowl to get it."

I didn't tour around with him much. The last time I met Tom Parker. He was a pompous type. But a lot of the guys went around with him. In the movie *Jailhouse Rock* a lot of those extras are my classmates. One you can recognize: George Cline, who was a disc jockey down here for a long time. His cousin Junior is in it, and a couple others. First time I saw it it was kinda weird, to see a movie where you actually knew the people in it. When I took the wife over to the house behind the hospital he built for his mother, he was coming down the road on a little motorcycle, with a little girl riding on the back. She turned out to be Natalie Wood. She stayed two days, and things must have been going good. But Gladys broke that up in a big hurry. She went home kinda rapidly. It was years before I put two and two together.

Why haven't I ever written any of this down? I'm not a writer. I've had a busy life doing my own thing. If I'd have thought of it 20 years ago I probably could have remembered a lot more. But I was just going through my stuff here. I want to kinda divest myself of some stuff, get that boat out of the water. Restore my own cars, take life easy. *(Kit Kiefer; Aug. 26, 1988.)*

Elvis Presley's first recordings for Sam Phillips were awkward. Phillips has been misquoted many times as saying he like Presley because he was a white boy who could sing like a Negro. The real attraction was that Presley was different. He was a raw talent, but he was a talent. And Sam Phillips had to struggle to find a style that could hold him.

Phillips tried casting Presley as a straight country singer. The experiment failed. Out of frustration, Phillips borrowed guitarist Scotty Moore and bassist Bill Black from a country band, Doug Poindexter's Starlite Wranglers, and sent the three of them over to the Louisiana Hayride radio show, a country show, in 1954 to come up with something. Phillips did not expect the sort of response the three received; he did not expect any sort of response at all. But they tore up the Louisiana Hayride, and returned to Memphis triumphant.

When Phillips brought them back to the studio, he had enough sense to just let the tapes roll. The result, in 1954, was a single, "That's All Right (Mama)." The record did not even carry Elvis' last name. It was credited to Elvis, Scotty and Bill.

The label that gave Presley his break started out as a blues label. When Sun was formed in 1952, Sam Phillips, a former disc jockey, had already discovered Ike Turner and Howlin' Wolf for Chess Records. When Phillips put on the first records on Sun, he was promptly sued for trademark infringement, and had to fold the label for a year. There had already been at least two Sun labels. Phillips' first signee was Memphis DJ Rufus Thomas; his first record was an answer record to Big Mama Thornton's "Hound Dog."

Phillips' independent label would take a chance on practically anyone, black or white. He made minor stars out of the Prisonaires, a group of inmates confined to the Tennessee State Prison in Nashville. He recorded country groups like the Ripley Cotton Choppers. He took chances on Carl Perkins, Jerry Lee Lewis, Johnny Cash, Conway Twitty, Charlie Rich, Billy Lee Riley, B.B. King and Bobby Bland, but he also took a chance on Howard Serratt, a crippled singer from Manila, Ark. Of all the artists he discovered, Phillips said he was proudest of Serratt.

There's a powerful argument to be made that Elvis Presley's most dynamic recordings were made for Sun from 1954 to 1955, and after Phillips sold Presley's contract to RCA in November 1955 for $35,000 Presley's records were never as good. Phillips has always considered the transaction a business decision.

Sam Phillips: I'm an artistic person emotionally. I played music from the sixth grade to the 11th grade in school. I never was a very good musician. I was a good conductor. I could always see the people that did have the talent, and I could get it out of them. And they would know that I was getting it out of them.

ELVIS, SCOTTY, BILL AND D.J. FONTANA: 'They couldn't make us mad, they couldn't afford to, 'cause by then, Elvis had the power.'

I had obligations all my life. I was the youngest of eight kids, lost my father early on. I had a deaf-mute aunt. I was trying to raise a family myself. I was at WREC and I had worked hard to get there. A little country boy that wasn't too good of an announcer, I guarantee you that.

I opened the studio in January of 1950. There was a vacant building and I worked on it from October of 1949. I quit my two regular jobs in June 1951. I knew what I had in mind. I was recording weddings and funerals and I was taking care of the PA system of the Peabody Hotel, which was a big convention center for the whole of the mid-South area. I was doing the Peabody broadcast every night at 10:30, and then was back at work at 7:30 in the morning. I was even doing the Sunday Symphony and concert orchestra. I was working seven days a week then. I was an 18, 20-hour-a-day person.

I found Howlin' Wolf. He had no voice in the sense of a pretty voice, but he had a command of every word he spoke. When the beat got going in the studio, he would sit there and sing, hypnotizing himself. Wolf was one of those raw people, dedicated, natural. His message was definitive. Wolf, Jesus Christ; he was a guy I hated to lose.

When I lost him, I knew what it was like to be cheated. Just flat cheated. I knew that I was emotionally not prepared for that.

I think that the names and dates have been represented fairly well. I'm more interested in the psychology, the psychological aspects of what made me and what gave me the gift that I had. What made me take this very brave step, to start a record company? Looking at it from a strictly business standpoint, I'm not sure anybody in their right mind should have done it.

I honestly feel that I can say I know what it is to have a baby. I literally mean this. This is what Sun Records was to me. Thank God, I didn't let anybody abort me. Tenacity is one thing, and I have that. Also a great insight into other people. I read people well. If I hadn't read them as well as I did, I would not have been able to do what I did. Now, I know that it wasn't just musical knowledge that did it. It was communication. It was the viability of stuff that people had rejected for social reasons that the world needed to hear. To me, a lot of that stuff did not become legend overnight.

The thread runs back to the Delta. The only other place you see it is Chicago. But even in Chicago, the creativity runs back to the Delta. This is borne out by the fact that almost every top blues musician in Chicago grew up in the Delta: Muddy Waters, Sonny Boy Williamson, Little Walter, Howlin' Wolf.

Keep in mind that there were a number of good rhythm 'n' blues labels on the market, but the base was not broad enough because of racial prejudice. It wasn't broad enough to get the amount of commercial play and general acceptance overall, not just in the South.

Even though I may have started recording [white] country music, I never left the kinship with the black man altogther. When you're on the road 65,000 to 70,000 miles a year, as I was in those days, you get a lot of input from the ground. On Monday and Wednesday when the juke-box operators, and Tuesday and Thursday when the smaller retail outlets, came in to buy their week's supply of records, I'd be there. They'd tell me, "These people" — the blacks — "are ruining our white children. These little kids are falling in love with the niggers." These were basically good people, but conceptually, as to what life is all about, as to the kinship between the blacks and whites, it was just not apparent to them at all.

As for Presley sounding like a Negro, that's not what I was looking for. I'm not the smartest person in the world, but I knew that wouldn't have worked. Even if it had, I wouldn't have wanted it. Not an imitator. I was looking for the feeling. And I knew if he could do anything at all, even toot a mouth organ, I had me my next star.

Believe me, before that [Jerry Lee Lewis' marriage to his teenage cousin] happened, Jerry was the hottest thing in America. The press tore him up in England over his marriage to Myra, and it rebounded back home. It was a devastating, unnecessary, stupid damn thing, but what could we have done about it? I think Jerry's innocence back then and his trying to be open, engaging and friendly with the press backfired. They scalped him. There's no question about it. It turned out to be a very ghastly thing. So many people wanted to do in rhythm 'n' blues, rock 'n' roll, and this was just what they were looking for — to point the finger of scorn at a rocker and say, "I told you so; rockers are no good." They picked on the first one they could. I don't say the press were entirely at fault, but they made so much of it. It should never have played a role of such significance in Jerry's life.

Jerry Lee Lewis has a superb talent. In my estimation, he is one of the greats that left Sun. I don't think Jerry has been able to achieve product-wise what he could have done. There's very few people that have the ability to take a great artist like Jerry and really maximize the man's versatility and ability in the recording studio. I just believe I was one person who could do that.

I saw Carl Perkins as one of the great plowhands in the world. There was no way Carl could hide that pure country in him, but that means an awful of soul, too.

Howard Serratt? Oh, that man! I have never heard a person, no matter what category of music, who could sing as beautifully. The honesty, the integrity, the communication, the unpretentious quality. It just had a depth of beauty about it in its simplicity. Just him and his harmonica and guitar. Oh, God almighty! That was a sad thing, because I could have just recorded Howard Seratt ad infinitium and never gotten tired.

It hurt when each one of 'em left. The one that hurt me the most was Johnny [Cash]. I had heard that Johnny was going, first to Capitol. My distributors had called because word was out and I didn't know it.

Still, even with these hurts, even losing all of these people, I cannot say that there was an artist who worked with me whom I disliked, even though some of them have said things about me that were untrue. But I cannot say that there's a one of them — and if there were one I thought was a damn shitass, I'd tell you. But even if there was, it still wouldn't have anything to do with me thinking that if he had talent, it deserved to be expressed.

I'm a very uncommercial person. At no point in my life did I approach this thing from a standpoint of commercialism. I knew that I was put on this earth for some purpose. As things worked out, I was able to do it and not starve to death. I was monetarily rewarded, but more than that, my rewards have been on the side of doing something I believed in fully when not too many people believed in it at all.

I knew I was going to be up against a society which required that some fortune come in or you wouldn't be in business for very long. For some reason, that freed up my mind so that I didn't feel pressured from inside or outside into making commercial compromises.

If I've got any forte at all — and certainly I didn't do everything right — it's my honesty and integrity. They're everything to me. They were back then, too. There were just very few people that I knew in the business that were as honest in their accountings as I was.

Recording was such an interesting thing with me that there was no way I would have a bunch of people around. I didn't want it to get too mechanical, and I didn't want to get too far away from any phase of it. I'm like that right now with this radio station. They say a smart man is one who can delegate authority, so I must be a dumb son-of-a-bitch! *(Hank Davis and Colin Escott; Aug. 14, 1987.)*

❧

Scotty Moore and Bill Black created a powerful sound for Presley, but it was a country sound. Country music didn't use drums; country blues didn't use drums. Popular music, jazz and urban blues used drums. Elvis Presley needed a drummer to enter the popular mainstream. D.J. Fontana filled the need.

Fontana learned his licks playing in strip joints, and worked on the Louisiana Hayride in 1954 just as Elvis, Scotty and Bill began to have a few regional hits. Fontana was the first drummer on the show. He stayed with Presley through his 1968 TV special, and never considered what he did for Presley as anything special.

D.J. Fontana: I worked with the Louisiana Hayride in Shreveport for a while around 1954. Elvis had had a couple of records out on Sun and they were getting airplay in Arkansas, Louisiana and Texas when the Hayride people heard them on the radio. So they called him in to do some songs.

First week they came in, I just happened to be there naturally, kind of like the staff drummer, because back then a lot of the country artists weren't using drums at all.

The manager of the Hayride called me into the office and said, "I want you to listen to these records, 'cause we got this kind coming in."

I listened and the records were great. That raw sound, you know, man. They were very different. I listened to them several times and they were great for just three pieces. So I said, "Who in the hell is this?"

"It's Elvis Presley."

I said, "Geez, what a funny name. He'll probably never make it with a name like that."

When they came in, Scotty came up to me and said, "You working here?" and asked if I'd mind working with them. I said, "I don't know what you guys are gonna do. I listened to your records a little bit, but let's go back into the dressing room and at least talk about it."

Scotty and Elvis and I got playing and said, "Let's try it," 'cause somehow or other, it laid right and it felt right and it worked. I don't think there's anything you could put your finger on as to why it worked, but I'd gotten to thinking, "Now there's such a unique sound; why clutter it up with drums and noise?"

So I just kind of laid back and stayed out of their way, and I think that's why I got the job. I just stayed out of their way.

Scotty had that little Echoplex guitar, Bill was playing slap bass and Elvis was playing that cheeky little rhythm. They just added me and I just learned how to stay out of their way and let them do what they had to. It sounded better to me that way, so I just kept the job. Kept it for 20-22 years.

And another thing: Elvis liked drummers to kind of underscore what he did, you know, man. Like if he moved a hand or whatever. Anytime he moved, well, he wanted some noise in there. Before then, I'd played some strip joints; they had a few little all-night clubs and strip joints in Shreveport. You know the type — strippers, comedians, and the band would play behind. Well, I'd watch the dancers and learned how to play that stuff. So I watched him, and I said, "He's doing the same thing!" and I played the same thing for him, and somehow or other it worked. At least, he liked it. Maybe they hired me because I started catching everything he'd do — legs, arms, hands, whatever. He liked that noise behind him. And again, it just worked.

ELVIS IN CONCERT: 'When he first started playing, he was scared to death nobody would come. We had to come; we were the audience.'

We worked out a few weekends, because he wasn't on the Hayride every week, mostly 'cause he started getting dates in East Texas and Oklahoma. Hell, we worked Texas for two years, might as well say it, before he ever got big. We were always in Texas, Louisiana or Arkansas, because that's where the records were being played. He was hot in those states, but mostly East Texas, Corpus, Beaumont, Tyler, Marshall, Texarkana; we'd always be driving there. Get in the car and go from town to town. You know, we were working six and seven days a week. Back then, it wasn't like now, where you have weekend tours; back then, you had a tour seven days a week for 30 days.

We were riding in a '54 Cadillac that Elvis had built a wooden rack on top with a canvas cover on it. That's how we travelled. One car with all the instruments, 'cause back then we didn't have that much, just one small kit of drums, one guitar, slap bass on top and our clothes. Usually there'd be four of us; sometimes he'd have Red West go with us, but we didn't have room for a lot of people 'cause when Elvis got ready to go to sleep, we'd let him go in back and then me, Scotty and Bill would sit up front. He'd take up the whole back seat.

Elvis was one of those guys that had a lot of nervous energy, a super-hyper guy, super-hyper.

79

Always jumping around or doing something. I just guess it was the body makeup. Some have it and some don't, but he sure did. He never got tired, but when he did, he'd just crash 11 or 12 hours straight in those days.

He was always doing something. We'd be driving down the road, we'd never get to a show date on time because we'd stop every 30 miles to buy firecrackers. He'd make us stop at every other stand, that sucker would. I'd say, "We've got a bagful," and he'd say, "Well, you know, man, we might need some more." We'd stop and buy more firecrackers, just for something to do.

We'd come by the house to pick him up before they moved to Graceland. Gladys'd always be out in the yard and say, "You be sure to take care of my baby." And no matter what, Elvis would call her twice a day. No matter where we were, he'd stop the car sometimes and call her, 'cause they were really close.

Bill was kind of the comic of the bunch. In fact, a lot of the shows when Elvis was fairly new, if Bill hadn't cut up, man, we'd have died. He'd get the people on his side by calling Elvis all kinds of names in a kidding manner. It helped, 'cause it would get the people on his side, and on Elvis'. A lot of the names for the band came from that time, too. See, we really didn't have a name then, but we'd show up places and there would be names on the marquee for us, like the Blue Moon Boys. One time we started out as E.P. and The Continentals.

Colonel Parker was a smart man, a shrewd man who wouldn't give you the time of day. Everything with him was strictly business, strictly money. He worked for Elvis, period. When he took Elvis on, we would book out and he wanted him out of that Hayride contract, even though Elvis still had 18 months to do.

On the road, Elvis would close the first half of the show, then there would be an intermission. When the rest of the guys would go back to play, then there wouldn't be anybody in the auditorium because everybody would be out back trying to find where the heck he was. So they had to finally put him on last to keep the people in the building. Nobody could follow him.

The crowds got bigger and then a lot bigger and there was more and more security. As the band, we didn't get out anymore. We'd drive up to the auditorium, play the show, there'd be security everywhere and then we'd rush offstage, through the backstage and try to get the hell out of there.

Girls on the road? You mean groupies? Oh, sure. Oh, yeah. Anytime you have an artist like that you'd have, well ... fans, they called them then. Yeah; oh yes, thousands of them. They were always trying to get backstage. That got to be a problem, and the hotels got to be the same way.

We started doing sessions for RCA in Janaury 1956 in Nashville, at a little Victor Studio on McGavock. It's gone now, but I remember flying into town then for the session where we had to run a microphone down the hallway for echo, so you know how modern that was. But it worked.

A lot of classics — "Heartbreak Hotel," "I Want You, I Need You, I Love You" — came out of those sessions, and you couldn't fix any of it up. You got what you got. If he was happy with his performance and the bands, that was it. Then we'd leave here and go out on the road for maybe 30 more dates someplace else. Then we started coming into Victor B around '57.

Elvis knew what he wanted. And since he was selling records, they weren't going to say something wasn't right because he'd already proved himself. He could pick material, and he had a keen ear for little commercial-type songs, such as they were, so they just kind of let him run it. You'd come in and there'd be stacks of tapes and acetates everywhere. He'd start going through them, one or two times through and he'd know the song; he was a quick learner. It made it easy for us; we'd work on the song and if he was happy with it, good or bad, that's the way he wanted it. We didn't have all the tracks you have now. There wasn't even a lot of separation. And he wanted everybody in the booth around him as long as he was familiar with them. So you'd have instruments and background singers on his heels with everybody using the same mike, because that's the way Elvis wanted it — and like I said, man, if he was happy, if it felt good to him, that was it. He was always telling us, "Boys, keep it simple 'cause guys working these little clubs out there can't play this complex stuff."

He warmed up four or five hours. We never went to work on time. Say, he'd call a session at Victor, usually Sunday at 6 p.m. 'cause he'd come over from Memphis. He might not show up until 11 o'clock, but we'd still get paid. Then he'd putter around and sing gospel songs for two hours, maybe three, and then he'd say, "Okay; let's go to work, let's make some records," 'cause he was ready.

He'd say, "Boys, how's it going today? You making any money?" I'd say, "No, man; you're going too fast." He'd say, "Well, we'll fix that," then he'd putter around for three or four hours, maybe go out to eat and keep us on the clock. Then he'd say, "How you doing, D.J.?" I'd say, "Okay, now."

The Gleason show with the Dorsey Brothers changed everything. We did six shows with them. They were a replacement show in the summer, and that was a powerhouse then. It started getting bigger right then. And then we sent to the Sullivan show, and that was the big move. Sullivan, for some reason, liked Elvis and treated him real good. Gave him a couple of good shots. And they treated us real good, too. Well, they had to, 'cause he had the power. They couldn't make us mad; they couldn't afford to 'cause by then, Elvis had the power.

Loving You was the first movie for the band. It was Elvis' idea. Like I told you, he wanted people around him that he was happy and comfortable with. If it had been up to the studio, they would have used West Coast musicians for everything 'cause they didn't have to pay their way out there or pay for their rooms. But he told the Colonel, "Tell 'em to call the boys." That was the end of it, 'cause he had the power, so they didn't argue with him. We only did four or five of them. After that we — the guys — got tired of that. Finally, we told him, "You do this, 'cause you're an actor."

Me and Scotty and Bill all felt this way. We didn't want to do that because it was too much of a hassle. After you do one film, it gets old. The first one you do is a thrill, seeing all these actors and people. After that it was just a job. He was pushed into it because of his popularity and all the studios wanted him because they were going to make money off the kid. That was the main reason for that. Hal Wallis [the producer] signed him for seven pictures, I think or something like that, and I think they offered him $100,000. The Colonel said, "That's all right for me, but what are you going to pay my boy singer? What are you going to pay him, nothing?" The Colonel was a shrewd old man; I have to give him credit. He had the power with Elvis. It was like, "Okay, I'll get you another studio." From the very beginning it was that way between them.

It was sort of like, "You take care of the business and I'll take care of the rest of it — the singing, the acting, whatever I have to do — just don't bother me in the recording studio."

Colonel would come in the studio some, but he wouldn't say anything, just walk around some. Then he'd be gone. Same on the set; he was around, but he wasn't around. Sit down to contract time, though, that was another story. Then he was everywhere. That's the difference, and I think that's why he and Elvis got along so well.

Scotty and Bill quit around 1958. I think we had just finished *Jailhouse Rock*. It was mostly a financial thing. They asked me about it and I said, "Well, boys, you know I started last and I didn't have this deal you guys got." 'Cause Scotty and Bill had a piece of the whole thing. When they started fiddling around after Sam Phillips got 'em together, they'd go over to each other's house and talk, and then once they were sitting on a curb and Elvis said, "You know, Scotty, if I get this deal on Sun I want to give you guys a percentage." Scotty said, "No, that's not part of the deal." *(Peter Mikelbank, Aug. 14, 1987.)*

Elvis Presley made an impression on young America that young America continues to feel. He got a generation rockin' and rollin', and if he didn't do it for subsequent generations directly he did it indirectly. He wrested the popular-music charts away from mainstream pop performers forever. He did more than anyone else to eliminate the class and age and race and regional distinctions and turn rock 'n' roll into a coast-to-coast, rich-and-poor social phenomenon. He did more than anyone else of that era to pit teenagers against their parents in never-ending debates over music and clothes, decibels and hairstyles and dancing. He was the first big rock 'n' roller. Rock 'n' roll needed him to do what he did.

And musicians remember. Perhaps not all of them realize how different things might have been without an Elvis Presley, but at some time even the hardest-core member of the latest new wave must hear something by Elvis — something early, hopefully — and hear a little of themselves in it. Because it's there.

Max Weinberg was the drummer with Bruce Springsteen's E Street Band. Roy Buchanan is a guitarist. Leslie West is best-known as the lead guitarist of Mountain.

Max Weinberg: My first recollections of Elvis Presley, like, I think, a lot of other people in this country, are rooted in his appearance that memorable Sunday night on *The Ed Sullivan Show*. I remember sitting in the family living room that night with my two older sisters, who were already very big Elvis Presley fans. I didn't know exactly where all the excitement about Elvis was coming from, or, for that matter, what it was really all about. But my sisters' excitement was definitely contagious. Without really knowing why, I was just as excited to see Elvis on television as they were. They thought that was pretty amazing; the fact that Elvis could have an effect on their little brother really amazed them.

Elvis was great that night, as anyone who remembers watching television that Sunday evening will tell you. But I've got to say it was D.J. Fontana, as well as Elvis, who had an impact on my life that night. When I saw and heard him play that opening drum roll of "Hound Dog," that's when I decided I wanted to be a rock 'n' roll drummer. Of course, I didn't fully understand it then because I was just a kid, but Elvis was affecting so many other people that night, too. That night, Elvis became the prototype for all future rock 'n' rollers.

I'll tell you a funny story. I remember my sisters dressing me up like Elvis, almost as if I was an Elvis Presley doll. They actually made me a cardboard guitar and used mascara to draw

ELVIS IN HAWAII: 'Even some of the not-so-memorable songs from the movie soundtracks — well, he just sang the daylights out of them.'

sideburns on the sides of my face. They would play his records and I would lip-synch the words to the songs. My favorite was "Hound Dog." This was what, when I was five years old, mind you. But regardless of the fake guitar and all, I wanted to be a drummer just like D.J. Fontana. Later it would be Ringo Starr. But the drums on "Hound Dog" really got to me. I can listen to that record today and still get totally excited about it. It's funny how certain songs will do that to you.

I like to listen to Presley's rockers more than anything else he's recorded, and I think my Elvis Presley record collection bears this out. I don't have any one particular period in his career that I go for. I love, for instance, "Jailhouse Rock," which I think is one of the greatest rock songs ever recorded. "Love Me Tender," though not a rocker, was a real early favorite of mine. When I was young I would lip-synch to that song, too. "Can't Help Falling In Love" was fantastic. The song "Trouble" I always liked.

These are some of the songs I'll pick out of my record collection — which, by the way, is mostly compilations when you're talking about Elvis, and play them time and time again. I don't have all the songs, but Gerry Tallent, the bass player in the E Street Band, has them all, plus all the Sun Records. He's a great Elvis fan and Elvis record collector.

Unlike, I think, other Elvis fans. I'll rank "Burning Love" and "Suspicious Minds" as Presley favorites, too. The incredible thing about Elvis was that on virtually every song he recorded, his personality came through; that's what really attracted me to him. Even some of the not-so-memorable songs from the movie soundtracks — well, he usually just sang the daylights out of them in most cases. He was great, for instance, on "Viva Las Vegas." His ability to put over a song got me like no one else did. His ability to make a lousy song sound great was a talent few other people have. If I hadn't been introduced to Presley's brand of rock 'n' roll as a kid, I don't know if I would have even considered rock 'n' roll a career. As it turned out, rock 'n' roll and drums have become pretty much my life.

Leslie West: The very first experience I had with Elvis Presley was a pretty unique one, as far as I was concerned. My uncle was a writer for *The Jackie Gleason Show*, for the part called "The American Scene Magazine." The summer replacement for that show was Tommy and Jimmy Dorsey's *Stage Show*, which was the first television program to feature Presley. I had gone down to my grandmother's to watch the show, and suddenly, Elvis was on the screen. Well, that was it. I mean, that was it! He tore me up. I mean it. He was on three weeks in a row, if I recall correctly. He was something.

My Elvis Presley record collection included the 78s of "Heartbreak Hotel," "Blue Suede Shoes," and "Hound Dog." I think I bought them on 14th Street in New York City, way back when. Actually, I bought them the day they came out. Presley, see, he looked so good playing that guitar. The guy could sing, no doubt about that. But he looked so good up there. I couldn't get over it; I really couldn't. Of course, when he started making all those movies, it wasn't the same. It was sad, actually. I blame that mostly on the Colonel. Elvis was a pretty good actor, but he never got loose at the right moments. Sometimes when he got loose, he got too loose. But he was definitely the King and he was definitely a big inspiration to me. I can listen to his records anytime, man, and get complete satisfaction out of them. Like I said, he was the King.

Roy Buchanan: I used to listen to a radio show called the "Lousiana Hayride," which came on on Saturday nights. I remember they mentioned this guy, Elvis Presley, who was going to be on the show. It took me a long time to learn how to pronounce his name right; I don't know why, but it took like about a year. When they called out his name just before he was gonna sing, the house went wild. I kept saying to myself, "Who is this guy?" I couldn't imagine what they were screaming about. It was only later I found out what he was capable of doing in front of an audience.

The first song I heard him do was a thing called "Mystery Train." I had never, I mean never, heard anything like it. It changed my whole world around. I was used to listening to hillbilly music and church-house blues, but nothing like what Presley was offering. The way he sang the lyrics, the tonal quality of his voice was just great. There's never been anybody in rock

— before or after Presley — that could sing like that. His talent scared me. I didn't think anybody could be that good.

I was 15 when I heard "Mystery Train." I remember I was laying in bed with the lights out and the song came on the radio. Darn near knocked me out of bed, I'll tell you. I left home about two weeks after hearing Elvis for the first time. He changed my whole life; I wanted to be just like Elvis. I actually thought I was Elvis for a spell. I went to L.A., got into a couple of pictures, played some gigs. It was a big switch from the life I was leading up around Bakersfield, Calif., where I was from. And I have to attribute all that to Elvis.

I bought a lot of Presley 45s in those days. I couldn't buy as many as I wanted to because back then, I didn't have too much money to spend on records. The records I couldn't buy, I would find out which one of my friends had them, and then I'd go over to their house and sit there playing the records until I learned all the guitar parts on them. I learned every one of Elvis Presley's records note-for-note, until he went into the Army.

Scotty Moore's finger style of guitar playing left a big impression on me. Someone hired Scotty to go to Chicago to do a session back in 1957, but he couldn't do it for some reason. So I got to do the job. And people could hear his influence on me. His style wasn't exactly a Merle Travis style, but it was along that line. It was more of a black sound.

"Hound Dog," "Heartbreak Hotel," "You're Right, I'm Left, She's Gone" were all favorites of mine. But when Elvis went into the Army, things changed. He changed. When he came out, he didn't use his same band. I just felt he didn't represent the teenagers anymore, to be honest with you. He used people like Glen Campbell on guitar, you know. Older people started to like him then. My mother, she went crazy over him. He lost some of that wildness he had before he went into the service. But I'll tell you, I think he regained the spirit of his wildness during his comeback years.

I think rock 'n' roll would have never made it had it not been for Elvis, because the only people who were around when Elvis started were people like Bill Haley and Fats Domino. They were good and all, but they weren't Elvis. They couldn't do what Elvis could do.

Going back to the "Louisiana Hayride," about three years after I heard Elvis on the show, I played the "Hayride" myself and used two members of Elvis' band: D.J. Fontana on drums, and Bill Black on bass. It gave me a little hint of the Elvis feeling back when I had first heard him. It was just a little bit, but it was fun.

❦

Elvis Presley in his later years, and especially after his death, became a symbol of everything tacky and plastic and bloated about America. Too many years in the public eye and too many years of a sheltered, pampered life reduced Elvis into a caricature of Elvis. Jerry Lee Lewis would later become a caricature of Jerry Lee Lewis, and Little Richard and Chuck Berry would become caricatures of Little Richard and Chuck Berry. But Elvis showed the way. He simply took Elvis to its logical conclusion, and when there was nothing more of a life on earth to leave, he died. He was fat and full of drugs and 42 years old.

It was all inevitable; Graceland and "My Way" and the deep-fried peanut-butter sandwiches, and the out-and-out devotion of so many people to the music that he made that expresses itself in black-velvet paintings and checkout-stand-tabloid headlines and the legions of Elvis impersonators who make good livings doing "Don't Be Cruel" and "Heartbreak Hotel" on Friday and Saturday nights were all inevitable. But it all began with the music. And you have to listen to the music. It was good music, mostly, some real rock 'n' roll, and the fact that it went from the fringe into the mainstream meant it could take a lot of people in at different times and then hold them there, and encourage their devotion.

Jimmy Ellis: I was born, or should I say raised, in Orrville, Alabama. When I was a little boy, I liked Eddy Arnold, Marty Robbins, Elvis, Ray Price and different artists like that, so I guess they were my major influences. I used to have a little plastic banjo and used to go around playing it, singing all the time. It seems like that's all I've ever wanted to do — be a singer. I don't recall anyone influencing me more than the other; I liked a lot of them, and I guess I drew a little from different styles.

Around 1963, I started singing a little. I played a lot of sports and would sing a lot in the shower. The guys seemed to like it and were always after me to sing at school functions. My graduating year, they had what was called "Religious Emphasis Week." That was my first public appearance as a singer. That really got me started, and I entered a talent contest later that summer. They were auditioning talent in several cities and counties all around Alabama. When they got to my county, there was a schoolteacher I knew involved, so I called her to tell her I wanted to audition. Well, I won the audition, along with about six others. All of us received letters and were told we had been selected to appear on a local television program. If we won there, we would appear later; on a Monday night we'd compete, and if we won there, we'd compete with winners of, like, 10 other Monday shows. If we won there, it was on to the finals at the Alabama State Fair. I was lucky enough to win the whole shooting match, which was a trip to the *Ted Mack Amateur Hour* and a $1,000 savings bond.

I sing like me, but people always have mentioned Elvis; it's always been that way. In fact, my first solo record was "That's All Right" and "Blue Moon Of Kentucky" — on the same label Elvis debuted on! Nothing ever came of it at that time that I know about, so I guess that was really my first "release." I forgot about it and went back to the horse business.

After Elvis' death, one of my records came out with no name on the label. They put it out later with my name on it. The only reason I can figure they didn't put it on the first time was the same reason I didn't get credited with the Jerry Lee Lewis stuff. Because of the similarity of my voice to Elvis', Shelby Singleton was trying to fool or tease the public into thinking it may be Elvis. At any rate, I'd been farming for years, and I think I just was waiting for the right opportunity. I hadn't been doing any club work or such and it got to the point where I either had to do music full-time or forget it. I couldn't forget it; the Sun thing was the first real opportunity I'd had.

Then I got involved with Boblo, with a guy named Bobby Smith. The label was in Brunswick, Georgia, not the hotbed of music. Bobby had managed Otis Redding and Wayne Cochran at one time. We cut several singles and were getting some reaction, a few bookings and such. Elvis died in 1977, and everyone started with the tribute records. There were impersonators everywhere, and not one of them could really sing. None could really display his vocal abilities. They just put on a white jumpsuit and performed. I don't think that's what Elvis is all about; he was an artist in the full sense of the word.

I just felt since everyone else was doing the Elvis thing while I was trying not to, I'd do something about it. I cut one single expressing my feelings, "I'm Not Trying To Be Like Elvis." In my shows, I'd do something like "Your Cheatin' Heart," and people would tell me that's how Elvis would've done it. I've never done an all-Elvis show, just a song or two as a crowd pleaser, which I still do.

I decided then I could do Elvis songs better than the impersonators, so I picked out 10 songs that I felt were the hardest Elvis songs to do, the most demanding vocally. I went to a little studio in Florida with my band and cut an album, *Ellis Sings Elvis*. I figured we'd sell them at my shows. As far as I know, only 1,000 or so were pressed, and they're hot collector's items. I have a few left I could sell, but I'm keeping them as antiques. I've heard of copies selling for $50-$100. The other Boblo singles are getting rarer, but they're all just decent songs that didn't make it.

The name "Orion" — well, I had already signed with Sun Records. From the very start, Shelby Singleton said he wanted to sign me and do some albums but he didn't know what to do to make me catchy, to draw attention to me. So I was playing at a little club in Atlanta. We'd already done the Jerry Lee Lewis album and it was selling very well. No one knew it was me on the album and everyone was commenting on how much it sounded like Elvis.

One day in Atlanta, I received a call at my motel from a lady. She was telling me about this book she'd written called *Orion*. It seemed there was talk of a movie being made from it, but that later fizzled. Several people were interested in the part, but no one was suitable.

She knew a little about me and wanted to meet to talk about the book and movie. At the time, I thought she was crazy and didn't pay much attention to her, but that night a group of people came up at the club and introduced themselves. She decided after seeing my show I'd be perfect for the Orion part in the movie. The original concept was that it was to be a movie based on the book, which was more or less a fictionalized, parellel version of Elvis' life.

We decided to change my name to Orion and go with the whole concept. Shelby then adopted the concept for my publicity; he even adopted the fictionalized characters from the book. I mean, the guy who drove my bus was nicknamed Tuck — his real name is Carl Schmidt — and the name of the guy in the book who was Orion's best friend was named Tuck. He adopted the whole thing and it went okay for a while, and then he came up with the mask for me. I think he had a thing with masks; he started out years ago by putting a mask on David Allan Coe, the "Mysterious Rhinestone Cowboy."

I made some good money in 1981, but I've had several obstacles that have stopped my career 'til now. Back to the mask thing, though; I think it worked to a certain point, but I think people are much too intelligent today, especially country-music fans. You can get by with more in rock music — dye your hair, wear makeup, dress like a girl. In country music, some people like to see rhinestone suits, but they also like to see blue jeans on singers. I think the mask was good to a certain point — it drew a lot of attention — but after about a year, we should have had a big show to unmask and went one from there, with some really good records to back it up.

To please the immediate public right now, they'd probably have liked to see me come out in a jumpsuit and do Elvis songs. However, to get to a certain plateau in entertainment like Kenny Rogers or Dolly, you have to get away from hype and come back to the artistry of the business. That means taking something original and making it belong to you, making it your identity. I could've toured many times as an Elvis impersonator, but I didn't and don't want to, because it's not the way to the top. Of all the Elvis impersonators who sprang up, I doubt there's more than 10 still doing it. I'm still here. As for the fans, there were probably some who didn't expect what they got. Some did think I was Elvis, even after talking to me; they thought he'd pulled a hoax about dying. I think they were misled to a certain degree by all the hype, but not by what was on the records; that was me.

Yeah, I'd do it all over again, because at the time I went the direction that was the only way I could go. When you're trying to get in the music business, I kinda look at it like a fellow getting on a fast train; there's no easy way to get on. You just grab what you can, and that's the way it is in the music business. People ask how to get in the business — who knows? You just try to do it anyway you can; you hope to find a little pathway. I found mine through Boblo Records in Georgia, up through Nashville and Sun Records. I give them credit; they did give me a lot of exposure and got my name around the business. I'm sure I wouldn't be this far in the music business were it not for the mask and Sun Records. The end result — what determines how big my career will be is the bottom line, a hit record. That'll make everything else worthwhile. *(Larry Stidom; June 7, 1985.)*

86

6. Down South in New Orleans

The center of the American musical earth is New Orleans. It was the birthplace of jazz and one of the birthplaces of rock 'n' roll and R&B. Zydeco sprung up from the nearby bayous, and folky Cajun two-steps still ring through Lafayette, west of the Crescent City. Music flowed up from the Caribbean and in from the Mississippi Delta and over from the rural parishes and into the port city of New Orleans. The city was a sailor's place, bawdy and wide-open; many of the city's best and most famous musicians played in whorehouses, after-hours joints and strip clubs. A lot of great New Orleans music was conceived in the brothels of Storyville.

New Orleans music is really about rhythm, about different kinds of rhythms mixed and laid over one another. Jelly Roll Morton would play songs with a shuffling Latin or Caribbean bear; 40 years later, that rhythm would show up underneath the songs of Professor Longhair or Huey "Piano" Smith. The marching-band, parade beat that was the underpinning of Dixieland was also the foundation for Fats Domino's "I'm Walkin'."

The rhythm produced hits. Roy Brown had the first with "Good Rockin' Tonight." Fats Domino had the most, and the biggest. Little Richard had the most influential. The Neville Brothers had the most recent. And all of them recorded for Cosimo Matassa at one time or another.

Matassa was a jukebox operator who began selling used records on the side. When customers asked for new records he began carrying them, and then opened a small studio in the back of his shop. It was the only recording studio in New Orleans for much of the late '40s.

Matassa's recording equipment was primitive, but the performances he put on record were legendary. In the early '50s a group of kids came into Matassa's studio and emptied their pockets, saying the wanted to make a record. The record was "I'm Gone," and it launched the careers of Shirley and Lee. Lloyd Price was discovered at the studio, and Fats Domino, Dave Bartholemew, Professor Longhair, Frogman Henry, Jimmy Clanto, Huey Smith, Irma Thomas, Lee Dorsey, Benny Spellman, Smiley Lewis and Dr. John recorded there. Creedence Clearwater Revival titled one of their albums *Cosmo's Factory* in tribute.

Johnny Vincent was a Mississippian who changed his name because Speciality Records president Art Rupe couldn't pronounce Vincent Imbragulio, Vincent's real name. He worked with Matassa and later launched Ace Records, one of the top New Orleans labels.

Johnny Vincent: I started in the jukebox business in Laurel, Mississippi, back in 1945 or '46, and basically from there I went to fooling with records in a little shop in Laurel. Then I got to the point that I wanted to get into something more what I liked, and I went to New Orleans to get into record distributing and finding out more about it. It's like a guy fixing to go to college, you know? I just basically fell in love with it.

I met Cos in 1950. Of course, I'd heard of him. I was with a company in New Orleans called William B. Allen Supply since '47. I got to know Cos good when I was with Speciality, but I had met him earlier. I began to do a lot of sessions in New Orleans. Well, I found out from analyzing all the sounds that I was listening to that the New Orleans sound was the sound I felt had the most potential of any sound that I would take to the kids, 'cause I began to watch them from a standpoint of when the records were actually being played. And, of course, being from Mississippi, you know that naturally you find out that the blues was big in here, but I just felt that the generation to come would be on rock 'n' roll. Rock 'n' roll is what I really started out in.

In Jackson we cut our first session that really got Ace started. We cut some stuff at Cosimo's, but they were very slow sellers. But when we cut some songs in Jackson, we basically cut what I consider our two big records there: "Lonely Nights" and "Rockin' Pneumonia." I think that's what really started Ace Records, what helped it become a great label. From there, we took off. We didn't want to go into one particular kind of sound; we wanted to go into all fields. A lot of companies became specialists, like Sun in rockabilly, but we tried to go into it all: New York sound with the doo-wop groups, the L.A. sound that we felt was catching on with the kids. But everything we did, we would always try and put a touch of New Orleans in it.

Frankie Ford heard "Sea Cruise" and liked it, and we were running with a hit by Huey ["Yockomo"], and we wanted to come back with something by somebody else. We took Huey off and substitued Frankie's voice on the that one.

Cosimo Matassa: At that point, it was probably two-track, with all the vocals on one track and the band on the other. Now, remember, we did a lot of bouncing and stacking and second-, third-, fourth-generation tapes. That tape was, oh, you've got to figure, it went about five generations. It's not a particularly great tape, I'll tell you.

Johnny Vincent: But "Sea Cruise" was a great, great song. Nobody could ever take the feel away from that song.

Cosimo Matassa: We're all victims of our own vices. You know, even when we were making records that — and when I say "we," I mean "me," I guess — but in New Orleans here we were making records that were million-sellers, literally, and we were working hand-to-mouth, ridiculous studio budget, and things like that. I mean, somebody made an awful lot of money, and it wasn't me, and it wasn't my artists a lot of times, either.

Johnny Vincent: New Orleans will be back. I'm hoping that we can get it back to where it was in the '50s. Tell your readers if there's anyone out there that feels like, "I've got the talent; if only I could get that one man to listen to me," tell him to send me a tape and I'll see if I can't do something for him.

If you listen to the rock 'n' roll singers today, a lot of the feel came from New Orleans. They had the feel; it was all there. It was basically a Dixieland jazz beat that they were putting together. It gave you inspiration when you heard it. This is what people just don't analyze today; when they hear these songs they say, "Well, good God, that was basically something taken from part of what we listened to 15, 20, 25 years ago." I'd like to see New Orleans get the feel they once had in this field, I think they will. I think rock 'n' roll in New Orleans will come back strong. Although my first records were blues, I started out with the idea that rock 'n' roll is here to stay, and it is here to stay. You'll never get rid of rock 'n' roll. It's a shame nobody ever went back and said, "Let's keep rock 'n' roll in New Orleans," you know, like country in Nashville. *(Mike Callahan; February 1981.)*

❧

In 1949 Dave Bartholemew led the hottest band in New Orleans and a chubby piano player named Antoine Domino was playing boogie-woogie and blues in a hole-in-the-wall club called the Hideaway. Within a year they would be recording together, and for the next decade they would be the hottest R&B act in the country.

Antoine "Fats" Domino grew up listening to boogie pianists on the jukebox and learning traditional New Orleans songs and standards taught to him by his father-in-law, Howard Verrett, a guitarist for Papa Celestin and other small jazz groups. One of the traditional songs he learned, "Junker Blues," became the basis for his first hit, "The Fat Man."

Bartholemew had been recording for three years before he met Fats Domino. He was a skilled arranger and an A&R man for Imperial Records, and he used his band in the studio to back his artists.

One of the first artists he recorded was Fats Domino, and the first song they recorded was "The Fat Man." It was one of the very first rock 'n' roll singles. Both Amos Milburn and Johnny Otis later said they wished they'd recorded it.

Bartholemew produced and arranged virtually all of Domino's recordings from then on, and there were a lot of recordings and a lot of hits. "Every Night About This Time" introduced the piano-triplet form that would become the basis of many R&B and swamp-pop ballads. His "Ain't It A Shame" topped the R&B charts 11 consecutive weeks. "My Blue Heaven" was a throwback to the Tin Pan Alley tunes his brother-in-law would play with Papa Celestin. It was one of the first standards to be set to a rock 'n' roll beat. "Blueberry Hill" and "Blue Monday" followed, and were two of the few crossover hits of the '50s, going to #2 and #5 on the pop charts while going to #1 on the R&B charts.

Domino's music had the beat and vitality of rock 'n' roll and the basic sound of R&B wrapped up for white audiences in a fun-loving, easy-to-take package. It sold records.

A third consecutive single, "I'm Walkin' ", made it to #1 on the R&B charts in 1957. It was one of seven #1 R&B singles for Domino. Only James Brown, the Temptations and Stevie Wonder had more R&B chart singles than Fats Domino.

The hits rolled for Domino until 1961 — "I Want To Walk You Home," "Walkin' To New Orleans," "My Girl Josephine" — and then stopped. But by that time Domino could afford to reprise his old hits in concert and re-record and repackage them on record. Bartholemew, meanwhile, continued as Domino's bandleader and arranger. Though he never had the solo hit he craved, Bartholemew co-wrote and arranged Smiley Lewis' "I Hear You Knocking," arranged "Lawdy Miss Clawdy" for Lloyd Price, and produced Huey Smith and Archibald. He was inducted into the Rock 'N' Roll Hall of Fame in 1990.

Fats Domino: I liked piano players like Amos Milburn. I liked his style of playing. Also Pete Johnson and Charles Brown, who I listen to all of the time.

I got my nickname back in the early days. I was playing around in a local band and the bass player, named Billy Diamond, gave me the nickname "Fats."

I did work in a factory making bed springs. Although I did scrtach my hand up a couple of times, it wasn't so bad that I couldn't work. I was still playing music at the same time. I was playing in New Orleans three nights a week while working at the bed factory five days a week. From there, I got lucky and got together with Dave Bartholemew and Lew Chudd of Imperial Records, who was looking for talent. Someone must have told him about me because they figured I had it. I got started from there and made my first record in 1949.

I wouldn't want to say I started [rock 'n' roll], but I don't remember anyone else before me playing that kind of stuff.

I remember my first session was at a little studio in New Orleans called the Cosimo's studio, where we did "The Fat Man" and sent it over to Lew Chudd at Imperial. He sent it back and told us to do it over, but in the meantime, he still went ahead and released it. He didn't like it because it sounded as though it was recorded in a big hall someplace. But then the record took off as it was, so Lew naturally changed his mind about redoing it. We sold a million or so copies of it, which was unusual because back then R&B music was referred to as "race" music, and we didn't have the number of record buyers we have today.

I made a couple of films, too. The one thing that I remember was that one of them forced me to get up at five in the morning. That was the first time I can remember getting up that early. *(Wayne Jones; February 1981.)*

❦

Dave Bartholemew: We were popular within a 500-mile radius of New Orleans, and one night we were in Houston and Lew Chudd [the president of Imperial Records] contacted me. He was selling every type of music except rhythm 'n' blues; he was in town selling Mexican records then. Six months later he was knocking on my door, and we went to see Fats Domino.

FATS DOMINO: 'I wouldn't want to say I started [rock 'n' roll], but I don't remember anyone else before me playing that kind of stuff.'

The first session I set up for [Imperial] had two million-sellers. It was a split session; we did Jewel King doing "3x7" and Fats Domino doing "The Fat Man." After that, I just let my name go down and become an arranger and producer.

All my men came from the swing era, but the kids couldn't relate to that, so we changed the bass line and added the backbeat and handclaps — anything to make it rhythmic. I only used saxophones — no trumpets — 'cause I wanted a mellow sound. I didn't want to bend peoples' ears too much. White folks didn't like the blues, so we give it to 'em gentle. It was sweet with a rough background, and that's how Fats got in there.

We made a lot of songs I thought was nothin', but the people pick the songs. The one I knew was gonna be a hit, though, was "Blue Monday." I think it's the best tune I ever wrote. It was a true story about the average man who wants to take Monday off 'cause he's been ballin' all weekend. The idea came up many years ago in Kansas City when they had "Blue Monday" and all the clubs would open up at four o'clock in the afternoon. I knew "I'm Walkin' " was gonna be a hit too. I just felt it. I went and got some kids off the street and said, "Listen at this; tell me what you think," and they were just jumping around.

We'd go to a music store, Fats and I, and I'd say, "Do you remember your mother singing this?" Fats had a brother-in-law who was very instrumental in music, and Fats knew a lot of those old songs. "Blueberry Hill" was all his idea; he'd heard Louis Armstrong do it. I remember throwing it on Lew's desk, and he said, "What you got?"

I said, "Nothin'," because I didn't feel it. A few weeks later, Lew had sold a million copies, and he called me and said, "Cut me some more of those nothin' records."

We used to be in the studio eight to 10 hours. We'd go in at midday and two o'clock in the morning we might still be there. The union wasn't really there, and the guys got no overtime. I'd take the tape home and if I wasn't satisfied with it, we'd go back and do it again.

We only had one track at Cosimo's studio. When you did something, you was married to it. We cut some with Bunny Robyn out on the West Coast, but we had the feelin' [in New Orleans]. I think the only hit we cut with Bunny Robyn was "Blueberry Hill."

Our drummers are born, not made. It was a beat you won't hear anywhere else. A teacher don't teach that. You wake up with that, and you have to be born here to have it. The drummers and piano players are what give New Orleans its sound. It's handed down from one generation to another. *(David Booth and Colin Escott; May 17, 1991.)*

Huey "Piano" Smith was pure New Orleans. He played the blues with Guitar Slim and played piano on Little Richard's first Speciality session, and on Smiley Lewis' "I Hear You Knocking." He hired Earl King for his first band and later played piano on King's biggest hit, "Those Lonely, Lonely Nights." His two R&B chart hits, "Rockin' Pneumonia and the Boogie Woogie Flu" and "Don't You Just Know It," influenced more people than they sold records. Smith's sound was rambunctious and piano-driven, with a powerful rhythm and disposable lyrics.

In the '70s Smith joined the Jehovah's Witnesses and stopped drinking. His comeback attempt in the '80s was stopped by his death.

Huey Smith: I'd try to hear all Louis Jordan's records. When I couldn't, we'd go down to the Lincoln Theater on Jackson Avenue and watch him in those short movies. If you ask me, that's where rock 'n' roll really started.

I had been fooling around with a friend of mine, Roosevelt Nettles, who played drums. One night I was coming home from Cohen High School and stopped over at Roosevelt's, and there was this guy there with a guitar. He was dressed in purple and yellow pants, a lime-green shirt and a straw hat. But Roosevelt said, "He sounds just like Gatemouth Brown." It was Slim. He started playin' "Have You Ever Been Mistreated," and I went right into it. He enjoyed it, and started callin' me his piano player from then on.

My voice wasn't that good, but I could get by with a couple of catchy lines. When I got to the studio, Johnny [Vincent] just wanted me to play the music and put vocals on later. I said, "No way." I didn't want another record out by someone else after I had put my music down. Fact [when I was recording "Little Liza Jane"], I got up from the piano at Cosimo's and went home. Johnny had to come get me and bring me back. As it turned out, I did a verse, Izzacoo [Junior Gordon] did a verse, and Dave Dixon did a verse.

Frank [Pania, owner of the Dew Drop Inn] used to send us out backing different artists. Anyway, Shirley and Lee came up hitting, and they were looking for a band so they could hit the road. So we got some uniforms and started rehearsing Shirley and Lee stuff. They had a hot record out, and we went to Atlanta, New York and the Brooklyn Paramount, and we did a show with Alan Freed.

So we came back to town one weekend and Johnny Vincent was in town, and he rushed me into the studio. I was always trying to pick up catchy lines, and Chuck Berry had this line, "I got the rockin' pneumonia, sitting at a rhythm revue," and Roy Brown had some line about "young man rhythm," so I started thinkin' about opposite lines like, "Kissin' a girl that's too tall." So we came up with "Rockin' Pneumonia" that night in the studio.

Well, I had to go right back on the road with Shirley and Lee. I was in Baltimore when I heard the record might be a hit.

Bobby Marchan's record ["Chickee Wah Wah"] was also high on the charts, and he was working the Royal Theatre with Shirley and Lee too. My record was starting to be a natural seller, so I figured I could start a group with Bobby 'cause he was a natural showman.

So Bobby said, "Yeah, why don't we go back to New Orleans and start a group?" Well, I didn't have enough money, so when Bobby got paid we got two tickets for New Orleans, and I gave my notice to Billy Diamond, the group's manager. They got Allen Toussaint to take my place.

We organized a group and Frank Pania booked us. In a matter of weeks we were playing the Apollo Theatre with Shirley and Lee. It was nice because I didn't have to play the piano all night. I'd just have to play three or four numbers. I was really enjoying the business then.

When I did the "Sea Cruise" track, I did the lead vocal with the other guys. In my mind, it was the one that was gonna throw me over the hump.

But Johnny and Frankie Ford's manager, Joe Caronna, liked it also. So Johnny came to me and said, "Let Frankie do this."

I said, "No way!" But Johnny said there was nothing I could do about it. It was coming out on Frankie. Now, the flip side was supposed to be called "Roberta." I didn't even know no Roberta. Johnny couldn't even hear it. He kept the voices in there singin' "Loberta" and Frankie's singin' "Roberta."

I never got any royalties from Johnny. He kept sayin', "It's comin', it's comin'." I'd get some little money, like two or three hundred, but I wanted some real money. So my contract ran out in 1959, and I decided I wasn't gonna record for him no more. But he had all the stuff I had already done, so he could put it out when he wanted to. *(Almost Slim; June 1982.)*

After Fats Domino and Little Richard, Lloyd Price was the biggest star New Orleans produced in the '50s. He wrote "Lawdy Miss Clawdy" and had a hit with it, though not nearly as big a hit as Elvis Presley would have when he covered it. He reworked "Stagger Lee" into a big-band R&B hit and made "Personality" into a top-five record on both the R&B and pop charts. He says he discovered Little Richard.

As his recording career began slowing down, Price became a club owner and entrepreneur. He met Don King when he was just a Cleveland bar owner, and the two eventually promoted a Muhammad Ali fight together. Price lived in Zaire for a time before moving to New York and going into real estate.

Lloyd Price: In my family we had a little shop and it was like a bar. They used to give me nickels and I would sing along with Louis Jordan, Charles Brown, Amos Milburn and Rosco Gordon, when they made records. I'd stand by the jukebox and they'd give me nickels and say "Sing, Lloyd." I'd sing and dance.

What really did influence me a lot was the early Professor Longhairs around New Orleans, the chords that they was playing. Amos Milburn was bigger than Charles Brown or Nat "King" Cole in our area. He had "Bad Bad Whiskey," and that was the town cry in New Orleans. The biggest of all during that time was Louis Jordan.

There was a disc jockey in New Orleans called "Okey Dokey" Smith. He was the biggest thing to hit town during my time there as a kid. Okey Dokey combined these two commercials into a little saying, "Lawdy Miss Clawdy, drink Maxwell House coffee and eat Mother's homemade pies." I sorta liked that saying, "Lawdy Miss Clawdy," and during our generation we just sorta used that when we were talking about girls. "Lawdy Miss Clawdy, she sure is fine." You know, that kind of thing.

One night I was playing at my brother's bar when I played an eight-bar blues and ad-libbed the words, "Lawdy Miss Clawdy, sure look good to me, please don't excite me, 'cause I know it can't be me." Dave Bartholomew, who was the biggest man in Louisiana at that time with his band, was in the bar. He asked me if I would be interested in making a record of the song. I said, "Why not?" and he replied, "Well, I got a guy coming to town and I would like you to sing that 'Lawdy Miss Clawdy' for him." Three weeks later Dave called me and said that the guy was here from Specialty Records.

Art Rupe: I had never been to New Orleans, but I heard that's where it's at. When I heard the first Fats Domino record I really flipped. I was just deludged with people who wanted to audition. So I listened for a week or so. They all sounded amateurish and quite poor. I remember on the last day, I had my plane reservations to go back home and a young fellow showed up just as I was getting ready to leave. Worrying about my plane, I listened to him rehearse, and finally told him it was time for me to go. I thought he was going to cry when I said that. The kid literally began to cry and I said, "Okay, I'll listen to it," and he sang — I should say, he cried — "Lawdy Miss Clawdy." He got to me, the way he did it. It was very emotional, very fervent.

Lloyd Price: Smiley Lewis was sitting in the control room and I sang "Lawdy Miss Clawdy." I sung it out to Fats and he picked it out once and said, "Let's do it." Two takes down we did it. I then had to come up with a B-side. I didn't know what they were talking about. I finally said, "Okay, fine. I have a song, 'Mailman Blues.' "

I was still working at the airport in the evenings after school, getting $26.40 a week. But then my brother said, "They keep saying a song by Lloyd Price on the radio. Okey Dokie Smith is screaming about this hit record." I asked him what it was called; he said, "Lawdy Miss Clawdy."

It didn't sound like me, 'cause I didn't know what I sounded like. But then the Dew Drop Inn called. They wanted to hire me for $50 a night! And I said, "Wow, this is the most money I've ever earned in my life." The record just kept getting bigger and bigger and within a month I went from $50 a night to $750 a day. From there it went to $2,500 a day — and remember, this was 1952. We then started taking 50 percent of the door plus a guarantee.

During that time in America it was really a race thing. The blacks and whites in the South did not go together. But from New Orleans to California I drew as many white people as I did black. All through the Carolinas, through Georgia, the record had no barriers; everybody bought it.

I had met Little Richard just before I went into the service, and I introduced him to Don Robey. After I got out, I told Art Rupe that Richard was booked by Don Robey and that he was out touring with Johnny Otis. I suggested that he should try to get in touch with Richard, and that he could probably be a big star for him. I knew that there was just something about him — the way he wore his hair, all kinds of makeup and stuff like that. I thought it was time for that. Art got hold of Richard in Texas and rest of it is history.

I had heard the song "Stack-O-Lee" all of my life. I sort of put "Stagger Lee" together when I was in the service. We had to have a 45-minute play for the officers and civilians attached to the Army. We had a tent for a threater that we were going to perform this play in. I had to come up with something, so I thought about writing a story around "Stack-O-Lee." It was easy for me to do; I just had to come up with some dice, a background and get some guys to do it. The play went over great with the soldiers and I'd completely forgotten about it until I got back to the States. I needed a song for the back side of "You Need Love," which I was sure was a hit. So I just threw "Stagger Lee" on the B-side. It was on the charts 18 weeks at the #1 position. So who knows? *[Ed. note: Actually, it was #1 for four weeks on both the pop and R&B charts.]*

I thought "Personality" would be a hit because we had set a pattern from "Lawdy Miss Clawdy" through "Stagger Lee'" to "Where Were You On Our Wedding Day?" It seemed as though the people were accepting these kinds of little gimmick songs. At that time Mitch Miller had a very popular television show, with Leslie Uggams. He would feature these singalongs and use a bouncing ball to point out the words. I said, "This is my hook; everybody has a personality." I needed to come up with something that everyone is familiar with. I sang, "Walk, talk, smile, charm" — all the things that go to make up someone's personality. The melody is taken from one line of the gospel song "Wade In The Water." I took it, turned it around a little bit and there was "Personality."

It took two takes. We knew that it was going to be a hit. It was on the chart 9 weeks and at #2 for about eight weeks. *[Ed. note: It was at #2 for three weeks.]* Johnny Horton's song "The Battle Of New Orleans," kept us out of the #1 position. The record just goes on and on. I just received an award for it from BMI [1986]. We're over 2 million performances.

I had this demo from a kid from Detroit named Wilson Pickett. The song was "If You Need Me," and I thought it was just an out-and-out smash hit. ABC said, "No, we will not distribute records. We want you to record as an artist and we don't think that you should have a record company at this time. You're building your own career."

LLOYD PRICE: 'Smiley Lewis was sitting in the control room and I sang "Lawdy Miss Clawdy." I sung it out to Fats and he picked it out once and said, "Let's do it." Two takes down we did it.'

I sent Al Bennett [at Liberty Records] the dub, and he flipped out. He said, "Let's go with it. What are you going to call the label?" The first thing I thought about were the first two letters in my name, double-L. Then my relationship with ABC started to fall apart, and when my contract came up for renewal, I decided I would just go with Double L. So there I was, back in the record business again for the second time.

We did two albums on Pickett. I imagine we were in the studio with him about six times, but Pickett was a very difficult person to deal with. He was very hyper, and above all he wanted to be big, to be gigantic. We had a four-year contract with automatic renewals but I chose not to renew his contract as I didn't want to go through any kind of hassles. I like Pickett, so I wouldn't even enforce the option.

We had Howard Tate, the Coasters, Baby Washington and both of Aretha's sisters, Erma and Caroln Franklin. We later placed Erma with [Shout] Records, and her first hit for them was the record that Janis Joplin took from her, "Piece Of My Heart."

94

Don King built a club, called the Corner Tavern, in Cleveland, just so my big band would come and perform. Don loved me; he loved the band. He would get up and direct the band. He decided that he wanted to get into the boxing business, and we talked about it. Muhammad Ali was a very dear friend of mine, and so I called him to come to Don's daughter's fourth birthday party in Cleveland. He came and Don said, just playing around, "Man, we can go into the boxing business. Lloyd knows all the entertainers; we could combine this thing, sports and entertainment, and take it all over the world." That's how Don King Productions started.

Muhammad Ali was the biggest thing in terms of entertainment at that time, and we decided to do it around the world rather than just North America. How could he be champion of the world and only fight in New York or California? Satellite and closed-circuit TV was coming in at that time, and we would be able to bounce the fight around the world. We were planning to use the same technique that the big shows are using now, but we thought of it 15 years ago. We wanted to rehearse it with fights because we knew Ali was good. I ended up going all over the world. *(David Booth; May 17, 1991.)*

Frankie Ford won a spot on the Ted Mack show when he was barely in his teens, and had his first band, the Syncopators, when he was in high school. His first professional group had Dr. John on guitar. After he had a hit with "Sea Cruise" he had another with "Roberta," and then a string of smaller hits and regional successes. In the late '60s, he became a fixture on Bourbon Street, and was singing "Tie A Yellow Ribbon" and "MacArthur Park" in piano bars well into the '80s.

Frankie Ford: I have a quote for you on this one-hit wonder thing. I'd like to go on record right here saying, whoever that disc jockey was that coined that phrase, well, he's a no-hit wonder! I mean, it can get rude. A jock did that to me one time in his introduction. I turned to him and said, "Well, then, you're a no-hit wonder. What have you ever done?" Some people have five records that sell 1 million each. Some sell none. I've had one that sold 30 million! And I've outlived that one record. I've been 38 years at this and it's still going.

I was singing in the backyard one day. I was in about the third grade, and the lady that lived in back of us said, "He sounds better than the kids on the radio. You oughta see about gettin' him some lessons." My ma took me and I auditioned. After about three months of lessons, I wound up on the program; like one Sunday each month. That was about 1948. Then, in August of 1952, I was on the *Ted Mack Amateur Hour.* I won, but it was the last show of the season and I was never brought back.

In high school years I had a group called the Syncopators. They're still around under a different name. Now they're called Touch. And Buck Baker has still got them gigging. We started out in 1954 as a stock band, you know, playing stock arrangements, "I'm In The Mood For Love" and the like. We were four horns and three rhythm players. We got to play weddings. Always during the last set after everyone had a few Dixie beers, some old apple-cheek woman would come up and say, "Doncha know 'Bony Moronie?'" And the sax player and I would say, "We certainly do!" By the time I was a senior, we stopped the stock stuff and just played rock 'n' roll.

The Syncopators couldn't tour behind me, so I formed a road band called the Skyliners, which had my cousin, Mac Rebennack. Mac's grandmother on his mother's side and my grandmother on my father's side were sisters. Got it? I think that means that we're twice removed. Whatever that is.

Now, "Sea Cruise" was cut to be the follow-up to Huey Smith's "Don't You Just Know It," but Bobby Marchan [then the lead vocalist for Smith's group the Clowns] was leaving. The track was cut. It was to be Huey's new release. It was cut while I was in Philadelphia promoting "Cheatin' Woman" and singing at the George Wood show at the Uptown Theatre. When I got home they said, "Well, let's try Frankie's voice on it." Huey heard me one night in a club and said, "Hey, he sounds like Bobby." So I agreed and went into the studio, not knowin' the song. I still have the piece of paper that Huey had written the words on for me, misspellings and all.

Now, we recorded it on this two-track Ampex. There was no punch-in. If you mad a mistake it was just there. We did about 13 takes on "Sea Cruise," I think. On "Roberta" the Clowns were actually in the studio. There was two microphones. I was on one and the four of them were on the other.

My manager [Joe Caronna] and the owner of the label [Johnny Vincent] said, "Huey, you don't need a release now. Let's put it out on Frankie." And it was set; I was to be the new lead singer with his group, too. Contrary to the Monday-morning quarterbacking, I was there when the agreement was made. Huey was to be listed as producer, and as to what was his deal with Ace Records, I don't know.

We're still friends. In a lot of books, it says that Huey was very displeased with me; and he was not, with me! We remained friends. We worked together and collaborated on a lot of compositions. And when things got as they did, we were instrumental in bringing him over to Imperial Records.

Actually, it was "Roberta" that was to be the A-side. Everyone liked it. I still have the original ads. Cosimo and I liked "Sea Cruise." I told them they should put out just one of the tracks and just put an instrumental on the back. That way we'd have two potential hits. I did suggest it, but they didn't listen to this 17-year-old. So, "Roberta" started happening, and then the record got flipped and we lost out on "Roberta."

I was coming back from somewhere in Mississippi and I was sleeping in the back seat when I first heard it. I remember, I said, "Oh yeah, they're playing 'Sea Cruise.' " And someone in the front seat said, "No, it's not *they're* playing, it's Hose Allen on WLAC out of Nashville." At that time, airplay on the station meant a lot of exposure. Then, Bill Randall at WERE in Cleveland picked it up. Bob Greene in Miami. And then Howard Miller in Chicago.

I was trained to do legitimate stuff. I write vocally. I was trained to be a crooner. I was getting a bit older and the trend then seemed to be going that way — you know, Bobby Darin, Bobby Rydell, and my good friend Jimmy Clanton were going in that direction — so I recorded "Time After Time" and "Chinatown"; stuff like that. I looked old enough and I could start working at the nightclubs, which was a lot better, believe me, than those rock 'n' roll road tours.

I had done the bus tours. One in particular started on January 3, 1960. We started out from New York City and criss-crossed the country. Now, the bus had no rest rooms, no beds, no anything. The tour ended on June 5th in Mexico. We only had two days off during those six months. It was quite drastic. We'd do two shows each, and at the big theaters we'd each do five shows a day.

Ace was getting so diversified and they weren't takin' care of their artists. Imperial gave me front money [reportedly $10,000] to go with them, and I took Huey with me. The first single actually made me more than "Sea Cruise."

Then I was drafted! And I wasn't terribly pleased about that. I mean, I had something going. When I got back to the States in 1965, it was all changed; the studio had moved. And sessions, there used to be one or more a day. Now, there was zip; nothing was happening. It was bleak. But, I was determined. I was gonna keep on working. There's a lot of clubs in New Orleans, and for years I worked them. Now, for the last 10 years I've been back on the road; did about a hundred shows last year.

You know, "Sea Cruise" meant absolutely nothing. I mean, think about it! I've heard Bobby Marchan's version. They always say they erased it, but they didn't. I'm not taking anything away from Bobby. He's a great singer, but it just didn't have that sensual thing, what *Rolling Stone* has referred to as the "marriage of rhythm and voice."

Our music wasn't made out of rebellion. But I did survive Catholic high school. I went to Our Lady of Perpetual Guilt. I couldn't wear jeans and T-shirts. I never did smoke, but I did roll the Camels up in my sleeve. At Holy Name — it was actually Holy Name of Mary in Algiers [Louisiana], that I attended — if you had too much grease in your hair and if Sister could grab it and it didn't squeak, then you'd have to go down and wash it right there with that greenish yellow soap.

Hey, my homeroom teacher as a freshman is still at Holy Cross College, here in Algiers. She is now the Mother Superior. I'll see her occasionally. She'll call me over — just for fun — and say, "Let me hit you, just for fun. I want you to remember the good ole days." *(Wayne Jancik; May 1991.)*

🐝

There are still links between the old New Orleans and the new New Orleans, more than in most places. The Neville Brothers still do "Mardi Gras Mambo" at the Jazz and Heritage Festival, and Fats Domino still sings "Ain't It A Shame" all over the world, with Dave Bartholemew leading his band. But the link to the past with the most stories to tell is Mac Rebennack.

Rebennack was exposed to New Orleans music at a young age. He followed his father around as he repaired jukeboxes; when he was 15, he was hanging out in Cosimo Matassa's studios, writing songs, and even producing a cut or two for Matassa's Rex label. James Booker showed him how to play the organ; Allen Toussaint, Professor Longhair and Roy Montrell taught him the tricks of the trade.

Rebennack started as a guitarist and played in bands until one of his fingertips was shot off. He moved back to keyboards and played sessions in New Orleans, played organ behind strippers, then moved to Los Angeles in the mid-'60s when the New Orleans club scene dried up. Rebennack played for Phil Spector and behind Sonny and Cher. In 1968, Sonny and Cher gave Rebennack their leftover studio time; the result was *Gris-Gris*, an album that tried to capture the flavor of New Orleans music and voodoo rituals. Rebennack became Dr. John Creaux, the Night Tripper; he wore outlandish New Orleans festival costumes and played with Mick Jagger and Eric Clapton. He had a rock hit in 1973 with "Right Place, Wrong Time" and continued to churn out albums and play sessions through the '70s and '80s. He played on Aretha Franklin's "Spanish Harlem" and Maria Muldaur's "Don't You Feel My Leg," and a thousand songs in-between. He recorded with Danny O'Keefe and the Rolling Stones and the Manhattan Transfer and B.B. King and Emmylou Harris and Van Morrison and Kinky Friedman and more. He made a comeback of sorts with an album of standards, *In A Sentimental Mood*, in 1989 and recorded the *Bluesiana Triangle* album with Fathead Newman and Art Blakey shortly before Blakey's death.

Dr. John: My father owned a record store, Rebennack's Appliance Store, and it was right next to Dillard University, which is a very hip black university in New Orleans. And most of the people that bought records there were from the college, so I got to grow up listening to a lot of R&B and blues — what they called "race" records in those days.

My father used to fix radios and PAs. He was very much into electronical stuff, phonographs and all of that, and I was lucky enough to go around with him to clubs when he'd be fixing the PAs.

My Aunt Dottie Mae and Uncle John used to have jam sessions a lot. My aunt would play piano, and my uncle would play bass. A lot of musicians used to come over, and they would have jam sessions. We had jam sessions at our house too, but not as frequently. There were bands around town that would rehearse at their house, but everybody would always get to be feeling pretty good, and it would end up being a jam session.

I played piano first and then I started taking lessons on guitar. But professionally, I began as a guitarist with the bands around New Orleans. Two of my teachers were studio musicians, and through them, I started subbing around on recording sessions.

And later, working with Wallace Davenport, I got hooked up with Professor Longhair, and got a gig working for Ace Records as a record producer and songwriter.

I knew Professor Longhair from when my father was fixing the Pepper Pot [club's] sound system. But then I got to know him better when I started taking guitar lessons from his guitar player. In those days, I hung out with those cats in the studios. Even if I didn't know what 'Fess was doing, I dug his rap; he was just so different.

Later down the line, I worked with Joe Ruffino [founder of Ric and Ron labels in 1959], and we talked about doing a version of "Mardi Gras In New Orleans" that was more in keeping with the spirit of Mardi Gras. So we put a band together with Longhair, John Boudreaux, Eddie

Hines, myself and others, and we recorded about six sides with Longhair, and I think it was a nice version. It's still the one you hear every year down there during Mardi Gras time.

I think what made that session real special to me, more than "Mardi Gras In New Orleans," was the version of "Hey Now, Baby," when Longhair sat down and showed Boudreaux the kind of thing he wanted on the drums. And I remember Boudreaux played it to death. I think that was one of Boudreaux's classic Professor Longhair moments in the studio. And I also think it was one of Longhair's fieriest moments, 'cause you could hear him so good, and the whole band was happening. On other records, you can hear him good, but the drums, or some other part wasn't happening. It was all happening on that record. It was all up there.

Professor Longhair used to call everything by different names. I used to love to hear him talk. One time he told me, "Mac, get your guitar down, you're gettin' too much *extortion* on your amp!" I loved him. He told the horns one time, "Now, when you get to this section I want to hear you guys make a *spew!*" And we said, "Fess, what is a *spew?*" And he says, "I want you to go, *Sppeeewww!*" (laughing) It was just his words. He would tell the drummer, "I want you to lay into your foot *propedaller* a little harder." He had all these great, descriptive words for everything. A lot of his dates were very off-the-wall.

A lot of Huey Smith sessions were very funny too. He had clowns with him, and you'd have to have seen them to believe them. And Gerri Hall [New Orleans vocalist, also a Raelette], who was the one girl in the group, used to kid them and say, "I'm more man than any of you!" It's very off-the-wall to try to dig it up now.

Back in those days, when we were doing stuff with Huey, in a funny way, he opened the door for Ray Charles to do the "What'd I Say" record. He had bought this prototype electric Wurlitzer piano that we kept in the studios at Ace Records. And Ray Charles used that on his gig, and "What'd I Say" and "Drown In My Own Tears" and all this other history went down through a real trick of fate. So many things like that used to happen in those days.

I actually began [as a songwriter] by writing songs for Famous Music, and I would rap with Harold Battiste a lot, and I think Johnny Vincent [founder of Ace Records in 1955], who ran the company, knew I wanted to do something. And Johnny knew I had a little office in Cosimo Matassa's recording studio, where I'd spend most of my days auditioning talent. So Johnny knew I could write songs and I was in touch with a lot of other songwriters. But he was one of them cats that always walked into a lot of good things.

I had decided long before that that's what I wanted to do. I wanted to get my foot in the door, and I had hung out at the studio since I was 14, with all the other guys — James Booker, myself, Leonard James. We just hung at the recording studio, and when the session was over, we'd just go and use the piano and write songs. Also hanging out at the studio were Allen Toussaint and Huey Smith, but of course, they were working already. We were just trying to get started in the business.

I was also a producer and A&R man for Ric and Ron. But I worked for Ace, Minit Records, all of the offshoot labels, and I did studio work for the Chess and Checker labels that were kind of out in the country in Louisiana and I did a lot of work for Mercury, and all of their different labels.

I had done an album that was half guitar and half piano, but I don't know what happened to it. Two songs, "Storm Warning" and "Foolish Little Girl," was all that was released as far as I know. "Storm Warning" sold a lot of records in the Cotton Curtain. The Cotton Curtain is like from Florida to South Carolina, and then across to Oklahoma and Texas.

Then in 1958 I did a record for Ace Records and around 1961 I did an album for AFO Records, but shortly after that, they went out of business. But they were all instrumental records. The album I did for AFO was half piano and half organ.

Harold Battiste, Melvin Lastie, Red Tyler, John Boudreaux and Peter Badie were five of your basic studio musicians in New Orleans in those days, and they decided they were tired of getting ripped off all the time, so they started their own label, AFO. They really lucked out, 'cause the first and second records they put out were Top 10 records. The second record, "I Know," by Barbara George, was a #1 record.

The only flaw with the whole idea was there was no businessmen in the cooperative. Even though Harold and Melvin tried to be businessmen, they really missed the boat in some ways, 'cause they had signed me and everyone that was involved in the studio session clique in New Orleans was involved with this label in one way or another. And it turned into a nightmare in some ways, 'cause when Barbara George got big she was lured to a bigger label, and all kinds of stuff that happens in the record business started happening. And by the time my record was ready to come out, they started going under, and all these bad things were happening.

DR. JOHN: 'We used to work 12 hours a night, seven days on Bourbon Street. We'd work four hours at one club, four at another, and four more at yet another.'

I was working with Ronnie Barron — he was a singer with my band —and I was picking him up at a motel. He was only like 15 years old, and his mother told me that if anything happened to him, she was gonna take a chunk out of me. I remember this guy was pistol-whipping Ronnie when I walked into the room. And I tried to get the gun out of the guy's hand, and I thought my hand was over the handle of the gun, but it was over the barrel. It went off, and shot the tip of my finger off. They sewed it back on, but there was no feeling left in it.

Obviously, I'm still able to use it on piano, but it affected my guitar playing. It's the fourth finger on my right hand, and it's awkward to bend strings, playing the blues with that finger, so I had to develop a new way of playing guitar. And I couldn't play chords the way I used to play them, so I developed another method, but it took me a long time to be able to do it.

But it was after that I got this gig playing organ with James Booker at these [strip] clubs like Madame Francine's, Poodle's Patio and Trader John's in New Orleans. We would work these 12-hour-a-night gigs, and it was real good, 'cause you really kept your chops up.

Booker had taught me how to play organ and how to play at these joints, and there were four

99

clubs that we'd work in for hours. We'd play three of the clubs seven nights a week or we'd play four of the clubs seven nights a week. It was good steady work, and I really enjoyed it. The first gig would always be backing up strippers and exotic dancers, the second gig would be more like a blues or R&B gig, and the last gig was like a jazz gig, a jam session. It was back in the days when New Orleans club owners would hire us for a certain kind of music, and they really didn't care if the audience had come out to hear us, if they liked it or not. We were just paid and told what to do, and it was fun, because some of the guys we worked for had real good tastes in music.

In the early '60s, Jim Garrison became the district attorney of New Orleans and started pad-locking all the clubs. Actually, first he started busting all the whorehouses. The people who owned the whorehouses also owned a lot of the clubs and the gambling joints. Well, he put a lot of musicians out of work. It caused all the musicians to get the hell out, including me.

But when I first went out [to California], there was this thing with the union. You couldn't just start working and settle right in. But I did work. I did sessions with the O'Jays, Johnny Watson, artists like that. I also did some work for Phil Spector. That's how I got in with Sonny and Cher.

But, jeez, I went from doing Irma Thomas and Professor Longhair sessions to the Electric Alarm Clock [sic] and Iron Butterfly. I didn't know what the hell I walked into. I remember being told at one session to just play "smiles" on certain tracks. The stuff New Orleans players were laying down was just too real. They wanted dragon-and-butterfly stuff. I did so many weird dates, man, it was incredible.

Sonny and Cher was out making a movie, and they weren't able to use some of their studio time, so I used some of their studio time to do the *Gris-Gris* album. Sonny's manager at the time, Joe DeCarlo, helped us hook a deal up [with Atco records]. But it really pissed Ahmet Ertegun off; all of a sudden he was stuck with a record he didn't want. But that's how it happened. They put the thing out, and I wasn't really expecting it to be much more than a one-off deal, but the record kept selling. It didn't sell real big, it just kept selling.

The *Gris-Gris* album was like bringing New Orleans to Los Angeles. I didn't intend to do the record myself. But I couldn't sell it to anybody else, so I did it out of disgust.

Then Atco sent me out on the road to do some promotion. I remember it was an ideal situation at first, because I always wanted to have a road band that was also the studio band, but it backfired on me, 'cause I was losing my guys to more money back in the studio scene. I was constantly re-putting the band together. The band we started off with in L.A. was a killer band, but when I took it on the road I kept losing the guys.

It helped that the whole hippie and psychedelic thing was happening then. All those love-ins and be-ins and freak-ins were happening at the same time. I got Chicken Man and some other guys who did a real voodoo show. That was a little too much for some people, so I toned it down a little. Basically, I kept the snake dancer and the backup singers and a small version of the band.

We all lived in one big pad. We all made our own costumes. We had people like the Diggers in San Francisco, cats that helped us get the material for our costumes. It was a cool scene. We didn't have any money, so this was an important thing for us.

I had made four albums for Atco, and I remember Leon Russell brought Jerry Wexler to the studio where I was making my fifth album. He found out I was a piano player, and that I was from New Orleans. Even though I'd been with Atco for years, and done a lot of other sessions work for them, and Ahmet and Nesuhi knew I was a piano player, Jerry just found out at that time. He found out that I knew how to play Professor Longhair and all of this stuff.

So we did this album called *Gumbo* and I got my first big single, "Iko Iko," off of that, and it opened a lot of doors, because Jerry did some really good liner notes on that record. And it turned a lot of people on to checking out the original records, you know, where all the stuff came from. It helped a lot of people and caused a lot of commotion for Professor Longhair. But they did reissue some of the stuff they put out previously in the 1940s and '50s on Longhair.

I'd have to say that Atlantic treated me very professionally. 'Cause I was there nine years, and there were ups and downs, but people like Nesuhi Ertegun, Ahmet Ertegun and Jerry Wexler really made me feel like I was part of a family operation. There was a real sense of family there. The sessions I did for Aretha, and whoever I worked for with that label, they were all really fun projects. I look back with fondness at those years. A lot of the people I got to meet and work with through that time were real important, whether it was Eric Clapton or Buddy Guy or Junior Wells or Duane Allman.

I had done a session with them when they were the Allman Joys, prior to the Allman Brothers, and I met Duane when we were both doing some studio work. He was a real special guy, very talented. I always looked at him and Eric Clapton as really — I mean, now they're appreciated for their phenomenal studio work, but at the time, these guys just contributed to a lot of things, and even today I don't think all of those old sessions have been dug up. I think they're putting together some composite records of Duane's. He did so much work, with Aretha and Wilson Pickett, some really nice, tasty things. And I lived in Macon, Georgia for a while, myself and the Meters, and we were booked by Phil Walden, who was managing the Allmans at the time. It was a real special time at first, when Otis Redding and the Allman Brothers were both happening.

I took the Allman Brothers out on one of their first tours, and they were one of the only bands in all the years I've been on the road, that, when they got hot, they took me out with 'em to open up for them. I really appreciated that because, over the years, there's been so many bands that I've taken to open for me, but when they got hot I never seen 'em again. That's one thing about the Allman Brothers, man: they're really *nice* guys. I saw all of them just recently and it was just a real good feeling to see them all still together, toughin' it out on the road.

And Dickey Betts and Duane just set a standard for a lot of other bands with the two-guitar thing, and a lot of other bands with two guitar players just don't have the chops that they had. And also, some of the things that Duane did with Eric Clapton, and the *Layla* album, there were some classic things that happened there.

I feel that funk music basically came out of an area of New Orleans music that happened in the 1950s.

Earl Palmer started a thing in the studio clique about playing everything funky. Earl started the whole funk thing, I believe. And when Earl left New Orleans for California to work with Aladdin Records, everybody back in New Orleans was still hot on this funk thing, and this was the middle of the 1950s. And the drummer who took his place in New Orleans was a guy named Charlie Williams; we called him "Hungry." Hungry was not a schooled drummer like Earl Palmer; he was just one of these street cats that played in a way that people call street beats today.

And all your music today, whether it's hip-hop or rap records, all of this came out of one guy. This guy Hungry would make everything funky and, whoever he played with, it was just funky. And he started a tradition that was passed down from him to John Boudreaux, Smokey Joe Johnson to Zigaboo, who played with the Meters. Those were the basic guys that did most of the studio work in those years when funk music developed. I think those are the basic guys that created what we now know as funk.

They established the basic alternatin' of the left hand and right foot, or your bass drum and your snare drum. The alternating of the rhythms is what made it funky. All of the drummers, they're all indebted to this one cat, Charlie Williams. He set the mold for the way it would go and is still going. *(Richard Skelly, May 17, 1991; and Robert Santelli, April 24, 1987.)*

7. Save the Last Dance for Me

Rhythm and blues music in the '50s was everything the name implied. Its rhythms were powerful and usually jazz-based, and it was bluesy. Its singers came from churches and its musicians came from big bands. It was distinctive enough to have charts of its own, and stars. Through the early '50s its stars were the Clovers, the Ravens, Ruth Brown, Wynonie Harris, Fats Domino, Lloyd Price and Johnny Ace; they had as much trouble maintaining their hold on the charts as pop stars did.

R&B was musically sophisticated but socially backwards. It developed under the shadow of segregation. Almost everywhere black R&B performers played for black audiences; in the South, it was forced and enforced. R&B records rarely crossed over on to the pop charts or were played on pop stations, though watered-down versions of R&B songs recorded by white artists were. The biggest stars of R&B from those days had something incomplete about their stardom, a bad taste to it. An R&B singer was up against it; to become a star he had to become a Nat King Cole and she had to become a Dinah Washington.

R&B record companies were usually small labels, and not scrupulous about their record-keeping. Session personnel vanished; masters were leased and released. Accounting was a sometime thing.

The paradox of R&B in the '50s was that the only way to make it big was to cross over to the pop charts, and the only sure way to cross over was to cross over to R&B. Only the most talented performers could pull it off. Jesse Belvin came close.

Belvin was Sam Cooke's equal. His voice was expressive and versatile, but rough-edged and bluesy. He could drop down and sing tough on something like "Confusin' Blues," and then he could soar on classics like "Goodnight My Love" and "Earth Angel." He started out recording in Los Angeles in the early '50s for the legendary record-store owner and all-around hustler James Dolphin, and later cut songs for bigger L.A. R&B labels like Specialty and Modern. Most of his songs were R&B hits. He signed with a major label, RCA, and that was supposed to be the start of his stardom. But RCA knew Nat King Cole, and as they did with Sam Cooke RCA tried to drown Belvin in strings and strip the soul away and create another Nat King Cole. It worked, to the extent that some whites began listening to Jesse Belvin. But blacks quit listening altogether, and it forced Belvin to sign up for a package tour of the South with Jackie Wilson and Little Willie John in 1960. After a concert in Little Rock, Ark., Belvin, his wife and driver were killed when their rented Cadillac crossed the center line and collided with another car. There were rumors than the KKK was behind the accident, but the rumors were never substantiated. But they made for a better legend.

His sister Honey, arranger and musician Rene Hall, local singers Buster Williams and Richard Berry, producer George Motola, singer Bobby Lewis, and friend Gaynel Hodge remember Belvin.

Honey Belvin: It was clear from the start that Jesse was the singer in our family. Our mother recognized how gifted he was, so she worked with him more. He was out there singing when he was only seven.

Gaynel Hodge: He would always get around with kids in junior choir and sing rhythm 'n' blues songs, but he'd change them into gospel to get away with it. Like, he'd change a word here or there to make the songs about the Lord; he'd change "baby" to "Jesus," and that's how he got away with it.

John Dolphin could put a record on the air the same day you recorded it, so you wanted to cut for him, even though you knew he'd screw you. Dolphin chewed cigars and growled all the time, and he carried a knife and sometimes threatened people with it. Finally, some young dude, Percy Ivey, a songwriter, blew him away with a gun. But back then he treated everyone like a fool. But he could get you on the air, man, and that's all we thought about in those days. He'd walk out of the record date with the first masters while we were still recording in back of his place, and by the time we finished our session and walked out of the studio, he was playing them on his show.

Dolphin would pay me for my thoughts, my songs. I think he did the same thing with Jesse. He knew how popular Jesse was and he appreciated the way Jesse's mind worked. Jesse could just sit down and write you a song like that, and sell it to you without a thought, and Dolphin took advantage of that.

Richard Berry: Man, we all learned so much from Jesse. He was the father of us all, of rock 'n' roll in Los Angeles. We were all trying to sing like Jesse so that we could get the girls like he could.

Gaynel Hodge: Jesse was like a big brother to all of us; we worshipped him, tried to sing like him, and we never questioned the things he did, even when it went against our interests. He would borrow our songs and nobody minded, because we'd take his songs, too. Like "Earth Angel."

I introduced Jesse to Curtiss Williams. Jesse was always writing songs on those thin cardboards the laundries put into folded shirts, and he had them laying all over his mother's living room. One of them was "Earth Angel," and I remember Jesse singing it, but the song wasn't fully developed yet. He was still working on it, so he asked Curtiss and me to help him. The three of us finished writing it just before Jesse went off to the army, and Cornel Gunter, who was a genius at arranging, worked out all the background vocal arrangements. One day Curtiss came into my house and started playing the piano, and he took our arrangement out of the piano stool and told me he and Jesse had exchanged songs. Curtiss had given Jesse "Baby Doll," which Jesse and Marvin recorded on Specialty.

Right after that, Curtiss and I went with the Hollywood Flames and we must've sung "Earth Angel" for nearly a year. We changed it some more. There was this lady in our neighborhood named Jessie Mae Robinson who had written "How Much Is That Doggie In The Window" for Patti Page. She hired us to do a demo for this new song of hers called 'I Went To Your Wedding' for Patti Page, and we sorta borrowed the bridge from that and put it into 'Earth Angel.' When Curtiss left the group and formed the Penguins, he took the song with him. He sold the publishing to several different people, which is why we later went into court to establish who wrote it. When Jesse came back from Germany in '54, the song was a big hit and Curtiss' name, not his, was on it — and Jesse at that time had a young bride and not a cent in his pocket!

Rene Hall: Jesse could sit down and write songs on the spot, but he'd always sell 'em outright for $100 or so. Sometimes he'd take me with him on his rounds [of the indies] so that I could play along on the guitar whenever he tried to sell his songs. He could go into a studio with a few musicians and compose on the spot. He'd just pull these songs out of thin air, improvise with the musicians, then do a demo. If he didn't like it, he'd run it down again, but change the song completely.

Gaynel Hodge: Jesse'd write these songs, but actually all he might have were six words on a piece of paper. He'd go into the record companies and start singing, just making up shit, and hypnotize them with his voice, because he had such a strong effect on people when he sang. But after he left with his money, the people would realize the song had been all Jesse and all they were left with was smoke. When Jesse wasn't there, that song that had sounded so good a few minutes ago suddenly wasn't anything.

Buster Williams: We were down at Austin McCoy's studio on Avalon, recording behind Jesse on "Deacon Dan Tucker," and we took a break out in Eugene's car, smoking some grass and singing this line from the song: "I'm lookin' for a pretty girl." Now that was Jesse's song, Jesse's line, but we started turning it around and we came up with "Pretty Girls Everywhere." A week or two later we recorded it as Eugene Church and the Fellows, and had a hit with it. But if you listen to the two songs, you can hear a lot of "Deacon Dan Tucker" in "Pretty Girls Everywhere."

George Motola: I had an office on Melrose Avenue, and Jesse would come in just to say hello. One day he said he was going to record for Jules [Bihari] down at Modern, and did I have any songs. That's when I pulled out "Goodnight My Love." I'd written and copyrighted it back in 1946 but it needed a lyric for the bridge, so I gave the song to Jesse to work on. He came up with the four lines, you know, "If you should awake in the still of the night ..." so I offered him half of the writer's credit, but he just said "Forget it; I'll take $400 for writing the lines." John Marascalco was standing there with me; he said, "I'll give you the $400." That's how John's name got on the record instead of Jesse's.

Bobby Lewis: I was on a tour at the time [February 1960] with Jesse, Jackie Wilson, Little Willie John, Lloyd Price, Arthur Prysock and several others. We finished a show in Little Rock, Arkansas, and were en route to Dallas when the accident occurred. I was riding with the baritone saxophone player in his car and we were about half a mile down the road behind Jesse's car. All of a sudden we saw a cloud of smoke go up in the air and at first, because there was a railroad running parallel to the road, I thought that someone was probably burning railroad ties. I mentioned that to "Beans," the saxophone player, simply because I had seen railroad ties burned many times. Well, the closer we got the more vivid things became. Beans then said, "Man, that looks like an accident ahead." We then saw Jesse's car down in the ditch folded up like an accordion and the car that collided with him was in the middle of the highway burning. We stopped, of course, and ran over to Jesse's car. He was in the front seat with his wife and his driver. In the back seat was his guitar player and one other passenger. Jesse was still alive at the time, after feeling his pulse and all. We were afraid from the way the car was crushed that it might explode at any minute so we decided to remove the people from the car. We found the doors jammed, and from out of nowhere somebody came up with a chain. Somebody else arrived on the scene with a pickup truck so with that and the chain we hooked it up to pull the doors off. We pulled everyone out from the car and immediately got them to a hospital. Jackie [Wilson], who was driving ahead of Jesse, didn't hear about the accident until he got to Dallas. So he immediately got back into his car and drove back to the hospital. And we stayed there for hours waiting to give blood or whatever was needed. And that was really the gist of what happened. *(Wayne Jones; November 1981.)*

Belvin was the first and best-known R&B singer to come out of Los Angeles, but there were plenty of others. There was a whole West Coast R&B style and sound, and groups and artists that had hits on the West Coast and never had their songs played east of Pasadena. After Belvin, the next figure that changed popular music at least to a degree was Richard Berry. Berry was one of the founding members of the Flairs, one of the first L.A. doo-wop groups. After recording one of the first teenage doo-wop sex anthems ("She Wants To Rock"), Berry became the bassman on Etta James' "Roll With Me Henry" and the Robins' (Coasters') immortal "Riot In Cell Block No. 9," and still later wrote probably the most misunderstood song in rock: "Louie, Louie." When he recorded it, as a calypso-novelty sort of number, you could understand the words.

Richard Berry: We started out in the music department [at Jefferson High], started out in a cappella choir. We just kind of got together to do some street-corner doo-wop stuff. Then we went on talent shows they had around the city. Hunter Hancock, who was a DJ at the time used to have talent shows at the old Lincoln Theater at 23rd and Central avenues. We'd go and be on some of the shows and we were singing some of the songs that the guys like the Robins and the Hollywood Flames had recorded — songs like "Young Girl." We would win first place which would be a certain amount of money. We got the idea we ought to try approaching a record company.

We also knew that John Dolphin had recorded Jesse Belvin. Jesse at that time was our idol. We didn't have any idea what we really sounded like, you win talent shows and everything, but you never have an idea what you sound like. We did go to Dolphin's and we told them we had a group. We told him we wanted to record for his company, so he took us up to a studio. He had a couple of musicians there; I remember Pee Wee Crayton was there. This really wasn't a recording; it was more of an audition, because John would never say, "Okay, I'll just record you"; he'd want an audition. So we did the audition, which was really a bummer.

We had been so used to that atmosphere of everybody, the kids and stuff; now we were in the studio without any of this, we didn't have that atmosphere of a live audience, and plus we had to wait so long that night to even start recording.

We did do the demo which was "I Had A Love." John Dolphin said, "You guys need to go back and rehearse because you don't really sound that good." We were dejected and we went back home. We did rehearse, but we always felt there were other record companies, so we just started looking in the telephone book and we came upon Modern Records up on Robertson Boulevard in Beverly Hills.

I told them we had a vocal group and that we wanted to come down so they could listen to us and talk about recording. We went the very next day and auditioned for Joe [Bihari] and he said, "Come back tomorrow and we'll record you," which we didn't believe. It was too good to be true.

We went back the next day and we recorded. We had the song "She Wants To Rock." Five days later they released the record.

We went through a couple of names, I remember the most important name we had was the Flamingos but this was before the original Flamingos even came out. Modern Records said the Flamingos are all right, but we should think of another name for you. We were on Flair Records, so they said how about the Flairs? Great. What better association can you have than being named after the record company? If we're on Flair Records and we're the Flairs, then at least they're going to try and play the record.

When the record came out, [it] immediately started selling. Everybody was familiar; when you're a local guy, everybody knows you, we were even known all over the Southern California area. When John Dolphin heard "I Had A Love," he released the dismal demo. So when people came in [to Dolphin's record shop] he said, "I'll sell them the Dolphin's Of Hollywood record." When they got home and played the record, immediately they said this isn't the record. We went down to his record store and told the man you gotta take that record [off the market]. He was playing it on the air rather than playing the Flairs record, because in a way they were similar.

It wasn't rock 'n' roll then. They were just starting to call it rhythm and blues, but the most people who came to hear this hadn't heard some of the stuff I was doing. It was danceable and it was just like a big family thing. They called it rock 'n' roll in those days, not rhythm and blues. Then all of a sudden there came a divider where rock 'n' roll sort of went off into a white pop market and rhythm and blues came in, which was predominantly black. But I was playing with mostly all rock 'n' roll artists at that time. I was playing with Bobby Darin and Ritchie Valens and all those guys. They were all at El Monte Legion Stadium.

The first mind-blower was when I did the tour with Bobby Blue Bland and Junior Parker, which was the early part of '57. They considered me rock 'n' roll. They put me on the show because "Louie Louie" was an attraction for all the white kids. So we had a mixed crowd. All the white kids were coming to see me, and all the black people were listening to "Further On Up The Road" and Junior Parker. It's funny how we were still categorized. The guy who booked me on the tour told me, "The reason why I'm putting you on this tour is that you are a great attraction to white audiences."

I was almost what you would call a flop because my music had a different type of sound. As a matter of fact, there was one black club I went to play in and the guy said I'd never make it in the club because my music "wasn't black enough," although I went back and played the club for four or four-and-a-half years. I had a majority of black artists come tell me, "Man, your music's so different, but we like it."

At that period of time we had only one radio station — actually only one *disc jockey*. I don't know if you remember Hunter Hancock. He was a white dude, but he was a guy who played all the black music. Even when I was in school, we did the record hops. We did the old show at the Lincoln Theatre and Hunter was the DJ. He was more respected than a lot of the black DJs. There were three or four black DJs. He had the market cornered before the stations started to change and started to get in all the other black DJs. Those were the days when you could take your record up to Hunter and say, "I've got a record out," and he would put it on the air. Otherwise, Huggy Boy and Johnny Otis were the only other two. Huggy Boy was white. A lot of people thought Johnny Otis was black, but he was white. It was never a racial thing with me. It was just an appeal thing.

I think what made the black music come into focus were the record companies — Chess Records, R.P.M., Modern Records, which I was on for a while. Back in the beginning, when I was with the Flairs, we were actually the first young teenaged group to come out with a record that didn't go nationally but went regionally. There were no teenaged groups then. After that, you had scores of groups coming out, like the Rainbows, the Crows, and all those groups. I don't say that we were the main impact, but it was good to know that we were the first ones.

I think we were at that time with one of the strongest West Coast record companies: Modern Records. Everyone who later became a heavy black artist was, at one time or another, on that label in their early years. If you look at their catalog, you'll see they had Johnny Ace, Ike and Tina Turner, B.B. King — they had almost everyone under contract. At that time, we didn't know how to get in touch with a record company like Columbia or Atlantic. And, of course, Capitol and Columbia and Decca and those companies were square — *square, square!* They were doing old stuff, like, they were recording groups like Jimmy Ricks and the Ravens. Ever hear of them? The guys I was listening to at the time were Sonny Til and the Orioles. I think the emergence of black music was primarily in the blues: Amos Milburn, Charles Brown and those guys.

I never received any writer's royalties. It was quite some time before I was hip to B.M.I. But then again, I was 17 years old, and if you went down and asked for an advance, they'd give it to you. And in those days if someone handed you $200, man, that was a lot of bread for a black kid. You could go out and buy a car for $400 or $500 — you know, the big '49 Buicks with convertible tops. I couldn't even drive. My cousin was driving me and he said, "Man, you gotta learn how to drive." But it was a lot for a kid who was in high school to have his own wheels, to be able to drive around school and hear, "Hey, there goes Richard Berry!" It was a real ego thing then. *(Steve Propes, Jan. 31, 1986; Aaron Fuchs, June 1983.)*

Two of the most important solo stars of R&B came out of the same group. The Impressions were a Chicago group that launched the solo careers of Curtis Mayfield and Jerry Butler. Mayfield wrote revolutionary songs like "It's All Right" and "Gypsy Woman" for the group, and later went on to write the influential soundtrack to the influential movie *Superfly*. Butler, "The Ice Man," was the voice that made the songs unforgettable.

Curtis Mayfield: Our intention was to go across the street to Chess Records. We're in Chicago, the snow is up to your waist. I guess it's five above. We're standing at the door of Chess. I guess there was nobody there but a secretary, who saw us through the window but who would not let us in. We had an appointment, but we were freezing standing there looking in the window. Someone turns around, right across the street, there was Vee Jay Records. We jumped across the street, and as we walked into Vee Jay, the first element we met was a Great Dane. We stood there. The dog held us toward the door until someone could come downstairs. That was our introduction to the people at Vee Jay. We performed "For Your Precious Love" right downstairs. Three more days we were in the studio.

["For Your Precious Love"] was something a little different, the high-pitched [tenor part] comes from the church. The basic mood could've been a nice gospel tune.

Guitar Red and Lefty Bates both played guitar on ["For Your Precious Love"]. Johnny Pate played upright bass and Al Duncan played drums. During those days, there were no charts. We'd go into the studio with Calvin Carter, who was the A&R man, and record things off the top of your head. You'd come in, group around who was the originator [of the song], and in 10 or 15 minutes you got the tune. You got the ending, the middle, everything. When the group is right there, it all locks in. You go for that, that's life. "For Your Precious Love" was done the same way; we made no changes. The only difference was we had a bunch of musicians to show the tune to. I wasn't even in the union. I was playing with a bunch of professional cats who added music to my ears.

Was changing the group name to Jerry Butler and the Impressions on "For Your Precious Love" a problem?

It was for the Impressions.

You hit on a sensitive note. It was so important to us to move ourselves as a group, the way things happened with Jerry Butler and the Impressions was no intention on Jerry's part. During all those years, all the labels would take the lead away after one or two hits and try to do that crossover thing. I guess they felt they could hit another horizon. When it happened the group would usually just dwindle away.

For one of the first times I can recall, the Impressions even surpassed the lead singer as an act. We'd do many shows where Jerry was "co-liner" and we were headliners. Of course, this was total fulfillment, knowing where we came from.

It's funny how songs flare from either titles or the lyrical content may lend inspiration to leave that and start something new. Many times, you may have written one song, you find yourself writing another to find the first song corresponds as the middle part of the second song you've written. Songs do come in all possibilities.

This is Nashville, Tennessee. You take forms of statements, it leads to inspiration. We were sitting out front. Myself, Fred [Cash] and Sam Gooden were just in one of those inspiring moods, speaking of how things may happen in our dreams and future. Fred just kept making the comment, "We're all right, it's all right." Before we knew it, we're putting this harmony together. I was saying, "Say it's all right." By the time we arrived back to change for the next show, we'd actually put the song together. I'd incorporated inspiring lyrics. We could've performed that song on that final show; put Bobby Bland licks by Johnny Pate and we had "It's All Right."

I've never lent myself to trying to be competitive in the music. I've always admired everyone for their own tributes and left it at that. Stax in Memphis and Berry Gordy in Detroit was to be admired. Let's face it: they had at least 60 percent of the airwaves during those times. Chicago locked itself in there; we were getting touch-and-go with the Philadelphia sound later on. There was a competitive ground; it was important to me to express myself. When we came together in concert, everybody learned and picked up from everybody. When they went in for recording, they had their own way to make it marketable. On stage, it might have been competitive.

In order to open yourself up to a larger consumer, you had to cross over. It meant you had to get the white business as well as the black business, which was only a small percentage of the business, you could only sell so many records. You always have the pressures of walking that line of your own personal needs and the fads and needs to sell your products. In concept, my music was totally new anyway. The statements were a little heavier than those that were into the Top 40 cared to play. Many times there was a controversy. There were stations that wouldn't play "We're A Winner" or "Choice Of Colors." Your whole intention is to deliver the message to the people themselves. In the long run, they make the choice. My intentions were never to be typecast.

Chicago having always been a heavy blues town, there was never anything stable enough other than Vee Jay or Chess Records. When Vee Jay and Chess began to disappear, that was all your studio work, production work. When that faded out, all the little companies, my company as well, just did not have the revenue or the distribution to handle the business. I even moved. It had nothing to do with the music. Maybe it did. *(Steve Propes; Jan. 25, 1991.)*

❦

Calvin Carter was head of A&R for Vee Jay Records.

Calvin Carter: Jerry Butler came in with a group with Curtis Mayfield, called the Impressions. They came to us on a Saturday. We were distributing our own label in Chicago, so we were open a half-day on Saturday. Jerry had been all up and down Michigan Boulevard in Chicago trying to record a record. So they finally came to us; these five guys walked in the door. They sang about five or six numbers, and sounded pretty good, so I said, "Do me a favor. Sing me a song that you wrote, one that you're almost ashamed to sing in public." So Jerry says, "Hey, let's sing that church-type song!" And Curtis says, "No, no, not that one." I said, "Well, let's hear it." The song was "For Your Precious Love." I signed them on the spot, and recorded them on the Wednesday after I signed them. Now I took the dub over to my sister Vivian; she put it on the air and we got immediate reaction. We also took it over to the record store and played it over the loudspeakers outside. Now at that time, there was a very big R&B singer named Roy Hamilton, who had had "You'll Never Walk Alone." Jerry Butler sounded just like him, and everybody came up and thought it was a new Roy Hamilton record. They asked, "Who is is?" and I said, "The Impressions." But they said, "No; who's the singer?" But I didn't even know their names then, so I called them into rehearsal and told them to sing the song and got down their names.

When I first put them out, they came out as "Jerry Butler and The Impressions." So the promoters picked it up, and they bought the group into the Apollo for their first gig. On the marquee was, in very big bold letters, "Jerry Butler," and down in the corner, "and the Impressions," and they screamed. It almost broke the group up. They came running in to me with it, saying. "What is this? We don't want it on the label; all for one and one for all." So I said, "Well, okay. On the next pressings of the record, I'll change it around." But I never got around to changing it. As a result, I got two acts out of that one act.

What had happened was, I had given the Impressions their release, because I was never really in love with Curtis Mayfield's voice; I didn't really like that falsetto voice. Well, I gave them a release because they were bugging me to record without Jerry Butler. I did a couple of things with them, and Sam [Gooden], who was the bass player, kind of sounded like Jerry Butler, but it was just pseudo. So I passed on it. Jerry was out on his own, and I told him that the best thing for him to do was to take Curtis Mayfield as a guitar player. I never met a guitar player who played the guitar the way Curtis did. Everything was on open strings, and it sounded very unusual. I don't care where you'd go, you'd always hear people say, "Play me some Curtis Mayfield-type guitar," and they'd know what you were talking about. Curtis was also a prolific writer, although he didn't write "For Your Precious Love"; that was Jerry Butler and two other guys who were singing with him, the Brooks brothers. Curtis wrote "I'm A-Telling You," and he and Jerry and I wrote "He Will Break Your Heart."

I usually did the lyrics. Like on "He Will Break Your Heart," they came in, Jerry came in, with the hook "don't break my heart" or something like that, and I turned it all the way around, told him, "No, put the triangle in there — he will break your heart." Now we have a hook, and

108

I'm trying to figure out the first verse, because I basically know we have a song. I would always try to go back and try to find a true story in life, and I tried to remember but couldn't come up with anything, so I started thinking about literature. When you think about literature, you got to think about England, and what's a famous line from literature in England? And it just popped into my mind: "fare thee well." The next line, "I know you're leaving for the new love that you found," we took because we noticed that on the road, we would come in and be strangers in town, and we could get all the local chicks. And the guys they would come with, they would be left outside the dressing room waiting for them to come out from getting autographs and whatever else they do in dressing rooms. *(Mike Callahan; May 1981.)*

🎗

Dance crazes helped R&B. There was the mashed potato, and "Mashed Potato Time," and the Monkey, and Major Lance's "Monkey Time," and Chris Kenner's "Land Of 1000 Dances." Most importantly, there was the Twist. The Twist was a product of Hank Ballard, a veteran R&B singer and leader of the Midnighters, who'd had a major R&B hit with "Work With Me Annie" in 1954. Ballard wrote "The Twist" in 1959 based on Clyde McPhatter's "Whatcha Gonna Do," and it was supposed to be his biggest hit. Instead, the song went to Ernest Evans, a Fats Domino-soundalike who recorded under the name Chubby Checker. The song was supposed to be a B-side, but it shot to No. 1 like no other R&B hit ever had. It made a star out of Chubby Checker, and made Hank Ballard bitter.

Hank Ballard: We were playing an amateur show at a theater in Detroit and we won first prize. Johnny Otis sent us to King Records in Cincinnati where we auditioned for Sid Nathan. I replaced the original singer of the group, who were first known as the Royals. Our first recording was "Every Beat Of My Heart" — the same tune Gladys Knight and the Pips later had a hit with. Then I wrote "Get It," which was a mild hit, and then I wrote "Work With Me Annie," which was a smash.

King Records wasn't afraid to record anything. Sid was the only one who had the guts to okay something like "Annie" for the market. The average company wouldn't have recorded it. Today, there's a different morality out there. Those lyrics are just mild stuff. The Rolling Stones make my stuff look tame, but with "Annie," people went around and they just pulled it off of all the jukeboxes. When they banned it, record sales tripled. The song went to the top in one week and stayed there for a year.

I knew there was a marketplace for something funky and lowdown. Everybody was sounding like Sonny Til and I said, "We gotta change that groove, man, and get funky." So I started writing suggestive lyrics, double meanings and then — boom! — overnight there was a marketplace for it.

I was working on the assembly line at Ford Motors and when King called me and told me the song was a hit, I left and didn't even pick up my check. I haven't been back since.

I played with James Brown for about a year-and-a-half. That was a total waste. I was the one who gave him his first date. I put him on my show because no one else would book him. I told the promoter the James was very excitable, a real crowd-pleaser ... but what an ego that man has.

We were doing the Twist for approximately two years before it caught on. We were in Baltimore, Maryland, on a 10-day engagement at the Royal Theater. The kids saw us doing the Twist there. There was a show in Baltimore, the *Buddy Dean Show*, which was similar to *American Bandstand*. Dean saw those kids out there doing the Twist, because they had seen us doing it at the Royal. So he called Dick Clark and said the kids over here are going crazy over a record by Hank Ballard called "The Twist," and they're not even touching. Dick Clark said something to the effect of, 'I don't want to hear the record because I know it is one of those dirty records by Hank Ballard and the Midnighters. But Dean sent him a copy of it anyway. We cut another tune called "Teardrops On Your Letter," which was the hit side, and the DJs never flipped it.

A lot of people think I should be angry with Dick Clark and Chubby Checker. But no. Man, they were a blessing to me because they enhanced my career. Brother, I made a lot of money from "The Twist." Not the kind of money Chubby made, but I'm still making money playing it.

Chubby was a good friend of mine even before he recorded the song. I thought it was me when I heard his version. Dick Clark did a magnificent job on the cover. They didn't miss anything at all — all the phrases, all the gimmicks, the yee-ows! The one thing that makes me angry is when people ask me why did you let Chubby Checker steal "The Twist." You can't steal a song. It's unfair to him and it's unfair to me. *(Robert Pruter, Aug. 12, 1988; Andrew Edelstein, November 1981.)*

❦

By the late '50s and early '60s, the style of black vocal music was evolving. Groups like the Drifters and the Coasters became popular, and their white-written, white-produced R&B became the new sound to emulate. Ben E. King became the lead singer of the Drifters in 1959, and his smooth, high vocal on "There Goes My Baby" became their trademark sound. Later King went on his own and had hits — real hits, national hits, hits on all the charts, not the limited regional hits R&B artists had been used to. King did "Stand By Me" and "Spanish Harlem" and became one of Atlantic's first big R&B solo artists. In 1987, the movie *Stand By Me* made the title song a hit all over again. And the song was every bit as bittersweet the second time around as it was the first.

Ben E. King: I never really thought of the music as anything except something to do because I loved doing it. As a matter of fact, when I started in R&B, I never knew that you got paid for doing it. The donations from the church were because we maybe had to come to New Jersey, or because we had to get dinner after the performance. So I never thought of that as pay.

My first group was the Four B's (Ben E., Billy, Billy and Bobby), which was a high-school group. I started with them when I was in James Fenimoore Cooper Junior High School, and then I went to Seward Park High, which in on Delancy Street. We did it just for school programs mostly, and we did a thing at the Apollo Theater. Of course, *Amateur Hour*, we came in second on that.

Later, I was working in my father's restaurant and I met a man named Lover Patterson, who managed a lot of groups. He managed the Five Crowns and a few other people; the Five Crowns were his biggest name. He came into the restaurant one day looking for a singer, and I volunteered. I was just singing baritone and second tenor. I wasn't doing any lead singing at all during all those years.

The Five Crowns were working at the Apollo Theater, and we were on the bill with Ray Charles and the Drifters and a few other very big names. The Drifters' manager, George Treadwell, came up to Lover Patterson and said, "The Drifters are going to break up at the end of this week and I'd like to get your guys to become the new Drifters." So Lover sat down and talked to him for hours and hours ... and on Monday we went into the office and became the new Drifters. I went on the road with the Drifters for about a year and that's when I wrote "There Goes My Baby." That was the first song I recorded.

Charlie Thomas, who was singing tenor in the Five Crowns and then, of course, in the Drifters, was supposed to be doing the lead. When I was in the studio, I was showing him how "There Goes My Baby" should be sung, and Jerry Wexler, who was the president of the company [Atlantic] at the time, came across on the mike and said, "Look, Ben, we're running out of time. Why don't you do the song if you know the song." And that's how my lead started. I was never doing lead, I was doing second tenor-baritone.

Then, of course, I got stuck as lead singer. I took over from Clyde, and then Rudy Lewis [featured on "Up On The Road," "On Broadway" and others] took over after I left. And it went on and on. Each [lead] singer had his own identity, and that helped.

When we were on the road and "There Goes My Baby" was a No. 1 hit, we were on salary, and we had to take care of our uniforms and things like that. I felt that we weren't making enough money, even on salary, to send any money home and to take care of all the little things we had to take care of on the road, such as feeding ourselves. We discussed asking George Treadwell for a raise when we got back to New York from one of the road tours.

When we got back, we were saying to George, "Whatever small raise we could get we'd appreciate, because we're working our buns off but not making enough money to take care of the small things." So he told me, "If that's your feeling, you stand up and talk for yourself."

So, as the lead singer, I stood up and spoke for myself. I was newly married and I said to George, "I find it's really hard for me to live on the road and send money home to my wife and feel like I'm really accomplishing anything out here." I was making such a small amount — $75 or $100 a week or some ridiculous amount like that. So, in a word, he couldn't pay any more money and it was up to me whether I wanted to stay with the group or not. So I stood up by myself, looked around the guys, and said, "Well, I'll quit." And I walked out.

Purely because of the money situation, I was working, before I started singing, with my father at his place. I was working as a process server. It was a terrible job; I hated it, but somebody had to do it. And I was making $34 a week. With $34 a week, and living at home, it was fine because I didn't have to spend any money. What hurt me more than anything was the fact that I did better on a small amount at home than I did as a singer on the road.

"Spanish Harlem" was my first really big solo recording. They [Leiber and Stoller] called me down to the studio and said, "We've got a song." So I said, "I guess you guys haven't heard that I'm not with the group anymore." They said, "That's okay. We talked it over with Atlantic and they'll sign you as a solo artist." It was all set up for the Drifters to do "Spanish Harlem," but they gave it to me.

It was so different that I said, "It'll never go!" Although we had done things with a Latin feeling, such as "This Magic Moment" and "Save The Last Dance For Me," this was super-Latin. So I said, "This is strange!" But they showed me how to sing it. "Spanish Harlem" had a lot of ups and downs and trickery; it was more involved. I was there with Jerry, Mike and Phil, and they helped me through the song more or less, because it was that new. They had the magic touch.

I remember my first engagement with "Spanish Harlem," which really tripped me out. I went to a nightclub in South Carolina from New York. I took the bus because I couldn't afford anything else. I rode all the way down there and got to the front door, where the guy said, "Who are you?" I said, "I'm working here tonight — my name is Ben E. King." He said, "What!" He paid me right there at the front door and said, "Not in this club!" They'd never seen a picture of me. They didn't know I was black.

I wrote the lyrics to "Stand By Me." The lyrics basically come from a spiritual that I haven't heard for a long time called "Lord Stand By Me." I did a little twist of the words of the spiritual and wrote "Stand By Me." To this day, it still hasn't been recorded the way I wrote it.

I showed it to the Drifters after "Spanish Harlem." We're still friends to this day. I went to their house and said, "I've got a song for you guys. It's really good." I showed the bass part and we did the harmony bit and I showed Charlie Thomas the lead. We went down to George's [Treadwell's] office, even though I wasn't a member, and the guys stood up and sang "Stand By Me" [for Treadwell] the way I'd shown them. After the song, I said [to Treadwell], "What do you think?" He said, "It's not bad, but we don't really need any more material right now."

So, one day I was in the studio with Mike and Jerry, and we had about a half-hour of studio time left over. So they asked, "Do you have any songs?" I banged away on "Stand By Me" on the piano as best I could, and they said, "Oh, great!" And they whipped it together like that [snaps his fingers].

I was fortunate to be involved at a time when everything was all built around the artist. When I was recording, I was right there with the instruments and I was singing, unlike it is today. And I found that they more or less used the voice as an instrument as well. They'd say, "Benny, this is where you're going, and the strings will be here and kettle drums will be there." Nothing really interfered, because everything locked in perfectly. They wrote it that way. I miss those days. It was great. On everything that you hear on the sessions I'd done from the '50s, right up until '65, I was right there with the orchestra.

I would go over the material with Mike [Leiber] and Jerry [Stoller], or with Doc Pomus and Mort Shuman, or with Gerry Goffin and Carole King. We'd all work through it with the piano, and we'd go to the lyrics. We'd talk about which way I was going to interpret a song, and "What's the best way to sing this line?"

Those were the most beautiful days of my life. When someone said, "I have a song for Ben E.," they would honestly come to me, present the song, and if I liked it, they would work with me, 100 percent. That song won't leave me to go to Teddy Pendergrass or whoever. There's no way that sound would leave me once I say, "I love that song, that's my song." They would stay right with me, and if I wanted to change a few lyrics here and there ... it was total respect for the artist.

I think that's what made the career happen — having those guys at our disposal. They were there. It was just one of those thing where you'd wake up in the morning, they'd call you and say, "Ben, we got a great song! We just finished it. Come to the city, man..."

And then we'd go into the studio, where the rest of the dream comes true. They would say, "The strings are going to do this, Ben, and then we're gonna have the drums here and the French horn." And then we'd go in there [the studio] and hear it all together.

I was in awe of those guys because I came from Harlem with no musical talent at all, to my knowledge, and when I came downtown to sit with people like Jerry and Mike and Doc Pomus and Morty Shuman, I found that their interest was much more honest than mine. Honest because they'd lived with what they wanted me to do longer than I would ever live with it; in other words, they started the dream.

I couldn't honestly say what was in the minds of Ahmet Ertegun, Jerry Wexler or Leiber and Stoller. They were constructing this whole thing to give a new sound to black music, which they did. I couldn't say that it was geared to a white audience, although it happened that way. But I think it happened because it was good music. *(Gene Kalbacher; August 1981.)*

Atlantic was the label that did it. Atlantic made R&B into "soul" music, and made soul music not only something that record buyers would listen to, but something record buyers craved, and wanted to hear more of. Atlantic had an unprecedented roster of R&B greats, starting with Ray Charles and including Solomon Burke, Sam and Dave, Joe Tex, Wilson Pickett, and Aretha Franklin. They took R&B without much adulteration and gave it to the public, and the public loved it. Motown might have been guilty of shaving a few too many edges off the sound in changing it from R&B to The New Sound Of Young America, but Atlantic never could have been.

One of Atlantic's biggest stars — literally — was Solomon Burke. Tipping the scales at better than 300 pounds and dressed in the robes of the King of Rock 'N' Soul, Burke put everything into his hits: "Cry To Me," "The Price," "Got To Get You Off My Mind," "Down In The Valley," and the revelatory "Everybody Needs Somebody To Love." His music shook the walls and still explodes today. Next to Otis Redding, no one could match Solomon Burke for dynamite soul and 100 percent R&B.

Solomon Burke: The church existed 12 years before I was born. I was the spiritual head under God of the church. It's kinda funny being head of a church at two years old and when you get to be seven years old someone says "Hi, bishop." These days, when I meet someone that knew me when the church was starting up, they find it hard to believe that I'm only 86.

We had a radio ministry, which still exists, and we traveled in trucks and vans with my godfather, the late Daddy Grace, who helped my grandmother form the church, the House of God for All People.

It started in 1954. The first song I wrote was called "Christmas Presents From Heaven," and I wrote it for my grandmother, who passed away on the 19th of December so she only heard it three times. Then the Lord blessed me to meet Bess Herman who owned Apollo Records. She was sitting in my church, and she said that she wanted to record me, so I recorded that song which was my first hit. While I was still on Apollo we had a big hit called "No Man Walks Alone" and "You Can Run, But You Can't Hide," which was written by Joe Louis.

Before I signed with Atlantic, I was on a little label in Philadelphia called Singular Records which was owned by Babe Shiveon and Artie Singer. Babe took me to Atlantic and Paul convinced Jerry Wexler that he should sign me.

Jerry said, "What do we do with him?" So we released the first record we had on Singular onto Atlantic and it didn't do too much. Mr. Wexler was so confused that he didn't know what to do with me.

He said, "Can you do country and western?" I said, "I certainly will try." So, we did a country-and-western song called "Just Out Of Reach Of My Two Empty Arms," which is a classic today. It's sold over 7 million copies. That began my era of country music. We did "Put Your Sweet Lips A Little Closer To The Phone [He'll Have To Go]," "Travel On" and many, many more.

Then we got out of that because Atlantic, at that time, was a totally R&B label. Jerry Wexler said, "We can't become the world's greatest country-and-western label. Ray Charles got very upset and said that he wanted to do country, and Jerry Wexler got very upset and said that there wasn't going to be any more country singing on Atlantic. That was one of the reasons Ray left Atlantic.

There I was for three years almost by myself on Atlantic. Lavern Baker left, Ivory Joe Hunter left, Clyde McPhatter left ... everyone left. There was just myself, the Drifters and the Coasters.

I would see the words on the paper and my own spiritual projection would come out. This would be a problem of mine. Mr. Wexler would say, "You have to say what's on the paper," and I would say to him, "But I don't *feel* what's on the paper because I haven't experienced that. If it's okay, can I just try doing it the way I feel right now?" And it worked, and I'm very grateful to Atlantic for allowing me to express my soulful feeling.

In those days, being a rhythm 'n' blues singer meant being someone who drank and smoked and cursed, and I didn't like that classification. There were a great many rhythm 'n' blues singers who weren't drinking and smoking and using drugs and using profanity, though. They were just great singers.

I asked God to give me some sign and show me how we could do it. Then, one day I was doing an interview in Philadelphia with a disc jockey, who was my manager, a man named Kae Williams, and he said, "Well, you're singing from your soul but you don't want to be a rhythm 'n' blues singer. What kind of singer do you want to be?" I said, "I want to be a *soul* singer" and that was the beginning of the whole thing.

Whose idea was it to open "Down In The Valley" with a tuba?

It was my idea. The tuba and the trombone are my pet instruments. I love marching bands and we have those instruments in my church. If you come to my church there's no way of sitting still because we have boys that can do "Precious Boy Take My Hand" on the tuba. So, when it came time to record "Down In The Valley," I said, "I've got to have a tuba there." It's also the New Orleans sound and feel, and "Down In The Valley" started a whole dance craze in New Orleans called the Popeye. I love that sound.

We were on a bus coming out of Mobile, Alabama, and one of the boys in the Falcons, I think it was Eddie Floyd, had taken Wilson [Pickett]'s seat, and Wilson had to squeeze in with me. Now you've gotta believe that being squeezed in with me is pretty rough. Anyway, Wilson's a little guy and he sat down there and said, "Listen, I've got to get out of this group, they're holding me back. We've only had one hit record and nobody won't even listen to our album." He said, "I've got this song. You've got to sing this song, man. Get me out of here."

Anyway, the next day, we were on the bus again and Wilson brought his guitar back and started singing "If You Need Me." I said, "I'm going to record that song, but you record it too." He got Lloyd Price and Harold Logan to record him and they brought the master to Atlantic Records but Jerry Wexler turned them down. Wilson was very upset.

Anyway, I demanded that Jerry Wexler give Wilson $5,000 for "If You Need Me," and Wilson became the first black artist to receive $5,000 for a song.

Anyway, I told Wilson, "See if Lloyd Price and Harold Logan will put your track out. I'm going to record it too." The record companies had a little feud going when both versions came out. I was supposed to go to the radio stations and say, "I am the original singer of 'If You Need Me.' Please play my record." I went to the stations and said, "Hi, I'm Solomon Burke, please play the Wilson Pickett version of 'If You Need Me,'" and, in return, Wilson would go to the stations and tell the people to play my record. That created a beautiful relationship between us, and we later became part of the Soul Clan.

The original members [of the Soul Clan] were Wilson Pickett, Otis Redding, Don Covay, Ben E. King, Joe Tex and myself. Arthur was voted into the Soul Clan after the death of Otis Redding because he was Otis's protege.

Otis was a dynamic, tall, handsome Georgia boy with muscles and keen features. The girls were crazy for him. He was like a black Tom Jones. Otis's speech was totally different. He had that Georgia accent, and you would often not understand what he was saying.

I first met Otis when he had a record out called "Shout Bamalama" and he said, "Why don't you take me on board with your show?" [Solomon imitates Otis's Georgia accent] I said, "I like your record, even though you only got but one." Then he said, "I got my boys, I got my boys. I got a band." So I took him on and he would come out and sing "Lord have mercy on my

SOLOMON BURKE: 'He said, "You're singing from your soul but you don't want to be a rhythm 'n' blues singer. What kind of singer do you want to be?" I said, "I want to be a soul singer," and that was the beginning of the whole thing.'

soul/How many chickens have I stole/10 last night, 12 before/Going out maybe steal 10, 11 more ..." Nobody knew what he was saying. I had Joe Tex on board, too.

I was constantly teaching them the meaning of soul. How to take the words and say them e-a-s-y. Like on "These Arms Of Mine," Otis couldn't pronounce "these" and I'd say, "Otis, say 'Dese' but say it e-a-s-y." He brought it out. It was beautiful. Otis and I discovered Sam and Dave playing in Florida doing songs like "You'll Never Walk Alone," but we didn't have the capability to take on artists' management in those days. But we saw the potential there.

"Got To Get You Off My Mind" was written for my first divorce. I wrote it coming back on the train from Los Angeles. Earlier that day, I'd sat in a meeting with Sam Cooke and his manager and then learned that Sam had been killed. It was a double shot. I didn't take the plane because I needed time to think.

"Everybody Needs Somebody To Love" is the march we use in our church, the money-raising march. All of the children in our church receive new blessed dollar bills, and this is the march they get it on. We teach them to save and make it grow. All the senior citizens get in line, too, to receive those blessed dollars. The song was stolen [by the Newbeats] for "I Like Bread And Butter" but we never bothered to sue. The Lord has blessed me.

The Rolling Stones recorded it and it appears on 11 albums. And, of course, the Blues Brothers recorded it; it plays for 28 minutes in the movie, which is beautiful tribute to me as an artist. They didn't put my name on the first prints but I love it when those BMI checks come. It's opened knowledge and wisdom to a lot of people about my writing ability.

Eighty percent of the songs I recorded during the '60s were about me. You could hear those records and know what was going on in my love life, my family life and how long it took me to grow up. When you fall in love, nobody can tell you anything. My mother told me that the marriage was wrong, she said, "I told you, fool, I told you." I was standing onstage at the Apollo Theater and I had just been informed that my wife had just smashed all the windows on my limousine and shot up all the tires. I had to go onstage and we made up "The Price" right there on stage.

It's very hard on the wife. The man has to say to her, "Look sweetheart, pay no attention to me kissing the girls in the front row and saying, 'Gosh, you sure do look good tonight.' " If you leave your wife at home, then it's even harder because then she really wonders what you're doing. If you're an entertainer and you have a good wife or girlfriend then hang onto her.

I was born into the sanctified church, the church that moved. I was born with trombones and tubas blasting as the doctor was spanking me and I've known rhythm and movement all my life. I feel that I've brought a new dimension of entertainment to many peoples' lives. I've opened up the door to hundreds of singers, black and white, and all nationalities from all over the world. I like that — and I hope that others profit from my mistakes. I'm trying each day to teach love, happiness, understanding and joy. It's not easy. *(Dave Booth and Colin Escott; Jan. 18, 1985.)*

❧

The soul sound culminated in Memphis. All the singing in the churches, all the singing in the fields, all the blues that were played, all the jive that was laid down, culminated in a little more than 200 singles that were released on the Stax and Volt labels out of Memphis.

The labels were subsidiaries of Atlantic, but the records that came out on Stax and Volt had a rural strength, a great big rough edge, that nothing that was recorded further north could match. Wilson Pickett's "Midnight Hour" came out of Memphis, along with the followups, "99½ Of Your Love Won't Do" and "634-5789." Sam and Dave's "Hold On, I'm Comin' " was a Stax product, as were "Knock On Wood" and and "Time Is Tight" and "Sweet Soul Music."

The greatest products to come out of Stax were the work of maybe the greatest soul singer ever. Otis Redding started out singing backup with Little Richard's band and was the driver and vocalist for guitarist Johnny Jenkins when he showed up at the Stax studios in 1963 and cut "These Arms Of Mine," starting a five-year career that would produce 10 top-10 R&B singles. Redding was a disciple of Sam Cooke who took Cooke's melodic smoothness and added a coarse punch. He cut Cooke's "Shake," "Chain Gang," and "A Change Is Gonna Come"; he cut Beatles songs and James Brown songs and the Rolling Stones' "Satisfaction" and had the original, pre-Aretha version of "Respect." But his greatest songs were his own, and the greatest of all was his last "(Sittin' On The) Dock Of The Bay" was written with guitarist Steve Cropper and recorded just three days before Redding's plane crashed into a Madison, Wis., lake.

Redding was a powerhouse live performer. He stole the show at the Monterey Pop festival. He brought down house after house in Europe. He had an electrifying style and a personal magnetism not even Sam Cooke or James Brown could approach.

Steve Cropper was the guitarist for the Mar-Keys, the group that became Booker T. and the MG's. The band was Stax's studio band — an integrated band — and Cropper was one of its busiest members. He wrote or co-wrote "Green Onions," "In The Midnight Hour," "Knock On Wood," "Time Is Tight," and "634-5789." Booker T. Jones was leader of the MG's.

Steve Cropper: Several people have asked me how I picked up the guitar, and I guess the definitive answer would have to be seeing a guy named Ed Bruce play around Memphis. He was a country 'n' western singer of sorts who had been around Nashville for a long, long time, but around the time I saw him he was doing Bo Diddley and Chuck Berry along with Jimmy Reed, like everybody else, and it just looked like a fun thing to be doing. One time I actually went backstage after one of his shows and said, "Hey, how do you do that?", and his answer was simple: "You've got to get a guitar and learn how to play it." That was when I was about 14 years old, and I began to pursue it from there.

Most of what I eventually learned came from hanging around with various guys that played, particularly a guy named Charlie Freeman, with whom I started my first band. He was taking lessons, and he would pass the things he learned along to me. He was sort of the lead player and I was sort of a rhythm player, and so the things he taught me were basically the things that would allow me to accompany him.

In certain instances, I was a little bit limited because I didn't start doing sessions completely knowing how to play the guitar. I learned on the job and had enough chops to keep me going. I was in demand all over town, as was Duck Dunn and a lot of the other players, until we got so busy at Stax that we just turned into the band that worked there exclusively.

There were writers who came through there that had certain specifics as to what they wanted, but they usually walked away fairly satisfied. I mean, when you get someone like Booker T., who was so forceful, it was just incredible. He could do anything. Whatever it was, whatever it took, it still came out the Stax sound.

If you can visualize a movie theater that had two aisles and you pulled all the seats out, you'd have a pretty good idea of what the actual space was. Then you cut it into thirds by drawing a line down the middle, about two-thirds of the way down. You use the third that's on the left for storage, and in the right third you put carpeting and you put up a wall and a big curtain to separate the space, and that became the studio, more or less. I think the measurements of the space were 17 by 23 or 24 feet, and two-thirds of the stage that faced this space was the control room. The old movie-theater speakers were used as our playback monitors. The other third was used as the Satellite record store.

In the actual room itself, about 15 feet into it, there was a piano, and then behind that was a drum riser. On the other side is where Duck and I would be located — and, y'know, the funny thing was the placement of the microphones. On the old Stax records, on some of the first ones to come out in stereo, the left mix was on one side and the right was on the other. Nothing was in the center, and all of the echo was coming back on one side and the vocalist was coming out. We didn't really deal with it until about 1965.

While we're talking about the actual Stax sound, I think that you've got to credit the whole thing to Al Jackson. He was probably the finest drummer for a session that I have ever worked with, and the only other drummers that I think were good enough were the ones who would walk in and say, "My favorite was Al Jackson; I loved him." Those are the drummers that would sit down and play the drums like they were supposed to be played. He just had a feel like nobody else I've ever seen. A definite artist within himself, he was the driving nucleus of that whole thing, and he knew dance tempos, he knew groove, he could listen to a piece of music and go, "It needs this." I mean, a song could be written one way, and within 15 minutes he'd have it completely turned around in another direction, and he'd be right. That's just the way he was.

Songwriters would come in with a definite idea of how they wanted a particular song, and we could begin to work it with their intentions in mind. Nobody was ever denied their creative input; it would be like, "Okay, what have you got?" "Here it is." "Okay, here are the changes." And we would beat it to death until we finally said, "Guys, give us five minutes."

So we'd sit down, Al and I, sometimes some of the other guys, and say, "Okay, where are we going with this thing?" We'd sit there and get a groove going, and then when we were ready we'd call the guys back in and say, "Okay, let's try this." And it usually happened pretty quickly after that.

We did that a lot. I would say that 90 percent of all the arrangements were "head" arranged. There were no charts, nobody had anything written out. Otis always came in with horn ideas, and I think that rubbed off on me too. I got to where I would write a song and the same night I'd be coming up with horn ideas. Maybe not million-dollar riffs, but something that the guys could take from there.

We would usually write three songs a night and record three hits the next day. Whenever we really got on a roll, Isaac Hayes and David Porter would work all week on songs for whatever artist was coming in, then they would rehearse the artist for a couple of days while we were cutting somebody else. And a lot of times it hurt us, because we couldn't get Isaac on the session we were working on. That's how it went for much of the '60s.

Otis always came in with ideas, and we'd sit down and start to jam. I'd play him things I was working on, and he'd play me some of his ideas, and we'd use whatever fit.

I've got pictures of him when we were on tour in Europe and he had a guitar in his hand; I mean, he never stopped. He'd get on the bus and the guitar would come out; if we were on the road for six hours, he would play for six hours. Y'know, he plays the guitar on "Sweet Soul Music," the Arthur Conley record. He produced it and is playing guitar on it. He also played his guitar on "Dock Of The Bay."

Eddie Floyd and I had been trying to write something for [Wilson Pickett], and we were goofing around with the idea of using a telephone number as the title of a song when we came up with "634-5789." We were really proud of it.

So the next day I go over to the airport and pick up Wilson and say, "Look, before I check you into the hotel why don't we go by the studio? We've got this hot song that we wrote for you last night that I'd like you to hear right away." So we get to the studio, go into the control room with Eddie Floyd, cue up the tape, and I hand Wilson a sheet with the lyrics on it, and he gets about half a verse into it when he wads the paper up and throws it on the floor. He says, "This is the biggest piece of shit I've ever seen." About this time I see Eddie Floyd fly across me and tackle Wilson, and the next thing I know they're rolling on the control-room floor and I'm thinking, "These guys are going to kill each other." I mean, I just knew I was in trouble. I had never seen anything like this in my life; I've been in a few bar brawls, but this was crazy.

I later found out they had been in a band together, and this was a fairly regular occurrence. Anyway, we finally get them apart and I said, "Forget this!", and we all left. About six o'clock that night I called Wilson at the hotel to see if he was all right, and he asked if we were going to write that night. I said, "I don't know; it depends on how you feel." He says, "Is Floyd around?" I said, "Yes." He says, "Well, bring him along." Now, as I'm pulling into the hotel parking lot I see this sign for Coca-Cola or something like that and it says 99½ percent real something or other, and I think, "Ah, now there's a good idea." So that night we wrote "99½ Of Your Love Won't Do," and the next day we cut both that and "634-5789," just like nothing had ever happened the day before, and they were both big hits for him. *(Danny McCue; June 15, 1990.)*

🍂

Booker T. Jones: I was with the staff band for a couple of years before I formed the group. We formed in '62, just out of high school. "Green Onions" was actually the start of the group. Steve was already working at Stax; both he and Duck were members of the Mar-Keys. Al I met through Willie Mitchell, who had hired me as a baritone-sax player when I was in high school.

Otis was a dynamic man in every aspect of his life. He came to us as a valet and a shoeshine boy, and I don't know how he ever got them to let him sing a song. But he sang "These Arms Of Mine," and he was a hit with us from then on. He had a lot of energy. He was a big man physically, but he was totally dedicated to what he did. It was easy to work with him because we could just go on his energy; we didn't have to rev up. We didn't have to try to remember parts or anything. He just guided us like a pilot.

Sam and Dave were the same thing. They were a little bit more energetic than Otis physically, but it was the same energy. It took two of them, though.

We were total, like a full circle. What one guy couldn't do the other could. Nothing had ever been heard like that before, especially from a small group. We were able to sound real big. *(Jeff Tamarkin; July 1981.)*

8. Teenage Idol

The people who had the most hits in the '50s were, outside of Elvis Presley, not rock 'n' rollers. They were pop singers and big bands and producers, Perry Como and Perez Prado and the McGuire Sisters, Mitch Miller and Gogi Grant, Pat Boone and Frankie Avalon and Paul Anka. Only the last group would argue that they were genuine rock 'n' rollers.

After 1970 there was little distinction between pop and rock. In 1950, there was no rock. In 1955 the rock 'n' rollers stood out on the charts because there were so few of them and because they weren't singing "Love Is A Many-Splendored Thing" or "Cherry Pink And Apple Blossom White." In 1960, pop and rock split the top of the charts. Elvis Presley had three #1s, but Connie Francis had two, and Percy Faith had the top song of the year with the theme from the movie *A Summer Place*. And despite all the monster rock hits that would follow it to the top, it was also the #1 song of the decade.

Pop music in the early '50s was dominated by the past, by songs of the '40s, by old radio acts and big-band singers gone solo: Dick Haymes, Margaret Whiting, and especially Frank Sinatra. Sinatra was the first musical teen idol. He drove teenagers crazy, first as a singer with Harry James' band, then as a solo act. In the late '40s his record company, Columbia, dropped him, and no one wanted him. But Sinatra came back on Capitol in the '50s, stronger and leaner than anyone could have expected. His albums were lean, swingy mood music featuring powerful arrangements and intelligent singing. Eighty percent of the rock 'n' roll that came out of the '50s couldn't match Sinatra for toughness and style.

Outside of Sinatra, the top records of the early '50s were cast albums from Broadway shows or movies. The only truly new sounds outside of rhythm 'n' blues were provided by Les Paul and Mary Ford, who double-tracked vocals and laid incendiary, surreal guitar work over pop standards; Patti Page, whose country-tinged ballads had a less lush, more personal feel that would later be copied by Patsy Cline, and a nearly deaf pianist and singer named Johnny Ray, whose intense, dramatic readings of "The Little Cloud That Cried" and "Cry" stood in contrast to the easygoing Como and Crosby.

Patti Page took her name from a dairy and sold more than 60 million records in her career.

Her version of a Wisconsin accordion player's country song, "Tennessee Waltz," sold more than 8 million copies alone. She was one of the first pop singers to have made a name for herself as a big-band singer prior to her solo career, and her career stretched well into the '60s. Her "Allegheny Moon" outsold Fats Domino's "Blueberry Hill" and Gene Vincent's "Be-Bop-A-Lula" in 1956 (though Nelson Riddle's "Lisbon Antigua" outsold all three). Her music was rooted in the big-band era but had an appealing freshness.

Johnny Ray started out singing Ivory Joe Hunter songs, and did his first recording for Okeh, an R&B label. His biggest hit, "Cry," was written by a night watchman at a dry-cleaning plant. It went to #1 on the pop charts and #2 on the R&B charts. To some people, he was a white singer who sang black; to everyone, Ray was the most provocative singer of the early '50s. Audiences rioted after his performances; girls swooned, and police had to be called in to restore order. He was the first teen idol since Sinatra, and the first teen idol of the '50s.

Ray was a movie star who never found a proper role and a performer under the thumb of his record producer and arranger. In 1951 and '52 he went through the same trials Elvis would go through three years later. Ray said he paved the way for rock 'n' roll, and he was right.

Johnny Ray died in 1990.

Johnny Ray: The degeneration of my hearing was so gradual, we didn't really notice it until my grades in high school started suffering badly. One of my teachers suggested to my parents that I be put in a school for retarded children. I couldn't pay attention. My mother and dad wouldn't go for that, so the first thing they did was ship me off to a specialist to find out what was wrong. I got my first hearing aid when I was about 13 or 14. Unfortunately, hearing aids are only manufactured for the reproduction of speech, and that has nothing to do with music. That's a cross I have to bear.

In 1951, I was working in Detroit, at a small nightclub called the Flame Show Bar. Unknown to me, a local disc jockey named Robin "Bobby" Seymour had seen me work at the club. This club was patronized by both blacks and whites; in those days, that type of bar was called a black-and-tan club. I was the only white entertainer on the bill. The show consisted of about five acts and Maurice King and his 12-piece orchestra. We all did about four shows a night, each act. I didn't know [Seymour] nor was I aware of his radio show. Somewhere along the line, he got in touch with Danny Kessler, who was employed by Columbia Records. Danny Kessler had been given the task of reactivating the old Okeh label, which had been very active in the '30s and '40s. Robin had told Danny Kessler, "There's a kid at the Flame Show Bar that you ought to hear." At that time, the type of material I was singing was very black-oriented — songs by Ivory Joe Hunter and basic blues.

When I signed with them, I was the only artist on the label. But it wasn't that simple. Danny Kessler came to hear me and offered me a contract with Okeh — which I turned down! That shows you how much guts you can have at that age.

I had recorded some demo records and sent them out to California, to Capitol Records. There were people like Stan Kenton, Nat King Cole, Kay Starr ... a lot of great artists were on Capitol at that time. That was the label I wanted to be on. So I told Danny Kessler, "I would rather hold off 'til I hear what Capitol Records has to say." He could have said, "Sorry, kid," and taken a walk. As it turned out, Capitol returned my records and turned me down. So I told Danny, "I'd be happy to sign with Okeh Records."

The first two songs were recorded at United Sound System in Detroit. They were "Whiskey And Gin" and "Tell The Lady I Said Goodbye." Those were songs I had written and was familiar with. We did them with "head" arrangements by Maurice King and his orchestra, and Okeh released them. I went back to work and continued doing my shows every night at the Flame Show Bar. A few weeks went by, and I started hearing strange things about those records of mine that Columbia had pressed and were being distributed in what in those days were very hot record towns: Boston, Philadelphia, Cleveland, Buffalo, Pittsburgh — places like that.

I was totally unaware that "Whiskey And Gin" had become a big hit in Cleveland. Columbia Records asked me if I would go to Cleveland, Ohio, to promote the record. So I got on a train to Cleveland, where I was met by a disc jockey named Bill Randall. He was the #1 disc jockey in

Cleveland. Unknown to me, he had put the name Johnnie Ray on the map, through his radio show. When I stepped off the train in Cleveland, there were anout 5,000 kids there. I had almost all my clothes ripped off. I really didn't know what hit me!

Back in New York, Mitch Miller found out what happened to me, and I was quickly whisked to New York. At 10 o'clock at night, at Columbia Studios, we recorded "Cry," "Please Mr. Sun," "Brokenhearted," and a song I had written called "The Little White Cloud That Cried." "Cry" and "The Little White Cloud" were released on the Okeh label, and the rest, as they say, is history.

The screaming, the tearing of the clothes, it was fun. I had a good time, but I kept a lot of security guards busy. I used to wear very cheap clothes because they would never last very long. This was especially true in England and Australia.

To me, whatever I was doing came quite naturally. I developed my style through the years while I was struggling to make it. It was not an overnight-success sort of thing. I had some pretty lean years, and I starved to death pretty good. I'd come to Los Angeles to break into show business, and I spent an entire year in Hollywood. I made about $500 for the year. Finally, I gave up in desperation. That's when I finally realized that if you want to make it in this business, the last place to come is Hollywood. That's still true. Your chances of being discovered are much greater right in your own backyard.

Right from the beginning, there was an awful lot of controversy. There was no such thing as being a middle-of-the-road Perry Como fan. You were either pro-Johnny Ray or you couldn't stand my guts. My work was very physical and demonstrative. It was something that was unheard of and unseen at that time, but it seemed quite natural to me. It caused me a lot of problems, because I had a lot of difficulty keeping jobs.

My only claim to fame was that I was an original. Before my success on records, television or film, or whatever media, the only thing that had preceeded me had been people like Russ Colombo, Perry Como, Dick Haymes, Bing Crosby, Frank Sinatra, people like that. They were, more or less, stand-up singers. I revolutionized all of that. I imagine that I opened the door or paved the way for what was to come, which was to be called rock 'n' roll.

I am a song stylist, a performer, a communicator and an actor. I apply all of this knowledge and experience into my performance. Unless it is basically a sincere offering, the audience can see through you like cellophane. *(Robert Cain; April 1983.)*

The next teen idol after Ray had his first #1 record with a Fats Domino song and his second hit with a song originally done by the El Dorados. He recut the Flamingos' "I'll Be Home" and Little Richard's "Tutti Frutti," Ivory Joe Hunter's "I Almost Lost My Mind" and Big Joe Turner's "Honey Hush," and sold more copies of all of them than the originals. But no one could ever accuse Pat Boone of being a rock 'n' roll singer.

Charles Eugene Boone was a descendant of frontiersman Daniel Boone; he was nicknamed Pat because his mother was hoping for a girl to name Patricia. He found religion at 13 in the family barn with the family cow, and eloped with the daughter of country singer Red Foley at age 19. Boone was a radio and TV announcer who had been on Ted Mack's show three times and won Arthur Godfrey's Talent Scouts competition before he cut a single record. He was a student at North Texas State when he cut his first side for Dot Records. It was "Two Hearts," a song first done by Otis Williams and the Charms. It went to #16 on the charts.

Boone was a crooner, a direct descendant of Perry Como who happened to cover R&B songs. As a teen idol, his appeal was limited — because he was married, not because of his squeaky-clean image. But in 1957, Boone was the second most popular entertainer in the country; Elvis Presley's "All Shook Up" and Boone's "Love Letters In The Sand" were the top two songs of the year, though Boone held down the #6 spot with "Don't Forbid Me." He was also attending Columbia University and making movies. At one point, Boone was on the charts for four years without a break.

Boone did an album of Elvis Presley covers, starred in a Rogers and Hammerstein musical, had his own TV show (sponsored by Chevrolet) and wrote religious books. His daughter,

Debby, had a #1 hit in 1977 with "You Light Up My Life."

Pat Boone: I'm looking at a picture of me and Little Richard — a wild, wild Little Richard and me looking, in contrast, very vanilla, but both of us looking pretty good. He's already in there [the Rock 'N' Roll Hall of Fame], deservedly, and I got to thinking, I sold 10 times more records during that period, and a lot of them rock 'n' roll records.

That music — R&B — had been around a long time, and it's still around, and there's still a gulf between R&B and pop music and even between just R&B and rock. It [R&B] is a distinctive kind of music; it doesn't appeal to everybody. So if it hadn't been for the vanilla versions of the R&B songs in the '50s, you could certainly imagine that rock 'n' roll, as we think of it, would never have happened.

PAT BOONE: 'If it hadn't been for the vanilla versions of the R&B songs in the '50s, rock 'n' roll, as we think of it, would never have happened.'

I don't think it was inevitable that R&B phased into rock 'n' roll, and that rock 'n' roll became the music of not only a generation but several generations. I don't think it was inevitable. There were other kinds of music, and there still are; it could've been country. Pop music could have veered into country rather than R&B — much more logically, perhaps. So there wasn't a conscious effort, a lot of suits in suites, trying to orchestrate this thing; everybody was just trying to get a hit record. It's always a chicken-and-egg with these things; you can't always tell who caused what.

It worked together is what happened. When two or three of these records were covered and did happen, there was a demand created for more. Then others jumped on the bandwagon and consciously promoted and drummed and tried to create or foster a demand for music they knew they could supply.

But what I started to say was if you look at those R&B charts of the '50s, you'll see many names of artists who had several big hit records and they've never been heard from since. What makes you remember them is that their records were covered by other artists. Those records first became big pop hits and eventually focused attention on the originals; people like Alan Freed and others were insistent on playing the originals. Then the fans began to demand, and there was a certain retroactive thing where they might not have known Little Richard's "Tutti Frutti" to start with or Fats Domino's "Ain't That A Shame" and then they heard mine.

Eventually my record was played and played and DJs would say, "Here's the record that started this; here's the original record of 'Ain't That A Shame' by Fats Domino." It did happen more and more. It took a period of several years, but I don't think it was inevitable. It certainly wasn't inevitable for a lot of the other R&B performers who weren't covered. They've unfortunately, perhaps — these good talented singers and songwriters — been phased out. Hardly anybody remembers them today except dyed-in-the-wool R&B fans. We did serve a very useful function and, for better or worse, made a huge contribution to this juggernaut that became rock 'n' roll.

I had to be selective and change some lyrics, but nobody seemed to care. It made it more vanilla, particularly 20-30 years later when you say, "That was so innocuous, why did he care?" Back then there was a hue and cry, not just on the part of ministers but even DJs and some of the kids themselves. We were living in *Happy Days* society then, and it was pretty innocent by comparison. The only things that kids got into then was beer and cigarettes, and some heavy necking.

A lot of Elvis' audience was my audience, too. Of course, even then, there was a growing subculture, counterculture, and rock 'n' roll, R&B was feeding into that and fostering that. He was representative — because that's what he actually was — of the sort of outcast kid that, for one reason or another, either economic or because he wasn't on the athletic teams or didn't have the latest clothes, was a minority in a lot of schools.

Most of us like to say I *can* do it my way and win, and Elvis was the supreme example of the guy who's doing just that. On the other hand, I was going to college, I was married.

Balancing all that was tough. I was busy. I was lucky that I had a supportive wife and good people around me to help me take care of the professional requirements. I would somehow manage to juggle taking a full load at Columbia University, making some movies, a weekly television series, always managing to make records and stay in the charts. More than Elvis did. That's one of the records I really cherish: For over 200 weeks I was never off the charts. That rode through several trends, ups and downs and changes in rock 'n' roll music. That included some pop, some movie themes, rock 'n' roll.

The question you asked before: Does Pat Boone consider himself a rock 'n' roll singer? I consider myself an entertainer who sang rock 'n' roll. It was one of the things I did, and I did it well enough to get in the charts and sell millions of records.

At the time, those who really were the experts — the DJs, the record buyers themselves, the trade publications — considered me a bonafide rock 'n' roller. It's only 20 years later that you look back and say, "Gee, he doesn't stack up against Screamin' Jay Hawkins or Jerry Lee Lewis or Howlin' Wolf or any of these other guys, even against Little Richard or Fats. He doesn't sound like a rock 'n' roller." Not now, but by hindsight, right.

How'd I get to be a rock 'n' roller? I was on national television, on some talent shows, the *Ted Mack Amateur Hour* and *Arthur Godfrey's Talent Scouts* show, which was a professional show, and I won them both. That didn't lead to anything except a handshake agreement to record for Dot Records. I went back to school at North Texas State and was planning to be a schoolteacher.

Because of the national exposure, which created tremendous excitement in my home states of Tennessee and Texas — I'd grown up in Tennessee and was now living in Texas, going to school — Randy Wood, of Dot Records, based in Gallatin, Tennessee, thought, "Gee, this guy's got a lot of national exposure, I think I hear some talent, so I'm gonna sign him."

He called me up in Denton, Texas, in March 1955 and said, "I've got a song I want you to record." This was eight months after we'd agreed to record, and I thought he'd forgotten all about me. He said he had a song he thought was a hit and wanted me to meet him in Chicago. I asked him what the song was and he said it was called "Two Hearts," by Otis Williams and the Charms. It was an R&B hit.

I knew that was just starting. I'd been listening to the radio and I knew about the Crew Cuts, the Penguins — I didn't know much about the original R&B artists except the Penguins. But I knew it was starting to happen, and now he wanted me to copy an R&B song and I just assumed "Two Hearts," it's a ballad, I can do that.

I get to Chicago and find it's a real rhythm 'n' blues jumper. First I said, "I don't know if I can do that." I mean, I could sing it, but I didn't think I could make it sound anything like the original. Well, we did it and we came away with a Top 10 hit, eventually a million-seller. And, of course, Frank Sinatra, Doris Day and others covered that same song. If you think mine sounds vanilla you ought to hear them. My record did capture a lot of the same feeling [of the original]. I tried my best to do it vocally, not having been very familiar with R&B. I tried my best to capture their flavor and feeling, and did.

I did discover in the early recording days that I did have a curious affinity for blues. I loved doing "Stormy Monday" and songs like this. I did record songs like "Drinking Wine, Spo-Dee-O-Dee," "Money Honey." I really felt at home with some down and dirty blues. I did some Jimmy Reed songs, songs like "Going To New York." I don't think they were ever released, but Randy Wood knew he could put a blues song in front of me and something very catchy and tasty would develop out of it. I would settle into this groove, and I really loved singing blues.

Now, this is weird for the ultimate WASP who grew up in a happy home in Nashville, Tennessee. But I somehow loved it — and that was also true of Elvis; he had a terrific affinity for the blues, and for R&B, as it turned out.

Anyway, Randy Wood sent me all over the country, knowing we had competition. He sent me to about 20 cities in 18 days: Cleveland, Detroit, Pittsburgh, Akron, Canton, Baltimore, Boston. He went to a lot of other cities and went to the radio stations and the dance-party TV shows, and we established my record as *the* record of that song, although there were several other cover records.

Then the next record was "Ain't That A Shame," which went right to #1. I didn't feel like I was a recording artist; I felt like I was a college student who was having a couple of fluke experiences. I didn't expect anything long-lasting to come of this.

But in August of '55 I was driving across town in Manhattan and I pulled up to a group of kids in a car. It was hot and the windows were rolled down and they were just bouncing up and down listening to — in my recollection it was Alan Freed — and they were listening to my record of "Ain't That A Shame." *(Jeff Tamarkin; Feb 22, 1991.)*

By the mid-'50s, television began creating teen idols in earnest. Elvis Presley could drive teenage girls crazy anytime he appeared on the Dorsey Brothers' program or *The Ed Sullivan Show*. Ricky Nelson had that opportunity every week.

Nelson was the son of bandleader Ozzie Nelson and singer Harriet Hilliard, who, as Ozzie and Harriet, had one of the most successful situation comedies of the '50s and '60s. The show ran from 1952 to 1956, and the Nelsons' two sons, Ricky and David, had to grow up on it in front of millions of households every week.

Ricky Nelson wanted a career in music, and he had a successful one, despite being a typecast TV child star. Nelson's first single, "I'm Walkin'," was a cleaned-up version of a Fats Domino song squarely in the Pat Boone mold. But unlike Boone, Nelson moved on from that to cut fresh songs, songs with as much depth and style as a good-looking teenager who was on TV every week could cut in the late 1950s and early '60s. If "Poor Little Fool" and "Lonesome Town" weren't exactly Jerry Lee Lewis, they weren't far removed from Elvis Presley. Nelson cut "Milk Cow Blues" as a B-side and did a convincing "I Got A Woman." James Burton, who would later play with Elvis, was Nelson's guitarist.

In the '60s, as Presley edged into self-parody, Nelson edged into obscurity. His last chart hit was in 1964. He cut Doug Kershaw's "Louisiana Man" in 1966 and Dylan's "I Shall Be Released" in 1970. In 1969 he formed a country-rock group called the Stone Canyon Band and made good albums with them. In 1972 he was back on the charts with "Garden Party," a misunderstood song about Nelson's misunderstood appearance at a '50s revival concert. The song finished just above Elvis Presley's "Burning Love" on the year's singles charts.

In the '80s Nelson covered John Fogerty's "Almost Saturday Night" and Graham Parker's "Back To School Days," and did them both justice. On Dec. 31, 1985, he and his fiance and his band died in a plane crash near DeKalb, Texas.

Rick Nelson: It wasn't like we had stage parents. We were kind of born into it, so that was our normal existence. We were exposed to a lot of things. I know the early shows we did on radio and then TV, when I was about seven or eight, were written around real things that happened to us. I remember going to school — we always went to public school — and the friends that I had. I always had a lot of friends outside of show business, so I had a life outside of that. The show-business part was just a job that we were doing.

I had always been around music. My dad started with a band and my mom was a vocalist, so we were always listening to music and I was always a fan of different music people. It started when I was in high school; that's when I first started to actively pursue it.

Recording was scary at first. I remember all these people there, and I had gone straight from singing in my bathroom to the recording studio. There was nothing in-between. Things were all in mono then. Then it went up to two tracks and then four, and everyone was saying, "Four tracks? Why do you need four tracks?"

It was a great time for me. It was really the beginning of rock 'n' roll and I was fortunate to be around then. We played places that had never heard electric guitars.

I had just signed to Imperial and was looking for a band. I heard an audition coming from down the hall, and I just heard this great guitar playing. So I subsequently got to know James Burton, and we started doing some things. Then I asked him if he wanted to be in a band. We stayed together over 10 years.

[When the Beatles came] a lot of people who had been around stopped getting airplay. You had to be English to get things played for awhile. But I was still under contract and it gave me a chance to do things, recording-wise, that I might not have had a chance to do otherwise, to experiment. I did production-type albums and country albums.

It was a different kind of thing to try, to use a steel guitar in rock 'n' roll and use those types of harmony. It was an idea I got when I saw Buck Owens on the old *Jackie Gleason Show.* There was something about it, that feel, that made me think it would work. So I contacted Tom Brumley, who was Buck Owens' steel player, and he hadn't been on the road for a year-and-a-half. He didn't want to go on the road at first, then all of a sudden he changed his mind, because he never had the chance to play music like that. Then I heard Randy Meisner with Poco; they were just getting together and doing the same thing I wanted to try, and it sounded great. I heard them at the Troubadour and Randy, at that time, wanted to do something else, so I was fortunate enough to get him.

I had to talk myself into being there [the Madison Square Garden '50s revival concert at which his show was poorly received]. It was actually kind of confusing at first because we had done all our songs in chronological order; we had to go back and learn them. At the time, I was involved in writing new songs. I felt weird being there; I thought, I knew I shouldn't have done this. It wasn't a frightening experience; it was more of a weird one. We had just come off doing a lot of colleges where there was no problem doing new songs, so it was weird getting that non-acceptance. But now when I look back at the pictures, my hair was real long at the time, so physically I guess it was a whole lot different than they expected. I had never been to one of those before.

At first, I just wanted to record, to be able to walk around and show my friends a record. I thought nothing beyond that. We did it on the television show as an afterthought. All of a sudden, that exposure helped a lot faster than anybody ever thought it would; in about a week's time, we sold a lot of records.

I've just thoroughly enjoyed the things I've done. And it's so important to like what you've been doing. It's never been work at all. It's always been a necessity for me to do what I do. Even when I'm home alone, I always end up doing something that has to do with music. *(Jeff Tamarkin; Feb. 14, 1986.)*

The teen idols of the '50s seemed to be interchangable. They shared a pompadour and a soft style of music, mostly gentle rockers and ballads. Most of them had musical talent. Few of them had a chance to really show it.

Bobby Vee was the fill-in act for Buddy Holly the night after Holly was killed. The opportunity did not produce overnight fame and fortune, but Vee persevered and succeeded anyway. His first albums were collections of R&B covers and tributes to Buddy Holly. Vee made movies, had a hit with an early Carole King song ("Take Good Care Of My Baby"), did an album of Beatles and Dave Clark Five covers at the very start of the British Invasion, and had Bob Dylan in his band for a weekend. Bobby Rydell was a child mimic who had his first hit at 16 and had a string of hits with the pop standards "Volare," "That Old Black Magic" and "Sway." He made movies and cut "A World Without Love" at the same time as Peter and Gordon. Joey Dee led the house band at New York's Peppermint Lounge, gave the Ronettes and the Rascals their start, had a hit with a remake of the Isley Brothers' "Shout," made movies, and had a massive hit with "Peppermint Twist." Freddy Cannon was the George Michael of the early '60s. He made dance music with a heavy beat — "Tallahassee Lassie," "Palisades Park," "Buzz Buzz A Diddle It" — remade "Muskrat Ramble" and "Sweet Georgia Brown" and "For Me And My Gal," and wasn't above cutting sorry singles like "Transistor Sister" and "Teen Queen Of The Week."

Bobby Rydell: Who knew, really? I must have been about 16 or 17 at the time, and couldn't tell what would be a hit more than anybody could. I guess if anybody could predict something like that he'd make a million dollars a week, just picking out hit records. "Kissin' Time," though, sounded good to me. It had a lot of gimmicks in it, like mentioning quite a few cities in the U.S., for example. It had a hand-clap-heavy beat to it. So when we recorded it, it sounded great. Actually, we recorded it with a local Philadelphia group that worked a lot of the shore resorts called Georgie Young and the Rocking Box. I put my voice on it, Bernie Lowe, Kal Mann and Dave Appell wrote it, and we put it out. Then, a disc jockey in Philadelphia called Harvey Miller started playing the record on WIBG, which was, at the time, *the* radio station in Philadelphia. He played the record three, four times in a row, just back to back to back. The record started taking off in Philadelphia, at which time Dick Clark became aware of it, and that sales on it were up to 100,000, 200,000 copies. This led to a guest appearance on his show, and from that appearance on *American Bandstand*, the record just took off.

My mother suggested to me that "Volare" be released as a single. I explained to her that it wasn't up to me. Bernie Lowe, though, did take the tape of "Volare" back to the studio and sweetened it up, adding whatever they had to add to it. It was mastered, then released. To me, it sounded good, but, my God, I thought, Domenico Modugno had already sold over a million copies with it; Dean Martin had a million-seller with it, so how many times can one song really be a hit? Ours, of course, had a completely different sound with the "wo-wos" and the "yea-yeas" — the Rydell sound. We put it out, and son of a gun, it became another million-seller. And it all came about from an album that was never released.

I think that most of my records related to a happy feeling, the guy-next-door kind of thing. Basically, I want to be remembered as an average around-the-corner type of guy who enjoyed what he did and is still doing today, and wouldn't change for all of the money in the world. I think I made a lot of people happy with the songs I recorded. *(Wayne Jones; August 1979.)*

Joey Dee: In the lounge we had the Ronettes. They were unknown at the time. They came into the lounge and sang a few songs. I had an engagement in Wildwood, New Jersey, at a place called the Ripcord, and my manager thought it would be a good idea to bring the Ronettes with me, which I did. This was the summer of 1963. And Phil Spector heard them somewhere along the line and recorded them. So we were commuting from New York to Wildwood each day. And one day, in the third week of the contract, I heard a record on the air — "Be My Baby," by the Ronettes. I didn't even know they were recording while we were working.

They were minors. They weren't old enough really to come into a drinking establishment. But they came in with their aunt and their mother, and so the management let them in. And they were so talented and so cute we though it'd be a nice gimmick to put them on stage, and they did very fine. And that's how they got in.

In 1964, I opened my own nightclub called the Starlighter, on West 46th Street in New York City. And I had to put together a band because the original band had disbanded. So I got musicians from different groups. Gene Cornish was the guitar player. Felix Cavaliere, he was our keyboard player. And Eddie Brigati was one of the original Starlighters' younger brother. And I put them together with another drummer. And they got so good and tight they told me they were gonna try and make it on their own, and I wished them all the luck in the world.

A year after I owned the nightclub, I sold it and decided to go back on the road. And I was very fortunate; I had a good ear and a good eye for talent, and my guitar player was Jimi Hendrix, in 1964. He stayed with me for a year and he had an engagement in London, England. He had somebody who was gonna back him. I wished him all the luck in the world.

We were working in Stockholm, Sweden, in 1963. We were the headliners, and our opening act was the Beatles. Brian Epstein was their manager at the time. He came to me and asked me if there was a possibility of their making it in the States, 'cause they were having a record release two months hence. And I said, well, all I heard them do was Chuck Berry, the Everly Brothers, Little Richard, Fats Domino, and that was all passe already in the States. So I figured it would be kind of hard to emulate any of these artists and make it. So I told him I didn't think they'd make it in the States. I didn't know they'd come up with some great material. And I didn't know that they were songwriters. The only song they had at the time which was a big hit in Europe was a song called "Please Please Me," and that was their entree into the music field. *(Randy Russi; Aug. 17, 1984.)*

&

A few teen idols had more of a chance to develop their talents, mainly because they weren't such teen idols to start with. Neil Sedaka started writing songs at 13 and was singing with the Tokens at 16. He was a classically trained pianist and a singer with a high, unusual voice. Sedaka worked in the Brill Building, wrote hits for Connie Francis, dated Carole King, and wrote his first top-10 hit about her. When he was finally allowed to have a solo career, he had hits with the soft but catchy "Breaking Up Is Hard To Do," "Calendar Girl," and "Right Next Door To An Angel." He quit recording in 1968, but then resurfaced under the wing of Elton John and had another string of top-10 hits. Gene Pitney wrote "Hello Mary Lou" for Ricky Nelson and "He's A Rebel" for the Crystals and had his biggest hits with two movie songs: "Town Without Pity" and "The Man Who Shot Liberty Valance." He wrote the Rolling Stones' first American hit, and with George Jones won a country-music award for best new group.

Neil Sedaka: I started as a pianist, so everyone knew Neil was going to be a concert pianist, get his Ph.D. in music and teach. It was a shock to my parents when I changed directions. I was going to Julliard and my parents said, "In six months, if you can show us that you can do it, fine." And in those six months, I just wanted it so badly that I knocked and broke down doors. I was a pushy little Jewish kid. At first my mother was very disappointed and said, "There are a million people who can sing and write songs; why are you going to be different?" As soon as she heard me on the radio and the royalties started coming in, of course, that changed.

I had been writing in the New York area since I was 13, so by the time I was 19, I had a reputation with such people as Jerry Wexler. It was really Mort Shuman and Doc Pomus who steered me to Al Nevin's and Don Kirshner's office. Connie Francis was a friend of Kirshner's and recorded "Stupid Cupid."

Was there rejection? I didn't accept rejection. I had a lot of confidence. When I have a collection of songs that are good, there's no stopping me. I just push, and I can sell myself very well. The enthusiasm is contagious to the musicans and everyone else. Sure, I was turned down by several record companies when I was 18. They felt my voice was too high; they thought I sounded like a chick. They thought my T's and D's were funny, lots of things. But I had built up my reputation as a writer. I was making demos, and at the time, the singer-composer was very new. There weren't that many: Sam Cooke, Elvis, Roy Orbison, Buddy Holly.

I discovered I had a good voice when I used to write the songs when I was 13. But I was embarrassed. I used to close the door because my voice was very high. I remember my Bar Mitzvah, when I had to do my Haftorah. They were crying, and the rabbi came to my mother and said, "He should be a cantor because his voice is so pure. My mother said, "Oh, no; he's going to be a pianist/teacher."

When I started writing and playing popular music in those days, I played all the wrong chords. I would read the classics very well, but when I started playing by ear, Uncle Karl said, "You play lousy pop, but you have a very nice voice." He was the first one to give me encouragement. Then when I started writing with Howard Greenfield, I used to make the demos and they would say, "Who's the girl on the demo?"

I was playing the piano in the Catskills at 13, and [Mrs. Greenfield] got me together with her son. When I was about 14 or 15, I was a camp piano player. Then at 16, I had the Tokens and we only sang local hops in Brighton Beach, Brooklyn. I met Carole King, and we went out for a couple of years there. I was 19 when "The Diary" came out on RCA Victor, and I wasn't really ready for performing. I played to 86,000 people in Argentina — 86,000 people. I said to my mother, "I'm not going out there." She said, "Oh, yes you are. This is what you chose; you wanted this." And I got out there, but I was shitting in my pants. "Oh Carole" was a tremendous hit all over the world, and they wanted rock 'n' roll all over the world. Not too many of us went to those crazy places.

I can remember exactly every moment and every detail [of my first songwriting session with Howard Greenfield]. After Howie's mother Ella had seen me, he came ringing my doorbell. We lived in the same apartment building. I was playing Chopin and he said, "My mother heard you play and thought we could write a song together."

"A song? How do you write a song?" He said, "Try it."

I sat at the piano sort of to pacify him. We never really got along because he was a little older, 16, and he was a big kid. My sister was in the kitchen laughing. It was the worst thing she'd ever heard. I had pop records in the house, and my dad used to take me to movies, so I sat down and improvised something that was probably from an old 1940 movie. I call it a "Ruptured Rhumba," something I had seen in a Betty Grable movie or something like that. It came quickly and Howie wrote a lyric called "My Life's Devotion." It was the worst: "My life's devotion is loving you only." The middle was, "My life is madness, it's sadness, it burns with desire, I'm yearning, just burning, my soul is on fire." Every line rhymed.

My sister was laughing and my mother couldn't wait for Howard to leave the house so I could go back to practicing. But I was fascinated. He had a wire-head tape recorder, and when I heard it back, I said to myself, "That's not too bad, and it makes me feel like I'm somebody." I lived in a two-room apartment with nine people, eight of whom were women. There was my mother, my sister and my father's five sisters and my grandmother. So I was a very, very babyish person. I lived a very sheltered life and I was made fun of all throughout public school. So I heard myself sing something I created, I loved it.

So we wrote every day. I would wait until my mother left the house, and I would call Howie and say, "The coast is clear. Let's write another song." And we wrote dozens and dozens of songs that first year, 1952. I knew then I could sing them, and I knew what I wanted to do. Yet I continued going to Julliard. I went every Saturday and then I went to the collge. And the teachers at Julliard were very straight. They would ask, "Are you developing? What kind of work do you do? Your mother tells me you're doing something other than Bach. How many hours did you put in? How do you interpret the Chopin?"

Every Saturday we would give a concert. One day my piano teacher, a great classical teacher, said, "Play me something." And I played "Stupid Cupid," because she heard through the grapevine that I had a hit out by Connie Francis. I sang it for her and she said, "Not only is it good, but you have a good voice. I might lose you to popular music, but never give up classical. Whatever you do, always be able to have a Beethoven sonata under your fingers." And she was right.

I remember I had the record by Mickey and Sylvia, "Love Is Strange." I scratched out their names and put down "Neil Sedaka," to see how it looked on a 45 record. The first song I ever wrote that was recorded was for the Cookies on Atlantic Records, called "Passing Time." I held that record coming home on the BMT subway like it was a diamond. My name as a writer was on that record! That was something that was so unbelievable. Hearing my voice on the radio blew me away. It still does. Then when you had a hit and you were on the beach and every transistor radio was playing it and you could hear yourself, it was incredible. *(Robin Flans; May 25, 1984.)*

🎙

Gene Pitney: I never had any intentions of getting on a stage singing, or taking any musical lessons, for that matter. After I got my driver's license, I went to a place in Manchester called Center Springs Ice Skating. Shortly after I got there, it began to snow quite bad, so I thought I had better leave back for home because I had no snow tires on my car. On the way back, I spotted a little music store called Dubaldo's. I stopped in and signed up for guitar lessons, and I have no idea why, because I never intended to. It was really strange.

That led to putting together a group at Rockville High School. There were only two guys that played guitar anyway, and at that time they only knew two or three chords, which was okay because most of the songs at that time only had three or four basic chords. We also included in the group the only piano player and the only sax player the school had. Our sax player could only play in three keys, so we had to transpose everything into a key he knew if we had a song we wanted him to play along with us on. We ended up playing a date down on the coast once, and the proverbial fat guy with the cigar came up and asked if I wanted to make a record. I loved the idea, and because at that time a lot of twosomes were successful, I was teamed up with a girl from New Haven named Ginny Arnell. That led to trips to New York and meetings with Jack Pleis of Decca Records. We eventually had two releases on Decca under the names Jamie and Jane. From there, I could see that I really wanted to go out and do it on my own. I didn't want to be influenced to the point where I would be tied down to doing things only suitable for duets.

Initially, I had been writing the way I felt like writing — i.e., writing lyrics, musical ideas, and musical formats that weren't acceptable at the time. If I walked in with a song that was something more unique the response I got was, "Well, that's good and it's interesting, but who would want to record it?" And that's how some of the biggest things I wrote came about. "Rubber Ball" by Bobby Vee, for example, was strictly a song written just to make money to eat. It was a very easy, unsophisticated, rock-type song. I would have preferred the other things to have become more successful, but Aaron Schroeder was in the business to build up his publishing companies. As a result, I knew I could write the type of product to work with.

After that, it seemed as though everything happened at once. "Hello Mary Lou," which I also wrote, came out at the same time I had a record on the charts. So it was great going out to promote not only a hit I had myself, but also hearing someone else having a hit with one that I had written at the same time.

Phil Spector came to New York and went to the publisher's office, where they would play him songs to consider. Every publisher would start off by playing their worst stuff first, and the go down the line. The publishers hoped, of course, that they could get away with their lesser quality first. Phil had a tremendous ear, and usually he would sit and wait until he heard something that he knew would be a winner, and then he would grab it. This was how he got "He's A Rebel." Also, at the same time he had the beginning of a new record company, Philles. In order to get Philles off the ground he had to get out from under a contract he had with Liberty Records. He was a producer there along with Snuff Garrett. Music publishers, being a sneaky bunch, which they have to be at times, used to give like nine people "exclusives" on the same song. Phil went to the extremes of saying he was ill and was moving to Spain, so Liberty finally released him from his production demands. Snuff Garrett, meanwhile, also had the song "He's A Rebel" and was cutting it with Vikki Carr. Phil ran around like crazy and cut it with Darlene Love on the lead vocal. But the funniest part of the story I heard later on, and that was when Snuff Garrett took Vikki Carr into the studio to cut "He's A Rebel." It was a night session, and they were waiting for the musicians to arrive when the guitar player came in. He sat down, looked at the music sheets, and said, "Hey, man, I just played this!" Snuff said, "Where?" So the guitar player said, "In Studio C." Well, what happened was Phil was in the next studio finishing up his production of the record, which shows what kind of crazy guy he was. And from that point on it was just a battle between Liberty and Philles on distribution on who had the better record.

Town Without Pity was a loser of a film at first. The song came out, and it took about six months for it to get into the charts. Once it did, they re-released the film. From that point on the film went into the black and became successful. Because of that, we had all kinds of songs flooding in for motion pictures. When *Liberty Valance* came in, the combination was almost impossible to turn down, with Bachrach and David as the writers, and then John Wayne, Jimmy Stewart and Lee Marvin starring in the movie. It was unbelievable because they paid me a bundle of money, and not only paid for the session but a lot of fringe benefits as well. Burt wrote for Famous Music, which was owned by Paramount Pictures. The only problem was that Famous Music was in New York and Paramount was in Los Angeles. By the time we finished recording the song, which was tailor-made for the film, the movie was released already in Los Angeles with incidental music. Well, at the time I thought it was incidental, until I found out that the music was from a 1939 film called *Young Mr. Lincoln*. Why in the world they used that I have no idea.

My affiliation with the Stones began because my publicity agent in England was Andrew Loog Oldham, who also managed the Rolling Stones at the time. As a result, a lot of places I appeared over there, so would the Stones. At that time they were just a struggling group. When I first met them, I don't believe they even had the record "I Wanna Be Your Man" out yet. Andrew had asked me to see them. This was the first time I had really seen long hair on a guy, but for them it was a common thing because of their background. So I went to see them and I can tell you that they were doing the same thing to audiences then, without any hit records, that they are still doing today.

They were writing at the time, and they had this song called "That Girl Belongs To Yesterday." I remember having to change it around completely. The song was written in the Rolling Stones' style, which was completely wrong for me at the time. So I had to change the melody to fit the track that had already been put down on tape. They came in and loved it.

I was on my way back from Paris and stopped over in London for one day. Andrew Loog Oldham called and asked if I could come to the recording studio where the Stones were working on a followup to "I Wanna Be Your Man." He was in a little bit of panic because Decca had wanted the song like yesterday. Andrew told me that he had the guys in the studio, but it was one of those days where nobody was talking to each other. So I told him that I would try to help out. I jumped into a cab and got to the studio on Denmark Street. Now, who's outside in his big Rolls-Royce? None other than Phil Spector. I mean, Phil looked even smaller than when he was in a big Rolls. Anyhow, Phil and I both ended up inside. As I recall, I had five fifths of cognac with me, which was the duty-free limit. We made up some fabricated story about it being my birthday and that it was a characteristic thing in my family to celebrate with a glass of cognac. In the end, they all got a little tipsy and made up with each other. I believe Phil played on an empty cognac bottle with a half dollar.

I felt I've left a mark, hopefully in a good way, with the people that have seen my performances and heard my recordings. I've had the option to be in a profession that lets me walk out and leave people with something. One person in millions gets this opportunity. There's nothing greater than walking off a stage after a two-hour show and just knowing that you did it and everybody else walked out with something as well, not necessarily that they loved you, but just maybe down the line you influenced them in some way.

I'll give you a good example of that. I received a letter this morning from a guy in Massachusetts. This fellow wrote that he had served in Vietnam, and while over there, one day he went into some sort of a bazaar in Vietnam where he saw one of my albums. Evidently, he was not only homesick but also down because of a major battle coming up. So he bought the record and quick converted it into a tape. He explained that otherwise the record would have melted in the tropical heat. He then went on to say that the record meant so much to him, having that little piece of home, and knowing that I was from nearby Connecticut, that he thanked me for helping him get through the war. That is the beauty of this business. *(Wayne Jones; January 1983.)*

The poles of talent for '50s teen idols were two big-city kids, one from Philadelphia and one from New York. Fabian Forte was spotted on a porch stoop by a record producer and turned into the hottest thing in the country in 1959. He had major hits with "Tiger," "Turn Me Loose" and "I'm A Man," played opposite Bing Crosby and John Wayne in movies, and was off the charts by 1961. By his own admission he was no singer, but he became a capable entertainer.

Dion DiMucci was a street-corner singer who took his doo-wop group, the Belmonts, to the top of the charts and then left them at their peak in 1960 to embark on an even bigger solo career. Dion's solo hits, "Ruby Baby" and "Runaround Sue" and "The Wanderer," had a shouting swagger and a street-tough beat. But when the Beatles came the hits stopped for Dion, as they did for everyone else. He cut "I'm Your Hoochie Coochie Man" and "Johnny B. Goode"; after he had a folk-flavored hit in 1968 with "Abraham, Martin and John" he covered "Both Sides Now" and "Purple Haze." He had drug problems, found religion, recorded gospel albums, and was coaxed back into the secular mainstream for a tour and the Dave Edmunds-produced *Yo Frankie* album.

Fabian: Do you remember what you wanted to do when you were 14? All I wanted to do was get laid a lot. I liked football and school, I remember that. I had some idea that I wanted to get into engineering.

I was a red-blooded youth. I was glued like the rest to rock radio. I was brought up on it; that and all the a capella groups that were all around in my neighborhood. It was all I ever heard every night in the summer.

My father had a heart attack. I lived in a row house in South Philadelphia, a house much like you'd see in Brooklyn. Anyway, I called an ambulance. He was being rushed out. I was sitting on the steps. I wanted to go, but my mon wouldn't let me. I had to watch my two younger brothers. I'm sitting there. There is a lot of people around, and this fellow, Bob Marcucci, who owned Chancellor Records, was driving by. He had a great friend — now if you can picture it, the stair stoops are like glued together, and the friend lived next or to us and his wife was pregnant. Marcucci thought that it was his friend's wife who was being taken. So that's how we met.

He introduced himself. He was rude enough to say, "Are you interested in being in the singing business?" I told him to go to hell. I remember that, real well. I couldn't believe the balls on this guy.

He kept bugging. And then as the weeks and months went by and my father came home and couldn't work, things were getting very desperate at our house. Compensation on disability was only $45 a week. My mother didn't work and I brought only $6 a week, that I got as a delivery boy. Marcucci started asking the friend next door to ask me again if I was interested. I kept saying no. When we got more desperate, he showed up at our door. I loved rock 'n' roll. All I asked him was that I make some money for my family. This is what I'm interested in. If I can do that, I'll be glad to go along with this. That's how it started. It was part love of rock 'n' roll, but it was mainly to help my family. I never made any bones about it. And the wonderful thing was I did get involved in making rock 'n' roll.

I picked the songs, most of them. There were a couple of albums — hah! — of those old standards where I didn't get to pick a thing. I didn't want to do those. I was coerced, forced into that. None of that was my choosing. The rock things were mine. "Turn Me Loose" was mine. "I'm A Man" was mine. "Tiger" was mine.

Very few people, prior to me, went through what I went through. I mean, Sinatra and, going back further, Rudy Vallee went through the experience. But the response was all new, you'll have to remember. I mean, I couldn't imagine me going through it. And it was quite an experience. You'd think it would be flattering, but it was unwieldy. It was out of control.

I've had time to think about it, and now and again people ask me of those crazy days, and I've had to piece it together in my mind. I had a manager who was an egomaniac. He was a frustrated dancer/performer. And he put it in the press this way: He wanted all the credit for manufacturing me and [Frankie] Avalon. So he presented it to the press that I was taught what to do. Consequently, the press got ahold of that and really killed me. It's like being stabbed in the back by your own. I didn't realize it at the time. I was too busy to read reviews and shit like that; you know what I mean.

I used to be bitter, but no more. I've come to terms with it. But believe me, I would do it all over the same way, if I could. I would have liked it if I had been older and more experienced. I wasn't prepared, and it was all like a dream world. *(Wayne Jancik; Dec. 28, 1990)*

❧

Dion DiMucci: I got this guitar when I was eight years old, but I was just plunking on it. Then when I was about 10, I heard Hank Williams. I started collecting his records and had about 250 Hank Williams songs. And I learned about 200 of them. I had them all logged, and what key they were in. That's what put me on the road, when I heard songs like "Be Careful Of Stones That You Throw" and "Honky Tonk Blues." I found out at an early age that I could write songs for a group of guys and girls and take them on a trip for four minutes. That just blew my mind and I got hooked, wrapped up in it. I guess I was motivated by all the wrong things to start with, like being accepted, getting the girls, being cool and all. Then you find out you can do it for a lifetime, and express yourself and your ideas.

I remember the morning I heard Hank Williams I was sitting and my mother was cooking the spaghetti, and I heard it in the back room. I heard "Be Careful Of Stones That You Throw" and I listened carefully, and then they played another. And I said, "I never heard this guy." It was the Don Larkin show from Newark, New Jersey. I don't even know why the channel was on, but that's the way it worked out. I went to the record shop on Fordham Road the next day and said, "Who's Hank Williams?" And they showed me that they had a couple of records. I just drove that guy crazy. I used to order all the Hank Williams catalog. He really helped me and got involved, and became a friend.

Then when I got into high school, groups like the Penguins and Crows were out, and I started running down to the Apollo Theater, hanging out at the back door trying to cop riffs off these guys — the Heartbeats and Cadillacs and guys like that. So I got taken up by that and it evolved. But I never lost those roots, because even songs like "Ruby Baby" and "Drip Drop" are like Hank Williams and the Drifters mixed. But within the Belmonts, there were different cells bumping into each other around a nucleus. Like Carlo [Mastrangelo], he was a jazz fanatic, listening to Miles Davis and Olatunji and some of the pianists and big bands. I liked rock 'n' roll and Hank Williams. Angelo [D'Aleo], who sang tenor in the group, liked arias and classical music. He was trained as a classical singer. And Freddie [Milano] was just an out-and-out doo-wop freak. So coming together, we just brought a lot of different expression.

We were the only group in my neighborhood. There was like one good group in each neighborhood. I remember the Mello-Kings were up in Yonkers, we were in the Bronx, and then you get to New York and you had the Cadillacs. We were in a group *and* a gang. We'd sing after the fights.

They used to call me Dee or Dion, so when I put the group together, with the best street-corner doo-wop singers that I knew, we were running through names for them, because I had already recorded a song for Laurie Records. So they said, "What street do you come from?" And we said, "183rd, Crotona." "Well, Belmont Avenue has the best sound to us."

The Schwartz brothers [Gene and Bob, the owners of Laurie Records] would look for songs for us. Some were submitted, some were commissioned. I would write a lot of them. Ernie Maresca and I would write a lot of them. He lived right across the street from me. He was the only songwriter in the neighborhood I knew. I never closed my mind to any avenue, like saying I had to sing only the stuff I wrote. I would sing standards and stuff like "Ruby Baby," which I grew up with. "Where Or When" came from the president of Laurie Records, Allen Sussell, a beautiful man. I loved this guy; he was a man's man, and his favorite song was "Where Or

When," by Rodgers and Hart. We decided to do that for our appreciation of him. We were out of our backyards — it was nothing we did naturally — but the expression of wanting to please him was an honest one.

After "Where Or When" [the Belmonts] wanted to do all this standard, smooth harmony stuff. It wasn't for me. We did a whole album called "Wish Upon A Star," and it just wasn't me. That's when I started recording "Ruby Baby" and "The Wanderer" and all that.

We were mostly a guys' group. We were good, we had good harmony, but we weren't threatening to the guys. But [girls] motivated us. Either she'd be this kind of girl or that kind of girl or you'd be in love with her or she left you. All these different situations. That was it; it was very simple. This way a least one girl would buy it; every girl named Sandy across the country, you knew you had a sale.

The Wanderer was this guy who used to hang out at George's Bar in my neighborhood. He had tattoos all over him — Flo, Mary, Janie. "Donna The Prima Donna" was written about my sister. Especially when I became a, quote, star, she used to hang out backstage trying to play the role of the sister of the star. She used to get all decked out. She used to wear sneakers and now she was wearing high heels. She was about 15 at the time. I wrote it kind of, you know, tongue in cheek. I wrote it with a lot of love.

"Runaround Sue" was written about a girl that every neighborhood has. I couldn't use the girl's real name because it wouldn't rhyme, so I used Sue. My wife would like to believe that it was her. Good for her image, you know; love 'em and leave 'em.

"Abraham, Martin And John" was written after the death of Bobby Kennedy because of the frustration. It was an attempt to make something good out of a bad situation, bring some solution to it. It was saying, here's these guys that have a dream, they believe in a state of love that does exist, and that we should work for it. But they died short of seeing the dream realized, so we should pick up on the dream and carry it further. That's what I was trying to say. When Dick Holler first brought the song to me it was like a shuffle. He was this guy that followed baseball teams, and this was practically the only song he wrote.

I wasn't involved in drugs at all when I put "Abraham, Martin And John" together. But it was a short distance from the drugs to that time. Actually, April 1, 1968, I was emotionally stuck and wondering why there was something missing from my life. I was trying to fill it with booze and drugs. It wasn't working. It got worse. So on April 1, I asked God for help. Somebody said ask and you'll receive, and here I am. I haven't had a drink since. So "Abraham, Martin And John" came like six months after that. But it seems to me it happened almost immediately after that decision, because I started working on it after that. It was like I was reborn and had a second chance, and it's been a process ever since, growing spiritually. *(Jeff Tamarkin; Aug. 28, 1987.)*

The most tragic teen idol of the '50s and '60s wrote the most haunting song of that era. Del Shannon was a carpet salesman and honky-tonk country singer named Charles Westover who wrote a minor-key song called "Runaway" and turned it into a classic with the help of a home-made instrument called the Mellotron. He had hits with "Little Town Flirt" and "Hats Off To Larry" but was restrained by his management from expanding his career. He was the first artist to have a U.S. hit with a Lennon and McCartney song, and one of many to suffer from the British Invasion. He was a sometime alcoholic who suffered from depression, but he made a comeback with a Tom Petty-produced album in 1981 and was supposedly in line to replace Roy Orbison in the Traveling Wilburys when he was found dead in his home. He had committed suicide.

Del Shannon: I didn't sell too many carpets. I hated to do anything but play music, and to survive I had to do a night job with the band and work in the day trying to sell carpets. But the carpet job was easy, really, because customers would come in and then they would leave, and the guy sold them bad carpet anyway. When customers came in to complain, the boss would hide under the desk. He said, "Don't tell them I'm here!" I was so embarrassed working there.

I was working a club in Battle Creek, Michigan. There was a guy who used to come in a lot that drank heavily. He was a big guy who was always saying that one day he was going to become a wrestler and that, well, Shannon, that's a great name. Well, anyhow, I knew he would never be a wrestler, so in essence I stole the name he wanted to use. Then, too, I always wanted a Cadillac because I was always poor. My friend had a Coupe deVille, so I took Del from deVille.

Strange how you get started in the business. First your mother likes your music. Then you go get a band and the drummer falls off his stool one night. It was some song I was writing and he said, "My God, I can't believe this song! It's unbelievable!" and he throws up his sticks. That was a great inspiration, because no one would ever say, "Love your music," and drop their drums. Then he said, "I know this guy, Max Crook, and he plays this weird, funny machine; get him down here."

I said, "I don't want a piano player, man." He said, "Just try him." So [Crook] came in and played that silly machine, and I hired him right away.

Max was a classic. I never saw him take a drink in his life. He used to drink Kool-Aid with cookies. He was a great baseball freak. He'd listen to the ballgame in one ear and play the piano with the other. When he was onstage he had this big box of Kleenex. Every 10 songs, he would blow his nose. He hated smoke. He was just unbelievable, but he loved to play music.

[We found this chord progression one night.] We played it for about 15 minutes. Got in trouble with the manager, too, who finally came onstage and told us we were nights: "Stop playing this! What are you doing?"

I ran away from myself, just wanting to get out of that town. I think everybody wants to run away. That's why that song seems to live on. I wanted to run away from the environment. I always want to run away from A to B, and then I get to B and I want to go back to A. I suppose everybody's like that, so that's probably why I write songs sometimes as neurotics. People are neurotics; the batch of new songs I'm writing are still neurotic songs.

We went to New York to record the song. It was about 10 degrees below zero, and the heater broke, and the muffler fell off. It was awful. I smoked cigars then, and Max hated smoke, so I had to leave the window open and blow the smoke out. We had our wives with us. We were totally broke. I had to borrow $60 from my manager.

It was insane. I didn't get to enjoy it, really. I was too anxious about the future. All of a sudden, you get what you want, and it isn't really what you expected. My first touring gig was on Broadway, and I'd make more there in a week than I was gonna make all year at the Hi-Lo Club. It was unbelievable. I was in total shock. I walk in and I'm working with Jackie Wilson, Johnny Burnette, Ray Peterson, Dion, Bobby Vee. And here's my first gig on Broadway: "Wow, this is amazing," after all these Hi-Lo gigs where there was bottle-throwing and knife-throwing. And I go to New York and here's these young, screaming kids, and five shows a day, and this little dressing room. I thought that when I'd go to Broadway, I'd have this Hollywood-dream dressing, with lush, purple carpets and white ceilings. I came in and it was cold and the window wouldn't shut.

Dion was there and I stepped on his foot. He said, "Hey, what are you doing? Where did you get those ugly pants? Look at those bad pants?"

I said, "Well, that's hip."

He said, "That's not hip! Pegs are hip!" I had red socks and a red tie, and a black suit. He said, "I can't believe what I'm seeing."

I was sober when I wrote "Runaway." "Hats Off To Larry," I was sober, I think. Then when I got three or four hits, I got to drinking heavy. When I found booze, I went crazy for it. I didn't write "Flirt" boozed, because Robert McKenzie was boozing and I had to be straight. But after that, when I wrote "Keep Searchin'," that's when things get a little foggy. That's when I was hitting the juice pretty bad. Booze can be good for you for awhile if you're a writer. After it takes you over, and you have no control over it, it's over, man.

But that's all changed now. I don't drink at all anymore. *(Wayne Jones, issue No. 11; Dawn Eden, March 23, 1990.)*

9. Oh Boy

The story of Buddy Holly the one single story of rock 'n' roll, the one legend that will be passed down before all others. Every kid with horn-rimmed glasses and a skinny neck wanted to play guitar, and form a band, and sing at the sock hops, and get a record deal, and make a record and have it be a hit, and then sing it on *Bandstand* and tour the country singing it, over and over again. Buddy Holly did it.Buddy Holly led a rock 'n' roll band when there were few rock 'n' roll bands and wrote his own songs when songwriters who fronted bands were a novelty. Holly's best songs — "Peggy Sue," "Everyday," "That'll Be The Day," "Rave On," "It's So Easy," "Not Fade Away" — are the pure stuff, quick and vibrant and so fresh they still sound like they might have been sung yesterday by the kid next door with the guitar and the wire recorder. They're fresh because they're good, not because Buddy Holly died young. Maybe the fact that the freshness never had a chance to get stale has something to do with the endurance and popularity of Buddy Holly beyond his music — the legend, if you want — but in the end, the songs make Buddy Holly special and keep Buddy Holly's songs forever running through your head.

Charles Hardin Holley was born in Lubbock, Texas, Sept. 7, 1936. He got the nickname "Buddy" from his mother, who thought "Charles Hardin" was such a long name for such a small boy. Buddy was singing in public from the age of five on. He took piano lessons when he was about 12 and could play songs by ear. A little while after that he started playing guitar.

He was elected king of the grade school when he was in sixth grade, and he was active in Boy Scouts. He didn't care much for school, and preferred rabbit hunting to studying.

Larry Holley was his brother.

Larry Holley: Oh, I just remember him as a common, ordinary, young fellow around Lubbock here. He worked for me, and I liked having him around. He was a good hand in the tile business, and many times we'd have him bring his guitar out to the job, and he'd sit on the tile boxes and play for us sometimes while we were working. He got out of work like that. I enjoyed going hunting and fishing with him, and we were frequently running around together. He was a bit younger than me, but we got along real good.

About a year before he put out "That'll Be The Day" we started really realizing that he meant business when it came to music, and he'd play just about every time he got the chance. He had his guitar with him a lot, and we noticed he could sing and play real good just about any song he'd ever heard. It seemed to us that he did them even better than the people who'd put them out. I know we enjoyed hearing him.

He was an overnight sensation in a lot of respects. We saw him coming up playing in small places like the fairgrounds or the high school, but then it seemed like he suddenly broke it big the second time "That'll Be The Day" came out. He recorded it at Norman Petty's place, and I was with him when he did that. We really thought he had a good one. It did take a couple of months before it really broke, but that's pretty quick, really.

Around Lubbock, no one really caught on to Buddy, except for the younger set that'd heard him play out in the clubs. The older people just took him in stride and didn't think much about it. Actually, he didn't gain a lot of fame here until after the movie *The Buddy Holly Story* came out. Now he has a lot of fans.

When Buddy left for New York City, that didn't faze us too much. He had bought a lot here to build his house on, and we were hoping he'd settle down in Lubbock, but he was hardly ever here anyway. He was on tour nearly all the time the last year and a half of his life, and we only saw him once or twice a year. So we didn't mind if he lived in New York or on the road; he wouldn't have been at his home much, anyway, no matter where it was at.

Buddy didn't want to go on that last tour, but he was hurting for money. He was about as broke as he'd ever been. His royalties hadn't started coming in; they were all tied up in different ways and he had other things working against him. He needed the money, and I think he was getting paid $1,000 or so a night for that tour. It was offered and he took it.

I remember listening to the radio the night that he got killed, February second. I call it the second, but everyone says it's the third; that's because the last night they played was on the second, and the crash took place a few minutes after midnight on the third. I knew he was up in Iowa somewhere, because I'd seen his itinerary. And I recall the radio saying that a snowstorm was moving into the Midwest, with flash advisories and all that. I remember saying a little prayer that they'd be all right. I didn't know he was flying; otherwise I'd have said a long prayer. I thought they were on the bus.

The next day I was checking out some of my tile jobs and my other brother, Travis, was working for me. I hadn't had the radio on that morning. It was a cold day, and I was wandering around checking jobs, wondering where all my people were. My brother wasn't on the job, and I couldn't find anyone. So I went up to a cafe to eat and the lady there said, "That was sure bad about the boys, wasn't it?" And I said, "What boys?" She answered, "Isn't your name Holley?" When I said yes she replied, "Well, Buddy Holly and them, they had a plane crash." I told her, "No; I'd have known about it if they had. It's surely not true." She said I'd better check with my folks and find out. Then I started getting excited; I knew something must have happened. Sure enough, I found out that the real bad thing had happened. And I thought, Lord, if you'll just help me, if he's still alive, I'll go up there, I'll fight the elements, I'll do whatever. But it was too late.

It's been hard for me to figure out myself why Buddy is still so popular. Buddy had a smooth, sincere quality to his voice. He sang plain where you could understand it, and nearly all of the time his tunes'll stick in your mind. I've noticed it seemed he was a bit ahead of his time, bridging the gap between country, rock and pop. He blended them together, and that caught people. *(Stu Fink; July 18, 1986.)*

One of the first musical friends Buddy made in Lubbock was a junior-high drummer named Jerry "J.I." Allison. They chummed around and played in little bands; later on, Allison co-wrote many of Holly's biggest hits.

Jerry Allison: I met Buddy probably around 1952 in junior high school; he was older than me by a couple of years. We started making music about '54 or so. I was playing with a group called

Cal Wayne and the Riverside Ranch Hands. We played some clubs around Lubbock and Buddy used to come sit in, and that was the first time we'd ever played together.

Sonny Curtis was around then playing guitar and fiddle. Don Guess played bass fiddle and steel guitar, and Larry Welborn played bass with the group some. When Buddy and all of us first started playing we were more of a country-western band, with Sonny on the fiddle and Don Guess on the steel guitar. Bob Montgomery was singing with Buddy at the time. In fact, he did most of the lead singing and Buddy sang harmony in that particular group.

Around 1956 we went to Wichita Falls, Texas, to Nishman Studios, I believe it was, and did some demonstration records. We sent them to Nashville to some people we ran into in Lubbock who came through on a show. They got in contact with someone who got the record deal, and they just picked Buddy out; Buddy's the one that got the contract. We did some duet records with Buddy and Bob both singing, and then we did some rockabilly, I guess you'd call it, with just Buddy singing. They wanted to sign Buddy, and he got the contract.

I didn't come on the very first session they did 'cause I was in school at the time. Sonny and Don Guess went. Then the next trip we cut the original "That'll Be The Day" and four other songs; that was in the summer. It was a real in-and-out, three-hour session, a real quick thing. We didn't have any time to fool around with it much. That was at Owen Bradley's studios. I was 17, Buddy was 19.

After those session, we went over to Norman Petty's studios in Clovis and recorded some more demos. We were going to send them to New York because we'd gotten involved with people who knew Buddy Knox — in fact, Buddy Knox's sister lived in Lubbock — and they were going to send the records to Roulette in New York.

"That'll Be The Day," the record we did come out with, was one of the demos cut at Norman Petty's studios. It was sent to Roulette, but they already had the Buddy Knox and Jimmy Bowen sounds, so they weren't interested in signing another rock-'n'-roll-type group. So Norman sent the records to Murray Deutch at Southern Records, who played them for Bob Thiele at Coral. Thiele signed us and actually put out the demo on "That'll Be The Day" and "I'm Looking For Someone To Love." That was the first record that did anything. It sure got us started.

On our first tour, we played shows with like 20 different acts. In fact, the first tour we played when we left Texas was 17 weeks long, and I think during that time we only had a week off, not all at one time. We went all over the U.S. and most of Canada. It was grueling, but he had a great time. And during that tour "Peggy Sue" came out, and so did "Oh Boy." All three records were doing very well while we were on that same tour.

The last tour we did was in October '58. Buddy wanted to move to New York, and Joe B. and I didn't. So we were going to try it for a while; none of us were really sure what we wanted to do at the time. Buddy and I had both gotten married, so there was another involvement there. He had married Maria Elena, and I married Peggy Sue Gerrow — just like the song. She was also from Lubbock. We were married for nine years.

Buddy, Joe B., and I discussed that we'd get back together if it didn't work out good, and it *wasn't* working out. So we were all sort of figuring on getting back together again. Waylon [Jennings] was on the last tour with him, and Buddy told Waylon before the crash that he was planning an England tour and wanted Joe B. and I to go with him. And I suppose Sonny, too, since he was working with us at that time. Buddy told him this not two days before he was killed.

On February 3rd, 1959, I was in Lubbock at my folks' house, and Sonny woke me up and told me. I had lost my best friend. *(Stu Fink; July 18, 1986.)*

The producer of Holly's first and best hit records was a piano-playing studio owner named Norman Petty. An unwary innovator and something of a maverick, Petty, by his own admission, fashioned the "Tex-Mex" sound, a spirited mix of rock, R&B, blues, and the gentler swaying rhythms of Mexico. The Tex-Mex sound was at its freshest, rawest and most commercial with Holly; later on it flourished in the good hands of producers like Huey P. Meaux and artists like Doug Sahm, Freddy Fender and Los Lobos.

Petty fronted a popular local trio and produced Buddy Knox, Roy Orbison ("Ooby Dooby") and a handful of other acts prior to hitting it big with Holly. Petty produced the *Buddy Holly*, *That'll Be The Day* and *The Chirping Crickets* albums and a string of singles and EPs. After Holly's death he produced the Crickets and many other singers and bands, but never quite hit it big the way he did with Holly.

Norman Petty died in 1987.

Norman Petty: Actually, the studio was built to record our trio, and we had a few hits on our own as the Norman Petty Trio. We sort of backed into the production business of doing rock records simply because we had good equipment here and then some of the kids didn't know what to do when they got into the studio. I more or less came in the producer's seat at the same time.

At first, we only handled the groups on a custom basis. When we saw that some groups didn't have a channel to promote and market their product, we started taking the demos to New York, California and Nashville. We evolved in much the same way as Sam Phillips of Sun Records. We were both independent producers who owned our own studios. Of course, that's nothing new now, but in that era there weren't many studios around that were doing excellent work.

Buddy had recorded in Wichita Falls and Lubbock prior to coming to see me. He came in and said, "If you can get Buddy Knox a hit, you can get me a hit." I thought that was pretty remarkable and I told him then that it was not the place, it was the artist. So he recorded his demos, took them to Nashville and actually landed his first record deal himself.

You know, many people lay claim to what they did to get Buddy started, but most of it was just his being willing to camp on doorsteps. He came to see me, recorded his demos, took them to Nashville, and was signed by Decca. He was with them for about one year. He tried to get the Decca people to let him record in Clovis at my studio and they just said, "Clovis, where?"

When Decca dropped his contract in the latter part of January 1957, they thought he was very uncooperative. He got his official release in February 1957 and we became officially associated, and I took his tapes to New York.

"That'll Be The Day" was the first demo that I had anything to do with, that I took to New York for him. He did some other things here prior to that, but I don't recall the titles.

I think the success of our trio opened some doors for Buddy in New York. One connection helped the other. I think the fact that we were connected to the records we brought to New York helped us place them.

It was a very exciting time for all of us, when "That'll Be The Day" became a hit. In my memory, it remains one of the most exciting times I've ever had. It was one of those nice things where I respected what he did and he respected what I did. It was one of those chemically right things — two people in the right place at the right time. I understood what he wanted to do, and it was easy for us to communicate ideas.

Making records was a lot more fun than it is now. I know that sounds like I'm getting old, and I am. But it seemed like the camaraderie among the musicians was really excellent. We had quite a few people coming in and out of the studio, and it seemed like back in those days everybody was interested in seeing that everyone became successful.

The technical structure of those early records was rather unique. Jerry Allison was and still is a very fresh and inventive drummer. He would do super rhythm patterns which were just excellent for such a young player. Anyway, at the end of a session he said, "Let's do a song for my old girlfriend." He came up with this beat and we sent him into this small room by himself. Buddy and Joe B. were in the main studio and I was potting the echo signal up and down in time with the beat. Everyone thought it was a mechanical contrivance, but it was just a matter of loading the chamber in time with Jerry's beat. That was pretty unique for that day and time.

There's an interesting story behind "Oh Boy" and "Maybe Baby." Our trio was playing quite a lot, but we were really winding down because it made more sense to stay with rock 'n' roll in a production role. However, we played country clubs, hotels and the like, and we were playing the Officers' Club at Tinker Air Force Base in Oklahoma. Buddy and the boys had some days off from a Houston gig, so they came up. I had brought my recording equipment with me, and we set it up after the club closed and recorded the basic tracks to "Maybe Baby" and "Oh Boy," took the tracks back to Clovis and added the echo and the voices.

Oddly enough, I was cleaning the storage area about a month ago and I found some of the original pressings of Buddy's records that were still sealed. If you compare those original pressings with the repackages on super-critical, excellent equipment, the originals are superior. They really are.

All the keyboards were played by either me or Vi, my wife. For example, Vi played the piano part on "Think It Over." I did the organ part on "Take Your Time" and "Valley Of Tears," and maybe some other things.

Five different people will give you five different versions of how the celeste on "Everyday" came about. Actually, the celeste was part of the instrumentation in the studio for the trio. It was used as an extra voice alongside the organ. It was an icing-on-the-cake instrument. Buddy liked the sound of it. He'd play around on it in the studio, and we both agreed that we should use it on "Everyday" because it's such a delicate song.

BUDDY HOLLY: 'He was a quiet sort of person until he got a guitar in his hands, and then he came alive ... He was a pile-driver on guitar.'

I helped him write songs. I would often write the bridge, because Buddy didn't like to write bridges. I wrote the bridges and the lyrics for it on "True Love Ways." It was a co-operative thing, where Buddy would come up with part of the words or part of the melody.

They moved around an awful lot, and they were always part of a show. For example, Buddy was part of the Irving Feld Shower of Stars or other packages, and the organizers of these package shows didn't want any setup or rehearsal time because they were on very tight schedules. There was simply no time.

Jerry Lee Lewis told me that Buddy went over very well on tour in Australia. He told Jerry, "I love Texas, but I could live here."

I was with Jerry and Buddy on that tour. You see, Paul Anka was actually top of the bill, Jerry Lee was number two and Buddy and the Crickets were number three. The first place they played was unbelievable. Paul didn't come off at all well, and Jerry Lee just tore the house down. It was always a contest between Buddy and Jerry Lee to see who could get the wildest reaction. It was a game between them. Paul never got a look in for the rest of the tour.

I didn't go on all of his tours. I went on the Australian tour and the British tour, and I would usually meet Buddy someplace along the line on a tour. For example, I would fly into Baltimore and I would be there when the bus got in and the suitcases were unloaded and the tired, angry, hungry musicians got off. They would hustle about to get ready, go on stage and then get back on the bus. The closest one-word summation of those trips is "futility." You just think, "Is it all worth it?" Then, of course, sometimes you have a great gig and the crowd tears down the place and, yes, it was worth it.

Many of the super-critical people, who have lint in their mouth when they talk, say that Buddy was super-awkward and he probably was compared with the polished acts with their choreography where you can turn to page 13 and see an arm go up at this time. That's very slick, and Buddy was not slick. He was very natural, and the outstanding thing about him was the lack of inhibition. That lack of inhibition came through on stage because he was often super-shy offstage. And he was a piledriver on guitar, too.

He was a ham. He loved to perform before people. All the boys did, especially Jerry Allison. They were all good hams. They loved for the audience to love them.

You might have heard that Buddy's marriage started to change things. I think that chronology is a little misleading, because Buddy was evolving in new directions prior to his marriage. The King Curtis titles, such as "Reminiscing," were actually done prior to his marriage. Buddy thought King Curtis was great, but he [Curtis] was doing a lot of television and radio out in New York so it was hard to book him. What happened was that we flew King Curtis into Lubbock, Buddy picked him up and drove to Clovis where we recorded all night, and then he took King Curtis back to the airport so that he could be in New York the next day.

I really think Buddy started to evolve when we did the string arrangements. They were remarkable demonstrations of what Buddy could do as an artist.

There have been pages and pages written about the split between Buddy and I, but it was simply the fact that Buddy was told that he wanted to go to New York, and I think once he got there his mind and ideas changed.

It didn't make any difference where the record companies were, because we were producing a lot of tape that was released and sold out of here to various record companies all over the world. But as far as Buddy was concerned, I think that he and Maria Elena felt they could get better publicity and do better things in New York than they could by staying here with me in New Mexico.

Jerry Allison called me the day he died. It was very early on the morning after the crash, right after they had called him. It was a terrible shock to everyone.

Buddy did some marvelous work that still stands up. The quality of the records and arrangements have held up amazingly well, perhaps even better than the early Elvis Presley recordings.

I think the longevity of anything is dependent upon how people can use whatever information they have at hand to fit in with what their own lives are. That's been one nice thing about Holly's music: It was not complicated, and it tends to be a good, fun thing for almost every generation that's come along. So I'd be very optimistic and say yes, I think that in 25 years Buddy Holly will still be remembered. *(Stu Fink, July 18, 1986; Dave "Daddy Cool" Booth and Colin Escott, Aug. 31, 1984.)* 🎸

The second member of the Crickets Buddy picked up was bass player Joe B. Mauldin. Like Jerry Allison, Mauldin was with Buddy Holly through the Norman Petty-Clovis days, then left when Holly moved to New York. After Holly's death, he re-formed the Crickets with Jerry Allison.

Joe B. Mauldin: The first time I saw him he was doing an opening for a tire store in Lubbock, Texas. They had a flatbed trailer out in front of the store. I was playing with another group at the time called the Four Tunes. This was probably '55, or '56 'cause I started playing with him in the summer of '56. He had a group and was working. He and Jerry Allison came by one morning and woke me up and said, "Man, we got a gig we gotta play tonight over in Carlsbad, New Mexico. We don't have a bass player. Do you wanna go over and play?" I think the only reason they came to me was 'cause I had a bass.

I had a bass, too. A big upright one, same one as I have now. Anyway, I went and played the gig with him, and on the way back from Carlsbad, Holly says, "Man, why don't you play with me all the time? We're gonna start a group called the Crickets. We're gonna make records and we're gonna make money and we're gonna be great!" I said, "Sure, I've heard that stuff before. How long do you think it's gonna take to make it?" He said, "How long did it take Elvis?" I thought, "Boy, that's a ballsy statement!" But you know, he was right, 'cause I started playing with him in '56, and then in '57 "That'll Be The Day" came out. It really started the ball rolling. In fact, I was still 16 years old when "That'll Be The Day" took off.

I was co-writer on "Well All Right" and "I'm Gonna Love You Too." Then there was a ballad called "Last Night"; probably nobody's ever heard it. Jimmy Bowen cut it when he was with the Rhythm Orchids. Of course, Buddy and the Crickets did it on the first album.

Petty was a real good mixer. He knew his equipment and how to use it. He knew his mikes really well, which mikes would get the best effect out of an instrument. But I think Norman Petty was somewhat overrated, in that he wasn't the beginning and the end of it, just like George Martin wasn't the beginning and the end of the Beatles. Well, maybe not, because Norman was responsible for getting us our first record deal. I'm talking about in the studio.

Jerry and I had just about as much say-so in what was used and what we did. Like I said, it was a group effort as opposed to a Norman Petty production. But you know, we were young and didn't know anything about it. All we wanted to do was play and go on the road.

Who knows? If we'd have moved to New York things might not have worked out the way they did. We might have gone on the tour, might have all been killed. Holly might not have taken the tour. Who knows? But, you know, you can't undo things like that.

I've tried to speculate on what Buddy would be doing now. I know where his head was going when we separated and I wanted to be involved in that, too, but I didn't feel comfortable and I chose not to stay with him. I think he would have been heavily involved in record production, writing. He was a real creative guy, and at the time he was making some drastic changes from what we had been doing along the way. He was taking some avenues that none of the other rockabilly artists were doing. He was kinda merging black rhythm-and-blues with the rockabilly stuff we were doing. He was getting King Curtis involved, Sam "The Man" Taylor, and he was getting black girl vocal groups behind him. When he came up with an idea he wouldn't turn loose of it 'til he had either made a success of it or realized that it wasn't going to work, period. But things really seemed to go great for him every time he got into something.

He was a great writer, and if you stop and think about it, even though Elvis might have gotten writer's credits on a couple of tunes, Elvis was not creative. Elvis was a performer. I don't mean to put him down; let's face it, Elvis was phenomenal. But Holly was a great writer. He was a superb guitar player. He never really had the opportunity to show people what he could do on the guitar. He could do Mexican guitar, flamenco-type stuff.

He had a unique style of playing guitar. Sonny Curtis says it over and over. Buddy always used down strokes on the Crickets stuff. Buddy just had a guitar in his hands all the time. If he didn't have it in his hands, he had it in the back seat of the car. When we used to go out and get in the car and buy a couple quarts of bootleg beer and just go out and drink beer at night Buddy had a guitar in his hand.

Buddy could roll with the punches. He started out playing country music. I don't know if you've heard some of the country stuff he did before the Crickets. Whatever's happening he could fit in with. Just like on that first album. He did Chuck Willis' "It's Too Late," which was an R&B ballad, and he just did his own rendition of it. It seems like everything he did he did really well. *(Argyle Bell; Feb. 10, 1989.)*

🎵

After the breakup of the Crickets in 1958, Holly recruited Tommy Allsup to play guitar with the tour band.

Tommy Allsup: I was working at a nightclub in Odessa [Texas], and Buddy came down and said he had a tour coming up in February, and wanted me to join in; he already had Waylon to play bass. He asked if I knew a drummer, and I knew a good one in Odessa named Carl Bunch. He's been referred to in all the books as Charlie Bunch, and I don't know where they got that. His real name is Carl. His mother owned a record shop, and she drove us up through Lubbock to pick up Waylon, and then took the three of us to Amarillo to get our plane to New York for rehearsals.

Most of the acts rehearsed in New York. Dion was there, and we were going to back him up. Frankie Sardo was also there, but I don't think we met Ritchie until we got to Chicago, where the tour left from. Waylon had never played bass before, so we taught him all the songs, and Carl knew all the drum parts.

Buddy really liked New York. He had a real nice apartment, and fit in real well. Waylon and I stayed there with him before the tour. Irving Feld of G.A.C. [the tour promoter] had just signed Buddy to be his personal manager. At that time, Feld had only handled Clyde McPhatter and Paul Anka. Buddy was to be his third act. He put together all the big rock 'n' roll tours and had us booked way down the line. So Buddy looked forward to New York and being in that type of situation. I didn't like New York, though; it was too different and strange.

We went from New York out to Chicago by train, where he had more rehearsals. We picked up a few horn players there. Right after the first day, we got up there in 25-below-zero weather,

BUDDY HOLLY AND THE CRICKETS: ' "We're gonna start a group called the Crickets. We're gonna make records and we're gonna make money and we're gonna be great!" '

and the buses started to freeze. Most of them had bad heaters. We'd complain and they'd get us another one. The bus company was out of Chicago, and they were sending the old junker buses, not the nice ones like they have now. One night we had a nice, warm ride because they'd chartered a bus from a school and it had a good heater. But for the most part, the buses we had were old and falling apart.

Buddy sang all of his records during the shows. He'd open with a more upbeat verson of

"Gotta Travel On," then a hit by Billy Grammer. We did a trio on that one. He'd do some of his own songs, then some Jerry Lee Lewis and Little Richard. He really liked that.

He did sing "It Doesn't Matter Anymore," because that was one of the hardest songs that we had to teach Waylon. It's got those little breaks in the bridge, and I remember having trouble showing Waylon those chords.

The worst night was after we played in Duluth, Minnesota. We were working our way to Green Bay, Wisconsin, by way of Appleton, and our bus froze up while we we going down the road. We waited for hours, and finally the sheriff's patrol came to get us in jeeps and trucks. Carl Bunch got frostbite and we had to leave him behind in a hospital. We didn't get any sleep that night, and had to catch a train to Green Bay right after that. There were always all-night rides, usually four to six hundred miles, but that was the worst.

Buddy'd thought of the plane that afternoon. We were cold, but the main reason was that we'd been out about two weeks, and we were running low on shirts and clean laundry. Flying would get him to the next date with plenty of time to get everything done. Waylon and I were going to go, but during that afternoon, J.P. [Richardson] had gotten a sore throat and thought he'd caught the flu, and he got Waylon's seat so he could get there and see a doctor.

I had already put my bag with the dirty shirts into the station wagon to go out to the airfield, and Buddy wanted me to check that we had everything loaded. He'd once lost a brand-new Fender amp and guitar, and was real cautious about that. So I went back in and Ritchie was still signing autographs, and he started bugging me to let him fly in my place. He said, "C'mon, guy, let's flip," and I, for some reason, told him all right; if he wanted it that bad. He called heads and won the toss. He went and grabbed his bag off the bus, and I left mine in the station wagon.

I gave Buddy my wallet to pick up a letter for me at the P.O., as my mother had sent me a letter with a check in it. He stuck it in his coat pocket, and it was found at the crash sight later that morning. As a result, the first Associated Press news that went out said I was on the plane with them.

It was really weird, because J.P. had bought a sleeping bag that afternoon, and I got to sleep in the sleeping bag. Those old buses used to have a seat all the way across the back of them, so I got to stretch out back there in that sleeping bag, and I probably got the best rest that night than on any ride that we'd made.

We weren't going to finish that tour, but we couldn't get a plane out, and nothing was moving. Then GAC talked us into it, offering us more than the salary we were currently making. But we never did get paid for what we were supposed to have gotten for those last two weeks.

Waylon started singing Buddy's, as well as some of Ritchie's songs. After that we brought in another kid from Texas named Ronnie Smith to help us. Bobby Vee worked with us that night, and I think his drummer might have worked with us also. Up to that point, Ritchie was playing drums behind Buddy, or sometimes Dion would play. We were switching around.

The very next day, Frankie Avalon came on, and so did Jimmy Clanton. They stayed on and finished the tour.

We just kept on with the same thing that we'd been doing. Waylon knew all the songs, and he'd sing them in the same key that Buddy did them in. Ronnie Smith handled all the cover songs, like Little Richard, Jerry Lee or Elvis, and Waylon sang Buddy's songs. He really went over big, and you could see that the kids really liked him.

When the tour was over, we took the train back to New York, and had found that Norman Petty had arrived with Jerry Allison, Joe B., Earl Sinks and Sonny Curtis. He had recorded a song with them with Earl singing, and had made a deal with Coral. We all got together and met at GAC, where Norman really chewed out Irving Feld. Feld told him that we had finished the tour for him, and said that he'd book the Crickets only if they used Tommy on guitar. That put me on the spot, because ol' Sonny was a good friend of mine, and he'd come up from Lubbock. So J.I., Joe B., Earl Sinks and myself would be the new Crickets, and that sent Ronnie Smith, Waylon Jennings, Sonny Curtis and Carl Bunch back to Lubbock.

We stayed in New York for about six weeks, waiting. We did a couple of TV shows, but they couldn't book us. We stayed there until about May of 1959, and I went back to Texas to find something else. *(Stu Fink; Feb. 10, 1989.)*

Bobby Vee was 15 years old when Buddy Holly was killed, just a North Dakota kid with a rock 'n' roll band called the Shadows. Vee's band wasn't even the best in Fargo, let alone North Dakota or the Midwest. But Vee and his band earned a shot at stardom and an asterisk in rock 'n' roll history by replacing Buddy Holly on the bill at the Feb. 3 show, just hours after Holly had been killed.

Bobby Vee: Today, the show would have been cancelled, but 30 years ago there was that tradition that the show must go on.

I think everyone was in shock. They didn't know what to do, including the radio station that promoted the concert. Everything had happened so fast, and the show was at 7 o'clock that evening. I got home from school that afternoon and turned on the radio, and they were asking for local talent to fill in. No one really knew what was going on. And one of the guys in our band — unbeknownst to me — called up the radio station and told them we'd play. There was no audition; we just showed up and they asked if we could do about 15 minutes. Of course, we said "sure," and ended up opening the show that night. The lineup was Dion and the Belmonts, Frankie Sardo, Holly's band, another local band called Terry Lee and the Poorboys, and us. There wasn't much of a show.

We did just that one night, but that particular tour did go on. It was grueling. I don't know how anyone could have done it; it was a terrible time of the year to be traveling through the Midwest, especially by bus.

My career really had nothing to do with that show. If I'd never made a record, that would've been the end of it. There was a guy in the audience who was kind of a local promoter that came up and introduced himself to us afterwards and apparently thought we had done a good job, but we didn't have people pounding at our door after that show. "Suzie Baby" was the first thing that really got us going.

The idea that I did some of Buddy's songs has been haunting me for 30 years. I did know a lot of Buddy's songs, but I didn't do any of them that night. I was 15 years old, but I was smart enough to know not to do that. *(Stu Fink; Feb. 10, 1989.)*

Buddy met and married Maria Elena Santiago, a receptionist at his music-publishing company, in a whirlwind courtship as quick and fresh as one of his songs. They were married in August 1958. Six months later he was dead.

Maria Elena Holly: I met Buddy in New York. I was working for Southern Music Publishing Company; I was the receptionist/secretary there. He and the Crickets came in one morning and asked to see one of the executives, Murry Deutch. I asked them to be seated, so they sat down and immediately tried to engage me into a conversation with them. They started trying to speak Spanish with me, you know, ending English words with a 'o' or an 'a.' So that was real hilarious, but I just took it that they were trying to be nice and funny.

We continued talking, and then Buddy asked me if I'd join him for lunch. I told him I was sorry, but I was too busy and usually didn't have time for a lunch break. He said he'd come back after his meeting and convince me. So they went in for about an hour or two, and when they came out he said, "Well, I'll see you later." And I said, "Okay, goodbye, good luck," and I thought that was it.

Apparently, he had talked to Murray Deutch's secretary, and arranged it in such a way that she'd ask me to go to lunch with her that day, and not mention Buddy Holly. So I figured, why not?

She took me to Howard Johnson's, where they had arranged to meet. When we got there there was a huge line, but off to the side I saw hands waving, and who do you think it was? Buddy Holly and the Crickets, plus Norman Petty, and they were calling for us to come over. So we went and sat down, and that's the first time I really got to know Buddy Holly.

After that lunch, he asked me to dinner. Of course, I told him no, so he asked me if I'd go with him to buy some guitar strings before returning to the office. So we walked toward the music store, and he tried to convince me to have dinner with him.

Of course, I liked him right away when I saw him, but I didn't take him very seriously in what he was trying to say to me. He told me he was going to marry me, and I said, "Oh, when? Right away?"

But after that we worked it out. I asked my aunt, and she opposed it right away. I worked on her for awhile and then she consented; she had found out that he was a nice guy. So Buddy did take me to dinner that night, and again he asked me to marry him. "Oh, sure," I replied sarcastically, "why not tomorrow?" I didn't know he was *that* serious, but he kept insisting that he wasn't kidding. So I told him to go see my aunt; it was not up to me. I was trying to get him to calm down, and suggested he talk to me when he came back from his tour. But he said, "No, I don't think so. I want to be sure that, before I go, you say yes." So I said okay, and made him promise that tomorrow he'd go and talk to my aunt. I thought that he just wouldn't show up.

But sure enough, Buddy Holly was there the next day ringing the doorbell. He came in and told my aunt that he wanted to get married, that we were in love, and he was sure I felt the same way. He wanted her blessing. And that's exactly how it happened. It all started at Southern Music Publishing Company.

Buddy was already considering moving to New York City even before we got married. He thought New York was the place to be at that time for the music and his career. He told me this that very first night when we were talking. He was discussing different things about his career and what he intended to do, and I told him he was right; New York was the place to be.

When we got married, we took an apartment in Greenwich Village on 8th Street and 5th Avenue. That's where the Mark Twain House used to be, until they destroyed it and erected an apartment house. We first lived there until we decided what we wanted to do.

I'd like Buddy Holly to be remembered as a person who really enjoyed people and wanted them to be happy. That was something he also conveyed through his music: happiness. Buddy will always be remembered as a good composer, a fine musician, and a good human being — as he was. That's how I see Buddy Holly. *(Stu Fink; Aug. 29, 1986.)*

10. Folk City

While the country was discovering rock 'n' roll, it was also going through a folk rush. Ever since a group of New York City folk singers who called themselves the Weavers hooked up with Frank Sinatra's future arranger, Gordon Jenkins, in 1951, and produced a surprise hit with "Goodnight Irene," the country had been rediscovering folk music. It found it liked catchy ethnic singalongs like "Tzena, Tzena" and "The Banana Boat Song." It found it liked Harry Belafonte, who was black and exotic and not at all threatening. It found it liked "This Land Is Your Land" by Woody Guthrie, who at that time was beginning to suffer from the awful, debilitating disease called Huntington's Chorea that would leave him hospitalized for the rest of his life, and incapable of realizing what his songs would do. It did not hear the other songs of Woody Guthrie, the angry songs like "Vigilante Man" and "Jesus Christ," the Dust Bowl songs like "Dust Pneumonia Blues." But it liked what it heard.

The public especially liked the clean, bright folk songs of groups like the New Christy Minstrels and the Kingston Trio, songs like "Tom Dooley" and "Michael, Row The Boat Ashore." From 1958 through 1967 the Kingston Trio were the most popular folk group in the country. They had a million-seller with "Tom Dooley," had hits with "M.T.A." and "Greenback Dollar," had two of the top five albums of 1959 (the other three were soundtracks), had five of the top 25 albums in 1960, and eased the way into the mainstream for less cheery, sadder, more strident folk acts like Peter, Paul and Mary and eventually Bob Dylan. They sold more records than either Chuck Berry, Little Richard or Bo Diddley.

Nick Reynolds was one of the founders of the Kingston Trio.

Nick Reynolds: Theodore Bikel, The Gateway Singers — these were the people who were motivating us, who we went to see or listened to their records. I imagine the first couple of albums were from those first people, who were where we'd heard them. It was a very democratic process. People would bring in or we'd have favorite songs, and the first few albums were things that we just put in the act. No one said, "Okay, we're going to sing this," because everyone would look around and say, "Oh, yeah?"

145

We'd all make up head arrangements, sit around and say, "Okay, we're gonna sing this song; you're gonna sing this verse." We'd more or less all decide on a song all the way through. We didn't take a vote or hold up our hands, but we'd say, "Hey, yeah; that's all right, that's neat," and we'd just go along with it. There was never very much argument about what songs we were going to sing, ever.

We just got together and banged the songs out. We'd just go in there and put our heads together and sing 'em. I could harmonize pretty well, and David was a great harmonizer. We used to have to tell Bobby what to sing — "Bobby, you sing this" — and he'd nod his head and his glasses would fall off. He was perfect. Bobby is the most majestic performer of all time! He was the main key in the whole thing.

David Guard, by the way, is the first person — and I'm putting this on record — that said we should go electrical. And I remember very well, because we went back to Cape Cod when John first joined the group and played there, and the Whiskeyhill singers were there and David was playing electric guitar. And he was the first one that I know of the "folk people" — before the Byrds, before everybody else — that ever wanted to go electrical. And he was right on ... if you want to evolve then you do this. Bobby and I just wanted to have a good time and have people accept us and not have to have any hassles, but David was very avant-garde and involved along those lines. He was right on as far as where the music was going to go. That was years before the Beatles. I never would have wanted to do it that way. It's hard enough getting my ass out of bed, much less getting me to an amplifier.

It was fun the whole time, really. When I talk about the ending of the thing, it became evident to me that I was going out on the road and paying more people at the office — secretaries, accountants, lawyers, PR men and stuff like that — than it was really bringing back to me emotionally and everything else. It got to be really big business. It just wasn't worth it and it just wasn't going to get any bigger at that time, so we sat down a year before we quit. In June of '66 we sat down — Frank and Bobby and John [Stewart] and I, and our accountant and lawyer — and said, "Well, work real hard next year and it can go down that way." And it was planned a year in advance. there was no sudden cutoff, breakup, fist fights. We knew exactly what we were doing at the time. As I said, it's like me beating my head against the wall emotionally, etc., to go away from my family for this, that or the other; certainly the financial gain is not there. And I've done it for 10 years! I've had my ego stroked; I've had my kicks. *(Jack Rubeck and Benjamin Blake; April 1980.)*

New York was the hotbed of the new folk revival. Around 1960 Greenwich Village was full of clubs, and poets, and young men and women with guitars. Richie Havens would come there, and John Sebastian and Judy Collins, and Phil Ochs, and Joan Baez, and Eric Andersen, and eventually a fresh-faced Minnesota kid with a nasal Woody Guthrie twang named Robert Zimmerman who had taken the name of a wild Welsh poet. Somewhere along the line, maybe not in the Village but somewhere, a young Steven Stills would fall in love with Judy Collins and write "Suite: Judy Blue Eyes" for her and his new group, and Joan Baez and Bob Dylan would fall in love and back out again, and Phil Ochs would die, and Richie Havens would open Woodstock, and Eric Andersen would find his shot at worldwide stardom thwarted by fate and death. But in the early '60s beatniks were in the Village.

The scene spawned festivals. The first rock festivals were folk festivals. The Newport Folk Festival in 1965 featured Richie Haven, Joan Baez, Bob Dylan, Phil Ochs and Tom Paxton, and drew nearly 10,000 fans. Eric Andersen was in the audience.

Havens had a knack for being in the right place at the right time in the '60s. He grew up singing doo-wop but picked up the guitar, wandered down to the Village and fell right in. He sang at the Newport Folk Festival and opened Woodstock. He covered the Beatles and played Indian ragas years before they did. He was one of the few black singers to come out of the new folk revival.

Richie Havens: I began fooling around with the guitar in 1960, but I didn't start to play until

1964 when I learned my fourth chord. I was living in Brooklyn, had odd jobs, like Western Union and in a florist shop for four years, and sang with an a cappella singing group. We thought that one day we would become professional, but we never did.

I have sung my whole life. Coming to Greenwich Village made me think about picking up the guitar. Traditional folksingers were around when I discovered the Village in 1959. The beatniks were around then. Beatniks and poetry brought me to the Village, and it was there that I discovered folksingers. Folksingers were an education for me. I learned that it didn't matter how far back in time you went, the stories were still the same. The same things that were happening then are happening now, which was truly a great education at that time in my life. I was leaving Brooklyn because my neighborhood was getting a little bit crazy, with the street gangs and all that craziness. I didn't know what I really wanted to do. I had quit school. I was intending to be a singer, but then I went to work.

I like anybody that does anything nice. I grew up listening to country-and-western every day in my life. My mother went to work with it. As far as the Village goes, the people who were guitar players that inspired me were Len Chandler, who was the first person I met in the Village and who was writing his own material at the time. "To Be A Man" was his big song then. It was a great song, too. And there was Noel Paul Stookey, who was singing by himself then. His name was Noel, not Paul, in those days — before Peter, Paul and Mary — and also Dino Valenti [later of Quicksilver Messenger Service], who was probably the most influential on my thinking about playing guitar, because he played the guitar like nobody else on this planet. He still does, but probably doesn't do it for anybody. He has always been an escapist sort of person. He also inspired me to sing by myself because up until that time, I sang with many, many a cappella groups. But I never really intended to sing by myself. When I went to Greenwich Village, I went for the poetry, and I did get to read a few poems and listen to a lot of poets read.

I never felt any indication that I was a black musician in a relatively white medium. I was always accepted as a musician. It had a lot to do with the way I grew up in Brooklyn. Fortunately, for me being born in 1941, I grew up with everybody in terms of nationality backgrounds, and I kind of give that as the reason that I am the person I am. I don't see such things as color, and I never did.

There has always been a representative amount of black folk singers throughout the times, from all the way back to Sonny Terry and Brownie McGhee, who started a long time ago, to Josh White Sr. and Josh White Jr. Josh White Jr. was my first contemporary. His was the first concert I ever went to. Someone bought me tickets to the concert because they wanted me to see him, and it blew my mind because he was one person on stage with a guitar. It was a confirmation that it could be done.

I opened [Woodstock]. I was supposed to be fifth. I said, "What am I doing here? No, no, not me, not first!" The reason I had to go on stage was because there was nobody else to go on first; the concert was already 2½ hours late. Michael Lang was going absolutely nuts. He didn't know what to do. Everybody was at the Holiday Inn seven miles away and couldn't get to the stage because the one back road they thought they could take directly to the stage was completely blocked with abandoned cars. That's why the helicopters were brought in: They had to get from the Holiday Inn to the stage. I got there by helicopter. It was a small helicopter and we had the smallest instrumentation to carry — two guitars and a conga drum.

Nobody knew what to expect, what it was going to be like. We thought it was going to be a regular festival, as far as anybody knew. I had done festivals before Woodstock. So it was going to be no big deal. I think they were expecting a couple hundred thousand people at the most. I had performed in front of 250,000 people in Hyde Park, England, at the free debut concert Blind Faith gave. We had also done a concert in California for about 100,000 people. We all expected just a little bit larger than normal. It was more than 400,000 in actuality — that was the figure the newspapers gave. I would say there were 800,000 people there during the middle of the second day.

My impression was that there were over a million people there. It was a completely unique experience. No one expected it. "Freedom" was written right on the stage; it never had been sung before! It was spontaneous. What happened on that day was that I went onstage a little bit reluctant because I felt they were going to throw beer cans at me for being late, for the concert itself being late. But that wasn't the case. They were happy something was going down in the first place. And it was beautiful because I got started talking about how beautiful the day was and how we are going to have a good time, how it's going to be real nice and how everyone is going have a far-out time. I just started singing, and I was onstage for about 2½ hours before any of the other performers came by helicopter to go on. I was only supposed to be on for 25-30 minutes, like everybody else.

The Woodstock film has taken me to places I haven't even really been yet. Woodstock has permeated the entire world much more than Americans even dream of or believe or understand. It affected the entire world. It has gone places I have never been before and preceded me in a certain kind of light. It was historically perceived as just a mere entertainment event, but it had historical repercussions to it, which really cemented me into a large section of people around the world. For instance, I went to Argentina about a year ago, and they had played "Woodstock" for 7½ years on Saturday nights at midnight. The reason was that the government didn't allow them to have anyone come into the country and sing. The government was so crazy, and entertainers were out. So the movie surfaced for 7½ years in place of the entertainment that would normally be there. Those groups that performed at Woodstock are indelibly written in the minds of the Argentinian people. It also gave them a sense of the camaraderie it gave us in the 1960s. *(Bob Grossweiner; November 1982.)*

Eric Andersen could easily have been another one of the decade's dead folk singers. He was a drug addict for a time, and went through as many career phases and experimental periods as all the San Francisco bands put together.

In many respects, Eric Andersen was the perfect folk singer. He was born on Valentine's Day, dropped out of Hobart College, and released his first album at the height of the British Invasion. By the time he released his second album he was a sex symbol. "He is what everyone who is 18 in the Village wants to look like," *Harper's* magazine wrote, and his lyrics had a deep romantic power. The *New York Times* loved him too, and called him an antidote to the Beatles. Later the Beatles' manager would ask to become his manager. But Brian Epstein died before he could make Andersen a star.

Andersen went through a psychedelic period, a country period, a lush pop period, and a disco period. He recorded one great album, *Blue River*, that can stand with the works of contemporaries like James Taylor and Jackson Browne. For the last several years he's recorded on small labels and played the coffeehouses again. Many of his current songs have undercurrents of bitterness and irony running through the gentle poetry.

Eric Andersen: I went to San Francisco. I got a gig at the Coffee Gallery, a place that Janis Joplin was playing in, and Dino Valenti, this crazy Italian guy who wrote "Get Together." And Howard Hesseman was the bartender. He vouched for me, that I was old enough to play.

I was living on Stinson Beach. I met a roommate from college. He'd gotten thrown out of school too, and his father was living out there. He had a car and a house on the beach. So I'd either stay in San Francisco or drive in.

It was [Robert] Shelton that did everything. He took me to *Broadside.* And then he introduced me to Maynard Solomon at Vanguard Records because Jac Holzman from Elektra was out of town, and he signed me to Vanguard. It was as simple as that. Tom Paxton let me have his apartment in New York because he moved and so there I was, doing business already.

I recorded for Vanguard, and they sat on the record for a long time. And there wasn't any reason. Maybe I'd gone in and done more songs, but the bulk was there. Vanguard was a very frustrating experience because you waited and waited. They don't have to compete in the mass market in terms of sales and charts. They weren't timely in that sense; they sold in the long run. That was their philosophy.

I was walking with Phil Ochs down 14th Street, and I sang a little bit of this new song called "Thirsty Boots." And he said, "That's a great song; you've got to finish that." So I wrote a couple of verses to it and he arranged a meeting with Judy Collins. And I only had two verses, and in those days you had to have a third verse, you couldn't just have two, so I just wrote it on the subway to Judy Collins'. That's when I learned I could write really fast. And I sang it for her and she did it. It was Phil, really.

I went down to Mississippi with Jack Newfield, who's a writer for the *Village Voice.* I stayed with a guy named Steptoe, who was trying to help civil rights. Near Liberty, Mississippi. And Jack Newfield was in a car and they got shot at. I had real short hair, and I went into a drugstore, and the woman said, "Hi, can I help you? What part of New York are you from?" Everybody knew where we were from. It was pretty scary.

I was playing Steve Paul's Scene in New York, and it reminded [Brian Epstein] of the Beatles in Liverpool at the Cavern, so he arranged to meet me through Bobby Colomby, who was the drummer in the band. I had a wonderful meeting up at his house. He was very proud of the Beatles. But he never took any credit; he was a very humble guy. He never said, "I made them." He told the whole story about how they badgered him to get into it. He was running a record store, he was a frustrated actor, he'd gone to the Royal Academy.

He never signed contracts, with the Beatles or with anyone. He just said, "I'll do this, you do that." He told me, "All you have to do is just write your songs and do what you do. Don't worry about it; I'll put you in the right places."

I liked the Beatles, but I was lyrically into realism. I saw Hendrix over there and he was all in velvet. I was in blue jeans. Paul McCartney was driving me around; I was going to clubs with Lennon, and I had really no money to speak of. I felt dressed really differently.

They were all smoking on the streets. I couldn't believe it, coming from New York. I thought, "You can't get away with this." I remember Lennon yelling at the cops one morning. Of course, Brian said they were already over. He was telling me things I couldn't believe — that they didn't need him, that there was nothing there to do.

Paul was telling me he wanted to do his own albums without the Beatles. He wanted to work with Elvis Presley. I could understand what he was talking about at the time, because Elvis Presley needed him. He needed something different. That was before he did that telecast [*Elvis,* the NBC-TV special, December 1968]. Basically, he was over the hill. I was with Phil [Ochs]. I went up to see Gloria Stavers. And Phil had a sort of fascination with the pop world. She was from the South. She's dead now, I believe. She ran *16* magazine. We went up to her house and she started playing Hank Williams' "Luke The Drifter." I'd never heard it before. It blew my mind. And I started listening to Hank Williams, and I'd been listening to Otis Redding, this real soul stuff, and Gloria Stavers was turning me on to Hank Williams. I'd heard such stuff, but it was so great. "A Picture From Life's Other Side," really spiritual — besides the sound, it was old-fashioned, just great.

Blue River I did in four different cities. I did part of it for Warner Brothers, actually, and then [Warner's president] Mo Ostin said, "We're not going to let you just do this experiment. So we're going to let you take the tapes." So then I took them to [Columbia Records president] Clive [Davis]. I did "Is It Really Love At All" in San Francisco with Roy Hallee and I did some stuff in Nashville with Norbert Putnam, but as a whole, the tone had a feeling of one thing.

Blue River was a horrible period. But I had a drive, I followed my instincts and pushed. You can push in the right way and push in the wrong way, and in that case it was in the right.

Somebody asked me about Tim Buckley tonight. They didn't know he had died. And I had known him in New York. He was sort of competitive; I don't know why, but he wasn't forthcoming. Maybe, Elektra/Vanguard, New York/Boston, you know, that kind of rivalry. But he died, he fell down the stairs or shot too much junk or something. I look at all the records and I think, "What does it total?" And yet a lot of people I know are gone, they're dead. I guess, still to me, I'm the one that's been sort of elected to keep on experimenting, taking my chances. *(William Ruhlmann; Jan. 17, 1986.)*

❦

No folk artist, from the Kingston Trio on up, would have been as popular as they were if it hadn't been for Bob Dylan. And few of the groups that would follow, the Byrds and Credence Clearwater Revival and the Band, would have been as popular if not for Bob Dylan. Bob Dylan was as important a force on the American music scene as the Beatles, and as enduring. And he was an even more important force on the social scene.

Bob Dylan was a paradox: a Jewish boy from the Iron Range named Bob Zimmerman, a fraternity boy at the University of Minnestoa who occasionally played at a coffeehouse called the Ten O'Clock Scholar. He wore slacks and sweaters and white oxford sneakers and a poplin raincoat and sang Odetta's "Another Man Done Gone." In the summer of 1960, no one expected him to evolve into a social force.

But over the fall and winter of that year Dylan changed. He listened to Woody Guthrie and Ramblin' Jack Elliott, traveled out to the New Jersey sanitarium where Guthrie was confined, and absorbed the wordplay and feeling that made Guthrie great. He began playing guitar and harmonica in Guthrie's style. He even started talking like Guthrie. By 1961, when he would play his songs in New York coffeehouses, people would think they were new Woody Guthrie songs.

Zimmerman changed his name to Dylan and moved to New York. Even before his first album was released he was proclaimed as the new folk superstar; "he was adopted by Pete Seeger, befriended by Joan Baez, patronized by *Broadside* and *Sing Out!*, proselytized by Robert Shelton, and signed by Columbia Records," David DeTurk wrote. And each by itself was grounds for folk canonization.

Dylan's first album was uneven; his second, *The Freewheelin' Bob Dylan*, was a smash. He was compared to Dylan Thomas, James Dean, Woody Guthrie, Huck Finn, Holden Caulfield, and Elvis Presley, all in the same sentence. People debated endlessly whether his lyrics constituted poetry; scholars and students were polarized, but everyone listened.

Dylan was a powerhouse songwriter, and a prolific one. His songs touched nerves the way few folk songs and no other popular songs had; "Elvis protested against potential violence to his 'Blue Suede Shoes,'" De Turk wrote. "Dylan wrote 'Masters Of War' and 'With God On Our Side.' Others have assured teenagers that they *do so* have the right to be necking on the beach in between surfboard rides; Dylan wrote 'It Ain't Me, Babe,' 'Don't Think Twice, It's Alright,' 'Sad-Eyed Lady Of The Lowlands,' and 'Girl Of The North Country.'"

Dylan continued to push the outside of the musical envelope throughout the '60s. He became a teen idol by doing everything the other teen idols didn't do. Dylan was banned from *The Ed Sullivan Show* for insisting on singing "Talking John Birch Society Blues." He protested the Vietnam war and social injustice, and students followed suit. He wrote protest songs, and other popular musicians followed. He came onstage at the Newport Folk Festival in 1965 and plugged his guitar into his amp, and folk-rock was born.

Everyone wanted to record his songs. Bobby Darin and Dion did; so did Fairport Convention, Sonny and Cher, the Turtles, Frankie Valli, Johnny Cash and Jimi Hendrix; later, Rod Stewart, the Grateful Dead and George Harrison would do the same. In one month in 1965, other artists recorded 48 of his songs.

Dylan was a force on the charts as well. Nine of his albums were top fives; four of his singles cracked the top 10. "Leopard-Skin Pillbox Hat" charted, as did "Just Like A Woman," "I Want You," and "Subterranean Homesick Blues"; "Rainy Day Women #12 and 35" made the top 10, as did "Positively 4th Street," perhaps the bitterest top 10 hit ever. "Like A Rolling Stone" was a #2. For a singer who produced anti-commercial songs, Dylan was a remarkable chart artist.

And Dylan endured. After going electric and alienating many traditional folkies, Dylan got together with a group of Canadians who had been backing rockabilly singer Ronnie Hawkins. As the Band, Robbie Robertson, Levon Helm, Rick Danko, Garth Hudson, and Richard Manuel provided Dylan with the instrumental strength he needed to record a classic run of albums: *Blonde On Blonde, John Wesley Harding, Bringing It All Back Home*, and a motley, remarkable collection of outtakes that later emerged as bootlegs and as the stunning *The Basement Tapes* album.

As the '60s ended, Dylan's output lagged. A serious motorcycle accident seemed to sap some of his creativity. His albums operated off the residual power of his previous efforts. After the Band broke up, Dylan staged the elaborate Rolling Thunder Revue tour. He made bad movies, most notably *Renaldo and Clara*. In 1975, he tapped the anguish of his divorce for *Blood On The Tracks*, one of his finest records; in 1979, he said he had found religion and released the religious-oriented *Slow Train Coming* album. Subsequent albums in that vein followed, and were increasingly less successful.

Dylan's music was based on poetry and power, and when they were lacking, as they were for many of his albums in the '80s and '90s, there was no music. But even if he stopped making music today he would have left enough of a legacy to last through the whole of the rock age.

For one thing, Dylan made the Byrds possible.

BOB DYLAN: In one month in 1965, other artists recorded 48 of his songs.

The Byrds created a crossroads between folk, country and rock and then stood there, despite more personnel changes than any other major band of that time. The Byrds that recorded the seminal *Sweetheart Of The Rodeo* album bore little resemblance in fact to the group that recorded the seminal *Mr. Tambourine Man* album, even though two of the group's original members, Roger (Jim) McGuinn and Chris Hillman, were still with the band.

The Byrds, along with Peter, Paul and Mary, gave Bob Dylan his first taste of chart success. Peter, Paul and Mary had a #2 hit with "Blowin' In The Wind" in 1963; two years later, the Byrds had a #1 with "Mr. Tambourine Man," and another #1 with Pete Seeger's adaptation of the book of Ecclesiastes, "Turn! Turn! Turn!" Those were the Byrds' only two #1 hits, and their only two top 10 singles. Cher had a bigger hit with "All I Really Want To Do" than the Byrds.

The Byrds were an indifferent live band. They were a much better album band, though none of their albums ever finished in the top 25 for any given year. But despite their shortcomings, they were the most influential American band ever.

The Byrds were formed out of three folksingers, a rock drummer and a bluegrass mandolinist, all looking to take advantage of the folk boom sweeping the country in the early '60s. Jim McGuinn had played in the Chad Mitchell Trio and the Limelighters, backed up Bobby Darin through his folk period, played guitar with Judy Collins, and worked a little with a duo called Tom and Jerry before they became Simon and Garfunkel. Gene Clark was a former member of the New Christy Minstrels. Chris Hillman played Bill Monroe songs in a group called the Hillmen. David Crosby was a solo folksinger. They were recruited into a band by a Los Angeles A&R man named Jim Dickson, who wanted to recast the spirit of the Beatles in a purely American fashion.

The Byrds began rehearsing in 1964. In September they signed with Columbia, Bob Dylan's label, and in March 1965 they released "Mr. Tambourine Man," a Bob Dylan song. The Byrds cut off three verses and concentrated on the chorus, stroking it over and over again with strong harmonies and surrounding it with a powerful, bell-chime riff played on a new-sounding instrument — a 12-string Rickenbacker electric guitar. The voice and guitar were Roger McGuinn's. Though their next hit would not be by Dylan, and though Gene Clark wrote and sang many of the group's best songs, the image of Roger McGuinn playing his 12-string and singing a Bob Dylan song became the image of the Byrds.

Actually, the Byrds *were* the most prolific coverers of Bob Dylan of any rock 'n' roll band. Their *Mr. Tambourine Man* album contained two other Dylan covers, "Spanish Harlem Incident" and "Chimes Of Freedom," in addition to the title track. Their greatest-hits album contained four Dylan covers, five originals and "Turn! Turn! Turn!" After seeing the Byrds perform electric versions of his songs at the 1965 Newport Folk Festival, Bob Dylan supposedly decided to try the same thing himself, changing the course of his career forever. Even in their straight-country period the Byrds managed to cover Dylan's "Nothing Was Delivered." After the Byrds broke up, Columbia was able to assemble and release an entire Byrds album of Dylan covers; after he left the band, Roger McGuinn became a member of Bob Dylan's Rolling Thunder Revue.

Despite their purely American roots, the early Byrds looked and sounded British. They were supposed to. Their first name was the Beefeaters. The electric 12-string had already been used by John Lennon, and despite the Dylan covers the band sounded closer to the Beatles and the Hollies than they did to Peter, Paul and Mary. The suits and psychedelic logos and Roger McGuinn's granny glasses all enhanced that image. In 1965 and 1966, the Byrds were teen idols, just like Gerry and the Pacemakers or the Mindbenders.

This disparity between sound and image made the Byrds a great band; it also hastened its evolution. Michael Clarke left almost as soon as he joined. Gene Clark lasted until 1966, when the pressure of touring became too much. He formed a duo with banjo player Doug Dillard, rejoined the group for a short time in 1973, and later in the decade wound up in another group with McGuinn and Hillman. David Crosby left the group in a huff in 1968. He joined forces with two former members of the Buffalo Springfield, Neil Young and Steven Stills, and former Hollies singer Graham Nash and formed Crosby, Stills, Nash and Young, the first great second-generation folk-rock band.

McGuinn kept the Byrds together. He joined an Indonesian religion and changed his name from Jim to Roger because he was told his first name should have an 'R' in it. He considered "Rocket" but changed his mind. He recruited Gram Parsons from the short-lived International Submarine Band and bluegrass superpicker Clarence White and formed a new Byrds playing a new sort of country rock. The first album with the new aggregation, *Sweetheart Of The Rodeo*, came out in 1968 and featured covers of the Louvin Brothers, Woody Guthrie and Merle Haggard as well as Dylan.

McGuinn was nonplussed. "We hired a piano player, and he turned out to be Parsons — a monster in sheep's clothing," McGuinn told an interviewer. "And he exploded out of this sheep's clothing. God! It's George Jones! In A sequin suit! He took it right into the eye of the hurricane and *Raaaaaaooooow* — came out the other side. It was Japanese."

Parsons left the band in a tiff over a South African tour, took Chris Hillman, and formed the Flying Burrito Brothers. Parsons went solo in 1972 and released an album, *GP*, that continued the country-rock fusion and featured backup vocals by a gentle-voiced folk singer named Emmylou Harris. In 1973 he released a followup, *Grievous Angel*. The next year he was dead of a combination of alcohol and morphine. Friends stole the coffin with Parsons' body, took it to the Joshua Tree National Monument in California, and set it on fire. His ashes scattered in the high desert wind.

Roger McGuinn and David Crosby were founders of the Byrds.

Roger McGuinn: We took one of the verses [for "Mr. Tambourine Man"], and changed the melody. We used to take songs that were written in time signatures that were more folk-oriented, and put them in a more rock-oriented time signature like 4/4.

[Dylan] liked it. He came to our rehearsals before we ever recorded, and his comment was, "Wow, you can dance to it."

One of the stories is that his inspiration for playing electric at the Newport Folk Festival in 1965 was his hearing the Byrds play his songs electrically. Do you know that to be true?

He never said so. I think there were a lot of things working on him at the time. He was obviously influenced by the Beatles and the Rolling Stones, as we were. Times were changing; folk music had kind of peaked out, and people were looking at alternatives in musical styles. Rock was opening up to embrace folk music and meaningful lyrics. And he knew that because we'd had a #1 hit with one of his songs, we were definitely one of his influences. But I wouldn't say we were the only one.

I was really very impressed by the Beatles. They were doing much more than anyone knew at the time. It was more than just a glossy pop group. Pop music, up to that point, had been kind of glossy, all that Philadelphia stuff. It was kind of a greasy, superficial medium at that point. And the Beatles came along and did things that they weren't even aware of, where they were melding folk music changes into their songs, and they were putting bossa nova in there, and various other things.

I started playing that kind of music as a solo artist in the little coffeehouses and things. And then I got a job out in California doing it at the Troubadour. That's where I ran into Gene Clark, who had just come out of the New Christy Minstrels. And he wanted to get something else together. So we wrote some songs together, and David Crosby came along.

I got a letter from [Pete] Seeger, and he loved "Turn! Turn! Turn!" He said, "Dear Byrds. I liked your version of 'Turn! Turn! Turn!' very much. My only musical query was, why didn't you repeat the chorus at the end?" And the answer is, obviously, for time. We were already running three-and-a-half minutes, and that was long for a single. We only did one verse of "Mr. Tambourine Man," which is a four-verse song, and a number of other songs we shortened up.

Peter Fonda flew to New York and screened [*The Ballad Of Easy Rider*] for Bob, and Bob didn't like it. He didn't like the ending, where Fonda got shot, and Dennis Hopper got shot. He thought that they should have gotten away with it, or gotten away not getting shot. So he wouldn't formally write the song, but he scribbled, "The river flows, it flows to the sea, wherever that river goes, that's where I want to be, flow, river flow," on a paper napkin, and gave it to Peter, and said "Give this to McGuinn."

So, Peter flew back to California, and gave me the napkin, and I took it home, and wrote the song with it. And I gave Dylan the credit, and then he called me up when he saw the LP, the first batch had the credit. And he was angry about it because he didn't want his name on it. He said, "I don't need the money, and I don't want the credit, and just take it off." And so I did, but somebody's still getting the publishing on it. I'm splitting it with somebody, but I don't know who. Some fantasy character.

I was going to this thing ... this Indonesian ... I'm not sure what ... some sort of religion. It was very difficult to pin down because there was no doctrine and no verbal speech within the worship services or whatever you call them. It was all non-verbal, so I really don't know what it was. But I believed in it at the time. And they offered this optional name change, and so I sent away to Indonesia, and the guru over there sent me back the letter "R" and told me to send him 10 names that started with the letter "R." I was a science-fiction buff, and I sent him names like Rocket, and Roger was the only name in there that, coincidentally, was a name that people used.

Rockin' Rocket McGuinn. I would have loved it, but he didn't send me that one; he sent me Roger, which I was delighted with because it's a two-way radio term, and I like radios a lot. I didn't have any fear about [the change]. It didn't concern me a bit. Of course, a lot of people did think that Jim McGuinn had died or moved to Brazil or something.

We all had freedom of speech in the group. We were very democratic, and we all felt that any of us could say anything we wanted to. However, [David Crosby] did embarrass us a couple times. What he said wasn't so much the Kennedy thing because that may or may not be true. It's possible that the Warren report was a lie; that's what he said. He also said that Paul McCartney said that everybody should take acid. Then at the stage in Monterey, I didn't think was our place to go advertising LSD on stage, you know. I didn't like the idea ... although we'd all experimented with it.

"Eight Miles High" wasn't a drug song at all. It was a song about an airplane trip to England, but we did experience with drugs, so people assumed it was drug song. The only songs we wrote about drugs were anti-drug songs like "Artificial Energy."

The Byrds is a good band name, and it's certainly something I could make money with. I could probably make more money doing that than I am doing what I'm doing, but I find that would be a compromise artistically to do a thing like that. And I feel my artistic integrity is more important than making money.

I don't really want to be in the Byrds anymore, and I'm happy being a solo artist. That's the way I feel about it. *(Peter Jones; July 1, 1988.)*

David Crosby: I used to make a joke that [burglary] was how I worked my way through school. But the truth was that we did it more for the rush and the excitement than anything else. We did it a number of times. I worked out a system. It worked pretty well. I did it until one time I had to confront a woman whose house had been ransacked, and she wanted her wallet back. It had the only existing picture of her old man who had died in the war. She was in tears, and it changed it completely. Suddenly, it was not just taking stuff, but somebody's precious things. I've never stolen anything since. I wouldn't mind swiping from the government or GE or ITT because I don't like them. But that made quite an impression on me and I would never take anything now.

I've been in jail, but that was a juvenile offense and I just spent a few days inside. I've never been in prison and done any time. I got probation. It was dumb; it wasn't smart at all. But it taught me, fortunately. The other time I got popped was for having dope on my bus, Sunset, with Elliot Roberts. It was a mess. I can remember the sheriff jumping up and down, saying, "Wow, a kilo of gold!" One time down in Newport, much later, some people were smoking pot on my boat and somebody called the law, and the law called the feds so that they could go on the boat, and they all arrived and busted everybody. Then I came back. This is an interesting story because it tells you to mind your hunches, and pay attention to them. Nash and I drove down there, pulled into the parking lot and I looked around and I saw all these four-door black sedans. And I said, "It's the feds coming to bust me, Nash!" Then I thought, "Jesus, I am really getting paranoid." We got out of the car and I said, "Well, maybe I ought to leave my bag in the car; it's got a bunch of dope in it." Then I thought, "No, I'm just being crazy." So I shut the car, locked it, and went down to the boat, only to be confronted by the words, "Are you Crosby?" A big shiny .357 was pointed right in my face. And that was that. They popped us. Nash didn't have anything on him so they couldn't bust him, and he was English, so they had to let him go. But I really should have paid attention to the hunch. I knew they were there. I even said, "Feds," and that's what they were. So how's that for paying attention to your hunches? If you ever get one — listen to it. That cost me a lot of money.

When "Tambourine Man" hit, we thought we'd have a great record, but we didn't have any idea that it was going to do that. McGuinn probably said he was absolutely sure it would happen, you know — "I trust it'll work out all right" — but I wasn't; I didn't know. I was really surprised. We were driving along in a black '56 Ford station wagon that we'd bought from Odetta. All of us were in the car. We were driving along and on the radio comes KRLA playing "Mr. Tambourine Man" three times in a row. We just sat there and drooled. We went crazy. It was so good. We knew we'd won. It was a good feeling.

There was never anything called raga-rock. It didn't exist. It was something that some idiot at Columbia thought up. "Mind Gardens" had nothing to do with raga or rock. It had to do with the words. And they're good. It wasn't excessive. They're just good words. What it was was unusual and not comprehensible by everybody because they'd never heard anything like it before. Everything was supposed to have rhyme and to have rhythm. And it neither rhymed nor had rhythm, so it was outside of their experience and they weren't able to get into it. The words are good. I used an unacoustic 12-string taped backwards. I did it. It wasn't a success because of the rhythm and the rhyme. It was just a little story and what it said was very true. It said that if you build walls around your mind to keep out the abuse and harshness of life and pain, you also shut out the joy and the love. That's all it said. There's nothing wrong with that.

As for my leaving the Byrds, let's get it straight. We're talking about McGuinn and Hillman and manager Larry Spector. Spector had those guys pretty well fooled. It was a bad mistake getting him in, but I'd already figured him out. He knew this, so he did his level best to set McGuinn and Hillman against me, all the time. But mainly it was just ego on their part. They felt me getting stronger. I think they either resented it or were worried by it.

I probably did encourage people to drop acid because I thought it was a good idea. It did sort of blow us loose from the '50s. And at the time, it seemed like a great idea. I don't know if I'd recommend it now. I did say something about the Warren Report as an introduction to "He Was A Friend Of Mine." That was why I said it. It was pretty relevant, I thought.

I don't think it's true or fair to say that I sang out of tune. There was a clash on stage, but it came from me feeling that the band was not good enough. Every time the Byrds went on, it was an embarrassing thing. It was never any good. I cannot remember us ever being good. That bummed me because I wanted to be in a good band. Also, the resistance of my material was like the resistance of the Hollies to Nash's material. It was just dumb. They were territorial; they were afraid. And I kept writing better and better songs. When they threw me out I had just written "Guinevere," "Wooden Ships" and "Laughing." Now, who the hell do you think was the best writer there? They can't fight it, man. There isn't one of them can write as good as me, and you know it. And that's the truth. I'm better than they are. I'm a better writer. And they can't touch it.

They came zooming up my driveway in their Porsches and said that I was impossible to work with and I wasn't very good anyway, and they'd do better without me. It hurt like hell. I just said, "It's a shameful waste ... goodbye."

I was pissed off ... I'm still pissed off. That was dumb, man. I played, I sang, I wrote on that record and they tried to make out that I wasn't even on it, that they were that good without me. That was the main thing that they were trying to say ... that they could be that good without me. And that was bull, because I was there.

McGuinn used to do that stuff regularly. He wanted to be the boss of that band. And I don't really allow anybody to be my boss. I won't have any bosses. I have partners, but nobody is my boss, ever.

Excuse me for being angry, but it was unjust what did happen. They didn't mean to do it. They didn't consciously set out to screw me over, and they're okay guys. I don't hate them. But it hurt, and it was so frustrating that you couldn't even believe it. I was writing good stuff and I wasn't getting credit for it, and I was doing good work and I wasn't allowed to grow. And I was growing. Look what happened afterwards ... what did they do next, man? Compare them. It's over 10 years later. What's the lasting worth of what they did in comparison to what I did?

I'm a little more bitter and cynical and a lot less utopian. I'm less hopeful for mankind. Why not? Look at where we are. Look at what we're doing. We've got ourselves at the end of so many ecological, sociological, economic, military and political limbs that it's just a matter of which one breaks first. I believed in human beings trying to help each other. I believed in all that stuff. I've just seen it fail too many times. *(John Rogan; October and November 1982.)*

11. He's a Rebel

If all the rock 'n' roll world's a high school and all its people its students, then Phil Spector is the boy genius. Phil Spector is the brillant one, the mysterious guy, the borderline nerd who eventually blows up the chemistry lab, and himself in it, on the eve of his greatest discovery.

But in another way, Phil Spector is just what his name implies: a spectre, a scary presence that drifted in, made some great records, and then drifted off again. Despite the records, with their big, crude, crashing echo and their mounds of vaguely black voices and their lyrics full of kisses for someone's sweet baby, it seems most of the time as if Phil Spector never really existed. Yet Phil Spector shaped music as no other record producer has before or since.

No other producer before or since has been so much more famous than the groups he recorded or the records he made. "Be My Baby" isn't a Ronettes song; it's a *Phil Spector* song. Spector interchanged groups and singers like they were different guitars, tuned to only certain pitches. He used people like sounds, and cast them aside when the song was over. He made every convention of music bend to his way of thinking and doing things, and the miracle is they did it for a time. The reality is they could never have done it for very long.

Harvey Philip Spector was a New York boy, born in the Bronx in 1940 but raised in Los Angeles by his mother. He got a guitar for his Bar Mitzvah and listened to every black-music station and R&B record he could get his hands on. He admired Leiber and Stoller, and tried to write songs feeling the way they felt and hearing things the way they did.

When he was 17, Spector formed the Sleepwalkers, with future Beach Boy Bruce Johnston and drummer Sammy (Sandy) Nelson. When that group broke up, Spector formed the Teddy Bears with his friends Marshall Leib and Harvey Goldstein. Goldstein dropped out, and was replaced by a friend of Spector's girlfriend, Annette Kleinbard. As the Teddy Bears, they recorded Spector's first big hit, a light, gorgeous song called "To Know Him Is To Love Him."

Annette Kleinbard is now known as Carol Connors — the writer, along with Bill Conti and Ann Robbins, of the *Rocky* movie theme. She has been nominated for two Oscars, four Emmys and a Grammy.

Carol Connors (Annette Kleinbard): The Teddy Bears came about because my girlfriend was dating Phil Spector. Her name was Donna, and we were in junior high school. I used to sing all the time — in the halls, wherever. He [Spector] asked me one day if I had $10, and I said, "No, I don't have $10, but I think my parents have $10." I got the $10 from my mom and dad, and we went in and we cut the flip to "To Know Him Is To Love Him," called "Don't You Worry My Little Pet," the most dreadful record in the history of records.

But what happened was that my voice kept shining through, because I was the girl. It was Phil Spector, Marshall Leib and myself, and Phil said to me one day, "I want to write a song for your voice." He fell in love with my voice. His father's epitaph said, "To have known him was to have loved him" and that became "To Know Him *Is* To Love Him," and that's how that song was born.

I was still in junior high school, Louis Pasteur Junior High School, and they were in Fairfax High School. We recorded it at Gold Star, with Stan Ross, the engineer. We did it in 20 minutes, two takes. Sandy Nelson played drums. It was the first [studio] thing he ever did in his life. One of the DJs once said to me, "Well, who were you thinking of?" And I said, "My father," because I was too young to have a boyfriend.

It literally did not sell one record at first, but it was the most requested record in Southern California, because every junior high school and high school was calling to request it. A disc jockey named Lou Reigert in Minneapolis, KDWB, flipped it over one night. He just happened to put it on, and he fell in love with my voice; he's told me this. And he played it and the lines lit up, and Dore Records got an order for 100, 300, 1,000, 3,000, 10,000, 20,000, within like two to three weeks. And we said, "My God! We've got a #1 record. Get to Dick Clark!" We performed it on Dick Clark's *American Bandstand* as the #1 record in the country, and the rest is history. It sold millions and millions of records.

Phil was one of the singers. He did the "Voh, doh, doh, doh's." That is Phil and Marshall, and I did it in two takes. One take for balance, one take on tape. That was it, and we rushed out of the studio. This was like a high-school get-together type of group. I was interested in music before this, but this was obviously the first thing any of us had ever done in our lives.

Then I had a terrible accident. When I had enough money to buy a car — even though we got ripped off for a lot of the money — I went off a 350-foot cliff, and it really ended the group. I had bought an MG, and I went off a cliff. I lost control of the car. Twenty-six stitches to put my nose back on my face. I was pretty much of a mess. But in the long run, everything has turned out okay. I'm very grateful. *(Michael Aldred; June 17, 1988.)*

After Spector graduated from high school and went into the music business full-time, he drifted to Phoenix, where producer Lee Hazlewood was in the middle of a string of hits featuring Duane Eddy, the king of the deep-stringed, echoey "twangy" guitar. Hazlewood was also a partner with a veteran record man named Lester Sill. Sill had worked with Modern Records and was associated with Leiber and Stoller. As a manager, a publisher, a promotion man and sometimes a producer, Sill had contacts on both coasts. Spector met Sill in L.A., and after the Teddy Bears' follow-up records on Dore and Imperial flopped, Spector hooked up with Sill.

Lester Sill: I had seen Phil in a studio on Fairfax Avenue, when he was recording the Teddy Bears. I knew the record would be a hit, even though I didn't have the time to really stay and listen. I was there mastering some Duane Eddy records. Anyway, Phil was in there working with the Teddy Bears, and I asked the fellow, Bunny Robine, who ran the studio, who he was, and he said, "He's fantastic!" And I said, "Gee, I love the record"; sure enough, it came out, and it was a hit.

I was on Argyle at the time. Some time went by, and I guess Phil got unhappy with the record company, and he came up to see me because he knew I worked with Leiber and Stoller years before. And we signed him to our company as a writer and as a record producer. That's how it happened. I can't give you a year, because shortly after that, Phil traveled with us to Phoenix when we were producing Duane.

Phil came along with us a number of times, and he also produced a couple of things for us; somebody by the name of Kell Osborne, and some other acts. He did the Paris Sisters for us. He did "I Love How You Love Me," which wasn't even a song and we had a hit with it, and then he did "Be My Boy," which was a hit, and we owned it. And then Lee and I parted ways, and I went with Phil and we started Philles Records. That's basically what it is.

Phil and I had some misunderstandings about certain people. I set Phil up in New York with Leiber and Stoller and Atlantic Records. After that, him and I just parted ways, and I sold my interest to him.

I felt that he [Spector] was a monster. He was a fantastic piece of talent. It's a shame that he's so neurotic. *(Michael Aldred; June 17, 1988.)*

❧

At Liberty, Spector heard the demo of a Gene Pitney song intended for Vicki Carr and loved it. He snatched the song from Liberty, said he was going on a European vacation, and flew back to Los Angeles to record it. But before he did, he bought out his partners in Philles Records, and decided to make the lead singer on the record someone who wasn't even in the Crystals at all: Darlene Love, then with the Blossoms.

Darlene Love: My father was a minister, and I used to sing all the time in the church choir. That's my favorite type of music, gospel music. I started working with girl groups professionally when I was 16. By professionally, I mean actually getting paid, not just gas money. You know, you'd be singing, running around town when you are younger and they'd say, "We'll give you gas money to come to record hops and whatnot." But at 16 I started recording with a group called the Blossoms in Los Angeles. We were recording at Capitol Records at the time, and our first background session turned out to be a date with James Darren, the actor. And so I actually started as a background singer.

Then that led to commercials, TV shows, those kind of things. Then people started asking us to go out on the road with them, because the Blossoms really had a tight, dynamite show. So they not only hired us for background, they hired us to open their shows also.

The singer I listened to most back then — and I tell people this all the time and they find it very strange — but it was Marian Anderson. I guess you'd call her a folk-gospel singer. I never met the lady, but I always admired her, and I came up, like, on her kind of music. Music was never banned in our house. Rock 'n' roll music was never banned, even though my father was a minister. We'd listen to Sam Cooke, and Nat Cole and those kind of people. We didn't have that hollerin'-and-screamin' rock 'n' roll, but rock 'n' roll wasn't banned in our house, so I got the chance to listen to all those rock 'n' roll singers.

The Blossoms started in high school. When I was in the 12th grade, I met them. They had been singing under the name of the Dreamers in Los Angeles, with a guy named Richard Berry. When I auditioned for the group, they were recording for Capitol already as the Blossoms, and they needed a lead singer.

It was four girls at the time. It was twins, Annette and Nanette, Fanita James and myself. But off and on the group changed around. If one member got sick and we needed a replacement or something, Grazia Nitzsche sang with us. She was Jack Nitzsche's wife, the arranger for all of Phil's things. Grazia was with us until we got *Shindig.* Then they wanted three black girls. They didn't want the group to be mixed, so we found Jean King. We continued to do sessions with Grazia Nitzsche, but Jean King became a full-fledged member of the Blossoms.

I knew Phil Spector's partner before I knew Phil. We had been doing a lot of background work for Lester Sill, and he knew I could sing. He didn't know I could do leads, but a lot of times we would do sessions and I would do what they call tag endings, where you'd do fadeouts and a lot of riffing on the ends of records. So Lester told me he wanted me to meet his partner Phil Spector, and he took me to meet him, and he had this song. I mean right away; I didn't rehearse any other song. He just had this song, "He's A Rebel," and asked me if I would be interested in recording it. I told him if he paid me triple scale, I would do it. So I got paid triple scale for going in one day at Gold Star and doing "He's A Rebel." Scale was $22.50 an hour, so I got about a hundred and something dollars an hour, so I made about $400-$500 for that session. I have to laugh at those things now. I was just 19 years old.

I knew "He's A Rebel" was going to be released under the name of the Crystals. We

158

had been doing things like this for years, under other group's names. This time it just made a difference, since this record became an overnight hit — and I mean almost overnight. It was a No. 1 record, which was a shock to me.

It really kind of launched his career. He really had the group, the Crystals, and they had had little success, but this was their first success, and it was weird because they couldn't really enjoy the success of it because they really didn't do it. They did enjoy it, but not really, because they knew deep down inside who actually did the record. They were in no way involved with that record at all. It was the Blossoms, myself and some more studio singers like Sonny Bono and Cher.

Once I got that record, other people tried to get me to do records like that for them. I didn't have as much success with other producers, but they were paying me a fortune to do the leads. You know, I could go in and say I wanted $3,000, and get it. That's probably the reason I never held a grudge against Phil Spector, because once they found out that I did that record and it was such a monstrous hit, I started doing those kinds of things for a lot of producers, and I never signed contracts with them, which gave me a whole lot of leeway. I would go in and ask for unbelieveable prices, and the records were never hits. Maybe they were mild hits, like Top 50 or 60, but I was enjoying getting all that money.

I recorded "Da Doo Ron Ron," and it was supposed to go out under my name. By then, I had signed with Phil and then he decided he didn't want me to sing it, because, I guess, he knew it was going to be a hit and he didn't want to pay anybody. So he flew in LaLa Brooks and she put her voice on top of what I had already done.

Nobody ever sees Phil. He could probably walk in here, and the only people who probably know him would be me and maybe Ellie [Greenwich]. But I know him so well, I know his physique, and I been around him when he tried to wear disguises. And if you know Phil, then you know it's the mystique about him, all the talk about him.

To be involved with Phil Spector is like ... I mean, we didn't know at the time that this was going to be great, so to be involved with him was like looney tunes. Here we are, 20 years later, still doing these songs, and they are great songs. He was before his time. You know, people used to talk about his music, and how he was the first person to ever decide to produce a record that was three minutes long — "You've Lost That Lovin' Feelin'." They told him they'd never play that record on the air; it was too long. But he said, "They'll play it," and they played it. And you know, he was the first person ever to do a rock 'n' roll Christmas album. He was the first doing all these things, and I think the Christmas record would have been much bigger than it was had it not been for the John Kennedy death and all the stuff that was going on at the time.

I don't have any bad feelings about Phil, because even though I wasn't getting paid the right amount of money that I should have gotten paid from him, I still had a lot of success, other things, because of my involvement with him. You know, on TV shows and because of Phil's mystique, they will always ask me about him because they knew I was involved with him. So I have no kind of grudges.

Some of the songs he put out were half-finished products. My voices were on it, but the background wasn't on yet and it wasn't completely finished when he just put it out. He knew he wasn't going to get back in the studio to finish them, so he just put them out the way there were. I was shocked, as a matter of fact, when I heard it. I hated it.

We did everybody's background. The Ronettes didn't do their background; Ronnie did the lead. Everything that came out of Phil Spector and Philles Records had us on it. We didn't have time to do our other sessions because we had so much work with Phil, and he paid us great. We'd ask for the money and he paid us.

Now see, "River Deep, Mountain High," I wanted that record and Phil wouldn't give it to me and he never gave me a reason. It was like, "No no, er, okay" ... and then I'd turn around and he had recorded it with Ike and Tina Turner — the only one record I really wanted to do.

Phil never recorded me after that, never recorded me, and the Righteous Brothers had started to come in very successful with "Lovin' Feelin' " and they used to bug him all the time. "Why don't you record this woman?" That's when he did "Stumble And Fall" and "Quiet Guy" and he pulled it back; whatever his reasons were, we didn't know.

There are so many people that enjoy my talent that I'm not aware of, and it's because of Phil. I didn't know Bette Midler was a Darlene Love fan, or Bruce Springsteen, and then I did a show in Los Angeles and they were all there, and I was more shocked than they were. I said, "What are you doing here? You mean you actually know me?" It's the same thing with people in Europe. They know me but I don't know them, but they're dying for me to come over there because I'm more of a mystique over there than Phil is, because the Crystals and the Ronettes went to work there but never Darlene Love.

It was really weird. I always had said, "Oh God, if I could ever get to work with Elvis or Tom Jones, the Beatles or the Rolling Stones." I've worked with the Rolling Stones because of the T.A.M.I. show but I never got the chance to really meet the Beatles. I met John, when he was at one of Phil's sessions when we were doing "Lord, If You're A Woman," but not the other Beatles. Oh, I met Ringo when I was working with Dionne. We went to Paris and Ringo came to the show. But actually the original group, the Beatles, I never got to meet them.

The songs today, the way that I sing them, are grown-up songs. There are not like I sang them on the records. When I sing them in person, it's a whole new attitude, and people enjoy listening to them the way I perform them now. It does have nothing to do with the teenage records; the way I do them now, everybody enjoys them. My audience is, my God, from 8 to 80, and you know, they actually enjoy it. *(Dennis Garvey and Edward Hawkins; April 12, 1985.)*

After "He's A Rebel," the hits started coming fast for Phil Spector and his groups. There was "Zip-A-Dee-Doo-Dah," featuring Sheen and Love as Bobb B. Soxx and the Blue Jeans; "He's Sure The Boy I Love," with the Crystals again; "(Today I Met) The Boy I'm Gonna Marry," with Darlene Love singing solo; and, best of all, "Da Doo Ron Ron," by the Crystals.

"Da Doo Ron Ron" is so simple and innocent, but so relentless. It seems to be powered by 10 different instruments all at once — a piano up high and a kick drum down low, saxophones and a big thumping bass.

Lala Brooks sang lead on the song.

Lala Brooks: I was on "Da Doo Ron Ron" and "Then He Kissed Me" and that's about all. Oh yeah, I was on "Little Boy" and "All Grown Up," too. I think Phil withdrew them. He was always doing that. One minute the record was released and then it wasn't.

It was crazy. We were on the road, and we didn't know if we were supposed to sing the songs or not. I think we did anyway; I know we did "Da Doo Ron Ron," and "Then He Kissed Me" and the other hits, like "He's A Rebel," and "Uptown." We'd have to sing those songs five times a day sometimes. Can you imagine singing, "Met him on a Monday and my heart stood still, da doo ron ron ron, da do ron ron," five times a day? I got sick of it in the end. I felt "Da doo ron ronned" to death.

Darlene and I did most of the tracks. Some of the girls only did the first ones, like "There's No Other (Like My Baby)" and "Uptown." After that, Phil took me to California when he knew I could sing. All of us were on "There's No Other (Like My Baby)" and "Uptown," because we did it in New York. But then Phil moved to California. After that was recorded, he didn't take everyone to California.

When I did my tape, Darlene would come along and do the background with other people. Cher would do the background. She would just sit there waiting to do backgrounds. It's true! I remember when I got off the plane one time. Sonny was a valet for Phil, and she had to go look for an apartment and she didn't have enough money to pay for the apartment. I think the apartment was like $300 a month, and she and Sonny didn't have a place to stay, so she and I went to look for an apartment. It was too much money in California, because she couldn't afford it, and then I went to her house, and she was living in this flat that was really cheap.

She was always dying to be on Phil's backgrounds. She used to sit in that studio for hours, waiting to get a chance to sing. I'll never forget it, and then as soon as we put the lead on, she would ask Phil if she could go in there and sing with Darlene and them, and he'd say, "Go ahead! Go ahead!" But she always waited for that opportunity, because she would be sitting on the side all day. They'd pick me up, maybe, 11 or 12 in the morning, and we wouldn't finish until at least maybe 8:30 at night. Sometimes the tracks weren't done. The men would do them first, and then when they finished the track, we would go in there after, and we'd be sitting around looking at them.

Phil was always nice to get along with, and I think my first gift from him was a poodle. He took me in his limousine, and he gave me a poodle, a grey poodle, and I was so happy for it. And he gave us luggage, whatever. But he never paid us royalties. Yeah, the royalty was my poodle and my luggage that I could put him in and travel with. DeeDee Kennibrew and him didn't hit it off, plus he was just weird. He liked everything in the dark, and he always turned off all the lights. He was very health-oriented. He could treat people kind of raw, though. Sometimes people would come in and say, "Phil, can I listen a minute?" and he would say, "Get out of here, goddammit!" When he was busy working, he'd sometimes tell people, "Shut this door and don't come back!"

The only reason I didn't do "He's A Rebel" was because at that time Barbara was the lead singer, and Phil didn't know that I could sing. I came in last, and when I popped up, I was the youngest. I sang background on "There's No Other (Like My Baby)," but what happened was when we performed on stage, Barbara got hoarse and I sang "There's No Other." I could sing so well, I started singing all the leads, but Phil Spector wasn't aware of it, because Barbara was always the lead singer. So he knew that when he got this record from Gene Pitney, "He's A Rebel," that Barbara's voice was too light to sing it. I was too new in the group to be recognized, and Darlene *was* recognized because she had been doing record dates with him, and so he recorded Darlene on "He's A Rebel." I could do it as well, but Phil didn't know it.

We were getting frustrated. Mary and Pat just dropped off because of Phil Spector, because we weren't getting paid. We weren't really making that much money. I mean, we were making nothing from the record company, and then when we started working with the tours — James Brown, Diana Ross and all of them — we were making $75 a week, each of us. That's all we made. And my money was supposed to be in a trust fund until I was 18. When I got to be 18, there was nothing there. The lawyers had been taking it, so I ended up with nothing. *(Michael Aldred; June 17, 1988.)*

By 1965 the Crystals and Darlene Love were no longer on Philles. Spector no longer needed their voices. In their places were the buttersmooth voices of two Californians, Bill Medley and Bobby Hatfield — the Righteous Brothers. They were white but sounded black; Hatfield's tenor overlaid Medley's deep baritone like nothing this side of Sam and Dave, and their unique vocal style fit perfectly with a Mann-Weil song, "You've Lost That Lovin' Feelin'." Spector took the song and the style and the Righteous Brothers to No. 1, and never made a better record. In fact, it might have been the finest hour of any record producer. Nothing soars and keeps soaring and *sounds* like "Lovin' Feelin'," even today.

Bill Medley: We were both raised in Southern California, Orange County. We both had small groups and had heard of each other, so we started going in and listening to each other sing. Then a mutual friend of ours took Bobby's drummer and Bobby from his group and myself and my guitar player from my group and formed a five-piece group called the Paramours. Bobby and I started singing a lot in that group, and some black guys used to come in and call Bobby and I "The Righteous Brothers" of the five guys. So when they kicked us out of the Paramours, Bobby and I said, "Well, let's go be the Righteous Brothers," and that's how it started.

Bobby Hatfield: We first met Phil at the San Francisco Cow Palace in a big, big show with the Supremes and Stevie Wonder and so many other acts, and he was up there conducting the orchestra. He had the Ronettes in the show. He was kind of aware of us through Moonglow Records, and somehow his lawyer started talking to Ray Maxwell and he ended up leasing our contract from Ray, who was Moonglow Records. And then we started getting telegrams from Moonglow Records; this was after "Lovin' Feelin'" and "Just Once In My Life" and "Ebb Tide" and some of those songs, saying that we could no longer record for Phil. And Phil would send us telegrams telling us, "Everything's cool, come on in and record," and all we wanted to do was sing. We didn't want to get involved in all this legal stuff and the disputes. It was a drag. Anyhow, MGM Records came in and bought the whole works, as Bill just mentioned, but our contract paid Phil Spector a whole lot of money and paid Ray Maxwell a whole lot of money. But at least we didn't have to go spend any more time in litigation.

Bill Medley: Working with Phil Spector was terrific. I guess Phil has a pretty famous reputation as being "out there," and he was terrific. He was terrific to us, he was a friend of ours and he was great in the studio. It got a little difficult every now and again because he was such a legendary producer that all the other producers wanted to come to the studio while he was recording. He had an ego just like everybody else, so he would let them come while he was putting the vocals on, and sometimes it would get a little carried away. It was basically Phil's time to show off. So there were a couple of times where we had to say, "Hey, you know, let's get down to this and get it over with." But he was great to work with.

Bobby Hatfield: I don't know how many takes we did of "Lovin' Feelin'," but it wasn't bad. I think we probably did more on some of those Ray Maxwell things, but mainly that's because we used to get the giggles in the recording studio and blow a good five or six hours in there just laughing at each other. And I mean, we would go out in the hall and take a walk and come back in and try to sing it, and we would just have to say, "Uh, we better pass on it today because we ain't going to get anything done." But he wasn't too demanding of us as far as doing that many takes.

Bill Medley: The single on "Lovin' Feelin' " is listed as being 3:05, but the song is over 3:50. Phil discussed that with us. He said, "We're going to have to do something, man." I know he chopped at least a minute off of it. He just threw it off there, 'cause I think Marty Robbins was the only one who ever attempted anything like a four-minute record. For some reason, it didn't seem to bother him too much, but it worried the heck out of us. We knew, from "Little Latin Lupe Lu." We kept those suckers right at about two minutes 20. I mean, you tried not to fluctuate. But, yeah, we were concerned about what he was going to have to splice out of there to get this sucker played. But he just changed the time on the thing, he didn't take anything out.

Bobby Hatfield: No, Not a second. Not one second.

Bill Medley: As a matter of fact, isn't there a fake ending there?

Bobby Hatfield: Yeah, left that in; left it all in.

Bill Medley: I mean, he could care less. I can remember some people, some of the distributors, and this is the truth, calling Phil Spector saying, "I got the record, I'm sure it's a good record, but there's something wrong with the speed. It's on the wrong speed." They thought my part should have been sung faster. They literally thought that the sucker had been slowed down. They timed it and it was "Bome, bome, bome" instead of "Bome, bo-bome," so that was a funny, funny record. I meant he went against every principle at the time, and it was the right thing to do. *(Len Scher; May 11, 1984.)*

Phil Spector lived to be in the studio. The studio was the one place in his life where he had the control; he pushed the buttons and slid the levers, and things happened just the way they did in his head. No one ever studied what worked in the studio harder than Phil Spector, and no one got together musicians and technicians and made them work quite the way Phil Spector did.

The two key people in making Spector's music were engineer Larry Levine and arranger Jack Nitzsche.

Jack Nitzsche: I had heard about Phil for a long time. In 1962, I used to hang out at Lester Sill's on Sunset Boulevard, when Lester and Lee Hazelwood were partners. I met Lee, and he had just split up with Lester. Lee asked me to come with him and help make and arrange records. I got space in an office; we had a deal that if the records were to sell I would have a small piece.

They didn't sell. Lester was still on the floor above my office; Lee had one downstairs. It was the same office where I had met Little Richard. One day, Lester came downstairs and said that

Phil Spector was in town and needed an arranger. I went upstairs and met Phil. He played me the demo for "He's A Rebel." We went to a rehearsal with the Blossoms; I introduced Phil to the Blossoms. I had been working with them for years.

I didn't have to do the lead sheet for "He's A Rebel," just the arrangement. I put the band together for the session, a lot of the same guys I had been working with for years. Phil didn't know a lot of these people; he had been in New York in 1960-1962. Leon Russell, Harold Battiste, Earl Palmer, Don Randi, Hal Blaine, Glen Campbell: a lot of the players came out of my phone book. Phil knew Barney Kessel. At one time he had taken guitar lessons from Barney, years before.

Phil was different than the A&R men and the record-company people I had been working with. In those days, A&R men would hire me to do an arrangement or arrange for a three-hour session, and no matter what, we had to get it done before the three hours were over. Phil Spector was the first one to go into the studio with one song, and if it needed two sessions to do the rhythm section, that's the way it happened.

My fee was $50 a song. I don't feel any bitterness about the money and payment whatsoever. The credits helped secure employment for years. Phil knew what he wanted. He put my name on many of the singles as arranger. I loved it. What an education! Phil understood the teenage record market. He could relate to their feelings and buying impulses. He was a kid. He would call me up at 4 a.m. and want to go out for ice cream. Phil's great.

Phil cared about people: Lenny Bruce, the outlaws. I met the songwriters; I heard the tunes in advance that we were gonna cut. Sometimes Phil played them for me at the piano, or I would hear the demos. There were a lot of visits to his house, and he would come over my house to work on the songs. In the beginning, he stayed in hotels and came to my house. We became friends real fast. We had a lot of laughs together. I always liked the tunes he played. Everything he played always sounded like a hit.

The "Wall of Sound" happened over a period of time. I don't know who coined the term. The sound just got bigger and bigger. One time we cut the Crystals' "Little Girl." Sonny Bono was the percussionist on the date. Always. He came into the booth and said it had more echo than usual, and wouldn't get played on the radio. The echo was turned way up high. Phil said, "What's too much echo? What does that mean?" Phil was smart enough to say, "Wait a minute; listen to this." If you notice, there's more echo on each song we cut. It really hadn't been done like this before. People on the business side, the promotional side of the record industry, felt it was different. He didn't listen to them.

The musicians played at once. Before that, I was working with compact rhythm sections and three or four players. This was groundbreaking for me. "Zip-A-Dee-Doo-Dah" and "He's A Rebel" sounded like great records. They had magic. There's a great Billy Strange guitar solo in "Zip-A-Dee-Doo-Dah." It was gonna be a horn instrumental. Phil said to me, "Just do something like 'I Know' by Barbara George," and I wrote a horn instrumental break. Half of it he kept; the other half was made into the Billy Strange guitar part. Phil said to Billy, "Just play a solo," and Phil pretty much told him how to play it.

I had met Don Randi, one of the piano players, a long time ago. He was a pianist at a jazz club on La Cienega. He was cool. He looked like a beatnik. His hair was right. He had the attitude. He didn't smile when he played.

Hal Blaine. I liked his work, but sometimes felt he overplayed. That's just the way he plays. A lot of fills. As it turned out, Phil and the people loved the breaks Hal took, especially at the end of the tunes, the fades. Hal had a big kit. I liked the fills.

Earl Palmer was the other drummer on the records. He's the best. Like a rock. A real good New Orleans drummer. Harold Battiste, Mac Rebennack. New Orleans guys were on the dates, so you had a good mixture of jazz guys, West Coast studio cats and New Orleans players.

Leon Russell. I met him with Jackie DeShannon; she introduced me. Leon, at the time, was playing piano at a bar in Covina. He was an innovative piano player. He was good. I heard him on a Jackie DeShannon record. In those days it was real hard to find rock 'n' roll piano players who didn't play too much. Leon talked the same language. You could really hear Leon play in the *Shindig* band. I put him in *The TAMI Show* in the band, and he's all over the soundtrack.

163

During the Spector sessions, a lot of the time we had two and three piano players going at once. I played piano as well. Phil knew the way he wanted the keyboards played. It wasn't much of a problem who played. Leon was there for the solos and the fancy stuff, rolling pianos. The pianos would interlock and things would sound cohesive. I knew Leon would emerge as a band leader.

I knew all the horn players. Steve Douglas on tenor, Jay Migliori on baritone, other horn players as well. I had met Steve through Lester Sill. We were friends for a long time. Phil had an idea about horns. It started on "He's A Rebel." Remember the horns on "Duke Of Earl"? Phil wanted something like that. The horns always had to figure out this thing. The thing that came out of it was the voicing. The trumpet was voiced real low, and the voicing of those horns made a big thing happen. The horn section would play quiet behind the rhythm section. Phil sure knew what he wanted. He had all the bases covered.

Percussion. Well, Sonny Bono. I love Sonny. He helped me get in the business. Julius Wechter, later of the Baja Marimba Band, was on a lot of the dates. Frank Kapp was on a lot of the sessions. He was a jazz drummer who used to play at Sardi's with Stan Kenton. I played percussion, chimes, orchestra bells. They weren't mixed way in the back. Phil would dream these percussion parts up at the session. They were his ideas. There were no formulas.

Guitarists. A lot of the guitarists were jazz players and weren't rock 'n' roll players, like Howard Roberts, Joe Pass, Herb Ellis, Tommy Tedesco, Barney Kessel. Dennis Budimir. A lot of the guitarists were very good and well-known session players: Carol Kaye, Glen Campbell, Bill Pitman. Most of the guitarists had to play eighth notes on Phil's records. There was a lot of acoustic guitar on the songs. Phil used to walk around to the guitar players just before we rolled the tape and would whisper in their ears, "Dumb. Don't do anything. Just play eighth notes." It was hard for any of the guitarists to breathe or stretch out on the records.

Bass players. Jimmy Bond and Red Callender were on most of the dates. Ray Pohlman and Ray Brown as well. The bass parts were written out and the players had to stick right with them. They were mixed low in the back, almost a suggestive element to the song. No one really had a lot of room with those sessions. Really, only the drummer had any sort of freedom. They weren't R&B records.

Vocalists. It would last all night. Background groups doubling and tripling so it would sound like two or three dozen voices. Phil would spend a lot of the time with the singers. I would split and he'd still be working on lines with the singers. The rhythm section and horns were done together. Vocals and string parts were overdubbed later.

We did most of the sessions at Gold Star Studios in Hollywood. I loved the rooms, but it was always too small for all the people. Larry Levine and Stan Ross were good engineers. Larry would never question anything that Phil wanted to try to do. There were four echo chambers, and I remember Stan Ross, who was also a co-owner, telling us many times that the echo chambers were acoustically and geometrically designed to get the right amount of balance and reverb. That added to the impact of Phil's recordings. I loved the echo. It's like garlic.

And — I didn't realize it at the time — Phil was doing business, even when he was producing a session. There were people at the sessions. Not hanging out; a lot of kids and people who ended up in the record business were monitoring the sessions. They learned a lot from Phil.

What was really unique was that Phil owned most or all of the record. That was different. I think Phil really knew what was going on in the record business. He made use of distributors and publishers. He understood the music and the heritage, as well as the people before him who were great producers.

Phil was tenacious. He sure learned a lot in New York. Leiber and Stoller must have been good for him. Phil carried the torch for rock 'n' roll. His attitude upset the industry. Phil plugged into the youth. He knew a lot. He had social feelings. He was good on TV sometimes. On TV, Phil had a way to always bring up the idea that he had more money and that was power, which it probably was. Phil antagonized some people. He had 13 hits in a row without a miss. Around "River Deep, Mountain High," people started to want him to fail. That's [how it is] with sports and everything. You get too good and people don't like it, too succesful and people don't like it. There was no competition for Phil in those days.

"Be My Baby." Ronnie Spector's voice. Wow! I was amazed at her vibrato. It got bigger with each record. That was her strong point. When that tune was finished, the speakers were turned up so high in the booth that people had to leave the room. It was loud. Ronnie also delivered onstage. She's still good. I loved her.

The Righteous Brothers. Early on, Jackie DeShannon and I wrote a song for them during their Moonglow Records period. Sonny Bono also wrote for them, "Ko Ko Joe." I did a session with them. I didn't arrange "Lovin' Feelin'" 'cause I was working as musical director for *The TAMI Show*. Gene Page did it. The Righteous Brothers could sing. Bill Medley had energy. He could sing. Looking back, they were good, but not great. They were the first white guys around L.A. that sounded black. They tried hard, and with Phil, had great, powerful songs to work with.

"Then He Kissed Me" was my favorite Crystals record. Listen to the percussion! Castanets and all. We had some room to experiment and make the records sound different. Phil would go into the percussion kit and say, "This song needs castanets."

I arranged the Christmas album. I'm glad it's been reissued. What a great Christmas album! I thought it was a great idea at the time to do a rock 'n' roll Christmas album. He mentioned it to me and we went right into it. Six, eight months of recording. Once again, Phil knew how he wanted the thing to sound. He always had a lot of lines. It turned out a certain way 'cause I was the arranger, but Phil was the captain. We had a lot of fun; we hung out a lot. Sonny Bono on percussion blocks. Darlene Love singing "Christmas (Baby Please Come Home)" blew my mind. I got chills. Powerful. She could always sing. Sonny always made everyone laugh. He was doing comic things then. It stands up.

The album never really took off. I think some of that had to do with the world after the Kennedy assassination. It affected the public. No one really wanted to celebrate Christmas in December 1963. *(Harvey Robert Kubernik; June 17, 1988.)*

In every Phil Spector song there's a climax sometime before the record ends, one amazing point where all that sound comes to a peak and then starts tapering and fading off. In Spector's own career, that peak came with "River Deep, Mountain High."

"River Deep, Mountain High" is still a tough record to listen to today. It sounds great, but at the same time it sounds like too much is going on. Tina Turner's voice soars too much; the wall gets a little too high and deep.

In other words, "River Deep, Mountain High" sounds like the musical milestone it is. It just doesn't sound like a hit.

Rodney Bingenheimer, now a Pasadena disc jockey, was at the recording sessions for "River Deep."

Rodney Bingenheimer: I had seen some of the Rolling Stones earlier in the day at the Hollywood Ranch Market with Jack Nitzsche and Denny Bruce, who was the drummer of the Mothers Of Invention. I was in Hollywood and went to Wallach's Music City on the Sunset Strip. I was listening to records in one of their booths and ran into Brian Wilson, who was also in the store. I told Brian that Phil was doing a session at Gold Star down the street. He said, "Let's go!" We jumped in his car and walked in. The first person I saw was Mick Jagger. He was wearing a mink fur coat. Mick kept leaving the booth to use the telephone and call a girl. I took pictures with my Brownie Instamatic camera. Mick said I should save some film and take a photo of the girl.

Brian and I never left the studio booth during the recording of "River Deep, Mountain High." You don't leave when you're at something like this. Jack and Phil were very tight. They were like co-pilots of the Concorde from a flight from France. Dennis Hopper showed up a few times. He later took the cover photo for the *River Deep, Mountain High* album that came out much later. Phil was screaming like a madman during the sessions. Tina was loud and sexy. She was wearing a wig and go-go boots. Very '60s. Phil was in control.

Brian didn't say a word. He soaked it in and sat there stunned. Tina's vocal kept on soaring. Some of the musicians were wearing alpaca sweaters. Phil and Jack dressed like kids. They wore

165

clothes from DeVoss and Sy Devore, where the Beatles shopped. Dark glasses and puffed-sleeve shirts, boots. They didn't look like record-company people. They were listening to the song as it was played over and over. Jack was cool. He liked rock 'n' roll, and any type of black music. I talked to him once before that at the taping of *The TNT Show*. He came with Denny Bruce to see Bo Diddley and talk to the Modern Folk Quartet.

After the sessions I walked home and couldn't sleep. I kept hearing the song over and over. Later, I could never hear it on local radio like all the other Phil Spector songs. I heard it a few times on KRLA when Johnny Hayes was the DJ. I wanted to hear it on KHJ, but it never happened. Something weird happened when the record was released. KRLA got to play it first, or had an exclusive copy, one of those things, and I don't think it went over well with the people who operated the RKO radio chain. Thirty million listeners. Radio consultants operated the chain of stations all over the U.S. I even had to buy "River Deep" as an import at a record shop on Hollywood Boulevard called Lewins.

Jack Nitzsche: On "River Deep, Mountain High," I went over to Phil's house and went over the arrangement note by note. Phil said, "I've got a song for Tina." I knew who she was. I had seen them (Ike and Tina) perform at the California Club. When he played me "River Deep, Mountain High" on the piano I knew it was a great song. We did the rhythm track in two different three-hour sessions.

It was amazing to watch "River Deep" grow. Even during the cutting of the track, when she was putting on a scratch Tina was singing along as we cut it and was so into it she was holding her crotch on the high notes. Oh, man, she was great, doing a rough, scratch vocal as the vocal as the musicians really kicked the rhythm section in the ass. Once in a while a vocalist would run through a song, but this time Tina made everybody play better.

I thought the song was unique, a little different. When I first heard the intro I didn't like it much, but once it was being recorded it all made sense. It was real good. Phil was a co-writer on the song. Phil embellished the song and was the producer. I've talked to Gerry Goffin about that a lot: Phil co-writing songs that he would produce. Phil would always have the writers come over and write in the room with him, and I knew he directed it. They all say the same thing, that without Phil Spector in the room that song wouldn't have been that way. He helped. He knew what he wanted it to be. I know Phil Spector helped write "River Deep, Mountain High."

I was a big Tina fan. I used to go over to Ike and Tina's house. I thought "River Deep, Mountain High" would be the biggest record Phil ever made. I thought it was an obvious #1. I couldn't believe it didn't happen here. I was happy it charted in England. But even before "River Deep," Phil felt that it was starting to come to a close. I remember I was in the studio with the Ronettes, and we were cutting "Born To Be Together" and "Is This What I Get For Loving You" and during the playback Phil came out into the studio and stood next to me and said, "It's all over. It's over. It's not here anymore." The enthusiasm was gone. He had done it so many times. The musicians were changing. They didn't want to work overtime for a deal. Everybody. It just wasn't the same spirit anymore. The spirit of cooperation started to change. And for Phil as well. It was a combination of things, and it just stopped being so much fun. The Beatles were coming. *(Harvey Robert Kubernik; June 17, 1988.)*

🦜

After "River Deep, Mountain High" failed, Phil Spector quit producing records for a time. He did a bad album (*Metamorphasis*) with the Rolling Stones and some questionable work on the Beatles' *Let It Be* album and John Lennon's *Rock 'N' Roll* sessions. Some people say those records are the better for Spector's work on them; others don't. He battled drug and alcohol problems and whatever other darknesses were in his head for most of a decade, was divorced by Ronnie, then came back in 1980 and produced a respectable album for four New Jersey three-chord bashers known as the Ramones.

In the late '80s, Spector was supposedly working on an exhaustive anthology of his records for Rhino Records. But at the last minute, in a crossfire of lawsuits, the anthology was cancelled. The tapes are still on the shelf. Supposedly, they sound tremendous.

12. Going to a Go-Go

It called itself "The Sound Of Young America," and for a time it practically was. The sound came from a record label, the most focused and singular record label of the rock era, run by the most focused and singular record executive of the rock era. The sound was the product of the executive, and it generated hit after hit and brought rhythm and blues music squarely into the American mainstream. And you could dance to it.

Berry Gordy was a song plugger, a songwriter, a photographer, a producer, an arranger, a promoter, a talent scout, an agent, a recording engineer, a smooth talker, an image maker, whatever the occasion called for to get a record made and out on the streets. He graduated from being just another song hustler peddling tunes to small Detroit labels to the head of one of those labels — Motown. It was called Hitsville first, and was a partnership between Gordy and his second wife, Ray. But the Gordys transformed Hitsville and some allied labels (one run by Gordy's sister Anna) into Motown, gave it an identity and began attracting acts to it, promising them better songs and better promotion of those songs. And they delivered on those promises, and that attracted more performers, and the word spread. No one worked harder for groups and records than Berry Gordy, long after the work no longer seemed necessary. That was why Motown succeeded where other labels failed.

Gordy never lacked ambition. He was single-minded and hit-driven. He had a powerful ambition to be mainstream, and big, the biggest record man of them all. The fact that he was black just made things a little more interesting.

One of the first to sign up with Gordy was a young singer who called himself Lamont Anthony, though his real name was Lamont Dozier. Dozier came to Gordy as a songwriter and was paired up with the Holland brothers, Brian and Eddie. Together they became a songwriting team as famous and talented as Lennon and McCartney: Holland-Dozier-Holland. Writing primarily for the Four Tops and the Supremes, H-D-H turned out acknowledged classics of the Motown sound: "Can I Get A Witness," "Baby I Need Your Loving," "Heat Wave," "Where Did Our Love Go," "(Sugar Pie, Honey Bunch) I Can't Help Myself," "Reach Out I'll Be

There," and more. Along with Smokey Robinson, Holland-Dozier-Holland created the music and lent the words to the Sound Of Young America.

Lamont Dozier: Jackie Wilson was a great influence on my singing and entertainment careers. Jackie was quite popular in the '50s when I was growing up with him and Little Willie John at the time, but they sort of inspired all the little rock 'n' rollers at the time that desired to go into show business. So we all studied Jackie Wilson and Little Willie John's techniques in singing. Willie John lived only a few blocks from me. We got together on several occasions and he taught me a lot about singing as far as singing technique goes, different riffs. I didn't know how they did that, how they slurred words; we call it musical acrobatics. It was fun and the techniques we found invaluable.

We used to copy the Spaniels' harmony. There were so many vocal groups on the street-corners of Detroit in the Jeffrey Projects where I stayed; we all sort of did our vocal gymnastics and we all learned a lot from the Spaniels — Pookie Hudson. I was the leader singer of the Romeos, and 15 at the time. Our record "Fine Fine Baby" was picked up by Atco. "Let's Be Partners" was on the back of that. Jerry Wexler at Atco took a little bit too long, I thought, on getting things to happen with the Romeos. So, being the lead, the businessman and the lawyer, I wrote him a letter saying, "Hey, get off the thing; do it or don't do it." He sent me back a nice letter — because actually I gave him an ultimatum — saying, "Gentlemen, good luck and you have your release." Needless to say, the group was very upset with me for my thinking, but the group disbanded shortly thereafter and we all went our separate ways.

I came in with a song "Just To Be Loved" with Gwen Mordy, who's part of the Berry Gordy Motown family. Shortly thereafter, I couldn't get arrested as a singer so I figured, well, let me go to Motown and see if I can started as a writer, which I did.

I wrote the lyrics to ["Come On And Get These Memories"] on a piece of Kroger sack. I didn't have any money. I used to cut these papers up and write, use it for writing paper. So I wrote this lyric "Come On And Get These Memories" on the Kroger sack, and that's how I took it to Motown.

I like to think this was the real tone or the real roots of H-D-H and the Motown sound as well because of the technique to writing. I came up with this idea purely out of feeling sick and tired about a lot of things and I think a lot of people think that way, a lot of girls I knew. I was the cause of making them feel that way. So I got some of these stories back from them from time to time, and this was one of them. A little bit from three or four different girls and I came up with "Come On And Get These Memories."

I think "Lock Up My Heart" by the Marvelettes was the very first one we did together. Actually, they were ideas and songs when I first came to Motown, and they were 75 percent finished, and we sort of finished them up when we got together.

"Can I Get A Witness" is a song that I guess is inspired by my churchgoing when I was a kid. This is a phrase often said in church. I thought it may be interesting to write a song about that phrase. Experiences people overlook, such as "Can I Get A Witness," came from your day-to-day life, in this case being the church. It was a phrase that was quite prominent in the church I attended and most black churches in Detroit.

Again, most of the H-D-H songs — a lot of urgency there, a lot of desperate need, again from old girlfriends and their troubles thrown upon me which I was partly responsible for — I took advantage of that and wrote songs from it along with Eddie and Brian [Holland].

When I first teamed up with the Hollands I wrote all my songs alone. I wrote the melody and lyrics, so it was quite easy to do. It was easier having Eddie as a lyricist — and a very good one — and Brian as a recording engineer and a marvelous melody man.

"Sugar Pie, Honey Bunch" was one of the lyrics Eddie and myself collaborated on, and when I came up with "I Can't Help Myself," that was the first thing that came out of my mouth as I sat at the piano, "Sugar Pie Honey Bunch" — bam, that was it — and Eddie took it from there. That's the first thing we muttered out and it stuck, so we finished it off.

The house band — the Funk Brothers, as they called themselves — included Bennie Benjamin on drums, James Jamerson on bass, Earl Van Dyke on piano, Robert White on guitar, Joe Messina on guitar, Eddie Willis on guitar, Clarence Isabel on vibes; James Gittens was another guy who played vibes as well. It was incredible how they knew each producer; they knew what H-D-H wanted. They knew all the producers, so if H-D-H came on the scene, they'd give us a little tease [*hums "I Can't Help Myself"*] — okay — which one will it be today? And they knew Smokey's style and Norman Whitfield and a couple other producers. Knowing that, they locked right into what we were about as producers and songwriters, which made our job very easy.

We knew that the Temptations were given to Smokey and then to Norman Whitfield, so we didn't want to venture over into their territory. We did a couple sides on the Tempts but they were album tunes primarily. We really didn't go out in a major way or give it a major effort because they belonged, so to speak, to Norman Whitfield.

Whoever had the best tune on a groove would get the release; that was the competitiveness of the Motown scene and kept all of us on our toes. One year we didn't have the release on Martha & the Vandellas. I think Ivy Jo Hunter did a song called "Dancing In The Streets" and we did a song called "Jimmy Mack." At the time, everybody thought "Dancing In The Street" was better so "Jimmy Mack" went into the can, and stayed there for about four or five years. "Jimmy Mack," when it did come out, was about five years old.

Berry Gordy was good and still is good at picking songs, being a songwriter extraordinaire himself. He knew songs, he felt them and he knew how to direct their release. That was a tremendous help to all the producers and songwriters and made us all look good.

The Primettes ... originally there were four — the other girl, Barbara [Martin], the fourth girl, how soon we forget. The group used to be sort of the low act on the totem pole at Motown. They quickly remedied that with a song called "Where Did Our Love Go." But before there were songs like "Run Run Run," that was top-20 at the time, it at least got their name out there and got them recognized as a force to be reckoned with.

The Supremes were sort of feeling their way as far as direction is concerned. Brian and I thought that since the Ronettes were hot at that time, that accounts for the "Run Run Run" sound so similar to the Phil Spector era. "When The Lovelight Starts Shining Through His Eyes" was another one that was influenced by the Phil Spector sound.

Berry gave us our chance to express ourselves and we tried out a lot of things. Being a songwriter, he wouldn't bug us because he understood creativity and he let us have our head in the studio. We tried all sorts of things and were able to come across with a variety of different sounds and musical directions. I thank him for that opportunity. "Reach Out I'll Be There" was quite exciting at the time because it was a new direction for us, something we were trying out and it was a breakthrough. It transcended everything we had done before.

We left Motown in '68 and we were responsible for 200 million sales; these songs have sold millions of records by other artists, so I'd say it's close to a billion records over a period of 22 years. That's a lot of songs. At the time we thought the stuff would be done and gone a long time ago. Now they are considered to be a whole other ballgame by say the standards of today. *(Steve Propes; June 20, 1986.)*

🍂

Part of the reason the sound sold was the attention paid to the songs by Berry Gordy and his staff. Holland-Dozier-Holland and Smokey Robinson were the most talented songwriters in R&B in the early '60s. Bob Dylan said that Robinson's "My Girl" was pure rock 'n' roll poetry. The house band, led by snakey, stylish bass player James Jamerson, put down a tough groove. And the A&R staff, led by Gordy and Hank Cosby, kept turning up acts that could fit the embryonic Motown sound, and sell. The acts were not always mainstream when they came to Motown. Marvin Gaye was a Nat King Cole soundalike; Stevie Wonder was a misdirected bundle of pure talent; the Supremes were a moderately talented group called the Primettes. But Gordy and Cosby were able to guide them and make them into distinctive individual acts but also hitmakers with a powerful overall sound.

Hank Cosby: Basically, Berry Gordy was the leader. He set the direction we would strive for. And the whole thing centered around songwriting.

It all starts with the songs. And therefore, he was looking for writers. We were very fortunate because we got the Holland-Dozier-Holland team going. We got a young Marvin Gaye going. We got Stevie Wonder. And there was a young lady there named Sylvia Moy. She was a fantastic writer. There were just so many writers, you know. And they would all collaborate together or do it individually.

This expanded over into the artists. They saw what was happening and they started to cooperate. We had the Temptations singing behind the Supremes. We had everybody cooperating.

It wasn't like going to work. It was almost like playing. Everybody loved what they were doing. It was all in one building. Everybody had little rooms. And they would go into their room and write a song, and then from room to room passing the song around. And everybody would express their opinion.

In the early days, Berry Gordy would [decide who should record a certain song]. Later on, as the company grew, it became the responsibility of the A&R director. And after we started having producers, they would say, "This song is great for Mary Wells," or, "This song is great for Smokey."

Stevie Wonder came into the studio, and I heard him the second day he was there. I just liked his way; he was amazing. He was about 11 or 12 years old.

We had recorded ["Fingertips"] in the studio, and we loved that track. I did the music completely but I had no lyrics. So I played it for Stevie and said, "Hey, listen to this; I like the music but I can't come up with any lyrics." Because I came up with the melody in five seconds. So we just goofed around on the track a little bit, and it was never really completed in the studio.

But, in the meantime, we had written up a big-band arrangement of it to put in the show. The reason we were calling it "Fingertips" is because he was playing bongos at the time. He was playing bongos to the music, and he just started ad-libbing and it came out.

He was at a live engagement in Chicago, and I think it was the first time he had ever performed the song. And he said, "Everybody say yeah," and the crowd just responded to him. As he was singing, half the song was ad-libbed right there.

In fact, back in the early days Berry Gordy said, "Hank, Stevie Wonder is going to be my greatest artist." At that time, Mary Wells and others were hot. "Fingertips" was a very difficult record to follow up. It was a live record first of all, and it was the first live record I know of to make the main selling mark.

I guess my greatest reward was when the great team of Holland-Dozier-Holland left Motown. Berry Gordy called me up in the middle of the night and said, "What are we going to do?" At that time, they were producing the Supremes, the Four Tops, Marvin, you name it. They were really hot. So, here was our greatest writing and production team leaving the company.

Berry Gordy's feeling was that the way Diana Ross went was the way the company went. At the time, it was true. When she had hit records, everything else would move. When she was cold, so were the other artists.

But anyway, this particular night he called me and said, "Hank, what are we going to do?" I told him I'd let him know in the morning.

I thought about it, and I'd realized for quite a while that the secret of Holland-Dozier-Holland was teamwork. What I mean is that Brian [Holland] would writer part of the song, Lamont [Dozier]) would write part of the song, and then Eddie [Holland] would write the lyrics. So the three together would create the song, and it was fantastic.

So I said, "Why can't we do that?." So the next morning I told Mr. Gordy I had an idea. Let's try it; let's take our three best writers, our three best producers, take them downtown to the biggest hotel, rent a suite and give them champagne. And let them stay in there until they come out with a smash!

And he did, and that's exactly what we did. We came out with "Love Child," which sold two million. So this was my greatest reward. Actually, I was a company man. This is why I was stuck in the background most of the time. Also, as a company man, I was responsible for damned near most of the creative part of the company. And it was really rewarding for me.

The hits came from all over from about 1964 to 1968. In terms of chart success, Motown was arguably the No. 1 record label in the country. Whenever the Beatles weren't there, its artists battled for the top spots, and dominated the R&B charts. Smokey Robinson and the Miracles had "Tears Of A Clown" and "I Second That Emotion"; the Temptations had "Ain't Too Proud To Beg" and "My Girl," and teamed up with the Supremes on "Someday We'll Be Together"; Stevie Wonder had "Fingertips (Part II)"; Marvin Gaye had "Too Busy Thinkin' 'Bout My Baby" and "I Heard It Through The Grapevine"; the Supremes had "Can't Hurry Love" and "Stop! In The Name Of Love" and "Come See About Me" and a host of others; and the Four Tops had "I Can't Help Myself" and "Reach Out I'll Be There" and "Baby, I Need Your Loving."

Think about that string of hits — by no means all the hits Motown had — for just a second. Turn over in your mind what those songs sound like, and you'll have some idea of the scope of the Motown sound. "Stop! In The Name Of Love" bears little resemblance to "Fingertips" on the surface — "Fingertips" even has one of the musicians shouting "What key? What key?" in the background — but both songs advance the concept of the Motown sound. It was black music made to sell to white teenaged audiences, without giving up its soul entirely. No other label, not even Stax or Atlantic, was able to pull it off as successfully as Motown. And Motown did it time and time again, until it almost seemed effortless.

The Four Tops had a powerful, earthy, direct sound that wears well, particularly the deep, raw, insistent voice of Levi Stubbs. Their hits were pulsating, undeniable; they came at you with the force of a linebacker and drove you hard for a good three minutes. "Reach Out I'll Be There," "I Can't Help Myself," "Bernadette," "It's The Same Old Song" and the others were songs of yearning, of irresistible love meeting immovable desire, of aching and living and hoping. They were classics.

Duke Fakir was a member of the Four Tops.

Duke Fakir: We've been together 27 years. We knew each other when we were growing up and became close friends during high-school days. We were all from a part of Detroit called North End, and we were singing in different groups in the area. It seemed like the thing to do. We were at a party and a girl just wanted to hear someone sing, so we did and thought it sounded pretty good. So, we thought we'd group together and try to win the $25 being offered at a local amateur contest. And a few girls!

When we were coming up we were just teenagers, and that's all there was; you either played sports or sang around town. It seemed like every street corner had a group.

We backed up Billy Eckstine for about two years. That was like going to college for music. He was quite a show-business character, and quite a nice guy. He taught us a lot about singing in key and about stage presentation. He was like a big brother or a dad.

We were interested in jazz, but we were really interested in all types of music, simply because that was the only way we could keep working. We had no records out, so we had to try to sing every type of music so we wouldn't limit ourselves to one type of engagement. But we did enjoy jazz more than the other styles when we started out.

We had known Berry Gordy for ages. Berry Gordy and Billy Davis used to write a lot of the hits for Jackie Wilson. Berry was a songwriter and photographer. When he started the company, he told us that if we wanted to record for him, he'd be more than glad to have us. After we looked at other companies, we found Motown getting stronger and stronger, so we told him we were ready to record for Motown.

When we first signed up, we did a lot of old, standard type tunes with big-band arrangements. We did quite a few of them, but I don't think any were released. "Baby I Need Your Loving" was the first release.

The guys who wrote the tune — Holland, Dozier and Holland — were good friends of ours, and they thought that the first record we did should be a big hit. So they listened to us for about a year, and watched us perform, and came up with that tune. They just said, "We got it." And they sure had it.

It was almost a science. They knew what they were doing. They had the right producers for the right people and they knew how to create those individualistic sounds. The producers knew what they were looking for.

It was just a super period. It was magic. Those seven or eight years were the greatest years in my life. To be part of an organization, and to see people like the Supremes, Stevie Wonder, ourselves, come in with no money and then overnight grow and have money and Cadillacs and homes — within one or two years — was just fascinating. We were all great pals then, and we still are. It was a magic period of my life. It's hard to explain, of course, but I could tell you about it in detail for hours.

There was one tour that I remember: when we went to England. We were still on cloud nine over a couple of hit records, but we'd never been out of the country. When we landed there were three or four thousand people waiting to greet us, and tell us how they loved us. And that was the first time I'd been so far from home and to have people clamoring over us was just something I never forgot. Here I was, 5,000 miles from home and people are telling me they love me when they don't know me from Adam. But it felt great! I just stood out there by the plane and started crying.

I wasn't surprised [our music was so successful] because Motown music was so different, and had its own impact. In fact, when we went to England to meet the Beatles, and as much as we liked them, they said they liked our music as well. They derived a lot of their music from American blues, and our music was great to them.

The first thing I remember about ["I Can't Help Myself"] was that it was one of the quickest sessions I had. I remember the night the tune was written. I was out with Lamont Dozier at a place called the 20 Grand, where the Temptations were performing. Lamont and I got pretty smashed, and he started telling me about this tune he had in his head. So I took him home and he started banging out this tune on the piano. After that, we went to the studio and did the song in about two takes. It was the same thing with "Reach Out, I'll Be There." I think we did that in one take. It seemed like the bigger the tune, the simpler it was for us to do. They were simple, and they stuck with us right away.

There was a great demand for us to record a quick followup to "I Can't Help Myself." I remember we went into the studio on a Thursday and ["Reach Out I'll Be There"] was out on Monday ! We were sitting around on the weekend helping to make label copies.

It's hard to say what happened to Motown, but I know we had to depart because it was time for a contract negotiation and we had to get our heads together on certain things. A lot of the personal touch was taken away when the company moved to California and began operating in a bigger sense. But that's the way this business has to be operated. Still, the move took away a lot of the working mechanism that helped produce that Motown sound.

Oh sure, we're still friends: Smokey, the Four Tops, Marvin Gaye, Stevie. I still see Diana a lot. I see Holland, Dozier and Holland when I go to California. We still see each other and chat a lot. Even the Gordy family; sometimes I go have lunch with them. All of them are part of a family we had, and no friendship has been lost at all.

I don't know what the chemistry is, but I can probably say that when we started out as a group, our heads were screwed on. We wanted to make this a career, something we'd do the rest of our lives once we got into it. And I think we just set our goals and said as long as we can sing, we'll be in this business. *(Jeff Tamarkin; August 1981.)*

The hits came from all over at Motown. Being signed to Motown practically guaranteed a hit, even for the second-line stars. Junior Walker and the All-Stars churned out sax-driven hits, including the classic "Shotgun," for more than a decade. The Velvelettes had a smash with "Needle In A Haystack" on Motown; they once beat the Supremes in a girl-group battle of the bands. Mary Wells was a teenage songwriter who hit first with "Bye Bye Baby" and then again, massively, with the loping "My Guy" (which stole its intro from, of all things, "Canadian Sunset"). And Martha Reeves came from the Motown steno pool to join a group called the Vandellas and cut the classics "Dancing In The Street" and "Heat Wave."

Mary Wells: I met Berry through Robert Bateman, who was the engineer at the time. And he was in a group, the Monitors — ah, the Love Tones, I think. He took me over to Motown as a songwriter.

I started out as a writer. But once I got into recording at that early age it took all my time to get into learning how to perform — you know, walk on stage and walk off. I stopped writing and got more into being an artist. Smokey wrote a lot of the hit records for me then.

During that time they had one-track recording. No one could make any mistakes. The singer, the musicians, you know, it had to come out perfect. We did 22 takes on "Bye Bye Baby," so I was pretty hoarse. But it came out great, 'cause it came out more church and bluesy.

I wrote "Bye Bye Baby" when I was 15. And I'll tell you during that time I was really admiring people like Jackie Wilson, Sam Cooke. And I wrote this particular tune for Jackie Wilson. I knew that Berry Gordy had been recording him and writing songs for him. So I wanted him to hear the song. I didn't think I could ever be an artist. I'd never thought about it, you know. I just wanted to be in the record business. So I went there and I couldn't read music. I couldn't play music. Nothin'. You know, I had to sing the song. And Berry right away said, "Why don't you record it?" I said, "Me?! Wow. Great." And I got a recording date with him.

When I got there, you see, it was Tamla Records. And Tamla was so huge in Detroit that I thought, "Wow, I'll be on Tamla." You know, it was like not that national then, but to the people of Detroit, they looked at Tamla like maybe Columbia Records. So, he told me, "I'm getting ready to start a new label and I want you to be the first new artist on there." It was a try. You know, he didn't have any money at the company then. And I was kind of disappointed about it, 'cause Motown wasn't nothin' then. But once the record was released it stayed out a year and a half, 'cause they didn't have the money to take it national. It was just released in Detroit. They played it there for six months. It was a smash there. Then they took it and put it out in Cleveland and so forth. It was on the top pop charts for a year-and-a-half, on and off. From there we did "I Don't Want To Take A Chance," which was a top-35 record. Then, "The One Who Really Loves You" came out and it went top-10. And I think then is when Berry transferred some of the other groups over to Motown; the majority of the other artists, the Supremes, Stevie Wonder, were on Tamla.

You take a great drummer, great bass player, people that are good and I'll tell you what: I've noticed when I tried to put a band together it's near impossible to find one guy per instrument that has that special something. It's impossible. But, if you got a band where each guy has a sound, a feel, you've got a winner.

It was a simple deal. Smokey would just call and say, "We got a rehearsal, I got some tunes." I'd go down to the studio and Smokey and I would get on the piano. He'd play it. We'd get the right key. And we'd go over and over the song. I'd learn the basic melody. He'd let me put a lot of myself into it; different ad-libs. He'd let me get myself into it. It was real simple, once you got the right people. It was no planned thing. Get those talented people and it's going to work.

In those days, see, I was young and didn't know the business and those companies just didn't know how to promote black acts. And even though I was a pop artist a lot of the records sold R&B and then went pop. My record buyers were a mix. That's why I had sold so many records.

I don't think of Berry Gordy as a dictator. I see him as a genius. Honestly, he knew how to run a company. And he was an artist. He could tell if you had talent or not. He knew how to take these people that were talented, the singers, the songwriters and even the businessmen to a certain extent and get the best out of 'em. He knew how to pick 'em well. He takes a person, figures them out, knows their capabilities and he takes the artist and makes him a superstar. To me, he'd have to have quite an insight to do that; to be able to turn 'em from nowhere into a big act, and then keep them there for years. He knows what the people like. He's an artistic person who knew enough to surround himself with genius, too. He wasn't on no ego trip. He was a great man, but he knew it took others to make it all work. He had a formula, a family company.

I've been at companies and I've seen how they work. They have no friendship. It's all business; not artistic people but people talkin' fast jive. You know, "I've got a great artist, blah blah and here's what I can do for you." They con. To me, a lot of artists that are out today would be openin' shows in the '60s. They would never be the top acts they are. These companies put a lot of money behind these acts and they end up losin'. A lot of these things I didn't recognize in the beginning. I now know that Berry Gordy is a genius.

A lot of old-timers, people in their thirties and forties, who were record buyers, know that I had been one of the first artists on Motown, and they look at me as being so connected with the company as if it was a part of me. I feel pretty good about being a part of something that proved to be so huge.

Ah, it was a pretty great time in my life, those years. *(Wayne Jancik; October 1980)*

Martha Reeves: I first debuted as a singer in my church at the age of three with my two older brothers. On that occasion we won a box of candy. That was the first time that I thought I could sing, perform, or whatever, and get approval. After that, in high school I was featured in many of the choirs that I learned to sing in. Upon graduating from Northeastern High School, I sang the Bach "Alleluia," the aria. Previous to this, I had sung it on four occasions and then on my graduation day, which let me know I had something to offer as a performer. After graduating, my girlfriends and I rehearsed diligently every day to become known first as the Delphis, where we recorded a song on the Checkmate label that I don't think anyone ever heard of. Later I went to Motown for an audition, but was told they weren't having auditions at that time and to come back next week. So I hung around and got a job as the A&R secretary. Mickey Stevenson was the A&R man at the time. From that, one thing led to another.

My job as the A&R secretary was to call people and schedule them for the studio, to arrive on time and to get out. Mary Wells was returning home from a tour and she was quite fatigued at the time. She had been requested for a recording session that didn't quite suit her schedule and was a little ill as well. So as a stand-in for the union's sake, I sang a song which became my first recording on the Motown label. They heard my demonstration record and decided to release it as a single. It was a song called "I'll Have To Let Him Go." Holland-Dozier-Holland took an interest in me and wrote "Come And Get These Memories," which got our name into *Billboard,* then *Cashbox* and *Record World* as Martha and the Vandellas. "Come And Get These Memories" became a top-20 record.

Vandellas was a name we decided upon after debating the company president, Berry Gordy, as to what we would be called. At that time we had a record, but no name. The girls were just out of school. One of them, Annette Beard, was married and dropped out of the group in 1964. Berry named us the Vandellas finally, after we refused to be called something like the Tillies.

Berry's a genius of a man. We, being so young and rebellious, crossed his path several times, and maybe even got on his bottom nerve at times. But I think the reason for the success of the Motown artists was because of him. He's a hard-working man who knows what he's doing, has a great ear, and if someone listens to him, they'll succeed.

"Heat Wave" was a big hit for me. And I'm proud to be the first to record it. I know a number of people have recorded it since then. It's a very good rhythm and blues song by Holland-Dozier-Holland. It was released right after "Quicksand," which was a big successful record for us, too.

The riots were happening all over the nation at that time. So, Marvin Gaye, Ivory Joe Hunter and Mickey Stevenson came up with [Dancing In The Streets] as opposed to fighting, rioting or looting, it was an effort to get everybody to dance and sing. Basically to spread music, because music has always been what soothes the souls of the world.

On our first big tour, I had to leave after just getting out of the studio and cleaning up my desk, putting away my things and giving instructions to the two secretaries who replaced me in the A&R department. I placed a quick call to my parents saying hello and goodbye and then got on the bus for 94 one-nighters. The show was headlined by Marvin Gaye and the Miracles. The Supremes opened the show, because then they hadn't had a major hit yet. They were just being introduced to the public and had a song out called "Let Me Go The Right Way Out." Sammy Ward was a fabulous blues singer on the show who I don't believe is around anymore. We had a 12-piece band with us as well. Now, mind you, this was all on the same bus. The Temptations, Stevie Wonder and Mary Wells were on the tour as well. So it made for quite a tour. The Marvellettes were not on the tour initially, but did join it later. It was a memorable tour because we went all over the United States and pioneered a lot of things.

We were chaperoned. Some of us were not 21, so it was necessary to have chaperones. I love Mrs. Morrison, who was our very first chaperone. We found her to be very influential. She taught us many things that we might not have been able to learn otherwise. She kind of kept us separated from the guys. Some of the girls did sneak through and did get married to some of the guys. I think one of the Marvellettes married one of the Miracles and one of the Contours married a Marvellette. It was difficult for us because we were basically sheltered.

I get tears in my eyes when I sing "My Baby Loves Me." I get a special warmth when I feel "Come And Get These Memories" coming on. And "Jimmy Mack" — well, I'll find him any day. I keep calling him. And "Dancin' In The Street" means that you can get a group of people together and enjoy music and dancing and to just let yourselves go. I think that was my basic reason for wanting to entertain; just to get people involved in happiness, love and joy.

I was speaking to someone the other day and I told them that no, I don't have a lot of awards on my wall, no, I haven't been nominated for a lot of Grammies and no, I don't have a collection of gold records. Also, I don't have this cash stashed away somewhere for my son's education, but I'm still able to perform. I've learned the business the hard way. I know how to read contracts now. I could produce myself. I feel show business has a lot yet to offer me and I have lot yet to offer it. I found that a voice can be trained and it can expand. My lows are lower and my highs are higher and I've got things that I'd just like to explore as far as vocals and music are concerned. I'm with the musicians union now, which makes a difference in one's career, and I'm also with SAG [Screen Actors Guild]. I've done a little bit of acting and I've been in a movie and also have done several film scores. There's a lot of areas that I would really like to get in and try to succeed in. I look forward. *(Wayne Jones; June 1981.)*

Motown's biggest group was the biggest American group of the '60s. If the fact that it was a black group, and a group of women, doesn't seem astounding, it's only because Motown and the Supremes made the astounding commonplace. They were the first black R&B girl group to cross over completely and score hits that were as big on the pop charts as they were on the R&B charts. They were the only group in history to have five consecutive No. 1 singles: "Where Did Our Love Go?", "Baby Love," "Come And See About Me," "Stop! In The Name Of Love," and "Back In My Arms Again" — and those were just a fraction of the Supremes' hits, and not even their biggest hits or their best songs. You can add to those "Love Child," "The Happening," "Can't Hurry Love," "Someday We'll Be Together," "I Hear A Symphony," "You Keep Me Hanging On," and more.

The temptation is to say that the Supremes were Diana Ross and the rest of the group were interchangeable, just dancers and backup singers. That might be the version that Diana Ross would have you believe, but the Supremes were really a vocal ensemble, and Mary Wilson, Florence Ballard and Cindy Birdsong were important to the group's success. Diana Ross had style and flair, and having her out front certainly didn't hurt, but the Supremes were a group.

Mary Wilson: How it all began? Florence and I went to the same elementary school in Detroit, and each year the school held a talent show. This particular year I was singing in the show. Florence was also on the same show. After the show, we met backstage and said to each other, "Wow, we were really great!" We really didn't know each other that well, but we became buddies and decided that if there were ever any offers to be in groups, we would call each other.

This was in about 1959, when groups were becoming very popular with teenagers. It was the "in" thing to do. About two months later, two of the Primes [who later became the Temptations], Eddie Kendricks and Paul Williams, approached Florence about starting a girls' group — the Primettes. One of the guys knew Diana and he asked her to join, we got Betty [Travis], and that's how we started.

When we first started, it was fun. We sang with the Primes at variety shows and record hops. We really didn't think too much in terms of money. But, after a year or so, we said to ourselves, "Hey, everybody else is making records; why don't we?"

Our first audition was with Smokey and the Miracles. Diana knew Smokey — they lived in the same neighborhood — so she asked him if he'd like to listen to our group. He said he would, so we went over to Claudette's house [Smokey's wife and a member of the Miracles] to sing for them. It was Smokey who suggested that Berry [Gordy] listen to us.

Well, at first, Berry said, "No more girl groups." He just didn't want to be bothered with us. So we just went and hung around the studios every day. We became friendly with the artists, and eventually, when they needed someone to add hand claps or whatever, they'd say, "Let's go get the Primettes." So, eventually, by hanging around so much, we more or less made them sign us.

When we signed a contract with Motown in 1962, we had to have a name. Berry didn't like the Primettes, and suggested that we get a new name. Florence went around the offices, getting suggestions. The name the Supremes was on one of the lists. Diana and I said, "Wow, that's terrible! It sounds like a male group." But, Florence said, "Well, we have to have a name, and this is the one." So that's how that happened.

We all agreed that Diana had the most commercial sound. We knew it would be to our advantage if she sang lead, so that's what we did.

After you had a string of flop singles, why did Berry Gordy keep you around?

By that time, we were part of the Motown family; we were like fixtures. And we were all very determined. We knew we were good on stage and that all we needed was the right song to hit. Berry really believed in us and really tried to get that hit record for us.

It wasn't that I didn't like ["Where Did Our Love Go?"], but we wanted a *hit*. I felt that particular song wasn't a hit. We wanted them to come up with a hit for us, not this teenybopper stuff. We wanted songs like Martha and the Vandellas and the Marvelettes. After "Where Did Our Love Go?" went to number one, I always said I could never pick a hit!

Well, it took us so long to get that first hit record, we really had a love and a zest for our music. And having Motown behind us and coming up with Holland-Dozier-Holland made for a very strong combination that worked.

Holland-Dozier-Holland did all the research and work. They brought songs to us, and the decisions were made by Berry and H-D-H. Berry always oversaw all our recordings. By the time they brought a song to us, it was already decided what would be released. And we were happy about that; it was their job. We had enough to do with touring, selecting our gowns, etc. In the beginning, we always knew what songs were going to be released. But after we became so popular and we were so busy touring, we didn't always know what was being put out.

In the beginning, it was wonderful. All the musicians were in the studio together, and it was just like a party. Recording is so different today; it can be very lonely. We recorded hundreds and hundreds of songs. I can't even remember them all.

It has always bothered me when people refer to me as "just" a background singer. I never thought of myself as *just* a background singer. The Supremes were a *group*, and every position was important. So I never saw myself as *just* a background singer. When people ask about that, I tell them that I was the *star* in the background.

Berry was wonderful to work with. When he was excited about a project, it was great. He was a genius, and his enthusiasm rubbed off on us. We wanted to know as much as he did. He was a great creator and he knew how to bring out the best in the people who worked for him.

I wouldn't say that we almost disbanded in 1966. But that was a hard time for all three of us. That was about the time that Diana began to think about her solo career. And I, myself, was trying to deal with Florence's departure.

There were problems within the group fairly early — as early as '66 or '67. We were doing so much and had so little time for ourselves. Schedule-wise, we were here, there and everywhere, doing shows and whatnot. We just didn't have time. Florence became very upset because she felt things were not going as they should. I felt that way, too, but it was worse for her. It was obvious that, for example, Diana was asked all the questions in an interview. The reporters were just primed to ask her all the questions. That bothered me, too, but it was just worse for Florence.

Those conflicts were just differences in personality. Florence and Diana really loved each other. We all loved each other. It was just one of those that happen whenever people get together. We certainly didn't argue all the time. But, I think that because we were so big, the problems were blown up more.

THE SUPREMES: 'The Motown Sound is difficult to explain. It's like trying to define love. There is no one aspect to it.'

We were all aware that Florence was leaving. I hated the thought that we were splitting up, that Florence was leaving and that Diana would leave, too. I never thought that one of us would not be there. When Florence finally left, I was terribly upset. Diana was, too, but it was different for me. Since we had shared the background, I felt closer to Florence. I felt like I was losing my partner and my friend. I was not very happy about it. But, I felt that if things couldn't be worked out, then perhaps it was better for us all.

Florence really didn't have the proper guidance and management in her solo career. Plus, I think she was still too closely linked with the Supremes. She really didn't have the same kind of push we had. Motown really helped us. They were really behind us. Most artists need that. It's very important to a career.

What were your feelings as you watched Diana getting more and more attention, though, at the group's expense?

That I don't have good feelings about — but it's directed at the company, not Diana. It was all a matter of packaging. You know, who was more marketable. Diana was just packaged more beautifully, while we were left sitting on the shelf.

177

The timing is something I'm not really sure of. I started hearing rumors as early as 1967, or maybe even late 1966. Naturally, hearing those rumors presented worry for me. What will happen to us? I wasn't ready for us to break up yet. I never thought about breaking up.

By that time, the Supremes were so far in the background — I mean totally in the background — we were so far in the shadow of Diana Ross that we were becoming obscure. We weren't a group anymore. After 1970, we had the chance to become the Supremes again, a whole group.

As far as I was concerned, I wasn't ready to quit yet! And no one could have made that decision without my okay. You see, we each had an equal voice in the group's decision-making. I really want to emphasize the fact that no one person was *the* "boss" in the group. We all shared equally in the decision-making. So I never even thought of quitting the group in 1970.

Just like the Four Tops had their own style within the Motown Sound, the Supremes had their own style. The common basis was with the musicians and the writers.

The Motown Sound is difficult to explain. It's like trying to define love. There is no one aspect to it. I think the Motown sound was a combination of a lot of different people with ideas blending into one expression. And it came out like love. We had ambition, drive, energy, and we all had love.

No one knows what all our dreams are. As far as the Supremes, that was my biggest dream. All of mine have been answered. My dream was to have children and a family. I have that, too. Diana's dream was to go out after her career. I think now she is trying to find her other dreams. So I got what I went after.

Of course, we all dreamed of having stardom like Diana. That's what I'm working on now. I want to make sure that the same thing happens for me. It's like I'm living a second life now. Most people only get one life. I've had two. *(Randall Wilson; September 1983.)*

13. Eight Days a Week

The Beatles changed everything. They changed the course of music, and the course of society. They ended one form of music cold and started up another, and though they were the same music they were nothing like each other. The Beatles shook the world with a force that on the scale of universal upheavals was somewhere between the Great Depression and Elvis. They made young girls swoon, ended careers overnight, and made new stars just that quick. Just when popular music was becoming a little more acceptable, a little tamer, a little calmer, a little more syrupy and orchestrated, just when the only threats to society's foundations were Bobby Rydell and Pat Boone, the Beatles knocked fear into the hearts of parents and drove the kids nuts all over again.

It was only rock 'n' roll, really. The Beatles went back to the roots of rock, the Carl Perkins shuffles and bluesy Chuck Berry rockers, and then went forward from there. They mixed free-form studio experimentation with a sense of melody and song structure that's still unmatched in popular music. Most current pop music goes back no further, and does nothing any better, than the Beatles. The Beatles were simply the best and most revolutionary musical group in history.

The Beatles started out as nothing more than another bunch of lads with guitars. They grew up in Liverpool, a dreary port town in northern England. You could compare life there with life in the American South in this respect: There wasn't much else for kids to do but listen to the radio, hang out at the dance halls, and buy whatever records they could afford. Liverpool kids grew up on Little Richard and Bo Diddley and Carl Perkins and Jerry Lee Lewis while their parents listened to big-band jazz, and yelled at the kids to turn the racket down.

The first contribution England made to rock was called "skiffle." It blended American folk with the British music-hall tradition, and produced a worldwide No. 1 record in 1961 with Lonnie Donegan's "Does your Chewing Gum Lose Its Favor On The Bedpost Overnight?" Skiffle was simple, easy to play, easy to sing along with, catchy, and not very much like rock. For a while, practically every British kid had or wanted to be in a skiffle band.

But skiffle was soft at its core, a sort of la-de-da music, and Liverpool kids wanted something harder, something more in line with the R&B they were listening to and the tough lives they were living in Liverpool. The music they came up with became known as "Merseybeat," after the Mersey, the dirty river that flows through Liverpool. It was really nothing more than American rock 'n' roll with a British accent to it, but it was loud and raucous and the kids could dance to it.

On Dec. 27, 1960, the Silver Beatles played at the Litherland Town Hall, filling in for a band that didn't show. Their pay for the evening was £6. It was the beginning of the Merseybeat explosion.

After the show, promoter Brian Kelly booked the Beatles for four months of solid work, and raised their fee to £8 a show.

But Merseybeat's roots go back farther, to the small clubs that opened in the late '50s and to the "beat nights" they began having in the summer of 1960. On May 25, 1960, Cass and the Cassanovas and Rory Storme and the Hurricanes shook the walls of The Cavern. In the months that followed, the Bluegenes (later the Swinging Blue Jeans), Gerry and the Pacemakers, Derry Wilke and the Seniors, and the Big 3, the remnants of Cass and the Cassanovas, came to power in the clubs. Compared to these groups, the Beatles were a second-generation band.

The early days of Merseybeat were wild beyond imagination. Rory Storme was known as "Mr. Showmanship," and drove the girls wild. Ringo Starr was his drummer. Derry Wilke, Liverpool's only successful black vocalist, wasn't far behind Storme. By 1962 there were more than 300 working bands in Liverpool, and many of the most popular groups didn't have recording contracts.

The golden age of Merseybeat only lasted from 1960 to 1963. "Like most crazes, the Mersey Beat didn't realize it was dead until about two years after it had actually died," the *Liverpool Daily Post* wrote in 1970. "Groups were jumping on to the almost static bandwagon in 1965 and 1966, but the magic had died."

In 1966 the club that started it all, The Cavern, closed and filed for bankruptcy. "The kids barricaded themselves in The Cavern all night," doorman Pat Delaney said. "When the police arrived, and the kids came out, a lot of them were crying." They might have known what they had lost.

Brian Kelly promoted many of the shows around Liverpool in Merseybeat's heyday. Johnny Gustafson, Mike Evans, Billy Hatton and Pete Clarke were three of the top musicians in the Liverpool scene. Elsa Goodlass was one of the first secretaries of the Beatles' fan club. Ray McFall owned The Cavern, the darkest, dingiest and best music club in town, where the Beatles took Liverpool by storm. Allan Williams was a club owner and band manager.

Mike Evans: At the beginning of the '60s, there was a distinct Liverpool style. It was a brash nasal scouse, a guitar-based approach that was applied to the bewildering diversity of material, the bulk of which was a common ground of rhythm 'n' blues and country-ish rock 'n' roll that everyone seemed to play.

John Gustafson: Just before that period, all there was were traditional jazz, skiffle groups, folk groups, 4,000 acoustic guitars. Then amplified rock 'n' roll groups appeared, and as the groups got better the kids got more interested.

Adrian Barber and John Hutchinson and myself formed ourselves into a group called The Big Three. The papers called us "the boys with the benzedrine beat ... the rockers with the heaviest sound."

Mike Evans: It was Barber who made the first significant contribution to the Liverpool sound. He pioneered and built the famous "coffin" speaker cabinets favored by all the Merseyside groups in those days.

Billy Hatton: Barber had the coffins all lined with sand and all vented and fluted with wood. It made them sound like a 50-watt amplifier. It was their secret weapon.

Mike Evans: Barber left the band to make speakers, and Brian Griffin replaced him. Brian was the Eric Clapton of the Liverpool groups. He was the first to bend notes and play rock 'n' roll as jazz/blues.

John Gustafson: We didn't compromise. As other groups got more popular, they gave in to certain demands being made on them. Once a week I'd go the NEMS and buy 10 singles, go and learn them and do them at The Cavern the next day.

Pete Clarke: We used to go to The Cavern, but one day this guy told me that he was going to a club called The Storyville. It was May 1961, and I never had experienced anything like it. I couldn't believe it. I was rooted to the spot. The atmosphere was great; there was a total communication between the people who went to the club regularly. They were playing R&B music; they took it from Chuck Berry and Howlin' Wolf. I really got into it. I started to go there with my friend Billy Kinsley. We used to go to The Cavern at lunchtime, but I could never bring myself to go at night. I thought we had a lot more going at The Storyville. We were loyal.

Elsa Goodlass: My first taste of The Cavern was in late 1961. I was 14 then. I'd heard of the Beatles and The Cavern lunchtime sessions through a friend of a friend. The first thing that hit me when I walked in was the darkness and bareness of the place, plus the smell of vegetables mixed with disinfectant. Entrance fee was one shilling for members and one and sixpence for guests. As sixpence meant the difference between a bowl of soup or starving, I had no hesitation in joining. I found a seat as close to the stage as possible, not realizing that had I stood in the back the sound balance would have been that much better. I was glued to my seat by that raw and beautiful sound that hit me from the stage. At 2:15 the lunchtime session had ended, as had my first taste of the Beatles; I was exhausted.

It was a very cliquish club, but I soon got to know everyone, and it felt great to be a part of it all. Liverpool stores must have made a packet of money off us, all in our black polo-neck sweaters. Everyone, including all the bands, owned at least one. And for the chicks, if you didn't own a leather coat you really felt like an outcast.

Every band that played at The Cavern had its own following of girls. It went by who you fancied, rather than the music. Every evening there were loads of girls hanging about outside, waiting for whichever band happened to be playing to ask them if they would take them in. If there were no takers, they would stand outside for ages asking passers-by for odd coppers until they had enough money to go inside. The evening session used to end each night at 11:15. Always the same record played us out: Bobby Darin's "I'll Be There."

Pete Clarke: I heard a lot of talk about the Beatles, but I hadn't seen them yet. There was a kind of energy in the air; all the kids at The Cavern felt it. When the band came on nobody said a word in the club, like everybody was petrified. I couldn't believe it; the band was so good. When they first started playing, I got instant shivers down my spine. I was shivering, and I was getting tingles through my spine, through my whole body. I couldn't believe that a band could do that to me. They were clowning around while they were playing as well. So I said to this friend of mine, "Listen, man; you've got to be out of your mind if you think the Beatles are better than that!" And he said, "They are the Beatles!"

Brian Kelly: We didn't take any notice of them. We were short-staffed and were more interested in controlling the front door. All of a sudden, we heard the sound of a lot of people running. We dived in and we could see people running like mad to the stage. I thought, "Oh, my God, we've got a fight on our hands." But one of the bouncers waved, meaning don't come forward. We all relaxed and looked at all these girls jammed against the stage, entranced by the Beatles.

Ray McFall: At times it was difficult to fill lunchtimes when these groups were away. Evenings didn't present the same problem, because I could call upon hosts of semi-professional artists who would do a day's work and race home to collect their instruments in time to take the bandstand by seven.

Pat Dawson-Hidgetts: I remember before the Beatles' final Hamburg trip, there was a feeling at the lunchtime session that it was one of the last times we'd see them like this. "Love Me Do" had been a minor hit and there was a certainty in the air that they were about to happen. John sang "To Know Him Is To Love Him," and when he finished the group could feel the sadness in the audience. Instead of fooling around, they were just fumbling around and looking at each other. Everyone was numbed. The night Bob Wooler announced as they were going onstage that "Please Please Me" had reached #1 was awful, because the reaction was the opposite of what they expected. Everyone was stunned. That was the end of it as far as we were concerned.

Pete Clarke: There were only three bands in Liverpool who ever did anything, and one was the Beatles. When the Beatles went, the Merseybeats, who'd always been playing rock 'n' roll and R&B, took over. We had a hard time getting the top place off them. You can forget the other people, just forget them. The only reason we got the Merseybeats' place off 'em was because they recorded and moved out of Liverpool. We were a lot younger than they were, and they were a lot dirtier than we were.

There was never a time if you were in the Escorts that you could walk down Mathew Street. I mean, I wouldn't walk down Mathew Street with a crowd outside. We'd get raped, the lot of us. We were the top band for three years because nobody ever came back and we never left. The reason we didn't leave was because of our recordings, which were just awful. But onstage we were the best.

Once, when we were leaving from the side entrance of The Cavern, we all got out and were about to get in the van. We all made it except for Mike Gregory. He was posing down in the back of the alley, slowing himself down while all the chicks were rushing down from the main entrance. There was no way we wanted to hang around for him, because as much as I like women, I don't like three of 'em grabbing me at once. He hung around for it, and he got it. He got it all right, because we jumped in the van and we took off and they'd already reached the van.

You never saw anybody run like he ran because we left him in the middle of Mathew Street, and those chicks were about three feet away from him and there was a good 150 of 'em, and he only had one chance: run — I mean, run! — and he ran right through the center of Liverpool. He went through the front door of Rushworth's Department Store and out through the back door into a pub. About seven of them ran into the pub and started ripping his clothes off, and I saw guys pull them off and throw them back out of the pub and Mike stayed in the pub.

Allan Williams: It was like a gold rush. And the money wasn't made by anyone in Liverpool, either. Every agent in London came running to Liverpool. They used to meet in the Blue Angel. The groups were all signed up by London agents; they were all whizzed away. It was like signing up football stars.

The chronology of the Beatles goes back before Merseybeat, to skiffle. In its early stages it was no different than the chronology of many Liverpool bands. It could make you think that some other band might have been able to rise up and become the Beatles.

In 1956 John Lennon, a student at Quarry Bank High School and a guitarist, formed a group called the Quarrymen. On June 15, the group played at a church picnic, and he asked an acquaintance named Paul McCartney to join. Six months later, The Cavern opened as a jazz and skiffle club. A year later, John Lennon began attending Liverpool Art College.

In 1958, John Lennon's mother was killed in a car crash. McCartney's mother had died two months earlier. George Harrison joined the band, which occasionally performed as Johnny and the Moondogs. The next year, all three dropped out of school, and took Stu Sutcliffe with them as a bass player. Sutcliffe was an art student, a friend of Lennon and McCartney, but not a musician. At the same time, Pete Best cleared out the basement of his mother's house, which she intended to turn into a music club. In late August the Casbah Club opened in the basement. The Quarrymen became the regular house band. In late November they broke up and became first the Moondogs, then Long John and the Silver Beatles, then the Silver Beatles, and finally, in 1961, the Beatles. George Harrison got a job in a Liverpool department store.

In the spring of 1960, the band returned from a gig in Scotland backing singer Johnny Gentle, and got a job at a local club backing a stripper named Shirley. When they got an extended engagement in Hamburg, Germany, at the Indra Club, they asked Pete Best to be their drummer. He accepted, and the first lineup of the Beatles was set.

Best stayed with the band through 1962, recording a number of sides with the group, and was in on the first wild stages of Beatlemania in England and Germany. While he was with the group, the Beatles became the top rock 'n' roll band in Liverpool, playing regularly at the Casbah Club and The Cavern. They won the *Mersey Beat* magazine popularity poll after Lennon and McCartney stuffed the ballot boxes with forms written under assumed names. He met Brian

Epstein, who became the Beatles' manager. He auditioned with the group for Decca and EMI, and played on at least one version of their first U.K. single, "Love Me Do." But just as the band was about to explode worldwide, he was kicked out of the Beatles in favor of Ringo Starr, the drummer for Rory Storme and the Hurricanes. Best never spoke to John, Paul or George again.

Pete Best: My mother was born in India. The family moved over there generations ago. She was working with the Red Cross over there. My father was from England and went to India with the forces. They fell in love, married, and I appeared on the scene. My younger brother was born out here, and at the end of the war, because my dad was born and bred in Liverpool, he went back home again. They separated.

My fingers were always tapping since I was two years old, so the logical thing to do was go and buy a snare drum. Because of that, and the fact that my mother had a club called the Casbah and I was meeting a lot of musicians, I decided I wanted to become a drummer.

The first time I saw what became the Beatles they opened my mother's club, the Cabash. They were known as the Quarrymen, and had another fellow with them called Ken Browne. He stood in on Saturday nights. I got to know them from when they came to the club, just as friends. Then they did an audition for a guy named Larry Parnes, who was the impresario, and disappeared to tour Scotland backing a singer named Johnny Gentle. By this time, Stu Sutcliffe had joined the band and they had a drummer named Tommy Moore. As it happened, by the end of this tour — which wasn't a great success as far as they were concerned — they came back and Tommy Moore had left. In the meantime, I started up my own fun combo, which played the Casbah. They were aware that I had a drum kit and played, and becase Tommy Moore left, I got a phone call from Paul. He said, "Look, Pete, I'll lay it on the line to you. We've had an offer to go to Germany and we need a drummer. Would you be interested in joining?" By this time, my group had folded — we were only school friends in it for kicks — and I said yeah, I'd be very interested. I played about six numbers with them at an audition.

I never thought that it would last beyond the tour of Germany; not in the least bit. But they had decided to go into it professionally, and their parents had said that if they were going to go into it, they should go into it wholeheartedly.

George was very much into his music. He practiced for hours, improving his guitar technique. All he wanted to do was become the best guitarist around; that was his aim in life. He had a mischievous smile, and a fan following, but music was his first love. Paul was, for want of a better word, the PR man of the group. He made sure everyone knew what the Beatles were doing in Germany. He was the one who corresponded with the local trade magazine. He was a talented musician, with a hell of a vocal range. You can't take that away from him; he could sing a slow ballad and then an out-and-out rocker. He played piano, guitar, sat in on drums.

John was the abrasive one. He was the one who really couldn't give a damn. There was always an attitude, a fiery temper. He was quite prepared to slug it out with people if it came to that. He was a natural wit. He threw away lines onstage, mixed things up on purpose. That was his sense of humor. He was aggressive. He'd give you a verbal whiplashing if you got on the wrong side of him. He could dress people down. He could blow up, and then simmer down and in a couple of minutes be the happy-go-lucky guy he was.

Stu Sutcliffe realized that his musical talent — he was the bass player — was more limited than that of the others. He persevered; he was part of the Beatles, but his first love in life was painting. First, he was an artist, and second, a show-business performer. But there must have been something else going through his mind all the time, because when he met Astrid [Kirchherr, the girl who photographed and befriended the Beatles in Germany], he decided to stay there. He quit the group in '61 while we were at the Top Ten Club. He'd made the decision to go back to his first love, painting. But he contributed a lot to the group. The five of us each had our own personal charisma, and that contributed to us being the Beatles.

Germany? Well, you have to imagine five kids of about 17 or 18 suddenly getting whizzed out to Hamburg, virtually overnight, and getting stuck in one of the hardest areas. It was sin city. The Reeperbahn [the name of the district where they performed] was supposed to be the entertainment capital of the world, but it was something we were apprehensive about.

We were deported from Germany. It was a little bit of a shock, being sent out the way we were, but let's put it in perspective. George was being sent home because he was underage. We had the offer to play the Top Ten Club, and we spoke to Bruno Koschmider [the promoter at the Kaiserkeller, where they'd been playing] and said we wanted more money, better living accommodations. But it wasn't forthcoming from him. So Peter Eckhorn [Koschmider's rival], who owned the Top Ten — which was *the* club in town at the time — offered us more money to play for him. But Paul and I had to go back to the digs first and get our stuff. When we got there, we sort of lit a few things up, because there were no lights in the place. We scorched a few things, but nothing really big. The place was grotty to begin with. It was like a dungeon; it was just the back of an old cinema, no electricity or anything. We thought nothing at all about it, got our stuff and whizzed away to the Top Ten. A couple of days later we were picked up by the Hamburg police and, in no uncertain terms, told that we tried to burn the cinema down. A couple of hours later, we were deported and sent back home to England.

We had an inkling that even though we had only conquered Germany we were going to go places. I mean, even they didn't know they'd become the phenomenon they did become, but we were gonna become big. We thought we'd become the #1 rock stars in England, and it was that inner belief that kept us going.

When we got back to England, first we played the Casbah, and then what we called the Brian Kelly circuit, which was three town halls: Litherland Town Hall, Lathom Hall and the Aintree Institute. It was around March '61, just before we went back to the Top Ten, that we started to break into The Cavern. We did a couple of dinnertime sessions, and Ray McFall was impressed by what he saw, and started to book us.

A typical Cavern gig *(laughs)*? Okay, you have to envisage The Cavern. It was an underground cellar, dark, acoustically terrible. The stage was at one end. As soon as the crowd got in there it was a sweatbox. It was dark, dank, gloomy, smelled of disinfectant. Once the kids came in and we started playing, the sweat rolled up the walls. It was like standing in water. But the atmosphere was fantastic! It was that atmosphere, and the acoustics, and the groups appearing onstage that lent it its excitement. Because of that, and the way the kids reacted, it became the rock 'n' roll mecca of Liverpool.

We'd taken the single "My Bonnie" back and played it at The Cavern, and the kids started requesting it. They were going down to Brian's record store and asking for "My Bonnie" by the Beatles, although it was actually by Tony Sheridan and the Beat Brothers. But Brian said, "Who the hell are the Beatles?" and people said, "Oh, you've never seen them? They play at The Cavern. They're Liverpool's #1 band." Brian promised the kids he'd get them the record, and then curiosity got the best of him and he went to the Cavern to see who were the Beatles. He watched us a couple of times, and then it must have gotten into his mind: "Hey, I'd like to manage them." So we got a message passed to us saying, "Come and see Brian." He laid it on the line what he wanted to do. He was quite honest and said, "I've never managed a group before, but I'm a good businessman and I know the record business. I have record contacts and I'm financially well off — a reputable person. Think it over and I'll help you to the best of my abilities." So we went away, had a couple of beers, thought it over and the final decision was yeah, we'll give him the go.

He was very apprehensive about how to handle us initially because we were explosive, a little volatile. Brian was sort of gentle, a suit-and-tie-brigade sort. It was only after he'd been with us for a couple of months that he started to be like a manager with us. He'd say not to drink or spit on stage. He started drawing up the programs we had to play, making sure we got the right billing. Then when we slowly adjusted to that came the big crunch bomb: "Okay, guys, I'm taking you out of leathers, and I'm putting you into suits." Everyone sort of went, "Aaarrgh! We don't want to wear suits!" But it was a good move at that time, because by then every other group in Liverpool was copying the Beatles. I guess he was trying to make the Beatles look different, and hence the collarless suits.

I didn't change my hairstyle when the others did, but let's get this straight: It wasn't a case of not going along with it. If they would've said, "Pete, we want you to change your hairstyle," I would've. Stu was the first one to change. George followed suit, and Paul and John didn't change for quite a while. Then they went to Paris, where they met a couple of friends from Hamburg and they came back with what they call today the Beatles hairstyle. If they had said that they wanted me to change too because they wanted us to be different, I would've most probably changed. But there was no mention of it.

I never thought I was the focal point of the group. It never became obvious. Okay, there were a couple of times I was singled out and mobbed while the others were pushed over to the side, but that didn't make any great shakes to me. The group was the group; they got more screams one night and I got more one night, and only after the incident [getting fired] happened, people told me that I wasn't aware of it because I was so involved with it, but I was becoming the focal point.

Girls were sleeping in the garden outside of my place. I can't deny that one. They used to camp out there. It was something I wasn't aware of; I'd come home and go to bed, and when I woke up the next morning there were kids in the garden.

Sure, I remember what they called me: "Mean, moody and magnificent; the teenaged Jeff Chandler." That was put into words by Bob Wooler, who was the DJ at The Cavern. He did a great write-up on us in the local trade paper *Mersey Beat*, and he highlighted the physical appearance of the group. So I was "mean, moody and magnificent Pete Best, the teenaged Jeff Chandler." It stuck with me after that, but it was a case of that while I was playing the drums I was very much into what I was doing. Whether people saw me as mean and moody, I don't know, but I was a laughing, enjoyable guy. I wasn't going to spit on people.

Let's take my firing step by step. Brian was having trouble getting a recording contract, so his ego was a little bit deflated by this time. When we heard that George Martin was interested in signing us up, the band started bouncing again. Brian told us to work on a tune that George Martin would be interested in. He sent us tapes of songs and said to work on them, but it was just a lot of rubbish as far as we were concerned. But when we first met George, he was just an A&R man, a natural guy. We weren't aware of his talents.

When we went down to EMI, I laid down the track for "Love Me Do." In-between the first recording and going back to put the finishing touches on it, George Martin told Brian he wasn't very happy with the studio sound he was getting from me, and that he wanted to use a session drummer, Andy White. In-between going back, I was kicked out. Ringo was in. So when the group went back, George Martin asked where I was, and the guys said that I left. So George said, "Who's this?" and they said "This is Ringo, the new drummer." Ringo sat down to play and did a couple of takes, and then George said, "Okay, Andy, you do 'Love Me Do.'" To this day, there's confusion — because it's been mixed — over what ever happened in the studio. No one really knows whether it's Pete, Ringo or Andy. Even George Martin says he's confused, but he believes it might be Ringo. Those're his own words.

To this day, it's hard to explain why I was fired. Taking everything into consideration, the hairstyle could've been changed. As for the drumming, a lot of people thought I was better than Ringo. Other reasons that may have materialized, like saying I wasn't part of the Beatles ... how can they say that when I was with them for two years? So the general consensus is that it was because I was starting to get more attention than the others, which, to may way of thinking, is stupid, idiotic stuff, because it doesn't matter who's popular in the group if the group's popular.

I didn't expect the fans to react the way they did. When the news got out, I just expected people to accept that. But the fact that the fans demonstrated in the way that they did brought a lot of compassion to the situation. It was good to realize that they liked me so much they would do this for me — violence, write petitions, you name it. They did anything to try to get me back in the group. But my inner feelings were that no matter how hard they tried, it was cut-and-dried.

There was bitterness, resentment. They caused me a lot of heartache. You name it; whatever trauma you can go through in a short period. It mixed my life up for quite some time. But I had to tell myself that I couldn't stay that way my whole life and that whatever happened with them, I had my own life to live. I have my own lifestyle and a close circle of friends that have stood by me. Now I've got contentment — though don't get me wrong, I did have to work at it.

I joined another band. I'd had offers to join other groups, but Lee Curtis and the All-Stars had a good reputation. They were different. They were a non-guitar lineup; they didn't have three guitars up front. And Lee was a lead singer as well, but the group had three singers; they weren't a conventional group at the time. The group felt I could do something for them and they were right, because in the space of 12 months we built ourselves into being the second biggest group in Liverpool. We knew we could never topple the Beatles, but it was nice to know we could come that close.

Lee Curtis put out a record by himself on Decca, with an orchestra, a ballad. But I wasn't on it. Then the studio decided to use the boys and we did a cover version of a song called "Let's Stomp." It got good airplay in England, but we never did anything else after that.

After Lee Curtis split with us, originally we wanted to retain our identity, so we just called our band the Original All-Stars. But when we landed a recording contract with Decca, they said, "Drop the Original All-Stars. You're now the Pete Best Four." We used that name for about two years, but then when we had the opportunity to record in America, I wanted a bigger sound, so we changed the name to the Pete Best Combo and added some horns.

After the record in America, I went back home to England, struggled for a couple of years. Things weren't working out. I decided to quit.

In a nutshell, by the time I decided to quit, I'd had a belly full of it. I didn't want to manage anyone, either. Managing would have meant that I'd still be involved in show business, and having to deal with people.

Yeah, I grew my hair long. I think everyone followed suit with that. I got a job. It was a case of having to, I guess, to be honest about it. I got a job in a bakery, stayed there for 12 months, and then a job came up with the government, and I've been there since. It's job-oriented. We call it Employment Services. It's finding people jobs.

I'm not really recognized from my days with the group. Possibly people around the same age as me know me as Peter who used to be with the Beatles. But usually they just know me as Mr. Best or Pete, whatever the case might be.

I did an *American Bandstand* anniversary a while back. Dick was putting together a bunch of old-time rock and roll stars like Chuck Berry, and he got in touch with me and asked if I'd like to do it. I said, "Well, I haven't played drums in 20 years." But he said not to worry about it, that there'd be 20 or 30 people up there and they were going to double up on each section. I had a lot of fun doing it, but it was terrifying, too. It made me feel good to sit behind the skins again, but I knew it was just a one-off.

For about two years after I left, the Beatles progressed as I'd expected them to. They were learning new ideas, but their music still sounded like the Beatles. Then they started to lose their identity with me.

I found John's death hard to accept, even though I hadn't seen him in 20 years. No matter what happened in the past, I did have a lot of fun; we spent fun times together. It was a senseless slaying that just didn't have any reason behind it.

He was a nutter. We used to dare him to do things onstage, and once when we were in Hamburg in the middle of winter, John went out in a pair of long johns. We came back about three or four in the morning after playing, and John was sitting in the back of the cinema in his bedroom with long johns. He was reading a newspaper he'd picked up, which was most probably about three or four weeks old by then. We dared John to go stand in the middle of the crowd like that. There was no word from John. He picked his paper up, put on a pair of sunglasses and his cowboy boots, and with a straight face, walked out in the middle of the street, which was still buzzing. People were dressed up, some of them were going to work, some were drunk; you name it. He was standing in the middle of the street in his long johns, reading the paper with these sunglasses on. You can imagine the reaction of the people. They'd just seen the Beatles perform onstage, and here was this guy, very stone-faced; he stayed there for about five minutes reading his paper. By this time we were breaking up. Then he walked back in and sat down on the couch.

My time with them's something that I look back on and see a lot of fun, hard work, laughs and jokes. It's two years of my life that are still locked up in my memory, two years that no one can take away from me. Apart from the ghastly deed that happened, they were two great years of my life. *(Jeff Tamarkin; October 1982.)*

It's hard to grasp today what the Beatles did to American kids when their first records hit the States. It was as if American youth was all one tightly coiled, adolescent spring, and the Beatles were the trigger that set loose all that compressed energy. Even today, people can remember how and where and when the Beatles changed their lives — pretty remarkable, considering that the Beatles were an ongoing phenomenon and not just a traumatic one-shot event.

Jim Carroll is a poet, author and musician.

Jim Carroll: I was about 12 years old and just starting to write *The Basketball Diaries*, which was published as a book when I was about 16. I had a friend who played guitar, and he wanted me to play the drums. He even bought me a drum kit. I was terrible. Fortunately, I broke my wrist playing basketball; I got caught in the net and they had to cut me down. That was the biggest break that band ever had. They then got another drummer who was good but ugly; he looked like Arnold Stang, who used to be in the Chunky commercials. Anyway, this friend of mine who wanted to start the band was really into the Beatles. So, when they were on *Ed Sullivan*, we watched it and they did "I Want To Hold Your Hand" and "She Loves You." And my favorite one they did was "All My Loving," because it sounded like it could've been a Phil Spector production. But the truth is that I really wasn't into music much yet at that point, just maybe some Dylan and "Louie Louie" and things like that. Later as I started getting more into music I followed their career and started to like them more.

Andrew Edelstein is the author of the book *'60s Mania: A Decade Of Pop Culture.*

THE BEATLES: 'We all lived together so close; we knew each other so well that it crossed over into the music. We knew exactly what the other was doing.'

Andrew Edelstein: "You won't believe this," said Mr. Johnson, my sixth-grade teacher, a guy in his mid-30s with a crew cut (he looked like John Glenn). "I saw Huntley and Brinkley on the news last night and they had a report about this strange new music that's sweeping England. You won't believe what these guys look like. Get ready," he said, laughing. "It's probably going to happen here."

I had never heard of these "Beatles," even though I had been a faithful listener of top-40 radio. So for the next few days I paid special attention to the radio so I could hear this "strange new music," which had the power to make my teacher laugh. When I heard "Surfin' Bird" by the Trashmen, I figured this was what he was talking about. It certainly had a strange new sound, a lot weirder than anything by Bobby Vinton or the Singing Nun.

But the Bird wasn't the word, because just a few days later you couldn't avoid hearing disc jockeys talking all about the Beatles and their groovy fab-gear language. But the first time I heard "I Want To Hold Your Hand" I was disappointed. I didn't think this new music was that different from the stuff I'd been hearing for years on Murray the K's oldies-but-goodies show. It sounded like speeded-up Everly Brothers and Buddy Holly.

I really couldn't understand what the screaming was about. Radio was going crazy; the local radio station became W-A-Beatle-C. I was a 12-year-old whose roots lay with the urban-macho sound of Dion and the Four Seasons, and I was immediately suspicious of these new guys who, frankly, with their collarless suits (what? no sharkskin?) and hairstyles (what? no Vitalis?) looked like fruits to me. They did have cool boots, though.

My classmates began talking in English accents; one nerd became Mr. Popularity with the chicks when he told them he had a cousin who had actually visited England. Girls debated endlessly who was their favorite Beatle.

But what really began to win me over to the Beatles was the fact that my parents didn't like them. I figured then that there must be something cool about them. (At least they aren't greasy like Elvis Presley," my father said.) You couldn't be a true teenager if you had the same heroes — like JFK and Glenn — that your parents had. So eventually I found that it was possible to divide one's loyalties between the Beatles and the Four Seasons. But it wasn't until 1966 that I had the courage to wash the Vitalis out of my hair and let my pompadour spill over my forehead.

Harry Harrison was a disc jockey on WMCA in New York City.

Harry Harrison: I was one of WMCA's "Good Guys" when I first heard of the Beatles. We played their records in 1963, before they went with Capitol Records, but nothing happened. We watched their popularity grow in England, and when Capitol did sign them for the United States, we played "I Want To Hold Your Hand" on the air for the first time in December 1963.

From that moment on, radio stations waged a tremendous battle for Beatles exclusives. Joe Bogard and Frank Costa of the WMCA music department did a fantastic job of getting the Fab Four's records on the air — and often exclusively.

When John, Paul, George and Ringo arrived in this country on their initial tour, it was our pleasure to be at their lively, fun press conferences, interviews and concerts. The Good Guys introduced the Beatles to New York and America at Carnegia Hall and Shea Stadium. Those performances were electrifying, unforgettable experiences. I had met and worked with many recording stars, but had never felt the excitement, enthusiasm and hysteria that the Beatles generated. Beatlemania had struck!

John Densmore was the drummer with the Doors.

John Densmore: I remember seeing their picture in *Time* magazine, and the mop-top look. I was real fascinated; I thought they were crazy. First I thought they were gay — faggots, as we called them back then. I was still a jazz snob, but when I heard "I Wanna Hold Your Hand" I thought it was real infectious. I was blown away when I saw the pictures of them with their hair over their collars. It was shocking! So weird! I went, "Oh, my God!" Then I became a fan. Two years later we formed the Doors. Did you know, by the way, that John Lennon died on Jim Morrison's birthday?

Don Paulsen was the editor of *Hit Parader* magazine.

Don Paulsen: "Just another fad for screaming pubescent girls" was my first reaction to the

Beatles in February 1964. Musically, they sounded inferior to the John Coltrane, Thelonious Monk, Miles Davis, Charlie Parker and Sonny Rollins I was listening to at the time. Back then, I was a recent art-school dropout — like Lennon, and many of the early British rockers — who free-lanced cartoons, articles and photos to pay the $48-a-month rent on my fifth-floor Greenwich Village walkup.

But just a month after Beatlemania erupted, I was interviewing the Fab Four on the phone. And a few years later, I partied with John Lennon and George Harrison in London. By then my jazz albums had been displaced by the rock music I now preferred.

The sudden revitalization the Beatles brought to the music business gave me my first — and in many ways best — job in March 1964. Through the recommendation of a high-school friend, who was an editor for Charlton Publications in Derby, Connecticut, I was hired as their New York editor for *Hit Parader, Song Hits, Rock & Roll* and *Rhythm & Blues* magazines. During the next four years, I interviewed and/or photographed virtually every major rock artist who passed through New York City.

My second week on the job, I was invited to a transatlantic telephone press conference with the Beatles to promote their first movie, *A Hard Day's Night*, which they were just completing. Later, I was part of the chaotic mob scenes known as Beatle press conferences held periodically in hotel ballrooms during their American tours.

In 1967, when the Lovin' Spoonful (who were good friends of mine from the Greenwich Village folk-rock scene) made their debut in England, I accompanied them as both their personal photographer and as a photojournalist for *Hit Parader*. One night, John Lennon and George Harrison left a recording session to see the Spoonful perform at the Marquee Club in London. Afterwards, the two Beatles joined about two dozen people, including the Spoonful and entourage, Spencer Davis and Yardbirds manager Giorgio Gomelsky, at a small party in the Spoonful's hotel suite.

Everyone sat in a large circle quietly chatting, drinking champagne and smoking hashish. Most of the conversations involved typical musician shop talk (i.e., "How did you record that track?" and "Have you ever seen an organ-guitar?") Then, Gomelsky, who, earlier that evening had called John Lennon "the greatest unappreciated intellectual in all England," brought the room to a stunning silence by asking, "Tell me, John, what is the meaning of life?"

Lennon cast a weary glare at Gomelsky. The Spoonful's producer, Eric Jacobsen, jumped to the rescue by saying, "Well, that's a question best left until morning." Everyone resumed their more subdued conversations. The two Beatles left around 2 a.m. and the party continued a few more hours. Everyone in the room felt exhilarated to have spent a few hours in the presence of two Beatles away from the hype and the hysteria that surrounded their public image.

And those, more or less, are some of my Beatle memories.

Ellie Greenwich was a Brill Building songwriter, and the songwriting partner of Jeff Barry.

Ellie Greenwich: I was working as a songwriter at the time the Beatles invaded, and I watched as they wiped out half the American artists. We certainly didn't know it was going to happen, and we felt that if a song was good, who cared? But the British Invasion really did happen, and most of us independent songwriters were sitting there going, "Oh, dear; what do we do now?" It was difficult to get our songs recorded by the British groups. Fortunately the year they came in was the best year I had, with songs like "Leader Of The Pack," "Maybe I Know," and "Chapel Of Love." Manfred Mann, which was a British group, had a hit with my song "Do Wah Diddy Diddy." So on one hand it affected me, and on the other it was, "Oh, well."

Marshall Crenshaw is a former John Lennon in the stage show *Beatlemania*. He later recorded a string of excellent power-pop albums and portrayed Buddy Holly in the movie *La Bamba*.

Marshall Crenshaw: When I was about nine or 10, my parents used to let me stay up on Friday nights and watch the *Jack Paar Show*. I know I learned more from watching his strange guests — Oscar Levant, Jonathan Winters, and so on — than I ever learned in school. I think Jack Paar had a bad case of Anglophilia. He'd have people like Malcolm Muggeridge or Beatrice

Lillie on all the time, and he was constantly babbling on about Great Britain. One week he showed a film of what was then England's top TV show, *Steptoe And Son*, starring Wilfred Brambell (Paul's grandfather in *A Hard Day's Night*). This show was the inspiration for *Sanford and Son*. Anyway, I remember reading one week in the *TV Guide* that Jack's next show would feature a look at "England's No. 1 rock 'n' roll group, the Beatles." The idea of a rock 'n' roll group from England seemed totally unimaginable for some reason, but I was real curious. Unfortunately, something happened that week, and I missed the show. Shortly thereafter I started to hear "I Want To Hold Your Hand" on the radio, and the idea of a British rock 'n' roll band didn't seem so strange anymore.

The Beatles were not only the most innovative group in rock, they were the most popular. They dominated the American charts their entire careers. They had 23 #1 singles; 44 of their 47 singles charted. They had 18 #1 albums; 34 of their 41 albums charted. As solo artists, they had another 20 #1 singles and 14 #1 albums. And they endured. More than 10 years after their breakup, in late January 1981, there were 18 Beatles-related albums in the *Record World* top 200.

The Beatles single-handedly laid waste to the record charts. In 1963 the top records in America were "Sugar Shack," "Dominique," "Hey Paula," "He's So Fine," and "Blue Velvet." In 1964 they were "I Want To Hold Your Hand," "Can't Buy Me Love," "I Feel Fine," "She Loves You," "A Hard Day's Night," and "Love Me Do." "Twist And Shout" was a #2 record. "Please Please Me" was a #3. "She's A Woman" was a #4. "And I Love Her" made it to #12 and "I Saw Her Standing There" to #14. "My Bonnie" checked in at #26, "Thank You Girl" at #35, "From Me To You" at #41, "You Can't Do That" at #48, "If I Fell" at #51, "I Should Have Known Better" at #53, "Roll Over Beethoven" at #68, "There's A Place" at #74, "Why" (with Frank Ifield singing) at #81, a Beatles EP at #92, "I'm Happy Just To Dance With You" at #95, and the German version of "She Loves You" at #96. They were also responsible for Donna Lynn's "My Boyfriend Got A Beatle Haircut," the Swans' "The Boy With The Beatle Hair," the Four Preps' "A Letter To The Beatles," and the Carefrees' "I Love You Beatles." The top Elvis Presley song that year, "Kissin' Cousins," peaked at #12.

The week of April 4, 1964, the Beatles had the top five singles on the *Billboard* charts ("Can't Buy Me Love," "Twist And Shout," "She Loves You," "I Want To Hold Your Hand," "Please Please Me") and the top two albums (*Meet The Beatles* and *Introducing The Beatles*). And the next year the Beatles had four more #1s and four more chart singles.

The Beatles had all the trappings of a fad. There were Beatles dolls and wigs and Band-Aids and bamboo trays and bongos and bubble bath and cake decorations and hairbrushes and lunch boxes and oil-painting sets and hangers and Thermoses and panties and talcum powder and wigs and four sets of trading cards and the Milton Bradley Flip Your Wig game. There was nothing to match the Elvis Presley Side Burns Machine, but it was an overnight commercial explosion of unprecedented proportions.

While the Beatles were not the first group to experiment with drugs, or confer with a maharishi, or include drug references in their songs, or hold a love-in, or protest the war, they were the biggest and most popular. Their behavior was a pattern for society's behavior. What they did society could somehow find a way to condone. When John Lennon said in 1966 that the Beatles were bigger than Christianity, this was what he was referring to.

The Beatles were a great live band, though few people after 1963 can say they actually *heard* the Beatles play, or heard anything more than what seemed to be a band playing Beatles songs buried by a tremendous din of screams, whines, shrieks and miscellaneous wails. The Beatles' last live performance was Aug. 29, 1966, at Candlestick Park. The rest of their career as a band was spent in the studio. The Beatles broke up in 1970. They had been together as a band 10 years.

The Beatles did not record the first concept album, but they established the album as a coherent form of musical expression. They did not invent any of the forms of music they did, but they made all the forms of music they did better. They were not the greatest musicians of most breathtaking songwriters, but they meshed better and sounded better. They never really tried to sound like anyone else.

All four Beatles had successful solo careers — Lennon with his wife, Yoko Ono, McCartney with Wings, Ringo Starr with various bands and as a solo act, and George Harrison as a solo act and most recently with the Traveling Wilburys. Starr and Harrison had surprising chart success; Lennon's hit singles were few and far between until his death. McCartney and his band, Wings, made one wonderful album (*Band On The Run*) and a handful of undistinguished ones, and played what most critics considered to be well-crafted, basically empty pop-rock.

John Lennon was shot and killed in front of his New York apartment Dec. 8, 1980. After his death he had twice as many #1 singles (two) as he did before his death.

Ringo Starr played drums with the Beatles.

Ringo Starr: My grandfather and grandmother were very musical and played mandolin and banjo, and we had a piano, which I used to walk on as a child. Being an only child and a spoiled brat, my mother would let me do most things, so I used to walk on the piano, but never actually learned it. Then when I was seven, my grandfather brought me a mouth organ, which I never got into either, and then they died, and I sort of ended up with the banjos, but never got into that.

Drums were just the ones I always felt an affinity with. At 13, in the hospital, we used to play on the little cupboard next to the bed, and then once a week, they had a band to keep us occupied, since we were in there for a year. So they fetched this band around and this guy would have these big green, yellow and red notes, and if he pointed to the red note, you would hit the drum, or the yellow was the cymbal or the triangle, and things like that. It was a percussion band, but it was just to keep us entertained while we were in bed.

They used to come once a week to the hospital, and we used to knit and do all stuff like that — anything to keep us occupied. So in the hospital, I wouldn't play in the band unless I had the drum. When I came out, it was always the only instrument I wanted. So at 16, I bought a $3 bass drum, made a pair of sticks out of firewood, and used to pound that, much to the joy of all the neighbors. I couldn't really play; I used to just hit it. Then I made a kit out of tin cans, with little bits of metal on the snare. Flat tins were the cymbals, and a big biscuit tin with some depth in it was the tom, and a shallow biscuit tin was the snare drum, and so forth.

Then my stepfather, Harry Graves, who came from the south of England (we're from the north), went down to see his family one Christmas, and one of his uncles was selling a kit of drums for £12 (roughly $30). It was a great old kit — a great trap and all the wood blocks and everything — so I had that. I got that kit in January 1958. There were two problems, though. One, I didn't have a car to carry it and, two, I wasn't in a band. But in February, one month later, I joined a band, although I couldn't play. Nobody knew, though, because they couldn't play well, either. We were all just starting out playing.

It was called the Eddie Clayton Skiffle Group. The guy next door used to play guitar, a friend of mine used to play tea-chest bass, and we played "Hey Lidy Lidy Lo" and all the skiffle songs. We used to play for the men at lunch hour in the factory. It was mainly, if you had an instrument, you could join a band. It didn't matter if you could play. But my problem was I was always traveling on the bus, so I couldn't carry the kit.

Then we started auditioning, and we did every audition in the world, every free show we could do. We had no sense of time, so we'd start with the count of "one, two, three, four," and then it would be like an express train because we'd get faster and faster and faster. People were just dropping like flies on the dance floor because it was like, "Can't you slow down, can't you slow it down?"

So we did a lot of free shows. In that band, I didn't really need the full kit, but I always wanted to play it. Anyway, I got the kit, and I set it up in the back bedroom like a professional, thinking, "I'll practice and everything." I only did that one night and we had all the neighbors yelling, "Shurrup [shut up]! Get out of here!" because we were in very close proximity to everyone else. So I never practiced since that day, except with a band. I made all the mistakes onstage.

The only drum record I ever brought was Cozy Cole's "Topsy," parts I and II. I used to like Gene Krupa, although I never bought any of his records. It was that type of drumming, though, heavy kind of tom-tom stuff, and Cozy Cole was another tom-tom person. But I was never really into drummers and I never did solos. I hated solos. I wanted to be the drummer within the band, not the frontman. The longest solo I ever did was 13 bars.

On the first professional gig, they offered me 10 shillings, which was about a dollar and a half in those days, and the guy got so drunk at the end of the night that he didn't pay us anyway. We were really down about that, but it was the first paying gig. We [the Eddie Clayton band] had done all the auditions and won a few competitions and stuff like that, but also still worked in the factory.

Then I joined a couple of other bands, a skiffle group, and I ended up with Rory Storme, which was basically a skiffle group, but we were going rock. We were the first band to be thrown out of The Cavern for playing rock 'n' roll because it was a jazz club. The only thing we used to have different was that our lead guitarist used to come out of a radio. That was his amp. He used to plug into this little radio onstage, so suddenly we were too rock 'n' roll for this jazz club, and they threw us off the stage. It was all in good fun at the time.

That was in 1959. In 1960, we all decided to leave our jobs and go real professional, where that's all we'd do. So I left the factory.

It was a major commitment, but it was all I wanted to do. The family said, "It's all right as a hobby, but keep the job." My mother still thinks that to this day, I think: "It's all right as a hobby, son."

Anyway, this is a roundabout way of saying how my names came about. We decided to go away to play Butlin's Holiday Camp in England, which is a camp where people go for two week's holiday. So when we went professional and bought the red suits and the shoes and everything, we all thought we'd change our names, because show biz means changing your name. That's what's so great about it; you can call yourself anything you like, like Zinc Alloy.

So the guitarist called himself Johnny Guitar, and in the end, I think because we're English, we all picked cowboy cames like Ty Hardin, Lou O'Brien, Rory Storme and Ringo Starr, because of the rings, which I always wore then. As children in England, your cowboys were great heroes to us. To an English kid, a cowboy was a fascinating thing, you know, in his leather waistcoat and his black gloves and all of that, so that's part of it.

But then I used to do a 20-minute spot with vocals. I used to sing songs, because we used to do hours, so anyone could sing, play a solo or anything. The guitarist would do a couple of guitar numbers, then the singer would come on, and then I'd do a couple of numbers and that's why it was called "Starr Time." So I'd do "Let's Twist Again," "Hully Gully," "Sticks And Stones," a Ray Charles number, and a couple of other numbers like that. God, it's all so long ago.

I never did any drum solos. Never have; never wanted to — even at the beginning. While we were still at this holiday camp, we used to play in the Rockin' Calypso, but on Sunday, the big night, they had a big theater there, and they'd have name acts, and the local people working there would be on the bill. So we were working with the Happy Wanderers, an English street band with a big walking bass drum, trumpet, clarinet, and they were like a walking jazz band. They used to walk around the streets of London playing songs, and then the guy would walk around with the hat. They became very well known. At the end of the show, it used to get to the solo and I used to let their drummer take the solo on the bass drum: "boom, boom, boom, boom." I would never do the solo, even then. Never liked them. So anyway, that's when we got our names.

Rock 'n' roll was very big here, and Elvis was out in 1957. We're talking about '59 and '60, so we were just getting into rock and away from the skiffle stuff. We suddenly got amplifiers and played different songs. Rock was coming in, and that's where I went; that was my direction. I was purely rock 'n' roll. Drummers or musicians were either going for jazz or rock.

I was playing with Rory about 18 months or two years. We'd all played the same venues and, at the time, Rory and the Hurricanes used to be top of the bill. There'd be all these other bands on and occasionally, the Beatles would play. It ended up that they were the only band I ever watched because they were really good, even in those days. One morning, I was in bed as usual; I don't like getting up in the day because I live at night. So a knock came at the door, and Brian Epstein said, "Would you play a lunchtime session at The Cavern with the Beatles?" And I said, "Okay, okay, I'll get out of bed," and I went down and played. I thought it was really good. I thought the band was good, and it was great for me to play.

They were playing better stuff. They were doing very few of their own songs then, but they were doing really great old tracks: Shirelles tracks and Chuck Berry tracks, but they did it so well. They had a good style. I don't know; there was a whole feel about Paul, George and John. And Pete, it's no offense, but I never felt he was a great drummer. He had sort of one style, which was very good for them, in those years. I suppose that they felt that they wanted to move out of it more. So I just played the session and then we went and got drunk and then I went home.

It was a one-shot, but we knew each other. We met in Germany when Rory played there and so did the Beatles, but we didn't play with each other. There was heavy competition because we used to play weekends, 12 hours a night between the two bands and we'd try to get the audience in the club, so there was a lot of competition. And then, at 4 a.m. or 5 a.m. in the morning set, if the Beatles were left on I'd usually still hang around because I was drunk, asking them to play some sort of soft sentimental songs, which they did. So basically, they were at one club and we were at another club and we ended up at the same club. That's how we sort of said hello. We never played with each other, but then out of the blue, Brian came and asked me to play.

This went on for about six months, where every couple of weeks I'd play, for whatever reasons. Then there was talk about me joining, and I was asked if I would like to. I said, "Yeah," and then went away with Rory to play this holiday camp again because it was good money for three months, and we just played what we wanted.

About five weeks into this three-month gig, Brian called and asked if I would join the Beatles. I said, "Yeah, I'd love to. When?" He called me on a Wednesday and he said, "Tonight." I said, "No, I can't leave the band without a drummer. They'd lose a six-week gig, which they have left to go." So I said I'd join Saturday, which gave Rory the rest of the week to find a drummer.

Well, I'd rather starve with a better band, and I felt the Beatles were a better band. By then, we weren't actually starving. We were making not great money, but enough to live on. And the Beatles were making a bit more; they were coming up real fast. But I loved the band so much. I thought it was a better band, and I thought I had done everything our band could do at the time. We were just repeating ourselves. So it was time to move on again, and that's why. And I liked the boys as well as the music.

I left Saturday, played on Saturday night, and it was in every newspaper. There were riots. It was okay when I just joined in and played a gig and left, but suddenly I was the drummer. Pete had a big following, but I had been known for years in Liverpool, so I had quite a following too. So there was this whole shouting match. "Ringo never! Pete forever!" and "Pete never! Ringo forever!" there was this whole battle going on, and I'm just trying to drum away.

But they got over it, and then we went down to make a record. I'm not sure about this, but one of the reasons they also asked Pete to leave was George Martin, the producer, didn't like Pete's drumming. So then, when I went down to play, he didn't like me either, so he called a drummer named Andy White, a professional session man, to play the session. But George has repented since *(laughs)*. He did come out one day saying it, only when he said it it was 10 years later. In the end, I didn't play that session. I played every session since, but the first session, he brought in a studio drummer.

There are two versions of the first tune ("Love Me Do"). I'm on the album and he's on the single. You can't spot the difference, though, because all I did was what he did, because that's what they wanted for the song.

I heard that Martin handed you a tambourine.

Yeah, and told me to get lost. I was really brought down. I mean, the idea of making a record was real heavy. You just wanted a piece of plastic. That was the most exciting period of records — the first couple of records. Every time it moved into the 50s on the charts we'd go out and have dinner and celebrate. Then when it was in the 40s, we'd celebrate. And we knew every time it was coming on the radio and we'd all be waiting for it in cars or in someone's house. We wouldn't move for that three minutes.

And then, of course, the first gold disc and the first number one! But like everything else, when you've had five number ones, one after the other, and as many gold discs as you can eat, it's not boring, but it's just that the first couple of records were so exciting. I think they are for everybody. It's like sweets every day, though. You get used to it.

So I was really brought down when he had this other drummer, but the record came out and made it quite well, and from then on, I was on all the other records, with my silly style and silly fills. They used to call it "silly fills."

Everyone put me down, said that I couldn't play. They didn't realize that was my style and I wasn't playing like anyone else — that I couldn't play like anyone else.

I think I drove George Martin mad, because we rehearsed for the next record and I had a tambourine in one hand and maracas in the other and played the kit with them. George was just flabbergasted. I didn't have a stick in my hand; I just had a tambourine and maracas, and I was hitting the cymbals and smashing the tom with the maracas, so he thought he'd better do something about it. So he said, "Well, if you use sticks, I'll let you play."

He never said that really, but I think he just thought I'd gone mad, so he'd better please me and let me play on the next record. And from then on, I played, except for "Back In The U.S.S.R.," which Paul played on because I wasn't there. We just carried on from there, and then it got to where John and Paul were always the writers and the bass player and rhythm guitar and George was getting some notice as a lead guitarist, but I was still getting, "He's all right," so it was a bit of a putdown at the time.

George Martin dictated a certain amount, and then it was John and Paul's writing to consider. See, what helped me a lot was that I had three furstrated drummers around, because everyone wants to be a drummer for some reason. John could play and Paul could play and George could play, but they each had one standard style. We all have one standard style, but they only had one sort of groove, where I have two or three.

John and I used to have, not arguments, but discussions, because we'd be playing all these records and he'd say, "Like that," and I'm saying, "But John, there's two drummers on there," and he could never hear there were two drummers. They'd play stuff with two drummers on it and the three of them each had their own idea of what the drummer should do, and then I had my idea. So all I would do was combine my idea, their three ideas, and the ideas of the two drummers on a record. They got what they were given, and it worked. But that helped me to play. Also, the long hours in Germany, you know, you soon get your act together.

I've read most of the stories about me. There was a guy in New York who said he played on everything. All that bull has gone down. You have to let those things pass. Some drummer in New York wanted to make a name for himself and said he played on everything, and I never played on anything. So what was I doing? I know on some sessions I wasn't all there, but I wasn't off completely away.

In a typical session, what would happen is that someone would say, "Well, I've got this," because it was very early on that John and Paul didn't write together. It was their own songs, and then a lot of them would start as jams and someone would put lyrics to them. "Helter Skelter" was a full-on jam, and "Birthday." Or one would have a verse and a chorus and they'd finish them, or anyone could shout a line and if the line was good, they'd use it. The roadies, the tea lady, if anyone had a line, it'd be used.

It was always open like that, and always the best line would be used. It wouldn't matter who said it. No one had the ego big enough to say, "I have to write this." [They didn't do this] all the time. They wrote 90 percent finished songs, but not musically, because they could only use what we could play. "Birthday" was one case. We went over to Paul's and came back and wanted to do a sort of rowdy rock 'n roll track because Little Richard had freaked us out yet again, so we just took a couple of chord sequences and played them sort of raucous and loud and there was a newspaper on the floor and it was about someone's birthday. So Paul started singing and we all just bopped on behind him. That's how that came about, but we never went in with anything. We just went in and I sat behind the kit and they stood behind their instruments.

On the finished tunes, they'd sit at the piano and play them. Then we'd go through several different changes of how we all felt it should be done. Mainly, the writer had the definite idea, but if anyone did anything to change it and it was good and moved into a place they enjoyed, that's how it would be. There was a lot of open-mindedness. There were very few tracks with the definite idea, this is how it has to be. Mostly, if someone came up with anything that was different and worked, then everyone would go along with it.

I was allowed to create anything I could as long as it worked, and it was the same with the guitar or the bass or the piano. It was all the same, but the difference was that it had to fit around their song.

First of all, I used to rewrite Jerry Lee Lewis B-sides and not really know it. I just put new words to all the songs. It took me years to fetch a song in because I, as much as anyone else, was in awe of our two writers, who I felt were the best writers around. So I'd write my little songs and I'd be embarrassed to fetch them in because of John and Paul.

So then I started fetching them in and they'd all be laughing on the floor — "Oh, you've written 'Crazy Arms,'" or something. So then I started writing a bit more, like, "I listen for your footsteps coming up the drive," some song I wrote, don't know the title any more ("Don't Pass Me By"). That was the first one that we did of mine. But they used to write songs for me, tailor-made, because they knew my range and it was like a personality thing I used to put across. Or then I'd pick the country song, because I always like country 'n' western. "Boys" I had done for years, then they started writing songs just for me. Then I started writing my own, and then I wrote "Octopus's Garden." I always mention "Octopus's Garden."

We were on this boat and they offered us this meal and we'd ordered fish and chips, and the fish came and I said, "What's that?" There were legs and things. And the guy said, "Oh, it's octopus," and being English and food-wise, that blew me away. "Are you kidding? Octopus? You've got be to crazy. Nobody eats that. Tentacles? It's not fish; it's jet-propelled."

Then I got talking to the captain, and he was telling me the story of octopusses building gardens under the sea. They find shiny rocks and tins and whatever and they build these gardens, and I found it fascinating. I was just sitting on the pier one day and I wrote "Octopus's Garden" for me and the children. And some days you really feel like you'd like to be there, under the sea, in an octopus's garden, because it gets a bit tough out here, and it was a tough period then. So I felt it would be very nice to be real quiet under the ocean.

The breakup came because everyone had ideas of what he wanted to do, whereas everyone used to have ideas of what we could do, as a group. Then we weren't really fulfilling John's musical ambitions or Paul's or George's, or my own, in the end, because it was separate. We weren't working for one aim, just the one band. Everyone wanted to do other things as well. So you could see it coming, but like everything else, we all held it off for a while.

Then it just got too silly and we had a meeting about what everyone wanted to do. You can't keep a band together. We never did it for the money; we did it for the playing. I mean, the money is very nice, but we were players first. As anyone will tell you, if we had wanted, we could have just carried on and made fortunes, but that was not our game. Our game was actually making music. So it became too strange, because there was a lot of stuff I didn't want to play on that I felt just wasn't exciting anymore.

John is the easiest to talk about. He wanted to do stuff which was avant-garde in its way. I had no place being on it and I wasn't on some of it. He wanted to do that more than play with the group, and Paul wanted to do another thing, and George was wanting something else.

I just wanted to play really good music — not that any of it is bad. I enjoyed the group thing, and then people wanted to do other things, which could have included us if we had wanted to. But half the time, we didn't want to get involved with certain tracks because it just wasn't what we were there to do as a group. We were there to do it individually, but not as a group. So the regression started about '68 and it was over by '70. So that was the end of that, and I did feel lost. I'd never played with a better band, you see, so I think that's the loss I felt.

It's not even just the best. A lot of it was telepathy. We all felt so close. We knew each other so well that we'd know when any of us would make a move up or down within the music, and we'd all make it. No one would say anything or look at each other; we'd just know. The easiest word is telepathy. The band worked so well, and we were four good friends a lot of the time. But like any four friends, we had rows and shouted and disliked each other for a moment.

We had all lived together so close, we knew each other so well that it crossed over into the music. We knew exactly what the other was doing. That's even the wrong way to explain it. We just knew that the chemistry worked! The excitement! If things were just jogging along and one of us felt, "I'm going to lift it here," it was just a feeling that went through the four of us and everyone lifted it, or everyone lowered it, or whatever. It was just telepathy. When I do sessions now, I'm playing the best I can and some sessions are really great. But I've never played on anyone's album all the way through, because I always felt it was boring, so I'd do three or four tracks.

We enjoyed the girls getting their hysterical needs out, because no one came to listen to our gigs. They bought records to listen to. They just came to scream and shout, which was fine, but after four years, I was becoming a bad player because I couldn't hear anything. Because of the noise going on, what I had to do was just constantly keep in tune, so we'd have something to follow.

If you look at films, you'll see I'm looking at their mouths. I'm lip-reading where we're up to in the song because I couldn't hear the amps or anything. We were becoming bad musicians, so we had a discussion about it. We could be in any town or country in the world and get the same response, but only the four of us would know if we played any good, and that was very seldom because I couldn't hear. So you're getting the same response for a bad gig and it wasn't any help. You only wanted applause if you did something that worked, so we decided to go into the studio. It was no fun playing onstage anymore.

We did 30-minute shows, and if we didn't like the place, we'd play a bit faster and do it in 25 minutes. We were getting real despondent playing live, so went into the studio for months and months. It got us playing again and exploring a lot of avenues of the technology of the studio, which compared to now, was Mickey Mouse. Eight-track was a big deal then, and we didn't have one. We begged for one because we did everything on four-track up to the *Pepper* album, and four-to-four, but EMI was technically a very, very good studio with their engineers and electronic wizards. When we went four-to-four, to go tape-to-tape, there's usually a loss, but the loss was so slight, because their engineers were technically so good that no one missed it. You can't miss it anyway because the public didn't know what they were missing, so they only got what they got. But we put the drums through phasers and things like that.

It was great, because it worked with the tracks we were doing and it was magic. Just like magic. And we put it through the Hammond speaker and it goes round and round, whatever that's called, and just tricks like that. We put the guitar through something going backwards and it was all experimental madness to us, but it was in the form of a song. It wasn't us just freaking out, playing, which we did quite a lot, but we never released any tapes like that.

After the Beatles, it wasn't that I didn't want to play drums; I didn't know what to do with my life. I'd been playing with the band for so long and suddenly it ended. I just sat there wondering what to do with my life, because I wasn't a producer and I wasn't a writer.

During the sessions for *The Beatles* album (the "White Album") I left for two weeks. I felt I wasn't part of the group. I felt that the other three were really together and close and I wasn't part of the group, so because of that feeling, I felt I wasn't playing well. I went around to John, knocked on the door and said, "I'm leaving the band, man. You three are really close and I'm getting out." And he said, "I thought it was you three." So I went around to Paul and said the same thing. "I'm leaving. I'm not playing well because you three are real close and I'm not in the band anymore." And he said, "I thought it was you three." I said, "Well, I don't know who it is, but I'm going on holiday," and I went to Sardinia for a couple of weeks to clear my head. That's when they made "U.S.S.R." which I wasn't on. Then I came back to the White Album, which I felt, for me, was a better album that *Pepper* for the group.

We were much more like a band [on the White Album]. We're like session players on *Pepper*, using all those orchestras and sound effects. I mean, it was good fun, but I felt we were getting more like a group on the White Album again, though it was a double album, and double albums give too much information for me, anyway. But that and *Abbey Road*, besides *Rubber Soul*, are a few of the finest albums.

*The music became a lot more sophisticated, and I'm sure you were called on to do more sophis-
ticated kinds of things.*

Never. You got what you got. I don't know if it got more sophisticated. I don't think you'd call
the White Album sophisticated, but I enjoyed it more than *Pepper*, which you could call sophisticated. But you'd only call that sophisticated because of what you put on top — the brass section
and such. The idea behind *Pepper*, which never got fully realized, was that it was going to
be a whole show, just a concept album of a show, but we only got into two tracks and then we
made it just a regular album. We segued from "Sgt. Pepper" into the next track with the
cheer, and there's Billy Shears, and then we did it for two tracks and we got bored with that and
just made another album. The White Album was not to do tricks; it was for us to get together, I
felt, and play together as a group, which is what we were, and best at.

There's different styles of playing I did with the group, though it's the one attitude. I still
think the finest stuff I did was on "Rain." "Rain" is, to me, my all-time favorite drum track.

Because of what I did; wherever my head was at the time. It is a vague departure for me. And
Abbey Road, and there's lots of things in between; bits here and bits there. "Get A Woman," by
B.B. King; I felt I played some real solid drums on that. "A Day In The Life"; I felt the drums
were as colorful as the song and the guitars. There's one, "It's been a long time..." ("Wait").
That has really fine tom-tom work on it.

It's fine on everything, really, but some of them knock me out. And it took me awhile to listen
to Beatle records without going through the emotions of the day — how we felt, what was going
on, who was saying hello to who.

After we broke up, it took me a couple to years to really listen. You know, you'd make the
record and really enjoy making it, and when it was finished, you'd enjoy listening to it in the
studio and enjoy having it at home as a piece of plastic in a sleeve, but then I would never play
them again. Only in the last several years could I listen to them as tracks. And you can also look
back and see the stages you were going through or you went through.

Can you define what you think makes a good drummer?

Yeah: me. It took me a long time to think of myself like that, but I am probably the best rock
drummer, because I play with emotion and feeling, and that's what rock is. Rock is not reading
— and I'm not putting reading down, although it's something that I don't do and something I
never wanted to do. I did have one lesson in the old days and the guy wrote all those dots on the
paper, but I felt it wasn't the way I wanted to play. I only wanted to play, and some days it's a
real bummer for people, because if I'm on a downer, I still have to play, and you only
get what's in my soul at the time. But that's life. We all make a choice. A lot of session guys can
go in and read and play five different sessions a day, totally different types of music. He just
reads it and plays it, but that's a different musician to me.

Highlights? There's too many. Well, there's high and high. How high do you want to get? You
know what I'm saying? As an act, which we were, the Palladium or *The Ed Sullivan Show*,
because they were definite moves in a career. I always thought, though we played music, we still
wanted to be the biggest band in the world. Not that we knew it would be a monster, but we
knew we were aiming somewhere, and the only degree of saying it is popularity. And we did
become the most popular group on Earth, so there's all those moves.

But like the "Rain" session, where something just comes out of the bag that just arrives, that's
exciting, it's not a conscious thing; it just happens, and some sessions can get exciting. Musically, sometimes you would be blown away with what came out, but not every time. Other times
you did the best you could, and if it worked, great. But sometimes a lot of magic, a lot of magic,
just came out of the blue, and it comes out for everybody. To play with three other people, any
other people, when it works is when everyone is hitting it together, no one's racing, no one's
dragging. The song is good or the track is good and the music is good, and you're all just hitting
it together.

If you're not a musician, I don't know if you'll understand that, when just that four, 10 of you,
a hundred-piece orchestra, hit it together for as much time as you can — because there's very

few times it goes through the whole track, never mind the whole album — there is magic in that that is unexplainable. I can't explain what I get from that. It's getting high for me. Just a pure musical high.

I've had to maintain my perspective some, but I think you're born with it. Also, at certain periods, I did go over the edge and believe the myth, but I have three great friends who told me, "You're fooling yourself." They were going over the edge as well, but they had their friends, too, to tell them they're fooling themselves. It's not that we actually all did it at once.

During all the talk about the Beatles reunion and all of that, was there ever a time when you thought if you get together for a night that ...

Well, we did. The four of us never got together, but at certain times after the breakup, three of us got together. We looked at each other and smiled. It was interesting. Now, it's impossible to put it all back together, of course, but I don't think any of us really thought we'd get back together. Everyone got too busy. No matter how much money they offered us, we never did it for the money, then or now. Then, when we were doing it in the '60s, and when they were offering us $5 million in '70s, it wasn't an incentive to play. Money is no incentive for musicians. It's nice to have, but it's not enough.

It's hard to say where I'd be if it hadn't happened. But it did, so I'm exactly where I feel I should be. Does anybody know what he would have done if he hadn't been doing what he did do at the time he was doing something? It's impossible to tell.

The difference would be that you wouldn't be interested in talking to me. I had just been playing some little club somewhere. But whether I would have been a different human being ... it's hard to tell. I'm sure I must have changed, but would I have changed had I gone through a whole different type of life? I don't know. The effect it all had from being born to today and everything that went on in between is that we're here in the garden, trying to say hello. *(Robyn Flans; July 29, 1988.)*

14. Catch Us If You Can

When the Beatles began the British Invasion in earnest in 1964, they were neither the first British band to have hits in the United States nor the most likely band to come over and have hits. Johnny and the Hurricanes, one of the very first British rock bands, had a #5 hit in 1959 with "Red River Rock"; Ray Davies and the Kinks would later salute the Hurricanes in their song "One Of The Survivors." Lonnie Donegan, the skiffle singer, had the biggest British cross-over with "Rock Island Line," a #8 in 1956, and "Does Your Chewing Gum Lose Its Flavor On The Bedpost Overnight?", a novelty #1 in 1961. But until the Beatles, the biggest British rock groups of the early '60s — Johnny and the Hurricanes, Johnny Kidd and the Pirates, Rory Storme and the Hurricanes — were nonentities on the American charts. Groups were playing raucous, up-tempo music based on American R&B on both sides of the Atlantic, but American radio stations would play American groups and British stations would play British groups. And it would stay that way until late 1963.

The group that was hurt most by the segregation was actually two groups. With a singer front-ing the band, it was the most popular vocal group in England, even through the Beatles' heyday. Without the singer, the group was the #1 instrumental band in England.

Cliff Richard was a teen idol and movie star in addition to being a singer. His first group was called the Drifters; his first British hit was in 1958. Renamed the Shadows, Richard's group had hit after hit in the early '60s — in Britain. In 1962, there was thought that Richard might be able to make it in the United States. He toured and flopped. His records did little on the charts. He would not tour again in the United States until 1981.

But in the late '70s, when every other act from the British Invasion except for the Rolling Stones, Kinks, the Who and the constituent members of the Beatles were either long gone from the charts or altogether nonexistent, Richard finally made it big in the United States. Recording for Elton John's Rocket label, Richard — still with the Shadows — had a #1 with "Devil Woman," and was able to follow that up with "We Don't Talk Anymore" and "A Little In Love." "Devil Woman" appeared on an album appropriately titled *Nearly Famous*.

Cliff Richard: I wanted to sing from the time I heard Elvis. The first thing I did was join a vocal group called the Quintones. There were five of us, and usually at the end of the show I'd be asked to do my Elvis impersonation. When I left school at 16½, I formed a band with the drummer and we did a few gigs locally, getting a certain amount of notoriety.

There was a cinema on the north side of London that used to have a talent competition every Saturday morning. We told the manager that we didn't want to do the talent competition, but we'd top the bill for nothing. The word nothing rings all sorts of bells with people, so he said okay. The next month we went back and made him the same offer, but we had an agent watch us, and he was impressed by the reaction. I took a little record we'd made to EMI Records, and my contract began in 1958.

CLIFF RICHARD: 'I wanted to sing from the time I heard Elvis.'

The amazing thing to me is that my first record actually made it. I'm aware that now someone can make records for years and never have a giant record, but for me the first one made it. "Move It" went to #2, then there was a nine and a 17 before the #1. So my career had started going downhill before the #1 record came along. It shot straight in at #14 and we were hysterical for a couple of days. That was my first gold disc.

My strongest memory is the continual touring. The U.K. isn't a big place, but we toured for weeks on end. We lived from record to record, from gig to gig. I couldn't survive it now. You have to be 18 to handle that kind of pressure.

I never really got my clothes ripped off. From the beginning, I was surrounded by a team that said it was okay to be available but not okay to be so available that people will actually get ahold of you. What 18-year-old guy is going to be bored having girls scream at at him?

The Beatles frightened a lot of people. I suppose I was frightened to a great extent. But the best way I can described what happened to me, especially to people in America, is that my career just kept going. I released 80 singles, and 76 of them made the top 30. This includes the period of the Beatles and the Rolling Stones. The media latched onto the Rolling Stones and didn't write about anyone else for ages. It seemed as though we'd all been left behind. But in fact, my band and I were still doing sellout concerts and still selling records. What they did was to take over the media, which made it look as though everyone else had died.

As to why I didn't have American hits, I would jokingly say that the Americans have no taste, but I don't really mean that. I did a tour here in 1960 called "The Greatest Show Stars of 1960." The headliners were Frankie Avalon, Bobby Rydell, Sammy Turner, Clyde McPhatter, Freddie Cannon, Clovers, Crests. I mean, it was packed with people and we were the British added attraction. But we did stop the show every night, along with Bobby Rydell and Clyde McPhatter. I thought we'd really won the States, but we hadn't. And I think the reason was because America had all these Fabians, Rick Nelsons, Elvises, and they didn't need any imported idols. So we went back with our tails between our legs and decided to go for the rest of the world. We then went through an extreme middle-of-the-road period.

America is the fatherland of rock 'n' roll, and to have credibility here is something I want to chase. In 1964, a poll was taken that found that without America, where I sold no records, I was the world's largest-selling solo male performer. At that time I thought that was fantastic. So I didn't come to America seeking fame and fortune; I already have that. I just came here to share what I've been doing everywhere else in the world. *(Jeff Tamarkin; June 1981.)*

The most enduringly creative group of the British Invasion never had a #1 record and only had four top-10s, but cut the definitive heavy-metal song a decade ahead of the genre, made a hit out of the first rock song about transvestitism and never even cracked the charts with perhaps the most beautiful ballad of the rock era.

The Kinks are fronted by Ray and Dave Davies, brothers who have fought continuously yet have been able to keep their band together for 25 years. Ray is a satirist, a performance artist and a sometime drunken sop with a keen idea of what consitutes a great pop song; Dave is an inventive guitarist and occasional songwriter. They began their career playing debutante parties in London and got their name because of Ray's sloppy dressing, yet later they affected maroon hunting jackets and were among the best-dressed groups in rock.

The Kinks played Chuck Berry and Little Richard and R&B, and later mixed in Ray's material. Their music was unabashedly British, and mocked British customs and concerns with vigor and vitriol. But it sold.

It sold more in England than America. There "Dedicated Follower Of Fashion" struck with as much power as "Masters Of War." But the power-crunch wallop of the Kinks' two bookend hits of 1964, "You Really Got Me" and "All Day And All Of The Night" was universal.

The Kinks may have been the worst live band of the British Invasion. Ray Davies wore a guitar but refused to play it. The American Federation of Musicians banned them from performing in 1965 until they publicly apologized for their crimes. The crimes were not specified. The Kinks did not tour again in America until 1969.

The band fought on stage. One night in Cardiff, Wales, drummer Mick Avory hit Dave Davies on the head and opened a gash that took 19 stitches to close. But the band fought equally well offstage. In 1971 Ray Davies told *Rock* magazine, "I tried to stab Dave last week. Stab him. With a knife. We were having eggs and chips after a gig and he reached over with a fork and tried to take one of my chips, and I could have killed him."

Whether because of or in spite of their differences, the Kinks made great music. They did theme albums — *Arthur* and *A Soap Opera* and *Lola Versus Powerman and the Money-Go-Round* — that spawned great singles. One critic called "Waterloo Sunset" the most beautiful single song of the rock era; "Lola" was a hit that cleverly walked an is-he-or-isn't-she tightrope of transvestitism; "Days" was an aching ballad covered by Petula Clark and Kirsty MacColl; the early "Stop Your Sobbing" was covered by the Pretenders on their first album. Ray Davies later married lead Pretender Chrissie Hynde; together, they wrote "Back On The Chain Gang" and had a child.

Even in the latter stages of their career the Kinks have kept their wits about them. "Rock 'N' Roll Fantasy" mixed satire with loneliness and an achingly pretty melody and was a hit in 1976; "Lola" even made it back on the charts in 1981.

Dave Davies is the Kinks' lead guitarist.

Dave Davies: There's a million reasons why you put a band together; I think you just do it. Obviously, I remember going to record stores and buying Chuck Berry records. I remember "I'm Left, You're Right, She's Gone" by Elvis Presley, "Big River" by Johnny Cash — those sorts of thing. Before that, Hank Williams. I think he had a lot more to do with rock 'n' roll than people ever gave him credit for. He projected the emotion of rock 'n' roll. And I liked the black blues people before that.

It was silly. It got to a point where we got to thinking that if we were lucky, maybe we'd only have to go onstage for 10 minutes. We had competition to see who could stay onstage the least amount of time. It was really sad.

I don't remember much about the TV shows we were on. It sort of whizzed right by. But I remember *Shindig* because the guitarist was James Burton, who was an old hero of mine from when he played with Elvis Presley and Ricky Nelson. For me to have James Burton as a backup musician was quite nice.

I really enjoy playing live. There were periods when I didn't. When our manager would say, "You're going to America for six weeks," I'd say, "Oh, shit." I think Ray is aware also that we're working better than ever as a unit, which seems strange after all this time.

I never thought I'd be doing this when I'm 33! That's a depressing thought. I remember a few years ago, we did a gig with Bill Haley at a college and I thought I must be really young. I think rock 'n' roll has helped keep me young. *(Jeff Tamarkin; April 1981.)*

In 1963, only one British performer, Frank Ifield, had a song crack *Billboard*'s Hot 100. In 1964, more than 20 British groups or singers were in the Hot 100. Ifield was back on the charts again, but so were the Dave Clark Five, Herman's Hermits, the Hollies, the Rolling Stones, the Searchers, Billy J. Kramer, Chad and Jeremy, Peter and Gordon, the Swingin' Blue Jeans, the Animals and the Zombies. Cliff Richard even had a #99 hit with "Bachelor Boy."

The charts were jammed with British groups and great singles. Songs we take for granted as being #1 hits in 1964 were lucky to crack the top 10. "Glad All Over" by the Dave Clark Five only made it to #6; the Honeycombs' "Have I The Right" only made it as high as #5. Gerry and the Pacemakers' "Don't Let The Sun Catch You Crying" was only a #4, and the Searchers' "Needles And Pins" and Herman's Hermits' "I'm Into Something Good" stalled at #13. "Hippy Hippy Shake," the Swinging Blue Jeans' classic, didn't even make the top 20.

The British Invasion came from all over England, not just from Liverpool. Gerry and the Pacemakers, the Merseybeats and the Searchers were Liverpool bands, and came up through the same clubs as the Beatles. The Dave Clark Five were from North London; their first hit was a blatant "Tequila" knockoff called "Chaquita." Dave Clark was the group's drummer, and neither the group's lead singer nor its primary songwriter. Billy J. Kramer was a Liverpool singer who was put together in uneasy combination with a Manchester group called the Dakotas by Beatles' manager Brian Epstein. Herman's Hermits were a London band; their lead singer, Peter Noone, was 15 when the group had its first hits.

All the groups had hits in 1964, and were able to perpetuate their careers beyond 1964 to varying degrees. Gerry and the Pacemakers never had a hit to equal "Don't Let The Sun Catch You Crying," though their 1965 followup, "Ferry 'Cross The Mersey" became better known. The Searchers' version of the Clovers' "Love Potion No. 9" jumped to #3 in 1965, though "Needles And Pins" was the more enduring song. The group re-formed with its original members in the mid-'80 and cut two overlooked, underrated albums, which included covers of John Fogerty and Ducks Deluxe songs. Herman's Hermits had two #1s in 1965 — "Mrs. Brown You've Got A Lovely Daughter" and "I'm Henry VIII I Am" — and a string of lightweight hits that lasted until the late '60s, when the band had a rancorous split. After 1967 the Dave Clark

Five were finished as hitmakers; Dave Clark became a theatrical producer and resisted all attempts to re-form the group. Billy J. Kramer split with the Dakotas in 1966, and neither the group nor the singer had a hit again.

Gerry Marsden was leader of Gerry and the Pacemakers. Mike Smith was the keyboard player with the Dave Clark Five. John McNally was one of the founders of the Searchers. Peter Noone was the lead singer of Herman's Hermits.

Gerry Marsden: There's always been music in Liverpool because it's a seaport. I started my first band when I was 11. It was a skiffle band. So I have a million memories of just playing music in Liverpool. There were thousands of places to play.

Brian Epstein used to sell records in his father's shop, and we used to get the obscure American records by Ray Charles, Fats Domino, Arthur Alexander and all that. They had a great rhythm and lyrics and we had a good feel for the music. We never played the Cliff Richard type of stuff.

The Pacemakers were formed in 1959 to go to Hamburg. One of them was my brother Fred and the other two guys we just met in clubs playing around. Hamburg was brilliant. The Beatles and us went over about 1960. They played the Kaiserkeller and we played the Top Ten. It was a wonderful eye-opener. We lived from day to day and hand to mouth. But it was fun.

We first met Brian Epstein around the end of 1961. I thought he was a great guy, very charming. He was a brilliant man, had a lot of charisma, dressed very smart. He didn't change our hair, but made us tidy up our suits and smoke real ciggies instead of Woodbine. It didn't matter a bleedin' thing to us; we just did it.

Around 1963, as soon as we did "How Do You Do It," it was all, "Aaaaahh!!" Suddenly we came from obscurity to millions of people looking at us. But you didn't notice it at the time; you just played.

[Being chased by the girls] gave you the shits, though. It was very frightening. Luckily, they didn't catch you too often. They'd be shocked that they actually caught you. They'd try to take things off you, like your tie or your hair, or your eyeballs or your teeth. And we didn't realize how bad it was over here. It was amazing over here. It was wonderful stepping off the plane and seeing all that. My memories of arriving in the States are very fond.

The group split up in 1969. We didn't have a top-10 hit in the U.S. after around 1967. I went straight to the theatre. I went into the West End for five years to do theatre. The I got fed up of being in one place and I wanted to tour again. So I re-formed the band and hit the road, and I've been hitting it ever since. *(Jeff Tamarkin, March 29, 1985.)*

Mike Smith: I was fortunate in that my parents used to pay for me to take classical piano from the time I was five years old. Of course, a few years later when I heard songs like, "Since my baby left me ...," my classical training went out the window, and I started playing rock 'n' roll. Then when I was about 13, someone asked me to play in their club for a weekend, and I couldn't believe I was actually being paid to do something that I loved. So it didn't take me long to realize there was money to be made just by sticking with music.

The only group I played with before Dave Clark came along was the Impalas, which featured drums, guitar, bass and keyboards. We were playing in a suburb of northern London, and after Dave came down and saw me sing and play a few times, he asked if I would care to join his band.

Before we turned professional, we were playing clubs and paying our dues, and we found that a sax was great because it added another dimension and could be very raunchy if we wanted it to be. I know if we just had piano, drums and guitars the scope would be limited, whereas with a sax it just opened up our sound.

We did some of our very first TV shows together with the Beatles, including *Thank Your Lucky Stars*, which I think was in October of '63. I remember turning up for the show and sitting in the stalls where the audience was going to be later, and there were a bunch of guys next to us who introduced themselves as the Beatles. They said they were performing at a place that was close to where I lived, so I suggested we get together. And for three weeks we were going out every night, imbibing a little, and playing rock 'n' roll. That's when we first sort of met. The rivalry business was all media.

I can't remember the exact date — I think it was March or April of '64 — the Beatles came in and did *The Ed Sullivan Show*, and then we did it the following week. Then we did a sort of mini-tour, and one place I remember playing was Washington, where we had to go through an audience of about 20,000 to get on and off the stage. And what I remember most about that tour is that Rick got knocked down the stairs and cracked his head, and busted a couple of ribs.

In those days we had to sell almost a million records to get to #1 to beat the Beatles, and interestingly, we did it with the first song I ever wrote. Previously we had recorded a cover version of "Do You Love Me," but David wanted to do an original song, so he asked me to go home and write one. Well, I had never written a song before, so I assumed the first thing I needed was a title. So I went back to my record collection — which ranged from the Contours to Lightnin' Hopkins to Hank Williams — and I took out my Hank Williams record and I saw the title "Glad All Over." Well, I thought it was happy-sounding, and it seemed like something that should have been loud and noisy. So I decided to do a song called "Glad All Over."

DAVE CLARK FIVE: 'The music was supposed to be fun. It had no message; it was just supposed to be about fun and good times.'

David didn't do everything, although it may have appeared that way. David doesn't pretend to understand music, but he's got a good ear, and he proved that by picking out quite a few good songs. But when it came to the musical side of it, that was left mostly to me.

In the first place, the music was supposed to be fun. It had no message; it was just supposed to be about fun and good times. And if people our age can look back and say, "Yeah, I remember the Dave Clark Five, and those were good times," then I've achieved what I set out to do. I didn't intend to write "Rhapsody In Blue," and I don't have the ability to do so. But if my songs bring fun and enjoyment to people, then why not be proud of what I've done? *(Sandy Stert Benjamin, Oct. 21, 1988.)*

🐦

John McNally: It started off as a hobby. Most bands start off as a few lads having fun in their spare time. We copied people such as Buddy Holly, Eddie Cochran and Gene Vincent. We took our name from a John Wayne movie and started off backing a singer from Liverpool named Johnny Sandon. We all switched off and played different instruments as well.

The early days were just a lot of fun, really. It all happened so fast that it's hard to remember. We just enjoyed it. We'd listen to American imports, preferably unknown things, stuff like

"Twist And Shout" by the Isley Brothers, and "Money." Of course, we were fond of "Needles And Pins," by Jackie DeShannon and the Clovers' "Love Potion No. 9." Ray Charles' "What'd I Say" was another. Those songs never really got the exposure in England that they should have. We used to pick them up as imports and do them in our own Mersey way.

The Beatles opened the door for everybody. The bands such as ourselves, the Swinging Blue Jeans, Merseybeats, Hollies, Gerry and the Pacemakers, Billy J. Kramer and the Dakotas, were all playing around Liverpool and the Star Club in Hamburg, Germany. Then we were internationally known.

There was competition, but it wasn't a nasty competition. It was a healthy competition. What would happen was that someone would find an American import, such as "Some Other Guy" or Money," by Barrett Strong. Then — let's say we had find it — we would do a version and the Beatles would hear it and say, "Where'd you get that?" They'd do their version of it, and then Gerry and the Pacemakers would hear it and do it, too.

America was an odd dream to us, and it was fantastic to go over there. It was so fast and so much it was hard to take it all in. [The adulation] was very good. There was no getting away from it; it was great fun. If we didn't get that, we might have thought we weren't as popular as we seemed to be. Once it stops, you feel something is wrong.

We did the *The Ed Sullivan Show* right after the Beatles did it. It was quite funny because it went out live and we had three amplifiers, for rhythm, lead and bass, and only two of them worked. So we went out on the air with only two amps working.

We did a Murray the K show in New York that was fantastic. They had the Dovells and the whole Motown revue — Marvin Gaye, the Supremes and others — and Dusty Springfield. There was one night when I got drunk and did a solo on the floor.

You had to develop your own ideas about how to look on stage. The Beatles were really cleaned up by the time they made it. They started out wearing leather jackets and trousers, black t-shirts and black boots; they were scruffy, but once the records broke and they started doing TV, they were clean-cut, and they got stuck with that image. We also had a casual look.

"Needles and Pins" was around by Jackie DeShannon for awhile. But we didn't realize that we should do it until Cliff Bennett and the Rebel Rousers did it in Hamburg. They were using brass, and we thought it was a great song but the brass was covering everything up. So we took it and did our own version of it.

"Love Potion No. 9" was found in Hamburg, in a little record store around the corner from the Star Club. Chris and I were walking home one afternoon and we popped in there, and they had all these imports. We just took that one home and learned it.

It's very hard to say how we came up with our guitar sound. That was just the way our guitarists played. Maybe it was just the guitars we were using, or the amplifiers. But we found that when the two guitars played together, we came up with that harmonic sound, which was like a 12-string. And then we used 12-strings as well. We never thought it would have an influence. All we did was record, and if we liked it, we used it. There are lots of English bands now that use 12-strings and say they got it from the Searchers.

Why did we stop having hits? Boredom. Mike [Pender] and I got fed up with the whole thing, and we wanted to get home to our families. We lost touch with the music; it changed so quickly and we never kept up with it. *(Jeff Tamarkin; June 1981.)*

Peter Noone: I got involved in music because my father was a semi-professional musician and he sent me to a school of music, so I would not suffer from the things he suffered from, like not being able to read music. While I was there I met people who were musicians. I had always been a musician in the sense of being a musician with a tennis racket in front of the mirror. Then suddenly I got into a $4-a-night group and we did a couple of Bar Mitzvahs and an uncle's wedding.

I was 15 [when the first Herman's Hermits records were made]. The first recording was "I'm Into Something Good." It became #1 in England, and then it was nonstop until 1974.

Herman's Hermits weren't as clean as everybody imagined. I didn't create the image. That was done by *16* magazine and Middle America.

It was the most incredible period of my life. I was whizzed around. I was straight out of school. It had taken me time to get up the nerve to ask a girl out, and suddenly girls were asking me out on dates. I enjoyed every minute of it. I'd like it again. Not the teen magazines, because they're too fickle. But that is what I'd like. It's strange, because I've never had any heroes except for rock 'n' roll heroes, like Elvis Presley, Gene Vincent, Buddy Holly. So I never wanted to do anything else but play guitar, be in a band, be a poser.

Our records were absolutely perfect, because they were the right record that week. It wasn't a study in how to make rock history. We lived from one day to the other. We didn't think of how it would look in 1980. Remember, I'm from the period of disposable rock 'n' roll, when you'd make a record and it would be a hit, and then it would be forgotten forever. There was no "oldies radio" or stuff like that.

It was the right way to learn about the record business. I got out when I realized that Herman's Hermits couldn't make the step into the '70s. The name and the image were wrong. Herman's Hermits were perfect for the '60s, but they weren't prepared for the '70s. We were a pop group. Album bands made it, like the Kinks. When you think about it, just the name alone wouldn't travel into the next decade.

It was never cool to be Herman. I wished I'd been Mick Jagger. The unfortunate thing about the Hermits was that parents started to like us. That turned the kids off. It was a nice, safe band to be in. I don't want to be Herman anymore. Anyone can be Herman now. *(Jeff Tamarkin; March 1981.)*

🎸

Billy J. Kramer: I didn't even want to sing in a band at first, but when I was pushed into it I knew I'd need a name. My real first name was Billy. It was William Howard Ashton, which would have been quite all right now that I think about it. I said I'd change it as long as the first name remained Billy, because it was the only name I'd answer to. They took a bunch of names out of the telephone book, and I chose Billy Kramer. Then it was John Lennon's idea to call myself Billy J.

I actually came over to the States before the Beatles on a short promo tour. But it was really a disaster; the British thing hadn't taken off yet.

I'd met Brian Epstein, and then I came in third in a poll taken by a very popular magazine, *Mersey Beat*. It was at that time that Brian saw me perform and offered me a very good contract.

The only way he changed me is that I used to wear outrageous gear onstage, like gold-lame suits. And I started wearing mohair suits, that's all. I didn't mind changing. Actually, it wasn't Brian's idea; it was more the Dakotas. They didn't like all that.

Brian put me together with the Dakotas. They were already an established band at the time. He thought he had to get me the best possible band. We had a rehearsal down at the Cavern and it sounded great. Brian said they could do their own thing as well as work with Billy, and that was it.

Brian gave me a tape of John singing ["Do You Want To Know A Secret"]. I liked John's voice on it, but I couldn't see it being a hit. After that, John said to me one day, "We've written a song for you." and it was "Bad To Me." We were doing that and then we did the B-side, "I Call Your Name," in no time. I wanted that to be the A-side but we finally got "Bad To Me" together and it was a No. 1. So there you go; you never can tell.

I was so young then. To put it bluntly, I didn't know my ass from my elbow. But then, after a while, I said to myself, "Well, I can't go on doing this forever, riding on these guys. This Liverpool thing isn't going to last forever." Then the next thing I did was "Little Children." That was by Mort Shuman. I found that by going through a big box of acetates and hiding myself away. Brian and everybody thought I was crazy. They couldn't see it. I did a TV show for children when that was released, and I sang it. It sold something like 76,000 copies in one day.

I was terrified when I came to America. It really frightened me; I wanted to call off the whole thing and take the next plane home. When fame happens really quickly, it's hard to handle.

I was in San Francisco and I wanted to go out and buy some cufflinks. We were on the coach at the airport and I said, "Please let me out. I'll be okay." Then when we arrived at the hotel I saw 15,000 kids rushing the bus as we pulled up to the side of the hotel. We got off the bus and went to reception and then to our rooms, and I remember the feeling looking out my window and seeing all those kids below.

I remember making [the movie *The T.A.M.I. Show*], but I've never seen it. All I know is that I was very fat at the time. I know it was fun. Quite honestly, I really felt sorry for Mick Jagger that day, because James Brown went on and tore the place apart. I thought, "Jesus Christ, I'd hate to go on after him."

I signed on for so many years [with the Dakotas], and when that gig was up I thought, well, that's it, I've paid my dues, goodbye. I wanted to leave them before I made my first record. I thought it would have been more of a cooperation, that there could have been a lot better material and we could have made a lot more records than we did. We got along okay, but it was no great buddies deal. *(Jeff Tamarkin; March 29, 1985.)*

The British Invasion continued unabated in 1965 and 1966. The Mindbenders, fronted by a singer named Wayne Fontana but led by musical whiz kids Eric Stewart and Graham Gouldman, had a #1 with "Game Of Love" in 1965. Also that year, Freddie and the Dreamers had their first #1 with "I'm Telling You Now," and a Birmingham all-star R&B band called the Moody Blues hit the U.S. charts for the first time with "Go Now."

Each these groups met with a different fate. The Mindbenders dumped Wayne Fontana in 1966 and had a #2 with "Groovy Kind Of Love" that same year. Later, Gouldman would write "Bus Stop" for the Hollies, and would rejoin with Stewart to form first Hotlegs and then 10cc, the wittiest British pop band of the '70s. Freddie and the Dreamers would never have another top-10 hit, but the Moody Blues, minus Laine, would become the lushest rock 'n' roll band ever, and would find lasting fame through songs like "Nights In White Satin," "Tuesday Afternoon" and "I'm Just A Singer In A Rock 'N' Roll Band." Laine would later join Ginger Baker's Airforce and then Paul McCartney's new band, Wings, and would provide McCartney with a worthy counterpoint for his talents.

Eric Stewart: It's the kind of story you only read about, or maybe see in the movies. I was down at a club in Manchester one night where a singer was being auditioned for this record company. His name was Glyn Ellis, who later gained fame as Wayne Fontana. Anyway, his backup group didn't show, so he asked if I could sit in with some other people and help him pass the audition. I said, "Sure," so we held a quick rehearsal in the kitchen of the club and then went on. The record-company guy liked us so much that he said, "Great; that's it. I want to sign you up." And Wayne said, "But this isn't my band." The record-company fellow replied, "Well, this is the band I want to sign. So within two hours I had joined a first-class recording group. The name was changed from Wayne Fontana and the Jets to Wayne Fontana and the Mindbenders. There was a Dirk Bogarde film in the early '60s called *The Mindbenders*. We saw a poster for it on the street in Manchester, and it looked so good that we just pinched the name.

"Game Of Love" was written by Clint Ballard Jr., and offered to us by a publishing company, as songs always were in those days. Hardly anyone wrote their own material back then. Instead, you'd go around to publishing companies on Denmark Street and ask them if they had any good tunes. They'd play six or seven samples and you'd pick one. We chose "Game Of Love" and took it into the studio. I remember that session very well because Jimmy Page was in the studio next door, and I had to borrow his guitar to play the lead parts. We didn't have anybody in the group with a low enough voice to do the "love" bit, so we called on an English folk group called the Spinners. They had a black guy named Cliff who came in and sang the word "love" for us. And that's how the whole song was made.

Wayne got to the stage where he felt he was bigger than the group and just wanted to go out on his own. It was left to us whether to disband completely or carry on. Our record company then came up with a song by Toni Wine and Carole Bayer Sager called "Groovy Kind Of Love." They played a demo of it for us; we liked it and decided to record it. It was #2 in the States, #1 in England, and many other countries. That was in the spring of 1966.

I think the Mindbenders broke up because "Groovy Kind Of Love" had locked us into such a definite bag. You see, we were a very heavy band onstage. When we came over here and toured, we played places like the Fillmore West in San Francisco. We were headed into psychedelic rock. But whenever we got onstage, people would cry for "Groovy Kind Of Love" and that sort of thing, and we hated those songs by then. They wouldn't allow us to do the rock 'n' roll we wanted to do. We had no choice. We had to split the band up. *(Gary Theroux; Jan. 16, 1987.)*

Denny Laine: I got interested in the guitar from listening to Django Reinhardt. Django Reinhardt and that whole free-form approach to jazz — the gypsy scene he was into — were my whole inspiration for taking up the guitar. It was only later that Buddy Holly and rock 'n' roll came along. We were into all that, and then we started listening to American rhythm 'n' blues.

The Moody Blues were formed by the five of us [Laine, Mike Pinder, Ray Thomas, Graeme Edge, and Clint Warwick] from the five top bands in Birmingham. We'd all been in these different groups, and decided to form a group together and go south and see if we could make it in London.

We were originally called the M&B Five. M&B was short for Mitchell's and Butler, a local brewery that sponsored our first shows together.

We had one advantage over a lot of the competition. We got a lot of American records ahead of other people with help from a friend — James Hamilton. He was a freak DJ with an incredible record collection, and he used to get American records, demos, everything, ahead of everyone and let us hear them. The records he had that we got to hear were incredible. We got to listen to every James Brown record, every Motown record. We did a lot of them first, ahead of everyone else in London.

We made a lot of money from "Go Now," and toured constantly for a year without a break, but we also spent a lot of money. We had a good manager in Tony Secunda; later, Brian Epstein became interested in managing us, but by the time that happened in 1966, he was really only interested in the Beatles. None of his other acts held his attention.

There was a vote to replace Clint Warwick, and I voted to keep him in the band. When that happened, I felt that the group had changed, and I decided to leave as well. I was very happy for them when they succeeded. *(Bruce Eder; Feb. 24, 1989.)*

One reason so many British Invasion acts were able to come over and score so many hits was because they had personalities — fresh, distinctive personalities. If they didn't have personalities, those could be created. And if they had connections to the Beatles, so much the better.

Peter Asher's sister dated Paul McCartney. That landed Asher and his singing partner, Gordon Waller, a McCartney song called "A World Without Love." It was a #1 record worldwide, and launched the careers of a duo that began singing in a London boys' school.

Peter and Gordon were a cover band that covered good songs rejected by other artists. They had hits with four songs written by Lennon and McCartney but not recorded by the Beatles ("Nobody I Know," "I Don't Want To See You Again" and "Woman" — written by McCartney under the pseudonym Bernard Webb — were the other three), a Del Shannon tune the Searchers didn't want ("I Fall To Pieces") and Buddy Holly's "True Love Ways." They also had a hit with the cloyingly cute "Lady Godiva" before the duo split and Asher began a second career. By the end of the '70s he was the hottest producer in music, responsible for the best albums of Linda Ronstadt and James Taylor.

Chad and Jeremy were acting students by trade. Their songs were gentle and smart, like pastoral Simon and Garfunkel, and their acting skills kept them visible. They were guest stars on *Batman*, *Laredo* and *The Dick Van Dyke Show*, and that helped songs like "Yesterday's Gone" and "A Summer Song" become hits. Later they would produce an early concept album, *Cabbages And Kings*, and dabble in art-rock before heading to the theatre (and, in the case of Chad Stuart, soundtrack arranging and scoring) for good.

Peter Asher: My own musical tastes were fairly eclectic. I was listening to a lot of bebop and folk music at that time; I was a big Woody Guthrie fan and a big Charlie Parker fan. Gordon was more a fan of the Everly Brothers and Buddy Holly. I mean, I was, too, but he introduced me to some Everlys' stuff I wasn't really aware of.

I came to [R&B] second-handedly. I remember Paul McCartney playing me the originals on some of the tunes they'd done, and I hadn't heard them. I like a lot of music; I just hadn't heard it as early as they did.

[Gordon and I] had already met at school, but I had already left school by the time the walls went up around the place,, so he had to do the climbing over. I was a year ahead of him so I'd left, but when he had a gig I would go meet him and he would climb over.

We actually met [Paul McCartney] about the same time, and he and I remained friendly and he was going with my sister.

We were singing in a club every night called the Pickwick Club and Norman Newwell, who was an A&R man for EMI Records, came down one night and very traditionally asked us over for a drink. He asked if we'd ever made a record and we said no. So he said, "Well, come and do an audition." He gave us his card, and it was all for real. We went to EMI Records and cut some of the tunes we were singing in the club. They said, "Great; we like it; you've got a record deal" — a terrible record deal, I may add! We didn't know that at that time.

Then, when we were choosing a song to record, we did a song that Paul had offered us. He said they [the Beatles] weren't going to do it and they'd offered it to Billy J. Kramer, who didn't want to do it. We said we thought it was great but needed a bridge, and we asked Paul to write one for us. He didn't for a while, so we went back to him and told him that we'd gotten a record deal a really wanted to do it, but it needed a bridge. So then he wrote one. It was written a few days before the session.

They brought in studio musicians to play on it. I remember a guitar player named Vic Slick, who was a heavy studio guy at the time. Jimmy Page played on a few of our records, but I can't remember which ones. So did John Paul Jones. On one of our albums we had Brian Jones playing harmonica.

We were on a tour of Australia with Del Shannon and the Searchers, and he was actually playing ["I Fall To Pieces"] to the Searchers, thinking they should reord it. But they didn't like it. We overheard him playing it to them and we said, "We like it; we'll do it." And he said great, so we did it.

Someone had written that the Beatles could write anything, and if it had their names on it it would sell. Paul wanted to find out if that was true, so he put the name Bernard Webb on ["Woman"]. He asked if we'd mind and we said no. And, of course, it did sell anyway.

I hated "Lady Godiva." That's the only one I didn't like. I was never particularly proud of that record; I thought it was pretty dumb. I said "yuck," but Gordon liked it and it was a huge hit, of course, so he was right. "Knight In Rusty Armour" was even worse. I was glad to be out of that year. The comedy year never did it for me.

I have fond memories, but I wouldn't want to do it now. I remember doing the Dick Clark bus tours, sleeping in a hotel every other night because you were on the bus the other night. We were all driven around in a Greyhound, around 40 of us. The shows, you were only onstage around 20 minutes, and you couldn't hear yourself at all. It was a lot of fun being a British rock 'n' roll star and being chased by girls.

We just got bored with it, though, and Gordon and I weren't getting on all that well — normal stuff. We didn't hate each other like the Everlys. We just became less interested, and Gordon was anxious to try recording on his own.

I did some producing first. I did a record with Paul Jones. Then Paul [McCartney] came to me and asked if I'd like to produce some things for Apple. He's heard what I'd done with Paul Jones and liked it; in fact, he played on it. It was a single, a Bee Gees song called "And The Sun Will Shine." We had an amazing band. Paul [McCartney] played drums, Paul Samwell-Smith played bass, Jeff Beck played guitar and Nicky Hopkins played piano. So Paul asked me if I wanted to produce for Apple, and I said definitely. Then a bit later he asked me if I wanted to be head of A&R.

It all still sounds pretty good. It had the Beatles as a foundation, of course, and they're still the best band in history. So it's got a lot of romance to it, and the '60s as a whole were a romantic period. The music retains its fascination. *(Jeff Tamarkin; April 25, 1986.)*

❧

Chad Stuart: Let's start at the beginning. Touchdown LAX. We found ourselves the first British act on the West Coast by sheer accident, actually. We had a record out, but we weren't from Liverpool or anything. Actually, my grandfather's from Liverpool. Does that count?

The record was at first going up the country charts, which makes it probably the first country crossover record, bless its little heart. But we found ourselves "Beatle people" by default, and here we are, landing at LAX and the radio stations have been broadcasting our flight number and arrival time. There's a humungous reception; everybody's read about those. We were chased to the hotel by this tremendous platoon of children in cars. Take it, Jeremy.

Jeremy Clyde: We arrive, pull up to the hotel in the limousine, and the record-company chaps open the limousine door and say, "Make a dash for it; we'll cover your rear." So we make a dash for it, in our little mod suits and Beatle boots, but what we didn't know was that coming out of the Beverly Wilshire Hotel — and entirely blocking the entrance — is a very large and very formal Beverly Hills wedding group. Mums and Dads and bridesmaids and wedding guests, all done up to the nines. And there was nowhere to go but *through*. So through we do. They manage to regroup from this unexpected assault from two Englishmen, and then they are totalled by the second wave.

Chad Stuart: I wonder: Did we ruin our wedding day, or did we make it for them? I wonder where they are now.

Jeremy Clyde: Speak to us, wherever you are! What happened? Are you divorced?

Chad Stuart: We've been remembering a number of funny incidents lately. There was the time I was entering a stadium through the passageway that the athletes use, running along with my guitar under my arm, when this girl just jumped down on me. I remember not giving a thought to her well-being or mine, just, "Don't you realize this is a priceless Gibson guitar?!" Thank God she didn't land on the guitar; she landed on me. And then I went out and did the show.

Jeremy Clyde: There was one promotional something or other, some nonsense before which our visit had been heavily touted. The idea was that we would sign albums at a department store, in the record/TV/hi-fi/washing-machine department. And then there was to be a radio remote from the department-store parking lot.

We arrive and are taken up the back stairs, and when we look through the main doors we can see that absolute chaos is reigning. There are 3 million people out there, all with sharp ball-points! We look around for security, and finally spot one aging rent-a-cop.

"Where's security?" we yell.

"I'm security," he stammers. No, no no!

We're pushed to the stepladder from which we're supposed to talk to the people and answer questions and such, and the microphone is ripped out within 30 seconds. And over the heads of the crowd, we can see that the looters have started, and are removing a great deal of the store. People are walking out with color televisions, people are walking out with hundreds of dollars of hi-fi equipment. The place is being trashed.

So we're now taken to the remote truck in the parking lot. The crowd is out for blood. They are *baying*. And we get into this little caravan number with glass sides, totally surrounded in this glass box by thousands of people.

Of course, the radio station went off the air immediately. They pulled the plug first, with, "We have a technical interruption," and they're playing records from the main studio. We're out of contact entirely, and the people start to rock the trailer. They are about to bodily pick up the entire remote studio. We were finally rescued by a flying wedge of very large promotion men. By the time we got out, quite a bit of our hair was missing, and a lot of clothes went by the board.

Chad Stuart: They used to do all sorts of stunts in those days, and we never questioned it. We would get up in the morning and ask, "Well, what are we going to do today?", and next thing you know you're being taken to a helicopter. It all happened so fast, you didn't question it or question the principle behind it.

Jeremy Clyde: The things we went through have been sorted out. The first two years, we didn't have a life outside of tour buses. Dates would be booked where you'd drive all night in a converted hearse. That's how we invented the Road Breakfast. It's been used many times by many people, but I think we invented it. You've been driving all night and you're going to catch a two-hour sleep before playing again and starting the cycle all over, and you pull up to a gas station at six in the morning because nothing else is open, and you have a Road Breakfast: a Mounds bar and a Coke.

Chad Stuart: We grew to hate the William Morris Agency, though it wasn't their fault. They didn't know any better. The worst part was they never checked out the venue. If someone would pay the money they got you. The Jaycees in some remote little community got us one New Year's Eve and stuck us in a barn in the middle of a field. They made our dressing room from half of the jerry-rigged coatrack, and as the kids piled their coats on the railing the walls of our dressing room got closer and closer together, like the trash compactor in *Star Wars*.

I think the lowest point of my touring life was going out to the station wagon in three feet of snow and opening the back to get my prized boots out, and discovering that a six-pack of Coke in there had frozen so hard that the cans exploded and Coke was caked all over my boots. Ah, that was the road in those days.

Jeremy doesn't think [*Cabbages And Kings*] was a very good album. This was 1967, post-*Sgt. Pepper*, and I went nuts casting off the commercial shackles of having to write every song two minutes and 30 seconds with a hook. But we went overboard, in retrospect.

Jeremy Clyde: I took the album back to England, where people were much less involved in the Summer of Love and all that, and it was gritty-reality time. I arrived with this hymn to the state of man, or whatever it was, and got, "Oh, yeah, it doesn't rock much, does it?"

Chad Stuart: After that, Jeremy just had to go act for the state of his sanity, and my ego wouldn't let me follow him to London. And I stayed on to learn my craft, which is what I really wanted to do.

Because the bottom line is, do you believe in yourself? So we're blessed, really, because we can come back now and look at one another and say, "I respect what you do and, more importantly, I respect myself." *(Ethile Ann Vare; April 13, 1984.)*

The British Invasion was mostly restricted to groups and duos. Solo artists had a rougher time of it. And the most successful solo acts were women.

Petula Clark had been a British film and recording star since the '50s, making vaguely nostalgic films and cutting vaguely nostalgic records and being forced by her father and manager to be a sort of Annette-Funicello-meets-the-Blitz character. In the '60s, under new direction and conducting herself as a full-grown woman for the first time, Clark became the biggest female recording artist in the world, hitting the top of the charts with "Downtown," "I Know A Place" and "Don't Sleep In The Subway." She cut songs by the Kinks and Bob Dylan and became famous all over again. Sandie Shaw dressed like the fashion model that she was and cracked the American charts with her version of "There's Always Something There To Remind Me." Shaw was a female Cliff Richard, more popular in England than she ever was in the United States. But she influenced a score of British new-wave bands, who brought her back on the comeback trail in the late '80s. Marie MacDonald McLaughlan Lawrie cut her first record at 14 with a group called the Luvers. As Lulu, she had a U.S. hit with the theme from the movie *To Sir With Love*, which she also appeared in. She hosted her own TV show, recorded with David Bowie, played Peter Pan, and married Maurice Gibb, one of the Bee Gees.

Marianne Faithful was an angelic convent-school 17-year-old when she was first spotted by Rolling Stones manager Andrew Loog Oldham in 1964. Oldham introduced her to the Rolling Stones and turned her into a star. The Stones gave her "As Tears Go By," and she took it to #22 in 1965. One year later, the Stones would take it to #6.

Faithfull had a tumultuous love affair with Mick Jagger and an equally tumultuous affair with heroin and alcohol. She battled depression and became suicidal and wrote the lyrics to "Sister

Morphine." But she got clean and hit the comeback with a series of stark, graphic albums that established her as the chanteuse of the '90s.

But the biggest solo act of the '60s was also the closest thing the British ever produced to Bob Dylan. Donovan Leitch started singing in small clubs; by the time he was 19, he had a British hit

DONOVAN: 'We all wanted to change the world, and we were looking for new and different ways to do things. But as it turned out, what we found wasn't so new, or even different.'

with the Dylanish "Catch The Wind" and was being whisked away to America and packaged on a Dick Clark tour. His first top-10 hit, "Sunshine Superman," was a U.S. #1, and established Donovan as a singer of lightly psychedelic folk-rock. Donovan's later hits — "Mellow Yellow," "Hurdy Gurdy Man," "Atlantis" — did nothing to dispel the image.

Donovan was serious stuff at the time. Paul McCartney sang backup on "Sunshine Superman," and Donovan sang backup on "Yellow Submarine." Donovan taught John Lennon how to play finger-style guitar, and visited the Mararishi with the Beatles to get a personal mantra. He sang about colors and lands below the ocean and recorded with the Jeff Beck Group. By 1969 he was through having hits.

Donovan: I was part of that whole youth explosion in the '60s. We all wanted to change the world, and we were looking for new and different ways to do things. But as it turned out, what we found wasn't so new, or even different.

You go into the whole thing with this wide-eyed, idealistic outlook, thinking you're in control of yourself and your music when, in reality, you're in control of neither. Someone else is, and when you find it out, it's a shock. You're being manipulated and ripped off, and the only thing you can do about it is to disappear for a while. So I did. I needed my private life back.

Music *can* change the world. Music did change the world. It has a tremendous effect. A songwriter has tremendous power. You can introduce dozens of new concepts and ideas to the world through lyrics. An idea can change the world.

My music's been the soundtrack to a lot of people's lives. It might be interesting for musical scholars to go back and take a look at my work in relationship to that of others and see what the impact has been. *(June Price; Dec. 5, 1986.)*

Marianne Faithful: I had the flu. I was had been working too hard and I just crashed for two days in a hotel, and by chance Jackie DeShannon was in the next room. She was having an affair with Jimmy Page, who was at the time a little session musician who had worked on "As Tears Go By." We were looking for my next record when I met them. I was a very sick, overworked, 17½-year-old girl taking antibiotics, and they sat in the next room and wrote ["Come And Stay With Me"] for me.

["Sister Morphine"] was the first proper thing that I wrote. As for my records, we compromised. I got to make two albums at once. One of them was a pop commercial album; the other was the album I wanted to make. But it didn't happen here as it did in England. What you got in America was a mixture.

Andrew [Oldham] was two years older than I was, and so self-assured. I actually realize now that he didn't know much more about it as I did. We were all learning as we went along. *(Marianne Meyer; February 1982.)*

The Rolling Stones called themselves the "world's greatest rock 'n' roll band," and for the time they were calling themselves that, the Stones came as close as anyone to the title.

The Rolling Stones had the reputation of being one of the roughest, rawest, rudest bands of the British Invasion, yet they were one of the most educated. Mick Jagger was public-school educated and won a scholarship to the London School of Economics. Keith Richards and Charlie Watts were art students. Bill Perks — Bill Wyman — was an office worker with a wife and family who had served in the Royal Air Force. Even Brian Jones, the true rebel of the group, had aced his public-school examinations and was in line for university when he gave it up for good for music.

Each one loved blues and R&B and early rock 'n' roll. Mick Jagger met Keith Richards when Jagger saw a Chuck Berry record under Richards' arm. Charlie Watts was the drummer for Alexis Korner's Blues Incorporated, a band Jones and Richards and Jagger and Wyman worshipped, and sometimes sat in with.

"It all boils down to the fact that the first band in the field produces all the leaders," Charlie Watts said. "When you consider Paul Jones used to come down from Oxford, Brian Jones from Cheltenham, and Eric Burdon from Newcastle — all to hear Blues Incorporated. And Mick, Brian, John Mayall, Graham Bond and Long John Baldry used to sit in on sessions ... I left because I really wasn't good enough for Blues Incorporated. The others were such fantastic musicians, and I couldn't keep up the pace."

Jones decided to form a band, and recruited Jagger, Dick Taylor, Richards, and Watts. Their first gig was at the Marquee Club filling in for Blues Incorporated, who were playing a radio broadcast that night.

The band played raw, energetic blues, but lacked direction. That direction was supplied by an ambitious 19-year-old former press agent for the Beatles named Andrew Loog Oldham. Oldham signed on as the band's manager and immediately began cultivating their image. Within a month after Oldham became their manager the Stones signed a record contract, recorded their first single and appeared on their first TV show.

Oldham was described as "a long-haired, gangling youth who uses makeup and swears like a dyspeptic drill sergeant. Some say he is mad as a five-bob watch. Others acclaim him a genius of pop." He carefully cultivated the Stones' image as rebels, and helped the Stones make hits.

Little by little, the Stones eased away from strict blues/rock and into the young rock mainstream. Phil Spector attended the session where they cut the Buddy Holly song "Not Fade Away." Gene Pitney wrote them songs and played piano, and they toured with the Everly Brothers. Most important, Jagger and Richards began to write songs together.

Jagger and Richards were the angry counterparts to Lennon and McCartney. They were the Glimmer Twins, and their songs always had a kick or a snarl to them. The best songs — "Satisfaction," "Get Off Of My Cloud," "Time Is On My Side," "Paint It Black," "19th Nervous Breakdown," "Ruby Tuesday" — were big hits. The worst songs were saved and reworked into better songs.

But In America the band got the same treatment as Freddy and the Dreamers or the Mind-benders. Girls went wild. The Stones appeared on *The Ed Sullivan Show* and the crowd rioted. Sullivan said afterwards, "I promise you they'll never be back on our show." And the fact that they seemed to be always rebelling against authority made them even more popular with teen-agers and less popular with their parents. If the Beatles were the first British group to put a wedge between parents and children, the Rolling Stones were the group that drove it home.

The mayor of Milwaukee called their concert "an immoral thing"; Jagger, Jones and Wyman were fined for urinating against a filling-station wall; Olympic gold medalist Lynn Davies critic-ized their behavior (to which Jagger replied, "The public rooms in this hotel ... were jammed with athletes behaving badly"); the Australian press assaulted Jones after he said "Christ" in a radio interview; and the hits kept coming.

By 1968, though, the cracks were starting to show. Brian Jones was less interested in the group and more interested in drugs and alcohol. His involvement on the *Beggars' Banquet* album was minimal. On July 3, 1969, he was found floating in his swimming pool at his Sussex country home. The Stones hired guitarist Mick Taylor out of John Mayall's Bluesbreakers and kept right on playing and making hits.

In fact, the '70s Stones were tougher than their '60s incarnation. Their sound changed to a driving, chugging rock 'n' roll that produced the classic albums *Exile On Main Street* and *Let It Bleed*, and more hits: "Tumblin' Dice," "Brown Sugar," "Angie." Richards became a heroin addict and Jagger an international playboy, but they were still capable of going into a studio or going onstage and making the sparks fly.

With former Faces guitarist Ron Wood replacing Taylor, the band settled into a sort of calcu-lated, polished roughness and coasted through the '80s with only the occasional kick ("Start Me Up"). In the '90s they toured again and recorded again, maybe no longer the World's Greatest Rock 'N' Roll Band but still surprisingly close.

Dick Taylor later founded the Pretty Things. Marshall Chess was head of Chess Records and the first head of Rolling Stones Records. Ian Stewart was the band's piano player and road manager.

Dick Taylor: I was at school with Mick Jagger. We were both interested in the same sort of music, and I was at art school with Keith Richards after. I didn't introduce Mick and Keith, but we were rehearsing around my house, a band with Mick and myself and other people. I was playing drums. I'm almost as bad a drummer as I am a singer. I really can't do anything on them now, but I did then and also played guitar sometimes. For ages we were playing in bands, and we were still doing that after I left school. Mick was still there at that time, and I met Keith at art school. Mick and Keith met at the station clutching their Bo Diddley and Chuck Berry records and started chatting. What I didn't know was that Keith really wanted to come around and play with my band wherever my band was, but apparently he was too shy to ask.

Anyway, then we started playing, with Mick, Keith, myself and some other people. Then we went to a club where Alexis Korner played and saw Alexis Korner and Cyril Davies. Charlie [Watts] was playing drums then. Everyone used to go down there and see Dexter Smith and Paul Jones and all those people. Paul Jones was introduced as P.P. Jones and his friend Brian Jones. They came up and played. Paul Jones had a pair of wraparound shades on, and Brian sat down with his guitar. They played some Muddy Waters stuff with some really nice slide guitar. There we were, saying, "Yeah, he's good." It was amazing, hearing this at a club in London.

Then we started thinking that we could do this, too. I think Mick and Keith got up on stage and sang and played. Brian Jones started a band and invited Mick to play, and Mick said he wanted Keith to come along. Keith was not liked because his guitar playing was thought to be a bit too rock 'n' rollish. So the band Brian started was with myself, Mick and Keith. Charlie kept turning up at rehearsals. We had another drummer, but he didn't turn up. Of course, Ian Stewart played the piano, and we just used to rehearse at a pub in London.

Brian was really the instigator of the band, but there was the nucleus of a band which had played before that, which was Boy Blue and the Blue Boys. That was the start of it, and then I just played a couple of gigs. We used to rehearse every week. Then I decided, well, I was playing bass, I felt like playing guitar rather than bass guitar. I was also trying to get some exams at art school and feeling a bit stretched trying to do both. I just felt it was time for a change and sort of departed. Then the Stones started doing the art-school circuits and clubs. *(Darrel H. Mullins; Oct. 6, 1989.)*

❦

Marshall Chess: I got a phone call from a guy named Bob Krasnow, who had Blue Thumb Records at the time. He called from California and said, "I know what happened with GRT" — Blue Thumb was half-owned by GRT — "And I heard that you're free. If something came up, would you be interested in moving to California?"

"Why?"

"Well, I heard the Rolling Stones were looking to get away from London Records and their manager, and because they had some kind of attachment to Chess, perhaps they'd consider going to a small independent label like Blue Thumb," and he wanted to give me a part of it. I was fed up with Chess; they were trying to put their own ego on top of what they bought. I'll tell you the truth: I didn't want to work with *anyone*. After GRT, I didn't want that, and I told them that. But I had met the Stones then they had come in [to Chess] to cut "2120 S. Michigan Ave."

A week or two later I got Mick Jagger's phone number. I called from Chicago and said, "Hello, this is Marshall Chess." And he said, "Hello man; how *are* you?" Very friendly, and I'll tell you the truth: At the time, I was no way a Rolling Stones fan! I think I owned one LP — *Under Their Thumbs*, or something like that. I was just a record man looking for product, and I knew they were funky. We established, in a quick phone call, that I was available, that Chess was sold and I couldn't get along with those people, and I was free, and I heard from Krasnow that the Stones were looking. I told him the whole thing. He said he was very interested in speaking with me, and could I fly over to London because he couldn't come to America because he had visa problems.

So a couple of weeks later, I flew over to London, and that's how it began. I had a meeting with him, which progressed to two or three meetings with him, then a meeting with the group. I was eventually hired as a consultant in getting rid of Allen Klein and London Records, and making a new deal. My marriage at the time was shit, so all of a sudden I was out of Chicago and into Europe and my whole world ... It was like switching channels.

I made a deal with Atlantic as *Ya-Yas* was being produced as the last London album. I formed Rolling Stones Records, the logo with the lips. *Sticky Fingers* was the first record I worked on 100 percent, and they just expanded and gave me what the never had at Chess, which was total freedom. It took almost a year to cut the deal, and during that time the record was being cut. I was president of Rolling Stones Records, and part of the situation was to design a system where they would not have a manager. They don't to this day; the system still works. They have a financial manager, Prince Rupert Lowenstein, a big merchant banker in London who knew nothing of the record biz and started about two weeks before me. So it was me and him; I did creative and he did financial, and we hired experts in every area for high money rather than have a manager that took a percentage. It worked, and I think it's still working now. I got immersed in that. That became my life. I became a very big fan of their music. We spent hundreds of hours in the studio, me as much as any one of them. That went along very fine, but the lifetsyle became very heavy. I began to take drugs heavy and get worn down. And after the *Black And Blue* album — I guess it was '75 — I quit. The reason I quit was it was just time to make another change.

It was all very interesting, so I have no regrets at all. It was just like a relationship that peaked out and I opted to end it, like you do in a marriage. It was an intimate relationship that was just very wearing on me.

We run into each other all the time. I think there's a definite love for each other. The label's still there. It was a very successful marriage that ended due to — I don't know, pure lifestyle choice. And luckily I wasn't a Rolling Stone! It isn't that easy for them to end their thing. They're like in the prison of being a Rolling Stone. *(Cary Baker; November 1982.)*

Keith Richards: The atmosphere in which blacks live in America hasn't really changed that much, but it's not the same high-pressure-cooker atmosphere of the postwar period, which tended to produce the incredible burst of energy in music. Our interest in it was purely due to the fact that when rock 'n' roll burst on the scene, when you happened to find out exactly who was doing the best records, it happened they were black artists. Apart from one or two white people, rock 'n' roll was played best by black people: Chuck Berry, Little Richard, Bo Diddley.

There still seems to be a real color bar in America. You would think that by the late '60s and early '70s that would be a thing of the past. But black people are not making an identifiable sound of their own now. Prince is hardly as mind-shattering or as interesting as when Little Richard or Otis Redding or Chuck Berry first appeared. It's quite a white-influenced sound. Black music is no longer as identifiably black as it used to be. [And new young white bands] don't think they're being influenced by black music when in actual fact, the music, being based very loosely on stuff we did and the influences of other '60s white groups, is — although they don't realize it — a once-removed copy of black music. It's white kids copying white kids copying black kids.

Now we're used to [bands modeling themselves after us], but there was a time when we used to say, "Let's spot the Mick Jagger and the Keith Richards character in that group." In a way, it's a mixture of cynicism and flattery. In a way you're kind of pleased about it; it's always great to know you've influenced so many people. It's also that you realize that what you were doing didn't come out exactly as you wanted it.

It's strange when you see these influences, because it doesn't seem we've been around that long. Sometimes it seems like a few days. When we actually started to cut our first record, we had the feeling that this is really the beginning of the end, because in the early '60s, even if you were a success, 99 percent of the recording acts lasted 18 months to two years. We felt that it would be over before we really got going, so it was very strange that we just kept going.

On ["Let's Spend The Night Together" on *The Ed Sullivan Show*], the rest of the band wasn't singing, so we didn't give a damn whether you changed a lyric. We didn't consider it to be an incredibly moral stand that we'd be selling out if we did it. But by telling us to do this, those people actually, in fact, enhanced the thing they were trying to avoid. That was typical of self-imposed censorship by the networks. By trying to avoid somebody, they end up tripping up everybody.

I always remember when we'd do the Sullivan shows, there'd be these hushed, reverent tones the minute he walked into the studio. And he'd say, "The Bible Belt, the Bible Belt." It's the one phrase that sticks in my mind: "Sorry, boys, we can't do it. We have to consider the Bible Belt."

If you think back to any given period, 90 percent of the music has been crap and has had a large following. Like when we started, the Dave Clark Five, Herman's Hermits — an awful lot of rubbish came out of that period. It's the other 10 percent that's interesting and makes you want to carry on.

I'd like to be playing as well as Muddy Waters and Chuck Berry when I'm 60 — and no doubt people will be asking me the same thing then. But as long as I can play well and improve my own life, then, damn it, I'll be playing. *(Andrew Edelstein; May 1983.)*

Bill Wyman: Phil Spector tried to buy us from Decca, because he didn't think they were doing a very good job on us at the time, which they weren't. He thought he could make us into an enormous American success, and he probably was right. He was ready for that, but Decca wouldn't release us.

There were a lot of other people in the studio. Two of the Hollies, Allen Clarke and Graham Nash, were banging bottles. It was all a lot of fun then. Gene Pitney called by and played piano on "Little By Little," "Now I've Got A Witness," "Can I get A Witness," and some other things. "Not Fade Away" was actually done then. We also cut a few naughty ones which couldn't be released, like "Andrew's Blues." Phil Spector was involved in that.

Phil was Andrew's idol. He tried copying him in the studio but didn't succeed. And the *Metamorphosis* album hardly had anything to do with the Stones. It was comprised mostly of Mick and Keith's songwriting demos for other artists. Almost no other Stones were on that album, even though it was released under our name.

No album we release is ever made up entirely of new tracks. Whenever we go into the studio we don't cut 10 tracks and stop. We might cut 20 tracks, and there'll be certain ones we can't use because they'll be similar to others, and you can't have four slow songs on one album. We're perfectionists, and unless something sounds shit-hot at the time we won't put it out. On reflection, some things we put out weren't very good, but we thought they were at the time. We put songs aside and go into the studio a year later and listen to see if they're still of use. We may add guitar, some lyrics, update a vocal, or just leave it as-is. Every one of our albums has songs from another era, whether it's only two to three years in the past. Which is why we just can't take the critics very seriously. Some guy'll get a new album and write something like, "The Stones have finally got it together. This is the album they should have made years ago. It's so totally contemporary." Often it *is* the album we made years ago.

Why should rock 'n' roll be the only music that is not played to mature people? Here are fantastic jazz instrumentalists in their '60s and '70s, great blues singers, classical instrumentalists. People reach their peak at different times, and the Stones just seem to be getting better and better every year. One of these days we'll probably make quite a good career out of it. *(Glenn Baker; May 1983.)*

Ian Stewart: R&B was a term used to encompass a lot of things, but nobody in the U.K. really knew what it was, because all of the minor American labels. Like Chess, had no distribution in England. So people only vaguely knew what R&B was all about. The stuff that Brian knew was the guitar stuff — Slim Harpo, Jimmy Reed, Bo Diddley and stuff like that. The R&B I knew were the Wynonie Harris things and the Louis Jordan things. We both had a different idea of what R&B was.

I was the second Stone, not the sixth Stone. I am actually company secretary. Road manager still applies. Call me anything you like.

I honestly don't like Andrew Oldham as a person. I just don't like his attitude. He's a brilliant guy, actually. And if it were not for him, I don't think the Stones would've gotten to where they are now. Mick and Keith would have made it no matter what. I mean, there would have been a Rolling Stones; there would have been a group exactly like the Rolling Stones, whether Brian and I existed on the face of this earth or not. Having said that, they would've probably, if not for the careful handling of the group by Andrew, burned themselves out in two or three years by playing too much. But Andrew was very careful about the exposure and image of the group. That was all handled very well. Andrew was very, very clever, actually. Andrew only slipped up when he tried to be a record producer. He knows nothing about music whatsoever. *(Bill German; May 1983.)*

Charlie Watts: Stew [Ian Stewart] would come up to you after the set and say, "That was *bloody awful!*", or, "It was *great!*" Stew had complete honesty, a strange sort of honesty. It didn't matter if everyone out there in the audience was screaming. He'd say, "That was *bloody awful!*" Sometimes with the Stones, you'd be playing for Stew, for him to say it was great. You would want to please him. Keith and I would actually be playing some nights for *Stew*. It had nothing to do with an audience. There'd be 40,000 people paying to get in, and we'd be playing to please Stew.

When I played with the Rolling Stones, and things were good, I used to imagine I was Ray Lucas, the drummer for King Curtis, or I'd imagine I was the drummer with the Temptations. I was never me. I never have turned into myself. I still imagine I'm so-and-so. *(Gene Kalbacher; March 27, 1987.)*

Mick Taylor: With the benefit of hindsight I can honestly say they were really the greatest rock 'n' roll band in the world. And also, you know, the Stones were one of the few English rock 'n'

roll bands that have stayed together as long as they have. I mean, apart from the Who and a couple of other bands, I can't think of anybody else that has been together as long as they have, and that have always been famous. *(Kit Kiefer.)*

The Animals were the only band that could match the Rolling Stones for scruffiness and power. And while the Rolling Stones' scruffiness was partly an act, the Animals' was not. They were bluesy and outrageous, and one of the most unsettled bands in rock 'n' roll.

The group was formed out of a combo led by keyboard player Alan Price and guitarist Hilton Valentine. Eric Burdon, a short, intense singer obsessed with John Lee Hooker, was leading a group called the Pagans and playing a place called the Downbeat Club. The groups combined and moved to the Club A Go Go.

As the Animals, the new group became notorious. Burdon onstage was like nothing else in England, and nothing this side of James Brown. Producer Mickie Most, who would later guide the careers of Herman's Hermits, signed them, cleaned them up a bit, got them a recording contract with EMI and sent them to London.

The disagreements started immediately. The Animals wanted to play and record blues. Most wanted them to cut pop singles and work with contemporary songwriters.

They compromised. The first single was a reworked Bob Dylan song, "Baby Let Me Take You Home." Their second single was also a reworked tune off the *Bob Dylan* album. "House Of The Rising Sun" featured Alan Price's churchy organ and Burdon's growling, screaming, typically daring vocal. It went to #1 in England and the United States, and launched the Animals' up-and-down career.

The first Animals were a cover band that chose inspired covers. While Mann and Weil's "We Gotta Get Out Of This Place" was written for them, "Don't Let Me Be Misunderstood" was an obscure Nina Simone song and "See See Rider" was a Ma Rainey chestnut. All three were hits. Original songs, like "I'm Crying" and "Inside Looking Out," were less successful. All were delivered with soulful authority by Burdon; in fact, the entire group had such a "black" sound that *Ebony* magazine gave them an unheard-of six-page spread.

But the Animals were falling apart from the moment they got together. Burdon fired Most in 1965; Alan Price, who was afraid of flying and tired of Burdon, left that same year. By the end of 1966 the only original Animal left was Burdon. Burdon kept the name, hired new musicians and took the new Animals in an entirely different direction. The group began playing a sort of psychedelic blues hash and covering songs like "Paint It Black" and "River Deep, Mountain High." Burdon emerged as a writer, penning hymns to LSD and gentler songs like "San Franciscan Nights" and "Sky Pilot." The band played the Monterey Pop Festival in 1967; Burdon moved to California and hung out with Jimi Hendrix (who was first brought to England by original Animal Chas Chandler.) By 1970, Burdon had hooked up with a black American band called Nite Shift. As Eric Burdon and War, they had a hit with the odd "Spill The Wine." Two albums later, Burdon and War split. The original Animals reunited for an album in 1973 and an album and tour in 1983. The tour ended with a bitter split that remains.

Eric Burdon: Both my parents worked, all their lives, and both enjoyed their work. My father was a electrician and my mother was a waitress. She was a waitress at the City Hall, which had a state-owned-and-run restaurant. So she got to serve the King and the Queen and the Duke of Edinburgh. They had a magnificent banquet room there. And the women who served the people in that banquet room were the best waitresses from all the restaurants in town. You had to work up to it. So that was her way of touching on show business. I used to love to hear stories from her about the people that she waited on — inside stories on royalty and all that kind of stuff. Yeah, we were a real working-class family.

I was very fortunate to live in the town that I did. Like any kid those days, I knew that if you stood in this certain doorway and waited long enough that the taxi with the artist had to arrive. And it was great to watch the arrival of these people. When Louis Armstrong came to town, he had this big superliner bus, three or four road managers, his physician and boxes of pills and all that kind of stuff. I got into his dressing room and met him when I was 14.

I was also highly impressed with Big Bill Broonzy, who walked up to the gig from his hotel, with his guitar on his back. He looked like, you know, a real bum off the street. But he was such a gentleman. He came back to a friend of mine's house and scrawled on the wall: "Big Bill Broonzy was here." This guy was such a fan that when they came to knock down his house, he got somebody to cut the piece of wall out and he took it with him. I once met Sam Cooke on the street in Newcastle and I knew exactly who he was. I walked up to him and said: "You're Sam Cooke!" He was on the same bill as Buddy Holly and the Crickets and Little Richard. Billy Preston was playing organ for Little Richard.

The background of the Animals has always been a screwed-up misconception, in terms of the press. It's a small town, Newcastle. And there were several bands in Newcastle that dabbled in blues, rhythm 'n' blues or were affiliated with jazz bands. John Steel and I were college students at the time, so there were various college bands. John played trumpet and I played trombone in a jazz outfit. And then he went into modern jazz and I got interested in rhythm and blues through seeing and hearing people like Joe Turner and Muddy Waters — they also came through Newcastle — and through makin' friends with Chris Barber, who worked with Lonnie Donegan's skiffle group.

Alan Price was working in a government facility. He handed out pensions to people. We knew that he was the keyboard player that we wanted. But he was in a band called the Thomas Headley Band, where he used to play bass and guitar, and Thomas Headley would play imitation Jerry Lee Lewis stuff. But I had heard Alan play piano, and I felt that he was better than Thomas Headley. So we tried to steal him from that band and get him to join us as a piano player. And Hilton Valentine was in another very successful band called the Gamblers. They were probably more successful than any other band in Tyne-side, verging on being one of the Liverpool groups, almost.

So there was a lot of different players at one point in time. A.P. got together his band called the Alan Price Combo and our other bands fell apart. I went to London, met Alexis Korner, saw what was happening in London and tried to convince Alan to come down to London. But he had to finish his trainee period until he was 21. He was only 19 at the time. He didn't want to give up his daytime job for a shaky future of goin' down to London and trying to make it as a musician.

I would hitchhike to London on weekends. I'd also go to Paris to get records that you couldn't get in England. During that period, I would jam with the local jazz outfits. There were a half-dozen traditional and modern or mainstream jazz bands.

So I freewheeled around the town as a singer, and A.P. had his nightclub kind of routine going, with the Alan Price Combo. And I just kept on realizing that he was the best piano player in town, and he was the guy I wanted to work with. So eventually, I started doin' gigs with him. Chas Chandler joined the band; he was the oldest among us. Hilton was the youngest, and he came into the band last.

Alan Price: What you really had was a cross-fertilization between the better groups of the area. It was like the law of the jungle: the better groups went on. Eric had a group called the Pagans before we founded this one. I had met Chas Chandler, who was much more of an organized hustler. He really wanted to get on, and he had his band and his gigs and kept it moving. He had a group called the Kon-tors, a nonsense sort of name, but he thought it was spunky, an aggressive sort of thing.

Eric had gone to London, and when he came back and had seen what was happening he was ready to work because he knew we could get a band together. So he came up and sang with this awful little jazz trio I had. So we became the Alan Price Combo, and then it had to be more commercial, so the name was changed to the Animals. So I became part of the group, and then it disintegrated very quickly when we became professional.

Eric Burdon: There was a gang, and unlike the American equivalent, they couldn't afford motorcycles. They got together on weekends and went from 80 to 100 strong. We joined them from time to time, but we weren't full-fledged killer members. We were musicians and they loved us. Anyway, they had a leader who was called Animal Hog. He had just gotten out of serving in the army and had flipped; he was your basic crazy vet. John Steel and I, in particular, worshipped him. His name was getting kicked around a lot. So one night when we were sitting

219

around having a pint after the show and we needed a name we came up with the Animals, after him.

We had a real unscrupulous manager called Mike Jeffreys, whose background was in the secret service. Actually, Graham Bond, who at one time in his group the Graham Bond Organization had Eric Clapton, Jack Bruce and Ginger Baker, came up to Newcastle and saw us perform. And he was so impressed that he went back and passed the word around London. Then Giorgio Gomelsky came up, who was the manager of the Stones at the time, with a recording unit and he recorded us at the Club A Go-Go, which is those tapes that keep goin' around and keep resurfacing everywhere. *Early Animals* — we've still never been paid a cent for that stuff. He came up and recorded us. Then Mickie Most got wind of the tapes and he and Jeffreys got together and they did a deal; Mickie came in and had a listen and said he was interested.

So when we left the clubs and ended up in Mickie Most's hands, he said, "Look, I think you guys should shape yourselves this way." And then we allowed ourselves to be put into the hands of agents who wanted to dress us up and make us look cute like the Beatles, which was not our character at all. And I was disgusted with the band for going for it. And from that point on, I wanted to leave the band. But then came success. And I got to tour with Chuck Berry and Bo Diddley and met Ray Charles and all those people.

So I toed the line and ended up lookin' like a Beatle, which was a big mistake. Because we were the first band to have a reputation that was far beyond the Stones' reputation as bein' tearaways — that's an English expression. But the Stones saw that gap and went, "Hey, let's go for it! Let's grow our hair longer than anybody can. Let's look worse than anybody. Let's slap the Beatles in the face."

We were sold and whored around in the worst way possible. We had the worst management, the most unscrupulous agents, and the band was just screwed completely from the get-go. And ultimately we started screwin' each other. Once we saw we were gettin' screwed, it was every man for himself. After about 16 months of non-stop touring in the United States and Europe, all over the world without a day off, just wrecking ourselves.

But right from the very beginning there was a split down the middle of the band, between the boozers and the acid-heads. And Chas always had the opinion that he was the boss. And I actually tried to get rid of him because I didn't think he was good enough — at the suggestion of the band. We all got together and said, "Hey, we see fame down the road. We think Chas should move over. We've got this other bass player." Alan Blackwell, I think his name was. He was a friend of Hilton Valentine's.

We all said, "Who's gonna tell him?" I said, "Well, I'll tell him, if that's the way you want it!" And so I went up to Chas and said, "Hey, Chas, we think you should get into management." Which is what he's doin' now, right?! I was just tryin' to tell him *then*. Then it hit the fan and everybody turned around and went [gesturing toward Eric]: "It was him. We didn't say anything. It was all him!"

So, from that point on, there was this *thing* between me and Chas. And I just looked for my own space within the band. And Hilton used to string along with me, because we used to do a lot of acid together and the rest of the band basically stayed straight and were boozers. That rift remained within the band forever.

It became very frustrating when we had a hit record. We saw the same thing happen to the Beatles. That's why we became close friends with the Beatles and we were like brothers-in-arms with bands like the Stones, because we all knew that we'd go through the same process. We were all crusaders tryin' to carry the spear forward of belief in rhythm and blues and blues music and get the kids to listen to the original stuff, and make them understand that we were just interpreters.

But then once you had a hit record, all that was over, and you got the adulation and the screamin' and the continual noise. I remember John Lennon walkin' out on stage and tellin' the audience to shut up, because, "This is a ballad, and Paul's really worked hard on this song — we want you to listen." But they'd scream anyway, and we'd really get pissed off and lose our rags. But then again, the Stones saw that and went for that and, like Jim Morrison did later, they placated that. They went out of their way to create mayhem. If it wasn't there, they'd engineer it.

But we were just dumb. We weren't that fashion-conscious or that future-conscious. We didn't have an Andrew Loog Oldham behind us that would hire girls to go mad in the TV studio, like they did when the Stones came on. We were stupid enough to rely on our own motivation to get over to people.

We were ridin' the crest of a wave, so it was easy for us to get on [*The Ed Sullivan Show*], but I know there were political games played, because Sam the Sham and the Pharoahs — they got on because of us. Yeah, those games were played, but fortunately for us we were on the up and up and on the winnin' side at that point in time. I think we did six *Ed Sullivan* shows, or more. We were regulars on there.

Ed Sullivan would always try to get us to do "House Of The Rising Sun." And we would have a new record out, and we'd get into arguments with him and his staff, because they wanted us to do the old stuff and we wanted to do the new. I've been a victim of that all my life. I think we gave in to him once. But they were disastrous shows to be on. I hate to speak ill of the dead, but he was a bastard of a guy to work with. He was an old man when we met him, and he was a real grouch. And no matter how much rehearsing you did with him, he'd always get it wrong. You'd rehearse for three bloody days, and when it came time to do the show, he would introduce us and point to stage right, and we'd enter from stage left and go crashing into him or a drum kit or something. It was always a disaster. And I remember that there were certain artists he would really put through the wringer. I remember the Supremes in tears: "We'll never come back to your show!" But you had to be on that show, along with the goats and jugglers and the elephants.

We copped such an attitude. We went back with such attitudes; people hated us. We smuggled half a dozen handguns and about a thousand rounds of ammunition back with us on one trip. We were walkin' around with pistols in our waistbands. One time Chas Chandler lost his luggage and there was a handgun in it. He was sweatin' bullets, because he thought the cops would arrest him. He got a telephone call: "We've retrieved your luggage; come 'round and get it." So, we went down to the police station, and we were standin' there and the guy went, "Three pairs of socks."

Chas says, "Yeah."

"Three pairs of underpants."

"Yeah."

"One shaving kit."

"Yeah."

"One toy revolver!"

"Yeah — let's get out of here!"

Alan Price left the band because he "nicked" the publishing to "House Of The Rising Sun" and set himself up for the future. He was in tow with our unscrupulous manager, Mike Jeffreys. This is one of the funniest stories in rock 'n' roll, period. It's so funny, it embarrasses the hell out of the band and they don't like to talk about it. But we had a meeting one day and Mike Jeffreys came along and said, "We've gotta rush to press the single to get it out really quick, because everybody wants it all over the world! And there's not enough space on the record for everybody's name. So, we'll just vote for one guy and put Alan Price on there, and we'll sort it out later, right?"

And we all went, "Yeah!" and that was it. He's still gettin' the royalties now. And I came up with the song, Hilton came up with the electric version of it, which had more lyrics to it than I had ever heard before. That's where the song came from. It was a mixture of Dylan comin' up with more lyrics and me knowin' it from way back.

It was the record company that forced me to keep the name Animals. I wanted to restructure the psychedelic version of the Animals, and totally rename them like Steve Winwood did with Traffic. I wasn't allowed. MGM said, "You keep the name, or we scrap the contract." And I was young and stupid enough then to say, "Yessir!", and take that as the party line and adhere to it.

Monterey was a good experience for me because I was there. I was in the crowd, and I met Jimi and I was right on the side of the stage when he did the famous act with burnin' the guitar.

And I hung out with him most of the weekend. That was the thrill of Monterey for me. But my performance ... We had just gotten together; it was a brand new band, and we hardly knew each other. It was one of our first gigs. That was the beginning of my writing phase, because I felt that I was cut free.

That was probably the happiest period of my life. Because Jimi was alive and he was a friend. I would see Jim Morrison a lot and we'd talk about cinema, and Hendrix would stop by after his concerts in town. I had this house up in Laurel Canyon. We socialized a lot. It was just before I got involved with War. It was a magical period. Laurel Canyon was really magic then. We loved it. John Mayall became my next-door neighbor. All that stuff is gone.

Everybody from the original Animals to my mother and my lawyer second-guessed me when I left the band. But I wanted to do other things. I wanted to be involved with film production. I wanted to make movies. Still do. That's why I live in Hollywood. I took one look at Hollywood and knew that it was the real center of power in America, not Washington, D.C. This town is the imagination of America. Lives and policies are shaped from this town. *(Steve Roeser; May 31, 1991; Jeff Tamarkin, October 1983.)*

The Who followed in the footsteps of the Animals, Beatles and Rolling Stones, and had their own sort of belligerence. The Who sang blues and craved R&B, too; their first album included two James Brown covers. But the Who took the feelings of that music, the alienation and anger, transferred them to rock, and kept them there. They were the unwilling leaders of a British movement called the Mods, a movement based on the proper motorscooters and clothes and music and attitude. They became an album band, and perhaps the most interesting album band of the British Invasion. One album, *The Who Sell Out*, was interspersed with fake commercials for Odorno and other bogus products; two albums, *Tommy* and *Quadrophenia*, were the first commercially successful rock operas. Onstage, they were a powerhouse, driven alternately by Roger Daltrey's prancing and screaming, Pete Townshend's masochistic guitar work and Keith Moon's over-the-top drumming. *Live At Leeds* is the best live album produced by a British band, and maybe the best produced by a rock 'n' roll band.

But the Who were not a force on the charts and they were not prolific. Only one of their singles, "I Can See For Miles," cracked the top 10; "My Generation," the rude whack over the head that introduced America to the band, stalled at #74. "Won't Get Fooled Again," their best and most pointed single, climbed to #15 and stopped. The band recycled ideas and songs and released a relative handful of complete studio albums.

Keith Moon died of an excess of excesses, but the band kept recording and touring into the '80s before splitting off into solo ventures for good.

John Entwistle — the "quiet one" — was the Who's bassist.

John Entwistle: The "quiet one" tag is a bunch of rubbish. I was stuck in that pigeonhole by a group of journalists when the Who first started. Keith was always flailing about madly at the drums, Pete was jumping up and down and Roger was singing. They looked for a pigeonhole to put me in and the obvious one was, "He's the strong, silent type." Eventually, I lapsed into a lazy attitude of thinking that if they want to say I'm quiet, I'll let them go on believing it.

I couldn't really get away from music. My mother and grandmother both played the piano. So did my aunt, and my father played the trumpet. So I was always surrounded by music. I was forced to play the piano at seven, and I was able to con my mother into letting me play the trumpet and give up piano. Then when Dixieland was dying out and rock 'n' roll was coming in, I decided I wanted to play the bass guitar instead. I thought it would be easier because it has four strings.

I was pretty much into rock 'n' roll. I enjoyed playing blues, but to me it was too close to jazz. I played a lot of Dixieland jazz when I played the trumpet, but I never really enjoyed it.

The first time we went into the studio there wasn't that much equipment. It was glorious mono; just one tape machine, one head amd quarter-inch tape. You had to do it all in one take or else bring in another machine at great expense. I was vaguely curious about where the other

222

end of the mike went, but I was mainly interested in getting the song right.

I think the Mods were just a fad, the way punk was, or glitter rock. But the kids really lived that whole lifestyle at the time. Every generation has to have its own lifestyle.

I remember how exciting it all was, because we were breaking new ground. We were the only band around using huge stacks of equipment. Everyone else was carrying around little combos. If we played with someone else, we were always louder than them.

Girls never did [rip our clothes off]. Ninety-five percent of our audience was guys. We really didn't make it until flower power and *Tommy*. Our early tours of the States were only a couple of gigs in Detroit and the Murray the K show in New York. It wasn't until *Tommy* that we did tours that made a profit.

Monterey was pretty comical. We had a lousy sound because we borrowed equipment. The whole drag was that we pioneered playing through stacks of Marshalls and cabinets piled high, but when we came here our managers tried to save money. So when we came over with Cream to do the Murray the K show, they had stacks of Marshalls and we had these diabolical little amps three feet high. When we did Monterey we used Vox equipment, and then Hendrix and the Experience were using Marshalls. We lost a lot of impact on the first trips by people trying to save money. We finally had to say, "Look, we don't care if we make a profit out of this tour," so we sent our road manager home and told him, "You bring our equipment or we're not going to do any more gigs. You couldn't be the Who with these toy amplifiers.

I have very fond memories of Keith, and I also have nasty memories of him. In time, the nasty memories will disappear. As a drummer, he could play things that no other drummer could play. But if you asked him to play something that any other drummer could play, he couldn't do it. He was completely unpredictable. I was the only bass player who could play with him. I've seen him get up with bands in clubs and the bands completely fall apart. It always turned into a drum solo.

Keith never drove a car into a swimming pool, ever. He accidentally went off the road and into a parked car once. He never learned to drive. He had a chauffeur, but he always insisted on getting into his cars when he was drunk. He drove up the steps of a hotel once. As for the TVs and stuff, my attitude is that if I have a dozen machines that I just bought and half of them work and half don't, most likely they wouldn't have been taken back but smashed instead. If I have a cassette machine and the tape gets stuck, I'll smash it. If televisions don't work, I'll throw them across the room.

Tommy was recorded over a period of six months and was originally going to be a single album. But as a single album the story just didn't make sense. So we stretched it into a double album. And it still didn't make sense. It didn't make sense until the film came out. We had intended to make a film of it from the beginning, but we weren't powerful enough to be able to say we want this director and we want it to go like this. We had to wait until we were a big enough band and Ken Russell [the director] came along before we could get such control over it.

Live At Leeds is still the album I enjoy playing the most. It actually captured the Who onstage, which had never been done, and wasn't done again until *The Kids Are Alright*. I think the Who are a very important live band. They're not particularly important as a recording band — plenty of people sell more records than us — but there's no on that we couldn't blow off the stage. *Live At Leeds* is a very important landmark.

Along with a few other bands, we completely changed the face of the rock industry. We've helped make it big-time as it is now. Up until us, the only band that played in a stadium was the Beatles. We turned it into something louder and bigger than it was. *(Jeff Tamarkin; December 1981.)*

☙

The British blues/R&B movement that spawned the Animals and Stones and Who started with Alexis Korner and Blues Incorporated. From there it passed to John Mayall and the Bluesbreakers, and the Animals, and the Rolling Stones, and a young Van Morrison and Them (who would have two raw, classic hits, "Here Comes The Night" and "Gloria," before Morrison would leave the band for a solo career), and the Yardbirds, and eventually Cream and Ten Years After and Led Zepplin.

Mayall was Korner's logical successor, and as shrewd a judge of talent as Korner. Mayall was a harmonica player, a keyboardist and a guitarist. He formed his first Bluesbreakers in 1962; by 1965, he had John McVie on bass and Eric Clapton, fresh from the Yardbirds and eager to play blues again, on guitar. The band recorded the classic *Blues Breaker — John Mayall With Eric Clapton* album before Clapton left with sometime Bluesbreaker Jack Bruce to start Cream. His replacement was Peter Green, who would later join John McVie and drummer Mick Fleetwood (a later Bluesbreaker) in the first Fleetwood Mac. When Green left, Mayall tabbed Mick Taylor, who would later leave to join the Rolling Stones.

Outside of the *Blues Breaker* album, Mayall and the Bluesbreakers never really made an album to equal their talent. Their singles were non-factors on the charts. But Mayall influenced the best bands of the second wave of the British Invasion, and supplied most of them with talent.

John Mayall: The first album [*John Mayall Plays John Mayall*, recorded live at Klooks Kleek in 1965] is a constant embarrassment to me. But at the same time, it is pretty hilarious to see the utter conviction and confidence in it, and playing all the wrong things. It's very amateur and very well-meant. Its heart is in the right place, but it leaves much to be desired in execution and knowledge of instruments and knowledge of how to hold a band together.

I think by the time we got to the Clapton thing that was such a marked improvement, and I think mainly because I found the soulmate in Eric's character and his playing. We were the ones who understood the most about the history of the blues and were able to make that the dominant force behind [the band].

The *Blues Breaker* album is the major one — not so much the album as the fact that I was able to get Eric and we were able to work together that year. The record just happened to represent it. The album was recorded just at the tail end of Eric's tenure with the band.

The success of the album just made Peter Green's life a little harder. Everyone was talking Clapton and the Bluesbreakers, and there's Peter on the stage. Then, when Peter left, it was the same old story: "Where's Peter Green?" One always has to live under the shadow of the predecessor, and they really set such standards that it was a hard act to follow each time around.

I've figured it out over the years that it's not the musicianship that's the most important thing when you put a band together. It's how they interact with each other on a 24-hour basis when you're traveling. If you've got any frictions, they will show up in the music, and ultimately they will be the death of the band. But the ideal, of course, is where you all get along together socially that you become sort of a family, full of these characters, but it works. *(William Ruhlmann; Feb. 23, 1990.)*

John Mayall begat Cream, and Cream was bigger than John Mayall ever had been or ever would be. Clapton was the focus; Cream looked like his group, and through Cream he became the guitar god of the '60s and '70s. But Cream was equal parts Clapton, drummer Ginger Baker and bassist Jack Bruce. All three supported one another. They had to; there was no one else in the band. Cream was the first successful power trio, and no one else after mixed blues, pop, rock, jazz and free-form improvisation as skillfully.

Cream was as stable as a three-legged calf. The egos of Baker, Bruce and Clapton were large and in constant battle. The band itself played at times like it was just on the edge of falling apart altogether. All three band members had or developed drug problems, and all three were capable of playing solos that verged on the interminable. But nothing else before or since sounded as powerful, as progressive or yet as basic like "White Room," "Sunshine Of Your Love," "Crossroads," or "Badge." The band lasted less than three years, from late 1966 to 1968.

Ginger Baker was Cream's drummer. Jack Bruce was the group's bassist. Felix Pappalardi produced the band.

Ginger Baker: I discovered I could [play drums]. It was as simple as that. I didn't sort of have to sit down and say, "I'm going to be a drummer," and start practicing and doing all these things. I could do it straightaway. I just did it. I sat on a kit and played.

I knew what to do, because I'd been watching drummers since I was a little kid. Every time I went to see a band of any description, I only used to watch the drummer, man. I didn't watch anybody else.

All the kids got me to sit in with a band at a party. There was a band playing, and somebody said to me, "Play the drums!" The drummer, of course, didn't want me to, and I wanted to but wasn't going to ask or anything. finally, I sat on the drums. The trombone player turned to me after the first chorus and said, "Great! A drummer!"

That was it, right? I got a kit the very next week, for £3.

Cream was a very short-lived band, and Cream didn't make it just like that. The first gigs we did, we got £45. I got Cream together because I couldn't take it with Graham [Bond] anymore. I'd been with Graham three-and-a-half years.

Eric used to turn around sometimes and say to me, "Where is it, man?" I'd say, "One! Two! One-two-three-four!" and it was away again. It did go like that sometimes. I would always like to know where it is. It's important if you play the drums.

We were actually two bands. Live, we were playing jazz; in the studio, we were playing music, much more arranged, obviously. Was it difficult to reconcile? No. Yes and no. No and yes. It's a problem because you get a sort of studio technique and a live thing, and it's wrong, really, because you should play the same in the studio as you do live. Then it's up to the engineers to make it sound right.

We didn't take our own airplanes [as it had been reported]. Sometimes it happened that somebody goofed out and missed a plane. Jack missed a plane. But that was a different story altogether. We did see our problems. Musicians are silly people, I suppose.

The bone of contention with me was the incredible volume. Having two guitars right beside you, man ... We didn't used to mike drums. In the beginning, we didn't. First of all, there were just small, little amps. Then they started building these big stacks. The Who and everything. Gradually these big stacks arrived. It started with one little box. Then two boxes, one as big as the other and standing on top of it. Then it was *four*. It got incredibly loud. Friends of mine would come to the gigs and say, "Yeah, man, it was great, but the only time I heard you was during the drum solo." The rest of the night I was completely inaudible.

There was this inaudible cacophony. It used to make me very bad-tempered. I know that. You'd come offstage and your ears are *ringing*. There's this buzzing in your ears. You're in bed, trying to go to sleep, and you've still got this *RRRRRRRRrrrrrrrr* going on. It's terrible, man. *(Gene Kalbacher; Oct. 11, 1985.)*

Jack Bruce: I had played rhythm 'n' blues with Alexis Korner. It was a translation of blues roots into a modern form of music. It was Eric who introduced me to the Delta musicians — Robert Johnson, Skip James, people like that. We felt that this was something that was important. We somehow related to it very much. We were moved by the honesty of it.

There was no blues scene at all in London before Cream. What people had been used to was the Shadows. That's what people expected in the clubs, small ballrooms and so on. With Alexis Korner we were playing this very strange ... we called it rhythm 'n' blues. There was us, there was the Rolling Stones, there was Manfred Mann's first group — the Mann-Huff Blues Brothers, I think it was called — and that was about it. I don't think there were too many groups playing in that vein. The Stones started off very much into Chuck Berry. It was just a different stream. Cream was much more of the original blues because of Cyril Davies. It was much more of Chicago blues and Delta-type, with influences from Charlie Mingus sort of mixed up with it.

I used to sing as a child — Scottish folk songs, which my family was very interested in. This was my background. Then I stopped singing. I used to sing a couple of songs with Graham Bond, but I never thought of myself as a singer. But when Cream got together, we thought, "Who's going to be the singer?" Eric said, "*You're* going to be the singer." So I was the singer.

There was a certain amount of — I wouldn't like to say — ill-feeling in Cream. Let me take it back further. When I was with Graham Bond, I was playing these fairly fluid and moving bass lines, which I had invented. I hadn't heard them; I was just doing it. And Ginger was saying,

"You're too busy! Stop it! Play more simple!" It built up to the point where Ginger said, "You're fired!" It wasn't his band. I said, "No, I'm not. I'm *not* fired." Finally, on one fairly traumatic night after a gig, Ginger drew this blade and said, "Come back and this will be in you." So I said, Okay, I'll leave." So I resigned.

I suppose the feelings we had carried over into Cream. But let me say now that I see Ginger quite frequently and we're good friends, now that we're not playing together. It was Ginger's idea to form a group with Eric, and he asked Eric if he'd be willing to do it. Eric said yes, providing that I was in the group. So Ginger had to come around and ask me if I'd join the group, which I enjoyed quite well.

When we were playing in Europe, we stuck very much to a short-song-type format with solos in the middle, very short solos. Then we came to San Francisco, right in the middle of the Haight-Ashbury thing, psychedelic, and went to the Fillmore, very nervous and diffident about the whole thing. We went onstage ready to do when we had been doing, but the whole feeling was just so amazing at that time. The people in the audience we shouting at us, "Just play! Just play!" And so we did. We just played. It was no conscious thing, nobody saying, "We are going to play long solos." It just happened on that first night at the Fillmore. And we became known for that. So we had to do it, but we enjoyed it.

What used to happen is that nothing was planned. We'd start off a song, then we'd go into the improvising, which would go on for some period of time, and you'd lose yourself in it. I was the singer, so it was up to me to come back and sing the end of the song. But I would sometimes have great difficulty remembering what song we were actually doing. The improvising, apart from what key it was in or the tempo, had very little relationship to *anything*. I don't remember actually going into another wrong song, but I used to have to think quite hard sometimes.

Towards the end, we used to travel in separate planes, separate limousines, and wouldn't see each other until we got into the dressing room just before the show. Paranoia in the extreme. *(Gene Kalbacher; Oct. 11, 1985.)*

Felix Pappalardi: Figures sometimes elude me, but I don't think *Fresh Cream* had done 20,000 copies when we went into the studio to do *Disraeli Gears*. The consummation of that which was Cream was not there until *Gears*. Nor the hit.

Eric was playing very liquid, incredible guitar. *Gears* was committed to tape in six or seven days. That's all the time they had. Gail [Pappalardi's lyricist-wife] and I wrote "Strange Brew" with Eric and Ahmet [Ertegun]. Gail and I wrote "World Of Pain" on a Tuesday night after a Tuesday session, and we recorded it Wednesday. The boys had some of the stuff nailed, and the rest they put together right there.

Disraeli Gears was like a party for a solid week. After that, I suppose, we had to get down to it. I had to get involved in some decisions that I think were key decisions.

For instance, when we went into the studio to do *Wheels Of Fire*, we came out with an LP that was very studio-oriented. It was a very natural thing to do. We had more time. We started to make records more. I saw, fairly early on, that we were dealing with two very separate great bands: One was a studio band and the other was a live band. Therefore, the double album: half studio, half live.

Jimi Hendrix had come by the studio the day we did "Tales Of Brave Ulysses." To the best of my recollection, he and Eric went down to Manny's [the Manhattan musical-equipment dealer] and got a wah-wah — which was fairly new at the time — went back to the studio, and that's what happened.

I do things very naturally in the studio. I'm not a gadget freak. Neither is Tom Dowd [the engineer]. So you're hearing a very natural drum sound, a very natural guitar sound. And Eric Clapton's guitar sound was very powerful. He had stack of Marshalls in the studio; so did Jack. It was very much the way we later recorded Mountain. It wasn't that the guys went on the road one way and recorded another way in the studio because it was hip to use small amps. The hell with small amps! If you want big amps, use 'em!

To be involved in the phenomenon of Cream was incredible. Nobody ever expects a phenomenon. You can tell when a tornado is coming better than you can predict such a thing. All of us were caught up in it, and couldn't believe what had happened. *(Gene Kalbacher; Oct. 11, 1985.)*

When Eric Clapton left Cream in 1968, it was to join another supergroup — Blind Faith, a combination of Clapton, Ginger Baker, violinist and bassist Rick Grech from Traffic, and another refugee from Traffic, a shy, red-headed 20-year-old singer and keyboardist named Steve Winwood with a voice that could conjure up images of every great soul singer from Johnny Ace to Otis Redding.

Winwood had already been singing in bands for eight years, and recording with important bands for four. He had been with the Spencer Davis Group, an R&B band led by a professor of German that leapt onto the charts in 1967 with "I'm A Man" and "Gimme Some Lovin'," songs that were to the British Invasion what the Rascals' "Good Lovin'" was to the American response. Both songs cracked the top 10 and made the Spencer Davis Group, for a time, the hottest British blues-rock band in the world.

It didn't last. After Steve Winwood and his brother Muff left, the hits vanished for Spencer Davis, though Davis kept recording well into the '80s.

Traffic, meanwhile, became the vanguard group of a second British Invasion. Their sound was like San Francisco crossed with London, a pastoral sort of jazz-folk-blues-rock punctuated by Winwood's gentle organ, Chris Wood's flute, and Dave Mason's guitar and sitar.

But Traffic was no less settled than Cream. Mason left the band under a cloud; Winwood left to join Blind Faith and then rejoined Traffic when Blind Faith collapsed under its own weight. The band became soporific in concert and dull on record. Like the San Francisco bands, Traffic produced no hit singles, though its albums sold modestly well. And Traffic was influential far beyond its commercial success.

Spencer Davis led the Spencer Davis Group. Jim Capaldi was the drummer for Traffic, and one of the group's founders.

Spencer Davis: Music was a hobby for me on the weekend — you know, like it was for a lot of university students of my generation. Most musicians were students of the arts.

Like Mick Jagger. Jagger was in another school studying economics, and Paul Jones of Manfred Mann was an English student at Cambridge. We were all serious students who turned on to American blues because it was considered *very* hip to do so. The next step in the progression was naturally to learn to play it. Basically, many of Britain's greatest and most popular musicians began in music as a hobby and as a way to show everyone else around that we were cool.

The band that I put together, which later became the Spencer Davis Group with Stevie Winwood, Muff Winwood, Peter York and myself, was put together in late '62 or early '63, while we were still in the university. We recorded from '64 though '66, but it took two years to get the first major hit record, which was "Keep On Running," a song that reached #1 in most of Europe. The other ones were minor hits and they later turned up on LPs, songs like "I Can't Stand It" and "Dimples," which was a John Lee Hooker tune.

As you can tell, we were really heavily into the blues, blues singers and blues writers. It took a good two years, and then we had that fabulous run from '65 to '67 when we had all the hits like "I'm A Man," "Gimme Some Lovin'," "Somebody Help Me," and "When I Come Home."

Chris Blackwell was our manager, and he was also our executive producer. Blackwell did all the business deals in America for me, and to be quite frank with you, I had no idea what was going on business-wise with my career. I left it all to Blackwell and concentrated on my music and the band itself.

That was a major mistake, but I was young and basically inexperienced and didn't know any better. Blackwell licensed the tapes we did to Atco in the States. I think the first one on Atco was "Keep On Running," and then he licensed stuff to United Artists. Half the time I didn't know what label I was recording for until after the record came out.

I think [Steve Winwood leaving the group] was one of the biggest blunders that was ever made, and that was due to management or direction. Although I sometimes tend to think otherwise, Blackwell claimed that he had nothing to do with it, and that the decision to leave was Steve's and Steve's alone. We are still really good friends.

But it was a very foolish time to leave the group, because the original lineup of the band never made any appearances in America. We would have taken the world by storm, and I believe if we were to tour America even today with the original lineup that we'd *still* take America by storm. I know that in my heart, and I think that everyone else knows that, including Steve and Muff Winwood. *(Tom Lounges; October 1983.)*

Jim Capaldi: I left Evansham when I was 16 to get a job in a factory in Worcester. I've had this wanderlust ever since I was a kid. I used to wander off and get lost, even when I was four, five years old. I couldn't wait to leave the nest. I met up with Dave [Mason] in Worcester. I knew all the guitarists and groups in the area — the Cherokees, the Jaguars. We were called the Sapphires. Birmingham was the big city, and there were hundreds of groups; London was the big, big city.

Anybody who was anybody, anybody who had a *head* and was hip and cool, ended up late at night at the Elbow Room. Traffic was incredibly aware of American music. Steve would wander in and was immediately attracted, I think, because Deep Feeling was innovative. Steve, credit being due, is very sharp and acute when it comes to listening to new things and wanting to get into new things. He was doing R&B and Ray Charles. They were doing their own songs, but Jackie Edwards wrote all the Spencer Davis hits. All Steve had written was a B-side, a 12-bar blues.

When Steve got up and jammed, I was in awe because he was the phenomenal force in England. We'd heard "Dimples," and when I saw the band, I suddenly realized that the record that was knocking me out wasn't done by a black guy from Mississippi but by a 16-year-old kid from up the road in Birmingham.

Steve was incredibly naive. I'll tell you something I've come to know about Steve after working with him for so many years. He only really, for me, comes to life when he's actually performing. When you hear someone who sings Ray Charles and sounds so *black*, you expect to meet someone who's a real character. He's not that way at all. It throws you sideways. To hear him and then meet him — they don't match. Steve was lightweight on the living side of life. I think he's not on this planet; he's somewhere else. A very aesthetic guy. So I realized his [blues shouting] was pure imitation up to a point. Then, suddenly, he came to a point with Traffic when he said, "I'm not going to copy the American accents and sing like that anymore."

The way he used to sing. He used to throw those scat phrases in, which he doesn't do anymore. You know, those blues phrases at the end of every Spencer Davis track. As the fadeout would go out, he would start riffing on the line, throwing the line around, howling, "Baby!" That was his blues hollering.

Steve has incredible gifts. He has a side to him that's very authoritative in what he does, but in dealing with the everyday life of the band and the outside world — he didn't really want to deal with it.

The band's name was mine. I hate to compare myself with someone so incredible, and I wouldn't dare to do it, but if you want to make a comparison, I was a sort of Lennon in the band. I was a bit of a — what's the word? — in England we say "tearaway." Steve is younger than me, and Chris was my age. I've done tunes where I've felt direct influence from Lennon. I love the way he *screamed*.

Chris was such a gentle, sensitive guy. An incredible character, Chris Wood. A lot of people don't realize the magic Chris added to the band. It was Chris who brought "John Barleycorn Must Die" into the band; he came in with an old LP by a family of a capella country singers named the Watersons. Chris sprinkled the magic over the top of the cake. He was there, he didn't have to say it. Poor Chris; he just went a little too far. He was intensely pure and honest in what he did and the way he did it.

Within the band, I was probably the loudest one. Dave Mason was a loner; his energy was too far in an adjacent direction for the group; it was a diversion. But a very strong guy, Dave. A great songwriter. I guess he had the darkest side of all of us.

Steve wanted to do other things, or maybe new directions, yet somehow he wasn't able to get out there on his own, like Dave Mason, and take up the reins on his own and drive along. It was all kind of crumbling in a way.

For instance, Townshend, Daltrey and Moon would boost each other or hold each other up. I remember nights on stage — I knew Keith quite well — when Townshend would turn around to him and scream, "Play faster, you bastard!" That great openness. Steve never wanted to project through the band personality-wise.

I was always trying to give that angle to the group. All through the eight, nine years of Traffic, I melted and blended myslf along with Steve and Chris. Steve would walk onstage, and being the great player that he is, he wanted to play. Nothing more! I don't mind that. When you're as good as he is, you don't need visuals. I just couldn't give it to him on the drums.

Honestly, if we only had that get-out-there-and-really-boogie feeling, and supported each other, I think Traffic could have gone on and been something phenomenally big. If we could only hang out together and boogie ... But then I realized, one man's meat is another man's poison. Yet for 20 years, the Stones and the Who held it together. *(Gene Kalbacher; April 13, 1984.)*

Steve Winwood: I took piano lessons at a very early age, and then I actually had some classical-guitar lessons. A bit later on, I went on a part-time basis to Birmingham and Midland Institute of Music. That was between the ages of 12 and 13. I started off playing piano, but very quickly I was told that I wasn't good enough to be a piano player. One of the reasons was because I was also playing guitar at the time. They said, "The ends of your fingers get hard, and you can't be a good piano player if you play guitar." Well, fair enough. Also, I didn't think I could sit right.

[My first band] was really a school band; it started as a school band. We used to want to play modern jazz. We used to play all kinds of mixtures, and at some point we used to try to do blues. All the time I tried to play a lot more blues, because I was hearing these records. I managed to get ahold of these American records, and I thought, "Why haven't I heard this music before? I want to play some of this music!" Our band used to play some colleges and universities and that kind of thing, and Spencer Davis used to play on his own — folk, folk-blues. And he sat in with the group. Some of the members of Muff's band were getting married or engaged or something, so we decided we'd put this band together with Spencer Davis.

Basically, what we used to do was more or less copy — or do our own arrangements of — blues and rhythm 'n' blues records, which at the time were fairly unheard-of. That's what Spencer Davis used to do, although toward the end, with "Gimme Some Lovin' " and "I'm A Man," which were really the last two things we ever recorded, I was writing and we were all, in fact, trying to write. We had an idea that we no longer wanted to actually copy, to write; we felt we could contribute ourselves toward the material.

Traffic decided exactly what we wanted to do. We wanted to use various forms of music, from country music to blues to even classical, and blend it with ethnic forms and also urban music, too. We also wanted to write *together*. When you say that maybe the first record has something more, I think it's because when you start from nowhere and you collaborate, everyone has the same idea.

We wanted it to be good, and we wanted it to be successful to a certain extent. And so we were all totally pulling together. I think maybe what happens is that later on, as soon as some kind of success is achieved, then the people who are collaborating get their own ideas of how they think it should continue. In fact, that's why Dave Mason left the group. He came with music he'd written; he didn't want to collaborate. He'd say, "I've written this. This is my song. I'll perform this, and you play what I want you to play."

When you look at the groups that do survive — the Stones or the Who — there's always one person in the band who's a leader and lays down the law, and everyone realizes that's the best and does it. Maybe that's why Traffic didn't survive; I don't know. On the other hand, had we done that, I don't think we would have achieved some of the things we did achieve.

Traffic was great fun and we were all friends. It's good when you can do something you like and enjoy and it's fun.

I was always a great fan of Eric's, and we used to hang out together in the early days. I'm sure that at some point we felt we'd play together. As far as feeling that [Blind Faith] would be dubbed the first supergroup, I didn't have the faintest idea that was going to happen. Not at all. I knew the band would be good. But it was almost a marketing kind of thing.

Blind Faith burned itself out. It came together with really good intentions, but Blind Faith really couldn't shake off an expectation. Everyone went to the gigs expecting something. They didn't go there and say, "We'll see what happens." The reaction was favorable, but we didn't always play that well.

I felt I was pretty good, but that wasn't having such a great effect on me. After all, I was supposed to be successful, but I was still sitting in a van and traveling somewhere. I'd always been doing that anyway, so, I mean, there's not too much difference in it. It didn't really fool me, and because it didn't fool me, I don't think it really bothered me. *(Gene Kalbacher and Lynn DeLotto; September 1981.)*

By 1969 the first British Invasion had almost completely run its course. The Beatles were on the verge of breaking up; the Rolling Stones were in a transitional phase, and not quite yet The World's Greatest Rock 'N' Roll Band; the Who were the hottest British band, but it was an album, *Tommy*, accounting for their fame, and a rock opera at that. The Hollies, their first group of hits two years behind them, were on the verge of even greater chart success; Rod Stewart was just emerging from the shadow of the Jeff Beck Group; and the Bee Gees were edging closer to a decade that would end with them on top of the musical world. In 1969 Jimmy Page, after studying the remains of the Yardbirds — consisting of Jimmy Page — and recruiting the New Yardbirds, went into the studio with his band. As Led Zepplin, they picked up where Cream left off and defined heavy metal for the ages.

But in 1969 the sounds of the second British Invasion were also the sounds of San Francisco. Groups like Procol Harum and the Small Faces drew as much from the Jefferson Airplane as they did from Chuck Berry or Ray Charles — or even the Beatles. The first British Invasion created; the second British Invasion adapted.

It was most evident in 1969 at Woodstock. A sandpaper-voiced, twitchy shouter named Joe Cocker and his Grease Band opened the festival's last day and sang R&B, but also interpreted the Beatles' "With A Little Help From My Friends" the way Janis Joplin might. A blues/boogie band called Ten Years After brought down the house with a breakneck version of "I'm Going Home" that spotlighted the guitar flash of Alvin Lee. But compared to what the Stones or the Animals or the Spencer Davis Group had done with the same sort of song just a few years earlier, it was only flash.

Cocker would go on to be the centerpiece of a big motley band called Mad Dogs and Englishmen. He would have out-of-character hits ("You Are So Beautiful," "Up Where We Belong") and be satirized by John Belushi on *Staurday Night Live*. Ten Years After would fizzle out to a breakup. The British Invasion was over. In a sense, the colonies had won.

Alvin Lee and Ric Lee were members of Ten Years After.

Joe Cocker: We had a lot of pubs around [Sheffield], so if we made about £20 a night playing, it was enough to get pissed with. We had a great following there; the town was pretty big, had a population of about 2½ million. I went through various stages when I started out. I went through doing straight R&B and went on to doing Four Tops-type of material.

I'd had an earlier band before the Grease Band, but when Chris Stainton and I went to London, we left the hometown band behind and put the Grease Band together. We met up with Henry McCulloch [guitar], Alan Spenner [bass], and Bruce Rowlands [drums]. Chris played keyboards and guitar. It was a good time.

Denny Cordell asked me who I wanted to work with on the [*With A Little Help From My Friends*] album, and I said, "Well, who've you got?" He said, "You name 'em, we've got 'em." Winwood played guitar, Jim Capaldi on drums. Albert Lee was there. Denny suggested that we get Jimmy Page and I said sure.

Someone had sent me a copy of the Delaney and Bonnie album, *Accept No Substitutes*. I asked, "Who is that monster on the piano?" Denny contacted him, and Leon [Russell] was interested in doing something. I had the idea of getting a small band together with Chris Stainton, but once I met Leon, he said, "I'll come out with you, and we can work with my guys." But we didn't reckon on how many there were.

I wonder if it's nostalgia to think about it, but I guess the part of being interviewed is nostalgia. I don't know if things move just move slower these day, but then it seemed like it was moving too fast and you never thought the feelings of the times were going to change. It was a good stage; I do like playing to big crowds. I remember about a week before Woodstock, we did a festival in Atlanta. The bill was Blood, Sweat and Tears, Hendrix, Janis. We were supposed to go on at four, and we were still kind of underdogs at that point. So as soon as these guys arrived we kept getting pushed back. We finally played at five in the morning the next day, and the kids were all blazed out on acid and all that. It was great, though, just to lay out on the terrace and hear, "Okay, you're next. Hendrix, you're on next." It was a good feeling, a relaxed feeling.

Woodstock, I suppose that for a lot of people today, that's how they know me. It's a reference point; they can see me in the movie. It was right at the end of our first tour and I was really exhausted. I was the only one who didn't drop acid that day. But you really find out who you are when you sing to 250,000 people. Suddenly my voice just sounded so much bigger to me, trying to reach this massive crowd. We went on pretty early in the day, and it took us time to get through.

You opened up the show the last day.

Did we really? I don't know, because we just dropped out of a helicopter and got whisked onstage. It really was something 'cause of the rain and all that. When it was raining I just ran into some people who said, "Hey, come on in here," and I sat in the back of this van with a bunch of hippies who were smoking drugs. I got to experience a little bit more of America than I'd seen.

The Mad Dogs band more or less ground to a halt. Leon and Chris and I went into the studio to try to do some stuff — we did "Wake Up Little Susie" — and we all just kind of said, "What are we doing?" There were a lot of ego problems. *(Jeff Tamarkin; November 1982.)*

Alvin Lee: Originally, we were the Jaybirds. For a short period, we were called the Blues Yard, but we decided that tied us down to one kind of music too much. The first happening thing in London was the Marquee residency, and that's when we decided we needed a name to take us through into the '70s, as it were. Ten Years After has got no real meaning; it's just a nice phrase. It's not particularly 10 years after anything. We did realize by accident it was 10 years after Elvis Presley became famous — to us in England, anyway. But we were nearly called Life Without Mother. That was the second one.

Ric Lee: Yeah, it could have been worse.

Alvin Lee: I quite like that, actually. So the name was picked and the Marquee residency led — it was the situation those days where we were getting a good name on the club circuit in London and we got approached by Decca Records. Did we want to make an album? And I think we were one of the first bands to make an album first, 'cause in those days you used to make a single, and if it did any good then they'd let you make an album.

Ric Lee: Funny thing about that was we did an audition for them a few weeks before, didn't we?

Alvin Lee: We actually did an audition for Decca and failed it, and then they called us up a few months later and said, "We want to make an album with you." We just got hooked with the wrong A&R man when we did the audition.

Mike Vernon, our first producer, was a pure blues fanatic. Remember the "blues boom" that John Mayall started? That was probably the turnaround for Ten Years After to take off. Because I'd been brought — my father used to collect chain-gang songs, very ethnic rural blues stuff, and of course, for the occasional one o'clock set in the morning when you do three sets a night we'd do a bit of the blues and a bit of jazz; there was no real outlet for it. And then when the blues boom happened, suddenly I had a whole list of great blues songs which I could start putting in the set.

Woodstock was not a particularly — it was an event, obviously. We were aware when we arrived. But we weren't ready for any event; it was just another name on the date sheet.

Ric Lee: We'd done a bunch of quite large festivals. It was just another festival.

Alvin Lee: In fact, we weren't even aware that it was going to be different when we left there. Obviously, it was special, be we weren't aware that it was going to be remembered so strongly. Had it not been for the rainstorm, we'd have probably flown in by helicopter, played, and gone out again within two hours and probably would never have even seen it.

But we were about to go on and the rainstorm broke. There was no way anyone could play with the sparks flying onstage. The rainstorm was actually the highlight of Woodstock for me. I thought it was better than all the bands. There's no way half a million people can run for shelter. So they just sat there and started singing, and I took a walk around the lake and experienced it first-hand, which was good.

But we didn't play that well at all, 'cause when we finally did go on there was a lot of brou-haha, 'cause nobody wanted to go on first 'cause of the risk of shock, and I think we took the plunge eventually and said, "What the hell. If we get electrocuted, we'll get good publicity." And we went out and actually had to stop playing "Good Morning Little Schoolgirl" and retune because of the atmospherics. The storm had done so many changes in the atmosphere, the guitars went way out of tune.

I actually had to say, "'Scuse us, but we've got to stop and retune." The audience didn't seem to mind; they were just having fun anyway. But it wasn't particularly a good gig. Playing-wise, we didn't rate it at the top. It's all in retrospect that it's such a huge event.

We went on for a year playing the same three-to-five-thousand-seaters. When the movie came out, we suddenly shot up from 5,000-seaters to 20,000-seaters. It crossed us over to the masses rather than a cult thing. It was the end of the underground. A lot of people say Woodstock made Ten Years After, but it only catapulted us into that mass market, and in a way, it was the beginning of the end. Going into the ice-hockey arenas, where you can't hear much, the sound's terrible, you can't see the audience, it wasn't that much fun and it was a decline of enjoying touring as much as we had done previously. Also, the sad thing about Woodstock: It seemed it was the peace generation coming together, and they never got together again. It dissipated afterwards. *(William Ruhlmann; Oct. 6, 1989.)*

15. Surf City

In the early 1960s, new sounds started coming out of California. It was rock 'n' roll for certain; it had that beat, but the harmonies were different and tighter and not quite doo-wop, and the songs were about the things that were important to California teenagers then and now: cars and girls and surfing. The songs came from two groups, basically Jan and Dean and the Beach Boys and the fact that the two groups sounded more than a little alike was no coincidence. Both groups were influenced by Little Richard and Chuck Berry on one hand and the Four Freshmen and the Four Lads on the other hand. They combined a rock 'n' roll backbeat with intricate four-part harmony and songs about running hot rods on dragstrips and shooting the curl all day and made unconscious, out-of-left-field music. It was a little far afield from Elvis Presley, but what the hell; it sounded great.

Both groups interchanged personnel and songs and arrangements. The Beach Boys' Brian Wilson wrote and sang the high harmonies on "Surf City"; Dean Torrence sang the lead on "Barbara Ann." "Sidewalk Surfin' " was "Catch A Wave" with different lyrics.

The creative genius behind the California surf sound was, in the words of one of his own songs, an adult child. Brian Wilson played with music because he understood music innately. Outside of Phil Spector, no figure on the American rock scene did as much with the music, took it more places, and got less good out of it than Brian Wilson. Wilson moved the Beach Boys from the freshly washed surf pop of "Surfin' USA" to a more complex sound, full of layers and layers of vocals enchanced in the studio and overdubbed with sounds and instruments to such an extent that it would have been impossible for a six-man band to play it in concert. "Good Vibrations," "Caroline, No," and "Heroes And Villains" were songs of creativity run wild, aural experiments of peculiar beauty and innocence. They sounded like a little boy's mind run through a recording studio, and that's just about what they were.

Wilson, like Spector, was a singularly troubled soul. He had a nervous breakdown in 1964, emerged from that with the classic *Pet Sounds* album, then went through 20 years of darkness. For 20 years Brian Wilson didn't write for the band and didn't tour with the band except for a few sporadic appearances. He smoked, drank, ate, took drugs, and rarely left his beachfront home. He ballooned to more than 300 pounds. Finally, in 1987, under the care of obsessive psychologist Dr. Eugene Landy, Wilson began to embark on a modest comeback that resulted in a solo album and a few personal appearances. It wasn't the Beach Boys; Brian's brother Dennis was dead, and Mike Love had alienated other members of the group. But it was still wonderful to have Brian Wilson back. The hope was he'd come further back. That's still the hope.

Jeff Tamarkin: What is the status of you and the group now? Do you still consider yourself a Beach Boy?

Brian Wilson: I still consider myself a Beach Boy, of course. I tour with them every now and then. What else do I do with them? I tour. I make records for them.

Jeff Tamarkin: But you've said you don't really get along with them.

Brian Wilson: No, no, no. We don't get along *real* well but we get along just enough to make it through. We save most of our stuff for the concerts and the recording sessions. We sacrifice a little.

Jeff Tamarkin: You recorded a lot of material in the '70s that never came out. One thing was an album called *Adult Child.* Do you know why that was never released?

Brian Wilson: No.

Jeff Tamarkin: Obviously, things have changed in the recording studio since you began in 1961. Do you remember what it was like the first time you went into a studio, to cut the "Surfin'" single?

Brian Wilson: Well, first of all, we did it at a movie-editing studio. It wasn't a regular recording studio. It was quite an event to go and do our first record. It was all mono, so we recorded it all at once. Backing tracks, everything; the whole record was mono. We practiced until we got to the point where we knew we had a hit.

Jeff Tamarkin: You're considered one of the greatest producers in rock 'n' roll history. How did you learn to produce?

Brian Wilson: It was like anything else. You just observe for a while, and then you get the knack of it yourself.

Jeff Tamarkin: Was the rest of the group quick to learn about recording?

Brian Wilson: Yeah. Over the years I could teach them things. Pretty soon the guys would be sitting there producing records, doing it all on their own. It was just amazing. Like I learned from Dr. Landy.

Jeff Tamarkin: Some of the people you were influenced by in the early days included Phil Spector, and you always mention George Gershwin. Do you think those influences showed up in your own music?

Brian Wilson: A little bit, yeah.

Jeff Tamarkin: Who else was important to you back then?

Brian Wilson: Burt Bacharach, Paul McCartney, Stevie Wonder, who I saw last night.

Jeff Tamarkin: Did you feel competitive toward the other groups that were around, especially toward the Beatles?

Brian Wilson: Toward the Beatles I did, yes. I felt competitive.

Jeff Tamarkin: Paul McCartney once said *Pet Sounds* influenced *Sgt. Pepper's.*

Brian Wilson: It inspired them, it didn't influence them. There's a difference. It wasn't a direct influence. *Sgt. Pepper's Lonely Hearts Club Band* was *not* an album that sounded anything like *Pet Sounds.*

Jeff Tamarkin: I'd like to run through some of the Beach Boys' biggest hits and hear what you have to say about them, the first thing that comes to your mind. Let's start with "Surfer Girl."

Brian Wilson: That was the first song I ever wrote. I was in my car, all alone, and I started humming this melody. Then when I got back to the house I went over to my piano — my grandmother's piano — and I finished out the song. And I said, "Whoa! Is this gonna be pretty!" After I completed the melody and the lyrics, then I started the harmonies. Four Freshmen harmonies, that modern sound.

Jeff Tamarkin: How about "I Get Around"?

Brian Wilson: "I Get Around" was done ... you know, that wasn't inspired by anything.

Jeff Tamarkin: The flip side of that was "Don't Worry Baby," which *Rolling Stone* recently called one of the Top 100 singles of the past 25 years. How about that one?

Brian Wilson: That was after I'd written the car lyrics, and sang the car songs with the high voice, I realized I was confronted with a funny kind of thing, a humorous idea. I sounded like a kid — my voice in those days was so high — and after I thought about, "I should've backed down when I started to brag about my car," I said, "That doesn't sound like a race-car driver, it sounds like a teenage ... whatever."

Jeff Tamarkin: "California Girls"?

Brian Wilson: That was inspired by ... good question. Just by California. I wanted to write a song about California.

Jeff Tamarkin: How about "When I Grow Up"? You were sort of projecting what you'd be like as an adult looking back on those years. Why did you write that song?

Brian Wilson: That was just spontaneous songwriting, totally spontaneous.

Jeff Tamarkin: "Good Vibrations" is considered one of *the* classics of the '60s.

Brian Wilson: That took six weeks to make. We used four different studios. A lot of producing. We felt very competitive at that time, because we wanted to prove that we could do something that sounded pretty good. It was a pretty good session.

Jeff Tamarkin: Did you ever expect that song to be the #1 hit that it was?

Brian Wilson: No, I thought it was too left field to be a big hit, but it turned out to be #1 in the nation.

Jeff Tamarkin: "Heroes And Villains" was supposed to be a step up from there. Did you feel it succeeded?

Brian Wilson: No, it didn't.

Jeff Tamarkin: That was originally going to be part of the *Smile* album, which, of course, was never finished. Why was that project abandoned?

Brian Wilson: It never came out because it wasn't finished; it was just bits and pieces of little tracks.

Jeff Tamarkin: Another song that was supposed to be on *Smile*, and which came out later in a different version, was "Surf's Up." Any recollections of how that came about?

Brian Wilson: That was written with Van Dyke Parks and it was supposedly a song about love.

Jeff Tamarkin: There's one song you wrote in the '70s that was hilarious and very atypical. It was called "Johnny Carson." Why did you write a song about him?

Brian Wilson: I just like Johnny Carson!

Jeff Tamarkin: Did he ever tell you what he thought of that song?

Brian Wilson: No, he never got back to me on that, but I'm sure he heard it.

Jeff Tamarkin: In the '60s, you also wrote and produced songs for other artists. Of all of them, I guess "Surf City" by Jan and Dean was the biggest. How did it feel seeing a song you gave away do so well?

Brian Wilson: That was written predominantly by Jan Berry, I only wrote part of it.

Jeff Tamarkin: Do you have a favorite of the old Beach Boys songs?

Brian Wilson: Yeah, "Good Vibrations."

Jeff Tamarkin: Any that you can't stand anymore?

Brian Wilson: Yeah, "Surf's Up." I don't like "Surf's Up."

Jeff Tamarkin: Would you like to start producing other artists again?

Brian Wilson: That sounds like a bet. I could go for that.

Jeff Tamarkin: Anyone in particular?

Wilson: Umm...my ex-wife. *[Marilyn Rovell, formerly of the Honeys.]*

Jeff Tamarkin: You've said that *Pet Sounds* is your favorite Beach Boys album. Why is that?

Brian Wilson: It was a very creative period in my life. A very spiritual time for me and my group, the Beach Boys. I was 24 years old, I was young and happy, energetic and creative. Boy, was I creative! Man!

Jeff Tamarkin: Do you see yourself being that creative again?

Brian Wilson: Yes.

Jeff Tamarkin: What was it like when you were making *Pet Sounds*?

Brian Wilson: I just remember that I took each arrangement very personally. I really wanted to get the arrangements right, so when you go into the studio you get that live-band sound.

Jeff Tamarkin: How did the Beach Boys feel about what you were trying to accomplish? It was a huge step forward from what you'd done before. Did they understand what you were trying to do?

Brian Wilson: They felt a little lost, because I did most of the singing on that album. The guys weren't really that much a part of *Pet Sounds*, but the next one they were.

Jeff Tamarkin: The next one would have been *Smile*, though, and you wrote that album with Van Dyke Parks. What was that collaboration like?

THE BEACH BOYS: '["California Girls"] was inspired by ... good question. Just by California. I wanted to write a song about California.'

Brian Wilson: Very good. A very heavy collaboration.

Jeff Tamarkin: Would you like to work with him again?

Brian Wilson: Sure.

Jeff Tamarkin: Even though you withdrew a lot after *Smile* fell through, you still contributed to most of the Beach Boys' albums. How do you feel about some of those records, like *Smiley Smile*, *Friends*, *20/20*, and *Wild Honey*?

Brian Wilson: I think they're kind of light, light-hearted albums. Easy to listen to.

Jeff Tamarkin: Did you feel, when the band started touring without you in the '70s, that they were living off of your creativity?

Brian Wilson: Yeah, I think they were. Ah, I don't know about *living* off my creativity but most inspired, most turned on [by it].

Jeff Tamarkin: You said in another interview that you didn't think today's music is as warm as the music of the '60s.

Brian Wilson: It doesn't seem to have a feel, but I'm sure the warmth is there. It's not inherent.

Jeff Tamarkin: Did you collect records when you were first starting out?

Brian Wilson: As a matter of fact, yes. I was a real record buff.

Jeff Tamarkin: Was there one artist whose records you would always buy?

Brian Wilson: The Beatles.

Jan Berry and Dean Torrence were less talented and more formulaic than the Beach Boys, but they had almost as many hits. Their best songs — "Surf City," "Little Old Lady (From Pasadena)," "Sidewalk Surfin'," "Drag City," "Popsicle," "Anaheim, Azusa and Cucamonga Sewing Circle, Book Review and Timing Association" — were a comic counterpoint to the increasingly serious Beach Boys.

Jan and Dean had top 10 hits in 1963 and '64. By 1965 they were out of the top 10. By 1966 they were off the charts. That same year, Jan Berry ran his sports car off a curve, much like the main character in their song "Dead Man's Curve." Berry suffered brain damage and was unable to perform in public for 12 years. When Jan and Dean finally got back together and resumed touring, they opened for the Beach Boys.

Jan Berry: We went to the same high school together and got to be friends. We were on the football team together and used to sing doo-wop stuff while clowning around in the shower room.

Dean Torrence: Jan had two home Ampex-type tape recorders that were just two-track stereo ...

Jan Berry: Two tracks is all it was in those days, so we started working with our music in the auditorium of University High, and then perfected it from there.

Dean Torrence: We started a band as a way to meet chicks. The band was called the Barons, and, boy, did we stink. You couldn't even say we were a garage band, because we didn't even have a garage to practice in. We would sing in the washrooms and shower room because it had great echo. So I guess you could say we began as a men's-room band.

We were really more interested in vocals and harmonies. It seems that nowadays young people tend to pick up an instrument first; the guitar players and the keyboard players are the stars these days. When we were starting out there weren't too many stars that were instrumentalists; the big hits were all by vocal groups. That was the era of doo-wop music and there was a minimum of instruments present on any of the hit records of that time.

Jan Berry: One of our early hits was "Baby Talk," and it was on the Dore record label which was owned by Herbie Alpert and Lou Adler. Herbie produced that record and helped us on some other ones, but we eventually did more ourselves.

Dean Torrence: Herbie evolved into his own situation. He was a jazz musician per se, and that is what interested him. After a while he pursued those interests. We worked together rather closely for maybe two or three years and then Herbie went his own direction. Lou stayed with us basically throughout our whole career.

Jan had met Lou through doing concerts with Arnie Ginsberg, who was Jan's singing partner before he and I got together. They had a record out at the time called "Jenny Lee," and they were doing some concerts with Sam Cooke. Lou and Herbie were involved with Sam Cooke at that time. So when it came time for us to look for someone to help manage and produce our records, Jan gave Lou a call because he had always been impressed by him.

At different times there were five, six, or seven guys singing. We'd lay down vocals every time we went to Jan's house, and then after we went home, he'd play around with the tapes for hours, combining different takes. So with that kind of a hybrid, we didn't really know who was on what by the time he'd put something together.

"Surf City" was written by Brian Wilson, who was also working on "Surfin' USA" at the time. He knew that the two songs were somewhat similar and that he couldn't use them both. And the one he had the most enthusiasm for was "Surfin' USA." Brian had "Surf City" partially finished, and to be truthful, I think he was tired of playing around with the song. He gave it to us when it was about half-done; the melody and the title were there, and a few of the lyrics. Brian was always writing, and he had tunes upon tunes upon tunes lying around. His publishing company was called Sea of Tunes for obvious reasons. He was tickled pink that someone else wanted to record one of his songs, because in those days people weren't exactly beating a path to his door.

They weren't too happy about [us singing on each other's records]. They often said if they could prove anything, they were going to hold up our royalties. But they could never prove it, and we weren't about to help them. We just liked to keep them confused.

Originally, the Beach Boys were going to record a party album, with a bunch of their musical friends. Because we were on different recording labels, I was not credited with singing on ["Barbara Ann"] because legally we couldn't swing the whole thing. But the whole thing was a lot of fun.

Jan Berry: I usually wrote the lyrics first and then built a melody around the syllables. "Little Old Lady (From Pasadena)" was inspired by a television ad we saw about this little old lady who drove around in a souped-up Dodge. But we later found out that it was only a local spot, and after Dodge learned that we had written a song about it, they pulled the commercial. Nowadays people would kill for that kind of a tie-in. Advertising agencies would probably give the writers a couple of million dollars for a song like that. But in those days they didn't want to be associated with rock 'n' roll. Maybe we were just 20 years ahead of our time.

"Jenny Lee" was written about a stripper that a friend of ours in high school had developed a crush on. "Honolulu Lulu" was inspired by an old Laurel and Hardy movie I saw where the two were supposed to have been at a business convention and instead went to Hawaii on a vacation without their wives. The wives saw them on television in Hawaii somehow dancing with a Hawaiian girl who I called Honolulu Lulu. Most of the songs have similar stories.

Dean Torrence: Recording-wise, we both agree that "Dead Man's Curve" is our favorite because it has all the elements. It had a great melody, it was satirical, we loved all the vocal parts, it's got a harp and strings in it, and Jan arranged some super horn parts. It was just a great song to record because it was full-bodied but yet not too busy. Sort of a blend between our sound and Phil Spector's.

The Beatles helped us. It boosted the sagging record industry here in the States. While it hurt many U.S. bands, those of us who had been consistently on the charts didn't really get affected all that much. It was like a revolution in the record business, but the top five or 10 American bands — the Beach Boys, ourselves and others — still did well and held our own. Rock music changed more between 1962 and '64 than it did over the next 10 years The British bands opened up the minds of many record executives and made it easier to try different things with music.

Jan Berry: It gave the music industry a real shot in the arm.

Dean Torrence: It broadened the range of teeny-boppers as well, and made rock and roll less of a teeny-bopper market. Shit, the Beatles came along, and all of a sudden 24-, 26- and 30-year-olds were digging rock. It opened up a whole new can of worms. Even Wall Street was forced to sit up and take notice of the music industry and because of that more money became available to bands. Everyone became conscious of higher quality sound.

You've gotta understand that not everything we did was *our* idea, but a typical stunt we did was the promotion we did for the newly opened Kinney Shoes. We went around to the stores signing autographs and lip-syncing tunes, and our manager — who realized that we needed to get publicity off of this — would go out of his way to make sure that a riot got started. Then he'd high-tail it down to a pay phone and call the police to tip them off that there was trouble at the local Kinneys. And then all these riot cops would arrive and find themselves surrounded by a bunch of 12-year-old girls.

Is there any truth to the rumor that you were involved with the kidnapping of Frank Sinatra, Jr.?

Dean Torrence: Well, it wasn't a rumor. We *were* involved. We just thought it would be a real challenge to kidnap somebody. I don't think any of us really thought our friends were going to go through with it, and we certainly didn't know it was going to involve Sinatra. We just assumed they were kidding, and it seemed like fun until they actually did it. Then it became very serious.

We were very lucky. Extremely lucky. I think the authorities finally realized that we didn't ever think it was really going to happen — that it was a fantasy that had gotten out of hand.

Jan Berry: As far as my crash goes, people have told me different things about it, but my memory is hazy. From what I gather, it was the day I had gone to the draft board, and I was on my way back to a business meeting afterward.

Dean Torrence: When I heard about it, somebody had come up to me in school and asked, "How's Jan?" And I said, "Fine, thank you." And he said, "Gee, it sure sounded serious." And I asked *what* sounded serious, and he said he heard that Jan was in a bad automobile accident. So I went to the telephone and found out that it was indeed true.

Jan Berry: It was, and I know that I will never be the same as before the accident. I had to relearn reading and writing, among other things. But this is the way it is, and the experience goes on.

Dean Torrence: Just before the accident we had sold a television series and it was going to be on the same time as *The Monkees.* We would've been on ABC and they were on NBC. And actually, we were all friends so we would've cross-collaterized our shows somehow. And I sense that our show would have been as zany — if not zanier — than the Monkees' in some regards. I'm sure it would have been a success for awhile, at least until we got tired of doing it. But then Jan crashed, and there was no reason to air the pilot.

We were signed to Don Kirshner and the Screen Gems Company, and they were *too* heavy-handed with us. So prior to Jan's accident, we were thinking of starting our own record label so we could have more control of everything. It was going to be distributed by Dunhill, which was run by our good friend Lou Adler.

Jan Berry: That was a dream of ours: to have our own label so we could do what we wanted to do and have control over our records and career.

Dean Torrence: We had just gotten out of our contract with Liberty Records and we were free agents. Then Jan had his car accident and things were put to the wayside. I had no idea what was going to happen with him or how long he would be out of commission. So I thought that while the name Jan and Dean still had momentum I would try to push the deal on through by myself. We had a hassle due to the small print on our contract with Don Kirshner and Screen Gems, and they wouldn't let us go ahead with Dunhill and form our own label. They had just formed Colgems and wanted us to record on their label, along with the Monkees. They thought I could be intimidated now that Jan was out of the picture, 'cause he would have told them to go to hell. So I did just that.

Columbia Records was pressing the record for me as a free-lance pressing client. They had heard the record and liked it and told me to be realistic about things and let them handle it for me. They said, "Sure, you've shipped thirty or forty thousand albums, but you haven't been paid for any of them." And they were absolutely right. I had never thought of it; all these records were going out but no money was ever coming in. I was getting scared and took their offer to let them handle everything. I got enough money to pay everybody I owed and then just about broke even. So I washed my hands of it and said goodbye. *(Tom Lounges, April 1982; Sandy Stert Benjamin, June 1, 1990.)*

There were two beach sounds, actually: Brian Wilson's bright choral beach sound, with everyone having fun, fun, fun until daddy took the T-Bird away, and the pulsating, big guitar sound of the Surfaris, the Ventures, and especially Dick Dale and the Del-Tones. The instrumental beach sound was more of an L.A. thing; few of the groups made it nationwide. Songs that are regarded as classics around L.A. are never heard anywhere else. But to surf-music fans, their stuff is the real sound of the California surf, and the Beach Boys are just easy-listening pap. And there is something tough and driving and enduring about Dale's "Pipeline" or the Surfaris' "Wipe Out," something that suggest bonfires on the beach, and catching that last wave, and a bleached-blond endless summer.

Dick Dale was called the "King of the Surf Guitar." His "Let's Go Trippin' " was the first true surf song, and his "Miserlou" and "Surf Beat" were classics of their kind. Dale appeared in the movie *Muscle Beach Party* and had a good run from about 1961 to 1964. He resurfaced on record in 1987, swapping licks with Stevie Ray Vaughan on "Pipeline." The surf sound was still intact.

Nick O'Malley, Art Munson and Barry Rillera were members of the Del-Tones.

Dick Dale: I was born in Beirut, Lebanon, as Richard Monsour. My family immigrated to the Unites States and settled in Quincy, Massachusetts, early on in my childhood. When I was about nine years old, my dad started me out playing the piano. I never had any private lessons, but I taught myself to play by ear. After that, I took up playing the harmonica. My uncle was impressed with my progress and gave me a trumpet. I took a few lessons but I learned how to play it by playing the songs I liked at the time. My interest in the guitar was spurred by my idol, Hank Williams, as I had always wanted to be a cowboy singer.

I remember there was this one kid on our block who had an old Harmony guitar. He used to sit down on the corner and strum on the thing while all of the girls sat around him. I once asked him if I could try it, but he wouldn't let me. That incident just inflamed my desire to play the guitar.

I started reading comic books at this time and I started seeing ads in the back encouraging kids to sell jars of Noxzema skin cream. For so many jars sold, you could get a ukulele. It was just beautiful and I wanted it. It even had a picture of the cowboy on it. I answered the ad and within a few weeks I sold $40 of the stuff. Happily I sent off for my ukulele and then waited for weeks until my uke arrived. I was really excited, but when I opened up the box, I just got sick! It was so cheap! It was painted green and you could hardly see the cowboy. What really made me mad was the uke couldn't even be tuned. I just smashed it to bits in the garbage can.

I started collecting deposit bottles and finally saved enough money to buy a cheap $6 plastic ukulele. I was having a hard time playing it so I bought one of these cord things you hooked on the neck and pushed down on, but it made the strings rattle. I finally gave up and bought a chord book, but that didn't help, because at the time, I didn't really realize I was holding the ukelele backwards. I finally just started strumming and moving my fingers around until I heard something that sounded right. The first two songs I ever learned were "The Wild Side Of Life" and "The Tennessee Waltz" in 10 different rhythms.

One day a friend asked me if I wanted to go see some guys playing the guitar. I said of course. He took me out to a farm somewhere in Massachusetts some distance from where I lived. It was just like the movie *Deliverance*, out in the woods. There were about 12 guys sitting in this big living room and they were all strumming and singing. It was there that I first heard that "ta dant it, ta dang it" sound I used later on. After some haggling, one of the guitarists sold me his guitar for $8. I really didn't know how I was going to play it with all of those strings on it until my friend told me to play it like I did the uke, but not play the top two strings, just muffle them. So for years I played my C, F, G chords like that. My strumming sounded so big and full after that.

Nick O'Malley: I lived in Corona Del Mar, but I hung out a lot on the Balboa Peninsula. I occasionally played folk songs at the Rinky Dink in their separate coffee room as a favor to the owner.

One evening, I was down there visiting friends and it was getting late, but I decided to drop in at the Rink and the owner asked me to set up and play for a while. I got out my trusty Fender guitar and amplifier and started playing. I remember the date well. It was April 6, 1961. Dick and Ray walked in and asked if they could jam with me. I told them it was okay. They brought in their equipment and we jammed almost all night. We agreed to come back the next night and do it again. That night Billy Barber showed up and jammed with us on the piano. I think it was that night that we decided we'd be a good group. The owner of the Rinky Dink hired us to play for eight bucks a night and free sodas and Seven-Ups.

Dick Dale: I started going down to Balboa so much that I finally moved to Costa Mesa to be closer. I opened up a little record shop across the street from the old Rendezvous Ballroom which was closed at the time. I sold records, repaired phonographs and gave guitar lessons. I could show someone how to play any song they wanted in one day.

I also started doing something new. Most of the kids who came to the Rinky Dink and into my shop were surfers. Soon, I found myself out on a surfboard being taught how to surf at the Santa Ana River Jetty by my girlfriend, Arlene. Soon I was surfing all over the place including Huntington Beach, Dana Point, Doheny and the Wedge. My daily routine was to have the shop closed in the morning so I could go out surfing. Then I would open up in the afternoon in time to sell records to the kids getting out of school. Then I would close up again and go surfing some more. Later that night I'd be playing over at the Rinky Dink and later the Rendezvous.

Everybody seemed to like us at the Rinky Dink, especially later, when I added drummer Jack Lake and a sax player by the name of Fred to our foursome. We really started drawing the kids, so I decided to ask the owner for a raise and he fired us!

I went next door to the Rendezvous and talked to the owner, Thelma Neufeld. I offered our services, and she liked the idea of us playing there. She said she couldn't pay us but maybe something could be worked out splitting the door. So there, on July 1, 1961, with Billy on piano, Art Munson and Nick O'Malley on guitars, Ray on bass and Jack Lake on drums, we opened up the Rendezvous Ballroom for free and in our bare feet to about 17 surfers!

Nick O'Malley: Prior to us playing at the Rendezvous, the ballroom had been a jazz and big-band dance hall where you paid a dime a dance. If I remember right, we were the first to start the idea of splitting the door. We were splitting the door 50/50 with the owners, with each of the band members getting an equal share, while Dick got double what we got. After all, Dick was the showman and the workhorse.

Dick Dale: While we were playing one night at the Rendezvous, I had a kid come up and ask me if I would play some instrumental songs instead of doing all vocals. I told him to come back the next day just to put him off, but then I realized that the kids might think I was a phony, so I came up with an instrumental the next day and the kids loved it!

As our audience grew, the city officials started giving us a bad time about our music and its supposed evil influence it was having on the kids. I guess our jungle beat was too savage for the city fathers. I decided what we needed to do was to get the word out to the kids before we got cancelled out, so I created the first musical assembly ever held at a high school. Up 'til then, there was no such thing as an assembly.

I convinced the principal at the first school I tried that what I was doing was the elevation of music. We played "Sunny Side Of The Street," "Sugar Blues," "Sentimental Journey," "Can I Get You A Taxi Honey? — you know, songs that he and the teachers could relate to. He finally allowed the assembly and we did as we promised. Then in the last 15 minutes, I would say, "This is what we are doing down at the Rendezvous," and boom! We immediately switched to our driving jungle beat and it drove the kids nuts. We did this at every school assembly, and soon the kids were flocking to the Rendezvous to see us, and with their support behind us, the city officials got off our backs.

The style of music I developed, to me at the time, was the feeling I got when I was out there on the waves. It was that good rambling feeling I got when I was locked in a tube with the whitewater caving in over my head. I was trying to project the power of the ocean to the people. Not everything I played was surf. "Peppermint Man" wasn't a surf song but it was backed by the sound of my surf guitar, so many people identified it as the surf sound. The kids really enjoyed this sound, and my following grew from 17 surfers to a much larger crowd every night within the next couple of months.

While I was playing at the Rendezvous, I met a man who designed guitars and amplifiers. My sound was getting real heavy and a lot louder and my amplifiers were not giving me what I needed.

I got to talking to Leo [Fender], and he seemed to like me right away. He liked my attitude about what I wanted and what I wanted to sound like. After a while, he told me he was going to have me try out some of his Fender amps he'd been making.

Leo started bringing me different amps, and I wound up blowing over four of them before Leo came up with one I couldn't. It was called the Showman. He also developed the JBL speaker because I kept blowing speakers too.

I remember this statement Leo once made: "If it's good enough for Dick Dale, it's good enough for the public. If it can stand Dick Dale, it's good enough to sell."

I got the first of everything from Fender. I got the first Rhodes piano. I tested the first mikeless guitar and the first outboard reverb unit. It was the reverb that gave me the sound I was looking for.

My first custom-built guitar was a right-handed, sunburst-finished Fender Stratocaster. I didn't like the color so I painted it white. Because I played the Strat upside down, I kept hitting the knobs with my hand, so I just turned the pots full and took the knobs off. I also had to play with the tremolo bar upside down and I eventually broke it.

I also got the first cream-colored Showman. Leo wasn't going to put it out, but my sax player Skip and I liked the color and we talked him into it.

There was this one instrumental we were doing and I really didn't have a name for it. So one night I asked the kids about it and they screamed "Let's Go Trippin' " and started doing the surfer's stomp to it.

These kids showed me a lot of respect for being the originator of the surf sound. It was a highly paid compliment.

Art Munson: Capitol Records sent the group on a promotional bus tour to Wildwood, New Jersey, Boston, Massachusetts, and surrounding areas.

At Wildwood we played on this stage that was located directly behind the bar and served as buffer between Dick and the audience that he liked to get close to.

But Dick's music seemed to confuse the kids. They were used to straight rock 'n' roll and rhythm and blues and with the combination of being away from the audience and the kids' lack of knowledge of Dick's style, the group did not go over well at all. For some unknown reason, the East Coast kids did not respond to Dick's surf music the way the kids did on the West Coast.

He preferred to play to local crowds in the Southern California area so he could be near his pet tigers and jaguars. This reluctance to tour probably prevented our material from getting more national exposure and led to the decline of Dick's popularity.

After that tour, we went back to playing Friday nights at the Harmony Park and Saturdays at the Riverside Armory and Sundays back at Harmony Park.

Then his dad made a move which in the long run really hurt Dick's popularity here at home. He moved the group from Harmony Park to Pacific Ocean Park out on the pier in Santa Monica. I think that was really the death of Dick's popularity. It was the night of the grand re-opening of the park.

What happened was that Dick's following was mostly people under 18. Well, the park would not allow people under 18 in, and there were just lines of kids waiting outside to get in that were turned away. Only a few kids came in, and we played to an almost empty dance floor. It was a very low point for the group.

After making the movie *Muscle Beach Party*, I finally left the group at the end of 1963. At that time Fred McNut was playing bass, Lee Farell was on sax, Bill Barber was still on piano and Barry Rillera was switching between sax and guitar.

It was a great period in my life. It's too bad that a lot of people had to miss out on that magical era. *(Robert Dalley; July 1983.)*

🐞 🐞 🐞

16. Where the Action Is

In 1963, as the Beatles were embarking on what turned out to be the first phase of the British Invasion, the United States was full of bands. The Embers were playing in a small country-western club in Fresno, Calif. Within two years they'd be known as the Bobby Fuller Four and have an immense hit with "I Fought The Law." Within three years Bobby Fuller would be found dead under mysterious circumstances.

In 1963 Tommy James was 15, but already had one hit single recorded. "Hanky Panky" had been recorded in 1961, when James was 13; four years later, it would be a hit, and would launch the career of one of the most successful pop hitmakers of the decade.

In Washington, D.C., in 1963 a group called the Mugwumps was playing spirited folk and blues in the clubs around the capital. When the group split up several years later it would launch the careers of two of the '60s most influential and happiest-sounding groups.

In New York in 1963, the group that would become first the Young Rascals and then the Rascals was playing with, of all people, the Beatles, while on the other coast, a young songwriter named P.F. Sloan was writing beach music and a group called the Crossfires was singing it. When they would get together three years later the group would be called the Turtles and the song Sloan wrote for them, "You Baby," would be a hit.

Also in Los Angeles in 1963, a German-Canadian immigrant named John Kay arrived from Buffalo and began working as a floor manager in a nightclub. Four years later he would be the lead singer of Steppenwolf and have the hottest, heaviest record in the country.

In 1963 the separate members of the Doors were still attending film school at UCLA, while Paul Revere and the Raiders had already had two hits and were renowned as the best band in Idaho. Along with their only competition for that title in the entire Pacific Northwest, the Kingsmen and the Wailers, the Raiders were recording a song that would become a smash hit for one of the three groups, and a minor hit for all three.

The Gentrys were playing together in high school in Memphis, the members of the group that would become the Chocolate Watch Band were handing out with members of what would become the Jefferson Airplane in San Francisco, one of the members of the decade's most famous blues/boogie bands was playing garage rock in Mexico City, while in Detroit an 18-year-old named Billy Levise Jr. was cutting the first songs with a sound that would shake the nation and kick out the jams once and forever five years later. And in a thousand smaller towns high-schoolers were hearing the Beatles and begging their parents for quitars or drum kits, and setting up in garages and playing. That was the state of the American rock 'n' roll scene in 1963. Two years later, it would be totally unrecognizable and altogether wonderful.

In Texas the memory of Buddy Holly was still strong. Bands would play Buddy Holly medleys and play their other covers with that spare, clean Buddy Holly sound.

The Embers were no different. The only difference with the Embers was their lead singer, Bobby Fuller. Fuller was talented, creative, ambitious, and shrewd. He was also domineering, insensitive and egotistical. But with Bob Keane of Mustang Records, the man who made Ritchie Valens a star, pushing every release, the renamed Embers, now the Bobby Fuller Four, made some great music. "I Fought The Law" was written by Sonny Curtis for the Crickets after Buddy Holly died. The Bobby Fuller Four made it a classic piece of American rock squarely in the Holly mold. The Bobby Fuller Four did a score of amazing songs, "Let Her Dance" and "Never To Be Forgotten" and "Susan" and a piece of derivative beach fluff called "King Of The Wheels" and more. At their best the Bobby Fuller Four stole whole chunks of their licks and sound from Jan Dean, the Everly Brothers, Eddie Cochran and Buddy Holly. But lots of other bands did, too, and not nearly as well as the Bobby Fuller Four.

On July 18, 1966, Bobby Fuller bought a Corvette. The next morning he was found dead in the front seat of the car, which was parked in front of his apartment, just down the street from Grauman's Chinese Theater. Fuller had a broken arm and other injuries, and apparently had been beaten up before he died. The official cause of death was listed as suicide, ostensibly from drinking gasoline. There were rumors that his death was linked to organized crime or a police coverup. Nothing was ever proven.

Jim Reese played guitar with the Bobby Fuller Four.

Jim Reese: I don't have any startling revelations to make about the Bobby Fuller Four.

I was raised in El Paso, where I played the trumpet in grade school and sang in the school choir. I've always had an ear for music and could play any instrument I laid my hands on. Because of this, I got ahold of a friend's guitar when I was about nine years old. When I found out I could play more than one note at a time, and loving the beautiful sound of the instrument, I soon forsook the trumpet and fell in love with the guitar.

About the same time, rock 'n' roll started coming out, and I knew this was the music I wanted to play. This was before top-40 AM radio, when all the stations played all kinds of music, and had different shows such as "Western Hits," big-band shows, and so on. At 9 p.m., one station had a two-hour rock 'n' roll show. I used to go into my room and get under the covers with my radio turned down low to listen to Fats Domino, Little Richard, Elvis Presley, Carl Perkins, Jerry Lee Lewis, and many, many others whose names have long since been forgotten. Does anyone remember "Death Of An Angel" or "Idol With The Golden Head?"

Anyway, I was soon trying to learn all the great songs by the great artists, and I was also teaching myself how to play the piano. We had an old, out-of-tune upright piano and I would pound on it for hours. I would sit in the bathroom for hours playing my guitar, an old-fashioned Silvertone f-hole guitar my folks got me for Christmas in 1955.

One day in April 1958, I was walking along a street when this car pulled up and a fellow known as a local tough kid came walking up to me, and I thought, "Man, I don't know what he's after me for, but I've had it." It was a guy named Willie Wilson, and he said he'd heard I played piano and wanted to know if I'd be interested in auditioning for a band he and fellow named Bobby Taylor were forming. I said, "Hell, yes!" That night I went to Bobby Taylor's house, where I blew their minds and became a member on the spot.

That band became known as the Counts and enjoyed tremendous success for about eight months; we were the top rock band in El Paso. When we started, there were three groups: the

Rhythmaires, the Rock-Kings and the Counts. By the time we broke up, there were at least a dozen new ones.

The group I was in formed up as the Royal Lancers and played its first gig at a local school. As a condition for me going with them, the others agreed I could play guitar — rhythm, not lead. Well, that was better than piano, so I agreed. We practiced with one of the singer's buddies as lead guitarist. And then, on our first gig, he got cold feet and quit. So, I had to become an instant lead guitarist, and to be honest, I really pulled it off and quickly became the No. 1 rock guitarist in El Paso — a position I enjoyed until I left for California with Bobby Fuller.

The band played together for about two years and the name was eventually changed to the Embers. Bobby Fuller had been playing for about a year with another band, whose name I don't recall, and in '61 or '62 I asked him to play drums with the Embers. We used to do things like have Bobby play a solo while the rest of us put down our instruments and mingled with the crowd. We entered a battle of the bands and won it, hands down, because we persuaded the promoters to have it in our part of town.

While he was in the Embers, I would have Bobby play guitar and sing a few Buddy Holly songs, and this caused great dissatisfaction to one of the other vocalists, who left the band. This was really all right with me; he remained mainly because we didn't know how to get rid of him. Anyway, Bobby nearly always brought a tape recorder to our gigs and recorded us.

Bobby eventually quit the group and tried putting together a band of his own, but apparently wasn't successful as I didn't hear much of him for a while. The one day in July or August 1962, he called me and wanted to know if I'd play guitar with him for a 10-day gig at a local bowling-alley lounge. The lounge lost its liquor license for 10 days and was going to operate a teen club. I needed the money for a down payment on a car, so I said okay. I was on lead guitar, Bobby on rhythm and vocals, Randy on bass, and Gaylord Grimes on drums.

We were on the top of the heap for a while then. We played mostly at the lounge and rehearsed. I was playing most of the lead, and the good old recorder was there. I think it was the spring or late winter of 1963 that we got a job at a country 'n' western club in, of all places, Fresno, Calif. We played there several weeks and then came back to El Paso. The group played a further three- or four-week engagement in Hobbs, N.M., and then broke up. Bobby had a habit of remaining distant from the rest of us and wouldn't communicate except when we played. He always seemed to be in a bad mood, as if he was mad about something. It beats me what it was.

Anyway, after that gig the band just kind of folded. We went back to El Paso and I played bass with a road band about eight weeks. Bobby and Randy started up another group, with Billy Webb on guitar and Larry Thompson on drums. They released a few records and were playing at the bowling alley on Sundays. Bobby had started his teen club and they mostly played there on weekends. Bobby wasn't happy with Billy and Larry, so he asked Dalton and me to come back, which we did. We played all around El Paso and its area until November 1964. We were, at different times, the Spiders, the Fanatics and several other names.

We were really nothing more than a human jukebox, except that we were playing mainly imitations of Beatles songs, Buddy Holly, and surf music. We were good at it, though. Bobby was a great imitator. He could sing just like Holly, McCartney, Lennon or Eddie Cochran. And he could imitate on the guitar, too. But Bobby never did Bobby. To me, the overwhelming impression I get from his singing is Buddy Holly, as well as his guitar playing, with a lot of Dick Dale and a smattering of Chuck Berry. And therein probably lies the real cause of the group's later problems.

Bobby wanted us to go to California, but I was leery because it always had been too one-sided with Bobby — he ran everything, hired and fired at the least whim, and didn't communicate well with other people. He was never able to understand that a musician, like other people, needs food, gasoline, clothes, a place to live, and so on. I often felt that Bobby thought we should follow him anywhere just for the thrill of it. Anyway, I wanted to try California. I called Bobby and told him okay, but only if it was understood and agreed that it was all for one and one for all, that we split everything evenly, that I got 25 percent. Bobby agreed and I told him I needed a week to check out of college and get all my business straight. Dalton couldn't go, so we got Dewayne "Querico" Bryant to play drums.

Bobby, Randy, Dewayne and Mrs. Fuller drove on out, and I came out one week later.

Initially, we all stayed together at an appartment and pooled our money from playing. Before Bobby left, I pleaded with him not to sign with anyone until I got to put my two cents' worth in, but he went ahead and signed with Bob Keane.

We played around L.A., and thanks to Kasey Kasem, we were able to play enough to stay alive. We released a few records, which has already been documented elsewhere. We also appeared on a few TV shows and were booked into La Cave Pigalle at the Ambassador Hotel. At the end of that engagement, because of personal hassles, I left the band and came back to El Paso. A week later, Bobby called me up wanting me to come back. I again repeated my conditions about equal treatment and he agreed, so I went back — probably the biggest mistake I ever made.

When I did get back, we had a booking to play in the lounge at a bowling alley, Carolina Lanes, near the airport. This was a real bummer gig, and while there we were booked into P.J.'s. All during this time we were in and out of the studio. We played at P.J.'s for about eight months, I believe. Sometimes around this time, it started hitting the fan. Bobby was under contract to Bob Keane, and they formed something called the Bobby Fuller Four, Inc.

Well, we were the Bobby Fuller Four, but only Bobby was a member of the corporation. They decided to put us under contract to Bobby. Well, this didn't fit in with my concept of the verbal agreement I had with Bobby, but at least it was better than nothing.

Ever since we had gotten to L.A., as far as Bob Keane was concerned, it was 100 percent Bobby Fuller and zero percent the rest of us. For every one picture they had made of the band, they had 50 of Bobby. They were consistently boosting Bobby and ignoring the rest of us. They even named the group the Bobby Fuller Four, leaving us out of it. And then they had the big Bobby Fuller night at P.J.'s, and the rest of us were literally shoved out of the picture. We weren't allowed to meet any of the people, get our pictures taken, anything. Any bit of recognition the rest of us got we had to bite and scratch for. So when I went to the office of Bob Keane to meet with him and Bobby about the contracts, I absolutely hit the roof when I saw them. They were only going to give us five percent or union scale, whichever was greater. I jumped up and down and finally got 15 percent, which I never saw. The best I ever got was union scale, and there's a bunch of recordings for which I never received that. Anyway, I put all that behind me and went on my way. We continued to play and record.

The rest of the story has pretty much been told — the happenings in New York, San Francisco, and then the last few weeks up 'til Bobby's death. But there are a few things I'd like to clear up.

We played out our full contract at the Phone Booth in New York, but the audiences there were hard to please. A problem we had was following one particular well-known group — who out of common courtesy I won't name — which didn't do a good job. We were in the position of having to prove that rock bands could also entertain.

Anyway, we got back to L.A. and I found a draft notice in my mailbox, which as far as I was concerned, eliminated any problems or hassles I had about the music business. I mean, I figured I was headed for Vietnam. Anyway, on July 16, I went out to Sepulveda Basin to watch some guys fly radio-controlled model airplanes. One plane disappeared in a corn field. The next day I went out there with Dalton and Rick and took a little airplane I had. Bobby came out there and we all tried to find that lost airplane, but didn't. I made arrangements to meet with Bobby the next day to sell him my Jaguar XKE, as I figured I wouldn't be able to pay for it in the Army. Bobby never showed up the next day, and the rest is history.

As far as the incident with the three men is concerned, I've never had any idea who they were or what they wanted. I believe this was the day of Bobby's funeral because I ran into a girl at the funeral whom I had met before and I went to her house that night. Dalton was staying with me at my apartment, and my place had become a refuge for all those who could get no comfort for their grief from the Fullers. Dalton and I found ourselves in the position of comforting people in their grief and I finally had to get away for a while. I went to visit that girl and her mother. When

I got home about midnight, I walked in the door and Dalton was standing there with a gun — mine — in his hand, trembling with fear. He told me about the three men who came by looking for me. We had already decided to go back to El Paso the next day, and this didn't change our plans. The only difference was that I had a loaded pistol in my seat all the way back. I had that insurance policy cancelled because I was worth a lot more dead to certain people, and I was taking no chances.

I added it all up a while back, and I figured that for "I Fought The Law" I possibly made about $150. The best paycheck I ever got as a member of the Bobby Fuller Four was around $450 for one month. My best year I made a little over $8,000.

And to all of you who would like to make it in the music business I'd like to say: Know your craft, know your instrument, and for God's sake, don't ever sign anything without the benefit of a good attorney. Don't trust anyone, especially in the record business, unless it is in writing. Good luck. *(Jim Reese; Jan. 1, 1985.)*

🐛

At about the same time Bobby Fuller died, the Buckinghams, a Chicago band that cut its teeth on James Brown and the Drifters, were five months away from away from enjoying their first taste of success with the quintessential lighter-than-air '60s pop single, "Kind Of A Drag." Gary Puckett was singing R&B with a group called the Remarkables and waiting for the man that would make him and his new group, the Union Gap, into stars, and records like "Young Girl" and "Lady Willpower" into hits. A New Jersey band called the Critters were recording and releasing their first two hits, the Lovin' Spoonful's "Younger Girl" and their own "Mr. Dyingly Sad." Just as the songs became popular, their lead singer was drafted and sent to Vietnam, where he remained for the duration of the group's popularity. The Association, a collection of California folkies and rockers, was on the top of the charts with the jazzy, uptempo "Along Comes Mary" and the delicate "Cherish." Two sons of famous fathers and one son of their real-estate man, Dino (Martin), Desi (Arnaz) and Billy (Hinsche), were in the middle of their three-year string of minihits like "I'm a Fool" and "Not The Lovin' Kind." And the string of seven consecutive top-10 singles was ending for the son of comedian Jerry Lewis and the only '60s pop band that featured an accordion. But Gary Lewis and the Playboys had a run of singles that included "This Diamond Ring," "Count Me In," "Sure Gonna Miss Her," and "Save Your Love For Me." They may not have been high art, but they were tremendous pop songs.

All of these groups specialized in light pop rock. Their songs were as milk-safe as Bobby Rydell's and Paul Anka's had been a few years before, but the difference was their British Invasion sound. Every song from each group contained at least a touch of the Beatles, something copped from "I Saw Her Standing There" or "And I Love Her" or "Eight Days A Week." They were as different from the late '50s ballads as they were from Sammy Kaye or Doris Day. And the groups that made them looked hip, even if they didn't always sound hip. Both the Union Gap and the Buckinghams occasionally dressed in mock-Civil War costumes. But by 1970, all of them except the Association would not exist. The Association would tough it out five more years before finally packing it in. Their sound was no longer hip.

Gary Lewis was the lead singer of the Playboys.

Gary Lewis: It was an accident, really. I was going to the Pasadena Playhouse College of Theatre Arts. The Beatles happened and it was Beatlemania everywhere, and I figured it would be fun to get the old drums out of storage for awhile, put a band together with the guys from my classes. I figured I'd make a little extra money for books and school. Then we started playing at Disneyland and that's where Snuff Garrett, our producer, heard us. He presented "This Diamond Ring" to us, and bam! All of sudden there were demands to go on tour and I was thinking, well, what about school? I said, "The hell with it; I'm going."

The first record I put out went to No. 1. I was excited; I couldn't believe it. Then Snuff Garrett said, "Don't be too excited about it, because there's a lot of one hit artists." He told me that most important song was the second one. If you can follow up a huge hit, then you're on your way.

He knew not only the songs to pick but when to put them out. He was a master of timing. Like right when one of the Beatles songs was starting to drop off the charts, he'd put out one of mine. He knew it would be rough trying to compete with a new Beatles song, or a new Beach Boys song.

We'd do the back tracks, and then the studio musicians were brought in for overdubbing. He used Hal Blaine on drums, Tom Tedesco on lead guitar, session singers. It was professionally done. At the time I was young and I thought, "My God, this isn't fair." I thought since it was Gary Lewis and the Playboys that we should do everything. Snuff and Leon would try to tell me that that was the best way, that I had to listen to them. And I did, and look what happened. I had no control. But I'm glad I didn't, because I wouldn't have known what the hell I was doing.

Sometimes I would get so upset with Snuff Garrett. It would be three in the morning and I'm singing and singing and he'd keep cutting me off, saying, "No, you're a little flat there." I'd keep saying "Damn, I'm tired of this!" He was a perfectionist; he wouldn't let me quit until he got it the way he wanted it. Now, of course, I'm glad he did it the way he did. But at the time, I thought he was tough.

GARY LEWIS: 'It happened so fast that I didn't actually realize the magnitude of what was happening. I wasn't prepared for it; I wasn't even prepared for life yet.'

"Count Me In" was submitted by Glen D. Hardin, who used to be the piano player in the group the Shindogs for the show *Shindig*. "Save Your Heart For me" was written by two guys in New York, Geld and Udell. Leon Russell and I wrote "Everybody Loves A Clown" and "She's Just My Style." "Sure Gonna Miss Her" was submitted by a guy named Bobby Russel from Tennessee. At the time, it didn't matter to us who wrote it. I never cared if I wrote the tune; I wanted the hit off it. "Green Grass" was submitted by two guys named Greenway and Cook, and "My Heart's Symphony" was another one by Glenn D. Hardin.

It happened so fast that I didn't actually realize the magnitude of what was happening. I was

248

only 18 and in my second year of college. I wasn't prepared for it; I wasn't even prepared for life yet, you know? And then all of the sudden here I was in the limelight, with a lot of money. Then I got drafted into the Army; that's when I learned about life.

I was a clerk-typist. They asked me to put together a group and sing for them and I told them to get lost. I said, "You cut my career right at its peak and now you want me to sing for you?" I was bitter, and I stayed bitter for many years at that.

We did *The Ed Sullivan Show* five times. People would work 20 years to get on Ed Sullivan's show, so doing that show at all, in the first place, let along five times, knocked me out. I loved doing *Hullabaloo* because it was the first network rock show. They had guest hosts, and I hosted it by myself one time; I also hosted it one time with my dad. That was kind of funny because he had to sing Beatle music with me. It cracked me up. You should've seen him trying to sing "Help!" I'd love to get a tape of that one. We also did a couple of cameo shots in movies, standard beach movies with kids dancing around a barbecue. And then some kid says, "Hey, everybody, look, there's Gary Lewis and the Playboys." And here were are out in the water on platforms.

I had two songs in the can before I went in: "Rhythm Of The Rain" and "Sealed With A Kiss." They were released while I was in the service, so I was able to tour off those for about two years when I got out. But then, after about six months, people like Jimi Hendrix and Janis Joplin started coming out. So all of a sudden there was no more market for Gary Lewis and the Playboys. I didn't want to play that kind of stuff just for the sake of staying in music, so I did nothing. I didn't care for any of that at all, and I decided not to do anything until music came back around to what I liked. That didn't happen, so I had to get out there and make something happen for myself.

The biggest pop hitmaker of the '60s cut his first record in 1961, and had to wait four years for it to become a hit. Tommy James was married and out of work in late 1965 when a song he had cut in Niles, Mich., for a DJ friend suddenly took off and went national. "Hanky Panky" launched the career of James, who with the Shondells cut perfect pop-rock songs like "Mony Mony," "I Think We're Alone Now," "Sweet Cherry Wine," "Crystal Blue Persuasion," and "Crimson And Clover." As a solo act James was able to extend his career into the '70s with his only #1, "Draggin' The Line," and "I'm Comin' Home" before his career finally fizzled in the mid-'70s. Subsequent revival efforts produced good albums and minor hits but no resurrection of the halcyon days.

Tommy James and the Shondells' songs rocked. They had strong beats and big, catchy hooks, and an occasional roughness that set them apart from the softer rock songs of the Association and Gary Lewis and the Playboys. They sounded like rougher, rockier Beatles songs. They were derisively called "bubblegum," but after the fact, after they were hits, and because they were hits. Rock 'n' roll from the outset was never really about anything more than a beat and a hook.

Tommy James was the lead singer of the Shondells.

Tommy James: My career actually started professionally in late 1965. I had recorded, in 1961, a song called "Hanky Panky," in my home town of Niles, Michigan, as a favor to a local disc jockey there. He was my good friend. I worked in a record shop; it was a small town and everyone knew everyone else. So the guy wanted to start an independent label. I was 13. I took the group, the Shondells, and laid down two or three sides. The record died a miserable death because we had no distribution of any kind.

The song fizzled out real quick but there was something about it; as bad as it was, there was something magic about it. I graduated from high school in 1965. I had been working in a record shop and playing local dates in colleges, etc., all through high school. Finally, I was married my senior year of high school. It was a matter of having to make a living at that point with music. In June of '65, we got together with some old fellows, went to Chicago and did Rush Street. We played up and down Rush Street in Chicago — the go-go lounges — you know, those kinds of places. In late November 1965, I was sitting home very depressed, very much out of work. I got this crazy call from Pittsburgh. A disc jockey there had a television show. I thought it was one of my friends calling me up and pulling my horn a little bit. I said, "Come on, who is this?" They finally convinced me that they were who they said they were. They said, "Your record is #1 here." I said, "What record?" I said, "You must have the wrong number" — my name wasn't Tommy James at that time. They asked, "Is this one of the members of the Shondells?" "Well," I said, "Yes, but that was the name of the group I had when I was in junior high school." They said, "Did you make a record called 'Hanky Panky'?" I said, "Yes, I did." What happened was that the disc jockey had played it, picked it up out of the record cemetery or wherever they keep records that die that kind of death, and played it as an oldie. Of course, nobody ever heard it before, so it was the old Cinderella syndrome. The old switchboards lit up and, "What's that record?" and all that stuff. Some guy had bootlegged 80,000 records and sold them in 10 days after this tremendous reaction to this oldie that went on. We were #1 in Pittsburgh. Only in Pittsburgh. My reaction was that I didn't believe it, so I went to Pittsburgh to do some local television. I didn't know what to expect or what I was going to run into. Sure enough, it was #1! We had a regional breakout in all the trade papers. I did local television there. I had to put an act together quickly because the fellows I had been playing with were just not interested in going on the road — thought I was nuts just for even trying.

We were doing semi-jazz rock, a long way from "Hanky Panky." Finally, it dawned on me that this was really happening. I got together with the original producer of the record and the promoter who got me into Pittsburgh. We came to New York and sold the master to Roulette Records. Four weeks after that, it was #1 in the nation. It was just incredible. It was just boom! I go from Niles, Michigan, my hometown, like a slingshot into New York. I had to compete with some pretty heavy dudes. Those early days were really something 'cause it was like watching somebody else's movie. This can't really be happening, and the Beatles were already coming into their own, and the English rock acts were really hitting heavy. I found myself in a strange position because here I found myself with a rinky-dink record. It was done on a mono tape — we had to play it and sing it at the same time. It was bad for '61! But for some reason then, the English acts coming in sounded like they were recorded in monaural. So "Hanky Panky" fit in. But it not only hit over here, but was #1 all over the world. It was just unbelievable. We did about 4 million units with "Hanky Panky." That was the beginning of close to 50 million records with Roulette. We had 22 gold records, 18 gold singers, four gold albums — actually, two were platinum. By today's standards, they did more than a million units. This happened between the years of 1965-1972.

We got away with it because we were the first ones to do that kind of sound. It was soft rock 'n' roll, but it was very chunky. It was not really very melodic. But "I Think We're Alone Now," "Mirage," and all of those started a very simplistic kind of music, as opposed to what was going on with the English acts. So, my feelings toward that are very simple. I'm glad. It's the highest form of flattery. I listen to a group like the Cars, and so many others, and I actually hear entire segments of the basic tracks we did in '65 and '66.

What happened, by late 1968, after "Mony Mony," I became very disenchanted, muscially, with the way my career was going. It was time to move on. Bo, Richie, and I parted company — although we're still friends today — as far as creating music together in the studio, which brought about "Crimson And Clover." "Crimson And Clover" was the first record I wrote and produced for myself, by myself. I sang all the voices on the record and played every instrument except bass and drums. It was the beginning of our second renaissance. "Crimson And Clover" was to date my biggest-selling record. We did under 6 million singles and 2 million albums. An amazing thing took place during those three-and-a-half years. A lot of the technology from the space program was finding its way into the studio and into all electronic media. We went from mono to four-track; actually, three-track was in the middle. Three-track to four-track to eight-track, to 16- to 24-track. In a period of three years it was incredible. Every week there was a new toy you had to keep up with. You had to re-educate yourself every week. I'm so fortunate. That period of time I made it in allowed me to be in the studio all the time. It allowed me to fool with sound effects, to play with the toys, the technology toys. Every toy that came in I learned immediately, so I knew them from technical aspects, from an electronic point of view.

I don't know if I coined a phrase or not, but I called our music "complex simplicity" because you can basically take the same format, and it was so wide-open for the technology. "Crimson And Clover" took five-and-a-half hours from start to finish. I knew exactly what I wanted to hear. The *Crimson And Clover* project was a milestone. It was almost an event, because the Shondells and I began to write. We had input from everybody. This massive amount of untapped talent, which I didn't realize was in my touring group, I didn't realize was around me. We began to come up with magnificent ideas. All the tunes off that project were magic. They really were; there were some magical tunes on that album. The funny part about it is that seven of the nine songs were released as singles, either by myself or somebody else, so it turned into a greatest hits album. I'm very thankful for that. I got my chops together that way as a producer. "Crystal Blue Persuasion" was off that album, and we had a cut called "Sweet Cherry Wine" that was in the middle, that I had done on my "Cellophane Symphony" album. We knew anything after "Crimson And Clover" was going to be a smash, unless the tape broke. We put out "Sweet Cherry Wine." We all loved the tune. But in the back or our minds "Crystal Blue" was kind of haunting everybody. That was the third single off that batch of tunes. Not off that album, but off that batch of tunes.

It has nothing to do with drugs. Everybody thought ... It's funny, I went to buy a car a few years ago. "Crystal Blue Persuasion" created something of its own. There was no color called crystal blue. I was reading the Bible in a Holiday Inn one night — the Old Testament. It had to do with the truth. What I was trying to say certainly wasn't "Let's take drugs, and let everything be wonderful." Anyway, in 1969, we had an incredible year. We put out five singles, two albums and got back five gold singles and two platinum albums. It was quite a year. It ended with the Woodstock thing. A whole chapter of my life was ended with 1970. In 1970, we had been doing this for five years.

When I was in Pittsburgh, I had no act. I went back to do "Hanky Panky." I had no group. I went into a bar one night and grabbed the bar band. They turned out to be the Shondells. I needed a group to go on the road with — fast. I didn't even have time to grow my hair long back then. And that was very important. The Shondells and I broke up in 1970, but it wasn't because of turmoil inside of the group. We had just lived the five years together so intently. We just looked at each other and said, "Oh, God, what is next?" We were regulars on the Ed Sullivan show, we did the Houston Astrodome, the festivals, there wasn't a whole lot more to do. We were all so physically and emotionally exhausted. I bought a farm in upstate New York — 3,000 acres of land — and I went up and stared at walls for 6 months. The unfortunate part was that I couldn't have picked a worse year to take off. I took off 14 months. The economy went to hell. The Woodstock thing was over. The whole industry was going through tremendous upheavals. At that time, the economy was getting so bad. In '69, bucks were floating around, albums were being made by the thousands and tossed out here. The record buying market was bascially from 12-18, and FM radio started coming in as a major musical force. FM was starting to break records and there was a tremendous polarization. FM would only play certain kinds of records by certain artists. All of that happened during the year I took off, so when I came back it was like "Tommy who?" I was so afraid of failure after seeing these things. All my friends in radio were fired. It was muscial chairs in the radio industry, and musical chairs in the record industry as well. All the faces were new; everybody was different. The whole concept of putting records together had changed. That was the one year I really shouldn't have been out of the studio. I should have stayed one more year, but I didn't. I was just too exhaused to carry on any further. I went up and I never stopped writing. The Shondells and I went our separate ways. I was going to be a solo artist at that point. I wrote a song called "Tight and Tighter" that I was going to come back with, and I had my studio crew lay down tracks. I had everything under control. Finally, when it came to doing the lead vocal, I freaked out. I said, "My God." I actually had chills go up my spine. The thought of failure just had not occurred to me. I said, "What if this just doesn't happen?" I was really frightened. I went out to Brooklyn. There was a group out there called Alive And Kicking. It was a guy and a girl with a rock band behind them. So I had all the tracks laid, and I brought the guy and the chick into the studio. They were all starry-eyed. I said, "You sing this set of lines and you sing this set of lines." It was a pre-fab record; they did it and had a #1 record with it. My fear of failure was over. We came back in 1971 with "Dragging The Line," and '72 with "I'm Coming Home." '72 was my last gold record.

I'll tell you the truth. You can take "Mony Mony" and "Crimson And Clover," they're worlds apart. Yet, there's something, I don't know if it's the voice of the production, I don't know what it is, but there's something they have in common. I think what we've done is simply to ... I wouldn't put it in the category of music, I'd almost put it in the category of persistence and determination, rather than music. We haven't done anything that spectacular except have a lot of hit records, which is an honor in itself. To put it in one phrase, our music is ageless. I can go on stage and play "Three Times In Love" and "Crimson And Clover" back to back, and suddenly there is no time lag.

The most famous of the teen-heartthrob, studio-created bubblegum groups were the Monkees. Michael Nesmith, Mickey Dolenz, Peter Tork and Davy Jones were assembled to star in a televison show and mouth the words to songs written and performed for them. Ability to play an instrument was not necessary. But as the group began to be portrayed as a group they began to think of themselves as a group, and sing their own songs and play their own instruments.

They won the battle. The Monkees began to play and sing their own songs. Shortly afterward, their television show and their careers began to slide. Dolenz, Tork and Jones vanished. Only Michael Nesmith was able to maintain a musical career through the '70s and early '80s. But by the mid-'80s a Monkees revival brought the group (minus Nesmith), back, with a best-selling greatest-hits package, a hit single ("That Was Then, This Is Now"), and perhaps the most popular '60s-revival tour in history.

The Monkees, whoever the Monkees were at the time, made good music. "Daydream Believer," "Last Train To Clarksville," Carole King's "Pleasant Valley Sunday," "Valleri," and "A Little Bit Me, A Little Bit You" were great pop songs. They were a cut above the usual radio fare, and they all sounded like they could have been cut by the Beatles or some other British band. As actors the Monkees were loose, brash, funny and fun to watch.

Peter Tork was a member of the Monkees, and continues to perform with them on their revival tours.

Peter Tork: So, how did the Monkees get together? Do you see much of the other guys? What are they doin'? How did you feel being a plastic pop star? Can you read and write?

Okay, answer all those questions.

No, no, yes, maybe, some of the above.

Going back to the beginning ...

Are you gonna ask me how the Monkees got together?

No, actually, I was going to ask you about your career before that.

Oh, I was a folk singer. Before that I was in school, and before that I was in the bosom of my family. I was in New York singing folk songs on the Greenwich Village stages.

How did you end up going out to California?

'37 Chevy. Broke down outside of Las Vegas. When it started to belch brown water out of the tailpipe I knew it was all over. We hitchhiked the rest of the way. I had a lady friend waiting for me, I thought. Turned out I was for more threatening in the flesh than at a calm, safe distance, so that didn't last long. But she connected me with the Golden Bear Cafe in Huntington Beach, where I got a job washing dishes. I did some work accompanying Steve Stills when he was with Ron Long and the Buffalo Fish. I accompanied this black trio called the Apollos, on the standup string bass.

No, actually I thought the world should make a place for dishwashers and people who jerk beers. No, I always thought I was gonna be an entertainer, I think. I think I thought. Acting was not out of that realm. I had no idea I was gonna break loose; that was out of the blue.

I would have gone to rock in short order. The Beatles were coming along and that was a thrill. I would have put down that acoustic guitar long since, anyway. I often wonder about that. Where would I be had I not joined the Monkees? But I think, all told, it would've been just the same. I think I would've been more consistent than I am now, but the overall effect would've been about the same.

Is it true that the Lovin' Spoonful were originally considered to star in the TV show that eventually became The Monkees?

That's what I hear, but I hear it about the same way that you do. The whole Spoonful was considered; there might've been a show called *The Lovin' Spoonful.* You might be talking to Zal Yanovsky instead of me.

Steve Stills tried out [for the Monkees] and was rejected for having hairy teeth, uh, for his hair and teeth. Stephen was the guy who looked like me on Greenwich Village streets. That's how I recognized him: I walked up to him and said, "You're the guy that looks like me." And he said, "Oh, you're the guy I'm supposed to look like." So, when they were looking for somebody like him but whose hair and teeth were better, Stephen instantly thought of his friend Peter, threw the bone my way, and took for a consolation prize the Buffalo Springfield and Crosby, Stills, Nash and Young. Poor guy. Not bad for second best.

Were you annoyed from the start that the Screen Gems people in charge of "The Monkees" didn't let the group write and perform the music?

Yep.

What did you do about it?

Squawked and screamed and squealed, actually to some effect, because by the third album we did play and we got that because we fought for it. We presented a unanimous front and the producer asked us if that's what we wanted to do and we said yes.

There's some evidence to indicate that without the show the records would never have sold. They didn't go beyond the show; they went with the show.

How were the musicians chosen? Did you have any say?

Of course not! On the first two albums, abso-fucking-lutely *not!* Come on! No, zero! It was all Micky and Davy, and Mike got his change because he wrote some songs, and he insisted on producing them himself. I was left out in the cold.

In Cleveland, we went across the street and bought the first copy of our record that we'd seen. We'd never seen it or heard it. The back liner notes were Don Kirshner congratulating all his boys for the wonderful work they'd done, and oh, yes, this record is by the Monkees. It was very hard to take and it blew my stack, so that's when we went in and insisted.

Our records certainly were correctly crafted. The most important thing that can be said about them was what happened as a result of their impact. As music I don't think they're anything great; there's nothing *wrong* with them, they're pretty good. The songs are good and I still like to do them.

We did the shows one at a time, and when we got hot, we did them in three days. Of course, they were 11½-hour days. When we did the pilot we got about 20 usable minutes out of about 10 days of shooting.

Tell us about the legendary Monkees tour with Jimi Hendrix as the opening act. How did that ever happen? That's amazing.

What's the amazing part? That he got on the tour or that he got kicked off?

Oh, that he ever got on in the first place. I know why he was kicked off.

Surely. Well, Mickey and I were at the Monterey Pop Festival and we went nuts! We never heard of him. Who was Jimi Hendrix? What is that stuff he's doing!? I saw Janis there for the first time, and the Who. Otis Redding: "This is the love crowd, right?" What an experience. I saw Ravi Shankar on a half dose of Owsley's purple acid. That was delicious — weeping with joy all the way through.

I had no notion of what was going to happen. We went early to catch his act, and mercy, what a musician! We had a lot of fun between shows on the plane with him. I learned how to play a guitar vibrato from Jimi. We were in the back of the plane with Jimi and the Experience and the [plane's crew] had to tell us to get out of the back of the plane because we were weighting it down. We were back there with the curtains closed smoking and doing tootsie. We used to smoke weed together, and we all congregated in the back because up front there were press people. We would desert them and leave them in the front of the plane. The pilot would call back and say he couldn't make up for the weight difference and would we mind coming back up front.

Nobody said anything. We only got popped once or twice by people who disapproved. I was the only head in the group to begin with. The damage I did to those poor boys' minds. I'm the corrupter that I read so much about, the one my parents warned me against.

We used to do what we called wall-crawling, which was leaping from wall to wall and slithering up and down the corridors. We felt like we were in a corridor. You'd go from your house to the limo, limo to the plane, plane to the hotel, hotel to the limo, then out on stage, explode, people go crazy, back into the tunnel underneath the stage, into the limo, the plane, the hotel. It was all corridors and stages.

It was obvious that the phenomenon had a life of its own and that this was going to go so far. I think there was a chance, given a certain amount of commitment on everybody's part, for it to revitalize at a later time, but it had to take its dip. All the great careers — Sinatra, Elvis — take modest slumps. I think we could've come back in another mode if we'd cared to. But there didn't seem to be enough energy for it. Certainly nobody seemed to care to accommodate me and my desires.

I wanted to be in a group. My goal in life was to be in a musical operation. I guess I'm as successful at that now as I've been ever since. I left, then they went on without me as a trio. Then Mike left and they went on as a duo. There was a rumor that Mickey was gonna leave and Davy was gonna carry on as the Monkee, but mercifully, that didn't come to pass. Then Mickey and Davy got together with Tommy Boyce and Bobby Hart and did a brief resurgence at Disneyland shows. I joined them once, with full beard, hair past my shoulders, looking very out of place with those four clean-cut guys.

There was one very real acid trip I took and they had to shoot around me. We had this Hawaiian thing and we were supposed to be wearing skirts and I just said, that's too much. So I shined them on for a day. Mike shined them on for three complete episodes.

We seemed to have affected TV awfully modestly. They're not doing it now, nobody's done it since. The biggest influence the Monkees had was on the Partridge Family. And the Archies, that was another one — Don Kirshner finding the Monkees too real and deciding he was going to go to a group he was absolutely certain he'd have no trouble with.

Yeah, time does heal a lot of wounds, and I think human beings have built-in forgetters, which I think is very healthy. There are certain bad habits you don't want to repeat and it's better to remember the results before you go back into the fray. You want to learn your lessons. You only have a certain capacity for pain; you don't want to hang onto resentments because you'll feel unhappy. So for me, I don't want to be cutting off parts of my past. It's like cutting off parts of my body, and there's no point to that anymore. I did think for a long time that it was a mistake to be involved and I didn't want to have anything to do with it. Hey, it really was my life and I really did learn a lot. Any mistakes I made were because I didn't know better. The only alternative I had was to never have run across those lessons, and that's no use to me. The trick is to not become involved in the things that hurt so badly. I'm certainly not averse to success and fame and a certain amount of publicity and promotion. I certainly don't decline any help if someone wants to do something on my behalf. It's strictly on a selfish basis, though, if you know what I mean. Don't give me any altruists.

The way I feel about the future these days is that I leave it alone. The less I think about what I can be doing and want to be doing, and the less I think about what I did wrong, the more I pay attention to what I'm doing now and the better I do it. It's a matter of concentration and focus, and I'm happy to say that a day at a time now I'm able to leave the future alone. *(Jeff Tamarkin.)*

🍎

The biggest and best of the TV-show bands started out as a band and performed as a band, though its leader and founder rarely performed on its recordings. Paul Revere and the Raiders had their first top-40 hit in 1961 and their last, "Indian Reservation," in 1971. They were the stars of the popular TV series *Where The Action Is* and the role models for countless bands. They had a hit with "Louie, Louie" at the same time as the Kingsmen, and hit with songs by Mann and Weil and John D. Loudermilk. They were the quintessential '60s American rock band, but their only #1 hit came in the '70s. And they started as an instrumental band.

Paul Revere Dick was running a drive-in restaurant called the Reed 'N' Bell when he formed his first band, the Downbeats, in Caldwell, Idaho, in 1958. Revere was a boogie-woogie piano player who loved Jerry Lee Lewis and liked to play rock 'n' roll. Sixteen-year-old Mark Lindsay worked in a bakery across the street and played saxophone.

The group coalesced in 1960, and had a hit with "Like, Long Hair" in 1961. The song was a piano instrumental based on Rachmaninoff. Revere was drafted in 1961, but by 1963 was back in the studio recording "Louie, Louie." The recording cost $40 and the song was a hit.

In 1963 Paul Revere and the Raiders were the hottest group in the Pacific Northwest. They dressed in 1700s fashion and played energetic, raw R&B with slick choreography. Their singles were covers of Allen Toussaint and Jesse Hill songs. In 1964 their act caught the attention of one of Dick Clark's secretaries, who got them an audition for the pilot of a TV show called *Where The Action Is*. They were hired on, and their careers skyrocketed.

Where The Action Is made the Raiders TV stars, but they also recorded strong material. They were never really a bubblegum band; they played rock 'n' roll, and their singles were some of the best rock 'n' roll of that period. "Kicks," "Hungry," and "Him Or Me," were powerful songs, and the Raiders were able and enthusiastic musicians, even though studio musicians played more and more of the Raiders' parts, with Mark Lindsay's vocals the only real Raider vestige.

The band began to disintegrate in 1968 and 1969. In 1970 Mark Lindsay had a solo hit with "Arizona." In 1971, the renamed Raiders had their only #1 with "Indian Reservation." Paul Revere toured the country on his motorcycle promoting the single, even though he didn't play on the song. It was the Raiders' last appearance in the top 10.

Paul Revere and the Raiders never really ceased to exist. They simply played smaller clubs and stopped recording. Revere continues to front a group of Raiders.

Paul Revere was the founder of the Raiders. Mark Lindsay was their lead singer. Roger Hart was their manager. Drake Levin, Jim Valley and Phil Volk were members of the band.

Paul Revere: I remember when I was little I would go to the movies and I would see the Hoosier Hotshots, and I would see Spike Jones and the City Slickers. The mixing of music and comedy together was, I thought, the best of both worlds. What do people love more to do than to laugh and to listen to music? Then, when rock 'n' roll came along, that was my music, and [I wanted] to make it interesting and crazy and visual.

I told Roger [Hart] the very first time I ever met him — 'cause I knew he had this sock hop over in Portland — I said, "There's this place that we can rent, the D Street Corral," it's a big old dance hall in Portland. I rented all the armories in the Northwest. I promoted all my own dates. I bought the advertising. I did it all: hired the policemen, counted the money at night, paid everybody. I was a promoter that happened to get onstage also. So I told him, "We can do this thing," cause I knew he's on the #1 radio station, and he's the #1 time slot, and I thought, hey, man you can sneak in lots of ads that we don't have to pay for, and we'll do this promotion.

So I said, "We'll split this thing." We did it, and it was a killer success. I got a circuit going, and he was a great partner because of his situation.

I told him, "Roger, anything you get me, you get 10 percent. That's all there is to it." And Roger Hart did the impossible. He was the guy that suggested that we record "Louie, Louie." He didn't know how to go about it, and I said, "Hey, I'll just get ahold of John Guss and he'll print you up some records. You can put it on your own label."

"You're kidding! I can have my own label?" So I showed him how to do it.

Roger Hart: We'd all essentially learned the song, or all the groups had learned it, because a disc jockey named Ben Tracy had brought the record down from Seattle, and it was the Wailers who really inspired everybody. Everybody wanted to be like the Wailers.

Paul Revere: I was so heartbroken when the Kingsmen beat us out on "Louie, Louie," and Columbia blew it because we were the first rock group with this label and they didn't know what to do with us. They didn't know how to promote the record. I promoted it myself. If I had known how bad they were, I'd have promoted it myself, because I made it #1 in the whole Northwest. I had assumed that Columbia, being the world's largest record company, would do a lot better than little old Paul Revere could. But they just sat on their hands. They really didn't believe in it. New York's a long way from Portland, Oregon.

Roger Hart: I remember when we went out and found Richard Berry. I found out somehow where he was, and we went on a scouting expedition to find him and see what else he had. We found Richard in a little bar in the Watts neighborhood. I hate to use the word "ghetto," but we were in a neighborhood we didn't belong in, and we just didn't know our way around. We were a bunch of green kids from the Northwest in a black neighborhood, a little rough and ready.

Actually, it turned out to be very pleasant. We go wandering into this bar, and everybody noticed us for some reason, and, "Is Richard Berry here?"

"Yeah; he's in the back, man."

And we found Richard and asked him if he had anything else. We were looking for a hit, and he got into either the piano bench or a briefcase and dug out a bunch of things, and we came away with "Have Love, Will Travel."

Mark Lindsay: Paul and I were walking down Southeast Broadway in Portland, Oregon, and we were playing that night at the Lake Oswego Armory, which we'd rented. We passed this costume shop, and here is this guy in a swashbuckling outfit and a guy in a George Washington-type outfit. By this time, our costumes were Beach Boy, La Jolla-type blazers. We stopped, and we were laughing and saying, "Yeah, that's the way the old guys dressed." I said, "Paul, what if we rented these costumes?" He went in and priced them; they were like 20 bucks. He said, "No, no." I said, "No; come on, man; we're gonna make a big thing. And we went in and made a deal with the guy, promised to have them back the next day.

The first half of the show at the armory, we went our in our regular collarless blazers. Everything was fine. We went backstage at intermission and dressed in these traditional outfits with the lace dickies and everything, and it was like looking at a clown. We got onstage, and the whole attitude changed. It was like suddenly the Marx Brothers were onstage. It's real hard to look over and be serious when you see somebody standing there like that. We had so much fun that night, and the audience had so much fun. Nobody had ever seen anything like it. Neither had we. After the show was over, Paul said, "I think we might have something here." So after that, I think we rented them a couple more times and then started having them made. It was a lot cheaper than renting them.

Drake Levin: We spent hours and hours dancing and working together in front of a mirror working together to get the steps like telepathic, and we used to change steps in the middle of songs, and we'd have names for the different routines. We were always changing the steps and trying different routines until we found just the right combination for a particular song. We got so smooth, and everybody thought it was spontaneous.

Phil and I would be running together across the stage and Paul would be jumping up and down, and Mark would be flipping around in the air, and then I'd be running one way, and Phil would be running the other way, and we'd be crossing each other. Then, the last verse [of "Oo Poo Pah Doo"], we would run around and jump up on top of our amps, which in those days would be six or seven feet tall, so we would be way up in the air, and Smitty would stand on top of his drums.

Paul Revere: Roger Hart is the guy who made the Dick Clark connection. He was in the right place at the right time when Dick Clark was planning this *Where The Action Is* thing, and he got us the show.

Roger Hart: Roz Ross was the key element at Dick Clark's office. She called me, 'cause I had an apartment in L.A. at that point, and said, could you come over and let's talk about this, and we pulled it together. Revere resisted, wasn't sure he wanted to do it. We talked him into it, essentially, and we did it. Or we did the hour special. That wasn't too much of a problem. But to extend it into a summer series, that was a little touchy, losing the whole summer of '65 and spending it getting union scale for a television series. But it was well worth it.

Paul Revere: When we were originally hired, we were like background. We were the band that was supposed to back Steve Alaimo and Linda Scott, and we were just there, and then occasionally, they would throw us a bone where we got to do a song by ourselves. Well, the group was so visual, with the three-cornered hats and all the craziness, we made what was originally thought to be the stars of the show just disappear when we were on the same screen, and the fan mail instantly poured in.

It was instant success. We were getting national response the same way we had become a big group in the Northwest, because of our personal appearances. Then when we started cranking out some good rock 'n' roll recordings to go along with it, we had a package that was hard to beat.

In the early years, before business got crazy, I loved sitting down and writing, working up stuff. But, boy, when the business got crazy and I didn't have anybody to take care of it — who can you trust besides yourself? I would have loved to dump all that on Roger, and me stayed in the creative end where I could have kept writing, and had I done that, I probably would have ended up the producer of the group, rather than Mark. But I pushed that. It was like, "Okay, let's divide things up here. You do this, you do this, you do this."

Roger Hart: I can remember Paul and Mark sitting in this hotel, before everybody had homes, working on "Stepping Out," and then, little by little, as we put "Just Like Me" together. But Paul became more and more — by either desire or circumstance — passive, but I don't think anything ever passed without him knowing what was going on.

It was important that everything could be put together so that the band could duplicate it. That was Paul's one prerequisite: "Nothing can get out of this room that we can't play onstage," and Paul was able to do everything. On the concert tours you knew a Raider hit, and it didn't need to be a Monkee tapeback kind of situation, where everybody and his mother had to contribute something to keep it together. No, the Raiders did their own music. Paul was involved and knew exactly what was going on.

Roger Hart: There was a controversy on "Him Or Me," and I think that didn't help cement relationships, in that the guys were on tour and Mark and Terry [Melcher] had put together a lot of the basics of "Him Or Me," just almost to help everybody out. That didn't go over too well with Phil and Smitty, for example, who were, "Gee, well, you know, I wish we'd've known; we could have flown home."

Paul Revere: So Phil, Smitty and Drake came to me and — I couldn't believe this, 'cause I had a 60-day tour booked — they came to me with no warning and said, "Well, we decided we're gonna start our own —" and I'm going, "I've babysat these guys for all these years. I made 'em a fortune." They were all driving brand-new cars and had big houses and everything, because I made sure I split up the pot with everybody.

I tried to talk them out of it. I said, "Hey, wait a minute. Let's just use common sense here. Where're you guys gonna go? What are you gonna do. You really believe just because you're in every teen magazine that if you'd go out and do your own thing you'd be an overnight success? What are the odds of that? Do you realize that it was lightning striking and hitting this band that we were in the right place at the right time with the right name with the right costume, just in time for the British Invasion, just in time when Dick Clark happened to have a television show where he needed something visual, colorful, with the three-cornered hats."

We had everything. I was total fluke, fluke, fluke, fluke. We just happened to get with the right record label just as they were shifting gears and getting into the rock 'n' roll market. We were their only rock band, and we were everywhere at the right time. Everything was perfect. And they really believed they were so unique and so special — that's what it was. And it was like, "Yeah, we were unique and special," but there's so much more to it than that. Come on, man!

It was the late '60s that got heavy. We'd go in the studio, and then I'd say, "Yeah, okay, that's good." We'd have the basics. "Yeah, let's go." I'd come back two weeks later, and they'd been in the studio overdubbing, overdubbing, mixing, overdubbing, overdubbing, remixing, changing things. I kept turning my head.

I always wanted the group to be a group. When Fang and Drake and everybody was in the band, they wouldn't let Mark get the last say. We were a band. When we got in the studio, people would argue and we would get things done, and I would love it. I would play referee. But as they got replaced down the line, and as Mark started using more and more studio musicians, Mark was more in control, and nobody was arguing with him.

Mark came to me with this brilliant idea of, "Paul, what if we change the name of the group to the Raiders?" I said, "What are you talking about?"

He said, "'Cause the Rolling Stones are called 'the Stones,' and we always referred to each other as the Raiders, 'cause 'Paul Revere and the Raiders,' that's a mouthful. So Mark thought this would be hipper. Maybe this would change our image, maybe, if we shed the Paul Revere, we'd shed the three-cornered hat along with it, and the costumes, and we would be hip.

Mark was obsessed with being hip. I didn't give a damn about being hip. We are what we are, we do what we do, and there's always going to be a market for us. But I let him talk me into this thing. I wasn't completely for it. As I remember this, it was like, "Well, this is interesting. Let me sleep on this *a lot*, see if this really has some merit to it. Is this really going to save our recording career. Well, in the meantime, Mark had all of Columbia in his pocket because he made sure that he was in everybody's office at all times when I was out of town. This is how I remember this, but it's been one of those things. Maybe I've been thinking it for so long that I believe it. But as I remember it, he let everybody that could make this happen know that this was something we agreed on, which, as I recall, I kind of did. All of a sudden, it was in motion. And then it was like, well, okay, no big deal, what the hell. *(William Ruhlmann; April 20, 1990.)*

Few of the groups that had hits in the pop-rock groove wanted to stay there. The Rascals started out playing out-and-out rock 'n' roll and R&B and wound up playing heavily orchestrated flower-power music. In between they had a string of hit singles that ranged from the sublime (their wild cover of "Good Lovin'") to the ridiculous (the swingy Italian "How Can I Be Sure"), with "Groovin' " and "Beautiful Morning" and "People Got To Be Free" in between. They were manipulated by their record company and overwhelmed by their fame. They have made no attempt to reunite.

Felix Cavaliere: There were various bands in high school, and then I went to college for a couple of years, where I was supposedly pre-med. But pre-med and I didn't get along: I started a band again and the band, once again, took over. Forget about studying; let's go out and play. We were in demand, since there were only two bands and we were the better band. In the other band were some of the guys in the Blues Magoos. We got to audition in the Catskill Mountains, so we went there in the summer of '62 as Felix and the Escorts. It was a period of time when the twist was happening, and there were also very strict dress codes when you always wore a jacket and tie when you played, which is how the Rascals' knickers came about. That was our way out of that.

After getting a taste of that life, the magic finger of fate called me. I got a call from Joey Dee's manager, whom I had met during that time. He really was one of those old-time guys with a cigar in his mouth, and he said, "What are you doing?" I said, "Nothing," and he said "You're getting on a plane and going to Europe." So I got on the plane for Europe. Then the real mad part of my life began, because I met the Brigati family. Then I really knew I should have stayed in school.

I got off the plane and there was no one there. That started it. There I was in Frankfurt, Germany, and no one was there and I didn't speak a word of German. I didn't know where I was going, I was 19 years old and I should have just turned around. The maddest thing started to happen to my life from that point. All the guys were from Jersey, and they were all like guys from the farm except David [Brigati]. David was like the farm inside, but outside he carried himself with a lot of class. Crazy good. Late all the time for gigs, and language I had never heard in my life. They tore me to pieces. But it was quite a shock to be exposed to that.

From that point on, my life was never real. It was a magical mystery tour. Here we were working, and who were we working with but the Beatles in 1963? I mean, I had my hair like Elvis, and I saw those guys with mops on their heads and saw kids going crazy in the clubs in Hamburg and Sweden. I couldn't figure it out.

But this was the music business, and I was miserable. There was no culture; there was no language. A lady came along at that point and helped me out of a confusing time. She said, "The reason you're so far in the back of the band is because if he lets you do your thing, you're going to make him look sick."

Meanwhile, this other lady I mentioned had been telling me about this drummer by the name of Dino Danelli. She said, "You've got to hear this guy play," so I went to the Metropole in New York, which used to be jazz and country-rock. I saw him play one song and said, "Wow, that guy is incredible!" So I told the singer I had one of the best drummers I had ever seen or heard.

The first time I played with Dino, it was amazing. Playing with him was like making love. He was an incredible player and he was just the person for me to play with. The job was horrible. I mean, it was the worst. We worked from 12:00 to 6:00 and she was so bad, but it was Las Vegas and I was making more money than I had ever made, and we were there for about six weeks.

I met Eddie during the period of time I was working in the club with the college band. He had a relative or friend who owned the club where we were working, and this little punk would come in, underage, usually on a Sunday night, and no matter who the band was on the stage, he would go and sing and bury the guy. I mean bury!

So one night I was there and he came in and started to sing and I started to sing, and it wasn't that far apart. It was like the battle of the bands, vocally, so we got to know each other from that. He said, "You're not bad; I'm bringing my brother next time." I love those guys. They corrupted my whole brain. You can't imagine the words I learned from them. What a great sense of humor! Unbelievable! And it's spontaneous. It just comes out of them. Incredible guys. We had so much fun in that band.

Then I went back to the only place I could go, Joey Dee's club, and I got my old gig back. This is where I met Gene Cornish. he had brought a band down from Rochester, New York, called the Unbeatables and they were real countryfied kids, so when they hit the city, they didn't last too long. But Gene stuck around and got a job with Joey Dee.

So now we've got Eddie, Felix and Gene in one place with another drummer. Dino was still in Vegas at the time. I said to them. "Guys, why are we doing this? We're making $50 a night; these guys are taking all the money and we're doing all the work. Let's do our own thing." Everybody said yes except the drummer, which was great because I wanted another guy anyway, the guy in Las Vegas.

When we sat down and played — those four guys — it was amazing. We didn't have the best of everything as far as musicians — maybe the best drummer, but the rest of us were average — but the first day we played at my father's home, which was right across the street from a high school, the place was mobbed. They came right out of school at 3:00, heard us and kept coming. And we knew, there was no band to compete with us. There was nobody who was doing what we were doing, so it was relatively easy. We didn't write our own material yet — we hadn't even attempted to — but what we could do with other people's songs was good.

When we were asked to sign up with Atlantic, we had been given two or three other offers, but Atlantic was the only one that would allow production. I was the one who basically wanted to produce the group. I felt very strongly about it, and at the time, I had been very influenced by Berry Gordy and Phil Spector, and the other two labels that were interested in us would not allow that. They wanted the typical A&R staff guy to take over, and I wouldn't stand for it.

I had to fight the guys in the group, who had become nervous about my stance. They felt I was overstepping my boundaries. I had an argument with Dino, and he got scared. Here was more money than he had ever seen in his life offered to us by RCA, and I'm pitching a fit. I can understand that, because Dino comes from nothing, and here's a guy who has never produced a thing in his life saying he's going to produce a band.

When we went to the studio the first time, there was a lot of experimentation. What Atlantic was hip enough to do was to allow this crazy kid to get his way and put two guys — what they called supervisors — in the room, and those superisors were two of the finest producers today in the world. That's Tom Dowd and Arif Mardin. So what they did was pacify me, and they got the groups, I didn't realize at the time what I was fighting for because there was no such thing as creative control, but that's what I was fighting for.

I had been writing all my life, but I had never thought to use it in the group until we saw things like Dylan and the Beatles. It wasn't done. Writing and arranging pretty much go hand in hand. When you take a song and do it on stage your way, that's kind of like creating, so I had this thought behind this band. I thought the instrumentation should be based around the Hammond organ and around good voices and an excellent drummer. That's what we were.

So I didn't want anyone taking that away from me. I was 22, but I knew I could do it. I had a musical education, so there was nothing in the music part that would throw me. I didn't expect to run the board, but I had had some experience. So when it started it was a joyous experience, from day one.

We started off with the "Good Lovin' " thing, which was basically a live band playing in a studio. In those days, a group was a live band, and they had to make the transition from a live band into a studio band, so there was always a period of time when the recordings sounded live. That's what the "Good Lovin' " hit was, a good feeling.

Murray the K came in while we were doing "Groovin' " and freaked out and said, "Hey, this is an absolute smash." Atlantic didn't even want to release it. They felt it was a mistake for us to do that, because we were going kind of soft. It wasn't the raucous rock 'n' roll band that the college kids could identify with. The thing was #1 for eight weeks.

"It's A Beautiful Morning" was at a period of time when I had this mad, mad love affair going on, which was really the inspiration for all those beautiful songs. It started from "Lonely Too Long" and continued through "How Can I Be Sure." It was just a blissful period in my life of love. I was the only one who even had a girlfriend at the time. Then it just ended. It was weird. It was like she was just supposed to be there for that period of time. So "Beautiful Morning" was just like getting up and saying, "Things are going so great. What more can I ask for?" Eddie really understood what I was trying to say because he really did a great job. He was able to bring out the themes that I was asking him to.

I brought a song to the studio with a title and an idea. For example, what's "Beautiful Morning" about? I would write the chorus like, "I think I'll go outside for a while and smile." Then I would send him home to finish it. He hadn't ever thought about being a writer until I approached him with, "If Lennon and McCartney can do it, why can't we?"

I would take his lyrics to the studio and correct them. I would say, "I can't sing this one." I had an instinct for it. I would force him to overwrite a verse so I would have another set of lines to choose from. They just blossomed. These beautiful words just came out of the guy, but he wrote reluctantly. He did not enjoy it, but I kept pushing him and pushing him and he got better and better.

By the time of "People Got To Be Free," we had a lot of songs and technique under our belt. I think from a lyrical point of view, I started realizing that Eddie didn't really want to work anymore. But that song was a major turning point because I think at that point in time I lost something and gained something at the same time.

It was No. 1. And it was also No. 1 in the greatest oppressed places in the world, like Berlin. It was an interesting record. This is one of the songs that I would like to leave behind that I feel strongly about. Unfortunately, it was also a situation where I chose to divorce myself from Eddie's leaning on, and he's never forgotten it, because I really felt he didn't contribute much at all, even before that. At that point, I wasn't going to allow any kind of unfairness, even in the group.

The pressure became the first problem. Today, groups have a certain status that we were fighting for in those days. We would do *The Ed Sullivan Show*, and they would treat us like Tiny Tim. People don't realize that we stood for so many things, and wouldn't take any crap. We had a policy for a while where we would not play unless there was a black act on the show. We had knuckled under too many times in the beginning. Like the whole name the Young Rascals. We didn't know anything about the "Young." The "Young" appeared while we were on the road. We were the Rascals, and it turns out there was another group called something like the Har-

THE RASCALS: 'When we sat down and played — those four guys — it was amazing. There was no band to compete with us.'

monica Rascals, and they owned the name. Our record came out and it had the "Young." Why that? Why not anything else? They had put us into a thing we would never, never get away from. So from that day, we were the "Young." After around "Lonely Too Long," I said, "Man, this is the Rascals. Let them sue us. Anybody on the street will know us and not the other group." But it was little things like that, little mistakes the management made in judgment that were bad for the group.

Then the contract was over at Atlantic, and we were free agents. We were still fairly successful, although we were kind of struggling at this point. We had come off "People Got To Be Free," and then it was kind of slow because the band was not the band anymore. But we still could have picked it up, enough for Columbia to offer us over a million-dollar contract. It was sitting on the table, there were airline tickets to the convention that year which was to introduce us as the new Columbia signed act, and that's when Eddie left. That day! It was an incredible way to end a band that was really close. We were really close.

But I try not to think of those times. When I think of the Rascals, I get sentimental. When I think of the Rascals, I think of the guy who lived in a room about the size of this glass, buying his family a house. It just blew my mind. And I think of the kids in Hawaii freaking out over the Rascals. I think of the joy of playing for the Martin Luther King benefit — the only white act in the place — at Madison Square Garden. I think of all those things that we were lucky enough to be a part of. I think of having Jimi Hendrix do his first American debut with us in Central Park. That's what it was to me. It was "People Got To Be Free," playing for the Hell's Angels. The Young Lords at the Apollo Theatre; it's not the rest of the stuff. I just block it out and let it go, because it was so beautiful. We were very lucky to have been exposed to what we were exposed to and to have been around at that time. *(Jeff Tamarkin; May 6, 1988.)*

Eddie Brigati: All our contemporary people were saying screw the government, take all the drugs you want, shoot it up, trip out, heroin is a cool. But as a writer, I felt I had a responsibility to humans on the planet, and that's something that I feel was special in Rascals, and that's why we're alive today and being played all over the world.

The most shattering thing was [Lyndon] Johnson arriving in California at our hotel, and the news media said, "2,000 hippies are out here protesting the president's arrival," and there were at least 30,000 people in the street. I was watching from my room, and the police came out of the two little holes in the something plaza of the Century Plaza Hotel, lined up and began to beat the people back with sticks. You could hear the bones crushing. And I watched the whole thing from my balcony, throwing up, watching the condensed media version on television and then watching the reality as they were splitting their heads. That's when I knew we were in a war, that we were against people who didn't want you to be yourself, who didn't want to know you any better, who didn't want you to question their power. I'm a believer because of that.

We had more friggin' toys and money and mobility and clothes and prestige, stacks of gold and platinum stuff, but the part I needed to thrive on was the personal thing, and that's a spiritual thing. The physical thing was that we rang all the bells and won all the awards and did everything that was expected of us, but the joy was the creating. The joy was doing a concert in front of 10,000 people and they dug it. The joy was signing an autograph, the joy was girlfriends and the joy was parties. *(Jeff Tamarkin; May 6, 1988.)*

Two of the most enjoyable and endearing '60s groups came out of the same group. The group was called the Mugwumps, and played around Washington, D.C., in 1963 and 1964. They played what they called "jug-band music," which was a little bit of John Hurt blues and little bit of folk, mixed together and played on electric and acoustic instruments and sung with a light pop lilt. Zal Yanovsky played guitar for the Mugwumps, and Denny Doherty and Cass Elliot sang. For a time John Sebastian played harmonica. When the group broke up in 1964 Cass Elliot and Denny Doherty joined up with John Phillips and his model-wife, Michelle, moved to the Virgin Islands and became the Mamas and the Papas. Zal Yanovsky and John Sebastian recruited Steve Boone and Joe Butler and formed the Lovin' Spoonful. Together they popularized American folk-rock.

The Mamas and the Papas had a vocal sound that had never been heard before. Michelle's soprano and Cass's contralto were blended with the men's voices in intricate arrangements that overshadowed the basic pop-folk orientation of the songs. It was a unique, bright, warm sound, and from 1966 on, it produced hits. "California Dreamin' " was first, followed by "Monday, Monday," "I Saw Her Again," "Dedicated To The One I Love," "Creeque Alley," and "Dream A Little Dream Of Me."

But as bright as the group sounded, the lives of its members were that dark. Cass Elliot was overweight and insecure. John Phillips was a drug user, and his marriage to Michelle Phillips was in constant turmoil. Denny Doherty had a drinking problem.

The Mamas and the Papas split in late 1967. Cass Elliot embarked on a basically successful, though erratic, solo career. In late July 1974, she was coming off her most successful concert appearance ever, a two-week engagement at the London Palladium. On July 29, she suffered a heart attack and died.

In 1982, a rehabilitated John Phillips recruited his equally rehabilitated daugher Mackenzie, Denny Doherty and Spanky McFarlane, of the Mamas and Papas-soundalike Spanky and Our Gang, and re-formed the Mamas and the Papas. The group, with Barry ("Eve Of Destruction") McGuire replacing Doherty, continues to tour.

Dennis Doherty: We had done everything there was to do in Washington. We stayed at that nightclub [Shadows] for six months just doing dance steps every night. Finally we decided we were gonna cut an album. We did part of the album in Washington and finished it off in New York. We closed the Peppermint Lounge; we were the last performers there, with the Coasters. And that was sort of the end of the Mugwumps. Cass went back to Washington with the trio — piano, bass, and drums. I went with John and Michelle for the New Journeymen, and Zal and Sebastian formed the Spoonful.

The Halifax Three had broken up, the Big Three broke up and the Journeymen broke up. But the Journeymen had some contracts to finish. Scott McKenzie left the group and Dick Weissmann left the group, and John and Michelle and Marshall Brickman and myself were the New Journeymen. Marshall was our accompanist. We did two weeks in D.C. and then the Doctor, Eric Hord, came up to be the accompanist. We finshed our contracts, and that is how I got together with John and Michelle.

We had six concerts at something like $1,500 a concert, and that took a month to finish that contract. So at the end of the month we had around $8,000 and an American Express card. One night on some strange drug, in an apartment on the lower east side, East Seventh Street, John and I blindfolded Michelle. And there was a map of the world on the wall, and we spun her around and told her to put her finger on the map of the world. Wherever she put her finger is where we were gonna go. It could have been anywhere. But she put her finger on St. Thomas in the Virgin Islands.

THE MAMAS AND THE PAPAS: 'People were ready to hear female voices together with male voices, a totally unique sound.'

John Phillips: It was that transition from folk music to rock 'n' roll. We didn't really plan that transition. It was right after Marshall had left the group and Denny Doherty had entered the group. We decided to get out of town for a while and find a place to go and sing and work without any pressures. And it turned out to be spending the summer in tents in the Virgin Islands.

I first met Michelle in 1961 at the Hungry i, in San Francisco, where we were playing with Mort Sahl. She was a runaway from L.A., she was 16 years old. And she had made friends with the guy who was the artist, who did portraits of patrons, and he introduced me to her.

Denny Doherty: After we were down there already, Cass came down with John's nephew, Billy Throckmorton; that was her pretense for coming down. She and John didn't get along too well,

263

so John didn't want her to sing with us. Two Virgos maybe, I don't know. They were both from the same hometown, they went to the same high school — only three or four years apart. She knew about him as the bad guy from the Del Rey Locals, a gang in Virginia. But she stayed and started waiting on tables in a club where we were working. We had gone electric at this point. It was a little bit of a trial to get John to pick up an electric guitar, but when he did he loved it.

John Phillips: [Michelle's] range wasn't high enough. She couldn't really sing the arrangements I was working on. Michelle has a very high soprano range and Cass had a contralto. She came about a month after we had been there and we were singing in a restaurant called Duffy's. She got a job there as a waitress, and she'd sing while she was waiting on tables and we were on stage. And it got better and better. Then Duffy's was putting in an air-conditioning system, and one of the copper pipes fell on her head. She went to the hospital with a concussion, and she came out three days later and her range was two tones higher. So that sort of decided it, I guess.

Denny Doherty: Cass had already left the islands and went back to New York and had taken off for California. She was staying with Jim Hendricks, who had gone out even before her. Then we arrived in California and we had nowhere to stay, so we were staying with she and Jim, and we started rehearsing there, and she started singing with us there.

We were signed through Barry McGuire. He was an old friend, and he came by to say hello. We were singing and he said, "It sounds great! I'm doing an album with this guy named Lou Adler; why don't you come down and sing for him." So we went to sing for Lou and he said, "Don't sign with anybody; what do you need?" and John said, "What we need is a steady stream of money from your office to our house, and we don't have a house yet!"

John Phillips: We sang the whole first album for Lou and he just freaked out. We had it completely rehearsed and there were just no mistakes. So Lou went crazy, and we signed the contract the next day. And Lou said he would like us to sing backgrounds on Barry's album that he was involved with at the time because he wanted to get a feel of what we did and how we did it. So we sang all the backgrounds. "California Dreamin' " is from Barry's album, and that's the exact same track that the Mamas and Papas used for their "California Dreamin'." All we did was substitute Denny's lead for Barry's lead.

Michelle Phillips: It wasn't hard for us to break in, I guess, because we did have a very, very well-rehearsed sound. By the time we even approached a label we had been singing together for five months without any interruptions whatsoever. And when we came to Los Angeles, the first one we approached was Lou Adler, and we were signed to Dunhill Records the next day.

Denny Doherty: They thought that we were freaks. They didn't know what to believe. We didn't have band uniforms, no choreography, we all looked very strange. There was a big tall Indian, a big fat broad, some angelic-looking thing, and a crazy Canadian.

John Phillips: We were so unconscious of what we were doing; it wasn't a conscious effort to be different. It was just a collection of people that all had very strong personalities.

Michelle Phillips: I think people were really ready to hear, first of all, female voices along with the male voices, a totally unique sound. Secondly, I think it was the vocal arrangements and harmony that were not a part of the scene; it was just a unique sound. Also, the contents of the lyrics of our first record, "California Dreamin'." It was a very optimistic record. I can't tell you how many people have told me over the years, the reason that they were in California was because they heard the song "California Dreamin'," they decided that they'd take a chance. It changed their lives.

John Phillips: "Go Where You Wanna Go" was released first, but Lou suddenly got cold feet and pulled it. He always believed in "California Dreamin'," but he wanted to go with something more commercial. There were 30,000 records out, and Lou called them all back and put out "California Dreamin' " the next week.

John Phillips: Michelle inspired that song. She came to live with me in New York later that year when I was on tour. We lived at the Earls Hotel on Washington Square. She was so homesick for California, and we had gone for a long walk that day. Later that night I wrote it.

Denny Doherty: We took the record over to Bob Cavallo, who was managing the Spoonful at the time. He was our old manager from the Mugwumps. And he said, "Oh, the horns are out of tune, some of it is flat. I don't think it's gonna make it. Who is the flute player? It's really shitty." He was wrong!

Cass Elliot: We decided that we wanted a name that would indicate that there were both men and women in the group, because it was the first group that was sexually integrated, so we were trying to think of a name. And we were sitting around watching a television special on the Hell's Angels, and one of the guys, Les Crane or somebody, asked them, "What do you call your women?" And this guy said, "Some call 'em cheap, but we call 'em Mamas." So it became kind of a gag. "Well, if the Mamas will cook the dinner, the Papas will go out and get the cat food." So it became the Mamas and the Papas.

Denny Doherty: The Magic Circle was the only other name really considered. That was the period when things were magic. Everybody was taking acid and talking about magic. We also thought of the name Mamas and Papas. So we talked to Bobby Roberts, our first manager, and said we had two names, Magic Circle and Mamas and Papas. And he said, "Look, if I call Ed Sullivan's office and say that I've got the Magic Circle, they'll hang up on me. If I have the Mamas and the Papas, they'll listen to me."

John Phillips: Michelle and I were having a lot of marital problems, and we just couldn't work on the same stage together without literally punching each other in the middle of the show. So we talked it over and we decided we would take sort of a hiatus from Michelle being on stage with us. They couldn't replace me because I was the arranger and the guitar player and the songwriter. I just said, "I'm not gonna go on this way, it is just too painful." Then Michelle and I came to better terms later, and she came back into the group.

Michelle Phillips: To put things into perspective, and I knew that I had to make the marriage with John work, if I wanted to be in the group. But also a lot was settled by the time I got back. It gave me the time to weigh things out. How much I wanted the group or how much I wanted the marriage to work out. I wanted the group more than anything else in the world. So John and I resolved our differences, and we had a better time the last year-and-a-half. There was just a better understanding all the way around.

We were always short of material. "Dedicated To The One I Love" was one that I had chosen. I really wanted to do "He's A Rebel," which was an old Shirelles song, but I couldn't get the group to go along. So then they'd say no, no, we've got to find something else. "Dedicated" was always one of my favorite songs, so we went with that. I do think that our "Dedicated" was better [than the Shirelles'] version. The situation of our voices gave us the opportunity to improve the song.

John Phillips: Lou decided for "Dancing In The Streets" and I just went along with it. "Dream A Little Dream Of Me" I had loved as a child when Frankie Laine had recorded it. There is a funny story about that. The guy who wrote it was named Fabian Andres and he had gone to college with Michelle's father in Mexico City when she was a child. He also wrote "Beer Barrel Polka," and then in the '50s there was a hit of "Dream A Little Dream" by Frankie Laine. He [Andres] talked to Michelle's father and said, "Tell the kids to record 'Dream A Little Dream Of Me' and make me some money!" So I talked to the group about it, and I sang the arrangement and everyone loved it with the whistling in the end. Then we recorded it. But the group broke up and it came out as Cass' single, when actually it was the Mamas and Papas.

Michelle Phillips: Creeque Alley was the name of the street that we lived on in the Virgin Islands. It was a small alley in Charlotte Amalie where we lived in Duffy's guest house. Within the context of the lyrics, we actually refer to "Duffy's Good Vibrations." John and I sat down one night and wrote that song. We wrote it very quickly. I think we wrote it in three or four hours. We were thrilled with what we had written, and when we got to the part where we say "No one's gettin' fat except Mama Cass," I fell down to the floor laughing. I was actually hysterical. I said to John, "That's really funny, but what are we really gonna say?"

I remember the Monterey Pop Festival, which I hated. I thought we were just awful. We hadn't rehearsed, we hadn't even sung together in over three months. We worked on the Monterey Pop Festival, we put it together, so we did everything for that concert except rehearse.

Denny Doherty: It sounded shitty on tape. But it was a crazy night to begin with. I arrived about 45 minutes before we were supposed to go on stage and close the show. And the Who was on stage, and I didn't know who the Who was. I had heard a couple of their records, but I'd never heard anything about their personal appearances where they blow up the stage and start eating their instruments and shit; I didn't know anything about that. When I arrived, Michelle was in tears because she thought I wasn't gonna show up. I was in the Virgin Islands during the whole time they were organizing it and putting it all together — the soundtrack and the movie, and I said "See ya! If you need me, here is my number." The day we were supposed to go on, I arrived about 8:00 in L.A., and I got in my car and drove up the coast. That took me about six hours. Then it took me a couple of hours to find the fairgrounds. I had no idea of where Monterey was or where the fairgrounds were. So it was nightfall before I found the backstage area. I finally got a backstage pass, parked my car, and made my way through the guards. Some guy was asking a cop if he had any speed, and I figured, "Oh, boy..." The cop said, "No, man, I think the guy over there does." This was about 45 minutes before the festival ended. I showed up in time to put some kind of Indian robe on, walked up on stage, closed the show, walked back to the car and drove home.

John Phillips: Some promoters came to me and they said they had an idea to do this one-day big show, and they would pay us x amount of dollars. Once they had us, they would get other acts to do it. It would be a 10-hour show, which then had never really been done. So I thought it over and just thought that the idea was just too good to pass by. I thought, well, why can't we get other musicians to come in and do a three-day show, and everybody do it for musicians' charity, to help other musicians. So I bought the original promoters out for $10,000, and then I contacted all my other friends, like Simon and Garfunkel, and other people. Everyone loved the idea and everyone cooperated. Acts came from all over the world; it was wonderful. I wasn't very happy with the performance, though. It was one of the first times we had sung together in some time, and Denny only showed up about 30 minutes before we went on stage, as usual. So it was pretty hard to get it together. We didn't have our normal band or anything. Everything was hodge-podge.

I hoped the group would all come back together again, that we could solve all of our problems and have a nice vacation. Instead it became completely broken up.

Michelle Phillips: We had no intention of breaking up at that time, when we left. As a matter of fact, we were going to do a European tour. But when we arrived there, Cass was arrested on some phony charges. [*Cass was arrested by London police on her arrival in Southampton on charges of larceny. They alleged that she stole the blanket and keys from her hotel room during a previous visit. She spent the night in jail, and was taken to court the following morning.*] Things just turned sour. I mean, I was five months pregnant, Cass was in jail. It just turned all around.

John Phillips: I recorded our last album in my house in Bel Air. The equipment wasn't the best equipment, and we mixed it there also, and we shouldn't have mixed it there. That's why I think it sounds sort of funny sometimes. We got along okay. It's just that everyone was on their own tangents, it was hard to get people together for any extended period of time. You remember that the Mamas and Papas had always been a group that rehearsed and lived in the same house together, up until that time, until 1967. Then in '67 we all got different houses, and that made a big difference in the group at that time.

Denny Doherty: Part of it was recorded in the studio and part of it was recorded in John's house, in Bel Air, the studio that never was. The Bel Air Commission couldn't find it. They knew there was one in the building somewhere, but it was behind a secret panel. They kept seeing construction workers coming up with building material and taking it into the house. But when they came into the house with their books and magnifying glasses and their checklists they could never find anything. It was all up in the attic behind a secret door. The Bel Air Commission doesn't allow you to renovate or put a commercial studio in a residential zone, especially in Bel Air. You don't do any construction unless you get it okayed by the Bel Air Commission. They just started building a studio without telling anybody.

The breakup just happened the same way we got together. Slowly people got together in California, and slowly the people who got together in California started to drift apart. Cass wanted to keep working. She wanted to keep busy and active. She finally had a shot at doing something she had always wanted to do — get in front of people and perform, sing, record, act, do TV, whatever. But nobody sat down and said, "We're gonna break up!"

John Phillips: I think Jay Lester and Dunhill Records thought we were so freaky that we could never stay together. They thought that Cass was the main ingredient of the group, and they would offer her a lot of money to leave it.

Michelle Phillips: I think that Cass should have talked about the group with more love. That's what people wanted to hear. They did not want to hear, "Oh thank God I'm out of that group!" I think she showed a little immaturity in that sense. Because no matter how well her career went, people would know that she came out of the Mamas and Papas, and that's what they remembered her by.

John Phillips: Well, Cass had the idea that she was Mama Cass, and she didn't want to be Mama Cass, she wanted to be Cass Elliot. She never liked being overweight; she was always going on these crash diets and hiding herself away in hospitals, and we would try to find her. It was an unfortunate case, I think. When the group first got together, Cass said she would never get on stage because Michelle was so beautiful, and she wasn't. Eventually, we got around that and Cass found that people loved her for who she was. But Cass could never accept the fact that people loved her for who she was. And that was her attitude toward the group — that the group had made her into a little caricature of herself, and she wanted to be free of it.

Jay Lasker had us all under contract still and we all wanted to go other places. We couldn't go unless we satisfied Jay Lasker's demands. So he said, "Give me a last album, and I'll let you guys go." I never had all four people in the studio at the same time for that album. Cass had come in with a private nurse, she was so ill. They'd take her blood pressure and say, "She can't sing anymore," just when I was getting the part I wanted. It was a complete frustration to me. It was so weird. Before I could talk to Cass I had to talk to her nurse first. "Can I talk to Cass?" "Ah, let me take her blood pressure first." It was really weird.

Michelle Phillips: I was shocked and terribly affected by Cass' death. She was a very, very close friend of mine and irreplaceable. She had just done the Palladium and she called me the night before she died. She was kind of crying, but she was flattered because she got a standing ovation at both shows and, "I know I'm on my way!" I really felt that she had accomplished something that she had set out to do, and after she died, I was really glad that she had accomplished it.

John Phillips: I was down at Montauk in a house that Hagger and I had together out there that Andy Warhol owns. I had been riding with Dick Cavett that day, and we came back from riding and the phone rang. It was Lou calling from California. Dick answered the phone and Lou said, "Look, I'd like to tell John that Cass just died in London. I don't quite know how to tell him. Suppose you tell him, and have John call me back." So Lou hung up, and Cavett told me that Cass had died. I was very, very calm for some reason, and I called Lou back and he gave me the circumstances and so forth. Then we flew to California for the funeral. And as soon as the funeral began, I completely broke down and went crazy. I was convinced Cass wasn't in the coffin; it was very emotional for me; it still is. I miss her very, very much. I never realized just exactly how much I loved her until she was gone.

Michelle Phillips: I wouldn't want to experience it all over again. I would do it differently; what, I'm not exactly sure. I was a kid during the Mamas and the Papas, and we were all pretty immature. I guess I would have improved my relationships with Cass and Denny and John. If I went back in time, and did it now, I'd know how to make things work. *(Jon E. Johnston; April 1982.)*

❦

The Lovin' Spoonful was not without its share of turmoil, either. The group at its peak was the brightest and most inventive of the American bands. "Summer In The City," "Do You Believe In Magic," "Did You Ever Have To Make Up Your Mind," "Darling Be Home Soon" and "You Didn't Have To Be So Nice" owed less to the Beatles than they did to the Spoonful's own roots. The songs were quick blasts of euphoria, and they were unique. "You Didn't Have To Be So Nice" was written in a taxi on the way to the studio.

The group broke up in late 1968 after a minor drug bust polarized Sebastian and Yanovsky.

In 1969 John Sebastian recorded a solo album. The next year he played Woodstock as a solo act.

Sebastian's solo career produced some good albums but no hits save for "Welcome Back," the theme song for the show *Welcome Back, Kotter* and one of Sebastian's least favorite songs.

John Sebastian: I lived in the Village, so I was able to kind of be a part of what you usually become part of when you're 18 a little bit earlier. The neighborhood was familiar to my parents; nobody was upset if I was down there. So I was playing on that street when I was about 16, and going out to Washington Square Park on Sundays, and so on. And I had been playing with people like Fred Neil and Timmy Hardin.

And then I went off to become a sailmaker one summer, just on a whim. I went up to Marblehead, Massachusetts, and worked up there for a little while until I discovered that I was allergic to the rust paint that comes off the bottoms of boats when you sand their hulls. Of course, most people are allergic to that stuff: most humans will swell up and look like they're dying if you put that on them. But I didn't know that. I was just sort of taking the job that I was able to get before they would let me in the sail loft.

But this is all a large digression. As I came back from my excursion as a sailmaker, the very day, I got a call from Stefan Grossman. He said, "Gosh, I'm really glad I reached you. You're in the new band. It's called the Even Dozen Jug Band and we need a harmonica player and you're it. And rehearsals start today, this afternoon," over in a lot right next to where Fretted Instruments used to be, which was a local folk hang-out and guitar store. Well, the Even Dozen Jug Band did assemble that day and began rehearsing material.

And that was for me two things: it was an opportunity, within a very few weeks, to hear a tremendous amount of jug-band music, because Stefan Grossman and some of his other friends, Peter Siegel, were collectors as well as being musicians. And so they were very well versed in this stuff. And I kind of absorbed a lot during that time. And I was also forming a friendship with the man who had been assigned production for this project, and that was Paul Rothchild. He'd had a few credentials as a producer of folk records in Cambridge and New York City, and I think he'd been working all over the place, and had just gotten solidified at Elektra.

The Even Dozen Jug Band was a fairly short-lived item. I don't know that it lasted more than about six months. But our very first gig was at Carnegie Hall. We had a lot of fun and there were a lot of very kind of seminal types in this band: The woman who was then Maria D'Amato [later Maria Muldaur]; Steve Katz, who went on to Blood, Sweat and Tears; John Rifkin, also a pianist who did a lot of work with Joan Baez and Judy Collins. But anyway, this friendship and musical aggregation — although the band sort of dissolved just out of being so large and hard to organize — was a kind of an infant jug band, and I got a chance to see what I liked about jug-band music.

I had become friends with Dylan playing in basements in Greenwich Village. He and I were never on a stage together or anything, but we used to run into each other and play, you know, in the back room at Gerde's [Folk City]. And when he began to try to assemble an electric group, because I was one of the few people in the Village that liked electric music at the time — I mean, this sounds really weird, but, there was a point in time when me and about four other guys I knew were playing electric guitars and thumbing our noses at the folkies. There were real camps of music in those days and they didn't interact. And I guess that because I fell in this electric camp, at one point, Bob asked me to come up and play bass on a session.

Well, I wasn't about to tell anybody that I didn't play much bass. I'd played bass — he'd probably seen me play bass once, because nobody else did, and I just would play anything that anybody needed to be played. I didn't say, "This is a bass and I won't play it." I just did it. So he asked me up to one of the sessions that became part of the *Bringing It All Back Home* album. And it basically was, "Play bass until the bass player gets here." And I did play on two or three cuts, then eventually Harvey Brooks came in. I still don't know to this day which tunes, if any, actually remain of the stuff I played on. I suspect it all was overdubbed by Harvey Brooks, as well it probably should have been.

But that began a musical friendship. A few months later, I had assembled the Lovin' Spoonful

— or an early incarnation, actually; we had not met Joe Butler yet — and we had gone out to Long Island to begin rehearsals so that we could become a band, more or less, and while rehearsing, the phone at this deserted hotel, where we had managed to talk somebody into letting us use as a commons room to rehearse in, rang. And I go and pick it up and the voice on the other end says [imitating Dylan's nasal voice], "Hi, John, this is Bob." He says, "Listen, I'm going on the road pretty soon, going to do a tour with this, and I was wondering if you wanted to be in the band."

And I just had to put my hand over the phone and just stand in the phone booth for a minute and say, "What is happening?" You have to remember the point in time. There was no important writer in the universe, at least in the United States, than Bob Dylan at that moment. And he was asking me to come and play with him, and I'm there rehearsing a completely unknown, unproven band, and it was like when you watch incredulously as your hand reaches for something. I watched incredulously as my mouth said, "Gee, I'm really sorry. I can't do it. I've committed to playing in this band and we're working up tunes and I can't just walk out on rehearsals now." And so that's how I never went to work for Bob Dylan!

I was a member, sort of an unoffical member, of the Mugwumps, for about two weeks. The way it was was this: I had already made a friendship with Cass [Elliot], and Cass had introduced me to Zal [Yanovsky]. We already, I think, quietly, had an idea that we were eventually going to work together, Zal and I. But, at that particular point in time, the group that was formed was formed around Cass and Zal and Denny [Doherty], and a fellow named Jim Hendricks, and a drummer named Art Stokes. And what happened was, they went to Washington, D.C., and called me up and said, "Hey, come to Washington, come for a couple of weeks, we all got apartments and we're yucking it up, and it's great; come to Arlington, the Arlington Towers, and party with us, and play with the Mugwumps." So, I went up there, and what happened was I had a lovely two weeks, as especially a harmonica accompanist; I didn't really play anything but harmonica in that particular configuration, and after about two weeks, the manager of that band decided to fire me because he thought that I was a bad influence on Zally. And the reason was, I would play little harmonica licks at Zal to incite him to riot on the electric guitar, and generally spoil the arrangements of the tunes.

But it was more a moment of enthusiasm for this new music by a group of people who were pretty much connected to this kind of hale and hearty folk-music tradition. And I don't mean the Jean Ritchie/Lightnin' Hopkins type, I mean the Brothers Four kind of thing. And it really wasn't until that group dissolved that Zally and I were able to start thinking seriously about putting together Spoonful. And it was a matter of wandering around the Village and talking to people in bands and finding out who was free.

We knew that there was a bass player who was the brother of a guitarist who worked in a group called the Sellouts, that was the first group to tour the Village. I bought Skip [Steve] Boone's Les Paul, which I still have. Steven was, at that point, in Europe on a motorcycle trip, and eventually he came back. I remember he walked in to the place that we had set up to rehearse, and Zally and I decided that he was the guy almost instantly. And then we said, "What do we do for a drummer?" and he said, "Well, I've worked with Joe Butler," who was, at that point, the drummer for the Sellouts. Well, we'd heard Joe, and we thought he was good, but we weren't sure he was the guy we wanted. But Steven said, "Well, look, you know, we've worked together, so we're already pretty tight." So that sort of settled that.

We were rehearsing at the Albert Hotel. Immediately preceding us, in the sort of television room that existed there, the only room large enough to rehearse in, was Paul Butterfield, and the Paul Butterfield Blues Band, complete with Sam Lay, who was one of the most devastating drummers in the world. So just to begin with, the sound coming out of the room, as we all stood around waiting to try Joe out, was so devastating. I can't imagine him being anything but horrified. I mean, I don't know how good I could have been as a drummer at that time, but I know no matter how good I was, I know it would have scared me to hear Sam Lay! We started our rehearsal and tried Joe out. He started playing it and dropped a stick at one point, and continued to play with his hand! Now, the end of the story is a bit gruesome, because the cymbal was one of those old-style sizzles with the rivets in it, and he proceeded to smash the rivets with his palm, and considerably bloodied his drum set! And so, at that point, we decided, "Well, that's as much heart as we could ask for, so the guy's got the job!"

We had been playing the Night Owl Cafe for a couple of weeks. We got booted out because we were so bad, went and played another place for six months, came back to the Night Owl Cafe, and were received with open arms because now we could actually play a 25-minute set and not be horrible. So we became the house band at the Night Owl Cafe. And shortly thereafter, Phil Spector came down to listen one evening. And this was after a little time had gone by and the teenage audience had begun to find us; it wasn't all guys with long beards playing chess in the audience anymore.

That's the truth; that's how it started. We go in, we're trying to play rock 'n' roll and there's women with ironed hair looking at us like we're crazy. But then, as time went on, we found our audience, and so, by the time Spector came down, it was packed and screaming and fun. We used to do eight sets at the Night Owl. So it was an all-evening kind of situation. And Phil Spector stayed the whole evening, most of the time with his ear to the wall, that is, *pressed to the wall.* And we never found out why.

Erik Jacobsen was tremendously important in the formation of the sound of the Spoonful. You see, Erik had been in a folk group himself, the Noblick Upper Ten Thousand, which was sort of a modern bluegrass quartet that made, I think, one or two records and then dissolved. Erik took what he'd learned from that and began making demos. And I was one of the first people he'd met right after he had made a demo with Timmy Hardin. He had been getting universal turn-downs from everybody who heard this and "I don't get it" kind of reactions. And he played it for me and I said, "I think this is the most exciting singer I have heard any time recently. He is an amazing stylist" and blah-blah-blah, on and on.

Jacobsen was so relieved that we became a kind of duo for a while, with him on one side of the glass and me playing all the instruments on the other side of the glass. And we had started attempting to make 45s, basically. And simultaneously, I was meeting Zal, the idea for the Lovin' Spoonful began to formulate, and Erik was there through the course of the whole development as a kind of fifth head as far as how the instruments should sound. He always used to make me sing a lot softer than I normally sang and he had all kinds of things that he particularly liked. And I think that his tastes are reflected in the Spoonful records pretty much.

I don't know if we really would have ever expected to reach the #1 slot straight out of the chute, but we were very happy with the response that we were getting, and to have a top-10 single at that point was just about as fulfilling as it could get.

There was never any apology for commercialism in the Spoonful. We were aggressively trying to be hits, in popular-music terms, not in commercial-folk, or traditional-folk, or anything-else terms. So every time, we were trying for one. We got a little luckier on that ["Summer In The City"].

I think we were pretty happy, especially in the beginning. As time went on, and we began to strive for further-reaching things, we were constantly at war with Erik to make them as commercial as possible. So it was a very fruitful kind of friction, really. You know, the best kind of chemistry.

In some ways, all our songs were fillers. It's the old song title: If they ask you, you could write a book, a song, whatever. The fact that there was the necessity was part of the stimulus for writing, and for having material. There were desperate moments. I remember I was only halfway through a tune or two that I had to finish in the taxi on the way up to the session. "Make Up Your Mind" I wrote in a cab on the way to the studio one day. So, again, it's all what's needed.

Steven came to me with the melody pretty much complete and the phrase, "You didn't have to be so nice." I filled it out. "Summer In The City" was originally a tune that my brother wrote, and he brought me a song that had a terrific chorus, and I didn't like the verses. I told him so and he said, "Well, geez, see what you can do." So I rewrote the verses, came up with the little piano figure and wrote the verses around that, then went to his chorus. We knew we need sort of a bridge section, and Steven came up with this [*sings*] "bum ba da da bum bum bum da..." section, and that kind of had a Gershwiny, New York-traffic feel to me, and that's how we ended up with this funny little old sound man, whose main training had been in films, listening to various car horns and pneumatic hammers until we got the right ones!

Some of the most memorable experiments were the "Summer In The City" session, where Roy Hallee was experimenting with sending the snare drum through the stairwell there at the Columbia studios, which is what the sound is on "Summer In The City." It's actually him "wowing" the volume on a speaker that was mounted at the top of the stairwell, and picking it up on a microphone at the very bottom.

Pretty much all the twos and fours were "wowed" that way; that is, the volume is goosed at the moment that the drum is hit, and then cut off so that you don't get the rest of the kit. Roy Hallee perfected that and went on and used it on "The Boxer."

One of the things that used to make us the craziest was, when we would finish a new album and we would put it out and some DJ would come in and say, "By golly, you've done it again! And it sure has that Spoonful sound, doesn't it?" And we would look at each other all puzzled and say, "How did this happen?"

What we were trying to do always was to come up with the most different sound we could from the last record. And, in fact, our intent was almost to sound like a different band than put out the last record. "How could these be the same guys?" Because we loved to draw both from a basically blues kind of a source and then do something that was drawing on a Nashville kind of source or what you've very accurately described, those various singles. They were all very different. We were trying consciously to sound very different song to song. And it sounds fairly mundane now, but at the time, this was a radical approach, because groups and producers were very conscious of, "If the last record has an electric sitar, boy, it better be on this record so they know who the hell this is." And we really were taking the opposite approach, and luckily it was untried enough that it was different.

We were going as fast as we could. I remember I was writing "(Did You Ever Have To) Make Up Your Mind" in the taxi on the way to the session because we needed another tune.

Zally and Steven were in San Francisco and purchased half an ounce of pot. Coincidentally, there was a squad car crusing the area that Zally and Steven were leaving. They were, we found out, answering a screaming-woman call. And when they saw two long-haired guys, they stopped Zal and Steven and searched them and searched their car and came up with the pot. This is, of course, already a situation that'd be thrown out of court nowadays to begin with. But it was just the right moment in time, and here we are again with this moment-in-time thing, because I think that that's pivotal.

Our perception of the police at the time was very different than what was happening in the country at large. There was polarity beginning between people of our age and hair length and the police. Zally and Steven had no idea when they got into this how ugly it was going to become. But they were taken into custody and they were informed that the only way that they were going to even keep Zally [who is Canadian] in the country was to tell where they'd gotten the pot. Well, this was also a point in time, as I say, when Steven and Zal were generally of the inclination to trust these policemen. They thought, gee, well, okay, we got caught, now these guys want something from us. What the policemen said was, "We don't want the guy that you bought pot from. We want Mr. Big."

Well, of course, marijuana at that point in time was infiltrating the country on a very grass-roots level, if you will. And there weren't enormous-quality dealers, or at least, none of us, or any of our friends knew them. Musicians usually were getting pot from other musicians. And in fact, in this case, I think the other guy was somebody that wasn't even an acquaintance, was somebody that had a little. So they figured, great, we tell the cops who this guy is, they find out he doesn't have any big connection, and we're going to be fine. Maybe we have to hire a lawyer and get the guy off and that'll be it.

The police, of course, turn around and bust this very normal family guy in San Francisco. And he, in turn, turns down our offers of helping him with a lawyer or something, and gets a lawyer who wants to legalize marijuana in San Francisco in 1967. So, of course, with that lawyer, he gets in trouble. And I think he had to serve a couple of months.

But it didn't take very long for the underground press to have a ball with it. Nobody ever found out the real facts. But suddenly we went from being culture heroes to going to concerts and reading things in *Rolling Stone* and the local papers about, "Groupies, don't screw the Spoonful." How presumptuous! How incredibly presumptuous! And bascially telling an incomplete story that had tragic repercussions.

It was very simply impossible for Zally particularly to continue with this incredible black cloud. And although I think it says a lot about our momentum that we were able to make another album [*Everything Playing*]. Zally quit, we made another album, we fired our original producer, Erik Jacobsen, and generally did some real strong writhing around before it killed us. But that was the blow, that was the mistake that made it possible to go on.

I could see that the Spoonful was now becoming a dead end. We were all anxious not to go off and play theme parks and be a "was" band. And, at the same time when I had done the sessions we were talking about earlier, these people were now becoming more visible. Some of them were becoming famous, and I was very anxious to rejoin some of my old friends and to get on with the business of playing with other people besides the basic four. The one hard-and-fast rule that the Spoonful kept for at least the first two years of our time together was nobody but the Spoonful plays on the records. And that was one of the things I wanted to throw out now, and I didn't want to do it by continuing the name "the Spoonful" and playing with other people. I wanted to end one thing and then go on to the next.

I got pressure from the record company. MGM wanted to put out what became my first solo album as the Lovin' Spoonful, and in fact, delayed it a whole year. And that's a crippling weight. And we had to go to court and extricate this whole thing. Warner Brothers eventually said, "Look, we'll take the weight here. We want to put this album out and we'll fight it in court." So we said, "Wonderful." We got the album out as *John B. Sebastian* and then, of course, MGM started putting out a second-generation master with old artwork and calling it *John B. Sebastian*. Suddenly, I was seeing the really seamy, unhappy underbelly of the record business.

So I was playing solo, but I was also kind of helping [David] Crosby and [Graham] Nash. They came out to Sag Harbor, where I was living at the time, and we started — I guess it was sort of helping them find themselves as a band.

Stephen [Stills] at one point asked me to come in. I'm an amateur drummer, always have been. So, he said, "Look, we don't need a great drummer in this band; we need somebody who can sing along and maybe provide another voice and just kind of keep time, and would you do it?"

And I said, "God." The timing was all wrong. I had just put out this *John B.* album, and I was waiting for it to get into the stores. I had no idea in the beginning that it was going to take as long as it did. So my judgment call on the thing was, it's too late. I've already committed to this solo thing for a while. I've got to at least put out the album, be John B. for a minute, and then, if this thing hasn't already popped, then I can go over and do this.

I'm particularly good friends with Nash and the idea seemed like a good one. But I couldn't take it seriously at the time. As a matter of fact, David said something very weird. I can't remember his quote, but it seemed to assume that I thought that I was going to get bigger than they were. Which wasn't the case at all; I saw the opportunity for them to be really big. But it just felt like my die was already cast and I had to go with it.

I came to Woodstock as a member of the audience. I was not intending to play and, in fact, I sort of got drafted as a backstage helper to try to keep the mud out of one of the dressing tents. I had been living in a Volkswagen bus tent at that point in time in a little semi-communal situation in California, where you can live in a tent. But I had found out from that tent experience how you keep a tent clean in water. The way you do it is, you take a cardboard box, you put it in a garbage bag and you put your shoes in the box as you're going into the tent.

I told that simple trick to Chip Monck [stage manager at Woodstock], and Chip Monck said, "That's it. You look after the tent, because you can explain that to people and they'll believe you." And I was sleeping in this tent with most of the acoustic instruments belonging to the Incredible String Band and just about any acousitc guitar in the festival. It was all in that one little eight-by-eight foot space. It was hilarious.

So I came completely unprepared to play. I had no instruments. I was not particularly conscious of bringing any stage clothes or anything. What I came in was just this Levi suit that I had tie-dyed, learning how to tie-dye in California from a woman that was teaching a number of people on this same property [where] I was staying. And so, when the rains became intense enough that the power was off the stage, Chip Monck came to me again and said, "Look, we need somebody to hold them while we sweep the stage, and we know you can do it with an acoustic guitar, so you're elected."

I said, "Chip, I didn't bring an instrument." At the time, I mooched a guitar from Timmy Hardin. Actually, Timmy had put this guitar in my hands, and he never collected it. Months later, I tried to get it back to him, and he said, "Nah, it's okay, never mind." This was a Harmony Sovereign, the kind of guitar that you can buy and leave at the gig. As reputed, Timmy used to do that quite regularly.

So, as I say, I was not prepared. I look at myself in that movie and I wish that I had known that I was going to perform, because I would not have been swimming around psychedelicized along with everybody else if I had known that I was going to play, because unfortunately it created a perception of this stoned-out hippie. Not only was it detrimental, but it really wasn't me very much. It was me that day, and you know how terrible it can be if your personality is conveyed by how you were on one particular day.

We were wonderfully lucky. We formed at a moment in time where there needed to be an American four-piece band that was self-contained, that wrote its own material, and that didn't sound like the Beatles. And we were there. And that much of it is just good luck. *(Bob Irwin Jr., July 1982; Jeff Tamarkin, Nov. 3, 1989.)*

The Turtles specialized in perfect pieces of pop-rock with a twist. They recorded songs like "Grim Reaper Of Love" and "Can't You Hear The Cows" and set them cheek-by-jowl with "Happy Together" and "She'd Rather Be With Me." In an era characterized by good-time music, they were one of the few bands with a real sense of humor.

The Turtles started as a surf band called the Crossfires that later became so taken with the British Invasion that the band members assumed British accents. They changed their name to the Turtles because bands with animal names seemed to be having some success. Their biggest hit, "Happy Together," was meant for another group. Their drummer eventually wound up with the Jefferson Starship, and the nucleus of the band, Mark "Flo" Volman and Howard "Eddie" Kaylan, left to join up with Frank Zappa's Mothers of Invention.

Between 1965 and 1970 the Turtles put out a gorgeous run of singles and a surprisingly good string of albums. "It Ain't Me Babe," "Let Me Be," "You Baby," "Can I Get To Know You Better," "Love In The City," "She's My Girl," "Elenore," and "You Showed Me" hold up. They still sound fresh and fun.

Mark Volman and Howard Kaylan were founding members of the Turtles.

Mark Volman: 1961 was the year we met in high school. The Turtles didn't even have their first hit 'til '65. We met in L.A., singing in a choir — an a capella choir — and we played in a band from 1962-'65, which changed its name from the Crossfires to the Turtles. We made a record called "The Fiberglass Jungle" and "Dr. Jekyll & Mr. Hyde." Oh boy, we had some real turkeys.

Howard Kaylan: In the latter days of the Crossfires, we were surf, but we were also doing top-40 material. We wanted to hold down a normal, responsible weekly job at a teen club, and in order to do that, we had to sound like everybody that was on the radio. We wound up backing the Righteous Brothers, the Drifters. We didn't know we could sing until we started imitating the songs off the radio and realized, yeah, we can sound like this group and this group. It was just a matter of us being in the right place at the right time that White Whale heard us doing folk-oriented material and said, "That's what we'd like to sign you to do."

Mark Volman: They saw us reproducing the Byrds, the Beatles, Freddie and the Dreamers and Gerry and the Pacemakers. That was happening about the beginning of '65, and we got asked to make this record about April. We did "It Ain't Me Babe" and we only did the other Dylan stuff like "Love Minus Zero" because we'd just bought 12-string guitars. When the record company heard us sing that, they asked us if we could come up with something original. We said we thought we could, and they financed us to record three sides. They brought in this guy named "Bones" Howe to engineer. Producers in those days didn't really have much to produce. It was on four-track; we played until the song ended and then we left.

Howard Kaylan: We were too ignorant to be thieves. That takes a certain amount of perception, and we thought everything we were doing was original protest folk. Part of what kept the Turtles going so long was a bit of the naivete of the band. In other words, we only made records we thought were good records, not that we thought were hit records.

Mark Volman: But by the time we did "You Baby," the Byrds were already moving into something else, their space-fusion thing. We were starting to do music that would become our niche, that fun music. That has yet to happen again. If you look at the lyrics of the songs that we were having our hit records with, "Happy Together" was an imaginary song. It had nothing to do with a real love affair.

"Happy Together" is a classic; "Elenore" will outlive me forever. "You Showed Me" ... Those records are gonna outlive me; they have already, I realize. I'm very happy about that. I feel Howard and I were in the right place at the right time. I feel that we're not responsible for their success, that the public made them hits. We were lucky enough to be involved with records that the people liked. When we made "Happy Together," it took us 15 takes to cut the basic track. It took us three days to get the vox together, and when we released it, it just as easily could have been passed over. Because it sold 10 million copies, people think I'm a star. And I say to you, "It's not my fault. We just made 'em." The public bought 'em, and we were lucky.

Oh, man, that record could come out today and be as big a release. I hear it once in a while and listen to it. I'm so separated from it now that I hear it and go, "My God, what a record." Then you think it was cut on an eight-track, that we didn't have the technical environment we have today, that we actually had to ping-pong guitars and overdub horns and then bounce them to other tracks so we could fit it all on the record.

There's a lack of those type of records being made today.

Howard Kaylan: The Turtles' albums were probably the most overlooked albums in history, as far as *albums*. Our record company was not capable of selling albums. We only had one major album and that was the greatest-hits album. No one remembers the great album we made with Ray Davies. He's only produced two outside bands in his life; us and Claire Hamill. That record he did with us, *Turtle Soup*, is a collector's item because of the fact that Ray Davies is well represented: not only in sound but that the material — "Bachelor Mother," "Love In The City" — was written around our love for Ray Davies.

Mark Volman: You have to realize that we were barely teenagers just holding onto our innocence at the time. We were an innocent bunch of high-school who signed for 5 percent of 100 percent and gave away all the publishing on any of those things.

I've been doing this for 16-17 years, making records, and I know one of the things that remains in my mind are the times I had in the studio making the records. The good times I had, 'cause I'll never have those again. I'm not ever gonna have those days of making records with Marc Bolan.

"Bang A Gong," the *Electric Warrior* album — wow ... He made another that never came out in the U.S. called *Futuristic Dragon*. But we did four records: *Jeepster, Futuristic Dragon, Electric Warrior*, and there was another I can't even remember. It was terrible when he died. He was young and his career was starting to get back on an upswing. He'd just signed on to do his own kids' show for Saturday morning. He'd kicked his drug problem. It was sad to see his life end in such a disastrous way as a car crash where he wasn't even driving. We realize as we get older — Howard and I are 32 now — that we've really known a lot of people. You start seeing people you've lived with and loved with and made records with and they start dying and you start going, "My goodness, I got to get it done. I gotta get all these things done. I gotta get known." I have to be accepted. I want to be known as more than just Mark Volman, former Turtle. That's forever, and they can't take that away from me.

Zappa wasn't hard to work for. In spite of what you read in the press, and in spite of what every other musician who's worked with him has said, I can probably ruin Frank Zappa's career

274

by saying that working with him was probably the most meaningful three or four years Howard and I ever did spend, learning the experience of music; not just performing but learning improvisation, acting, doing films, the ability to not only be counted on onstage but for writing. I know what I've brought to Frank Zappa and it was a lot and he gave it back to Howard and me in a lot of ways. I know how much of the *200 Motels* story was written around what we told Frank. That's all I need. It's not really important to us that we're in the news; it's important that we know what we're doing.

We see our lives as an education. We never got the chance to go to college. When we left high school we were swung into another kind of college. We were in the Turtles for five years, went through seven managers and much litigation, a lot of deposition, and learned a lot about business management, law, a little bit of everything. When we joined Frank Zappa for three or four years and five albums and a film, I felt like that was our master's. The Turtles was my bachelor's degree. That's our main regret, that we didn't go to college. We could've gone; we had the ability and the grades. If there's a regret, it's that we didn't have the time.

To me, there is no success or failure. Success is in the eyes of a much bigger being than Flo and Eddie or Robert Christgau. Robert Christgau's opinion of me hardly means anything when I'm sitting at the foot of Jesus. And I really take it that far; I'm afraid that I'm that far gone. And I'm not a Christian, either, I just believe, as does Howard, that if there's a success in life, it's in working and thinking and creating.

I don't hate record companies, but the motivation of the people there scares me. If you confront a guy with the fact that he's there because he's looking for a better job next year with another company, it scares him. But I don't want to lie to them. I don't want to tell them one thing on a Tuesday and then have them sign me on Thursday and then I come back next week and say, "Now, let me tell you what I'm *really* gonna do." I don't want to be a phony, but yet if I shut up and was less critical of the system, I'd be lying. If they told us that they wanted us on their label because we're smart, and that we could make two albums a year and just turn them over to them, you know what? I'd probably give them the most commercial album we've done in 15 years.

And it's the same situation in radio. I have a tape of a guy who's a field representative telling his home office how he needed four pounds of steak to get a record on a major station. In a way we're Robin Hoods because we have to suffer for talking about this stuff and not doing it.

It takes guys like you to irk me off enough to remember why I'm not in the music business. The last thing we can say, though, is that we still have a great time doing what we do, and we hope people are still interested in us — even if we button our shirts up all the way and we never married Valerie Bertinelli. *(Cary Baker, April 1980; Jeff Tamarkin, December 1982.)*

By 1967 new sounds were taking over the charts. The Beatles, the Yardbirds, the Animals, the Rolling Stones, and the Kinks were starting to experiment, and so American groups began experimenting, too. Some of the experiments even became hits.

The new sound was based on the blues, roughened up and stretched out and given a powerful rock backbeat. It was a little like Chuck Berry on an acid trip, and it featured oblique drug references and socially proper lyrics. Some of it, like the Iron Butterfly's opus, "In-A-Gadda-Da-Vida," was horrible. Some was quite good.

Steppenwolf was somewhere in between. Much of what Steppenwolf did in the '60s and early '70s sounds dated compared to the Kinks' "You Really Got Me" or even the pop-rock of the Turtles or the Lovin' Spoonful, but "Born To Be Wild" was a revolutionary sound to be hearing on the radio. It was almost too loud and heavy to be a hit on AM radio, but on the newer FM stations it ruled. Steppenwolf was a polarizing group. You either didn't like them, or went underground, listened to them on FM radio, and loved them. They helped create a rift between AM and FM radio that still exists.

The group was together for seven years but only produced hits in four. By 1972 they had split up, though they reunited in 1974 and again in 1980. Their sound had passed them by, though it was their sound.

275

John Kay was the lead singer of Steppenwolf.

John Kay: When I emigrated to Toronto from Germany with my mother and stepfather in 1958, I was 14 and couldn't speak much English. I liked rock 'n' roll then: Little Richard, Chuck Berry, Bill Haley. I was learning English through rock music on the radio. One day, I came across a country-music station and became hooked on country music. In Canada at that time, mostly all you had to listen to was country or rhythm 'n' blues. I bought a Hank Williams songbook with chord instructions included. After much pleading with my mother, she bought me a guitar.

I started learning three or four chords, then began playing in two or three different keys — the way most guys started, I guess. It didn't take long before I was performing in amateur shows and on radio. No money, but a lot of experience. By the time I was 18, I got sidetracked into rhythm 'n' blues and moved across the border into Buffalo. The folk period was going strong about the time I moved from Buffalo into Los Angeles, in 1963. I started singing in small clubs and kind of slipped into the folk revival movement. I worked at the Troubadour Club as a floor manager, and played with Tony Mafia in Mafia's Men when I had the chance.

Mafia's Men allowed me to pursue my musical dream, but things didn't pick up speed 'til Sparrow. When I met Tony Mafia, he had just left a group called the Men [most of whom later became the Association]. So we formed Mafia's Men. We lived on peanut butter sandwiches, having no money, and only did two performances. One was a political rally for Lyndon Johnson, the other for Barry Goldwater. I stayed in Los Angeles for a while, then decided to return to Toronto. And that was where I met Sparrow.

A band called Sparrow was playing the club next door to me. They were in the middle of changing band members with another group called the Mynah Birds. Bruce Palmer left Sparrow and went to the Mynah Birds, who later added Neil Young. Eventually, Bruce and Neil ended up in the Buffalo Springfield. Nick St. Nicholas went over to Sparrow, and later to Steppenwolf. Sparrow wanted to change to a more rock 'n' roll sound, so we decided to join forces.

We had just finished playing a club in New York called Arthur's, at 3 a.m. — in fact, we did five sets that night. Columbia called us and said, "We want you to do some demos at 9 a.m." So they dragged us into the studio at 9 a.m. and said, "Just set up all your stuff real quick, and we'll throw a mike on you. We want to get all your songs on tape so we can make a decision on which to record." Later, they put all the pieces on that album. Even though I didn't sing on any of those Sparrow singles, it was the first time I was involved with recording.

Well, the Sparrow had stayed for the summer of 1966 in New York, but I felt New York wasn't the hotbed for emerging groups. Even though there was lot of recording activity going on, there were only a handful of things coming out of New York that were making any noise. Most of the things happening were coming out of California, bands like the Byrds. I was constantly badgering the band to move to California, because I had lived there and was familiar with the music scene.

We arrived just as the Sunset Strip riot scene was starting. It was also the period of psychedelic music. Los Angeles was really where psychedelic music happened first, that whole underground movement of alternative lifestyles. Later it happened in San Francisco. The Strip was busy with a whole bunch of clubs, bands like the Byrds, Donovan, and the Airplane were playing.

At the same time, groups of street people were beginning to form. Groups like Vito and his freaks, who totally defied description and who were striving to remain outside the mainstream of society by their lifestyle: the way they looked, the drugs they used, the clubs they frequented, and the bands they championed or patronized. They themselves began to be a tourist attraction, and they were bringing in young people from all the outlying areas. By the late summer things came to a boil.

Between all the clubs and the bands, all the freaks hanging out and all the young people they were attracting, this element began to have a sense of power. The cops didn't like it, and the straight establishments didn't want this element congesting Sunset Strip, they wanted their Grey Line busloads of tourists with cameras. The result was the closing down of the clubs for a while, as a means of removing the gathering places. The Sparrow went up to San Francisco, out of necessity.

We now came to a point in our career where it became very obvious that we were not getting anywhere. We couldn't make ends meet financially, and so everyone was attempting to figure out what the problem was and what could be done to rectify it. Essentially, that split the group into two factions. Two people felt that we should cater to the viewpoints and the desires of the record company. They said that once we satisfied the straights, we would have an opportunity to get our real stuff out. The rest of us felt that the record companies didn't know what was going on because they were of an establishment nature, used to dealing with Perry Como and Harry Belafonte and people like that. They still viewed rock 'n' roll as the black sheep of the family.

So that caused the rift in the band that finally broke us up. The three of us stayed in touch with one another after the band broke up, and got together to form what turned out to be Steppenwolf, which was really a logical extension musically of what the Sparrow had started.

After Sparrow broke up, I moved to another apartment. My neighbor was Gabriel Mekler, producer of ABC/Dunhill records. He heard my Sparrow tapes, and wanted to do a demo for the company. I called the members of Sparrow that stayed with me and a couple of others about the idea. We got together, found an abandoned nightclub in L.A., and rehearsed. Dunhill liked the demo and we came up with the name Steppenwolf. Actually, Gabriel Melker picked that name for us from the Herman Hesse novel. It was now the summer of 1967, and we had our first solid single/album recording contract.

I quite often hear people refer to "Born To Be Wild" as a classic or timeless hit. We didn't look at it that way when we put it on that first album [*Steppenwolf*]. That first album was recorded in nine days, mixing included, for $9,000. It was produced by Gabriel Melker on an eight-track machine. There were 11 songs on that album, and all we knew was these were good songs, otherwise we wouldn't have them on the album.

The first song released from *Steppenwolf* was "The Girl I Knew," one of these softer songs. That song stiffed right out of the bag. The next tune was "Sookie Sookie," which received some respectable airplay on the West Coast. It was drifting into the South, but then it hit the Bible Belt and they weren't sure what the lyrics meant, so, rather than chance offending somebody, they dropped it from the playlist.

We had lost valuable time through that winter of 1967 and spring of 1968. So, at the beginning of the summer of '68, we were confronted with having to make a decision on what the third single from the album should be. The album was doing well; by summer it was in the Top 10 nationally. Yet we had no national single hit. We were pressed. The record company wanted to put out "Everybody's Next One." The band felt "Born To Be Wild" had a good chance at being a hit single. It was a long discussion. We compromised: both songs would be put on the 45, and radio would make the decision. The record company was not to tell them which was the "A" song and which was the "B" song. Within 10 days, most all radio stations had picked "Born To Be Wild" and it was a big hit.

The music shapers put us in the hard-rock category. The record company wanted two or three albums per year from us, wanted us to tour as long as we had product out. They only wanted one approach to songs, and that was: make it a hit. So we used *For Ladies Only* to expand some musical barriers. Now I realize we needed to take some time off. Not push so hard.

I got to the point where I didn't want to tour anymore. I was bored. I wanted to do a solo album, something other than doing gigs and then going back home. Secondly, the hard-rock audiences in those days were really rowdy. People were throwing things. They didn't have enough courtesy to listen for 45 minutes to the opening acts play. Then there was the whole image thing: the leather and dark glasses, "Born To Be Wild" and being in *Easy Rider*. There was a one-dimensional image about the group as far as the public was concerned. We were supposed to be a biker band with political overtones when the "Monster" and "Pusher Man" came along. That may have been a realistic appraisal of us in terms of aggression.

But that's not all there was to us. We had a strong visual image, and the music was expected to drive with that image. Things like "Renegade," which were melodic, acoustic and sensitive were not appreciated — only tolerated at best. It was discouraging, 'cause when we were ready for musical expansion, we were met with lukewarm response. I felt confined with what we were doing. So we made an announcement [1972] that Steppenwolf was retiring. I went and formed the John Kay band with George and Ken. *(Nathan Pyle; Dec. 21, 1984.)*

The career of the Doors lasted barely five years and produced only a handful of chart singles, yet the Doors are as well remembered as any '60s group, and to many people typify the '60s. Nothing could be further from the truth.

The Doors represent the sound and style of the late '60s, 1968 and 1969. They represent rebellion and creativity and wretched excess and death. They wanted to be thought of as a blues band, but were remembered for the poetic ramblings of Jim Morrison and his Christ-on-the-cross persona. Their best-known songs are straight ahead pop written by guitarist Robby Krieger.

Morrison did set a standard for the age, though. Brought up in a strict military household, he rebelled against it all and studied film and wrote poetry at UCLA. He married a practicing witch in an informal ceremony and was arrested in Miami for supposedly exposing himself on stage. He was a heavy drinker and battled weight problems. While he was a commanding stage presence, he wasn't much of a singer. But the Doors created a mystique. Joan Didion wrote about them in *The White Album*; Oliver Stone made a movie about them. Morrison was treated as a major poet.

Krieger and Densmore later went on to form the Butts Band, one of the first white groups to play reggae. Manzarek made a string of inspired solo albums, including one based on Carl Orff's *Carmina Burana*.

John Densmore, Robbie Krieger and Ray Manzarek were members of the Doors. Paul Rothchild was their producer. Danny Sugerman wrote the book on which the Doors' movie was based.

Ray Manzarek: We were attending the UCLA film school, where we hung out together and became friends. And I remember at the time of graduation, Jim said he was going to New York to pursue a career in avant-garde experimental film, so I told him I'd see him around if I ever got to New York. This was in late May or early June, mind you, and about six weeks later, after graduation, I was sitting on the beach in Venice, California, wondering what I was going to do with myself, when who comes walking down the beach but James Douglas Morrison. So I said, "Jim, what are you doin' here? I thought you were going to New York." And he said he decided to stay in California, and that he'd been keeping himself busy writing songs.

Well, I thought *that* was interesting, 'cause I knew Jim was a poet and he knew I was a musician. So I asked him to sing me something he wrote, and he launched into a verse from "Moonlight Drive." And when I heard those words — "Let's swim to the moon, let's climb through the tide, penetrate the evening that the city sleeps to hide..." I said, "Holy cow! This is incredible!" 'Cause at the time you've got to remember that the Beatles were doing "She loves you, yeah, yeah, yeah," which was all well and good, but that wasn't really saying anything. So to hear Morrison say, "Let's swim to the moon," and then hear in my head all the chords and music I could play behind it, I said, "Let's get a rock band together, and we'll make a million dollars!"

I *firmly* believed in what we had. I knew we had something that people would want to hear and enjoy. And at the time, Morrison also looked absolutely fabulous. At UCLA he was a little on the pudgy side, carrying about 160 pounds. But when I saw him on the beach, he was down to about 135 and looked like an Adonis. His hair had grown out, his cheekbones and jawline were just incredible, and although I never told him this, I was sure that the girls were going to go crazy over him.

I used to play with my brothers in a bar band called Rick and the Ravens, and we did a few rehearsals with Jim, but it didn't really work out. And at the same time, I was involved with the Maharishi's meditation, and in the same meditation class were John Densmore and Robby Krieger. So when I talked to John about putting together a band and needing a drummer, he said he was interested. And when I told him I also needed a guitarist, he introduced me to Robby and suggested we all get together to hear how we sound.

When we first got together on the beach, I asked Jim what we should name the band and he suggested the Doors. And initially I thought, what a ridiculous name ... like the windows, the floor, the chairs, the doors. Then I thought for a moment and said, "You mean like the doors in your mind, or the doors of perception?" And he said "Exactly," and then I started thinking it was a really great name.

It took a long time for it to develop, not to mention having enough material to hit the Sunset Strip. We played a place called the London Fog where there was barely a soul in the place, except for a go-go dancer, and maybe 10 people in the course of a five-hour night. But being on the Strip was where Morrison developed his performance. In the beginning, he would invariably face the band, but little by little he began to feel the power and the energy, and develop the strength to look at the audience. Then when we became the house band at the Whisky-A-Go-Go; that's when Morrison really blossomed into the great performer that he eventually became.

We were fired for improvising on "The End." In that particular performance, Jim decided to tell the whole story about "the killer who awoke before dawn." And when he got to the part of "Father, I want to kill you...Mother, I want to fuck you," management of the club freaked out and said, "You guys are fired!" They accused Morrison of having the filthiest mouth they ever heard, and told us that we had to get out of the club immediately.

The funny thing was, during the performance, it was as if Morrison had hypnotized the entire crowd. People on the dance floor stopped in their tracks; waitresses stopped serving tables; the bartender stopped serving drinks...and at the end of it all, we lost our jobs. But a week before that, we had signed our contract with Elektra Records, and two weeks later we went into the studio to begin work on our debut album, *The Doors*.

Robby wrote a lot of the Doors' songs, including "Light My Fire," and that team effort was a part of the group's magic. We all contributed to the structure and dynamics of the music. And one day when we were rehearsing at our beach house, Robby said that he had a new song for us to hear, and then started playing this sort of folk-rock song that had a lot of great elements to it. But it was more in the vein of something that Sonny and Cher or the Mamas and the Papas would sing. So we made some alterations on it, and it turned into the "Light My Fire" that we know today.

I've got *lots* of favorite stories, but one of the best has to be from December of '67. The Doors were finally making it; our first real royalty check had come in, and we had to hire an accountant to help handle our finances. So, being the end of the year, my accountant asked if I was planning to marry my girlfriend, with whom I was living, because if I did I could get a real tax break. So I thought that was as good a reason as any to get married; and after all, we were in love. So we booked some time with the justice of the peace, and got married on the judge's lunch break.

Anyway, Jim and his girlfriend Pam came along as witnesses, and beforehand, I had gone to the dime store to get the most garish, outrageous snake ring for $2.98, and when I put it on Dorothy's finger, Jim just fell to the floor, laughing. Well, from that day on, Pamela started bugging him ... "When are we gonna get married? There's nothing to it. It only took Ray and Dorothy five minutes." And about six months later, Jim said, "I don't know if I should kill you or kiss you. That ceremony was so funny, but now Pam won't leave me alone." For some reason, Jim just didn't want to get married, and as it turned out, he and Pam never did.

There's the story about Jim pulling it out in Miami. It was really a strange story of mass hypnosis, with some 15,000 people sort of having a vision of Lourdes, you know — seeing a cross on a tortilla or something. Anyway, the Doors had gone to Miami, where we were perceived as strange, otherworldly creatures, and the audience was waiting to see something happen. You could just *sense* it. So Morrison said, "You're not here to listen to the music. You're here to see something you've never seen before. So how about if I show you my cock?"

Well, the audience started screaming, so Morrison took off his shirt and held it in front of him like a matador's cape. And then he started fiddling with his fly, and quickly moved his shirt aside and said, "Did you see it? I'm gonna do it again!" And I thought to myself this is ridiculous — he didn't *do* anything. No one would ever fall for it. But he *told* the audience what he was planning to do, and as a result, they "saw" something. So to this day the talk persists that

Morrison exposed himself in Miami, but he really just hypnotized the crowd into believing he did.

John Densmore: Morrison was always saying at first that it wasn't happening fast enough. He said he wanted to be thought of as a shooting star: a big flash and then it's all gone. But look what happened to him; it happened too fast.

Robby Krieger: We always knew we had the potential to be big. But Jim was always disappointed it took so long. Even though we had a smash the first time out.

Danny Sugerman: It was hard to talk to Jim about the Miami incident and New Haven before that. To him they were just concerts that got out of control. The impression I got at the time and still retain is that he felt trapped on one hand by everyone pushing and encouraging him to do something more outrageous, making the Doors more controversial and therefore more successful, and then taking the brunt of the punishment and nobody sticking up for him. He was feeling damned if he did and damned if he didn't.

Then he had his frustration about not being taken seriously as a poet, especially when he was being taken seriously as a sex symbol. I think his hope was that if he did something outrageous the band would get attention and once people listened to the music they'd have to listen to the words.

Ray Manzarek: After Miami, I think Jim fell back on his upbringing, as we all do when we get older. Some of his father's tendencies started to come out. I think he needed to be an authority figure himself; that was the irony of it. But it became too much for him and he couldn't hold on; he was too far out there.

Robbie Krieger: It got to the point where the vice squad started coming to every show waiting for something to happen. It didn't bother me that much, but it sure did Jim. He was the one getting busted all the time.

Ray Manzarek: Jim became a figurehead. They were going to stop all of rock 'n' roll by stopping the Doors. As far as Americans were concerned, he was the most dangerous. It was more dangerous coming from him than from Janis Joplin or Jimi Hendrix. Joplin was just a white woman singing about getting drunk and laid a lot and Hendrix was a black guy singing let's get high. Morrison was singing "We want the world and we want it now."

What could you say to him? "Jim, don't have too many drinks? You're killing yourself"? He'd say, "It's my life and I'll do what I want." And you'd say, "Yeah, I guess you will." You couldn't tell him it was affecting his work because it wasn't.

John Densmore: Not long ago a kid came up to me, and said I must not have liked him or I wouldn't have let that happen to him. I said I loved him for his art and his words but I hated him for his self-destruction. But there were glimpses of that coming on from the beginning. And Jim's circle of friends was just patronizing him because he was a star. It makes me real sad.

Danny Sugerman: There was much unsaid around Jim. People tended to keep their mouths shut and just hope; he wasn't the kind of person you could say no to. I don't know if I was real ignorant or too blinded by my worship to see that he was killing himself with his booze and behavior. But that was part of his game: to keep people guessing what he was going to do.

Paul Rothchild: I left because I was bored with what was going on, except for two tunes: "Riders On The Storm" and "L.A. Woman." The rest I thought was boring shuffles and sounded like lounge music. I told them the only way they'd get it back on track was having to do it themselves. It turned out that my read of the situation was exactly right, because they did turn out a very good album, although to this day I still think those two songs are the only good ones.

By *Morrison Hotel* it was already hard to work with him. The three other Doors were at their wits' end by that point. Jim wasn't interested in being in the studio anymore. He was comfortable in his position as rock star and sex symbol and was becoming more involved in his poetry.

Ray Manzarek: I was at home having breakfast when I got a call from our manager who said that Jim was dead. And I didn't really believe it, because I had heard all kinds of rumors before, like Jim died in an automobile accident, that he fell out of a window, and on and on. So I told him to check it out and make sure it wasn't just jive. So he flew to Paris and called me back a couple of days later to say it's true, Jim was dead, and he was buried in a Paris cemetery with other artists and poets.

So I asked him what happened, and he said he didn't know — that the death certificate was in French and he couldn't read it. Then I said, "Well, how did Jim look?" and he said he never saw the body. So I asked how he even knew Jim was in the casket, and he said he just *knew*, that Pam was broken up, etc., etc. Then when Pam died a short time later, whatever she knew, she took to the grave with her.

Robbie Krieger: I wasn't surprised by his death. In fact, I was surprised he lasted as long as he did. I guess I prepared myself for it a long time before it actually happened.

Paul Rothchild: It was like hearing a news report. It almost didn't affect me. But somewhere along the way I knew that the bottom line to Jim's excessive drinking was either going to be very impaired health or his death. I started to steel myself against those emotions because it was just too painful. It was one of those things when you sit down and shake your head and say, "Well, what can you do?" I mean, how many times can you get hit in the face? By the fourth or fifth you're groggy but it no longer means anything.

Danny Sugerman: "L.A. Woman" had just come over the radio and the guy said, "Hey, did you hear that Morrison died?" I had heard that all the time; he was always dying. But when I heard that Bill Siddons had confirmed it, I just walked over to the Doors' office. I didn't know what I was going to do; I'd planned the rest of my life around him.

John Densmore: For a while, I kept thinking, "Jesus, this guy is going to go at this rate." But then I'd think that maybe he was just an Irish drunk who'd party with a red nose 'til he was 80. When he went, though, I was dumbfounded. I'm really starting to miss him.

I feel that Jim was meant to pack it all into 27 years. But I want people to know that you can't just drink and wear leather pants and be immortal.

The idea of replacing Jim was ridiculous. I mean, we thought about it and talked about possibilities, but, you know, we didn't. Whoever would have replaced him would have been compared like crazy, so we went on without him and had Ray sing. We went on because after you've played with the same guys for six years you get a musical tightness. But after the first album, we started to fight.

Ray Manzarek: Jim tapped into the spirit of rebellion that all young people have. What does it mean to be alive? Where do I come from and where am I going? When you get to be 15 or 16 you start saying, "I'm alive; what's it all about?" Up 'til then you're a kid running around. The Doors were addressing that question of what is life all about, and that's why people will continue to pick up on that.

Danny Sugerman: They don't sound like anyone else. They weren't like the Dead or the Airplane from the San Francisco sound, or the Mamas & Papas from the L.A. sound. In the '70s, they didn't sound like the Eagles, and even now there's nothing else like them. Today, without Jim's personality to get in the way, once people get into the music there are no distractions.

Ray Manzarek: I think America is ripe for a new Doors today. I don't think that was so eight or 10 years ago but now, yes. I don't know what they'd make of Morrison, though. I think if the Doors were just coming out this summer, it would take about two years before they were all over Morrison again, trying to stop him.

John Densmore: It's like another life. I mean, it's incredible and weird. Here I am, I have a kid, and she knows the Doors. She knows Jim was a singer but nothing about the destruction. But it's a whole other world. I don't know ... I can't look at it objectively. But yeah, it does seem like something that happened a long time ago.

Robbie Krieger: I have a Morrison dream at least once a month.

John Densmore: I think he's dead. But, you know, no one ever saw the body except Pamela. It's ridiculous. But if anyone could've pulled off an escape he could've. All I can say is that if he's in Africa, I hope he's content.

Ray Manzarek: I have dreams about Jim Morrison coming back. Every once in a while I'll dream that I run into him and the conversation goes something like this:

"Hey man, where ya been?"

"Oh, I've been around."

"I thought you were going to New York."

"I did, and I also went to Africa, India ... I've been all over the place."

"Well, you wanna start writin' some songs again?"

"That's *exactly* what I wanna do."

"Then let's get a rock band together, and we'll make a million dollars!" *(Jeff Tamarkin, July 5, 1985; Sandy Stert Benjamin, April 5, 1991.)*

Bands were everywhere in the 1960s, and most of them were lucky to have just one hit. The Gentrys were a high-school group in Memphis that spent 35 minutes of a seven-hour recording session cutting a B-side, the Avantis' "Keep On Dancin'," that eventually became a #5 smash in 1965. Their followup, "Spread It On Thick," was also a B-side. The group managed five more top-100 singles in six years before disbanding.

The Blues Magoos specialized in the garage-psych sound and had no hit singles. They wore battery-powered suits which they plugged into their amplifiers and called their music "Total Re-Creation." Their lead guitarist, Peppy Castro, later wrote songs for Cher and Rex Smith. Cannibal and the Headhunters had a tough garage-band sound, too, and one hit — an almost wordless reworking of Chris Kenner's "Land Of 1000 Dances" that got the band tours with the Rolling Stones and the Beach Boys and a chance to open for the Beatles. They were also one of the first Mexican-American rock 'n' roll bands, along with ? and the Mysterians, who had their only hit with the classic "96 Tears." Canned Heat's drummer, Fito de la Parra, cut his chops playing in wild Mexican garage bands like Los Sinners in Mexico City, and auditioned for Bill Haley's south-of-the-border Comets. The American group he joined became famous for 20-minute boogie jams on classic blues and a unique sound keyed by the harmonica of Alan "Blind Owl" Wilson and the gritty vocals of Bob "the Bear" Hite. Canned Heat paved the way for the Allman Brothers Bands and Foghats that would follow. Alan Wilson died of a barbituate overdose in 1970; Bob Hite died of a heart attack in 1981.

The Music Machine had a #15 hit with the raunchy "Talk Talk" in 1966. Their lead singer, Sean Bonniwell, went on to make Christian records. The Cyrkle had pop hits with Paul Simon's "Red Rubber Ball" and "Turn Down Day," and toured with the Beatles on their last U.S. tour. Brian Epstein managed them for a time, and John Lennon came up with their name. The Left Banke were the prettiest of all the pop bands of the '60s. Their music was classical rock and their biggest hit, "Walk Away Renee," was a lush, gorgeous thing written for a girl two men in the band loved.

Larry Raspberry was the lead singer with the Gentrys. Fito de la Parra was the drummer with Canned Heat.

Larry Raspberry: We started in 1963. We were all in high school except for Pat Neal, the bass player. He was 27 or 28, a married man who worked for the railroad. The rest of us went to Treadwell High in Memphis and were all in the class of '65.

Rock 'n' roll was a big presence in Memphis. We were around Memphis in grade school when Elvis was on the scene and Sun Records was so big. My parents encouraged me to sing and play. and they had me take some music lessons. Larry Wall and I had been in school together since the first grade. He took up the drums, and I learned the piano and the guitar. At around 12 or 13, we decided it would be neat to have a little combo. My next-door neighbor — he never became a Gentry — was a guitar player. He was very good friends with Larry. We put together a little trio, and pretty soon we added a piano player from down the street.

We were young kids and not great musicians. We didn't know anything about tuning drums or even tuning guitars or how to make things really sound good. We just tried to recreate our sound onstage, and the music died terrible sound deaths in the studio. Back then recording studios were very dead acoustically. They were padded, and that changed the sound of the room.

The Gentrys did "Sometimes" for Youngstown, and Chips [Moman, their producer] talked to us about eventually getting a record deal on a major label. When we cut our second record, it was the only time I had sung. "Keep On Dancing" was done as a B-side, so there was nothing to be lost with my not having a very good voice.

We used to do gigs with the Avantis in Memphis. They were friends of ours, three black guys who modeled themselves after the Isley Brothers.

We very much changed "Keep On Dancing" but did keep the words and the background vocal part. The Avantis' version was very much like "Twist And Shout," very mid-tempo, like cha-cha. The Gentrys were used to doing things like "Little Latin Lupe Lu" and "Do You Love Me?" We were going to do "Keep On Dancing" with a tom-tom beat like Barrett Strong's "Monkey," but later we opted to take that out.

"Keep On Dancing" took about 35 minutes from the time we decided to cut it until Chips said, "That's the take." For the A-side, "Make Up Your Mind," we went in after school one day, at around 3:30. We started doing the record at five in the afternoon. We recorded until midnight.

We got a take on "Make Up Your Mind" that Chips was satisfied with, so he said, "Let's cut a B-side and go home. Do something I've got publishing on." We were excited about doing "Keep On Dancing," because it was a song we liked. Our version ran out at 1:30, which was too short even for a B-side, so Chips taped the beginning over and stuck it at the end of fadeout. It sounds as if the song starts all over again; really, what you hear is the beginning a second time. At least it made the record longer — two minutes and 10 seconds.

Back in those days, if you got good local record sales, you found some way to let the regional guy in charge of A&R know about it. Nashville had a special regional guy [Jim Vienneau]; I guess Chips contacted him. "Keep On Dancing" had sold enough units by then to chart on WHBQ, the local AM rock station.

We all really enjoyed the excitement. We got to experience scenes at the local movie theaters where little girls would cry and the police would have to be called and we'd be whisked away from the crowds.

There had been only the Watermelon Festival or the White River Water Carnival or the Cotillion dance in Grenada, Mississippi, or whatever for us. Our world broadened when "Keep On Dancing" hit everywhere.

We made our first appearance on *Ted Mack's Amateur Hour*. Then we did *Shindig, American Bandstand* twice, *Where The Action Is* at least twice. We had pretty high TV visibility, but we couldn't get on Sullivan or Carson. We were a one-hit act. By the time we hooked up with an agency and got a manager in a major area, everyone was watching to see what the next record would do.

We opened shows with Jerry Lee Lewis, then the Beach Boys and later for Paul Revere and the Raiders. We were offered a *Where The Action Is* tour. It was to be 28 out of 30 days and was to pay a total of about $10,000, or about $300 a night. It wasn't even a bus tour; we had to provide our own transportation, pay for our own hotels and buy our own meals.

It was the Searchers, the Shangri-Las, the Zombies and the McCoys, or some such configuration. At that time, though, the Gentrys had become stars in the South. We could make $750-$1,500 a night. We were getting a lot of work and practically lived at teen clubs in Alabama, Georgia and northern Florida. We turned down the Dick Clark shows, which played to bigger halls — 5,000-seat places — but didn't pay much money. *(Randal C. Hill; May 6, 1988.)*

Fito de la Parra: A few of the [bands I was in] are very famous down there. One was Los Hooligans, another was Los Sinners. I also had the first Sparks in Mexico in 1958.

Basically, we copied American groups, but about 30 percent of the material was original. We sang in both [English and Spanish]. At the time, we thought that English had to be the natural language for rock 'n' roll.

I recorded with Los Sparks, Los Juniors, Los Sinners, Los Hooligans, and Javier Batiz. "Despeinada" was a gold record for Los Hooligans. "Despeinada" was written by Paolite Ortega, a famous Argentinian pop music writer of the late '50s and early '60s. He wrote several million sellers in Latin American rock 'n' roll.

When I was barely 16, I was working professionally in the top groups down there. I considered myself extremely lucky, but still my minds was on the black side of music — into jazz and blues.

As soon as I had a chance to join a real music band, I abandoned the pop scene and joined a band from Tijuana, Javier Batiz and the Finks.

At that time, the bands from Tijuana brought the "new sound" down from the borders of northern Mexico and the U.S. into southern Mexico. That "new sound" was American rhythm 'n' blues. In southern Mexico, we could get top 40 stuff from the U.S. on the radio, but what was hard to get was R&B. The only source for R&B was Wolfman Jack, who was on a Mexican station, XERB.

The Finks were basically a rhythm 'n' blues band. I found myself musically when I played with these guys from Tijuana who had black teachers. I also played with another group from Tijuana, the TJ's. These bands are quite famous, because they introduced R&B to Mexico.

At that time, the rock 'n' roll scene in Mexico was flourishing. Those were some of the best years of my life. I was working in three clubs at the same time. I would go from one to another in my old BMW. It was all very innocent. I was playing music in coffee houses which had developed from beatnik jazz joints into R&B and blues and rock 'n' roll places.

I came with Los Sinners in 1965. We were from Mexico City. I'm not talking about bands from the Tex-Mex border or California, Chicanos like Rosie and the Originals or Sam the Sham. I'm talking about kids 3,000 miles south of the border.

We went to the U.S. for about six months of touring and working illegally. It would be impossible to do that now, but we crossed the border in a Chevrolet filled with the six of us and our instruments. When we reached the States, an Italian manager who didn't care that we were illegals got us gigs. We played fantastic places like the Troubadour, PJ's, and a private club called the Daisy. In Los Angeles, we played the Lazy X, which was popping with great things like Bobby "Blue" Bland and Tina Turner.

We changed the name from Los Sinners to Los Tequilas when we came to the U.S. We thought that sounded more Mexican and more commercial. We did fine until we got caught by the Border Patrol. We were playing at a place in Cathedral City, which is near Palm Springs. They gave us 24 hours to leave. It broke our hearts, but we were homesick, too. When we returned to Mexico, we kicked ass. We had that American attitude. We knew that we had played rock 'n' roll up there in "El Norte."

One day, without reason, they closed all the rock 'n' roll joints. Basically it was a government decision, as it often goes down in Latin countries. That was a shock to all of us who were starting to make a living out of rock 'n' roll. Then I married an American girl who had an opportunity to go to a university in California. And I wanted to come to the source of blues and R&B. I wanted to play in places where black people went and to jam with black musicians, getting to the nitty-gritty feeling of that type of music.

I found myself in Los Angeles a couple of months after I got married. Before I could even speak the language, I was in a band called Larry Barnes and the Creations playing this great place in Torrence named the Tom Cat Club. We played behind some of the greatest R&B artists of the time: the Coasters, Ben E. King, Jimmy Reed, Etta James, Mary Wells, the Rivingtons, the Platters.

That was a great experience for a Mexican kid who came here for that reason. I didn't come to be a star or join a bunch of hippies. I came to play five sets a day in a black club. I was in heaven.

I was almost placed by destiny in Canned Heat. There were three sources which brought me to Canned Heat.

I met the original Canned Heat drummer, Frank Cook, in Mexico City when I was with Javier Batiz and the Finks. This was before he was with Canned Heat. I let him sit in with my band and play a couple of Jimmy Reed numbers. When I came to L.A., I visited him. He had joined Canned Heat and invited me to a gig. He used to sing a couple of numbers, so I asked if I could sit in while he sang. I had just come to the States and was dying to play. He refused, claiming that it was not an American custom to let people sit in. That disappointed me because I had let him play with my band. But I was shy and in a strange country, so I sat down and enjoyed the show. The ironic thing is that a few months later I would take his place.

Another source was that I started to build a name for myself among the L.A. music community. I was playing in three bands when I joined Canned Heat. I kept my steady R&B job and joined two newly formed blues bands in L.A.

One of the blues bands was the Sotweed Factor. We recorded a chain-gang 45, "Bald Headed Woman," for Original Sound, a famous studio on Sunset Boulevard. The Sotweed Factor needed management, so a couple of the members appraoched Skip Taylor, Canned Heat's manager. People were starting to talk about Canned Heat as L.A.'s equivalent to the Paul Butterfield Blues Band. So Canned Heat's manager knew about me through the Sotweed Factor.

Source number three involved a bust and a gig. Canned Heat was busted in Denver during their first tour. They started talking about replacing Frank Cook during the bust. They wanted a drummer with more punch and a greater blues orientation.

When they got out of jail, Canned Heat came back to L.A. to play a gig at the Magic Mushroom. A band I was playing with — Bluesberry Jam, which eventually became Pacific Gas and Electric — was also on the bill. We played with Canned Heat on a night when Canned Heat was not happening, and we destroyed them. The whole myth of Canned Heat being L.A.'s top blues band was shattered by Bluesberry Jam at that Magic Mushroom gig. All of a sudden, there was a blues band with a black singer that made Canned Heat look like a Mickey Mouse band.

At three o'clock in the morning, the night of the gig, Canned Heat's manager called me and asked if I'd like to audition. I can't tell you how happy I felt. From the moment I first saw them — when Frank Cook wouldn't let me sit in — I knew that they were going to make it. I wasn't sure that blues would make it, but I was certain that Bob Hite would.

I was a fan of Junior Wells and Buddy Guy. I showed up for the audition with a Junior Wells album. Bob Hite opened the door and noticed the album. He told me later that he respected that commitment to blues. Bob was a blues record collector first and then a performer. He thought that bringing the Junior Wells record was heavy. In his mind, that got me in the band.

After the audition, I talked to their manager, Skip Taylor. He asked if I would join the group. I answered, "I was born to play in Canned Heat." The statement put me in the manager's heart, because at that time, music was not a business. It was a family which you got your heart into. They were looking for that kind of commitment. They didn't want a mercenary.

The name comes from an old blues record, "Canned Heat Mama." Canned heat is really Sterno. During the Depression, black people in the South used to squeeze canned heat in a handkerchief and drink it mixed with soda. They used to catch a buzz. That's why those blues records came out. It's a great name and an American institution. *(Joseph Tortelli; Sept. 12, 1986.)*

🍎

Certain cities had certain sounds at certain times. Detroit had two sounds at once. The commercial sound was the black sound. While Motown was in the middle of its unprecedented string of hits, white artists like Mitch Ryder were struggling, covering R&B and Little Richard and laying the groundwork for the sound of the next decade.

Mitch Ryder, a/k/a Billy Levise Jr., started singing R&B in the clubs around Detroit in 1962, when he was 17. By the time he was 19, his band, Billy Lee and the Rivieras, were headlining local clubs *above* Motown acts. Producer Bob Crewe heard a tape of the band, and the next year Mitch Ryder and the Detroit Wheels were recording artists. Though their only hit was a cover — a wild cover of "Good Golly Miss Molly" and "Jenny Take A Ride," the Wheels' reputation carried over. Bob Seger, another Detroit product, took his inspiration from them; Bruce Springsteen covered them; John Cougar Mellencamp produced Ryder's 1983 comeback album.

One of the Wheels' managers was a publicity-loving avowed radical named John Sinclair, whose main talents were rock criticism and getting thrown into jail. Sinclair was the leader of the revolutionary White Panthers, but in-between revolutionary acts he managed the career of the loudest, roughest, foulest, and ultimately one of the most influential groups of the late '60s: the MC5. The MC5 were the first punk band; their music was raw and angry and anti-melodic. Their stage shows were chaos; their audiences were mayhem. The MC5 were followed by the Stooges, another loud, offensive, influential band led by drug user and habitual weightlifter Jim "Iggy Pop" Osterberg. They cut anthems for the alienated like "I Wanna Be Your Dog" and

"1969," and influenced the careers of David Bowie, the Clash and the Sex Pistols. They were major bands not for what they sang but for what they did. They gave the British something to follow for a change.

Dennis Thompson was the drummer for the MC5. John Sinclair was their manager. Ron Asheton played lead guitar for the Stooges.

Mitch Ryder: We did, like, Moose lodges of all-black audiences, and we did insurance parties. We were hired for banquets and stuff. We were just a vocal group. Then we did The Village, which of course was a regular gig. That was the Peps. Prior to the Peps, I had been signed up to a black gospel label — Carrie. That took me to a lot of black churches, you know, I got to cut my teeth on some of that for a while.

I didn't get real heavy into soul until I started messin' around with some Sam Cooke numbers. I used to be able to sing "Who's Lovin' You Now," by Smokey Robinson, in the *original* key! That was a tough one.

In the very beginning, the whites weren't privy to [soul] too much. And then as I got into the Rivieras, we played the state fair in the Battle of the Bands, and we did James Brown and Isley Brothers covers. Not real soul covers, but sort of R&B/pop covers — tunes of the day, more or less. Except the Isley Brothers; everybody was doing "Shout," and we were doin' a tune like "Your Old Lady," which was an Isley Brothers tune.

The hits, the medleys took off and became popular so fast that we were immediately called into the studio. And, naturally, there wasn't that much time to learn new tunes for the first album. We just did anything we could think of out of our club act.

After that first session, what a lot of people don't understand is that we had a constant flow of guitar players and bass players. The stable personalities in there were [Jim] McCarty, [John] Badanjek and myself. The rest of the band kept changing faces all along. Even before we had a hit record, one of the members was preparing to leave because he was going to get drafted.

The Who opened for me in New York at the [now-defunct] RKO 58th Street Theater. Not only they, but Eric Clapton and Cream as well. On the *same show!*

We were the only white group to come out of the city at that time. If you wanna look a little later, there were some groups. They were signed up, not to Motown, but there was this recording thing on Davison around Livernois. I'm trying to think of that guy's name. They had groups that came out with songs like "Just Like Romeo And Juliet." They were white guys and sounded black for the time. But there was no serious competition [for the Wheels] from Detroit. We were definitely a hot item back then.

We were the first self-contained rock group to make it into the top 10 of the R&B charts. It shows that we got respect from the black record buyers.

I'm not bitter about the public. I'm bitter about the opportunities and the monies that were taken from me when I was a success. Over the years, in pursuit of my career, that money would have been a nice cushion for me to ride on. But in any case, money or not, I would have continued to do what I'm doing. I understand why people aren't being exposed to the music I do, but I still feel that one day, my time will come again. Who knows how or what it's gonna take to get there? To me, this is a lifelong career. To feel bitter about having something at one time, the only way I can feel good about it is that is a level that would be nice to attain again. I have been able to squeak out a living doing this and I'm appreciative of that fact. I'm thankful for that opportunity. *(Ken Settle; May 20, 1988.)*

John Sinclair: The various bands were the products of different neighborhoods, each with little followings. Everyone played all the time, whether in high school or in teen clubs. By playing a lot you developed followings and received exposure through your performances.

It's not like today. Back then you would go hear a band from your school or neighborhood, or hear some band from another part of town that you heard about. Two hundred or 500 people would be a huge crowd. That was entertainment; it was much more localized.

It was the heyday of Motown. Black music was being produced right here, and all the kids into rock 'n' roll were all Motown and Beatles freaks. On Detroit Top 40 radio you would hear the Beatles and then the Supremes or Junior Walker and the All-Stars.

Ron Asheton: The Grande was our favorite place to play. It was where you could feel free to talk about drugs and counterculture. We wanted to be musicians and get our ideas across in order to express ourselves. I'd like to do what we called "let one go" — putting on a show and doing whatever came into your mind. With our limited musical capacity, we had to get it out theatrically.

Our stage act was a natural process. We'd build to this climax and then we would leave the stage. Maybe one guy would stay longer or we would put our guitars down and they would be feeding back in harmony. Iggy might stay on and recite some poetry off the top of his head.

Our lives were pandemonium every day, a brush with death, either getting kicked out of restaurants for our long hair, being searched by dope agents or even almost getting hit by jocks when trying to cross the street in Ann Arbor.

We played our first gig on Halloween 1967. It was our manager's house, and of course the people invited were the MC5, John Sinclair, and local friends. We just played in the living room and people laid on the floor in front of us, getting high in various ways. We played until we blew all the fuses in the house; it was kind of a shack house and the fuses couldn't take all the power. So when the guy ran out of fuses, the show was over. It only lasted a half hour.

We were playing the Silver Bell in Oakland County. The MC5 was the headlining act, the UP opened up and we were the middle act. Iggy swore on stage and when we got off there was a bunch of county sheriffs there and they are going to arrest him. So John Sinclair said, "If you arrest him, our band is out of here." And the club owner is in sheer panic because there is a place full of kids out there that want this music. Because of this, the cops didn't bust him. Ah, the power of the people, the power of the music had this straight-laced club owner worried about his club being torn apart or [us] never coming back and [him] getting a bad reputation. *(Gil Margulis; Dec. 4, 1987.)*

Dennis Thompson: I listened to Chuck Berry, Ricky Nelson, Elvis Presley, all the early Motown, the vocal groups, the Ventures, and all the instrumental groups of the time, California surf music, right up into the Beatles and Stones.

Nobody was popular in Detroit then. Mitch Ryder was doing something around Detroit then; Seger was starting out.

We played all sorts of creepy places. We met Sinclair in '66. I was in college, so it was the winter of '66 or the following spring in '67; I remember because it was my first year at Wayne State University. Sinclair was in charge of the beatnik community then; he was the head man. Basically Tyner, Kramer and Smith realized it would be a good thing to get a line with John, because John was a powerful figure in the beatnik community. This was the same time as things were happening in Frisco, we were getting vibrations from Big Brother, the Grateful Dead, bands that were forming out there. It was like, "Hey, let's get something happening back here."

We moved to Ann Arbor early in 1968. The first band house was right above the *Fifth Estate* [an underground newspaper in Detroit]. We got involved with Sinclair. Everybody by that point realized we were working together as a unit, and it was not a radical situation at that point in time. The credo was exactly as it was on the first album, and that was: rock 'n' roll, making love in the streets, etc. We were just moving with the mood of the times. Vietnam was going on, civil-rights movements, and all that.

Our first album was recorded in 1968, under the influence of every conceivable drug that was available at the time! I'll tell you — there were so many great bands then, when we first started playing the Grande Ballroom. Russ Gibb wanted to open the Grande Ballroom, and it might have been Sinclair who connected up with him, or Kramer or Tyner, I'm not sure. We got Russ to come down one night to a party that was being held at the Fifth Estate and we wanted to convince Russ Gibb that we should play at the Grande. At the time, the Fillmore was starting to become known out here; there were writeups in *LIFE* magazine and such about the Fillmore in

San Francisco, and we figured that Russ Gibb could do the same thing for us out here. He came to the party, we played for him, he liked it, and he said, "Yeah, I want you guys to be the house band." He didn't have much money then at all; many weekends we played for free.

We were broke. We washed Russ' hands and he washed ours. First time we played the Grande Ballroom there were 20 people out there, bowl haircuts, frats, greaseballs, you know. But week by week, it steadily built and built, using all local acts, until Gibb had enough money to bring in national acts, knowing it would bring in a crowd. We had built up a reputation as a great band to go see. You know, "If you like to get high, party down, go see the MC5 'cause they'd definitely blow your mind!" The loudest, hardest, fastest and the craziest. The other bands all started picking up on the same thing, too. The SRC, the Frost, started jumping on the bandwagon ... the Stooges, etc. They all realized this was a goldmine. Everybody loved it; there were no restrictions. As long as people got off on it, that was all that mattered.

The band was sort of hesitant about putting "motherfucker" out on our first album, because we figured it would alienate a whole lot of people. Jack Holtzman says, "No, no, the time is right, the climate is perfect for that sort of thing. He's that kind of guy, he thought it would be pretty cool. Hell, he had Jim Morrison and the Doors. He made the final decision; he said, "Let's do it."

He wanted to do it, and the band was holding back, because we figured it would be a Lenny Bruce kind of situation — harassment, etc. We knew we could say "motherfucker," but wanted to dub something in to avoid maybe not selling a hundred thousand records. As it turned out, when we finally did it and Holtzman went ahead with it he found out how much flak he got back from releasing it. Rack-jobbers were getting busted, distributors were getting busted, store owners were getting busted, parents were getting irate and calling up radio stations. All of a sudden this was happening, and Holtzman realized he had his neck stuck out; then he had it chopped off. The thing built and built, there was all this tension. The album was selling well. We were getting all sorts of national press, I got a drum endorsement with Ludwig, things were going crazy. We were on the cover of *Jazz and Pop*, got write-ups in *Time, Newsweek, Playboy, Cosmopolitan, National Enquirer*, etc., all down the line. While this was happening, Holtzman started to get cold feet. We played the Fillmore East in New York City. The first-ever free concert at that Fillmore and there was a total melee that ensued and developed, people went crazy and started to destroy the place, Bill Graham got punched, and forever hated the MC5 from that point on. It was Holtzman's idea once again to have the free concert. It turned into an absolute catastrophe. Hudson's [a large Detroit department store] wouldn't stock the album, so Sinclair took out an ad in the paper saying "Fuck Hudson's." That was the final straw for Holtzman; that's what he needed for an excuse to drop the band. He dropped us. Danny Fields, who got us signed to Elektra, said, "Don't worry, Atlantic Records is interested and we'll get a good deal." We went straight from Elektra immediately to Atlantic. No problem.

While we're crossing over to Atlantic, Sinclair has got his jail thing, his two-joint trial. The 10-year trial, at the same time as all this is going on. So we're getting signed up to Atlantic, Sinclair is going to jail, Jon Landau is being appointed by Jerry Wexler, Ahmet Ertegun and John Sinclair to be our guru, our producer, and take care of the band while we're in this transition period. Danny Fields has got us connected with Frank Barcelone and things began to happen quickly. We worked on *Back In The USA* for six to eight months, way too long. We waited a whole year before we released our second album, which is the dumbest mistake you can make in the whole world. You got a hot album, you gotta follow it up six months later! We had so many problems, Sinclair in jail, etc., just an avalanche of problems. So as a result we ended up signing with Dee Anthony before the release of *Back In The USA*. They were going to set up the tour, etc. We finally got the album finished. Sinclair was in jail writing bad things about us, calling us a sellout. Dave Marsh was in the middle and all confused, didn't know where to stand on the whole thing 'cause we bought Corvettes and everything was in a total state of chaos and confusion, obviously because the heavy hand of the law was breaking it all up.

We just symbolized the total rebellious underside of the youth revolution and the civil-rights movement. We sort of embodied all of it. Just before Sinclair went to jail, he had begun to super-radicalize because, I think, he knew he was going to lose his trial. So what did he have to lose? He was going to go down as a flaming martyr for the cause. In the process, he took along the MC5's name and made it as radical as he was. That's when he was interviewed on Channel 7 on the TV and called the Establishment "pigs," said he was going to beat these pigs, etc., and people out in TV-land are going "poor boy"; John knew he was going to be sent up. So the MC5 as a group had been affected by all this, and it caused a lot of dissension amongst the band. I think all this was the beginnings of the downfall of the band. When Sinclair went to jail and all this began to happen, we lost our focal point. The focal point wasn't Sinclair; it was just that so much confusion and chaos ensued as a result of the law coming down on us. They busted us in many cities; they were out to get us. So everything came down on us, 'cause we were supposedly Sinclair's band and carrying on the traditions while he was in jail. So *Back In The USA* turned out to be the antithesis of *Kick Out The Jams*.

The first time, yeah, we had a great time. Every place we played was sold out, people were nuts. We headlined every show except Wembley, which was a rock 'n' roll revival. It was a tactical error on our behalf; people were throwing bottles and stuff at us. We saw the show, saw 65,000 people out there and said, "Hey, look at this, look who's playing. All they got is Jerry Lee Lewis, Little Richard, Chuck Berry, Bill Haley, and they got all these people who are really into the Fifties and the only contemporary bands playing were the Move, Screaming Lord Sutch and us." So the guys got together and decided to pull a rock 'n' roll revival trip, but we probably went too far and came out really looking nuts. That got us the bad reviews. The Teddy Boys saw us and they expected us to come out in Levis and tee-shirts and our leather jackets. Sometimes we dressed up and sometimes we didn't. We always played with the image, 'cause we knew the whole idea of an image was a joke. So we came out and flaunted it, a real tactical mistake. There were ninety or a hundred of these fanatics dancing around with their suede jackets and velvet collars tearing up the dust, the hard-cores. Basically our show at that time went over fair, but had we gone on in a greaser image, we probably would have destroyed the place, 'cause it's the same music. But it was a mistake in image.

We had signed a two-album contract, and they dropped the option after *High Time*. We had no machine together. The energy was totally scattered and fragmented, so as a result, we got dropped. *High Time* got good reviews and no sales; we were disorganized with no manager in the United States. We were managed by Ronan in Europe. We would go back and play in Europe for a while, then come back to the States with no management and no one to head up the enterprise. We just lost our whole head of steam.

I quit the group first. We had some dates to do back in Europe still, but I figured if I went over there again, I'd never get out, so Tyner and I had a big argument and he quit too, for no real reason. So Wayne and Fred went back with Derek, a German bass player we had picked up, and Puerto Rican guy on drums and finished that tour. That was the effective demise of the MC5. This was in 1971 or '72. A matter of months later, I wanted to put the band together again, but couldn't get these guys together. *(John Koenig; May 1979.)*

17. San Francisco Nights

By 1967 some of the rock 'n' roll music that was being made was scarcely recognizable as such. In England the Beatles were experimenting with tape loops and backwards guitars; the Rolling Stones were expanding their blues-based vocabulary into sitars and drug hymns; the Kinks were becoming more theatrical and ever more satirical; and the second generation of the British Invasion, groups like Procul Harum and the Small Faces, were beginning to come over and hit the charts with frequency.

In England in 1967, Eric Burdon, still riding high on the charts with his group, the Animals, released an unusual song where he chanted like an airport P.A. announcer, "Save up all your bread and fly Trans World Airways to San Francisco, U.S.A." The song, "San Franciscan Nights," was a hit.

In the United States in 1967, Jim Morrison was setting his deathless poetry to the bluesy rambling and riffing of the Doors and scoring their first #1 hit with "Light My Fire"; an ever-changing, motley assemblage that called itself, among other things, the Jefferson Airplane was in the top 10 for the first and only time with "Somebody To Love" and "White Rabbit"; guitarists John Cipollina of Quicksilver Messenger Service and Carlos Santana were stretching out further and further on improvisational jams that owed more to John Coltrane than to Chuck Berry; the poet and essayist Richard Brautigan was recording narratives with a folk-rock group called Mad River; Moby Grape was about to record the flurry of albums that would ultimately ruin their career; folksinger Scott McKenzie was climbing the charts by informing people that if they were going to San Francisco, "Summertime will be a love-in there"; and a former paratrooper from Seattle was redefining the art and the experience of the electric guitar as a studio rat from Cucamonga was redefining music itself.

Most of what was going on was going on in San Francisco.

If the whole world went completely mad in 1967, the center of the madness was San Francisco. It was close to Berkeley and the University of California; the university was a magnet for artists and free thinkers of all stripes, and many of them naturally migrated to San Francisco, before or after graduation. Drugs were easy to get in San Francisco. For a time LSD was legal. It was in many places until local officials realized what it could do, but in San Francisco it was available. Marijuana was as common as tobacco. Whether or not it was ultimately good for them, musicians got stoned and made music; some of it was amazing. Some of it even wound up on record, and by that time the record companies were willing to put out the experiments, because many of the experiments sold.

Not as singles but as albums. The top songs of 1967, the year of the Summer of Love, were the Doors' "Light My Fire," Lulu's "To Sir With Love," the Association's "Windy," Bobbie Gentry's "Ode To Billie Joe," and Frank and Nancy Sinatra's "Somethin' Stupid." Scott McKenzie's "San Francisco" made it to #4. The Jefferson Airplane had a #5 hit with "Somebody To Love" and a #8 with "White Rabbit." The Electric Prunes were at #11 with "I Had Too Much To Dream Last Night" and at #27 with "Get Me To The World On Time." No other San Francisco band or psychedelic song cracked the top 50. It was the best commercial year San Francisco would have. In 1968, Jimi Hendrix's "Purple Haze" would make it to #65 on the charts. Dion's cover of the song would make it two notches higher. In 1970, Quicksilver's "Fresh Air" would struggle to #49 on the charts, and then the group would vanish from the lists forever. The Grateful Dead, the most enduring and consistently popular of the San Francisco bands, did not have a top 10 single or album until 1989.

The first band to come out of San Francisco and make it big was a pop band. The Beau Brummels sounded like the Lovin' Spoonful or the Turtles or any of a score of feel-good bands with a vaguely Californian sounds. They had two sprightly hits in 1965, "Laugh, Laugh" and "Just A Little"; Sly Stone produced their first album, and their manager, Tom Donohue, introduced FM rock radio to the world. But by 1968, after a disastrous all-cover album for Warner Brothers, the group was reduced to a studio duo.

Dec Mulligan and Tom Valentino were founding members of the Beau Brummels.

Sal Valentino: I was playing in a band with Ron Elliott and John Petersen.

Dec Mulligan: I was playing in an Irish hall and they were playing in another. I happened to go to an Irish dance one night and saw Sal, Ron Elliott and John Petersen playing. I thought I should pursue the group thing because the Beatles were just getting big around that time, so I approached the guys about playing and we got together, just like that. Sal had been singing solo and he knew a lot of people around the North Beach section of San Francisco. We played there and then moved down the peninsula. There were clubs on every block around that time.

There were hundreds of clubs. That was originally called DJ's, and it was the last club the Beau Brummels ever played in, before they embarked on the recording. Tom Donahue was also our manager. After us, the Lovin' Spoonful came in and played there.

Sal Valentino: We were playing down on the peninsula, in San Mateo, four nights a week for the summer. They guy who owned the club, the Morocco Room, took us to L.A. to do some demos. We did "Stick Like Glue" and "Still In Love With You Baby." Anyway, while we were playing the Morocco Room, someone told Tom about us. And also, I think the guy who owned the club had taken the demos to Tom. He was interested and came to see us, and he liked us. His record company had released Bobby Freeman's "C'mon And Swim," which Sly Stone had produced. When Tom came to see us we were doing "Laugh Laugh," so he made plans to record it. We were on the second album.

The Beatles were the biggest influence at the time, along with the rest of the English bands. We liked what they did, and it's difficult not to be influenced by something that you like. We didn't think we were comparable or anything; we didn't think we were stars. We were still in the stage of listening to music and liking it, although we were also playing it. It's hard to imagine how big an influence they in particular were. Maybe they were the biggest and maybe not much at all. Elliott had been writing since he was 13 or so, so it didn't inspire him to write or anything like that.

Dec Mulligan: Ron had written "Laugh Laugh" before the group was formed. I was there the night that he wrote "Just A Little." In fact, I had suggested some of the chord patterns. I still have the original copy of the typed lyrics for "Just A Little." There really isn't much to say about them. Ron said he had some original songs and these came up.

Tom Donahue really liked Sal singing "Laugh Laugh" in A-flat minor, as opposed to A minor, which is how we do it now. A-flat minor is kind of a crazy key to be playing a harmonica in. At the time, I wasn't very proficient on harmonica, and I remember Bobby Mitchell, who was Tom Donahue's partner at the time, came to me when we were recording the song and said, "C'mon, you can play the thing." I asked him, "Did you ever try playing a C harmonica in A-flat minor?" That's why all those wrong notes came out.

Sal Valentino: Sly was great. He was only about 19 at the time, and he made the six of us — including Tom and Bob — a great team. Sly had a lot of energy and was real enthusiastic and made us feel like we were doing something. He was appreciated as a producer. We were pretty well set with what we were doing when we went into the studio, but he suggested things, minor changes.

Dec Mulligan: One thing about Sly was that the British music influx wasn't injurious to him, like it was to a lot of black musicians. He was always very into that British sound, very excited by it. In fact, he was the one who tried to make us sound more British.

Sal Valentino: Yeah, that was Sly and Bob and Tom's doing. The thing about Sly's producing was that we were basically a country and folk-influenced act, and our drummer was a jazz drummer. Sly probably kept us a little more conscious of the bottom, the rhythm end of it. I'd been playing with Elliott since he was 13 — he was 19 or 20 when he recorded — and he's never really played any rock 'n' roll before. Sly was subtle in his suggestions, although there were some things that went down between him and Elliott that I wasn't aware of, because Ron was pretty much the arranger.

Dec Mulligan: He was a forceful personality, Sly, but somehow he didn't ram it down your throat. You couldn't say no to him; he'd talk you into it. I remember I was singing a song on the first album and I wanted to sing it alone, and he said, "No, Dec, you've got to double-track it. Everyone's doing it, even the Beatles." So I said, "Okay, Sly, sure," but he was right.

Sal Valentino: Tom and Bob were the ears. At the time we worked with them, Bob Mitchell was rated No. 3 in AM radio and Tom Donahue was No. 6, so that was directed by them.

We played in Mother's for about three months, and once the record was up there we started to go out and do concerts, and we hardly ever came back.

Everything happened while we were away. It was going on in a small way while "Laugh Laugh" was becoming a hit, and by "Just A Little" it was in full swing.

They never seemed to include the Beau Brummels because we were pre all of that. I remember Tom taking me and Sly out one night to see a band play, the Great Society, with Grace Slick and her husband. Those bands, like the Airplane, played around town all the time.

Dec Mulligan: I had left the group after the first album and went back to England. Then I came back to San Francisco and went to the Avalon and saw bands like Creedence Clearwater Revival and the Youngbloods. They hadn't made it yet; this was 1967.

It's nice to be remembered, but like a lot of "elderly" musicians, we'd like to get something new going too. It'd be easier to live with. I don't want to play the old songs too much longer. Twenty years is long enough. *(Jeff Tamarkin; March 14, 1986.)*

The band scene in San Francisco in the mid-'60s was the closest thing to perfect anarchy ever achieved. Band members would leave overnight, form new bands, go back to their old bands, go solo, form another new band, and then finally go back to their old band. Marty Balin pulled the Jefferson Airplane together out of thin air, and then watched it go through more changes than a kaleidoscope. Skip Spence, the Airplane's original drummer, had never played drums in a band when Balin approached him. He left to play guitar with Moby Grape. Jorma Kaukonen and Jack Casady were in and out of the Airplane, in and out of Hot Tuna, and solo. Grace Slick was a model at I. Magnin's who had a band called the the Great Society with three other Slicks. She joined the Jefferson Airplane and gave it what it lacked: balls. No other female rock 'n' roll singer could match her for sneering angry power.

The Jefferson Airplane were the standard-bearers for a new and unclassifiable kind of music: acid-rock. Everyone in the band was using drugs in huge quantities and drinking to excess; Slick and Kantner led the way. The Jefferson Airplane was always one step away from breaking up, and they made some mediocre records. At one point, they even made commercials for Levi's jeans. But at their best — "The Ballad Of You And Me And Pooneil," "Volunteers," Balin's "It's No Secret," "Wooden Ships," the *Surrealistic Pillow* album — they were brilliant.

They were also surprisingly flexible. Slick, Kantner and Balin worked on outside projects but kept the core of the their group intact. The Airplane was able to evolve into the Jefferson Starship, and enjoy something the Jefferson Airplane had never really enjoyed: commercial success. "Mircales" was a huge hit; their *Red Octopus* album was the best update of the San Francisco sound ever put on record. But by 1978 Grace Slick was out of the Starship: Marty Balin left a year later. Paul Kantner's role in the band diminished as the band became more and more commercial. Even Grace Slick's return to the band in 1981 couldn't stop the slide. When the word "Jefferson" was dropped from the band's name in the mid-'80s the transition was complete, and the last evolutionary trail of the band that created acid-rock had vanished.

Grace Slick and Marty Balin were members of the Jefferson Airplane.

Marty Balin: I did folk, and before that I did rock and roll. Before that I did street-corner harmony singing. Before that I sang in church, and before that I'm told I could whistle before I talked. I was born in Ohio and went to Frisco when I was about four.

I wanted to get some money together to go to Europe. I thought the quickest way to do that would be to get together a band, because people always used to hire me to sing. I was studying to be a sculpture designer, and I wanted to go to Venice and study glass. I was playing a gig in this club and some people came in who were fans, and they had $3,000 each. They were looking for an investment, so I said, "Give it to me and I'll start a club and a band. You can have the club and I'll take the band." So they did, and I went out and found a place and built the band.

I went out looking for people. I went to this hootenanny and saw Paul come in with a 12-string guitar in one hand and a six-string in the other. I'll never forget that: he came to the door and the guy there said, "Sorry, we're full tonight." So I ran over there and told the guy to give Paul my spot because I wanted to see what he did. He didn't know this was happening. So he went up to the microphone and started to play, and then he said, "Ah, I can't do this," and started packing up his stuff. I thought, "That's the guy I'm looking for, right there." I go by vibrations, intuition. I went backstage afterwards and asked him if he wanted to get something together, and he was hesitant at first because I came on pretty strong. We went to his house and went through some ideas, and it worked. Then about the second or third time, Jorma and his wife were there and I asked Paul who he was, and when he told me Jorma played guitar, I said, "Man, that's our lead guitarist." Paul said, "Jorma's really good; he wouldn't play for us." I said, "That's what we want, someone who's really good." We asked Jorma to come by and he was super-cool, as always. And we played. Then he didn't come back for a couple of weeks, so we called him and asked, "Why didn't you come back? Didn't you like it?" And he said, "Oh, I didn't know you wanted me to."

We tried a bassist and a drummer and they were nowhere. So Jorma said, "We have to have a good bass player. I used to play second guitar to a lead guitarist back in Washington. His name was Jack Casady and I heard he switched to bass. He was a great guitar player so he must be good on bass." Jack was in college and we didn't know if he'd come, so we began calling him at three or four in the morning — we'd make sure to wake him up because we wanted to make an impression — and he'd go in and wash his face and hands. Then I'd tell him, "Hey, man, we're making all this money and you gotta come out." We jived and jived and he finally did come out, and he was great. He looked a little strange, but he was a perfect bass player. He had a handlebar mustache and I told him he had to take it off. It was his pride and joy. He kept it until the first week we played and then, when we were in L.A. for all these meetings with the record companies, Casady came in with half his handlebar cut off. None of the record-company guys ever said anything about it.

I saw Skip Spence at the Matrix. He was a guitar player, and I walked over to him and said, "How'd you like to be my drummer?" He said, "Well, I'm a guitar player." And I said, "Well, that doesn't matter." He looked like the drummer we needed. I told him to get two sticks and

I'd call him in a week. He thought I was crazy, but a week later I called him up and asked him if he was ready, and he said he'd give it a try. He joined in and he was perfect. That was the band.

No one was doing what we were; I was counting on it taking off. It mushroomed, so after a while there were a lot of other bands and a whole scene developed. Plus, traveling musicians would all come to San Francisco to play. It wasn't just us.

It was certainly a wonderful period in my life. There are stories galore, but it would take hours to tell. It was like Paris in the '20s, with the writers all in one place. I'd always studied scenes like that, and then I found myself in one. I think it'll happen again. Just take the right music, the right chemists, the right people.

They developed drugs that there were no laws against at the time. That brought visual artists into it, and other people. We'd go out and play free in the parks and they had no laws against that then. We'd be throwing these drugs out to everyone, and there were no laws against the drugs. They had to quickly pass laws against LSD. It was pretty interesting for a while.

I've never believed in Timothy Leary and that you should go around giving acid to the world. I thought everyone had an individual right to decide things like that. I didn't want to get labeled the "kings of acid," or whatever they kept calling us at the time. I refrained from taking part in speaking out on that. I personally was exploring like everyone else was, but I didn't feel that just because I was doing it that it was right for everyone else to.

Do you remember the Monterey Pop Festival in '67?

Are you kidding? That was a thrilling show.

The film had the classic version of your song "Today."

Yeah, except they kept showing Grace while I was singing it. I was like a dummy act. After that show, it all exploded. It lasted all the way 'til Woodstock. It all happened for us, the Who, Otis, Jimi, Janis, Ravi Shankar.

It was like a balloon, and like a balloon, it had to burst. Altamont was a sign of it bursting. It was a big rumble; yeah, that was scary.

People were dying and times were getting dark. The night Janis died, we were playing at Winterland. The next morning someone told me she was dead. That stopped me right there; I wouldn't go on anymore. I wanted to get back to ground level zero for a while.

It was kind of a high cocaine, methedrine, crazy drug playing; loud, raunchy, crappy music as far as I was concerned. I didn't like the sound of the music and I didn't want to go on. One thing I liked about the Airplane was that we always improvised; there was always one good number that was total exploration. That developed into such a good high for us that we ended up putting each song into that improvisational state. But it did get out of hand by the end.

In the '60s, we tried to get out of our contract. There was something in it that said if we did anything crazy they could let us go. Well, we did everything we could, and they wouldn't let us off. We were doing all the protest and jive. Finally, we met the big boys in the company, and they showed us this pie, and the record company was less than one percent. The rest was like napalm bombs, guidance missile systems. And these were the people that owned us; it was embarrassing.

We'd say obvious things like "shit" and "fuck," and it wouldn't bother them. But then they'd find meanings in things that didn't have meanings. They used to watch us and police us; it was very funny. *(Jeff Tamarkin; April 1982.)*

🐛

Grace Slick: There was a chunk of time there — about a year — where I was going to be a spiritual housewife. I tried and I thought, "God, this is boring!" I quit Starship and thought, "Oh, screw the music business. I'm gonna be quiet here and take care of the house," but I just hate it. I kept trying to act like I wasn't hating it, then I thought, "This is ridiculous, I have to go back to the recording studio and do what I like to do."

The first music I ever heard as a kid over and over was "Peer Gynt Suite" by Grieg, which is semi-classical. And that stuck in my mind. And when I was about 16 or 17, no, later than that, I took about eight million mics of acid and listened to Miles Davis' and Gil Evans' record of "Sketches Of Spain."

Playing in a band was a lot more fun than standing up for eight hours a day modeling at I. Magnins, which is what I was doing. It was the third floor, which is the couterie department, and there were a lot of 40-year-old women who weighed 200 pounds and who would come up there and try to buy Dior suits that were a size four. And we'd squeeze 'em in there. It had its comedy level, but only to a point.

And then I went to see Jefferson Airplane, and they worked for maybe three hours a night, one or two sets a night, got paid for it, it was in a bar, had a great party, everybody's fooling around and I'm going, "*That* looks like the kind of job to have."

My mother was a singer, so she sang around the house. And my father sang around the house, but it was no big deal. I didn't start off thinking that I was gonna be a singer when I grow up. I didn't have any particular channel until I saw them do that. Then I started a group called the Great Society, and it was breaking up around the same time that Jefferson Airplane's girl singer [Signe Anderson] was having a baby. I had opened for them several times and more or less knew their songs, so the switch was sort of natural.

I was aware of the band's finances. A lot of them went up my nose. I just didn't care. And I'm still really not concerned with finding out. I mean, if I wanted to spend my time ... Let's put it this way: The more money you invest the more you gotta look out for it, so the more time you have to spend looking out for the guy who's looking out for your money. I don't have any money, meaning that I don't have any savings and bonds or property or anything. I've got a house, I've got an Aston Martin which I bought in 1969 — I still have the same car, which is on about its third or fourth engine — and I own part of the Starship corporation. I have this feeling that I'll always be able to weasel enough money to live out of somebody or something.

There are more musicians going into rock because it *looks* like it could be big bucks. Unfortunately, there's probably *less* bucks simply because if you get 800,000 people wanting to be a guitar player, there's only going to be one or two of those who are going to come out on top. If you only have a hundred guitar players, then there's going to be more than that who make it because they're scarcer. In other words, Airplane, Grateful Dead, Rolling Stones, Eagles, and the people that were around at that time, we made a lot of money because there weren't that many of us. There was no competition.

We didn't have the vaguest idea that we were gonna make any money. We thought it was gonna just be a party — playing the Matrix and other clubs in San Francisco. It got blown *way* out of proportion, and we just thought it was funny. We didn't believe people were saying and writing all the stuff they did, and that they were paying money for this kind of weird music. *(Jeff Tamarkin; April 1982.)*

The crowning event of San Francisco's Summer of Love never took place in San Francisco. From June 16-18, 1967, 30 groups took the stage at the Monterey County Fairgrounds for the first Monterey Pop Festival. Every major San Francisco group was there, along with many national groups. The Association, the Paupers and Johnny Rivers opened the show; the Byrds, Booker T. and the MGs and Ravi Shankar closed it. In-between may have been the greatest uninterrupted rock concert ever.

Eric Burdon and the New Animals, of "San Franciscan Nights" fame, were on fourth. Simon and Garfunkel, whose biggest hits lay ahead, were on next. After that, the bands never quit coming. Big Brother and the Holding Company, the Electric Flag, the Paul Butterfield Blues Band, and Canned Heat appeared in a row; after an intermission with Hugh Masakela and Country Joe and the Fish, the Steve Miller Band and Al Kooper's Band followed. Rings jammed on her fingers, bracelets tumbling down her arms, Janis Joplin, the lead singer for Big Brother and the Holding Company, single-handedly blew away the rest of the blues-rock bands.

Jimi Hendrix was a virtual unknown when he was introduced to the Monterey crowd. By the time the set was finished, everyone knew about him, and he was a guitar star of the highest magnitude. The Who, over from England for the first time, were stunning. Otis Redding brought down the house. The Grateful Dead, caught between Hendrix, the Who and Redding, were miffed.

Monterey was the first rock festival. It was the only big rock festival that really worked. It was meant to be a charity event, and it largely was. Most of the groups that appeared were not paid. People who attended the festival said later they had never experienced anything like it.

Lou Adler was the promoter of the Monterey Pop Festival.

Lou Adler: The original idea came from some promoters that wanted to do it as a commercial venture. Benny Shapiro, Alan Pariser and Derek Taylor were involved in it originally. I'm not sure where they got the idea from, but John Phillips and myself got involved about two months later. When they started to go after talent for the show, they came to me. At the time, I was managing and producing the Mamas and the Papas. They wanted the group to play the festival.

It was the first festival, and it opened the way to outdoor shows with more than one or two groups. It was the purest of all rock festivals. It showed that you could organize an event with considerable talent and actually make it work.

In booking the Who, it was either Paul McCartney or Andrew Oldham, the manager of the Stones, who had told us about the Who. The reports about the band that we had heard prior to the festival were something like the drummer had put his drums over the head of the guitar player, that sort of thing. Speaking to McCartney or Oldham, I can't remember which, one of them told us about the onstage act. There wasn't surprise on my face when they did it, but excitement. You can see it in the film, *Monterey Pop.* The camera also shows the audience. It's amazing.

There was a general philosophical difference between the San Francisco groups and all the other groups as well as the festival management right from the beginning of negotiations to do the festival. They [the Dead] threatened to put on their own festival across the street on flat-bed trucks.

I think some bands went down the football field where a lot of people were camping and performed there. They were into causing whatever commotion they possibly could.

Especially the Grateful Dead. We had a back fence where a lot of people were sitting. The fence was real wobbly and looked as if it might go at any time. The Dead, as a group, they were doing their best to provoke the emotion that they were interested in provoking.

The deals for albums were made wherever they were possible. Ravi Shankar had one of his performances at Monterey come out on Liberty Records. Hendrix was offered to Warner Brothers. They worked it out to have the Otis Redding side because, I believe, Otis' manager had something to do with Warners, though, I'm not sure.

The point that I was making is that artists were given the opportunity to use these things. The Byrds' performance was offered to whatever label they were on. Johnny Rivers was offered. All the tapes were offered to all the companies that the Monterey artists were signed to.

There were two or three acts that stole the show, and Otis was one of them. Janis Joplin, the Who, and Hendrix. Those four artists made the greatest impact. The Who and Hendrix were new from England. Otis hadn't ever played before in front of a white audience that size. Janis Joplin hadn't played much outside of San Francisco.

The police reacted differently in different stages. The first reaction was nothing because they didn't know what was happening, nor did they know how many people would be coming through. They didn't know a hippie from a Hell's Angel. The captain of the police department was retiring in two years and didn't want any problems. There was another officer, a lieutenant, who was very pro-festival, though. That's the way it was; the pros and cons of the Monterey townspeople were just split. For the first festival, we were almost able to sneak it through. We had all the contracts signed. We had negotiated the police costs, etc. When we went back to investigate the prospects of doing it again the following year, then they knew what had happened. The charge for the police quadrupled, that kind of thing.

What Monterey was, was a culmination of four or five years of music which was one of the most creative periods from the standpoint of the introduction of new groups and songwriters and the freedom of artists, similar to the turn of the century and the art nouveau when art went back to the artists. That was the point of Monterey. Although the festival was being promoted, it was promoted, in a sense, for the artists. The exchange between the audience and the artist was just real pure. These were artists who were at the top or would get to the top shortly. They had come together to exchange music with the audience and with other artists for nothing but the idea behind it. *(Robert Santelli; July 17, 1987.)*

When Janis Joplin electrified the Monterey crowd, her band, Big Brother and the Holding Company, did not even have a recording contract. They were just one of many San Francisco bands that played, hung out and played, in the San Francisco area. They were an intense group fronted by a transplanted Texas powerhouse named Janis Joplin. Joplin guzzled Jack Daniels from the bottle and sang like her lungs were on fire. She stayed with Big Brother for three years and two albums, one arguably the best thing she ever put on record (*Cheap Thrills*), the other a throwaway. When she left she was a star. In another year she was dead of a heroin overdose. Big Brother kept on for several more years before breaking up. They outlived Janis Joplin.

David Getz was the drummer for Big Brother and the Holding Company.

David Getz: It started out at a place in the Haight-Ashbury in 1965, called 1090 Page St. It was kind of a notorious crash pad. One of the guys who later became the bass player in Big Brother, Peter Albin, his brother Rodney Albin, who was also a musician, started a series of jam sessions there.

Peter and James [Gurley, Big Brother's lead guitarist] had played in clubs in North Beach in the early '60s, and they knew about [Janis Joplin] then. She had come to San Francisco and played in clubs, and then she went back to Texas. The suggestion that we get her back from Texas to join the band came from Chet Helms.

We were specifically looking for somebody that could carry their weight with the kind of band that we were. We couldn't have somebody like Grace Slick and Signe Anderson. They had pretty voices, they had most crystalline, folky, kind of clean voices. We needed somebody with more intense energy, because that was the kind of band we were.

We were completely naive. The first album, we didn't have a producer or anybody to teach us. That first record wasn't really intended to be a record. We went in to record, live in the studio, our songs, and hopefully come up with some singles.

There were two sessions; more specifically, maybe a total of eight hours in the studio for that whole album, and it was just recorded live in the studio. It was mostly stuff that was not released; it was not released until almost a year after it was made. It wasn't meant to be an album, but after we played at the Monterey Pop Festival in 1967, and became well-known, Mainstream decided to put it together as an album and get it out real fast.

Cheap Thrills was a good one ... that was done live; that was real live. But some of the stuff that is supposed to be live on *Cheap Thrills* obviously isn't live. It was recorded in the studio and room noise from live performances is mixed in, but "Ball And Chain" is live. "Combination Of The Two" is one I know we tried to do live, and we never could get a good version of it live.

Jack Casady, the bass player for the Jefferson Airplane, he was at a rehearsal of ours one day and just said, "Hey, there's this song you guys should do this." It was "Piece Of My Heart."

Janis was strictly blues and country-folk, and she had some great stuff; she was a great folk-singer. It's really a shame, just to put this in, that there are no really great recordings of Janis singing really what she ... a lot of people know that she sang like Bessie Smith, and there's stuff like that. There's some stuff that she did with a trad jazz band in San Francisco, and there's some stuff she did with guitar that's kind of Bessie Smith, but she also did stuff that was very much [like Joan Baez], kind of very lyrical, folky kind of thing. She wrote some songs that she would play once in a while, that never got recorded, that were beautiful and very lyrical, and mystical.

I remember this one song Janis wrote called "Pathways." I guess you could say it would be like modern folk music, rather than Bessie Smith or country-type folk music ... more like modern folk style, Peter, Paul and Mary, Ian and Sylvia, Richard and Mimi Farina, that kind of folk music, particularly Richard and Mimi Farina; she had a style that was something like that. I remember one of the first songs Big Brother used to do back then was a Richard Farina song called 'Ticket To Ride.'"

We kind of like were a group in the beginning, and Janis herself, if you listen to the *Cheaper Thrills* album, she's kind of phenomenal but she's awful too, in the sense that she sings and she screams out of tune, and sometimes she's in the wrong place, and stuff like that. We were all subject to that because we were all primitive in the beginning.

JANIS JOPLIN AT MONTEREY: 'It was the purest of all rock festivals. It showed that you could organize an event with considerable talent and actually make it work.'

What happened was that she got better real fast, and she had a certain kind of sensibility and ambition to really clean it up. Within about a year after she joined the band she kind of became much more tasteful, and learned when to sing and when not to sing, and how not to scream out of tune, but how to scream in tune, and how to hit the notes. She was listening to a lot of black music, soul music, Otis Redding, Aretha Franklin, and she was able to get her act together. With the rest of the people in Big Brother it took longer. Eventually it did happen. Eventually, by the time we were doing the later albums without Janis, the critics were saying how wonderful we had all become as musicians. There was an odd irony to it. We all kind of became good musicians eventually, but by that time it was too late.

After doing *Cheap Thrills*, there are a lot of tapes recorded after *Cheap Thrills* was made, from our last road tour in about September, October 1968, where we sound great. Making *Cheap*

Thrills, actually learning how to record and to listen to what we were playing...made everybody play much better. Some of the tapes I have of late performances, right before Janis left the band, are great, just great. The musicianship is excellent, everybody's in tune, and in time, and playing great, and it's wonderful.

The early days, the changes are absolutely true. In 1967 we played Monterey Pop and during that time, when we were first making it, the musicianship was awful, just awful. It was very inconsistent. It would be good; we would play great like one out of five times, and we were great, we were fantastic, the energy was unbelievable, because that's the kind of band we were. It was just an energy band. There was some kind of magic that would sometimes happen where the whole stage would just lift off. But if you listen to Monterey Pop, if you listen to it now, you'll see that even Janis is not that good in it. Everybody at that time was saying, "Oh, she's wonderful, she's fantastic, but the band sucks." If you listen to it now, or go see the movie, you see she sucks, too. She's terrible. She's out of tune, and she's just singing in the wrong places, and she's too frantic, and just all too hyper. Compared to the black singers at that time, she's awful. She's an amateur. But after Monterey, she started getting good very fast. She knew she was gonna be a star, she knew she had it, and she really started working at it, and getting good.

I don't think anybody resented her for it. There was a certain kind of disappointment in that she — even though everybody knew that the writing was on the wall, and we knew it was all coming — I think there were certain people in the band that felt that she couldn't have done it, and that she was succumbing to outside pressure. The band was receiving a lot of negative criticism, and there was a lot of pressure on Janis.

Within the band, we were all very close, actually. We liked each other a lot, but there was a truth that the band wasn't keeping up with her, in terms of development. So it was inevitable that she would leave. I felt that way. *(Eric Eberwein; July 19, 1985.)*

The trademark of the San Francisco sound was the electric guitar. The San Francisco electric guitar sounded like it was made of rubber and could stretch around the world and then snap back into shape. The bent notes of bluesmen were bent further and longer, and some of the jazz overtones that had been filtered out were put back in. The result was sometimes brilliant and sometimes unlistenable.

In the hands of Carlos Santana, it was magical. Santana started his career in 1966 fronting a blues band. The band bore his name only because the musicians' union required it. They didn't record a song until 1969. In August of that year the band played at Woodstock. At the end of the month their first album was released. It stayed on the charts for two years and spawned a top 10 single. In 1970, after the *Woodstock* film was released, Santana released a second album, *Abraxas*. It spent six weeks at #1 and spawned two more top 20 singles. Their third album sold a million copies. Santana was the biggest commercial band to come out of San Francisco.

Santana's sound was commercial but uncompromising. They played rock with a Latin beat and jazz overtones. They stretched out songs into double figures but kept the energy level high. And they could endure as long as Carlos Santana kept his name out front.

Carlos Santana changed directions frequently. He found religion and recorded with Mahavishnu John McLaughlin. He recorded with Buddy Miles and Alice Coltrane. He brought in Leon Thomas, a former vocalist for Count Basie, and kept him in the band for two albums. He recorded a Brazilian album and an album with Herbie Hancock and Wayne Shorter. He continues to record interesting music.

Carlos Santana: I grew up with Bola Sete and John Handy and Charles Lloyd and the Monterey Festival, which was Ravi Shankar and Jimi Hendrix. Mongo Santamaria, Willie Nelson, all this stuff was being played on one radio station. Watusi, or Chuck Berry. Thank God I never really associated with the San Francisco Sound. I have a great relationship with Jerry Garcia and all those people, but I don't belong to that clique of the Grateful Dead or that stuff. I respect it for what it is, but I never wanted to be part of that, and thank God, we're not.

CBS didn't start coming around til '69. Ahmet Ertegun from Atlantic was interested in us before CBS. I didn't want to be with Atlantic, even though I love Aretha. I wanted to be with CBS because Bob Dylan, Miles and people like that were over there. Actually, what got me wanting to be on CBS, they used to put out posters for Christmas with all the artists that they had on the roster. It would be a poster with Miles and Paul Simon and all those people, and I said, "I want to be on this poster."

So I held back. I blew a session with Ahmet Ertegun on purpose. Sure enough, CBS came to a concert. We were opening up for the Grateful Dead in Santa Barbara and this guy representing CBS says, "Man, the company's going crazy about you guys." So that's how we got hooked up with CBS.

Our first album came out a week to two weeks after we played in Woodstock. We had recorded. We recorded it in a week and we mixed it in about three days, like most starting bands.

We had played a lot from Phoenix all the way to San Diego all the way up to Seattle, but that's about it. So Bill Graham called some promoters because they were having those huge festivals already, Atlanta Pop and Texas Pop and Atlantic City, and then the Woodstock. Bill got involved with Woodstock through Michael Lang, who was Joe Cocker's manager, and he told him, "I'll help you if you put these cats in there."

It was very different from anything that I had ever done or have yet to do again in the sense that you could feel all the tribes coming together. The consciousness was very different from any other concert. Most people in the country, the biased people who look at any hippie as nothing — in other words, the system, the system that was sending everybody to Vietnam to get killed — they were saying that it was a disaster area and the pigs had their day.

But we weren't really the pigs; they were the pigs, because, even though they called it a disaster area, I didn't see that. I saw people sharing and coming together, sharing clothes, sharing food, sharing warmth, sharing all kinds of things. Without cops and without all the other kinds of stuff that big cities have. Two people died and two people were born. So I didn't see it as a disaster area. I see everything outside of Woodstock as a disaster area.

For me, it was a very, very supreme existence because of just being on the bill with Jimi Hendrix and Sly Stone and all those people. For us, we're still just about a year, two years right out of high school — especially me, because when I came to this country I couldn't speak English, so they sent me back in school.

I wasn't hot, not until we got to Woodstock, and that's because I took some psychedelics. When we got there, first of all, it was around 11:30 in the morning and one of the first people there I saw after I got out of the helicopter — because you couldn't drive in, you had to fly in because it was a mess, the freeways were closed — but, when we got there I saw Jerry Garcia. And he said, "Hey, man, what time you go on?" I said, "We're supposed to go on two bands after you guys." And he goes, "Well, make yourself comfortable, because we're not going on until eight or so." Eight o'clock at night. I said, "Oh, man!"

So next thing I know — I know he didn't give it to me — but somehow, I took some mescaline, or LSD, whatever it was. And as soon as I came on — I mean, *on* — they told us we have to go on. And all I could hear was some guy saying, "If you don't go on right now, you just ain't gonna play at all." So I just started playing. I said, "Lord, please keep me in time and in tune." It was like a mantra; I'd just keep repeating that.

And when I listen to tapes, I wasn't really that on until I sweated some of that stuff out, which was around "Soul Sacrifice" and maybe "Persuasion." The rest of my stuff, my guitar was like a rubberband, all over the place. "Gee, stand still!" The neck was moving around like a duck neck. But all in all, I think it takes a lot of guts to go out there and see an ocean of hair and teeth and hearts and arms, to go out there and still try to project.

Since we were out of high school, nobody was thinking about me being the leader or musical director or anything like that. We were all sharing together. And being in a hotel, if I would go to some cat's room, he'd be listening to Sly and Jimi Hendrix; another guy to the Stones and Beatles. Another guy'd be listening to Tito Puente and Mongo Santamaria. Another guy'd be listening to Miles and Coltrane. So every room that I went, to me was like being at a university.

And once the band hit national attention, within a year or two, after we got two or three platinum albums, all of a sudden, the band — we weren't rehearsing, everybody was catting, just basically acting stupid and out of our minds. And I remember saying, "Look, we got a couple of platinum albums collecting dust, we haven't rehearsed. That doesn't mean crap to me. Why don't we start getting to the music?" Then people started thinking I was bringing everybody down for trying to get to the next thing.

In essence, it's like the Super Bowl. Once you get to the Super Bowl, a lot of guys, they either become more professional or they become total flakes, in the sense that they think they achieved something. Where, to me, I've never been for the adulation. That to me is bullshit, just like Liberace and all that kind of Hollywood crap. To me, I'd rather hang out with people in the street. People around Macy's at Christmas time, they play infinitely better than any people that I've seen on MTV. And I still have that attitude about it.

And so, that created the separation between the band and myself. Michael Shrieve pretty much stayed on my side because, he and I, we love Miles and 'Trane. And you can't love Miles and 'Trane and not be a serious musician instead of a cat who's catting. Everybody's got talent, but some people's motives are different from others for playing. I never played to get the rent. I never played to get Grammys in Los Angeles. That doesn't mean nothing to me, because it's a bunch of politics, just like Mafia and unions. That stuff doesn't mean anything to me.

I never was interested in being like Herb Alpert, keep cranking out the same crap. Not that my stuff was crap, but I just don't like people to tell me what to play. I grew up in a family of mariachi musicians. My dad is a mariachi. Even though people pay your bills by asking you to play a song, they pay you. When I was a kid, I used to see drunk people pull out a whole wad of money and give it to my dad and say, "Play that same song 15 times in a row." And I said, "I ain't gonna do that shit." My mom said, "What's wrong with you? They're paying you." I said, "No. When I grow up, I want to play what I want to play. And they're still gonna pay me, or I'll be doing something else."

So all that stuff, I think, is a part of my conviction. I'm not a nasty person or a negative person, but I have a feeling that it's important to transcend every time you wake up. Yeah, I can play with Mongo Santamaria or Tito Puente or Eddie Palmieri. But I don't want to do that the rest of my life. There's still Jimmy Cliff. There's still Jimmy Page. There's still Otis Rush. There's still Milton Nascimento. I want to learn. And at that point, if you listen to *Caravanserai*, you hear all kinds of things in there, because we were listening to everything all the time, 'Trane or Miles or Freddie Hubbard.

To this day, people still don't know what to call us. They started calling us mariachi psychedelic rock music. I started laughing. I said, "Boy, these people must be really hard up to try to put a label in here." It didn't stick, and it won't stick, because I love music, music, *period*.

Again, to me, the San Francisco Sound was an amalgamation of the '60s, the Monterey thing with Ravi Shankar, and the combination of everything coming together in there. It was more like Bob Dylan says, "bringing it all back home," and not fusion. I hate fusion. That's like TV dinners. I hate TV dinners, man. Somebody gives me that, I'm throwing it back in their face. Give me something you cook by yourself, or I'll cook by myself. I don't like TV dinners, man.

So I don't see commercial as a negative thing. I see the people who try to control and they are in charge right now and they make everything sound the same. That's what I'm against. But commercial music is not bad. So my priorities are in the right place, and I feel really solid about what I'm doing and how I'm going about it. I don't want the acclamations that a lot of people are always looking for in Hollywood. I would throw up, man, in Hollywood. I don't even want to be buried in there. I like the sense that it houses a lot of creative juices and a lot of talented people. But I don't like the ultimate result. They make everybody into an okey-dokey thing. So as you can tell, I'm still a revolutionary, man, and I want the streets. That's really basically what I want. Show business? I was never interested in that stuff. So that's really where it's at. *(William Ruhlmann; March 24, 1989.)*

The greatest electric guitarist ever was a paratrooper in the U.S. Army who learned to play guitar upside down and backwards. Jimi Hendrix made the electric guitar sing and pray and weep. He coaxed a language of new sounds out of it, and played them in a stage show that defined guitar pyrotechnics forever. Hendrix fused jazz and rock and blues and soul, wrote songs with oblique titles and dense poetry, and dazzled everyone.

Hendrix backed up Little Richard and the Isley Brothers, and played in a group called Jimmy James and the Blue Flames with a 14-year-old Randy California, who would later go on to form Spirit. In 1966, a former member of the Animals, Chas Chandler, brought Hendrix to England. Chandler hooked up Hendrix with two British musicians, bassist Noel Redding and drummer Mitch Mitchell. Together they became the Jimi Hendrix Experience. They dazzled England.

Hendrix finally came back to the United States in 1967, for the Monterey Festival. Two years later, he formed the Band of Gypsys with Billy Cox and the former lead singer of the Electric Flag, Buddy Miles. The band survived on and off until Hendrix's death in 1971.

Almost every electric guitarist who has played since has been influenced by Jimi Hendrix.

Eric Burdon was lead singer of the Animals. Buddy Miles was in Jimi Hendrix's Band of Gypsys. Randy California was the lead guitarist for Spirit.

Eric Burdon: Just to set the story straight, Jimi Hendrix was introduced to Chas Chandler by Linda Keith, a girlfriend of Jimi's in New York. I knew who Jimi was and what he was months before I ever met him. I heard the stories comin' down the line from the chitlin' circuit about "this black guy": "He'd been in prison and he'd killed somebody! And he played guitar behind his neck! And he'd been fired by Ike Turner and Little Richard, because he was too good!"

So when I met him, it was like I knew him already. I went, "Hey, you're the dude everybody's talkin' about!" You know, I got offered the part of his management. I hung out with Jimi long before Monterey. We flew the Atlantic together to Monterey. Monterey was a good experience for me becuse I was *there.* I was right on the side of the stage when Jimi did the famous act with burnin' the guitar.

He told me he was going to kill himself long before he ever did. I think he had the perception to see what had happened to guys like John Lennon and myself, and the bands in England that had become victims and pinned themselves in a corner. He knew that he was painting himself into a corner — with bright psychedelic colors. Once he had that "act," he was cornered there for life. He was no dummy. The guy had a lot of courage; he was in the 101st Airborne. He was a paratrooper before he was ever a rock 'n' roller.

When I first met him, he still had a very military/politicized mind. You know, it was all anti-military and anti-Vietnam and all that shit, and he was still like, solider boy. I'd say to him, as we looked out his apartment window over Grosvenor Square in London, "Lookit, Jimi, what do you think of those riots against the U.S. Embassy?" And he'd say, "Well, when the Chinese hordes come screamin' down from China through North Vietnam and South Vietnam, you'll understand why we're trying so hard to stem the tide of Communism."

And to watch him drop acid and pick up a guitar, instead of a machine gun, and go through these changes was phenomenal. He was like a caterpillar changin' into a butterfly. One night he just sat down and said, "I'm gonna take off on a magic carpet, and a lot of people are gonna be sucked along in the jetstream. And you're gonna be one of them." I said, "How can you tell me that? How can you involve *me* in your traumas? I like you, Jimi, and all that, but this is a bit much."

I've been carrying that around inside me for a long time. I've only just recently met another person whom he said the same thing to: the lady who made the movie *Rainbow Bridge.* She's the only other person I've met who knew that. You've gotta understand about Jimi, that comin' from Seattle, he wasn't really a ghetto kid. There's a little bit of a ghetto in Seattle but there's always Mount Rainier in the distance.

So he was always in touch with some special thing that other black kids in this country didn't have. And then comin' to New York, and seein' a *real* ghetto for the first time, and really becoming a "brother," and doin' the chitlin' circuit. And then being transported to England and being treated like a prince, the black Elvis and all that shit, and really believin' it. And then goin' back to New York and havin' the Black Panthers tell him, "Hey, we know you're just another nigger off the street. And if you don't support us, we'll make sure that the rest of the world sees through your facade." It was a very special mental trip put on that guy. And he knew he couldn't get out of it.

There was only one or two people around him who understood it. Rahsaan Roland Kirk knew what kind of problems he was in; John McLaughlin knew what kinds of problems he was havin'. Those people understood that Hendrix was systematically murdered by the sytem, because he was too damn good. When he came to England, man, he just rocked England completely. He rocked the establishment to its roots.

And I think the biggest pity is we still haven't learned how to keep people like him alive. It's still happening to artists, it's a lack of love, you know? It's a lack of love and understanding. There's a lot of times when I've wanted to go up to Seattle and talk with Al Hendrix [Jimi's father] about this. But I find it tough; it's hard to rake over those coals. I've often thought about writin' a book about Jimi. I just want him to lay down and stay under the ground, or on a cloud, where he belongs. A good song would do it. I found a song — not mine, somebody else's — and I intend to make it into a musical comment on Jimi. And maybe it'll start there; I don't know. At least it'll help *me* to get over it. *(Steve Roeser; Sept. 21, 1990.)*

Buddy Miles: The first time I heard him play was in Montreal, Canada. I was in Ruby and the Romantics, and he was in the I.B. Specials, which was the Isley Brothers' band. We were at a club called the Grand National.

JIMI HENDRIX: 'Hendrix was systematically murdered by the system, because he was too damn good. When he came to England, man, he just rocked England completely. He rocked the establishment to its roots.'

I went nuts. We heard each other play, but we didn't have a chance to work together until about three years later, right after he had Jimmy James and the Blue Flames with Randy California. Then he went on to England, and our first jam took place in 1967, right after the Monterey Pop Festival.

As time went on, he didn't want to continue being a flaunter. He didn't want to do cheap tricks, and he got tired of being called a "wild man of Borneo." He was fed up with people saying that he was, quote, "F---ing his guitar." He wanted to stand up in front of an audience, play his music, and sing. But even still, when we played the Fillmore, I'll never forget our first set. He tried to come out and be real modest, but when we jammed for about three or four hours, you could see this whole thing building up, and when we hit "Wild Thing," all hell broke loose.

Jimi started bending and squatting, and picking his guitar with his teeth, and the audience went nuts. I understood where he was coming from, but it really didn't make any difference because the people just loved him. The man wasn't just an innovative guitarist; he had that *look* about him. And people everywhere enjoyed it — and that's why so many performers still emulate him today. *(Sandy Stert Benjamin; Sept. 21, 1990.)*

🦋

Not everything that was wild or psychedelic was from San Francisco. No group was as musically wild or as innovative as the Mothers of Invention. They were led by a studio prodigy with a wicked sense of humor named Frank Zappa, and they were weird. The Mothers played rock like it was free-form jazz, but with almost every note calculated by Zappa. It was the most tightly orchestrated music of the day, and it sounded like the loosest.

Zappa began composing music when he was in high school; by the time he was 20, he had a group called the Soul Giants and had already scored his first film. Two years later, he appeared on the *Steve Allen Show*, playing a duet with Allen while riding a bicycle.

Zappa was signed to Verve, a jazz label. His group was just called the Mothers; Bob Dylan added "of Invention" to the name. The group parodied the Beatles' *Sgt. Pepper's Lonely Hearts Club Band* with something called *We're Only In It For The Money*. *Lumpy Gravy*, another Mothers album, was recorded with a 50-piece orchestra. In 1967, the group rented the Garrick Theatre in New York and put on avant-garde shows.

The Mothers added former Turtles Flo and Eddie to the band, and then broke up in 1971, after Zappa was thrown off a stage in London. Zappa recorded a typically eclectic series of albums, drew the wrath of record collectors by re-recording parts for the compact-disc versions of his first albums, and fought against music censorship. The Mothers sued Zappa but largely went their separate ways.

Jimmy Carl Black was a member of the Mothers of Invention.

Jimmy Carl Black: I went to the Air Force in 1958, and started playing professionally in Wichita, Kans. I stayed there for a couple of years after the service and left in 1964. I went to California and joined a band called the Soul Giants with Roy Estrada and Ray Collins. Our guitar player got drafted and we needed a guitarist, and Ray knew a guy named Frank Zappa who he played with before. So he asked Frank to audition with us, and he liked the way we played and we liked the way he played, so he joined the band. Three days later, he took over, and the rest is history ... the beginning of the Mothers of Invention.

There's been a lot of stories, man! But there is this one. It was in Germany during a tour in 1968. We got to Berlin and found our concert was at the Sports Palace, where Hitler gave his first speeches. It's a round building and the stage is in the middle, so you're surrounded by people. Now, I didn't know that, but the S.D.S. [Students for a Democratic Society] had approached Frank and said, "We want you to get the people all worked up tonight, Frank, and then tell them to go down about four or five blocks and burn down the Allied supply dumps. That's what we want you to do." And Frank said, "Well, we can't do that, we didn't come here to do that. We came to play music. And besides that, we're citizens of the United States, and if we did something like that, we could never, ever go back to the U.S. As a matter of fact, they would probably send the C.I.A. out to do us in." And so they said, "Well, we'll just destroy your concert then." The band really had no idea anything was going on. It had been, up to that point, a terrific tour. So, then, we're on the stage playin' the first three songs, and pretty soon, we're getting showered with eggs! I mean, really showered from all sides. Then, they start throwing those big hard pears, you know, that feel like baseballs when they hit you.

Yeah, I'm playing the drums, and I'm supposed to be watching Frank, but I could give a damn about Frank! I'm going to watch out where the next ... I don't know what they are gonna throw next. And I thought, "If gunshots start going off, I'm going to hit the ground. I don't care; the hell with the music." And all of this was going down for the first 45 minutes of the show.

So we ended the first set. We went upstairs to the dressing room, and that's where all 75 of the cops were. They were supposed to be protecting us and we couldn't even get in our dressing room. They were hiding because there was about 10,000 people in the audience, but only about 800 S.D.S. agitators.

Then they sent a message up to us saying, "If we didn't come down and finish the show, they were going to come up and get us." And the dressing room was on the second floor, with about a 30-foot drop to the ground. So, we went and played the second half of the show, with 200 people standing on the stage! We couldn't even see each other. And that's when the cherry bombs started flying. They were blowing more of their own people away than anyone else. Well, we finally got out of that gig right then and there. And, we found out later that about 8,000 people ganged up on the S.D.S. bunch and I mean, did a trip on them.

Well, we did at least 10 shows with Jimi Hendrix and numerous after the show jams with him. We also did lots of shows with the Grateful Dead, the Jefferson Airplane, the Doors, Janis Joplin, Cream and John Mayall's group. The Stones and the Beatles used to come and see the Mothers play in London, and they had box seats at the Albert Hall.

That made us play good! You know, "We'll show these guys we know what we're doing. We're weird, but we *do* know what we're doing." *(Jack Ortman; Jan. 16, 1987.)*

Frank Zappa: I was introduced to Paul Buff, the guy who owned the studio, by Ronnie Williams, a guitar player that I was working with in some local bands at the time, and we would just go up there and record. And Paul — I think he's a genius guy. He invented a number of pieces of equipment that are standards of the recording industry right now. But before you can understand the studio and how I got it, you'd have to know how Paul got it. He was a local boy from Cucamonga who had decided he could go into the Marine Corps to learn about electronics, and he did. He got out and decided he was going to be a recording artist and he was going to make his own studio. He built his own five-track recorder at a time when four-track was an absolutely exotic piece of equipment in the industry. Three-track was something that they used for filmwork. Four-track was rare.

And the only person who had a machine that was truly capable of overdubbing was Les Paul. He had that eight-track. Well, Paul Buff built this five-track recorder and then proceeded to teach himself how to play just enough notes on the bass to play a bass part, just enough beats on the drum to keep a background beat, just a little bit of piano, little bit of organ, little bit of guitar, little bit of alto saxophone, and taught himself to sing, and proceeded to make pop records that were clones of hits.

I don't know how he met Ronnie Williams, but Ronnie had joined him up there and was putting guitar parts on some of his things and then Ronnie brought me over and I worked with him on some stuff, and I brought in Ray Collins, who wound up doing a lot of singing on some of these things. So Paul got into debt. He was many months behind in his rent, on his lease payments for the studio. And I came into some money because I'd done a film score for a western, and so I made a deal with him where I would agree to take over his payments on the studio, and that's how I got it. He showed me how to work the stuff, and I went from being kind of an incompetent commercial artist to a full-time obsessive overdub maniac, working in this studio.

[We were signed to Verve] because of Tom Wilson, who was the staff producer for — they called it "blue" Verve. The regular Verve label was black and silver, but blue Verve was for the rock 'n' roll and/or underground stuff. And Wilson was an interesting guy. He's dead now, but he would take a chance on just about anything. I remember one day he came in and announced that he had just signed a Japanese psychedelic artist named Harumi, and Harumi was making some kind of a flower-power album. I never heard the album, I don't know if it was in Japanese or what. But it was the idea that, "Okay, today we're gonna record a Japanese psychedelic record."

A lot of the credit for the odd stuff that went on the label has to go to him because he was the one who would stand up to the people that wrote the paychecks and say, "Yeah, I wanna record and/or produce these things." Without Wilson, we never would have got a contract.

They had no idea what kind of band it was. As a matter of fact, when I went to New York for the first time and was taken to the MGM/Verve office, they had a cafeteria in the building for the employees. They wouldn't even let me in, 'cause I had long hair. That's the kind of a world it was; it was just bizarre. And I went in there with Wilson, and they threw us both out. He was black and I had long hair.

There's a lot of people who write about me that have this image that if I do a concert that the people who are coming there are dressed up like Grateful Dead followers and there's just old hippies and stuff. First of all, we never had a hippie audience. The hippies went directly for the Dead. And they stayed there and God bless them. Our audience has always been really mixed, in terms of age, in terms of geographical backgrounds, whatever. We have strange appeal, it's really hard to describe.

Basically it's always been an employee situation, even with the earliest group. They had an employment contract. I was the one who had to guarantee them a weekly salary whether they worked or not. We're not talking about the Beatles here. It was run like a business, as much as you could run something like that like a business during that period in American musical history. I had to, one way or another, come up with the cash to pay people to be Mothers of Invention. This was not a cooperative, voluntary association.

I wrote the music, I paid the bills, I took the risk. This is called capitalism. And for those of you who don't like capitalism, please consider the alternatives.

The tour at which the Mothers stopped existing as a band, and we're talking about that original bunch of guys, the end came in 1969 after a concert in the Carolinas. We were on a George Wein jazz tour and we were booked with Roland Kirk, Gary Burton and Duke Ellington. And I witnessed a situation backstage with Duke Ellington begging the road manager of the tour for a $10 advance. *Duke Ellington ... begging ... for a $10 advance.*

And we were booked into a hall — it was one of those large, circular halls like an arena, big place — and the PA system was jukebox speakers around the room. And there we are, a 10- or 11-piece band that I had then. And I started the tour off, I had to take $400 out of my bank account to eat on while I was doing the tour and I was still responsible to pay the weekly salaries of the band and crew that was out there. At the end of that tour, I was $10,000 in debt. I felt like, I'm Duke Ellington here, in that sense of the word.

So after that gig, I just said there's no way I can continue this because, to be honest about it, with very few exceptions, most of the people in the band didn't want to rehearse. It was just a job to them. You couldn't get them to put in extra effort to make the group move forward to do anything spectacular. They didn't have any faith in it, it was their gig.

And when I said we're not gonna do this anymore, they were upset. It was like somebody cancelling their social security. There's no way I could have afforded to give them more money to keep them going. It's not coming in to me, what am I supposed to do? And one of the last things that I did as that group broke up was, Jimmy Carl Black came to see me; he had five kids, and he came to me and said, "Look" — at that point, his playing had certainly gone into a slump since the first time I saw him playing at the Broadside in Pomona — and he said he wanted to take drum lessons. And I said, this is good. I gave him $100 to take drum lessons. I don't know whether he ever took the lessons. I'd done everything I could with those guys to help them out, but there's no logical way you could expect any employer to just keep shoveling out money for no services rendered.

You don't make as interesting music, I don't think. But if you want to have a band with a lot of guys in it and be able to produce music with those kind of tone colors to it, you have to be just a little bit crazy. And I learned the same lesson all over again on this last tour. It was an 11-piece band. We rehearsed for four months, we toured for four months. I lost $400,000. But the tapes are unbelievable. And the audiences that saw the show really got a big thrill out of it. They liked the band. But there's no way I could keep it going. *(William Ruhlmann; Jan. 27, 1989.)*

18. The Hitmakers

For many great rock 'n' roll records of the '50s and '60s, the performers were the least important people involved. Songwriters were more important. A&R men found the right talent for the song. Producers and label owners called the shots. Disc jockeys could make a record a hit or doom it. The people who got credit for performing on the record might never have performed on the record. And if they did, their role was a supporting one.

The people who actually made the records weren't always the most scrupulous people, and they didn't always have the best interests of the performers at heart. Their motives were sometimes Machiavellian; they could make the record business legalized prostitution. But they made records with the same passion that the performers did. They wanted hits as badly, and did everything they knew to get those hits and keep them coming, and keep the royalty checks flowing. Some of them might even have harbored a thought or two about art.

And records were never more important than they were in the early days of rock 'n' roll. Records were made in greater quantities than ever, to fill jukeboxes and be played by kids over and over until the grooves were worn smooth. More records were spun by more DJs on more radio stations to fill the gap left by the demise of old-time radio. Records were spun at hops and played between features at drive-ins. And thanks to improved technology, there were more different types of records than ever before: 45s, which were easier to store and less likely to break, and could be played to death on take-anywhere portables; LPs, which gave performers more room to stretch out and explore the medium (and more of an excuse to record cover versions and filler); and EPs, which were billed as having the best qualities of 45s and LPs but never sold as well as either. Later there would be newer media, like eight-track and cassette tapes, to further enhance the portability of music. But rock 'n' roll and the black-vinyl record will always be linked — as they should be. Records made rock 'n' roll, and rock 'n' roll made record companies rich.

All the record companies and the people who made records descended from John Hammond. Hammond created more of the modern record business than any other single individual. He was the first A&R — artist and repertoire — man, the first record-company talent scout in history.

He either discovered by himself or had a hand in discovering and recording Billie Holliday, Bessie Smith, Benny Goodman, Count Basie, Lionel Hampton, Teddy Wilson, George Benson, Pete Seeger, Aretha Franklin, Bob Dylan, Bruce Springsteen, and Stevie Ray Vaughan. He made Columbia Records into the world's largest and best-known record company, and brought many more great performers onto the bright-red label. He arranged and promoted the legendary "Sprituals To Swing" concerts, and legitimized the musical cross-pollination — blues to jazz and folk to blues and country to jazz — that eventually spawned rock 'n' roll. He was a music critic, a disc jockey and a tireless campaigner for civil rights. He was the sort of musical renaissance man the music industry had to find to exist. Everything that's good about records and music and the music business has something to do with John Hammond.

John Hammond: I was a record collector. And later, I played the viola in a string quartet. I was wild about classical music, but the first record that completely knocked me out was James P. Johnson, "Worried And Lonesome Blues," which was an early blue Columbia record. That's really the record that changed my life, 'cause I didn't know anything about blues until I heard that. Then of course I got to listen to Bessie Smith, whom I later recorded.

My mother was a Vanderbilt. And her mother and father insisted that she have a home just as elaborate as her sisters' homes. One of them was my cousin Fred Fields, who later went to jail as a Communist in the 1950s. He was born at 645 Fifth Avenue. Then my aunt, Mrs. Burden, was given a house at 7 East 91st Street, and we had the house next door, at 9 East 91st Street. In fact, it was so elaborate a house that I used to go in through the servants' entrance in back, 'cause I didn't want to be seen going through these huge oak doors, you know.

I started out in Harlem. I started to know black musicians, and black artists in general, and this really was the start of my life. And as soon as I was 21 I was able to move from 9 East 91st Street to the Village.

My first recording was made in 1931. I had heard a piano player up at Covan's Morocco Club, called Garland Wilson. He wasn't nearly as good as I thought he was, but he was flashy. And so I decided I was going to try and get into the record business anyway, and the only real way to do it in those days was to pay for it yourself. So, you know, I guaranteed to buy 125 12-inch records, and I recorded Garland. And it wasn't bad! As a matter of fact, it was good enough so that the Okeh subsidiary of Columbia immediately recorded Garland on their own.

But the most important thing that happened to me was the following year, Columbia was in bankruptcy in those days, the way all record companies were hurting, even [RCA] Victor. And so I became the American correspondent for *The Melody Maker* and *The Grammophone*. I was able to talk about black musicians, which I wasn't allowed to do in *any* American paper. So I became a sort of chronicler of what was happening in the world of big bands, which were people like Fletcher Henderson for me, and Elmer Snowden, who had a magnificent band up at Small's Paradise [a club in Harlem], which I was never able to get into the recording studio, 'cause they weren't in the union!

But later, in 1933, I signed a contract with English Columbia to make a couple of hundred sides, and I told them all the people I'd get for them as a band around Benny Goodman, whom they knew of only as a sideman clarinet player, and Fletcher Henderson's band, and Coleman Hawkins, and Joe Sullivan — a whole bunch of people, you know, everything I wanted to do. Of course, I didn't get paid for this, but I got a lot of experience, you see.

English Columbia had taken over American Columbia, which was helplessly broke. Then they sold it to the Grigsby-Gruno company, which made Majestic radios. At this time, there was the Depression, of course, and there was no money for anything.

CBS Columbia didn't come along into the record business until December of 1938, the offspring of the American Record Company.

And so I was hooked, I was in, and my father was a banker and a lawyer, and he thought I was absolutely crazy because "radio had *obviously* signalled the end of recordings." And I said, "No, this is what I want to do." And so I did it. The money had very little to do with it, actually, and I was determined to integrate the music business.

Luckily, in the early years there were more successes than failures. I had heard a piano player in 1933, I guess it was, named Teddy Wilson. He was substituting for Earl Hines at the Grand Terrace in Chicago. I was so impressed when I heard him on the radio, that I called up WMAQ in Chicago, to find out who was playing piano in his band. And they said his name was Teddy Wilson, but they didn't know who he was.

In the summer of 1933 I became very good friends with Benny Carter, and Benny was working for Irving Mills in those days. He had made some records for Irving Mills under his own name, King Carter, and his orchestra. "I'm Left With The Blues In My Heart" was that first record of Benny's that knocked me out. And so, Benny and I became friends.

Irving was a song plugger, a person whose job it was to convince bandleaders and singers to record certain songs, and then to get the radio stations to play them. So one of the first big bands I signed was the Benny Carter Band. And then Fletcher Henderson, who had such people as Red Allen, Rex Stewart, J.C. Higgenbotham, Sandy Williams, Coleman Hawkins, all these great people. And so, I'd record the bands, and then record small groups from the bands, 'cause there was more room for improvement, you see. It was freer and all.
see. It was freer and all.

So I started getting bands together, and then, in 1933, I really got started with Benny Goodman. Benny was a wonderful clarinet player. I twisted Benny's arm one day 'cause I'd heard a girl named Billie Holiday at a speakeasy up in Harlem. There were still speakeasies in 1933, even though Prohibition hadn't been repealed — enough states hadn't ratified — so that you couldn't get much more than 3.2 beer in New York in those days, and that wasn't enough to satisfy most people's tastes.

I heard Billie one night at a Harlem gin mill that was fronted by a friend of mine, Monette Moore, and the irony was that I went up there to the opening of her new club, and she was working in a Broadway show and was late. They had somebody substituting for her, and that was Billie Holiday. She was the best singer I'd ever heard.

And with the rise of Benny Goodman, I finally did get Billie down to a Columbia session. She made two sides, "Your Mother's Son-In-Law" and "Riffin' The Scotch." And I guess this was the first time that Benny had ever worked with a black musician on record, because he was scared that he'd never be able to get another job in radio in New York if he was known to hang out with black musicians. The only other person who had been able to do that before was Eddie Condon, and Eddie had done some things with Louis Armstrong, and others.

And so, I started doing this, and I remember Benny liked Billie, but he wasn't wild about Billie. But I had to wait some time before we could get Billie on records. That finally happened in the fall of 1933. By that time, of course, Teddy Wilson had come, and he had joined the trio.

Since I had close connections with the Brunswick label, I was able to get bands together under Teddy Wilson's name. And I remember the first session I ever made for Brunswick was with all my favorite people: Benny, Ben Webster on tenor, John Kirby on bass, Roy Eldridge on trumpet, Cozy Cole on drums. And this was a hell of a little group!

I remember there were terrible problems making records in those days, 'cause you couldn't really do it with pop tunes. There was really only one publishing clearing house, and that was ASCAP. And they wouldn't allow their tunes by Gershwin and all the other good standards to be altered in any way. You had to play the melody at all times.

But jukeboxes were just coming in at the time, and the first Teddy Wilson record that hit the jukeboxes was "I Cried For You," with Johnny Hodges and various other musicians. And it had a gigantic sale — it sold 15,000 78s! Which, for Brunswick, was unbelievable, you know. Usually only three or four thousand were sold, 'cause they had people like Eddie Duchin and Ben Bernie, you know, all the square bands in the world.

I was so convinced that Teddy Wilson was a genius that I was able to persuade Harry Gray to put Teddy on a regular weekly salary whether he made records or not. And so this sort of helped Benny, 'cause although Teddy was making records with the trio, he couldn't work with Benny, 'cause there was no such thing as mixed groups before the public. So, Teddy was the first, and then Lionel Hampton was the second black musician we had, which was in 1936, for the quartet, and by the end of the '30s Benny had as many as six black musicians in his band. So, in the early part of my career, my lobbying was fairly successful, I guess, because it made money for the record company and it made money for Benny.

I had my first paid job in the record business in 1934. I had a little title as Irving Mills' recording advisor. And for doing that and for being managing editor of his little house organ, called *Melody News*, I'd asked for 100 bucks a week. He said, "Well, I'll pay ya' half for half time" and so, I got 50 bucks a week, and that was something. That's really how it started.

The most exciting experience I ever had in the recording studio was really in 1936. I'd heard a band out in Kansas City called Count Basie. And somehow or another, I was double-crossed, because Basie was supposed to have signed with Brunswick for a royalty. I was looking for royalties for artists in those days because only Bennie Goodman among jazz artists was payed royalties up to that time and he was on Victor. But Decca, which had a 35-cent record, didn't pay, except for two royalty aritsts, Bing Crosby and Guy Lombardo.

And so Decca just didn't believe in paying scale, if they could help it. And they signed up Midwest territory bands. So they signed up Count Basie right out from under my nose. Dave Capp, who worked for Decca, said he was representing me, which he wasn't.

Basie was to open at the Grand Terrace in Chicago in 1936, and so I figured before they got to New York, I'd record them in Chicago.

And so, I called the band Jones-Smith, Inc. It was the first record Jo Jones had ever made, and Buck Clayton had a split lip that morning, so we had a substitute trumpet player, "Tatti" Smith, and so that made it Jones-Smith and very mysterious, you see. And it was Lester Young's first experience in the recording studio.

Basie had recorded in the studio before, and so had Jimmy Rushing. And it was just a little five-piece group with Jimmy on the vocals, and we did this at 10 in the morning after their first or second night of opening there. And it was very tough because most of the guys couldn't read very well, and they were reading strange arrangements. We started at 10, and it was the first perfect recording session I ever had! Nothing was blown! Every single note was perfect! We did "Shoeshine Boy," "Boogie Woogie," we did "Lady Be Good," we did four tunes in three hours, and we sort of loved doing them so much we did second and third takes. But the first take was always the best.

I've had so many sessions, you see. That first Bessie Smith session I did was one of my best, which was the last she ever made. I remember I asked Jack Teagarden if he'd be on it and he said, "Would I be on it?! I've worshipped her all my life, and it would be the greatest privilege!"

I remember we had Frankie Newton on trumpet, and Chu Berry on tenor, and I had hired Big Sid Catlett on drums. She said, "I don't want no drums. I make my own time." And so she did. And that was "Gimme A Pigfoot And A Bottle Of Beer," and all those wonderful tunes.

There's still a lot of mystery surrounding her death. Chris Albertson got in touch with the doctor down there, who finally treated Bessie at the hospital in Memphis. This was in 1937.

I used to have great friends in Huntsville, Alabama, and one summer I was down there and I spoke with the owner of the show, who was a very light-skinned man, and he told me what he thought was the correct version of the story, that she and Richard Mogan — Lionel Hampton's uncle and her boyfriend — were driving on a narrow road in West Memphis, which is in Arkansas.

There was a terrible accident; they ran into a slow-moving truck and her arm was nearly severed. She was bleeding heavily, and a number of ambulances came along and wouldn't pick her up because she was black. Finally, the third one did, but by that time she had lost an awful lot of blood. And they figured there was nothing they could do for her at the Clarksdale Hospital, where she was finally taken, so they sent her on to Memphis and by this time she had lost so much blood that she was practically dead. Horrible story. And typical, of course, of what happened in the South in those days.

How were you able to handle people in New York in the 1930s, who would call you "nigger lover" and all of that nonsense?

I'd laugh at them! I'd laugh at them. I'd say, "You think you're insulting me? This is an honor!" And in those days I served on the board of the NAACP, and I covered the Scottsboro case for *The Nation* and *The New Republic*.

I have fun. That really is the simple part of it. I've had my share of failures and bad records. Think of all those years I was working with Mercury, when occasionally I had the great fun of working with Big Bill Broonzy and Albert Ammons, but most of the time I was dealing with Vic Damone and Patti Page, you know, all of whom were good artists, you know. But at CBS Columbia, I used to have to record Lawrence Welk and Dick Jurgens, and Orrin Tucker. In fact, that was my first big hit for them — Orrin Tucker with Wee Bonnie Baker, "Oh, Johnnie, Oh." And that hit almost a million copies within the first couple of years.

I had decided I *loved* recording, as such. Actually one of the great saxophone players I ever came in touch with was the third alto man with Lawrence Welk, Buff Estes. One day I said to Buff, "What in the world are you doing with this 'band'?"

He said, "Well, it's a job; you got any better suggestions?"

I said, "Yes — Benny Goodman is looking for an alto man," and to this day, Lawrence Welk has not forgiven me.

I've just joined the Rock And Roll Hall of Fame Advisory Board, and now I find myself saying things like, "Look, Bo Diddley has got to be recognized." Because, I mean, after all, this all came from the blues! And Chuck Berry! I mean, rock 'n' roll never horrified me at all.

After all, one of the first big rock artists was big Joe Turner, whom I'd brought to New York from Kansas City in 1938, in those original *Spirituals To Swing* concerts, and he made "Rock Around The Clock," and all those things for Atlantic. But I never had any real trouble with rock 'n' roll.

I did have a little trouble with Bill Haley's band, to be perfectly frank with you, 'cause they were among the first big rock records made on Decca in the early '50s. They didn't swing! And it seems to me that it's very important for good blues or good rock to have an exciting beat, and they didn't.

Pete Seeger is one of the great men of all times. As a matter of fact, if it hadn't been for Pete, I would never have been able to sign Bob Dylan.

In 1960, I had persuaded Goddard Lieberson, who was by that time my boss, that we should sign Pete. At the time he was with a very small label called Folkways. And he was blacklisted, you see, and he was blacklisted by CBS, which made it worse. So I said to Goddard, "I would love to sign Pete," and Goddard said, "Well, go ahead and sign him," and I said, "No, because he's still blacklisted by CBS, and you better get clearances. I don't care if I get into trouble but I care a great deal if you get in trouble."

So Goddard called one of the vice presidents at CBS, and said we had a chance to sign Pete Seeger. I was there during the phone conversation, and I could hear a gasp on the other line. And so, the CBS guy said, "Well, do you think he'll sell?" And Goddard said, "I wouldn't sign him unless we thought he could sell." So he said, "Go ahead, we're big boys now." So we signed him, and he was *still* blacklisted by CBS!

A couple of years after this [1961], I heard Bob Dylan at a rehearsal for a Carolyn Hester date, and I just decided that this guy was outrageous enough so that it might do something to help erase the square image that CBS had in those days. Luckily, I had heard Bobby alone before that. But we weren't in folk, and we weren't in rock, and I figured that Dylan was such a brilliant lyric writer, that there was a place for him. So I signed him.

He did some standards: Jesse Fuller and others. The only terrible thing that ever happened with Bobby was after about a year, Broadway started to take notice of him, and so Ed Sullivan decided he was gonna have Bob Dylan on the *Ed Sullivan Show*. And one of the things he was gonna do was "Talking John Birch," which was this really magnificent demolition of the John Birch Society. And the CBS lawyers decided that this was so libelous that any member of the John Birch Society could sue, for defamation and the rest. That's the only time I have ever encountered CBS censorship. And they *never* interfered with anything else we did, and I've recorded people like Len Chandler and Malvina Reynolds, and all sorts of fairly leftward people, because I thought that they had something to say, and it needed saying.

I had practically guaranteed Bobby that he'd never have to worry about censorship on CBS, and this was the only time that it ever happened. But by that time he had written so many great tunes and he was one of the big-selling artists. That's when they decided he wasn't "Hammond's folly."

This kid [Bruce Springsteen] is over in the corner, with a real funny, quizzical look on his face. And the first tune he played for me was something which absolutely knocked me out — it was about motorcycles and the rest, life on the road and everything. He played wonderful guitar, not very good piano, but wonderful guitar. And so I said, "Is there anything you've ever written that you wouldn't dare record?"

And so he said, "Well, I'll try something on you." It was something called "If I Was The Priest." And this was a really *wild* song, and very, very anti-Catholic. And I said to Bruce, "Bruce, were you raised by nuns?" He said, "Of course." And with the name Springsteen, you see, I had assumed he had the same racial background as Bob Dylan, which of course he did not have. And so I recorded "If I Was The Priest" at the first session, which Columbia didn't put out and which, actually, there's a bootleg thing out on it, you know, from my first session. Still, though, we got it done; I fought for Bruce. And his first album, I think it's finally gone gold, but it took a long time to go gold. But on his second and third albums, his genius as a performer comes through, and saved his recording career.

How has the industry changed since you first got involved?

Well, we've gotten big.

Has it gotten worse?

Well, yes and no. It's going to be saved by one thing, really. The new compact discs are the greatest technical advance, really, since the long-playing record. And Columbia still makes good records, but they don't have their own studios anymore, which is a real tragedy.

What's happened now is that, you see, in the early days of radio, people wouldn't broadcast anything that wasn't acceptable to majority tastes. Now, that's no longer true. *(Andrew Skelly; Sept. 7, 1990.)*

Not every record man was a social pioneer like John Hammond. Some were cigar-chomping hustlers from the backwoods who knew where to find the talent and only cared about getting that talent on a record and getting that record out — damn the formal contracts, damn the proper publishing, damn anything else that stood in their way.

Jay Miller certainly qualified in that regard. Huey P. Meaux, too. Miller and Meaux are bayou boys, short on book-learning but backwoods shrewd. The records they made may not always have produced the best financial outcome for the artists involved, but they were authentic, steamy slices of the South, whether it was one of Miller's blues artists or one of Meaux's Tex-Mex-Cajun specialties. Miller recorded classic sides on Slim Harpo, Lightnin' Slim, Lazy Lester, and Katie Webster, but also recorded the legendary Cajun fiddler Harry Choates and some of the best zydeco ever laid down by Clifton Chenier and Rockin' Dopsie. Meaux recorded Joe Barry, Jivin' Gene, Barbara Lynn, Freddy Fender, Doug Sahm, T-Bone Walker, Roy Head, Jerry Lee Lewis, Doug Kershaw, and Rockin' Sydney. Both Miller and Meaux made an awful recording on occasion, but they didn't make a habit of it. They couldn't afford to.

Jay Miller: I was born on May 5, 1922, and moved to Lake Charles, Louisiana, at an early age.

I tried to trace back and see if maybe I inherited some muscial ability. All I found was my old grandpa, who scratched a little on the fiddle and that was it. He was far from being a good fiddle player, but he could play a few tunes. That's the only person I know of in our family that had some musical talent.

In my childhood days, I was a big Gene Autry fan. What little I learned on the guitar, I started with a 29 cent Gene Autry instruction book which my parents got me from the Sears and Roebuck catalog. I played guitar, banjo, mandolin, and I played a little fiddle, something like my grandpa — pretty poor.

I started playing what you might call professionally at the age of 15. Actually, when I was 13 years old I entered an amateur contest over at Lake Charles, Louisiana, where we were living at the time, and for some reason I happened to win the contest. First prize was a one-year contract with radio station KPLC for a 15-minute program every Saturday morning. I was still going to school, but every Saturday I would broadcast a 15-minute program. Then we moved to Crowley in 1937 and I started playing with groups that played local dances. I did that 'til I got married in December 1940; after that I quit playing dance halls completely.

When I came back from the service, I went into the electrical contracting business, for which I rented a building. We had more space than I needed, so I set up a little record department. I had numerous people ask for French records, and at that time there was only one French record out on the market besides the oldies, and that was a record by Harry Choates called "Jole Blon." Of course, Harry and I had played music together for some time and I knew him quite well, but that was the only French record we had available to us. So I said, by golly, I think we can sell quite a few records. I suppose if we cannot buy them, we go ahead and make some.

My first artist was Happy Fats LeBlanc — I am sure you have heard of him — Happy Fats, Doc and another fellow by the name of Lewis Noel. I called the guy in New Orleans who recorded all the Fats Domino hits, Cosimo Matassa, and he was the one that cut our first session. We came back to Crowley and waited for about four weeks, and we had two new French records. Actually that's how it started, and then I recorded a number of additional French records. My third French artist was Jimmy Newman, who is now a member of the Grand Ole Opry. I used to write most of the songs for him.

Then I decided to get a tape recorder. Tape recorders had just come in, so I went to Houston and bought a little PT-6 Mag Recorder. We came back to Crowley and started cutting records and we have been cutting them ever since. We broadened out into the country and the blues and now we do just about everything.

I knew absolutely nothing about it. I had never been inside a recording studio. I just stayed in the background and the boys got behind the mike. There was only one mic at that time and one track. Actually what we cut was a plate-disk, and there was not too much producing at that time. Putting the switch on was about it.

The records sold pretty good. They were sold within a limited area, of course, but as I said before, there hardly were any new French records available. Every time we came out with a new single there was a good solid demand for it.

Do you believe that I have never gone out to look for talent? I have been fortunate enough for people to come to me. It's worked out better that way because you are in a better position when they come to you. It is quite costly to put out records; at least it was for me, because I was very limited on funds. I didn't have much money, and like I said before, I like all kinds of music. Good talent is very tempting to me, so probably had I gone out I would have heard more talent than I would have been able to take care of. The way it was worked out real fine.

Of course, there are many stories around about Jay Miller. I read one the other day which I got very upset about to some degree. Someone wrote that Lightnin' Slim got sick, went to Detroit, and I would not help him or record him. Now, I spent quite a big of time and money trying to find out where he was, and I finally found him and I called him on three occasions and just about had him convinced to come down to Crowley for some recording when somebody frightened him. Lightnin' Slim's story is long and complicated. A lot of people have written about my relationship with Lightnin', but every time it seems like someone has to twist words around. Lightnin' Slim was my favorite blues singer. I like him as a person and I did a lot for him. He recorded for me for a long time, and I have heard said that I did not pay Lightnin'. I bought him six automobiles ... I advanced him the money for six cars!

If an artist is dissatisfied with me, there is really no reason why I should keep them with me. They are just a problem then. Sooner or later they make the rounds and they come back. It has happened lots of times that way with us. You know, there is nothing magic about this business. We do not have a magic formula, nor does anyone else have one, and with the small companies like ours, some of these artists are the big fish in the ocean. They go with a big record company and they mean absolutely nothing to them and they learn.

I do everything by ear, and I play the whole thing by ear. I try to get the sound that I want. Most of it depends on the material you are recording and the artist.

I will be quite honest. Most of the artists I've had have relied mostly on my suggestions, and certainly at times I feel I have made the wrong suggestions. 'Cause goodness knows we've made a lot of records that did not sell, and we made a lot of tapes we did not even put on record. Still, overall our track record is fairly good.

We don't have a big promotional plan. We are a speculative label. We speculate hoping that we'll record something that will get enough notice, whereby we might be able to get a lease deal from a large company. We broadened out one at a time with our specialty records and we had up to 22 or 23 distributors, but you can lose a lot of money having distributors when you are a small operation.

A distributor is like a store. About the only thing they pay attention to is demand. They don't know anything about it, and don't care anything about it 'til people start asking for the record. You cannot walk in there with a record and say it is a hit because they will laugh at you.

Apparently it is just so much easier for those radio stations to pick up a *Cashbox* or *Billboard* and play top 40 of country, rock or whatever it may be, and so difficult to get them to play local and new artists, whereas it used to be the opposite. Of coure, I think it is very short-sighted on their part, for the simple reason that at one time all those artists in the top 40 were unknown and new artists. I think the DJs are doing a big injustice, even though I don't want to blame them totally. This thing has gotten out of hand; you got program directors, simply too many hands in the pot. Years ago, it was left up to the DJ what he played; now you have to go through the command and they figure it is easier to pick up a *Billboard* and *Cashbox*, and take it from there.

Oh, I like everything about the music business. I cannot think of anything I don't like about it, with the exception of the bad publicity and the bad stories that have been told, not just about me but most every other producer in the country. We are just in one hell of a shape; we get it one way or the other.

Of course, I am not gonna sit here and toot my own horn or anything like that. Whether I made a contribution or not is for someone else to judge. But I have devoted quite a few years to the music business and if I haven't made some kind of contribution I have certainly wasted some good years. But I have enjoyed every minute of it. *(Adriaan Sturm; December 1981.)*

Huey P. Meaux: I was named after Huey P. Long. Me and a lot of other people. He got back and met the people back in the swamps. He gave free books back there. Still have one of them cups that they sent to any family that named a boy after him. The inside was gold and the outside was silver. It had your name engraved on it. There was a bunch of Hueys in Louisiana. The people there loved that man.

My father couldn't read and write. Even when he died in 1979, he couldn't write his name. I was born in the Depression and my daddy worked for the WPA. I remember my daddy standing on the levee when I was a little boy. He worked for this farmer who had 100 acres of rice and gave my daddy 10 acres. Like sharecropping, you know. I remember watching him cry — one of the few times I saw him cry. He was looking at that 10 acres and he couldn't cut it. It wasn't worth the money to haul the distance to Kaplan, Louisiana.

We finally moved to Kaplan, where my grandfather gave us a Jersey cow which we could take out into the pastures around Kaplan. The government gave us cheese once a month. I remember my brother and me breaking our legs and arms because we didn't have enough calcium. My daddy was getting $3 a week on the WPA and my mom took in washing and ironing. We lost a sister between me and my brother. Finally, my daddy decided he could make more money in Texas shucking rice so we moved to Winnie, Texas, when I was 12 years old.

I used to love New Orleans. It was a better place when I started going there in the '50s. You could lay down on the sidewalk in the French Quarter and no one would beat you up. Now it's a tourist trap and you have nasty boys from other parts of the country in there. In those days, the French Quarter was *really* the French Quarter. You stepped over Canal Street and you was in another world. A peaceful world. So much music I thought I was in Heaven. Everyone would play. I remember the Dream Room. Sugar Boy Crawford was there. I loved it so much I stayed three months without going home. My old lady used to say she was gonna come and drag me out. The music was *so* good and I loved it *so* much. Everything was just flowing and rolling. It was like taking dope 24 hours a day and feeling pretty.

I always wanted to play, but I was never worth a damn. I used to play drums in a band with George Jones. I couldn't sing either. I tried to make records but then I'd play 'em back after I'd sobered up. I'd say, "Who's that?" They'd say, "Huey Meaux." I said, "Oh, my God. I can't believe I did that." It would just embarrass the shit out of me.

I knew I loved music so much that I just had to get next to it somehow. I could *hear* music because I held teenage hope and I was a DJ on KPAC. I could feel the rhythm that people liked — and it all starts with the rhythm track. If you ain't got that you ain't got shit. It's like a railroad train going without a track.

I started this barber shop in Winnie but I couldn't keep out of music. I got a tape from a guy in Beaumont. It had been recorded over. This guy wanted to sell me an act by the name of T-Baby Green. In between the T-Baby Green cuts was this girl they had recorded over. It was knocking me o-u-t. It was reaching at the roots of my heart. I just wanted to meet that voice. I had a guy named Big Sambo recording for me. I played him the tape and said, "Who's this?" He said, "That's Barbara Lynn. If you want her, I'll get her."

So I kept cutting hair, and he came back around 6:30 with Barbara Lynn. She was about 15 or 16, I guess, and she limped a little because she had one leg longer than the other. I said, "Barbara, if you'll pay the expenses for you and your mother, I'll meet you in New Orleans at Cosimo's studio. I'll pay for the musicians and the tape." She went for it, and we recorded "You'll Lose A Good Thing."

I asked her how she came to write that song and she said, "I used to go out with Sylvester LeBlanc and I caught him out with my best friend. I told him that if he messed around, he'd lose a good thing." She told the same story to Dick Clark on television.

Anyway, I didn't have no money. I had to use cheap tape, $1.98 a reel. Mono. I left the tape with Cosimo Matassa and I told him, "If anybody ever comes from up north, play these tapes for them." About six months later someone from Jamie-Guyden Records called me at my barber shop. He said, "Huey, I want to lease that Barbara Lynn record. Cosimo just played it for me." I just like to drop my clippers. He said, "How much do you want?" I said, "$650 for front money," which was like asking for the moon. If I'd got $50 I'd have thought I was a big shot. He said, "Stay right where you are in your barber shop. I'm gonna drive over from New Orleans." And that's how I leased Barbara Lynn and got in with Jamie-Guyden Records.

Me and Floyd Soileau put out Joe Barry's "I'm A Fool To Care" on Jin. It became very big. We couldn't press it fast enough. I wanted to lease it to Mercury. They were hot as blazes. Pappy Daily helped me lease it. I called old man Green from Pappy Daily's office. Pappy's standing there, cigar in his mouth, telling me, "Go on, son. Tell Mr. Green you want $5,000 or you'll give it to MGM." It was my first lease deal. Pappy was nudging me with his knee because I was freezing.

Anyway, old man Green said, "Could I send Charlie Fach to see you?" He was their field rep in Atlanta in those days. Charlie asked me if I would take a gamble with them on a new label because Mercury was so hot, they couldn't put another act on the label. I said, "What label will it be on?" Charlie said, "I don't know; we'll just make one up." I said, "Well, the Barry record's a smash. Let's call it Smash."

The Barry record was the first hit on Smash. I remember "I'm A Fool To Care" was running up the R&B charts and sellings in every market — even downtown Harlem. The minute I put Joe on *American Bandstand*, he dropped off the black charts completely. One week — boom! As soon as they found out he was white, man! I remember walking into the big black station in Philadelphia with Joe and Jivin' Gene. They was expected to go on the air, and then the DJ saw

316

them and said, "Oh, no! Don't tell me! Why you do this to me, Huey?" You see, I'd never told no one that they was white.

I used to sit at the record player in the pressing plant and I'd listen to other people's records. I could pick hits — and I was good at it. I could pick them damn hits like that — bam! bam! bam! I picked up Bruce Channel's "Hey Baby" like that. I leased it to Smash for Major Bill Smith. I kept the record for Texas. I picked up "Hey Paula" in the same way.

Doug Sahm always liked that South Louisiana sound we had. He was always crazy for it. He was always a nervous cat and had long hair even at that time. He had thick hair and a big long comb and he'd be combing it all the time. Drove me crazy. He would drive to Winnie, Texas, where I had the barber shop and pester me to record. He'd play something and say, "What do you think about this?" He really wanted the South Louisiana sound — Joe Barry, Fats Domino — he was really into it. Bugged me for five years.

Then the Beatles came along, wiped everybody off the map, including me. I had to get into the beat. I went to San Antonio, rented three rooms at the Wayfarer Motel, bought a case of Thunderbird wine and a little Philips plastic record player. I had a stack of Beatles records and I thought, "I gotta get into this goddamned music. It's so simple, I'm just missin' it." Really, the Beatles had a beat like a Lake Charles two-step.

I'd told Doug to go write some tunes like that and grow him some hair. I called him up on the phone and said, "You're gonna think I'm crazy, but come over here and bring your guitar." He come over to the motel. I was drunk on my ass. Full of that Thunderbird wine, but I needed to get into a subconscious state of mind and get into this beat. I'd given Doug some of my daddy's records and said, "Listen to the beat, Doug, not the accordion. Write me some songs like that." That's how we got "She's About A Mover" and "The Rains Came."

On the session we used a Vox organ. It came from England, and we had the first one in North America. It gave the record a half-Mexican, half-Cajun overtone. Doug loved that stuff. His idol was the late Papa Link Davis, you know.

We named his group the Sir Douglas Quintet because the DJs in those days were playing anything from London or anything that had an English sounding name. We thought that "Sir Douglas Quintet" would fool the American people into thinking it was English — and it did!

We cut those songs in the Gold Star studio in Houston. Doug had grown his hair. They were the first long-haired guys in these parts, and the fellas in the studio gave me so much trouble, calling them "faggots," "queers." They was messing up the groove. I had to ask the manager here to throw everyone out of the damned building. Hell! I was paying for the session. They thought we was crazy, though.

I went to Walt Maguire at London Records. I said, "Walt, I don't want my name on it or nothin' else, just put it out. 'Sir Douglas Quintet. Distributed by London Records.' Don't tell nobody nothin'. Make people believe it's from England."

And it worked. The DJs all thought it was British because it came from London Records. They jumped on "She's About A Mover" like gangbusters, man.

"Treat Her Right" was a thing that Roy used to start off dances. It was based on "The Mashed Potato." Roy would start with his "Treat Her Right" routine and then lead into "The Mashed Potato." People got off on "If you start real slow," you know, so we decided to cut that intro as "Treat Her Right." It ends kinda suddenly on the record, and that's because they were just getting into "The Mashed Potato."

Me and Charlie Booth cut that record. We needed the money and we couldn't find nowhere to place it. Then Don Robey at Duke/Peacock took it. He had an ear, but he didn't really believe in the record. He gave us $2,000 advance and, on the way back from the R&B DJ's convention in Miami, I said, "I'll show you what you're not pushing." I stopped in Atlanta, New Orleans, all the stops back from Miami, and by the time I got back the record was happening.

Old man Robey got sued by whoever owned "The Mashed Potato." They got me as an expert witness to go to court and say where it come from. Robey had never paid us a dime on that record, because he never paid nobody. I called him one night just before we were due to go to court. You didn't just go down there on Erastus Street, because he had his henchmen. They might pull a Jimmy Hoffa, you know. So I called him up and told him to keep his henchmen away. I might have been crazy, but I always had balls. I told him I wanted a business talk.

I got over there about 7 o'clock. It was drizzling rain and the sun had just gone down. I went in his room, and he had a deer rifle on his desk. He was polishing it with his handkerchief. I'd brought my .38, and I got it out and started polishing it. He'd take his handkerchief every once in a while and he'd wipe his bald head with it. He said, "How's it goin', Hue?" He called me "Hue" and I called him "Chief." I said, "Everything's fine, Chief. How you doin'?" He said, "Oh, everything's great," and he was polishing that deer rifle. "Chief, I come to talk to you. Tomorrow when I go to court I'm either on your side or them other people's side." He said, "What you talkin' about, Hue?" I said, "You know what I'm talkin' about. I want my Roy Head money: $40,000. I want it in a briefcase in *cash* when I got on that witness stand; otherwise, being an expert witness, I'm gonna be for the other side."

He got nervous. He said, "Oh, Hue, you know that damned thing didn't make no money." I said, "Oh, sure, it didn't! It ain't my first hit record and, like the man said, I didn't just ride into town on no mule!" I told him I was either on his side of the other people's side. I wanted my money. That's just the way it was. He said he'd talk to his lawyer.

He called me later and said we had a deal. Said I should meet him the next morning at his lawyer's office on San Jacinto. I got over there and Robey says, "Give Hue a check for $40,000 from the trustee account or something," then we got into his limo to go to court.

I said, "Let's just drop by the bank and pick up the money." Robey said, "Oh, Hue, we don't have to do that. You can trust me." He was gettin' all shook up. I said, "Look, Chief, I said I wanted this $40,000 in this briefcase." He got pissed off, man, but he said, "Okay, take him by the bank." So I went in and cashed the check and put the money in my briefcase. We went right to the courthouse.

When I was sittin' on the witness stand I had that briefcase right beside me. I'll never forget it. Afterwards, I got up to take a leak. I had Eddie Ilroy working for me at that time. I said, "Eddie, I'm going to take a leak in a few minutes. You meet me out in the hall by the bathroom. I'm gonna hand you a briefcase and you take that s.o.b. back to the office." I wasn't taking no chances. Could very well the briefcase *and me* disappear after the court.

You see, old man Robey was a gambler. He loved cards and he had racehorses. If you stood up to him and beat him, he respected that. But you had to come a long ways to beat him.

T-Bone Walker was great, man. He lived in Oakland, California and he had a girlfriend in Conroe, Texas. Her name was Leah. When he wanted to come see her, he'd call me up and say, "Huey, don't I still owe you an album for that last contract we got?" I knew he wanted me to send him $1,000, an airplane ticket, bring his girlfriend up and rent him a motel room. He'd come in, cut an album's worth of material and then party.

He couldn't hit a lot of his old licks and had Joey Long playing guitar for him. It would blow T-Bone's mind. He'd say, "Show me how to hit that lick." He was tanked up most of the time. I had to put him in a corner and box him in with the organ and piano, otherwise he'd go strolling out among the musicians.

It's not often that a person's job can be his hobby and his love too. Money don't bother me. It's not good to worry about eating tomorrow but above that it's all crap. All headaches and worries. Music always came first. I had to learn the business part of it and I learned it by getting screwed — it's that simple. I had eight million-sellers and I was still hitchhiking. You learn the tricks 'cause they been used on you. I hate the business and I love the music. I love putting songs and people together and seeing if I can come up with something that rings bells.

I like getting big checks, but my real love is taking somebody who ain't got nothing, finding a good songs, winding him up, dressing him up and making a star. I remember when Barbara Lynn was performing in Philadelphia I was the only white guy in the crowd. The crowd would get up and applaud and Barbara would get a standing ovation. This big old fat lady would punch me with her elbow, saying "Ain't she great?" That thrill. Those goosebumps are what it's all about. If you offered me a million bucks for that feeling, I'd look at you like you was crazy.

Simplicity is where it's at. Look at "My Toot Toot." It whupped 'em all. It was cut on a Teac 4-track. I laughed and laughed when I was promoting that record. I'd walk in this place where they had $1 million or $2 million dollars tied up in equipment. Nine people to run the board 'cause it's so long and you walk in there with a $1.95 session that's beating them to death. And then people would be trying to guess what "Toot Toot" was. Some thought it was a piece, you know. Some thought it was coke, but it's just an endearment term in Louisiana. We sold 100,000 copies in Louisiana before anyone would take it. No one would recognize simplicity. They just don't realize that you can push everything to the extreme but you always have to come back to Plan A — the song and the simple sounds, brother. *(Colin Escott; April 22, 1988.)*

Records begin with songs, and songs, now matter how old or well-known they might be, have to eventually come from songwriters. Early rock 'n' roll derived much of its material from reworked public-domain songs, or R&B songs where the publishing came cheap and the real songwriter could be easily shortchanged. But soon rock developed its own songwriters. Some were good. Jerry Leiber and Mike Stoller were great. Leiber and Stoller took the basic beat of rock 'n' roll and the basic themes of the songs — being young and in love, being young and out of love, dancing — and added humor and sophistication and street smarts. The results were some of the slyest, wittiest, swingingest songs ever: "Hound Dog," "Charlie Brown," "Kansas City," "Searchin'," "Ruby Baby," "Jailhouse Rock," and hundreds of others. Leiber and Stoller provided the words and the music for a class of artists and a time where the song sold the record. They were the models for the Ellie Greenwiches and Carole Kings and Barry Manns that would follow.

Jerry Leiber: We were fans first. We went down to Watts, down to Central Avenue. We used to go to the Five/Four Ballroom to the dances. We loved it.

This was in the very early '50s; 1950 or 1951. I remember early Fats and Little Richard, the Clovers, Amos Milburn. I loved "Bad, Bad Whiskey" and Charles Brown doing "Black Night."

One day a man came to the record shop who was the national sales manager for Modern Records. His name was Lester Sill. He dropped in to check the sales on the R&B records, because this record store was not in a black neighborhood. I happened to be working there after school and we were talking about the records that were selling. We got to talking and I told him that I was writing lyrics and he asked me to recite some of the lyrics to him. So I did and he said, "They're great but you need music, right?" I told him that I was in the process of hooking up with a composer and he said, "Well, when you get it together, call me and I'll take you around to the small record companies." And that's what we did. Lester Sill was responsible for introducing us to Aladdin, Modern, Specialty and all the little companies that were doing well in R&B at the time. Lester really got us into the business.

The Biharis were great! They were funny people. These were family-owned businesses. The Biharis were four brothers — Lester, Joe, Saul and Jules — and they ran it like a little family business. It was very casual. If you came up with a song they liked, they'd say, "Well, let's get a session together, call so-and-so, get a rhythm section together and make a record."

Oh yes, there were key people. In fact, some of the arrangers that they used were the unsung heroes of those days. There was an arranger and tenor player on the West Coast named Maxwell Davis who was responsible for arranging and actually producing a lot of those hits. We virtually learned how to make records by working with Maxwell Davis.

He would just call local cats, but he knew them all — the best bass players, the best guitar players, the best drummers. He knew everything. In almost every region in the United States where they had small labels, there was a Maxwell Davis, Bumps Blackwell, Dave Bartholomew, key men.

Johnny Otis helped to create access to the younger white audiences. He had a great blues band and great singers. In fact, he gave us our first assignment. After we had written for the Robins, Johnny Otis gave the assignment to write for three singers in the band: a great blues singer named Mel Williams, Little Esther and Big Mama Thornton. We went down to rehearsal and we heard everybody sing, then we went home that afternoon to Mike's house and we wrote "Hound Dog" for Big Mama Thornton. We went back and taught her the song and I think that we recorded it within a week. It was our first unofficial production.

In the rehearsal Johnny played the drums. When it came time to record, Johnny put his road drummer, Dope, on drums. I was listening to it and the beat had changed, the feeling had changed and the rhythmic pulse had changed and we didn't like it. I stopped the take and I said, "John, we're going to blow it. Go out and play the drums the way you played in rehearsal." He did and we got it in two takes.

Mike Stoller: We had heard of Elvis Presley, but the only record I really knew was "Heartbreak Hotel," which I thought was a terrific record. That was early in '56, and I went to Europe for my very first trip and I was gone for three months. I came back on a ship called the Andrea Doria, which almost made it to New York. We were in a collision with another ship, the Stockholm, and I got into a lifeboat and was eventually picked up by a freighter. After I got back to New York, Jerry said, "We have the No. 1 record. Elvis Presley did 'Hound Dog.' " It registered on me a couple of days later that that was not a bad thing to have happen.

I have eight or nine country records on that song from 1953, cover versions of Big Mama Thornton's record.

Jerry Leiber: Homer and Jethro did it.

Mike Stoller: That was after Elvis. A lot of West Coast companies did it. Someone on Imperial, and Ramblin' Jimmy Dolan on RCA.

Jerry Leiber: Elvis was no problem to be with. We could write for him. We knew what he sounded like.

Mike Stoller: He could do anything.

Jerry Leiber: That's right. He could do anything that James Brown could do, anything that Little Richard could do or anything that Bing Crosby could do. The problem was that the movies required certain songs in certain scenes and they became so repetitious.

Mike Stoller: And *boring.*

Jerry Leiber: We just couldn't do it after a while. We couldn't keep doing that. We just ran out of gas.

Mike Stoller: It was demoralizing. As Jerry has often said, it was a license to print money. They'd show us these scripts that were just godawful and they got *worse* by the time they got to the screen. We were offered every movie but we stopped after a few. We did a couple of songs for *Loving You* and most of the songs for *Jailhouse Rock* and a number of songs for *King Creole,* and then we quit. After that, the only songs we submitted were songs we had already recorded with somebody else like "Girls, Girls, Girls" or "Bossa Nova Baby."

Jerry Leiber: We discovered Linda Hopkins.

Mike Stoller: Right! We recorded her in 1953. We brought her down by bus from Oakland to Los Angeles when we were A&R men for Crystalette Records. They hadn't quite gotten into 45 rpms. We were so knocked out by Linda — we had seen her in Oakland — that we paid her bus fare out of our pockets, which were pretty empty at the time. Then we waited to get reimbursed by Crystalette Records.

Jerry Leiber: We're still waiting.

Mike Stoller: The big problem in those days was this: they'd say that if you got a big hit then you were in trouble because the distributors would not pay you in time to pay the pressing plant. You could go out of business with a big hit.

Jerry Leiber: The distributors wouldn't pay at all on a big hit until you had another hit coming. They'd figure, "They're going out of business anyway. Why pay 'em?" That aborted a lot of companies.

Mike Stoller: We wrote a song called "Kansas City" in 1952. We had recorded the song with Little Willie Littlefield under the aegis of Ralph Bass, and we had taught the song to Willie at Maxwell Davis's house. By the way, people frequently ask, "What is he saying in the middle of the record?" And he's saying, "Well, alright, Max." Wilbert Harrison never caught that and says something else just before the instrumental break. Anyway, Ralph Bass said to us, "Listen, Kansas City, Kansas City, alright. But what's really hip is 'K.C.,' so I'm changing the title of your song to 'K.C. Loving.' " We were disappointed, but we were happy that the record was coming out. When Wilbert Harrison did the song at the tail end of a record date in New York seven years later, he couldn't remember the title because nobody could.

King Curtis told us about that session on a Coasters date. He said, "We had a session the other night. We were recording a session on two kids and they'd promised their friend or brother that he could do a number at the end of the session. So this guy comes out and does this song called 'Kansas City' and it's a smash." That was the first we'd heard of it.

The funny thing was Jerry and I were saying that we'd love to get a song to Joe Williams, who was with Basie back then. I said, "You remember that old song 'Kansas City'? That would be ideal," and we put in a call to Teddy Reig, who was producing Basie and Joe Williams for Roulette Records. It was a Friday night and we couldn't get to him, and the trade papers came out on Monday and there were seven records on "Kansas City." The song hadn't been done in seven years.

*Jerry Leiber:*The first time I saw Wynonie Harris was in a concert at the Shrine Auditorium in Los Angeles. He sang "Good Morning Judge" and knocked me cold. He was very funny and very personable. We had a song for him and made an appointment to see him. He lived in a hotel on Central Avenue and we were only 17 at the time. This was a strange hotel; it had one of those old-fashioned fans, the kind you see in *Casablanca* and there were characters in the lobby in white Palm Beach suits and Panama hats reading the racing form. We went up to his room and knocked on the door. He let me in and he was wearing a process because the style at that time was marcelled hair. He was wearing a stocking on his head. He was a dandy, dressed beautifully like Sugar Ray Robinson. We sat down on the edge of his bed and read him the song when all of a sudden we saw this arm shoot out from the other side of the bed and reach for this half pint that was on the coffee table. Wynonie's hand smashed this arm and he said, "Bitch, don't you ever do that. You're in the presence of very young people!" That was Wynonie. He was marvelous.

"Riot In Cell Block #9" was done live in the studio. The only thing we added afterward was the sound effects, the siren, the machine guns, etc. We'd play the tape, bounce it over then splice at the point where we were finished with the sound effects so that the balance of the record would be first generation rather than second.

On occasion, for special effect, we even slowed the record half a wrap — and this was before electronic variable speed control. To speed up the tape we'd wrap a little piece of tape around the capstan. It was only years later that we were able to slow things down.

Mike Stoller: The "Searchin' " session was done in Los Angeles at Master Recorders with Bunny [Robyn], who was the engineer there in those days. "Searchin' " came at the tail end of the session. We had cut three sides and we had maybe five minutes left, so we said, "Look, maybe we can get two takes." We had rehearsed it, but it was an afterthought that afternoon.

I played piano on almost all the Coasters' sessions right up until almost the end, when we were trying Latin stuff. Jerry was always in the booth dealing with the vocal performances.

We picked everybody by hand. We used Gary Chester and Panama Francis on drums. Great drummers. On "Searchin' " we used the guitar player they traveled with called Adolph Jacobs, and when we were on the West Coast we always used Barney Kessell, the jazz guitarist. On the East Coast, we always called Mickey Baker. On the West Coast, we always used tenor-sax player Gil Bernal, an old buddy of mine from Los Angeles City College, who later worked with Lionel Hampton. He was our featured honking tenor man.

The first Drifters session was on the West Coast in 1955. Clyde McPhatter had left and Johnny Moore was singing lead. We were set to record "Ruby Baby" and "Adorable." It was at either Radio Recorders or United in Los Angeles and Neshui Ertegun was the A&R director. He was generally in charge of the album and jazz division, but as he was on the West Coast — in fact, he was teaching a course on jazz at U.C.L.A. — he undertook to do that session. Neshui came and asked us for a song and we gave him a song ["There Goes My Baby"] for a song.

They brought the song to us, and we worked on it. I wrote a little theme and I think it was Jerry's idea that the theme would work well with violins. We hired a very small string section; I think it was five violins and one cello. I was a little insecure about writing for strings, all the bowing and so forth, so we hired a very talented man called Stanley Applebaum who wrote the charts and another theme. They tell us that was the first use of strings on an R&B record.

Another thing we put on that record was a Brazilian rhythm that Jerry and I had always liked called the bayonne. We also used a tympani that was sitting in the studio. The drummer was not a percussionist, so we tuned it as best we could to the first chord and he played it throughout the record on this one pitch. As Jerry has often said, it was like listening to two different radio stations at once because the drummer was playing this tympani through all the different changes on one tone.

Jerry Leiber: The Drifters were not a legitimate group like the Coasters. They were a "name doing business as..." The personnel was constantly changing because the group was on a weekly salary.

Ruth Brown was a sweetheart. LaVern Baker was *TOUGH.* Dinah Washington was the *TOUGHEST,* but Ruth Brown was a sweetheart.

Joe Turner was the blues. We only did three sides with Joe. One of them was "Chicken And The Hawk."

How many songs would you write a day during the '50s and early'60s?

Jerry Leiber: Anywhere from three to five.

Were people lined up for them?

Mike Stoller: You know what? We wrote them for ourselves. Sometimes we were asked for songs and we couldn't imagine what to do. However, we knew what to do in terms of the people we were working with. The Coasters, for example, were like a little company of players, a vaudeville troupe.

Jerry Leiber: People would call us up sometimes to write a song for, say, Perry Como, and we would wrack our brains. We had a crack at getting a record out by Vic Damone or Damita Jo or Julius LaRosa, but I just couldn't think for those people.

Mike Stoller: What do they eat? It was a different world. *(Dave Booth and Colin Escott; Oct. 26, 1984.)*

Doc Pomus: I come from a ghetto-type neighborhood, a very respectable middle-class family. My father was a neighborhood lawyer, a captain of a political district. Consequently, we never had any money, but say he had a butcher client; we could get a free meal. Yet we had to live a certain kind of life. So, consequently, it was a very proper life. And here I was 15 years old, playing saxophone in the little joints in the neighborhood. The family never knew about it. Suddenly I said to myself, "They're going to see my name somewhere and there's going to be plenty of trouble." That name [Doc Pomus] was invented, and my family didn't find out about me. I started working serious gigs in Greenwich Village when I was about 17 and I started recording when I was 18, so they found out accidentally. They never even realized I was doing this; they didn't know what I was doing. So that's how it happened.

Originally, I was a singer — and you must realize I was making records from the time I was 18 years old, which was strange in those days. I was one of those people that didn't understand making records. Some people, like Joe Turner, knew how to make records. Later in life, there were certain people like Andrew Tibbs who never learned, and he was probably the greatest to ever make records. So I wasn't the only person guilty of that.

I first started playing saxophone, but I gave it up. So the way I used to write songs was with a tape recorder, or else I'd keep them in my head or fool around on piano. After a little bit, when I was around 17 or 18 years old, I quit playing saxophone completely because I couldn't do what I wanted to do on it. With the singing, I found I could do more. And the songwriting came very hard to me, in the sense that it initially took me a long time to write a song.

I wrote a song called "Boogie Woogie Country Girl" which ended up being the other side of "Corinne, Corinna." So I had a windfall. I gave a guy 15 percent of the song for writing the lead sheet, and I've had about five records of this song and this guy always makes a couple of hundred dollars on this song because of me.

Then I started writing with Mort Shuman. When I was about 29 or 30 years old, I decided I wanted to write a lot more songs. So a cousin of mine told me about this kid, Mort Shuman, and I got together with him. Morty was going with this cousin of mine, and he knew a lot about young kid's songs, and I was just starting to get into it. So I told him, "Listen, you sit in the room while I write. I'll give you 10 percent of every song I write. You sit in the room." So he sat in the room. After about two years, he started contributing. Meanwhile, I was giving him 10 percent, 15 percent, and then he started contributing, and I'm giving him 25 and 30 percent. About two-and-a-half to three years later, I made him a full partner. It was really weird. By this time, I had mastered the technique of writing with somebody.

I got married when I was 32 years old. Now, we were really in bad shape. On our honeymoon, we almost came back broke. We just had money from friends in the business. And Morty and I had been writing as full partners for Spier Music. We got a little record for people like Richard Hayes, those kind of people. No hits. Then I got married, and Spier Music gave me some money. Herb Abramson, an old friend of mine, gave us some money. We got an old car from my brother, and we just traveled until the money started running out. When it started, we were in upstate New York and we went to a little luncheonette where they had a jukebox. I put a dime in the jukebox, and I saw a song called "Youngblood." I called my wife over and said, "Listen; I believe this is my song." Sure enough, it was a song that sounded like my song. See, it wasn't the song that I had originally written. I never knew what it was when they finished with it. I said, "You know, this is the song that I gave to Leiber and Stoller. If it's on a jukebox, you can bet this is selling." I called up Atlantic Records and I got one of the people and they said, "I bet I know why you're calling." I said, "I want to know if I could get a couple of bucks." They asked, "How much do you want — a thousand, two thousand?" I had never heard of this. I said, "Well, send me $1500." I knew I was going to take over my mother's old apartment in Brooklyn, because I had lived in these fleabag hotels in Brooklyn for years. My mother had moved, so we came back, that's where we lived. We had this $1,500.

Now I'll get into the Ben E. King story, which is really funny. Right at this time, this joker I know tells me he's got a scam going. There's a guy who married a millionairess — a woman about 25 years older than he was. He met her when he was a teacher at Arthur Murray Dance Studios or one of those places. He sold her lifetime dancing instructions and ended up marrying her. So now, he wanted to get away in the daytime, so he told her he started a record company. The guy who told me about it said they were going to give a salary to somebody who would do the running around. That was going to be Morty. So I got Morty $40 a week, I think. This other guy made $100 a week. And I was the president of the company, but with no salary, just a couple of bucks. We had a little office space. We shared an office with some film company that was never there.

So I had this little record company. We were on Broadway, and when we put record company on the sign in the lobby, the strangest assortment of characters would knock at our door. One day this guy knocks at my door and he's got a group called the Crowns. That was how I met Ben E. King. So we get a session with the Crowns, and the first record is a sudden hit. But we can't get paid because in those days the distributors had a practice of not paying 'til the second record.

It was called "Kiss And Make Up." But Charlie Thomas sang the lead on it, not Ben E., because it kind of suited Charlie. Meanwhile Ben E. used to sit in the office and sing to me all night. He always thought he was one of the best singers in the world. When the record company folded because we didn't have any money, Ben E. went over to George Treadwell, who owned the name Drifters. Treadwell said to him, "Listen, man. I'll make you a full-fledged member of the group. You'll get a salary every week. I'm giving you a group. I'll put them on a salary basis. They'll be working all the time." And Ben E. said "Great." While they had that string of records with Ben E. King, the band was on a salary basis. That's why Ben E. left the group. He didn't leave the group for any artistic reasons, but because he wasn't making any money there. He couldn't even survive.

After we were married about nine months, the record company I told you about messed up. And Otis Blackwell, who I knew from my Brooklyn days — he's another Brooklyn blues singer

— had written "Fever" and "Don't Be Cruel." Otis always was my friend. If you ever get us in a room together, you'd crack up, because I've known Otis since he was a kid. So Otis got this gig with Hill and Range. Otis said, "Listen, let me get you over there, give you a build-up." And Morty and myself never had any records that meant anything. But Otis took us over to this guy by the name of Paul Case, who was the professional manager of Hill and Range, and, man, this guy signed us up.

The way they hired us was, I said that I needed $200 a week to live and Morty only needed $100. Because I had a pregnant wife, I needed $200, and he needed $100, and they gave it to us. The only record I had that meant anything to them was "Youngblood." Now, along the way, when I had this little record company, Neil Sedaka, who lived in the same building as Morty did, used to hang out at the office, and I knew Donnie [Kirshner], because Donnie was dating a cousin.

Donnie used to ask me what I thought of his writing. And I used to have a review: "Better off being a publisher," and that's the truth. He didn't know anything about being a publisher 'til I told him to be a publisher.

So he started a publishing company with Al Lewis that folded. Then he got one with Al Nevins, and they opened up these offices. Now, when they opened up these offices, Donnie came over to us first — Morty and myself — and wanted to sign us up. But I told him, I've got to have $200, Morty's got to have $100. I've got a pregnant wife. He said, "I can't afford to pay that kind of money. Could you send me someone?" So I sent over Neil Sedaka and Howie Greenfield.

Donnie didn't know either of those two people. He has only recently acknowledged the fact that that's how he got into it. But this is the real story. Bobby Darin used to make demos for us. So I said, "Listen, Bobby's great, Donnie, but you can't write songs, why don't you become a publisher? You'll make some bread out of it." Because he asked me, "What about publishing?" I said yeah, because he's a con artist.

How'd you make that transition to rock and roll?

Hard to figure. I will tell you this: Morty is greatly responsible because he made me aware of young people's songs. But I really made a study. After I heard Frankie Lymon sing "Why Do Fools Fall In Love?" I took the record home and studied it. And after about 20 times, I started to like it. And then, while I was working the gig, I got this record by Elvis Presley called "Mystery Train." And that completely destroyed me. I knew he was something different that was going to happen. And then I saw him on the Dorsey Brothers TV show, and he looked like somebody who had just come up from the swamp. He really killed me. But everybody was laughing, same as with the Beatles. And he was going to be the No. 1 star in the country.

Now, let me put some other stuff into perspective, because I jump around; try to bear with me. Now, all the time, I thought this music was second-class. Why? Because, first of all, in America, nobody paid attention to the people who were writing the songs. And the places where it was done were bad places, man; people who were robbing kids. And there were no rock critics. The only rock magazines were magazines that had lyrics in them. And a rock critic at a newspaper? Forget about it. So I was really very self-conscious. It was the way I was making money, doing something I liked to do.

It was only many years later that I put this in perspective. Here's what happened. We went to England, Morty and myself, and there were three records of "Teenager In Love" in the top 10 in England at the same time. Now this is something that never happened before or since in any area of the world in the music business.

The Dion record, the Craig Douglas record and the Marty Wilde record were all in the top 10 in England. Again, that doesn't mean shit to me. Anyway, we got to the airport in England, and boom. There's a mob of photographers. And suddenly I see it's different here than it is in America. Not only that, but older people knew us. People knew songwriters, period. And rock music was music to them; it wasn't apologetic. So, man, I suddenly started thinking there may be something here that I'm just subconsciously aware of. In fact, it was like that with me and the blues. I think I was just doing it because I could do it, that was it. So, I stayed in England for some time and was treated like royalty. I never got treated like that in my life.

But when I got back to America, the first day I was back, I went into the Brill Building — at that time, I got around on braces and crutches — and the elevator operator says to me, "Hey, I haven't seen you for a few weeks." And it suddenly hit me, I'm back in America, man.

And then it was downhill. It was almost with relief, seriously. I took a bad fall, ended up in a wheelchair. My wife left me. She told me while I was in the hospital that she didn't want to be married to me anymore. Morty decided to move to Europe. And it was almost a relief. I was in a state of shock from all the shit that happened at once. My father had a heart attack, and ended up in the same hospital I was in. Then my mother broke her hand. So, at the same time, in the same hospital, my father, my mother and myself. Years later, I realized I was in a state of shock.

So I got out of the hospital, and drifted around, really drifted around. And I did nothing. I always used to get a contract to a publishing company, but I didn't do anything.

Donnie Kirshner signed me up to Screen Gems and then he left; he left me there with some guy who couldn't do anything. He left before I actually did the first song; he was gone. He knew he was leaving. He bullshitted me. So that was it, until four or five years ago. But I left out a lot of stuff. To backtrack: along the way, when I was working the Brill Building, Phil Spector would work during the week in Leiber and Stoller's office and a lot of times stay at my house out on Long Island. And he was always bananas, but he was great. The main problem, let me put on the record, was that he had a complete inability to cope with the world. If you go from there, you understand everything. He's one of the thinnest-skinned people that I've ever met. And also one of the great, great pure talents.

He did something like the way Otis Blackwell did. They both had the ability to take the air. Nobody ever wrote a song like Otis did before. Whoever produced a record like Phil Spector before? That to me is real genius. It's like they're giving birth. And I'll tell you, Leiber and Stoller did it to a degree. But the geniuses, really to me, were Spector and Otis, doing certain kinds of things.

For different reasons, I like a lot of songs I've written. "Still In Love," that I wrote for Joe Turner; in a certain way, it was just what I wanted it to be. See, that's another thing. "Lonely Avenue," just what I wanted it to be. It's funny, those are the only two songs I wrote by myself. "Still In Love" was interesting. I'll tell you why. I was only 24 years old when I wrote that and to look back at it 20 years later, 30 years later, I realize that if I would do it now, I don't think I could do it any better. Maybe some of the language was different, but what it was supposed to be. Like, "You loved me, then you left me, you helped me, then you used me." Structurally, it was just perfect and simple. And I loved it. When I hear it today, I really like it as much as I did then. And "Lonely Avenue," the same kind of thing. It was exactly what I wanted it to be. I like a song that Elvis recorded called "Best Of Blues." I forget the reason I like a lot of songs.

I liked "Boogie Woogie Country Girl" with Joe Turner. I liked it because that was what it was supposed to be. Then there was a song of mine that I liked again, that I wrote with Mort, that was just what it was supposed to be, called "No One." "Teenager In Love," I liked because it was what it was supposed to be. "Save The Last Dance," yeah, because it was my Latin kind of translation, and, again, it was what it was supposed to be.

I don't know if you know, but there's a funny story attached to that. We did the song with the Drifters, and Jerry Wexler of Atlantic never liked the song. No matter what he tells me, he never liked it. And they recorded it; it was laying there. So Jimmy Clanton was coming up for a session, and I was rehearsing with him, with that song. So Wexler called up and said, "Listen, you've got both sides of the next Drifters record. 'Save The Last Dance For Me' is the B-side, and a song called 'Nobody But Me' is the A-side." So I said, "Great." So now I had to get out of Clanton's rehearsal. So I said, "Jimmy, you can't record this song; somebody recorded it without us knowing about it." So I told him we've written the song for you, we were going to spring on you, called "Go, Jimmy, Go." It was really "Go, Bobby, Go," and we wrote it for Bobby Rydell, but it never came off in the session. So I gave it to him, and he did it. And the Drifters record came out, and they were running with "Nobody But Me," but "Save The Last Dance" started catching on in certain areas. They had it broken in about three areas. Now, it was time for Dick Clark to do it. Dick Clark tells them they're on the wrong side. So that's how it got turned over to "Save The Last Dance." On their own, those schmucks would've never done it. It's typical about record people and publishers; they don't know.

I will help blues people. I mean, that's my obligation. I'm not doing them a favor. Let me tell you what happened with Joe Turner. I don't even know if I ever told you this story.

As years go by, there's less of a difference in age. Whereas, now, Joe's in his 70s, and I'm 56. It's not like when I was 20, and Joe's older. So as the years went by, we kind of drifted into it. It really started in earnest when he was working at the Cookery, a New York jazz club, and we started hanging out together almost every night. He felt alienated, for whatever mysterious reason, from the people who came over, but we got tight. Now, Joe has had mixed years because of what happens with the blues in America. Blues people aren't doing as well as they should be doing.

So one day Joe was here, and we were talking. We were sitting talking, and I said, "Hey Joe, you're going to make some money now because the Blues Brothers recorded 'Flip, Flop and Fly'." Now Joe didn't even know who the Blues Brothers were, but he said, "I don't get any royalties on these songs. I haven't gotten any royalties since I left New Orleans 10 years ago." I said, "Are you serious?" He said, "Yeah."

So now, these songs were in a publishing company called Progressive that Joe had. They were all in the same firm as my song; I had some songs with Progressive. So I called the accountant. Nice, nice man, an old friend of mine. I said, "Listen, Joe Turner told me he hasn't received any royalties in 10 years since he moved from New Orleans." So he checked it out and said, "Doc, but we've been sending the royalties to New Orleans, his ex-wife over there, we send them to his old address, and they get cashed all the time." So I checked into it. His ex-wife was getting those checks and cashing them. Her brother was Joe Brown, the ex-fighter, and he had a lot of businesses. So he could cash them through his businesses. And at that moment, they had sent out a check for $26,000 to Joe Turner. But they stopped the check. But now, Joe had to prove that he wrote the songs. Because they were written under his wife's name, Lou Willie Turner. And the reason Joe did that was because he always thought he would die before her. And he wanted, if there was any trouble, for her to have it.

But he outlived her. He said that Ahmet Ertegun was in the room a lot of times when he wrote the songs. And Ahmet knew about it. I called up and Ahmet said, "Absolutely, Joe." So he [Turner] ended up getting that $26,000 and subsequent monies, and they're still trying to collect old monies.

After they got that $26,000, Joe, for the first time in his life, or rather the first time at this stage in his life, was secure. And he got subsequent monies since then. He sent me over a check. This was a way of, like telling me, because he wanted to return some of the money I sent him. So he sent me a check for $200. And it was very sweet.

It's the same with Spector. I feel like he's a son of mine or a young brother. I mean, I talk to Spector; nobody'll talk to him the way I talk to him. One time, I didn't talk to him for a long time. But I love him. When he comes to town, he comes over here. When I knew Phil, he'd come over to the office; he used to have an attache case and have a loaf of bread in it, and comb and paper. And that's what he used to carry in this attache. He always remembers I bought him his first steak when he came back to New York. He always talks about it. The last time I went to California, I hung out with him every night. I went to his place and hung out. We don't even have to talk. He comes here and we talk a lot of silliness.

See, Phil, if you really, really know him, he's one of the funniest guys in the world. I mean most people don't play this fact up. I'll tell you one practical joke that we pulled. You'll get an insight to Phil Spector. There's a guy who became a hotshot since then, Artie Ripp. He was the head of Buddha Records. When I first knew him, he was a flunky for George Goldner. Now, George Goldner was the owner of Gone Records. And at that time, George's hottest act was a guy by the name of Ral Donner. Ral Donner was an Elvis Presley clone, who sang exactly like Presley and had hit records. His biggest record was "The Girl Of My Best Friend." Now, during the week, I kept a place at this hotel. And Phil would hang out with me every night. You've got to get the physical layout. The hotel is in the middle of a block. All the way to the right is this little candy store that was open all night long, where you could buy all kinds of stuff. And if you stand in the lobby, you could see somebody all the way over there. Now, once you get in the lobby, there's a long desk on the left and at the end of the desk is a telephone operator. And she's got her back to us.

So here's the scam that me and Phil got set up for Artie Ripp. It's late at night, and we knew Artie would always stop off at this candy store. So me and Spector were in the lobby and the way we got it fixed with the telephone operator was that after Ripp came in the lobby, none of us are going to talk, but wait for 10 minutes, and pretend there's a call for me, a long-distance call. I'd ask you where the call's from, and you'd say, from Memphis. So that's what happened. We see Ripp coming. Me and Spector are sitting in the lobby, just wasting time. Then suddenly Ripp comes in, and she presses a button. We hear a buzz, she says, "Doc, it's for you." "Ask where it's from. Long distance? So where's it from?" I said, "Who is it?" She said, "Colonel Parker." So I picked up the phone. Now, Ripp is looking over there. I said, "Colonel, how are you doing?" I said, "No kidding. It's too bad." And I had told her after the call, wait a half hour and repeat the same thing.

So Ripp was talking to us, and Spector asked me, "What's it all about?" We plotted it this way ... I say, "It's nothing." Half an hour later, same sequence. I said, "Wow, what? No kidding. The guy's name is ... I can't remember now. I'll check it out for you, I promise." I hang up. Now, Ripp is — "What's this?" I said, "You've got to keep this to yourself. Presley lost his voice, and they wanted Ral Donner to sub for him in the next session. They'll give $100,000 for him to do it."

It's about two o'clock in the morning. Artie Ripp gets a taxi. Now, his boss, George Goldner, is all the way out somewhere, and by the time he gets there, it's four o'clock in the morning. He wakes Goldner up at four o'clock in the morning to tell him this long story. It went down so perfect. This is the kind of stuff Spector and I would do. We were hysterical. We thought it was the funniest thing. And you have to know Goldner, this tough street guy. Imagine Ripp waking him up four o'clock in the morning to tell him this story. Before he's halfway through, Goldner realizes he's been had. So that's the kind of thing Spector and I would do.

I've got a responsibility to the blues. And I've got a responsibility to young people. But I've got a responsibility to myself. I'd really like just to keep going. *(Joseph Sapia; November 1982.)*

The second generation of great rock 'n' roll songwriters, if there ever was such a thing, worked out of the two buildings that collectively were the Brill Building. It was a songwriters' sweatshop that produced literally hundreds of classic songs, songs that defined the sound of rock 'n' roll for almost five years. Carole King and her husband/partner, Gerry Goffin, wrote "He's In Town" and "Will You Love Me Tomorrow" and "(You Make Me Feel Like A) Natural Woman"; Ellie Greenwich and Jess Barry wrote "Leader Of The Pack" and "Chapel Of Love"; and Barry Mann and Cynthia Weil wrote "Uptown" and "You've Lost That Lovin' Feeling" and "Hungry" and "We've Gotta Get Out Of This Place" and many, many more, right up to present-day hits like the Pointer Sisters' "He's So Shy." The songs that came out of the Brill Building never had a particular Brill Building sound to them; they had some musical sophistication, but otherwise they were just great songs, and the fact that so many current performers go back to them and record them over and over again proves that good songs can be hits and still be good songs. Mann and Weil's dedication to the craft was typical.

Barry Mann: I began writing as a kid, when I was 13 or 14. But I never really attempted to go into the music business at that time. I used to work as a busboy at the resorts in the Catskills because I was going to go to college to become an architect. While I was up there, I'd sing my songs at talent shows. I'd always run into these guys, typical music-biz people with the big cigars, saying, "If you ever decide to go into this business, look me up." For some reason, I took the names. Then I went to school for about a year, but I couldn't see myself as an architect. So I looked up the names and went to one of them with four of my songs. He took one, and said I should go cut a demo. This was about 1958. I asked him, "What's a demo?" So I went in, and with three musicians I cut one of my songs. That's how I got started. From there I went into playing piano on demos.

Cynthia Weil: It was horrendous. You'd hear about people selling songs for $50. I found it hard to believe that anyone was paying for doing this in the first place. I could've been taken advantage of in a minute.

Barry Mann: I remember my mother copyrighting my songs by sending them to herself in the mail. She was aware of that angle.

The first one we wrote together, but it didn't sell, was called "Painting The Town With Teardrops," by a guy named Vinnie Monte. The first hit we had, in 1961, was by Tony Orlando, a song called "Bless You." That was the first hit we did together. I had one by myself that was a hit for the Diamonds in 1959, "She Say (Oom Dooby Doom)." I had a Steve Lawrence record called "Footsteps." Then I met Cynthia.

Cynthia Weil: Most of the singers didn't read; they took the songs from demos, so you just taught it to them.

Barry Mann: I began to meet a lot of people, one of whom was Don Kirshner, who was starting a publishing company. I forgot about it for about a year, and then a friend of mine suggested I go see him. I did and he heard my songs and said, "Great, I'll sign you." I thought he was kidding. I said, "Well, for how much?" He said, "I'll pay you $150 a week," against royalties. I said great!

That was the most positive aspect of that period, because there's nothing like it around today. There were cubicles with pianos in them, and there was always a lot of activity, but we weren't forced to write; we wrote because we wanted to write. Basically we'd write at home, and then come in there and play it. It was an electrified, competitive atmosphere.

We were so competitive, and so were Carole King and Gerry Goffin, trying to beat each other out on a record, but we also helped each other. So we got out a lot of records because of it but I do wonder if all that competition wasn't in the way. I tend to think it helped. But we didn't have any lives; our lives were writing, cutting demos, never going on vacations, because we just wanted to get those records. The money had nothing to do with it.

It was the challenge of getting the record. We never even thought about anyone outside the office getting it. If Goffin-King didn't get it, or we didn't, it didn't matter who did. It was a sibling rivalry, with Kirshner as our father figure, and we all wanted to please him. If Don called and said someone was recording, you went to the piano and tried to write for them, whether it was country, R&B, rock.

There were actually two buildings, the Brill Building and 1650 Broadway, which we were in. But Leiber and Stoller were in the Brill Building, so if we were writing a Drifters song and they were working with them, we'd grab our lead sheets and go over there.

Cynthia Weil: We wrote a song that's never seen the light of day called "Up From The Streets," which was the history of that time. The subways and all that was part of you. It had to show up in your music, because it was your life. We wrote one, again that was never recorded, called "I'm A Man," which was the story of the whole racial situation at the time. "Uptown" was probably one of the first sociological songs in that sense.

It was purely a matter of wanting to say what we did. What's interesting was that at that time Kirshner was into romantic songs; they all had to have positive endings. I remember playing it for him and feeling horrible because it didn't get a reaction. If he loved a song it made your day. But after it was a hit he took me aside and said, "Write more of those ones I don't understand."

Barry Mann: It was easy in those days to write a follow-up. But I have to say I was never very good at writing a follow-up. In some cases, we just wrote a song. "Uptown" was just wrote, and then the Crystals had the hit. "On Broadway" was originally written for the Cookies. It originally had a female lyric. When Leiber and Stoller said they wanted to do it with the Drifters, we had to change lyrics. "You've Lost That Lovin' Feeling" was sort of tailored for the Righteous Brothers.

Cynthia Weil: Phil Spector told us he'd signed them and we heard some earlier records they'd made, heard the high and low voices and the song was just right for them.

Barry Mann: We've always been able to sort of become the artist we're writing for, to pick up their essence. It's a matter of sensitivity.

We were involved with all aspects. I played piano on "Blame It On The Bossa Nova." I played piano on "On Broadway," and Phil Spector played guitar, the solo.

Phil Spector was incredible then. So were Leiber and Stoller. They were the best there was so you didn't have to worry about your songs being done badly.

Cynthia Weil: There were always a lot of strange people drifting through. Now I would be paranoid to walk those halls at night, but we never even thought of that. It was really a hotbed of creative craziness. I remember we used to wait around for Kirshner to see if he needed a song for someone. We used to wait for him in front of the men's room because we knew that sooner or later he'd have to go. But then the men would grab him and talk inside. Once I grabbed him and said, "Okay, I've been waiting here for three days," and he finally said, "Okay, come with me," and we started to walk into the men's room together. Then we both looked at each other and said "No!" But that's where our consciousness was — totally into the music. There was nothing in our lives except those people and our work. We had absolutely no friends outside the business because no one understood our hours.

[In 1964] we wondered what was going to happen to us, because everything British was being played on the air. Somehow we just stayed, and had more hits: "Lovin' Feeling," "Kicks," "Hungry," "We Gotta Get Out Of This Place," "Soul And Inspiration." We'd actually written "We Gotta Get Out Of This Place" for the Righteous Brothers and it got sent off to the Animals.

As for classics we might have written, "Uptown" and "On Broadway," some of the other Crystals things, like "He's Sure The Boy I Love." I wasn't too hot on "Walking In The Rain." I felt that it was a cop of Ellie Greenwich and Jeff Barry. It was a great pop art record, though. "Lovin' Feeling" was good. I can tell you the one I don't like: "Blame It On The Bossa Nova." I kind of liked "My Dad," which Paul Petersen did. I like "Kicks." "Patches" doesn't stand out to me; that was part of the learning experience.

Barry Mann: "On Broadway" was originally written from the perspective of a small-town girl coming to Broadway.

Cynthia Weil: It was recorded first by the Cookies but it didn't turn out so well, so we had the song and were wondering what to do with it when we heard the Drifters were recording. We thought that melodically it could fit the Drifters, but the lyrics were wrong because it was for a girl. We played it for Leiber and Stoller and they said they wanted to cut it the next day, so we could either go home and rewrite it or work with them. The thought of working with them was pretty incredible, so we sat down and worked on it together.

Barry Mann: "Uptown"? We just sat down and wrote a song, with nothing in mind, and that was it.

When we went out to California, Phil Spector said he wanted to write with us. He played us this record by a group he had from Orange County: "Little Latin Lupe Lu," by the Righteous Brothers. He said he wanted to cut a ballad with them. We were influenced by "Baby, I Need Your Loving," by the Four Tops. So by osmosis we turned out "Lovin' Feeling." I wanted to change the title but Phil liked it.

On "Only In America" we were working with Leiber and Stoller again. That started out as something completely different, with lyrics like, "Only in America/Land of opportunity/Can they save a seat in the back of the bus just for me/Only in America/Where they teach the golden rule/Will they start to march when my kids want to go to school." It was originally written that way for the Drifters. They said it would never get played, so we changed it to fit a WASP, and for them it rings true: "Only in America/Land of opportunity." If the Drifters had cut it that way no one would have played that either, because it wasn't true! So Jay and the Americans cut it.

Cynthia Weil: I think those [Brill Building] days are behind us now. The young writers are too smart now and too business-oriented. Everyone is too isolated; they're all at their own cubicles at home not hearing anyone else, doing their own thing.

To tell the truth, there were only pockets of fun. I never found the music business fun.

Barry Mann: I found the writing fun. Working with someone like Jerry Leiber was fun. Watching his mind work was so incredible. The process is frustrating and anxiety-producing and fun at the same time. The business part has never been fun. It never will be, 'cause it's giving up control of your baby, turning it over to someone else, hoping they'll be good to it. Probably the most fun is working with talented people and watching the process.

It's still rewarding. When you get a hit that you really like, that's it. *(Jeff Tamarkin; August 1982.)*

It's hard for anyone who doesn't remember at least a couple of shreds of life and music before 1970 to grasp how records became hits and artists became sensations in those days. An obscure, scuffling artist would go into a recording studio and spend a couple hundred bucks on a record. Then the artists' record company would send the record out to disc jockeys, with or without a little greenbacked incentive for him to play the record, and the record would start getting airplay — maybe just regional airplay at first, but a lot of it. The regional airplay would suddenly explode into national airplay, and then the artist would find himself on the set of the most influential music program ever, *American Bandstand*, mouthing the words to the little record he had cut in that cheap studio what seemed like a century ago. Suddenly he had a hit record; the dream had come true.

That is just how it happened. *American Bandstand* shaped popular music in a way no other program ever did, ever could or ever will. It was the simplest program imaginable, just a good-looking DJ spinning records while kids danced, but for kids around the country it was a crash course in what was cool. The way that kids on AB danced was the way they had to dance. The way the kids on AB dressed and wore their hair was the way they had to dress and wear their hair. And the songs that were played on AB were the songs they had to have.

The "disc jockey" on *American Bandstand* was a fresh-faced Philadelphia kid named Dick Clark. Clark stayed with the show, refusing to age, from its inception in 1952 until its network run ended in 1987. He organized the legendary "Caravan of Stars" tours of the late '50s and early '60s that packed star-studded lineups in buses and took them around the country to school gyms, theaters and auditoriums, so that kids could see their current icons up close and hear their favorite songs straight from the stars. He spun off *Where The Action Is*, which made stars out of Paul Revere and the Raiders. He formed a television-production company that's made millions off lowest-common-denominator shows like *The $10,000 Pyramid* and *TV's Bloopers and Practical Jokes*. He still does syndicated radio shows, and continues to keep his hand on the pulse of the American music scene. Whether it's been good or bad, no single figure has had as much impact on current American musical culture than Dick Clark—and all because of a simple little show on Philadelphia TV.

Dick Clark: I looked in a diary I had the other day and every other page was, "I listened to the radio." As a sub-teen, I was hooked on the radio. There wasn't any TV at that time; when I first entered the business, it was all radio. I was in television about the time it was created. I started in radio about 1947 and by '49 or '50 I was appearing on televison, regularly in '51.

I was just there at the right moment in time.

Bandstand went on the air in 1952 and was an immediate success with two other hosts, so it could've happened in Cleveland or Buffalo or Dallas or Dubuque. It just happened to be in Philadelphia, which is propitious because not only was it in the East, it was close to New York, and it had its own music industry. It did well probably because in those days I think Philly was the fourth- or fifth-largest city. It might not have happened in a tiny little town.

The secret was that everyone said that *Bandstand* was a powerful promotion vehicle for music, when in truth we did have a huge audience and what caused the power was most of the ... I don't even know if they called them top-40 radio stations in those days, but the ones who played the popular music of the day, would copy the [*Bandstand*] bandlist, then immediately jump on [the records played on the show]. So you got this double whammy where the radio and television were playing the same songs and they hand't even entered the charts yet. So it was tremendous clout, and we were the folks who got the credit, and not totally justifiably.

When did the Rate-A-Record concept come into the show?

That was from the beginning. It was there from the first day and was there in 1956 when I took over.

You've been quoted as saying you were puzzled by the whole idea.

DICK CLARK: 'When I first entered the business, it was all radio. I was in television about the time it was created. I was just there at the right moment in time.'

I'm still puzzled by it. They still talk about "I like the beat and it's easy to dance to." They've been saying it for 37 years. It never seemed to affect the outcome of the success of the record, because some of them that were just butchered by the kids went onto great success, while others that were praised to the skies disappeared.

There's another story. That's the story of how, in my youthful enthusiasm, I went with a representative of WFIL, which is now WPVI, to New York to present a kinescope — we had no tape — of the show, which was getting 67 percent of the audience in Philadelphia. We said this could work nationally, and [the network's] response was, "Who the hell would want to watch kids from Philadelphia dancing to records?"

So they sent a guy down to investigate the phenomenon and he said, "I don't understand what they've got here but I think they're right and you oughta do it." They eventually gave us a five-week trial. It worked.

I missed the point, though. He wrote me a letter which inasmuch as said don't call us, we'll call you. The letter is in my office. I ran up there [to New York] and in my enthusiasm said, "You're gonna love our show," and I guess we must've overwhelmed them.

There were all kinds of people. I still work with people I knew 35 years ago, which is the greatest joy of my life. I'm now into exchanging photos of their grandchildren and talking about their personal lives, and that rarely ever happens in the entertainment business. I just got an invitation to Rod Stewart's wedding. It goes from the '50s to the '90s. It's kinda nice. You hang on to the people you run into along the way.

The easiest thing to write, for the most part in the late '60s and early '70s — young people who had no touch with the business and hadn't grown up with it — was that all we ever did was play Philadelphia artists, not realizing that two-thirds of the people in the Rock And Roll Hall of Fame made their debut on *American Bandstand*. They paid no attention to the Chuck Berrys, the Little Richards, the Platters, the Penguins, all the roots people who were on. They always said it was the white teenage idols.

The show was integrated in terms of artists from the first day in 1952 or '53. They didn't have artists on the first day but that happened within a week or two. One of the earliest was Dizzy Gillespie. Blacks were always represented. They were not in the audience till '55, '56.

When I was involved with the show in '56 we began to integrate with a greater purpose in mind, because it was obvious that was going to happen. Before that it was obviously a segregated show — it had a white audience, a white *dancing* audience. And the fact of the matter is that when it became integrated, there wasn't a ripple. Nobody cared, there were no outcries, there were no nasty letters, there were no fist fights. It just happened. The whole world should've happened like that.

There's a poster here on my wall — I collect things — that says "Notice. Stop. Help save the youth of America. Don't buy Negro records." It goes on with some more wonderful racist remarks that, in the '90s you say, "God, I can't believe these things were hanging around on lampposts." We would trail into town and be confronted by one of these things. It's scary stuff.

Right under that, I have a picture of the first integrated concert in Atlanta, Georgia, that we put on, with Sam Cooke as the black artist on an all-white bill. He was playing in front of an integrated audience, which had never happened before.

You're probably sick to death of talking about the years 1959 and '60 [the years of the payola scandal].

No; never. Those were good years.

In spite of having to testify before Congress at the payola hearings?

That's the dark side.

This was absolutely founded upon here's-a-threat-to-my-pocketbook. And the people who held the pocketbook strings in those days, the publishers, the old writers, the artists, the record companies, they were concerted in their effort to squash this new form because they were going to lose money.

And they used as their excuse, and bamboozled enough people into thinking, that this was going to cause the moral decay of American youth. And a lot of people were swept into that, including a lot of Broadway actors and actresses, writers, popular singers of the day: Mitch Miller, Frank Sinatra, Helen Hayes. Here's a wonderful quote from 1960 [*reads*]: "Congressman Tip O'Neill demands that the FCC investigate payola and protect America's youth from rock 'n' roll, which he called a type of sensuous music unfit for impressionable minds."

The whole world changed in 1964. Kennedy was assassinated, the English came in and took over the music world, *Bandstand* moved from Philadelphia, Californians were rising to the top of poularity in music and the whole world turned around. Then the Vietnam War came on not too long after that.

There's a story in your book about the first time you played a Beatles record, "She Loves You," on Bandstand, *and it just didn't click. The kids didn't think it was anything special and you didn't see what was coming.*

No, I couldn't figure that at all. I was at the dentist this morning and he said, "Dick, you always had a good ear for hits and know when people are gonna be stars," and I said, unashamedly, "Yeah, I'm pretty good at it." I don't point out the two or three I'd like to forget. That's one I certainly missed.

And logically, too, because most of that music that was coming to us from overseas was a reworking of stuff I'd already been through and I couldn't understand. But it was new to the public. And if they hadn't looked that way, if the German girlfriend of Stu Sutcliffe hadn't cut their hair that way and made them dress in leather initially, would it have been as impactful at that moment? Probably yes, but it certainly didn't hurt.

Did a record ever skip on Bandstand?

There are a lot of stories like that, but I don't remember any of them. There have been stories written about artists who say it happened to them, so I presume it did. The only one I remember distinctly was Jimmy Dean appearing and we played the wrong record; we played a Dee Clark record. Paul Anka tells a story that he came on once and the record skipped. I'm sure an artist would be much more aware of that than an onlooker or even I. I might've been turned away or talking to the control room or whatever.

Where The Action Is was developed as a CBS summer replacement for Jackie Gleason. It had been turned down for a variety of reasons and a guy at CBS asked if we'd do it five days a week as a half-hour vehicle and we said yes. It was a wonderful vehicle for a lot of the English artists and American artists. We took it out of doors and did skiing sites and beach sites and parks and nightclubs. It was quite an undertaking.

Hubert Humphrey was on the show once. I've got a picture of Mark Lindsay with Hubert Humphrey. It's just the funniest stuff I've ever seen. Here's this guy with a ponytail talking to the vice president of the United States, running for president, who did the kids show to try to garner youth votes or something. Who *knows* why?

You've said that you started losing touch with the music in the '60s. Which music did you not take to?

That was during the first psychedelic period. I couldn't figure it out. I wasn't into drugs so it left me behind. We still presented the artists but I couldn't tie into it because I didn't know what the hell they were talking about.

We lived through the folk period and the psychedelic period when dancing wasn't all in vogue. The show wasn't really based on whether you liked dancing or not; it was whether you liked people of that age. What were they wearing, what were they doing?

You don't stop being a fan. Being a fan of music doesn't necessarily mean you're a fan of all music. What your own personal taste is has nothing to do with what you're called upon to present.

Being called "America's Oldest Teenager" is like being America's oldest living Civil War veteran. That was first written in *TV Guide* over 20 years ago, as a dig, no less. I said that's a great piece of business. It works very well in introductions, whether you're giving a speech or making a personal appearance. It brings a smile to people's faces; it's obviously tongue-in-cheek and the silliest thing, so it breaks the ice.

I'm proudest of *Bandstand* because it proved a point, it stayed on the longest, it's the longest-running variety television show in history — that's in the *Guinness Book Of Records*. It's been a part of almost four generations. You can't get much better than that. *(William Ruhlmann, Dec. 28, 1990; April 20, 1990.)*

Jerry Wexler is John Hammond's bookend. Both are renaissance men with interests that range far beyond music. Both grew up loving jazz but were able to open their ears and spread their appreciation of music to the wider stage. Both had their hands in some of the legendary recordings of all time. Wexler joined forces with Ahmet Ertegun and his Atlantic label in the early 1950s; at his first session, he recorded Clyde McPhatter. From there Wexler went on to record LaVern Baker, Joe Turner, the Clovers and Ruth Brown for Atlantic in the '50s; in the '60s, he produced the definitive soul sides of Solomon Burke, Ray Charles, Wilson Pickett, and

Aretha Franklin, and put together a distribution deal that enabled Atlantic to distribute the Memphis sound of Otis Redding and other artists on the Stax label. He later got the Allman Brothers onto Capricorn Records for their greatest recordings, and signed the B-52s to Warner Brothers.

Jerry Wexler: I was a record collector, a devout record collector. I used to hang out at the Commodore record shop and I used to make the local music scene on 52nd Street, down in the Village, in Harlem, after hours and so on, and I always had a band of record-collector friends who were into the same thing.

We would collect records, which is not the same as going over to Sam Goody's or Tower Records with their stacks and stacks of records; in those days you really had to search: Salvation Army stores, places that had "Mad Dog" signs in the window. You'd have to yell through the crack of the door, "I'm the record guy." So, the grounding was tremendously motivated. You also tended to specialize in those days, defining for yourself where your area of interest was, and that had to be discriminating.

I don't know what the answer is, except that I can tell you this: In those days, the early '50s, people were coming to pop with their own ideas and sensibilities independent of the record companies. That's pretty much what we're talking about here. Somebody once asked me to what did I attribute my success at Atlantic Records, was it management? No. Was it this thing or that thing? No. Well then, what were the qualities? Well, the qualities were taste, probity and intelligence. That's a mighty big brag, right?

But, as Dizzy Dean once said, "If you can do it, it's not bragging." Those were the attributes, I think, that people who endured in this business had. Look at the competition Atlantic had. In the beginning, there were so many: Aladdin, Specialty, Modern, I could go on and on. Chess ... they're all gone. There isn't one that's still around and has its own identity.

I came to Atlantic in 1953.

What did you learn from Ahmet Ertegun?

Oh, a great deal. Let me put it this way: There was no state-of-the-art in production at that point, so what I picked up from Ahmet were the rudiments, the technical part, tracking, layering, setting up the microphones, because that was all there was at the time. What we were able to learn, we learned strictly from actually recording people like [Ray] Charles.

When it came to recording, we had two jobs: to nurture what was going on out there in the room on the other side of the glass and to catch that on tape. Now, that second one is really an engineering function, having to do with fidelity and microphones, seeing that there is no tape hiss to interfere with the sound. Much of that was handled by Tom Dowd. I never got very good at that. I mean, I'm not a hands-on person on the board to this day, but I didn't have to be because I had Tom Dowd. My emphasis and focus was on seeing if I could help it happen out in the studio.

The other side of that, quite frankly, is that we owned the company. We signed the checks, but that still doesn't cut it with musicians; you have to win that confidence from them, so that when you tell them something, they should take it very seriously, and ponder and deliberate.

I don't think we could fight the system. The most you could do was rage and rant. It was an absolutely racist system in which he had one simple, irreputable difficulty and that was that white radio stations wouldn't play our black records. Now from a historic perspective, people say, "Oh, man, I used to love those LaVern Baker records." That's a damned lie, because they didn't buy them.

Something like 90 percent of the people who bought those records were black, except for highly evolved blues and jazz fans and record collectors, and that was not enough to sustain them. Society had to become educated to this music, and it was educated by some British boys with long hair. They were the ones that brought Muddy Waters' music and Ivory Joe Hunter's music to the masses of American kids. They went out and found Bo Diddley, and Ike and Tina, and B.B. King, and presented them. Muddy Waters thanked them publicly.

What we are dealing with is a constituency of basically insentient squares. That's our record market and the evolved few, as is always going to be the case, are the keepers of the flame. That's why all those record companies disappeared, because that's not enough.

It's an article of faith not to have too much going and have conflicting lines going against each other. This is going to get a little technical. You sit down with the harmonic structure of the song after it's written out in chords, chord changes, so you can jump from one chord to another. In the early days that was maybe all that people did when backing up, say Elvis Presley.

You didn't do all that much except lay down the harmonic substructure, but music required more later on as it got more involved; it required rhythm patterns and texturing. The texture is what nourishes you. The high and low ends of the spectrum and what's in the middle, but now you have to be careful to have enough fabric to cut yourself a suit, while not allowing it to turn it into a tent. So when we recorded down in Muscle Shoals and Memphis in the mid-'50s, you'd come in with a song for the musicians, you'd give them the chord changes, they'd start playing with that and then somebody would come up with a riff and we'd start working off that.

The obverse of all this is Phil Spector's wall of sound. Now, that was another way to go, and Phil made it work by having a tremendous amount of lines going at once. The key was to realize that you couldn't just make any kind of sound; you had to have a known overtone with its own resonance and limitations. Even with Phil, you have to have the substructure to make it work.

Phil Spector always had the ability, the brilliance; he always had it. It was just a question of luck, or bad luck maybe, that it didn't emerge during the period he was with us. Maybe we didn't provide him with the proper framework that would keep him nourished, maybe we just didn't have him at the right time.

I don't know what A&R is anymore. A great record producer, Ralph Buss, called it "finding the bodies." That's the prime function in the record business, because if you find the right body, somehow the record will get made. You know, today, all the kudos go to the record producers; I think that's arrogant bullshit. I mean, Seymour Stein, they should give him the earth for finding Madonna and the Talking Heads and all those other people. I think the credit should go to the people who found Louis Armstrong, Bessie Smith and Hank Williams, Ray Charles and Bob Dylan. Those people are the ones that deserve the awards; that's why John Hammond stands above everybody else. Look at the enormous amount of talent he found. The industry is moving away from recognizing that now. A&R, is you want to call it that, is now under the domination of the promotions department. To me, that's outrageous.

Why do you think there was that twist that enabled Motown to be sold directly to white teen-agers?

That was Berry Gordy's genius. He saw this thing and somehow knew how to do it and he knew that these little mini-soap operas, these 36-bar songs, would have great power and he found a way to put it together.

I always thought maybe a record would sell, maybe it wouldn't, but as far as thinking in terms of a timeless masterpiece for the ages, never. I mean, you got more exciting about some records than others, but that's only a question of degree. One of the records that turned me on instantly, not a record that I made, but a master that was cut in Muscle Shoals, was "When A Man Loves A Woman," by Percy Sledge. I got super-excited when they came in. I called Ahmet in Europe and said, "Man, you won't believe this." *(Danny McCue; March 10, 1989.)*

About the Author

Kit Kiefer is the former managing editor of *Goldmine*, and continues to write for the magazine periodically. He is the author of *The Top 100* and *The Post-Nuclear Collegian* and the editor of *Baseball Cards*, *Fantasy Baseball* and *Baseball Cards Presents* magazines. He has written on travel and music for many national magazines. His favorite artists are Bob Wills, Buddy Holly, Ry Cooder, Otis Redding, Fats Domino, Richard and Linda Thompson, and the Raspberries.